Burkina Faso

the Bradt Travel Guide

Katrina Manson & James Knight

Updated by Gill Harvey

www.bradtguides.com

Bradt Travel Guides Ltd, UK
The Globe Pequot Press Inc, USA

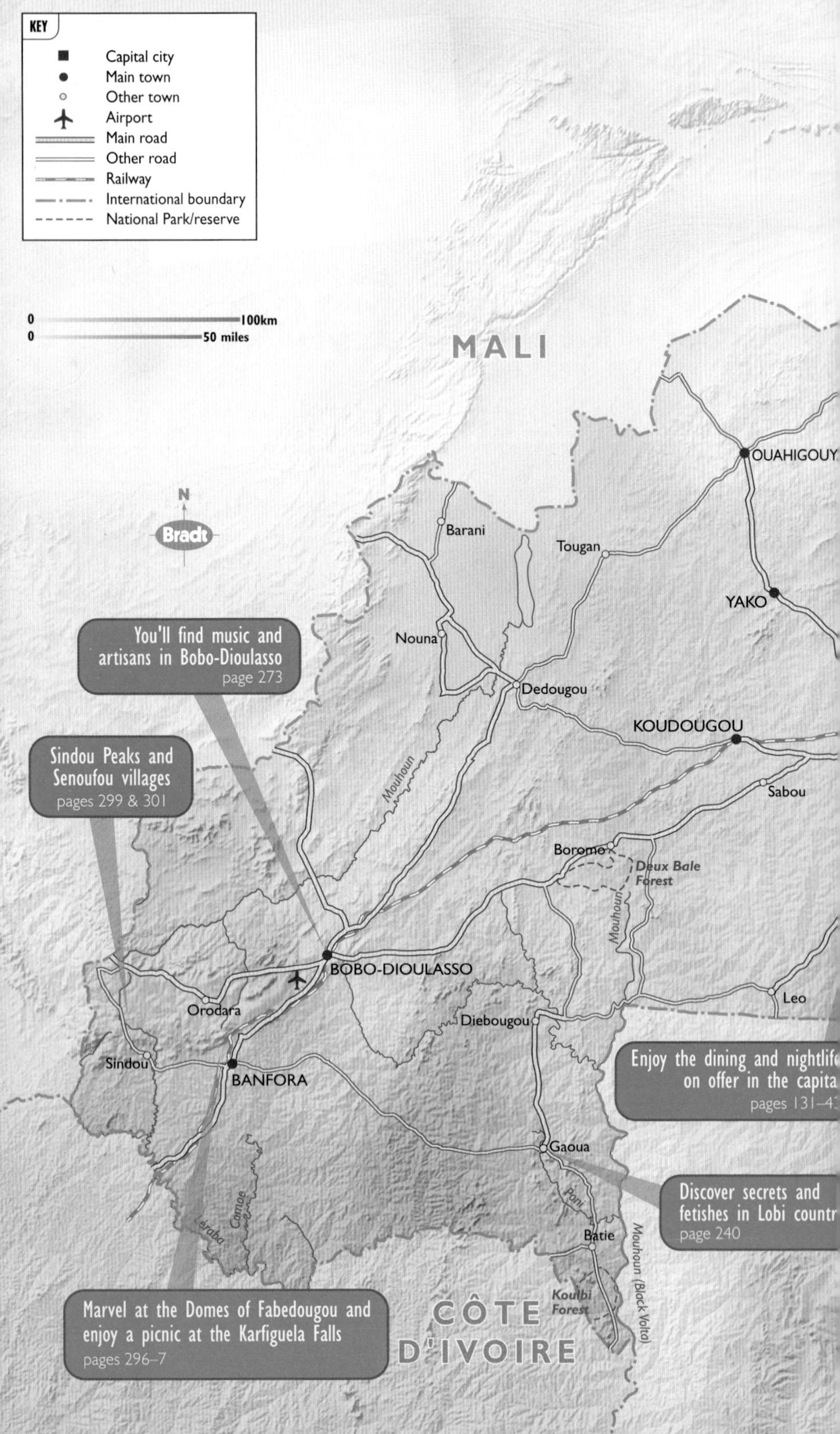
KEY
Capital city
Main town
Other town
Airport
Main road
Other road
Railway
International boundary
National Park/reserve
0 100km
0 50 miles
N
Bradt
MALI
OUAHIGOUY
Barani
Tougan
YAKO
Nouna
Dedougou
KOUDOUGOU
Sabou
Mouhoun
Boromo
Deux Bale Forest
Mouhoun
BOBO-DIOULASSO
Orodara
Leo
Diebougou
Sindou
BANFORA
Gaoua
Poni
Comoe
Léraba
Batie
Mouhoun (Black Volta)
Koulbi Forest
CÔTE D'IVOIRE
You'll find music and artisans in Bobo-Dioulasso
page 273
Sindou Peaks and Senoufou villages
pages 299 & 301
Enjoy the dining and nightlif on offer in the capita
pages 131–4
Discover secrets and fetishes in Lobi countr
page 240
Marvel at the Domes of Fabedougou and enjoy a picnic at the Karfiguela Falls
pages 296–7

Visit the colourful markets and dunes of the Sahel
page 174
Tin-Akof
Markoye
Oursi
The Sahel
GOROM-GOROM
NIGER
Dori
Take in the mud mosques at Bani
page 173
Bani
Kongoussi
Faga
NIAMEY
Kanbi
KAYA
Sirba
OUAGADOUGOU
Kantchari
Koupela
Kombissiri
FADA N'GOURMA
Tapoa
Diapaga
Tenkodogo
Garango
Oulé
W National Park
Nazinon
Arly
Reserves
Nakambe
Pama
PO
Tiebele
For wildlife parks and the stunning Gobnangou Escarpment
pages 217–220
TOGO
BENIN
GHANA
Experience romantic lakeside retreats at Pama
page 211
Take a look at Kassena housing and the Nazinga Game Ranch
pages 229 & 236

Burkina Faso Don't miss...

Market day at Oursi
One of Burkina's undiscovered pearls – a spectacular natural setting on an enormous lake, the Mare d'Oursi
(GH) page 185

Elephants bathing at Nazinga
With 800 elephants in this smallish park, be prepared for an encounter
(KM/JK) page 236

The Domes of Fabedougou
This hauntingly beautiful series of rock formations dates back 1.8 billion years
(GH) page 297

Barani's annual horse festival
Cultures from across the Sahel prove their horsemanship, and *griots* regale the village with the lineage of the visiting chiefs
(KM/JK) page 194

Geometrically painted Kassena houses
The small market town of Tiebele is the best place to see well-preserved Kassena architecture, painted by women
(GH) page 231

top left **Young girl in Dori's weekly cattle market; her facial scars denote her village of birth and social rank** (KM/JK) page 39

above left **Fulani boy: the traditionally pastoral Fulani are Burkina's second-largest group** (GH) page 40

above right **Kassena man dressed for a funeral** (SS) page 41

below **Fulani girls in northern Burkina Faso** (KM/JK) page 40

above left Mossi dancer and her baby; the Mossi account for about half the population, making them the biggest group in Burkina (KM/JK) page 39

top right Traditional archer's dress at the village of Tiakane (KM/JK) page 235

above right Bella girl: the Bella are one of several ethnic groups that live in the Sahel region (GH) page 41

below Village elders meeting up on market day, Songo (GH) page 235

top Lobi woman participating in fertility dance (SS) page 242

left Masks tend to represent ancestors, animals and spirits (KM/JK) page 100

bottom In Burkinabe society, the function of musical instruments carries deep spiritual and cultural significance (BR) page 48

AUTHORS

Katrina Manson and **James Knight** are freelance journalists and photographers. They have written for Reuters, the BBC, *The Sunday Times*, *The Economist* and *Business in Africa* magazine, among others, and their pictures have been published by the BBC, Reuters and national newspapers. They are editors on *Africa Investor*, a quarterly magazine assessing investment opportunities across the continent. Their work covers news, travel, business, technology, lifestyle, health and science, arts and culture.

UPDATER

Gill Harvey is a fiction and travel writer, and has made west Africa her second home. Her fiction has been published by Bloomsbury, Scholastic, HarperCollins, Hodder and Barrington Stoke; her travel writing by the *Independent*, *Travel Africa* magazine, Rough Guides and *B-Spirit* magazine (Brussels Airlines), as well as Bradt. Before embarking on this update she was already familiar with many countries in the region, but had never been to Burkina. It didn't disappoint. She found the Burkinabe people to be endlessly humorous and hospitable, the food delectable, the landscape beautiful and varied and the cultural talent staggering. She spends part of the year in Guinea-Bissau, but now she wishes that she'd discovered Burkina earlier.

PUBLISHER'S FOREWORD

Hilary Bradt

This is a splendid book. Until I read the manuscript, the only thing I knew about Burkina Faso was that it hosted an amazing African film festival. Now I know a lot more – and have concluded that this country must genuinely fit the cliché of 'best-kept secret'. When I'd finished reading through the manuscript I noted: 'The book has everything – a seemingly effortless writing style that is utterly professional, masses of unique information, plenty of interesting boxes, loads of insider advice, and an appropriate sensitivity to local customs as well. I really can't fault it.' And you can't get much better than that!

Second edition published October 2011 First published May 2006

Bradt Travel Guides Ltd, IDC House, The Vale, Chalfont St Peter, Bucks SL9 9RZ, England; www.bradtguides.com
Published in the USA by The Globe Pequot Press Inc,
PO Box 480, Guilford, Connecticut 06437-0480

Editorial project manager: Jen Haddington

British Library Cataloguing in Publication Data
A catalogue record for this book is available from the British Library
ISBN-13: 978 1 84162 352 8

Photographs Corbis (C): Finbarr O'Reilly/Reuters (FOR/R); Dreamstime (D): Djembe (D); Gill Harvey (GH); Christoph Herby (CH); Katrina Manson/James Knight (KM/JK); Photolibrary: Das Fotoarchiv (DF), Linear (L); Boaz Rottem (BR); SuperStock (SS)
Front cover Grand Mosque, Bobo Dioulasso (BR)
Back cover Kassena house, Tiebele (KM/JK), Smiling boy (BR)
Title page Sculpture in Place Naba Koom, Ouagadougou (BR), The road near Sindou peaks (GH), Traditional mask (D/D)

Illustrations James Knight, Katrina Manson, Annabel Milne, Carole Vincer
Maps David McCutcheon; colour relief map base by Nick Rowland FRGS

Typeset from the authors' disc by Wakewing
Production managed by Jellyfish Print Solutions and manufactured in India

Acknowledgements

SECOND EDITION

Huge thanks to Gill Harvey for her excellent updating work on this guide. She achieved amazing things on an incredibly tight schedule and budget, and her contributions, always sensitive and well judged, help understand the country more and make the guidebook better.

Two thank yous and farewells to mentors who since the first edition have gone on to other adventures. Tricia Hayne, our first commissioning editor; without you we would never have had the amazing chance to start on a journey that, in a sense, is still going. And Hilary Bradt, you were the guiding light and inspiration behind a range of guidebooks that was never afraid to let each author write without a straitjacket.

Thanks also go to: Alan Mates at Afriqiyah Airways; Flora plus motorbike; Xavier Chaniot and Hamidou; Franca and Moctar; Tiemogo Soulama; Amadou Dicko; Zachariah; Abdoulaye 'Pasteur' Ouedraogo; Nabarwe Dieudonne; Abdou 'Rasta'; Bouba 'Papa' Kambou; Drissa Sawadogo; Ali, knight on shining motorbike; Charles; Ounpoungla; Adama Sawadogo; Edem 'Winner' Assignon; the guys at Jackson, Koudougou; Seydou Traore; Richard Traore; Ibrahim ag Rissa; Ouoba Ounteni; the teacher in Diapaga; Tiemoko Ouattara; Xavier Bougma; Carlos Boutureira; Andrea Cefis; Akash Devendra; Christoph Herby; and last but by no means least, Kemba and Sal.

FIRST EDITION

Nausher Ali; Ancien, Gorom guide; Hamidou Bella; Osseni Bella; Eric, Paula, Emma and Molly Benjaminson; Janie Elliot Bini and Alessandro Bini; Ambassador Francis Blondet, Christophe Boutinout, Emilie Constable and Jean-Louis Roth at the French embassy; Judith Boyden; Sarah Chalmers and Katie Hulme at Air France; Commandant Moussa Cisse; Michelle Cormier; Daniel and Pascal, Burkinabe cinéastes extraordinaires; Korotimi Diallo; Sambo Diallo; Mohamed ag Alhatab Dicko; Dominique Dulieu; Penny and Sjon van Ee; 'Guida' Amadou Hamadou; Jennifer and Todd Haskell; Mirsad Hodzić and Selena Imeroviç; Ivan and Maria; Carla Jauregui and Frank Ayine; Keri and Tim Johnston; Gaston Kabore; Karen from Kaya; Bernadette Kuijpers and Arnold Sikking; Christopher and Merrill Knight and Elizabeth Knight; Jean-Pierre Marchive at the Ministry of Arts, Culture and Tourism; Angelique Moss; Moumouni, tennis star of tomorrow; Janet and Trash Manson; Chris Mullen; Paulina Neira-Julia; Noufou, best boutiquier in Ouagadougou; 'Showbiz' Omar; Albert Ouedraogo; Idrissa Ouedraogo; Karim Ouedraogo; Kassim Ouedraogo, young gentleman; Christoph Pelzer and Cecile

Tassin; Matthieu Petit; Andrea Reikat and Sadou Sidibe; Alassane Ida and Akim Sawadogo; Djibril Sawadogo; Souleyman and Osseini; Eva Stoffels, kindest of readers; Giri Tapsoba; Ben Idrissa Tarnagda; Sekou Traore; Ahmed and Issa at Verdoyant; Victor, Eric, Anouk and Dominique, diplomatic drinking companions; Maurice de Villepin and OK Raids; John Warehand at Inmarsat; Roger Wilson; Senator Marc Yao; Paul Young, George Magson and Charlie D-H; Siaka (Veille) Zerbo and all the strangers who found time for a kind word.

Many thanks too for the generous loan of hardy and high-tech equipment (laptops, cameras and satellite modem), books, maps and flights from: Air Afriqiyah, Air France, Casio, IBM, Inmarsat, ITMB Maps, James Currey Publishers, Pentax, Sony Corporation, Stanfords.

AUTHORS' STORY

Katrina had wanted to go to Ouagadougou ever since she was nine. On attempting to learn all the capitals of the world, none sung out with as much charm, mystery and beauty as the vowel-tastic centre of Upper Volta (the ancient map, stuck to the bedroom wall, recorded only Burkina's old colonial name).

More than a few years and several airport tequilas later, off we were to this magic land. The more we read up on the country, the harder we found it to believe that so few people had heard of it, let alone visited. Several of our friends thought we were going not to Burkina Faso, but to a place called Bikini Fastener. One artistic and supportive soul even made a T-shirt reading 'Haven't you heard of Burkina Faso?' to jolt London's busy passing streetwalkers into cognisance. A couple of months in, when we celebrated New Year's with mojitos at a street cafe in the tongue-twisting capital that was now our home, we knew we had found somewhere special.

Part of the anonymity of Burkina arises because it is not full of checklist tourism – the kind of spectacular one-off attractions or feats that act as international calling cards. It does not have Mali's Bandiagara Escarpment, Uganda's gorillas or Botswana's Okavango Delta. This is also its greatest strength. The infancy of the tourist industry means there is a remarkable absence of barriers between you and anything you come across. The hypnotic, breathtaking dances and frantic contortions of a mask festival, for example, are not put on for the benefit of visitors – they exist for the village, and the ancestors.

Many a memory stays with us, like turning up at an unknown village and sleeping on a roof instead of under one, canvassed by the stars. Or the way a game of table football on virtually any street corner acts as an icebreaker. And the taste of perfectly cooked garlic chicken as you watch couples on an open-air dancefloor accompany the night-time into the early hours.

When we first started this project there was no 'trail', meaning we had to make up the rules as we went along. The good news is so will you. No wonder another pal thought BF stood for Bloody Fantastic.

Contents

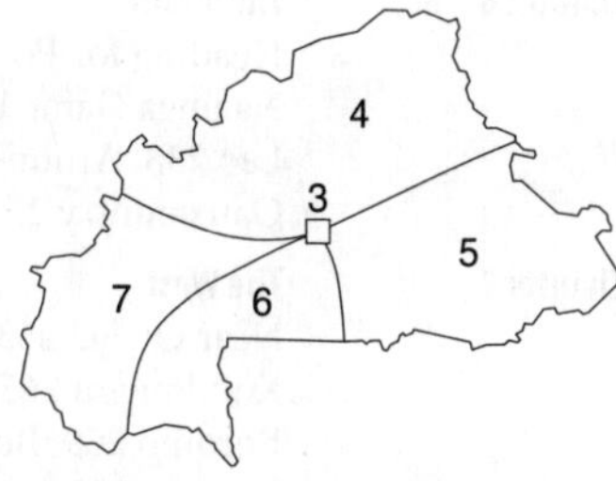

LIST OF MAPS

Introduction

The Land of Honourable Men (the translation of Burkina Faso) has a nobility borne from much more than its name. It comes from a shared identity that unites 60 ethnic groups in religious and social harmony, a love of talk and tradition, and a sense of hospitality that embraces the enthusiastic and the curious. Unrest in the first half of 2011 means that travellers to the country will have to be more wary than they have needed to be in the past, and at the time of writing it is difficult to know what will happen.

Celebration through art is something of a mantra here. Burkina's long relationship with cinema has given birth to the magnificent biennial film festival Fespaco, the Cannes of Africa, and the craft fair SIAO. Both are the largest events of their kind on the continent. However, Burkina does much more than one-off events. Its cultural traditions are still alive today: throughout the year live venues will struggle with the dodgy local electricity supply to pump out music for as long as there is anyone left to dance; galleries will spring up in restaurants and houses to showcase the work of up-and-coming contemporary artists; craftsmen on the side of the road will practise and cherish the artisanal secrets passed onto them by their fathers and grandfathers; new troupes will organise their own festivals to portray their updates on sacred mask dances; and bronze workers will shape their wares in the ashes of a village compound.

Firmly held links with the past lead to a fantastic variety of beliefs, practices, dress and even architecture: small, rounded, earthen homes tucked into the cliffs of the Senoufou; brick-like windowless fortresses of the Lobi; Mossi round huts capped with straw; brightly decorated death-traps of the Kassena; and bulging Sudanic mud mosques stuck with wood as if under the acupunctural care of the gods. To the north, there is the romance and heat of the semi-desert Sahel, home to nomadic herders. You can watch furious trading at camel and cattle markets and sleep in open-sided Tuareg tents, or lie among dunes under the stars.

On the subject of landscape, we'd read books, guidebooks even, that said Burkina was flat, dry and boring. Look hard and you'll find domes, crags, waterfalls, escarpments and lakes. Its savanna scrub is home to the largest number of elephants in west Africa, and nose-to-trunk encounters with the big grey beasts in its parks and reserves are common. Game is on the increase and wildlife viewing is as good as anywhere in the region, with hippo, antelope, crocodile, warthog, baboon and monkey easily spotted. Lion, leopard and, exceptionally, cheetah are harder to spot, but nevertheless present.

Village life remains at the heart of the country and centuries-old practices are easily glimpsed: karite nuts crushed until they ooze the cosmetic magic of shea butter; the first taste of freshly brewed millet beer; goatskin hides pegged on washing lines to dry.

There's no need to be intimidated by the language barrier, either. Yes, you will need at least basic French to get the most out of Burkina, but none of your efforts will go unrewarded. And forget any stereotypes you may have of linguistic snootiness here – there'll be a warm welcome for any efforts to engage and a few Burkinabe twists on the language along the way.

The country gives the independent traveller the chance to be just that – independent. There is no tourist trail, no tyranny of the 'must see'. If you want to visit a goldmine, or track down some hidden cave paintings, scale a nearby hill for sunrise or find a village of exceptional potters, then it's down to you. Sound out local information, get hold of a moped, and just go.

NOTE ABOUT MAPS

Several maps use grid lines to allow easy location of sites. Map grid references are listed in square brackets after listings in the text, with page number followed by grid number, eg: [110 C3].

UPDATES WEBSITE AND FEEDBACK REQUEST

Every effort has been made to ensure that the details contained within this book are as accurate and up to date as possible. Inevitably, however, things move on. Any information regarding such changes, or relating to your experiences in Burkina Faso – good or bad – would be very gratefully received. Such feedback is priceless when compiling further editions, and in ensuring a pleasant stay for future visitors. So if you have any comments, queries, grumbles, insights, news or other feedback please contact us on 01753 893444 or e info@bradtguides.com. Alternatively you can add a review of the book to www.bradtguides.com or Amazon.

Periodically our authors post travel updates and reader feedback on the website. Check www.bradtguides.com/guidebook-updates for any news.

Part One

GENERAL INFORMATION

BURKINA FASO AT A GLANCE

Location Lies on Greenwich meridian, between 9°N and 15°N
Neighbouring countries Clockwise from north – Mali, Niger, Benin, Togo, Ghana, Côte d'Ivoire
Size 274,200km^2
Climate Hot. The dry season runs from October to February, with temperatures of 29°C in October–November, falling to the year-round low of 25°C in January, before beginning the ascent to 32°C from March to May, although temperatures in the north can reach beyond 45°C. The rainy season runs intermittently from June to September, with heaviest rainfalls in August.
Status Parliamentary republic
Population 16.7 million (2011)
Capital Ouagadougou (1.5 million)
Other main towns Banfora, Bobo-Dioulasso (second city), Dori, Fada N'Gourma, Gaoua, Gorom-Gorom, Kaya, Koudougou, Ouahigouya, Po, Yako
Life expectancy 53.7 years
GDP US$8.6 billion
Languages French is the official language; Moore, Dioula and Fulfulde are national languages; there are dozens more local languages
Religion Animist; Muslim; Christian
Currency Communauté Financière d'Afrique (CFA) franc, also used by Benin, Guinea-Bissau, Côte d'Ivoire, Mali, Niger, Senegal and Togo and pegged at 656f to the euro
National airline and airport Air Burkina, Ouagadougou International Airport
International telephone code +226
Time GMT
Electricity 220V
Weights and measures metric
Flag Two horizontal bands, of red and green, united by a five-pointed gold star in the middle
National motto Unity, Progress, Justice
Public holidays 1 January (New Year), 3 January (Soulèvement Populaire, also known as SOUL POP), 8 March (Women's Day), March/April (Easter Monday), 1 May (Worker's Day), May (Ascension Thursday), 5 August (Proclamation of Independence/National Day), 15 August (Assumption), 1 November (All Saints' Day), 11 December (Proclamation of the Republic), 25 December (Christmas Day).

1

Background Information

GEOGRAPHY

Burkina Faso is a landlocked country, about the size of Colorado, between 9°N and 15°N latitude. It borders Mali to the north and west, with Niger to the north and east. To the southeast lies Benin and Togo; Ghana lies directly south and Côte d'Ivoire is situated to the southwest.

The popular perception of Burkina Faso's 274,000km² is its unrelenting flatness. There can be times, as one gazes out across the scrubby central plain that makes up three-quarters of the country, that this may seem true. Half the land lies between 250m and 350m above sea level, with a maximum variation across the country of 600m. The central plateau gives way to gentle hills, and occasionally granitic inselbergs.

A large sandstone massif occupies the southwest of the country, rising to 150m between Bobo-Dioulasso and Banfora. This culminates in Burkina's highest peak, Mt Tenakourou, which rises to a slightly undizzying height of 749m. Where the massif loses its rectilinear form towards the Malian border, bulbous rocky outcrops reach upwards like fleshy fingers pushing towards the sky. In the southeast, the smaller Gobnangou massif rises to around 100m, dominating the central plateau for a distance of 90km.

RIVERS Burkina's rivers belong to three basins. The largest and most important is the Volta basin, which stretches over 120,000km² from the centre to the west of the country, and gave Burkina its colonial name Haute-Volta (Upper Volta). This contains three principal rivers. The Mouhoun, formerly known as the Black Volta, originates on the north face of the Banfora Escarpment, flowing northeast before doubling back sharply north of Dedougou to begin the long, slow-flowing path south to feed into Lake Volta, in central Ghana. The Nakambe (previously the White Volta) rises east of Ouahigouya, crosses the Mossi Plateau north to south and feeds into the lakes around Kaya before continuing into Ghana. The Nazinon (previously the Red Volta) originates northwest of Ouagadougou and merges with the Nakambe in northern Ghana.

Like the Mouhoun, the Comoe rises in the Banfora Escarpment and takes a dramatic path south to Côte d'Ivoire, interrupted by falls, rapids and perennial pools such as Lake Tengrela. The surface area of its basin is 18,000km². Finally, the 72,000km² of the Niger basin takes in the small, seasonal rivers in the northeast of Burkina Faso, such as the Beli, which feed into its downward course after the Niger bend.

The major lakes in Burkina are Lake Bam, near Koungoussi; Lake Bagre, between Tenkodogo and Zabre; and Lake Kompienga, close to Pama.

CLIMATE

West Africa does not really have weather, in the sense of the daily changes experienced in temperate regions. It has climate instead, created by enormous air masses shifted by global forces across the region as a whole. Burkina sits across three climatic zones, which experience a decline in rainfall and shorter wet season as one moves from south to north. The **Sudano-Guinean zone** covers the southwestern bulge of the country that extends towards Côte d'Ivoire. This is the wettest part of the country, where the rainy season runs for a full six months from May to October, with maximum rainfall of up to 1,300mm a year. The **Sudano-Sahelian zone** is the largest climatic region, covering half of Burkina's surface area, and generally receives between 600 and 1,000mm of rain each year. Here the rains tend to finish slightly earlier, in September. The **Sahelian zone**, situated in the northernmost quarter of the country, is the driest region of all, seeing as little as 150mm of rain each year. Although the arid semi-desert of the Sahel currently covers 25% of the country, it is reckoned to be encroaching by 5–10cm each year, as overexploitation of the land and the destruction of plant cover, coupled with worrying trends in overall global warming, hasten the onset of desertification.

Generally speaking, landlocked Burkina escapes the debilitating humidity of its coastal neighbours, although daily temperatures tend to be slightly higher, averaging around 35°C. During the cooler periods, the temperature can drop sharply at night, down to as low as 5°C in the Sahel. In general, count on temperatures rarely falling below 30°C. In the dry season, the major metereological feature, apart from the unrelenting heat (which can hit 45°C), is the Harmattan wind, which blows from the northeast, bringing with it the sand of the Sahara. This peaks in February and early March, with the sun becoming completely obscured on some days.

Despite uniformly high temperatures, there are a number of seasonal variations, although these vary slightly between the three climatic zones.

EARLY DRY SEASON (SEPTEMBER–NOVEMBER) Following a period of sustained rainfall, rivers are usually full and flowing strongly, vegetation is lush, and there is still a touch of humidity in the air. This is also harvest time, and the quantity of rainfall will determine the stock for the year ahead.

MID DRY SEASON (DECEMBER–FEBRUARY) A layer of cool, dry air arrives suddenly from the northeast (the Harmattan), bringing clear days with little humidity and cool nights. This is what the Burkinabe call winter, digging out bulky overcoats and bobble hats in temperatures that would do a European summer proud. As the season wears on the Harmattan brings dust from the Sahara and by the end of February, remaining water sources are beginning to dry out. As the harvest period comes to an end, this is also generally the time of important cultural celebrations, of masks and dancing, marriages, feasts and baptisms, as time and temperature allow for a period of thanks for the year past and planning for the year ahead.

LATE DRY SEASON (MARCH–MAY) The hottest, toughest period of the year, when temperatures regularly top 40°C. The Harmattan reaches its zenith in March, before retreating to the Sahara, leaving a stillness that is oppressive and debilitating. Occasional fronts of humid air, outriders of the approaching monsoon, bring sweet but temporary relief with what is known as the *pluie des mangues* (mango rains), most notably in the southwest. Towards May reservoirs have reached rock bottom; frequent power cuts and the introduction of water rationing are common.

WET SEASON (JUNE–SEPTEMBER) The monsoon front arrives slowly from the southwest, bringing with it much-needed rain, to a land that is by now gasping. Winds can reach up to 120km/h at the start and end of the wet season as the monsoon front advances and recedes. Some villages can remain untouched by rain, however, while others a few kilometres away will be well watered. After a month or so the monsoon season becomes established, signalling frequent rain, often in the late afternoon. The change in the landscape is dramatic, as scratchy-looking land explodes in a profusion of colour and life. A rich green carpet of annual meadow grass rolls out across hills and valleys, almost literally overnight, and perennial grasses grow to over head height. Fields of maize, millet and sorghum start to shoot upwards. Insect populations, particularly mosquitoes, take advantage of large pools of standing water to breed profusely. Local incidence of cholera and diarrhoea also increases. This is the most important and intensive agricultural period. Entire villages can seem deserted as all but the most elderly and infirm are out in the fields planting.

NATURAL HISTORY

PLANT LIFE Vegetation can be divided into three zones, which roughly correspond to climatic variations. Plant cover is generally sparse, and steppes, savanna or open woodland tends to predominate. Following is a brief overview of some of the most common trees and plants. The Latin binomials are given not to confuse or bamboozle, but simply as backup for the avid naturalist, as any plant guide is likely to be in French and it will help referencing between English and French.

The harsh conditions of the Sahelian domain mean that small trees and shrubs dot the landscape, the most common of which is the **gum tree**, *Acacia senegal*. Its sticky residue is still used in paper-making, cooking and the pharmaceutical industry today. The **jujube**, *Ziziphus mauritania*, produces a sweet fruit beloved by Fulani and Tuareg, and pastors. Of spiritual and material importance are the gnarled branches of the **baobab**, *Adansonia digitata*, which are a regular sight in the region of Djibo and Aribinda. Virtually every part of the tree has a purpose. The fruit, known as **monkey bread**, hangs down in enormous oval sacs, and its sweet, slightly acidic pulp provides a welcome sugar jolt; the calcium-rich leaves are used in both cooking and traditional medicine, and fibres from the bark are employed to make baskets and twine. **Wild fonio**, *Panicum laetum*, is a type of common grass that can be eaten in times of drought.

The Sudano-Sahelian zone contains many of the 'trademark' trees of Burkina, none more important than the **karite**, *Butyrospermum parkii*. Shea butter, extracted from the fruit of the *karite* tree, is used in cooking or eaten raw, and both butter and oil are used in the cosmetics industry, locally and abroad. Rich in vitamins A, D, E and F, it protects and softens the skin without being greasy. The wood is particularly resistant to termites and used in construction and to make *djembe* drums. The fruit of the beautiful **nere**, *Parkia biglobosa*, is beloved of young children, while its seeds form the basis of *soumbala*, used to flavour *tô* and sauces. The **mango tree** and the **tamarind** both provide wonderful respite from the heat of the day with their thick canopies and plentiful fruit. The **caïcédrat**, *Khaya senegalensis*, is found towards the south of the region, and favoured by carpenters for building furniture and canoes.

Much of the open woodland that once made up vast tracts of the Sudanian zone has given way to savanna, owing to widespread deforestation by the Mossi population. The **Senegalese rosewood**, *Pterocarpus erinaceus*, and the **afzelia**, *Afzelia africana*, are still found, although the **siiga**, *Anogeissus leiocarpus*, is the most widespread species.

SAFARI TIME

For anyone prepared to swallow their preconceptions, armed with a spirit of adventure, west Africa offers some of the most unusual wilderness safaris in the world.

'What you lack in tourist infrastructure you gain by the authenticity of the game environment and the fact that you can get really, really close to the animals,' says Eric Benjaminson, a 45-year-old American veteran of west African safaris. 'Also, they are not overwhelmed by visitors.'

He draws a telling contrast. 'When I went on safari in Namibia, I always had the feeling that giraffes were walking out of the bush at us because the next truck along would be throwing giraffe treats at them. They seemed habituated.

'Here it's real. You can see elephants and they trumpet and protect their young and do all the things you would expect. At night here you need a flashlight, not to pick your way through the gravel path, but to see the elephant that's in the shadows.'

He admits that the standard of accommodation will come as a culture shock to those accustomed to tented-camp luxury. 'Basic' is most definitely a watchword.

But the service cannot be faulted. 'Like everything else in Burkina everyone is really nice. No-one is trying to rip you off. You can also hire a guide without booking in advance, they are very knowledgeable, and there's a clear tariff list of prices.'

As for authenticity: 'We got to the gate at Nazinga and got asked if we could give a young woman a lift at the nearest big town. We ended up with six guineafowl in the back that she was going to sell to market.'

Burkina's fledgling safari industry still faces problems. Poaching is constant – often simply as a source of meat for villagers during lean times. While visitors may have to wait for robust structures, tarmac roads, fully trained guides and palatial camps, the surface drawbacks are also the pulls that make a safari in Burkina so exciting. There are fewer rules, and often you have to track animals to see them, making it much more satisfying.

In the southwest, the Sudano-Guinean zone contains the most luxurious foliage and the greatest variety of plants, including many ligneous species. Forest galleries are a prominent feature. Palms include the **oil palm**, *Elaeis guineensis*, and the **ronier**, *Borassus aethiopum*, which in the regions around Banfora and Gaoua is heavily tapped for its palm wine, and also used in weaving.

In the southernmost reaches of Burkina, pockets of ancient dry dense forest, such as the forest of Koulbi near Batie, have microclimatic conditions similar to equatorial rainforest and include the **iroko**, *Chlorophora excelsa*. They line perennial rivers and permanently humid valleys.

WILDLIFE There are not the same opportunities for game viewing in Burkina that exist in the savanna of eastern or southern Africa. There are fewer animals, and the nature of the vegetation means that those animals are more difficult to spot. Nevertheless, its parks and reserves offer some of the best and most exciting opportunities in west Africa, and Burkina has four of the traditional Big Five (elephant, buffalo, lion and leopard).

Burkina is blessed with one cross-border national park, W, which contains the bulk of the best game, including six endangered species. The Arly Reserve has slid from what it once was, but the tracks through the park are receiving attention and the range of animals is good. Along with W and Pendjari park in Benin, it will be getting a chunk of EU funding over the next few years. The Nazinga Ranch and Deux Bale park, both within easy reach of the capital, offer a high likelihood of spotting elephant, and the former contains a magnificent selection of antelope. There are also 23 hunting zones throughout Burkina, with the majority in the east of the country bordering either Arly or W. Safari visitors are also welcome in these private reserves.

There are a few animals that will not be found in Burkina, including black and white rhinoceros, wildebeest, giraffe and zebra, and large primates such as gorilla and chimpanzee.

The groupings below are not taxonomically accurate, but we have tried to group animals loosely according to a combination of 'excitement value', regularity of occurrence and habitat.

Larger predators The **lion**, *Panthera leo*, never fails to set the pulse racing. W National Park is the best place to see one, although they are also present in Arly, and tracks have been found in Nazinga. The distinctive roar, often emitted at dawn and dusk to mark territory, can carry for 8km. Despite their reputation, lions are in fact incredibly lazy, sleeping for up to 20 hours a day, so your best bet for spotting them is on the hunt very early in the morning, or under trees in the afternoon. In traditional medicine, boiled lion bones are used to strengthen the bones of children.

Robust and elegant, the **leopard**, *Panthera pardus*, is a master hunter and a rare spot in W National Park. The best bet is around watering holes, as leopards drink frequently. Shy and elusive, the leopard prefers to hunt at night with its excellent sense of smell and hearing. During the day it retires to the shade and shelter of treetops or rocks, to rest or eat, and can haul carcasses of up to 120kg into the treetops. Leopards are not fussy eaters, most likely hunting primates or bush-pig, small antelope or carnivores, birds and their eggs, and reptiles. It is distinguishable from the cheetah by a slightly heavier, stockier build, and by its distinctive patterning, which consist of broken black circles enclosing smaller yellow circles.

Leopard

W National Park is the last refuge of the **cheetah**, *Acinonyx jubatus hecki*, in west Africa, although the chances of an encounter are slim. Diurnal, they hunt in the morning and the early evening, or occasionally under a full moon, and like to lounge at the base of trees during the hotter hours. The fastest animal on earth, reaching 100km/h in only a few seconds, the cheetah relies on speed and stealth, getting as close as possible to its prey before pouncing. It cannot maintain its speed over long distances and needs half an hour to regain its breath fully. Easily confused with the leopard, the cheetah has a much smaller head, a more streamlined build, a coat of black spots and distinctive black 'tear tracks' running from the eyes down either side of the muzzle.

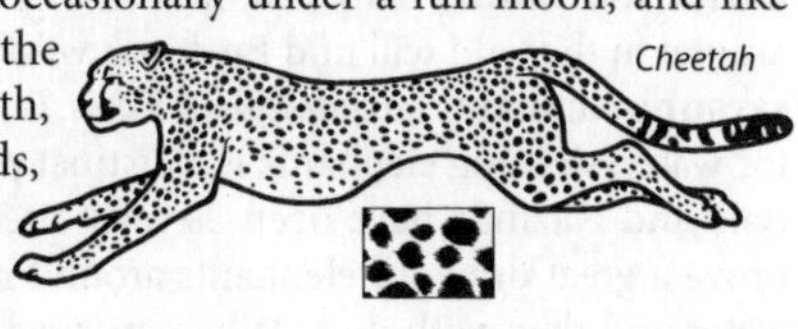

Cheetah

A dirty yellow coat, marked by irregular spots, long neck and sharply sloping back give the **spotted hyena**, *Crocuta crocuta*, a distinctive silhouette. Although mainly nocturnal, it is seen occasionally in W during daylight hours, grouped either in couples or in packs of eight to 20, with the stronger, larger female hyenas in charge. With a reputation for rather ignoble habits, particularly a fondness for carrion, the hyena is extremely well adapted to its environment, with a resistance to the toxins present in putrifying meat. While they will occasionally steal prey from other carnivores, hyenas are also fearsome hunters of live prey.

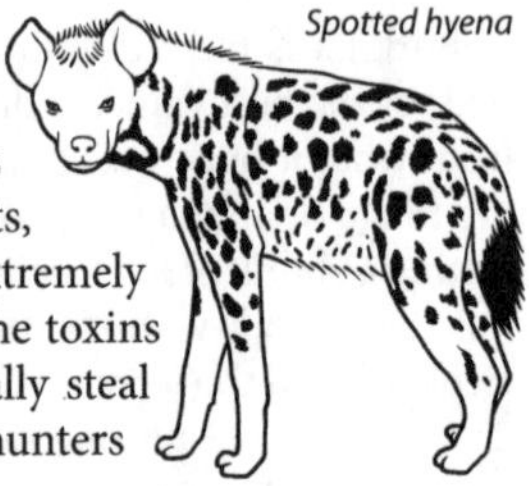

Spotted hyena

With only 3,000–6,000 left in Africa, the **African wild dog**, *Lycaon pictus*, is one of the continent's most endangered species, and has been hunted almost to extinction in west Africa. At least one pack survives in W. By nature highly sociable, they are organised into packs as large as 90, although 20 is more normal, and recognisable by a splodgy coat of black, cream and beige, and large rounded ears. They tend to attack small game such as gazelle and oribi. Extremely hardy and tough, the hunt has a terrible inevitability, as the dogs identify an isolated herd member and chase it to exhaustion before bringing it down.

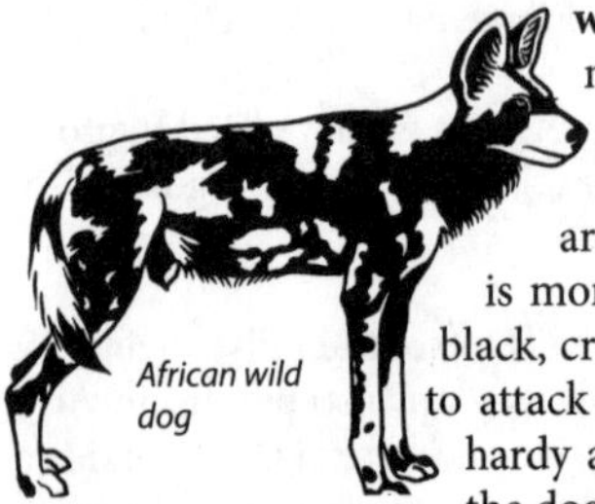

African wild dog

The **common** or **golden jackal**, *Canis aureus*, is slightly larger than the rare **side-striped jackal**, *Canis adustus*, and much more likely to be seen, most often towards the end of the day at watering holes. They share an omnivorous diet, although the latter usually only comes out at night. Common jackals often hunt antelope in pairs, one distracting the mother so that she charges while the other picks off the unprotected juvenile. Both species look conspicuously dog-like, but with enlarged ears and bushy tails. The side-striped jackal is recognisable by a white and black streak running along its flanks. Despite being relatively common, the beautiful **pale** or **sand fox**, *Vulpes pallida*, is a little-seen hunter, slightly smaller than the jackal.

With its distinctive, sleekly pointed ears, the **caracal** or **African lynx**, *Caracal caracal*, resembles a large cat. Discreet and solitary, it is considered rare in west Africa and usually hunts at night. Slightly larger but lighter, the **serval cat**, *Leptailurus serval*, is similarly elusive, with rounder ears and a spotted coat and striped tail.

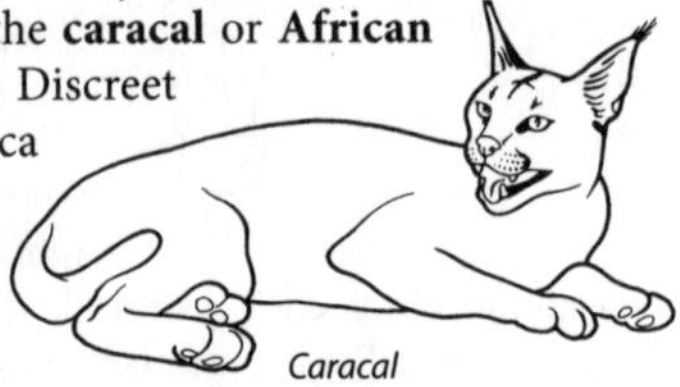

Caracal

Other mammals Any visitor with high hopes of seeing the world's largest land animal in the wild will find Burkina's wildlife parks a common home to the **bush** or **savanna elephant**, *Loxodonta africana*. Because of their regular habits and fondness for water, sighting elephants is a distinct possibility, especially since camps at Deux Bale and Nazinga have been cleverly sited around popular watering holes. These prove a great draw for elephants around midday when they come to cool off, with water and then with dust. When enraged, elephants will first charge to intimidate their adversary, with ears out, trunk raised and tusks down, although 90% of the time they will stop short. The second time, with tusks raised, will be to kill. Do not approach females with young calves too closely, as they are easily angered protecting their young. Hunting of elephants is prohibited in all three countries of W National Park, although around a dozen are estimated to be poached each year. Although there is a ban on ivory, elephants are also important in traditional medicine – in Burkina, elephant sperm is used to counter sterility, and the skin is used to improve physical endurance. Adults can consume up to 200kg of foliage each day and can drink up to 300l of water. Old males are often found wandering alone, although normally elephants form herds of ten to 100. Within these, the females with the youngest calves (one to five years) are placed under the command of a matriarch, while the males tend to patrol the outside of the herd.

As the name suggests, the **dwarf** or **red buffalo**, *Syncerus caffer brachyceros*, is smaller than its cousin of the east African savanna, and more reddish-brown in colour, resembling a fearsomely well-built, short-legged cow with sharply curling horns. Occasionally seen in groups of three to 20 under the shade of trees during the hottest hours, the best time for a sighting is at the beginning or end of the day as they make their way to water. When hurt or angered, buffalos charge readily, and can occasionally become spontaneously bad-tempered at dusk.

The **common warthog**, *Phacochoerus africanus*, is a common and comical sight across the gameparks of Burkina, with its pert little trot, protruding tusks and upturned tail like a radio antenna. Warthogs, so-called because of the growths on their faces, generally organise in family groups consisting of a father, mother and one or two youngsters, while older and juvenile males are solitary. Unperturbed by the approach of vehicles, it is sometimes possible to approach them quite closely. Their main predators are lion and leopard.

Warthog

Antelope The magnificent **roan antelope**, *Hippotragus equinus koba*, is the largest antelope in this part of west Africa, and Burkina has the highest concentration. In addition to graceful, gently curving horns, its coat, ranging from reddish-grey to yellow-brown, lengthens to a mane around its neck. Males have a black face, with white eye patches and snout; this is lighter on females. Sharpened horns have been used in scarification by numerous ethnic groups.

Roan antelope

The **western hartebeest**, *Alcelaphus buselaphus major*, is easily recognised by a long, horse-like face with a white chevron across the eyes that gives it the appearance of wearing glasses. Its athletic body, ranging in colour from reddish to sandy brown, and sloping back are also distinctive, and it tends to evade predators by running in a zig-zag fashion. The hartebeest is relatively common in the parks of Burkina, grazing in groups of five to 15, and often found around other antelope.

The **topi** or **Senegal hartebeest**, *Damaliscus lunatus korrigum*, is superficially similar to the western hartebeest, but sports much longer, strongly swept-back horns and a large black splodge above its hind haunches, over a rusty brown, almost pinkish coat. Groups are formed into harems, with single males taking up to 20 mates. Another species threatened with extinction, it is fully protected within W National Park.

Despite its timidity, the **oribi**, *Ourebia ourebia quadriscopa*, is easily observed, and enormous ears and eyes on top of a petite, elegant frame make it a Bambi lookalike. Often mingling with herds of larger antelope for protection, the male oribi will also turn to attack predators in an attempt to allow mothers and offspring to make their escape.

The powerful, elegant outline of the **western Buffon's kob**, *Kobus (Adenota) kob kob*, and the beautifully curving horns on the male, make it one of the most attractive members of the antelope family. It is also the most commonly occurring antelope species in Burkina, usually found close to watering holes throughout the day. The **Bohor reedbuck**, *Redunca redunca*, is often confused with the western Buffon's kob, although it is smaller, with a slighter form. Populations have been in decline in Burkina for the past few years, although it can still be seen in W.

Bushbuck

The **bushbuck**, *Tragelaphus scriptus scriptus*, is a fairly regular sighting in Nazinga and W, particularly around watering holes at the end of the day. Two prominent, complementary white stripes sweep its flanks, criss-crossed by finer vertical white stripes and white spots around the hind flanks. The squarely built **Defassa waterbuck**, *Kobus ellipsiprymnus defassa*, is also common, distinguished by its cow-like head and a

KNOW YOUR AGBA FROM YOUR DINDISGA

Now you have the English names, and the Latin binomials. In the Burkinabe bush, however, these are unlikely to count for much, as your guide will probably only know the French, or even a local word, for the animals of the west African savanna, if that. So below are French, Moore, Gourmanche (most useful in W and Arly since they're in the east) and Fulfulde names as well (in that order). Next time you hear your guide shouting 'wobgo', you'll know to get out of the way.

LARGER PREDATORS
African wild cat – *chat sauvage d'Afrique, chat de Libye* or *chat ganté; wegnouga; ki mudiga; genefeneru*
caracal or **African lynx** – *caracal* or *Lynx africain; dindisga; pyapebri; safandu*
cheetah – *guépard; dindisga; dyulali; marukopta*
hunting dog – *lycaon, cynhyène* or *chien chasseur; digdingnidiga* or *gingembaga; o fwasangbanlo; dondu* or *mbohu*
hyena – *hyena; katre* or *swasa* or *naniri; o namunu; fowru*
jackal – *chacal; webaga; tambwaga; kongoru* or *sundu-kongoru*
leopard – *léopard* or *panthère; abga; o gambo; kyirgu* or *dobbu*
lion – *lion; guigemde* or *bongnega; o yangbalo; biladde* or *rawandu ladde*
pale fox – *renard pale; wagha; fwabwaga; wagaru*
serval – *serval; sulufu; tyoromwanli; musurou lade*

OTHER MAMMALS
buffalo – *buffle; wenafo* or *padre; monwa; eda* or *m'bana*
elephant – *elephant; wobgo; o luomo; gniwa*
warthog – *phacochère; we reogo; fwadwolo; guirho* or *gadduru ladde*

ANTELOPE
Bohor reedbuck – *rédunca* or *nago* or *cobe des roseaux; beko; o gubo; mbillal*
bushbuck – *guib harnaché; gneogo; o twabro; dyabatiwa*
duiker – *céphalophe; gnismiga; bwalmwandiga; yabadiguel*
gazelle – *gazelle; nyaka; o pyacarbwano* or *o pwagnogo; leula*

white band circling its nose. A strong swimmer, this antelope is never far from water and will not hesitate to dive in if under attack.

The **grey (common) duiker**, *Sylvicapra grimmia*, with a vertical black band running along its snout and brow, is more commonly seen than its smaller relative, the **red-flanked duiker**, *Cephalophus rufilatus*. Both are most active in the early morning and late afternoon, but the grey duiker is unique among the antelope in occasionally eating guineafowl and francolin.

Common duiker

Found in the northern reaches of W, but also in Nazinga, the **red-fronted gazelle**, *Gazella rufifrons rufifrons*, is much rarer than on the plains of east Africa. It has been overhunted in west Africa, and the scrubland it inhabits has disappeared. A prominent black stripe between the haunches marks it out.

Small mammals Other carnivores include the **African civet**, *Civettictis civetta*, the **African wild cat**, *Felis silvestris libyca*, the **common genet**, *Genetta genetta*

oribi – *ourébi; walaga; o pyapyeno; dyabare* or *dyabagoude*
roan antelope – *hippotrague* or *antelope cheval* or *koba; wilpelogo* or *walpelogo; o kwa; koba*
topi – *damalisque; sib sablega;* n/a; *luindu*
waterbuck – *cobe defassa; webwanga* or *burugumdi; o djibri-bwano; yabakiwa*
western Buffon's kob – *cobe de buffon; monofo; o pyamwano; m'badde*
western hartebeest – *bubale; sibga; li kabro mwanli; dadi* or *daoura*

SMALL MAMMALS
aardvark – *oryctérope; tanturi; o balmando; hyendu*
porcupine – *porc-épic; syemde; o gnano; sangalde*
honey badger – *ratel;* n/a; n/a; *dagamere*
hare – *lièvre; swamba; dyakpewonga* or *dyapelga; wodyerhe*
rock hyrax – *daman de rocher; marawa; dyamabrhi; djabalawdere*
Senegal bush baby – *galago du Sénégal; lwanfulugu; o lando; armanga*
African civet – *civette; parignego; o tumbagu; wudyukuru*
genet – *genette; piffo; kpenmwanga* or *kpebwango; fifyo* or *ngusuru-lade*

PRIMATES
baboon – *baboun* or *cynocéphale; wam miga; o kpado* or *kpwaro; wandounkoru* or *wandubaleru*
green or **tantalus monkey** – *singe vert* or *tantale; puguwamba; gmankadaga; wandu*
red or **patas monkey** – *singe rouge; wam miga; o gwalmo; wanduwoderu*

WATER DWELLERS
crocodile – *crocodile, caiman*
hippopotamus – *hippopotame; yemde; o libo; ngabu* or *gabbu*
manatee – *lamantin;* n/a; n/a; *emsiel*
otter – *loutre;* n/a; n/a; *bossaru n'diyam*
tortoise – *tortue*

African civet

senegalensis, and the **large-spotted genet**, *Genetta maculata*. All of these are principally nocturnal and rarely seen during the day, with the occasional exception of the civet at sunset. On a night safari, however, the chances of seeing all of them go up, and the African wild cat even likes the rubbish bins around the camps in W and Arly.

The **ratel** or **honey badger**, *Mellivora capensis*, is another little-known nocturnal predator. Powerfully built and low to the ground, it has developed a partnership with the honey guide, also known as the indicator bird, *Indicator indicator*, which will direct it to honey with its calls and behaviour. The ratel is a good climber and can destroy a bees' nest with its sharp claws, protected from the fury of their stings by its thick skin and coat.

There are four species of mongoose in Burkina: the **Egyptian** or **large grey mongoose**, *Herpestes ichneumon*; the solitary **white-tailed mongoose**, *Ichneumia albicauda*; the **marsh mongoose**, *Atilax paludinosus*; and the **red mongoose**, *Galerella sanguinea*. Of these, the Egyptian and red mongoose are the most easily spotted on account of their diurnal habits, the latter often in tree branches. Known for its exceptional ability to hunt snakes, the mongoose has to rely on its speed and endurance to wear down the reptiles, as it has poor resistance to venom.

The **striped polecat**, *Ictonyx striatus*, and the **Libyan striped weasel**, *Poecilictis libyca*, are two closely related but exceptionally rare inhabitants of W. Little is known about their habits, except that they are exclusively nocturnal and bad climbers.

With its distinctive long snout and ears, the **aardvark**, *Orycteropus afer*, is easily recognised but rarely seen owing to its night-time habits. Grand engineers of the bush, aardvark tunnel construction is second to none, with warrens 3m deep and up to 30 separate entrances. Abandoned tunnels are used by other inhabitants. The tunnel mouths, usually around 50cm in diameter, are easily visible. The aardvark is a fully protected species, being favoured in traditional medicine. The right paw is used to detect bad characters and to transmit bad luck to others, the intestine is used to combat stomach ulcers, and the Bissa and Gourounsi use the animal in a concoction to make babies into good wrestlers, owing to the aardvark's ability to secrete an oil that makes it difficult to grab hold of.

Aardvark

The **north African crested porcupine**, *Hystrix cristata*, is a well-known but little-seen inhabitant of the savanna. Its distinctive, needle-sharp spines protect the porcupine from larger predators such as lion and leopard. The **lesser galago** or **Senegal bush baby**, *Galago senegalensis*, is a kind of evolutionary mix-and-match, with the body of a monkey, the head of a cat, and enormous circular eyes which can be seen like beacons by torchlight at night.

Easily startled by the approach of vehicles, the **striped ground squirrel**, *Xerus erythropus*, is often seen darting across the tracks and up into trees, detectable by its white-striped flanks and bushy tail, while the **rock hyrax**, *procavia capensis*, which looks like a bulky fat rat without a tail, can be easily seen on the face of the rocks that house its large colonies of 30–60.

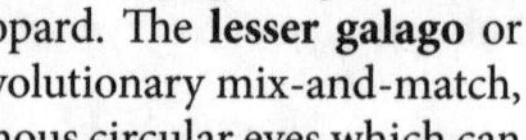

Rock hyrax

The **giant Gambian rat**, *Cricetomys gambianus*, and **cane rat** or **grasscutter**, *Thryonomys swinderianus*, are two rarely seen large rodents, the former with its long body and tail, the latter much more squat. The **scrub (Crawshay's) hare**, *Lepus saxatilis*, and the **cape** or **brown hare**, *Lepus capensis*, are the two species of hare found in Burkina Faso, and the **four-toed hedgehog**, *Erinaceus (Atelerix) albiventris* is another rarely seen ground dweller.

Primates The **anubis** or **olive baboon**, *Papio anubis*, is the primate species most often encountered in W. It is easily distinguished by a downward-hanging tail that looks like a bullwhip, and a dog-like face. Omnivorous, baboons roam in troops of as many as 200, and have a highly organised society that relies on matriarchal lineages. Between two and four dominant males have charge over the group, and any other male not respecting this authority is pursued and attacked. In Burkina, the muzzle of the baboon is pickled and used in traditional medicine against scorpion stings, as baboons seem to eat them without any apparent ill-effects.

Another common sighting is the **green monkey**, *Chlorocebus (aethiops) tantalus*. Essentially a creature of the savanna, enjoying close proximity to water, it is recognisable by a coat of grey or olive green and a black face bounded by distinctive pointy ears. It enjoys an uneasy relationship with its near-neighbour, the baboon – they will warn each other of danger and tolerate each other at watering holes and in the trees where they sleep, but baboons have also been known to prey on the green monkey.

Slightly less common is the **patas** or **red monkey**, *Erythrocebus patas patas*. Larger but lither than the green monkey, the dominant male is usually the most visible, as he tends to place himself on the top of termite mounds as a kind of lookout for the troop, which can be dispersed over as wide an area as $100m^2$ in order to avoid attack. The patas is readily identifiable by a red or ginger back and black brows running from ear to ear.

Patas monkey

Water dwellers Extremely sedentary, the **hippopotamus**, *Hippopotamus amphibius*, is easily found at watering holes, although during the day the visitor is unlikely to see much more than a pair of nostrils and ears and the occasional yawn. Hippos tend to leave water only at sunset to search for food, sleeping on land before returning to the water the following dawn. Despite their enormous bulk (up to three tonnes) they are capable of charging at 45km/h over short distances, and are also good swimmers. Society is organised around dominant males who are ready to defend their harems of females to the death, and mothers are particularly protective of young calves. Extremely easily agitated, particularly if its route to water is barred, the hippo is responsible for more deaths than any other animal in Africa. Since the 1990s, poaching of hippos has been on the increase in west Africa, and some suspect this is due to the trade in hippo teeth. Slightly rose in colour, they are used in handicrafts as an alternative to ivory. Hippo lakes can be found across Burkina Faso, and not only inside official wildlife parks: other notable ones are at Tengrela, near Banfora, and at Bala, 60km northeast of Bobo-Dioulasso.

The **African Nile crocodile**, *Crocodylus niloticus*, is the most common of the 13 crocodile species throughout Africa, and is considered sacred in Burkina Faso. They are a regular feature of wildlife parks, and of small lakes and pools throughout the country, most notably at Bazoule and Sabou, both west of Ouagadougou. For this reason crocodiles are much more readily approached in Burkina than in other countries. The Nile crocodile can grow up to 2.5m, averaging 30cm a year growth, and live for a century or more. The female lays a batch of 15–100 eggs deep in a nest hole in the bush, away from any possibility of flooding. She returns them to water 65–115 days later, balanced on her back or in her mouth. When descending into the water (to hunt or copulate), crocodiles can bring a transparent nictating membrane over their eyes – the croc's version of goggles. As well as being powerful swimmers, they are fast over short distances on land.

The **African manatee**, *Trichechus senegalensis*, looks like an enormous sea cow with front flippers and a tail, and is one of the animals on the W logo. They are incapable of moving on land and spend all day resting on the water surface, feeding at night on water plants and other plants overhanging the river, with a fondness for water hyancinth. Owing to their sedentary nature, they are extremely easy to hunt, and populations in the Niger River, which passes through W, have been severely depleted. In addition to being celebrated flesh popular in the bushmeat industry, their oil is used in traditional medicine to treat ear infections. Pollution and irrigation projects have also diminished their habitat. The manatee is considered at risk of extinction, having seen its population decline by one-fifth in the last five years, and is classed as a 'fully protected species' by the three countries that share W.

Other reptiles The **spurred African tortoise**, *Geochelone sulcata*, is the largest continental land tortoise. Shell lengths can reach 83cm, and the maximum recorded weight is 105kg. Their broad, oval shells are brown to yellow in colour. They enjoy an omnivorous diet of grasses, leaves, fruits and cadavers, can go without food and water for many weeks, and live in burrows. Occurring across the Sahelian region, their habitat has been squeezed by desertification, and they are heavily poached, making them a threatened species.

It is impossible to walk around a town or city without becoming quickly attuned to the scuttling of the **red-headed rock agama**, *Agama agama*, an ugly lizard that seems to be perched on every wall or roof or tree. The males are brightly coloured, often with orange or yellow heads and bodies that are blue-black in colour, while the females are a uniform tan. They also have a distinctive press-up movement, bobbing their heads up and down in the sun. **Geckos** are much more welcome residents of numerous hotel rooms. Their otherworldly appearance, with webbed suckers on their feet and translucent skin and bulbous eyes, makes them excellent night-time hunters of mosquitoes and other insects, often only giving themselves away with a distinctive clicking noise.

BIRDWATCHING For the birdwatcher, Burkina's prolific farming and grazing lands are very rewarding, making up in diversity what they lack in 'special' species. More than 360 species are known in Arly and W parks, with some 35 species of birds of prey in W alone.

Relatively few species (about 20%) are resident. All this movement results in an avifauna in a constant state of flux, with composition, abundance, habitat use and behaviour changing significantly from month to month. As a result many bird species are either thinly distributed and/or present for brief periods and therefore known only from a handful of sightings. This is an area where visiting birdwatchers can make a great contribution to ornithological knowledge.

The wet season is a fascinating time of year but access tends to be restricted. National parks are generally open between November and May, when seasonal roads can be used.

Much of the information and suggestions here have been kindly provided by bird expert Roger Wilson, who researched W National Park as part of the Ecopas

PLAY SAFE

Birdwatching in Burkina can be exhausting and is potentially dangerous given the stresses of the environment. It also needs strategy and patience for the most rewarding results, so if you mean business you should dig in for the long haul. The following advice is simple enough, but crucial to having a good time while you search.

- Wear a hat
- Keep the skin covered (long sleeves, long trousers)
- Wear good shoes
- Take enough water for the day – at least four litres – and drink regularly
- Do not go alone and take an experienced guide whenever possible
- Keep your group in sight and do not approach thick cover on your own in the park, especially near water
- Carry suncream and keep spare water in the vehicle
- If you feel faint, do not force yourself. Stop, rest in the shade, and drink. If it does not pass you could be in trouble and your companions will need to help you

project. His book on birds, *Les Oiseaux du Complexe WAP (W, Arly, Pendjari)* was published in 2007 by CIRAD (Montpellier, France) and makes an excellent field guide for the enthusiast. Don't forget your binoculars.

What to see Among Burkina's hundreds of species of winged fellows, look out for: Abdim's stork; Abyssinian roller; black kites; bronze-winged coursers; cattle egrets; Egyptian plover; fish-eagles and other raptors; fox kestrel; grey hornbills; grey pratincoles; helmet-shrikes; herons; lappet-faced vultures; Namaqua doves; nightjars; overwintering black storks; owls; Pel's fishing owls; rock pratincoles; starlings (several species); storks (including saddle-billed stork); thick-knees; Verreaux's eagle owls; waders; waxbills; and yellow-bellied fruit-pigeons.

Start early Birds are most active from dawn to mid morning and again from late afternoon to dusk, so it is imperative to start early. They are often hard to spot so actively searching is usually not the best approach. Waiting a few minutes and letting them show themselves is far preferable. Many small birds travel in mixed flocks and the most interesting species always seem to lurk on the fringe. During the rest of the day, searching for birds is hot work, tiring and frustrating. The trick then is to find a congenial spot near water and settle in – they will come in numbers and variety.

Chase the watering points The rainy season is the main breeding season, with many species in bright nuptial plumage and widely spread across the landscape. With the dry season, birds move as water levels fall, concentrating on where it is still available to profit from the sandbars, mud banks and the easy prey trapped in the shallow water. Pools on the point of drying up briefly offer some of the most interesting concentrations of birdlife in the park.

Vary your watchpoints Check out as many different habitats as possible. Wetlands and gallery woodlands, especially those with shaded pools, are top spots and always worth attention. Patches of open ground and short grass should also be scanned. Flowering baobabs and *bombax* are very attractive to a wide range of species, as are fruiting trees, especially figs. Crags and tall trees, particularly dead ones, merit a routine scan as do fires, which can afford a real spectacle as mixed flocks of birds of prey, rollers and bee-eaters snatch up the insects driven from cover by the flames.

Go out at night Take a night drive at every opportunity. This is normally not possible in W, but it is just as good on the periphery. The results are variable but this is the best way to see owls, nightjars and, given luck, thick-knees and bronze-winged coursers.

Check out specific sites In addition to the sites below in W National Park, ornithologists should also consider **Oursi** and **Darkoye** lakes in the north and **Deux Bale** park near Boromo.

Tapoa trail This runs along the northern edge of W from the Tapoa Hotel in Niger to Tapoa Djerma (and thence to Diapaga) in Burkina Faso. This is a good trail for general birding, passing through the full range of habitats typical of the northern part of the park – old village sites, open ground, and low gallery and savanna woodland. It is extremely good in the middle of the dry season when the last pools are drying up, with herons, waders, storks (including saddle-billed stork), fish-eagles and other raptors attracted to the trapped and stranded fish.

Koudou Falls and the Mekrou trails The Koudou Falls are a beautiful site on the Benin–Burkina frontier, accessible from both countries with a permanent pool and an excellent gallery forest. This is definitely a place to pass the heat of the day after working the roads and the waterholes on the way. Among other things there is a Preuss's cliff swallow colony in the rocks and a full range of gallery forest species including violet turaco. It also offers opportunities for Pel's fishing and Verreaux's eagle owls. The Mekrou is in fact extremely good along its entire length, with trails from Burkina Faso, Benin and Niger culminating in Point Triple. A warning though – do not swim in the pool because you are liable to be severely lacerated by siliceous algae growing on the bottom.

Atacora hills The road between Kondio (Burkina Faso) and Banikoara (Benin) is for the very adventurous in possession of a good all-terrain vehicle. It also possesses one of the very best birding places found so far in the W National Park – a permanent spring on the frontier that provides the only water source for a wide distance around. The ideal spot is in fact not the spring itself, although that is indeed good, but the small shaded pools in its outflow and their surrounding gallery woodland. These attract a wide range of small birds, notably starlings (three or four species) and waxbills. Again, do not swim in the pool. It is small and inviting but contains crocodiles and a population of enormous catfish. It is also sacred.

HISTORY

BITS OF THE JIGSAW Telling the definitive early history of Burkina is a difficult game, with few written sources to rely on (see box, page 18). Books about Burkina's history generally pull their punches about the same time the French colonials started throwing theirs, at the end of the 19th century. That's because the French were clever enough to write down their imperial musings, whether wittering on about just how pointy was the Mossi king's chin or the decadence of local jewellery. Without many historical documents, oral accounts dominate. There are lots of versions flying around – of marauding invaders, of Mossi brilliance dominating even fabled Timbuktu, of sackings and winged horses and head choppings and all sorts of gore.

The puzzle gets more complicated every time a new piece of the jigsaw is thrown in. Newly discovered 1,000-year-old ruins overthrow old ideas; similarities among mask carvings suggest ancient geographical and familial ties; Burkinabe historians fight to resurrect a time predating French arrival; and minority groups assert their stories in the face of Mossi dominance.

There are many stories to be told, and where possible, we have tried to give a taste of them in the individual chapters that come later in this book. Below we have tried to give an idea of how Mossi civilisation – 'one of the great civilisations of west Africa' according to historian Michel Izard – came to be so important in the region, and how, although the Mossi influence remains the strongest, it is by no means the only factor in creating a Burkinabe nation.

LEGENDARY BEGINNINGS Surviving oral traditions place the Mossi as one of the groups emerging from the Mamprusi Kingdom, which also gave rise to the Nanumba and Dagomba formations of what is now northern Ghana. The Mamprusi crossed the Niger from Lake Chad.

The Mossi believe themselves to be descended from the line of Nedega, a powerful Mamprusi chief who ruled the Kingdom of Gambaga, in northern Ghana. Exact details of the story vary, but the prevailing yarn is that Nedega refused to give away the hand of his eldest daughter, Yennenga, in marriage because of her considerable fighting prowess. Accounts differ as to whether she fled her father's overbearing court, or whether her horse bolted while she was out riding, but she soon found herself lost and alone, far from home in a forest. Here she encountered Riale, an elephant hunter said to be of Mande origin. They fell for each other and the lovers named their son Ouedraogo ('stallion', in memory of the horse that brought them together), who became the first of the Mossi. To this day, Ouedraogo is the most popular surname in Burkina.

WHAT'S IN A NAME?

The Mossi are animist first and Muslim second, but confusion over their name nearly saw them labelled as fully signed-up Christians as early as the 16th century.

The earliest European reference to the Mossi is thought to be from the Portuguese author João de Barros, in his *Decadius da Asia* (1552–53). He referred to them as the 'Moses' people, after hearing the testimony of a Wolof prince named Bemoy given to the court of Dom João II. Bemoy claimed that the territory of the 'Moses' extended east from Timbuktu.

The listeners, thrilled to hear of a tribe of adherents to Moses, were convinced the people were Christians, and assumed that the king of the 'Moses' must be the legendary Prester John, the supposedly Christian founder of the Ethiopian monarchy. The mistake nourished European dreams of African Christianisation, although the glut of missionaries arriving in the 19th century found they had their work cut out.

SPLIT IDENTITY?

In a puzzle that has stumped historians for the last two centuries, a fascinating discrepancy exists between written sources concerning the Mossi, and what Mossi oral history has to say about its own origins.

The earliest written references come in the important Arabic historical texts, the *Ta'rikh al-Sudan* and *Ta'rikh al-fattash*. These refer to a warlike but highly organised people who were based in the territory of the Niger bend and who set out on a series of large-scale conquests north of the Niger with the aim in mind of capturing its lucrative trading centres.

The *Tarikh al-fattash* speaks of Mossi incursions into the Islamic Songhay Kingdom of Gao in the middle of the 13th century. A century later, Mossi menace had increased. The *Ta'rikh al-Sudan* refers to a sacking of Timbuktu, considered to have taken place around 1337: '...the sultan of the Mossi, at the head of a powerful army, launched an expedition against that city. Terror-stricken, the people of Melli took flight and abandoned Timbuktu to the assailants. The sultan of the Mossi entered the town, pillaged it, set fire to it, reduced it to ruins and, after putting to death everyone he could lay hands on and seizing all the wealth he could find, he returned to his country.' This *Ta'rikh* also refers to raids on Benka (west of the Niger bend, upstream from Timbuktu) in the 15th century.

The *Ta'rikh*s recount that the accession of the Songhay emperor Sunni Ali in 1464–65 marked the beginning of a sustained period of pressure on the Mossi, in which they were pushed back. With the reign of Askia Mohammed (1493–1529) and his successors, Songhay offensives against the Mossi were conducted as *jihads* or Islamic holy wars. After three centuries of fighting for control of the Niger bend, the Mossi were defeated.

The first European historians to study the Mossi, including Leo Frobenius, Delafosse and Tauxier, were convinced that the Mossi of the *Ta'rikh*s and the Mossi that they found further south were one and the same. Yet Mossi oral history contains no mention of forays against the Songhay Empire, or of an occupation of the Niger bend, nor, for that matter, of defeat. The dominant Mossi oral history puts their arrival in the central plateau in the 15th century, too late to have achieved the feats recounted in the *Ta'rikh*s. European historians attempting to corroborate the *Ta'rikh*s had to either elongate considerably the average reign of each of the Mossi kings, or acknowledge genealogical gaps.

In the 20th century, historian J D Fage refuted this one-and-the-same thesis, drawing distinctions between the Mossi of the Niger bend and the Mossi of the Volta basin and accepting the chronology of the oral traditions. To have sufficient capacity to launch attacks on Timbuktu in the 14th century, the Mossi would have needed to have set up shop on the central plateau some time earlier, which does not square with what the Mossi bards say about themselves.

None of this resolves the conundrum of who was raiding Timbuktu in 1337. Either the oral history is wrong and the Mossi have been kicking around Burkina since as early as the 12th century or so, or the *Ta'rikh*s are wrong, or there is more than one lot of Mossi. Go figure.

Some sources recount that Ouedraogo returned to his maternal grandfather, where he fought with distinction at the head of his armies. Fired by dreams of his own empire, he left, accompanied by a clutch of his grandfather's horsemen, to conquer the vast lands to the north. His first base was at Tenkodogo ('ancient earth' in Moore), considered the cradle of Mossi civilisation.

Ouedraogo is said to have had three sons: Rawa travelled northwest to found the Kingdom of Zandoma; Diaba Lompo went east to Pama and founded the Gourmanche Kingdom; and young Zoungrana remained on the throne in Tenkodogo and consolidated power.

FROM MYTH INTO HISTORY Zoungrana's importance is as the 'father' of Naba Oubri, the first of the great Mossi rulers that we can be fairly sure actually existed, and the founder of the Ouagadougou ruling dynasty, from whom today's Moro Naba takes his lineage. Others say Zoungrana was not the father, but variously the cousin or brother of Oubri. Whatever their relationship, Oubri took Mossi origins from myth into history, by establishing a new kingdom at the end of the 15th century.

Oubri inherited his grandfather's thirst for conquest and embarked on a series of campaigns against the indigenous populations of the region. Gourounsi and Nyonyose farmers could do little to resist well-organised Mossi cavalry. Loumbila, Boulsa and Boussouma, to the north of Tenkodogo, yielded to Mossi expansion before Oubri turned west to take La and Yako. Finally, he assaulted the Nyonyose capital of Kombentinga, capturing it after a bitter fight.

Installed there, he renamed the capital Wogdgo ('come and pay tribute'), which over time became Wagadugu, and later – under French influence – Ouagadougou (pronounced '*wagadoogoo*'). He crowned himself the first Moro Naba ('king of the world'). His kingdom was known as Oubritenga ('land of Oubri'), which is still the name for the administrative district in which Ouagadougou falls. The third son of Oubri, Naba Nasbire, moved the royal capital to La, the place of his father's death, before Oubritenga relocated to Ouagadougou again.

INFIGHTING The first major schism in Mossi society was a power struggle between two grandsons of Oubri – Naba Yadega and Naba Kumdumye. Yadega came off worse, and made up for it by heading off to found the Yatenga Kingdom with his elder sister Pabre (see page 162). Meanwhile, Naba Kumdumye consolidated the central Mossi Kingdom, which was to reach its zenith in the 18th century. Tenkodogo's political clout dwindled, although even today the town is venerated as the birthplace of Mossi culture and society. The Kingdom of Zandoma, founded by Rawa, was subsumed into the upwardly mobile Yatenga Kingdom.

EMPIRE FLOURISHES Highly organised and hierarchical, the Mossi were robust enough to withstand external pressures, whether military, political or religious. Djerma invaders from the east, while quite happy terrorising the Gourounsi, did not dare venture into Mossi territory, while the Songhay emperor Askia Mohammed met with little success in his mission to Islamise the Yatenga Kingdom.

For the Mossi, their organisation and fighting prowess meant a stable existence for more than three centuries, while all around them civil war was raging. As the French historian Tauxier wrote at the end of the 19th century:

> The Mossi empire was centralised. The internal struggles often seen with other groups, between villages, neighbourhoods and even compounds, do not exist with the Mossi. Therefore they have internal peace and security. In addition, the centralised power,

> which prevents anarchy, ensures the country is not devastated by opportunistic conquerors...
>
> One is struck upon entering Mossi country by the absolute security that the population enjoys, where everywhere else war and slave-raiding parties desolate villages. One notices with envy the Mossi peasants who go out alone to their fields, axe on their shoulder, where among other groups the head of the family must have, night and day, his arms in his hand...

Most of the population was engaged in agriculture, but the Mossi were also traders, taking advantage of lucrative routes between desert and coast, and exporting cereals, slaves, donkeys, bronze, copper and gold.

COLONIAL INCURSIONS The greatest danger to Mossi stability was internal, since the system of power transfer from elder brother to younger brother made it very easy to covet the throne. As external pressures on Mossi stability began to build in the 19th century, particularly in the Yatenga Kingdom, outbreaks of vicious civil war increased.

Following the emergence of Yatenga, other fiefdoms sprung up, claiming independence from Ouagadougou. These included Mane, Riziam, Boulsa, Bousouma and Yako. The rulers also claimed lineage from Ouedraogo and Oubri. By the beginning of the 19th century, these were in open conflict with each other and with Ouagadougou. Arriving Europeans capitalised on this.

The first European to set foot in Oubritenga was a German called Kraus, visiting Ouagadougou in 1886. He was closely followed by the French explorer, Gustave Binger, who arrived in 1888 at the court of Naba Sanem (1871–89). There he was received at court, although his diary entries show little respect for the Mossi ruler, and reveal the route French occupation was to take.

Not only had Binger thought he could happily take over the north – the *naba* took care to tell him that Yatenga belonged to the Mossi and no Frenchman would be given permission to continue on such a route – he also refused to go prostrate before the Moro Naba.

> I believe that no white man travelling in this country, whoever he may be, should prostrate himself before a black king, however powerful... If ever, in the future, Europeans are to come here they will have to come as masters, and to form the superior class of society, without having to bend their heads before native chiefs to whom they are in all respects superior. In any case, a European is certainly as good as a Muslim, and such people do not prostrate themselves before the Naba.

As colonial interests in the region grew, the French most coveted the territory. While Burkina Faso did not have much to offer in terms of goods, it was of vital strategic importance as a geographical bridge. The French had a promising stranglehold on west Africa, but the isolated colony of Dahomey (Benin), interests in Côte d'Ivoire, and the interior territories of Soudan (Mali) and Niger lacked a reliable link. Burkina Faso was it. The problem was the intractable Mossi Kingdom.

In 1895, Captain Desteneves led an expedition south from Bandiagara, in Mali, with the aim of signing protection treaties with the Mossi Kingdom. Having passed through Yatenga and made an alliance with Naba Bully, he was stopped at Yako and his column prevented from going any further. When he sent his emissaries to Naba Wobgo (1889–97) of Ouagadougou, the 30th Moro Naba, he received the following response:

> I know that the French want to kill me and take over my country, although you insist that they are going to organise it. I think my country is fine just the way it is… I do not need them. I know what I want and what I need. So, think yourself lucky that I don't have you beheaded. Go away and never come back.

It was left to the brutal French captain Voulet to take Oubritenga by force, and he arrived at the city on 31 August 1896.

In the ensuing battle, the Mossi were resoundingly defeated, their cavalry cut down by French rifles. Naba Wobgo managed to flee the city, and after hiding out in the bush tried to prepare a takeover of Ouagadougou from Koupela. Initially, Voulet wanted to reinstall Wobgo on the empty throne as puppet leader to keep the kingdom together, and pursued a campaign of torture and execution to deliver the deposed leader, but found no success. Eventually, he decided to put a different emperor on the throne and at the beginning of 1897 the youngest brother of Naba Wobgo accepted the poisoned chalice to become Voulet's Moro Naba, known as Naba Sigri. As a final show of strength, Voulet publicly executed the Naba of Lalle, a long-standing enemy of Ouagadougou.

Meanwhile, Wobgo was preparing a return to Ouagadougou, having fled to British territory in the Gold Coast. He was willing to sign a treaty of protection if the British would supply him with the men and arms to retake his kingdom.

The battle to reinstall the *naba* never came. While camped in Kombissri, about 30km short of Ouagadougou, Lieutenant Northcott met with the French captain Arminion to discover that politicians in Europe had carved up the region. Ouagadougou was for the French and the British were to return to the Gold Coast, leaving Naba Wobgo without a throne. Heartbroken and homeless, he settled in Gambaga, the old home of princess Yennenga, and died there in 1904.

In the era preceding colonisation, there were a number of other powers exerting themselves outside Mossi territory, which both circumscribed the extent of Mossi power and contributed towards Burkina's heritage today. These included the Fulani emirates of Liptako, based around Dori, and Jelgodji, based around Djibo, in the Sahel region. The Udalan Tuareg, nomads originally from Algeria, also penetrated the Sahel. To the east, the Gourmanche struggled with armies from Benin and with Fulani incursions from the north, while the Gourounsi people in the south struggled hard against Djerma slave raiders. To the west, the kingdoms of Guiriko and Kenedougou vied for control of Bobo-Dioulasso. These histories are covered in greater detail in the later sections of this book.

UPPER VOLTA IS BORN, AND UNBORN The territory that was to become Burkina Faso was something of a colonial oddity. In the 20th century, its name changed five times as it was pushed around various systems of colonial administration like a problem child that no-one quite knew how to handle.

In 1904, it was made part of the Colonie du Haut-Sénégal-Niger, an amalgam of parts of Mali, Burkina Faso and Niger controlled by the Governor-General of l'Afrique Occidentale Francaise (French West Africa, or AOF) from Dakar.

The onset of war in Europe at the beginning of the 20th century did not spare west Africa. Like her francophone neighbours, Burkina surrendered many young men to the *tirailleurs senegalais*, the black regiments conscripted to fight in the killing fields of France and Belgium during World War I. For the Marka and Bwa populations of northwest Burkina, this was too much. The Bwa in particular found it difficult to adjust to French administrative structures, hit by tax increases and the severe famine of 1911–13. Taking able-bodied men, desperately needed

VOULET'S DARK HEART

Captain Paul Voulet was a prime mover in France's colonial expansion. His patriotic zeal and military prowess made him an ideal choice for the difficult missions of western Soudan. He was the first to subdue the Mossi Kingdom of Oubritenga, a feat that had not been managed in 400 years. Yet his descent into madness and death in Africa offers a chilling real-life version of Colonel Kurtz, the tortured officer at the centre of Joseph Conrad's *Heart of Darkness*.

Signs of a bloodthirsty zeal are revealed in the 1896 Mossi mission. He left the Bandiagara heights in July armed with 50,000 cartridges, hundreds of soldiers, porters and horses to exact revenge on Yako for having had the temerity to stop a previous French expedition. Continuing his mission, he set about summary executions and a scorched-earth policy – burning villages and crops – in his relentless march on the capital.

On arriving at Ouaga, his messenger – sent forth with the final offer of peaceful takeover – was badly beaten and the French flag lacerated. Despite concerted resistance, Voulet found his way to a violent victory thanks to a 'superhuman energy' he felt had evaded all others.

'It is not without a certain well-earned pride,' he said, 'that we make ourselves masters of this Mossi capital, the first among Europeans.'

After subduing the Mossi, securing Ouagadougou for the French and seeing off the British interest in Upper Volta, he returned to France in 1897 covered in glory.

Back in Africa in November 1898, the 32-year-old Voulet left Bamako to lead a mission into the heart of central Africa. By December he was short of supplies, low on water, and imagining Tuareg marauders at every turn.

The French colonial authorities in Mali became increasingly concerned about the methods he employed in the name of France. Grim reports of village

in the fields, off to fight in a war they neither knew nor cared about sparked a popular uprising.

At the end of 1915, the revolt spread rapidly in the region of Bona and Safane, in the heart of Bwa, drawing in Samo, Bobo and Gourounsi fighters. It was put down within six months by the French colonial administration, with the help of Fulani mercenaries, after a series of bloody battles which saw hundreds of villagers killed and fields and villages razed.

The territory was renamed Haute-Volta (Upper Volta) in 1919, because it was home to the upper course of three rivers: the Black Volta, the Red Volta and the White Volta, which feed into Lake Volta in Ghana. It joined, for the first time, Mossi, Gourmanche and Fulani kingdoms with mixed groups in the west and was administered from Ouagadougou by a lieutenant-governor.

Economically insignificant, Upper Volta was of value to the French as a land mass to link its richer colonies, and as a vast source of labour. In the name of progress, millions of workers were deported to maintain lucrative cocoa, coffee and sugar plantations in Côte d'Ivoire, or set to work on road and railway construction.

It came as little surprise when, in 1932, the territory of Upper Volta was dissolved, and its land and people were split between Mali, Niger and Côte d'Ivoire, which got the lion's share. This carving up of their land was a particular affront to the Mossi. Having fought off hostile takeover by rival local powers for so long, they were simply handed over by the colonial powers.

massacres were beginning to emerge that rocked the idea of the country as a civilising influence.

Lieutenant-Colonel Jean-Francois Klobb set out in May 1899 to relieve Voulet, trailing across the Sahel in his destructive wake. The journals kept by Klobb and his second-in-command Meynier tell of fire and blood that continues for hundreds of kilometres: villages burned, twisted bodies piled at the bottoms of wells. On 11 July 1899, Klobb rode into the burned village of Koran-Kalgo, southern Niger, and found it 'full of corpses'. Two little girls hung from a branch.

'It pains me to think that officers could command such horror,' Klobb wrote in a letter dated the same day. By now his expedition had almost caught up with its source. He sent four soldiers ahead to tell Voulet he was relieved of command. Voulet sent back a letter: 'I will treat you as an enemy if you continue your march against me. I am resolved to sacrifice my life.'

Three days later the two men met outside the village of Dankori on opposite sides of a field. Klobb flew the tricolour and appealed to Voulet to stop. He told his men to hold fire. Voulet didn't, aiming a pistol at his soldiers to ensure they obeyed the order to shoot. Klobb died of a bullet wound to the head. Several of his men were killed. Klobb was buried with honours in Timbuktu, where an inscription reads 'Died for France'.

After the fight, Voulet declared himself a 'black chief', and founder of a bush empire to rival that of the French motherland. Two days later his soldiers, angered at another threat to shoot deserters, shot both him and his number two, Lieutenant Chanoine.

The authorities were quick to lay Voulet's deterioration at the feet of Africa, in the shape of *le cafard* or *la soudanité* – a kind of nervous psychosis brought on by prolonged exposure to external factors of unrelenting heat and illness.

Following the German occupation of France in World War II, French West Africa allied with Vichy France for a brief period in 1942–43, before siding with the Allies. During this period, any African wanting to fight for the free French against the Nazis risked imprisonment and execution, while forced labour increased dramatically. Yet the African Empire was the first to rally to de Gaulle's Free French cause, providing military and economic support to the war effort against Nazi Germany.

ROAD TO INDEPENDENCE World War II had a profound effect on the relationship between France and her west African colonies. On the part of politically active French-educated Africans, there was a new determination to use the rallying call of freedom to press for a say in their own affairs, and a growing acceptance by France that things needed to change.

Even so, France felt it was too much to win the war only to lose its empire. 'How can she recover her vigour, her self-reliance, and, consequently, her role,' said General de Gaulle to President Roosevelt, 'if she is excluded from the organisation of great world powers and their decisions, if she loses her African and Asian territories – in short, if the settlement of the war definitely imposes on her the psychology of the vanquished.'

France was keen to tie in the political workings of its colonies to the French state, and offering minimum representation in a French parliament in Paris achieved just that. For the colonies, however, it was a first step on the path to self-determination. At the 1944 Brazzaville Conference it was decided that French West Africa would have ten seats in the new French Constituent Assembly, five of which would be elected by Africans.

Party politics in the region was dominated by the African Democratic Rally or *Rassemblement Démocratique Africain* (RDA), a pan-regional movement created at the October 1946 Bamako Congress. Felix Houphouet-Boigny, future leader of Côte d'Ivoire, was its president.

The RDA, and its Ivorian predecessor PDCI, saw a strong hegemony as the only basis on which a smooth eventual transition to independence could take place. Ouezzin Coulibaly, the first leader of the RDA movement in former Upper Volta, stressed the need for unity, telling the inaugural conference of the Convention Africaine: 'No underdeveloped country which has reached political maturity has done so without granting primacy either to a single party or to a party which had such a large majority that it controlled all the sectors of social life.'

Yet this did not suit the Mossi, who had spent centuries building up a hegemony of their own. They saw Houphouet-Boigny – and his likely domination of the African contingent of the French Constituent Assembly – as a platform for Côte d'Ivoire. So to its chagrin and surprise, the PDCI met with opposition from Mossi traditional leaders when it sought their support. In elections in Côte d'Ivoire in 1946, the Union pour la Defense des Interêts de la Haute Volta (UDIHV) captured four districts, on a platform of the abolition of forced labour (achieved that year) and a reconstitution of Upper Volta. This Mossi political grouping resulted from an unprecedented alliance between Naba Koum of Ouagadougou and his fellow *nabas*

ANYONE FOR A COUP?

Since independence in 1960, there have been six coups, with a particularly turbulent period in the 1980s. The November 1998 re-election of President Blaise Compaore was the first time an elected president had reached the end of his term of office without being overthrown. For date lovers everywhere, here's a quick timeline:

Independence 5 August 1960

First Republic 1960–66 Maurice Yameogo, leader of the RDA, becomes president.

Coup 3 January 1966 Army seizes power. Lieutenant-Colonel Sangoule Lamizana becomes head of state. Unrest follows strike supported by some political parties.

Second Republic 1971–74 Sangoule Lamizana still at the helm as head of state. Gerald Kango Ouedraogo is the new prime minister after his party, the People's Voltaic Union of the African Democratic Rally (UDV-RDA), wins legislative elections.

Coup 8 February 1974 Crisis within the ruling UDV-RDA leads to dissolution of government by Lamizana and suspension of all political activity. Military back in power.

Third Republic 1978–80 UDV-RDA supports General Lamizana's return as president, elected on the second ballot.

Coup 25 November 1980 Colonel Saye Zerbo seizes power following a teachers' strike, with Military Committee for National Recovery and Progress (CMRPN).

of Tenkodogo, Ouahigouya and Fada, which breached royal protocol – tradition demands that the top *nabas* should never meet.

Colonial authorities were sympathetic to the idea of recreating Upper Volta as a way of checking the spread of Houphouet-Boigny's radical nationalism in Côte d'Ivoire. Equally, African politicians recognised the strong Mossi claims to sovereignty, while acknowledging anxiety among the other groups of Upper Volta, namely Lobi, Bobo, Samo, Fulani and Gourounsi populations, who feared a return to Mossi subjugation.

The Mossi won out, and the law recreating the Upper Volta colony was passed in the French National Assembly on 4 September 1947. The new country elected three deputies to the assembly for the first time the following year, bringing African membership to 16 seats.

An intense period of jostling for position in the likely run-up to independence followed. Political parties came and went. Despite Mossi success in lobbying for a return to Upper Volta, the UDIHV became less of a force at the ballot box as the local wing of the RDA gained momentum.

The influence of African deputies in Paris helped press the case for independence, and the 1956 Loi Cadre established that each of the eight French West African colonies should have its own Governmental Council. So following Upper Volta's 1957 elections, the triumphant RDA, led by Coulibaly, formed the country's first-ever government.

In September 1958, with de Gaulle as the new French president, the empire was further watered down. Countries in French West Africa were given the chance to

Coup 7 November 1982 Zerbo is toppled. People's Salvation Council (PSC) assumes power, under army medical officer Major Jean-Baptiste Ouedraogo, who takes on role as president.

Coup 4 August 1983 PSC toppled by the National Council of the Revolution. Captain Thomas Sankara becomes head of state.

Name change 4 August 1984 Sankara renames Upper Volta Burkina Faso – 'Land of Honourable Men'.

Coup 15 October 1987 Popular Front seizes power, 'with a view to straightening the Revolution'. Captain Blaise Campaore becomes president, and announces 'an opening up of the political spectrum'.

Referendum 2 June 1991 Constitution of the Fourth Republic is adopted by the Burkinabe people, making Burkina 'a democratic, unitary and secular state'.

Election 1 December 1991 Blaise Compaore re-elected for a further seven years.

Election 11 May 1998 Blaise Compaore re-elected for a further seven years.

Election 13 November 2005 Blaise Compaore re-elected for a further five years.

Election 21 November 2010 Blaise Compaore re-elected for a further five years.

become members of the French Community in a referendum. Knowing which side their bread was buttered on, each country voted to stay with France, bar Guinea, from where France made an unceremonious and speedy retreat, even ripping telephones from bureaucratic walls. Burkina voted 'yes' to the referendum, by 99.18%, second only to Côte d'Ivoire in its endorsement.

Following Coulibaly's sudden death, Maurice Yameogo replaced him at the helm. A one-time member of the UDIHV, he had split off to form an independent party, and built a coalition of smaller parties that collaborated with, then joined and finally took over the RDA, renaming it the Voltaic Democratic Union (UDV). Following approval of the constitution in September 1958, Yameogo found himself the country's first president. Two years later, on 5 August 1960, he was signing the accord in Paris that gave Upper Volta its independence.

DEMOCRATS AND DEMAGOGUES Post-independence Burkina see-sawed between civil rule (in the shape of four republics) and coups (six) installing military rulers who always claimed they were working to return the country to civil rule. While in recent years Burkina has been one of the most politically stable countries in the region, the 1980s were a particularly turbulent period.

For the green Yameogo government, it was difficult not to become a little giddy with the trappings of power. This was perhaps understandable following the long, hard battle for independence, but in a country as poor as Burkina there was even less room than usual for a honeymoon period. Yameogo inherited a desperately impoverished country that, right from the start of its colonial existence, lacked the kind of French investment in even basic infrastructure that poured into its neighbour Côte d'Ivoire.

He banned all political parties other than the UDV-RDA, which made winning another election in 1965, on 99.98% of the vote, much easier. With an economic crisis looming, he unwisely slashed civil servants' salaries by a fifth as part of a cost-cutting exercise – a bitter pill to swallow when politicians were seen enjoying the high life. In addition, non-Mossi groups, particularly the Lobi, felt neglected by the Mossi-dominated Ouagadougou government. In the face of mounting opposition, Yameogo was deposed on 3 January 1966 in a military coup led by Colonel Sangoule Lamizana. This is still celebrated as a holiday in Burkina.

The new military junta wanted to set the country back on the democratic path as soon as possible. Lamizana got the economy back on track with tough austerity measures and managed to organise, on paper at least, the first multi-party elections in West Africa, in December 1970.

Like Blaise Compaore, Lamizana successfully made the tradition from *putschist* to president by being elected head of Burkina's Second Republic. But the ruling party, the UDV-RDA, was crippled by infighting. His government was paralysed, and faced with drought, strike action and growing inflation, Lamizana was forced to revert to military rule.

The junta embarked upon a period of consultation, with trade unions, political parties and traditional chiefs, to draft a new constitution reflecting the views of Upper Voltans. In elections in 1978, Lamizana was again elected president, on a UDV-RDA ticket, but without an overall majority in parliament. Internal strife and external pressure ground the administration to a halt. The military once again stepped in. Colonel Saye Zerbo led a bloodless coup that toppled Lamizana on 25 November 1980.

Despite the problems he faced and the fact that he twice overthrew a democratically elected government, Lamizana is fondly remembered in Burkina as a leader who strived for consensus, even if it ultimately eluded him. Much later, when called to give an account of his premiership in front of one of Thomas Sankara's public courts in 1984, he was acquitted of any political wrongdoing or corruption.

Zerbo's mission, once again, was to purge the political elite of its wastrels. It was a thankless task, not helped by draconian measures such as the closure of all drinking joints during the day to prevent absenteeism among civil servants. The prohibition was unsuccessful, hiding rather than stopping the practice and causing widespread resentment. Zerbo's increasingly authoritarian methods (he banned membership of political parties and abolished the right to strike) led to schism and he was replaced by another band of radical young army officers, led by army doctor Jean-Baptiste Ouedraogo.

Ironically, Ouedraogo's first political appointment proved to be his undoing: he named Thomas Sankara as his prime minister. Sankara already had a reputation as a charismatic officer and leader. He enjoyed cultivating the cult of personality built up around accounts of his exploits in the 1975 war with Mali, and his humble origins.

A self-confessed ideologue, Sankara was fired by a zeal to lance years of corruption and decadence among Upper Volta's political elite. He had been an architect of the overthrow of Saye Zerbo, backing Ouedraogo. Yet the new president quickly found himself in danger of being overshadowed by a popular hero. Matters came to a head when Sankara invited the Libyan leader, Colonel Muammar Gaddafi, to visit Upper Volta. Intrigued by this young pretender, Gaddafi did not even stop for Ouedraogo, who was furious. Ouedraogo arrested Sankara and this triggered action by military loyalists across the country, including another military captain and friend, Blaise Compaore. Stationed at the army barracks in Po, he seized control and began an advance towards the capital. On 4 August 1983, it was actually Compaore who deposed Ouedraogo and declared Sankara chairman of the National Revolutionary Council (NRC).

AFRICA'S CHE GUEVARA Thomas Sankara was a remarkable figure, and a continent's idol. Virulently anti-corruption, lean and good-looking, he was a charismatic dictator. Despite arbitrary and authoritarian rule, he remains an icon in Burkina and beyond, for his fierce ideological commitment and for forging the country's modern identity.

He turned what could have been his biggest weakness – his origins – into one of his fledgling nation's greatest strengths. He was a Silmi-Mossi, with both Fulani and Mossi roots. For two proud peoples, such unions are not always viewed favourably, yet he harnessed his mixed heritage to create a new identity for Burkina Faso, based on unity. A year after coming to power he renamed the country, unyoking the French appellation of Haute-Volta. 'Burkina Faso' combines elements of the three languages Moore, Dioula and Fulfulde. 'There is not a Burkinabe who does not remember an uncle or a father who died so that France could be free,' he once said. He gave the country a new flag, a new national anthem and a new motto – 'Patriotism or death, we will triumph'.

Sankara quickly embarked on an impressive programme of social welfare reform. A champion of women's rights, he appointed women to a quarter of the ministerial posts (including key education and finance ministries) and banned prostitution. He decreed 22 September 1984 a national day for husbands to do the family shopping. He took beggars off the streets, establishing 'solidarity compounds' in which they could learn trades. Within 15 days, three million children were vaccinated against killer diseases – yellow fever, measles and meningitis. In an effort to boost domestic production and consumption, he decreed that servants of the state should wear outfits made only from local cotton.

In public courts, members of the public and civil servants were encouraged to testify about previous examples of government excess and corruption. Ex-president Zerbo was ordered to repay US$200,000 in public funds he had embezzled and was sent to prison, as was Gerard Ouedraogo, former UDV-RDA leader. Sankara also appealed for people in towns and the countryside to set up Committees for the Defence of the Revolution (CDRs), to be known as 'shock troops'.

He was also determined to circumscribe the feudal power of the traditional chiefs, making sure they submitted to the same laws as everyone else. 'Many people respect the Moro Naba,' said one citizen at the time, 'but I believe that Sankara was right to oblige him to pay his electric bills.'

SANKARA: THE INSIDE STORY

Anonymous reflections from a retired American diplomat

My wife and I arrived in Ouagadougou in the late summer of 1983, just a few days after Captain Thomas Sankara's coup d'état. It was not an altogether comfortable experience for an American diplomat. This young apostle of radicalism delighted in taking pokes at the US, often offending our bosses in Washington, many of whom had barely heard of Upper Volta. The reaction resembled that of a bear being bitten by a mouse, and precipitated a gradual deterioration of relations (including eventual withdrawal of the Peace Corps), which didn't shed credit on either side.

Although Sankara was a mild despot by African standards, he nevertheless killed opponents on a scale never before experienced in Upper Volta. He shut down the best newspaper (*L'Observateur*, now back in business). He used fear as a political weapon. We will never forget the show trial of some hapless functionary for having owned a refrigerator, deemed prima-facie evidence of corruption. He had an unnerving habit of keeping a revolver on his presidential desk, even when receiving foreign ambassadors. He made the civil servants work on a never-completed railroad that was supposed to tap manganese deposits in the north. Much of this was pure theatre, and perhaps it wasn't such a bad idea to discomfit the bureaucracy, but some of it was quite nasty.

There was the day when we woke up to the sound of heavy machine-gun fire from a guard post just down the street from our house. It turned out that Sankara's revolutionary guards had decided to pretend that imperialist-backed mercenaries were attacking Ouagadougou. We were disturbed by so much firing of live ammunition. We protested in a diplomatic note to the government, pointing out that bullets fired into the ether had to come down somewhere, maybe in the nearby Bois de Boulogne where many US embassy families lived. The government was not amused by our complaint.

Yet somehow it was hard to take Sankara's anti-imperialism altogether seriously, despite his passionate words. He did none of the things which an African radical of the previous generation, like Sékou Touré of Guinea, or Modibo Keita of Mali, would have done. He did not expel the French, or the Lebanese business community, or end Upper Volta's membership in the franc zone, or even nationalise foreign holdings. It was as if he yearned to be revolutionary, but couldn't quite figure out how to do so without doing more harm than good. The spirit of his polity was summed up by a billboard that faced the airport. 'Welcome to Burkina Faso,' it said, 'the tomb of imperialism.' In the middle of the billboard, set off in a circle, was a Coca-Cola advertisement.

He maintained frosty relations with Europe, particularly France and America, and broke protocol to berate President Mitterrand, during an official visit to Burkina in 1987, about his foreign policy, especially towards South Africa and Chad. He lambasted the record-breaking Live Aid money-raiser 'We are the World' for failing to donate to Burkina. And after being refused permission to overfly US air space following a trip to Cuba in 1984, Sankara snubbed US dignitaries, preferring a visit to New York's Harlem. 'Black Harlem is my White House,' he explained to rapturous crowds.

Burkina was officially part of the non-aligned movement, although it maintained good relations with Libya and the Soviet Union, receiving money, weapons training and a dusting of Marxist dogma.

The man was also infectiously charming, and armed with a wicked sense of humour. Early in his presidency, before the departure of the Peace Corps, he received its director, Miller Beer heiress Lorette Ruppe, who despite her millions was a dedicated public servant. She and her party met Sankara in his office, and proceeded nearly to die of the heat. At the end of the meeting, he asked, 'I suppose you wonder why it is so hot in here?'

He then explained that a few years earlier, when he had been briefly prime minister before his coup d'état, he had been visited by a pair of Peace Corps volunteers who had known him when he was still assigned to a provincial town. Glancing around at his big, cool office, the volunteers had suggested that he was putting on airs and forgetting the peasants among whom he had lived. 'Ever since then,' he explained to the perspiring Lorette Ruppe, 'I always turn off the air conditioning when I have Peace Corps visitors.'

Toward the end of our stay Sankara starred in a novel by Gerard de Villiers, a French author who writes an endless series of spy novels full of sex and violence. The title was *Putsch à Ouagadougou*. It featured the James Bond-style hero of the series, an eastern European count in the employ of the CIA, in mortal combat with Sankara and his evil chief of security. Villiers had sent a team to Ouaga to research the book. Many business and civic leaders were flattered and co-operated fully, much to their subsequent regret. When *Putsch à Ouagadougou* appeared, they discovered themselves identified by name, sometimes awarded starring roles which graphically portrayed them in and out of bed with the CIA hero. The security chief, the arch-villain of *Putsch à Ouagadougou*, was moreover a real individual who enjoyed trying to pick fights with the Marine security guards at the US embassy and was a source of real fear in the expatriate community. Sankara said nothing, but after the book appeared he sent a signed copy of it to the American ambassador.

His death came under somewhat mysterious circumstances. He apparently became increasingly arbitrary and no longer consulted the other members of his ruling circle, including Blaise Compaore, now president. In October 1987, they eliminated him.

Today Sankara has achieved iconic status far beyond the borders of Burkina Faso. There are at least three biographies of him in print. He remains intensely appealing to African youth. His anti-corruption campaigns and emphasis on self-reliance, whether or not they seemed futile at the time, are today credited with contributing to Burkina Faso's image as a land where people work hard and keep their word – a land indeed of upright men.

Relations with other African leaders were often strained. Niger's Kountche and Togo's Eyadema thought Sankara behind coup attempts and Burkina went to war, disastrously, with Moussa Traore's Mali in 1985. Sankara took against Côte d'Ivoire's Houphouet-Boigny, thinking Burkina's neighbour took the lion's share in taxes accruing from the joint railway and arresting and imprisoning an Ivorian official who had defrauded ECOWAS (the Economic Community of West African States). He did enjoy a good relationship with Jerry Rawlings of Ghana, and they even discussed the possibility of political union by the end of the 1990s.

SANKARA'S DOWNFALL Thomas Sankara's zeal to radicalise ordinary people proved his undoing. The CDRs often terrorised local opponents, invoking the revolution to justify settling old grievances over family feuds and chieftainship conflicts. While Sankara vowed to curb the CDRs' excesses, he remained a stubborn believer in their role. Conflict between the CDRs and Sankara's original stalwarts, the trade unions, also brought problems. Teachers went on strike in 1984 in protest at the sacrifices demanded of them by Sankara's regime; Sankara dismissed them.

In 1987, as his grip on power began to weaken, he executed seven ringleaders (drawn from unions, civilians and the military) for plotting a coup in May 1985. Increasingly paranoid, Sankara attacked trade unions, accusing many of being reactionary and 'directly or indirectly at the service of imperialism', later reaffirming that CDRs were the backbone of the revolution.

His old friend and ally Blaise Compaore, now Minister of Justice, refused to follow the CDR leader's wish to have two trade unionists executed. Divisions deepened within the revolutionary council as it seemed Sankara's commitment to the CDRs was losing him popular support. Increasingly Compaore was seen as a possible successor to the man he had gone to war to liberate. In the face of rumours about his future, Sankara remained stoical, telling a journalist: 'The day you learn that Blaise is preparing a coup against me, it won't be worthwhile to try to resist or even warn me. Because by then it will be too late.'

It already was. On 15 October 1987, Sankara was killed in a gun battle with soldiers allegedly acting on behalf of Blaise Compaore and two other revolutionary comrades, Major Jean-Baptiste Lingani and Captain Henri Zongo. It is not thought this was a cold-blooded killing, rather an arrest attempt that went wrong. The tragic outcome shows how isolated and deluded Sankara had become.

State media were quick to denounce him as a traitor, and the coup that deposed him became immediately a 'rectification' of the revolution. The journal *Jeune Afrique* provided a fitting epitaph: 'His country was too poor and too small for the revolution that he launched to have been taken seriously. He tried to accomplish a great deal, and he devoted too much time to foreign affairs. But power itself is a school, and Sankara learned quickly. The pity is that he had so little time to prove himself.'

A survey of his personal effects shows that he died with an old Renault, a refrigerator, a few guitars and bicycles, US$560 in the bank, a weekly salary of US$100, and an outstanding mortgage of US$2,200 on a house. His cheques bounced regularly.

THE MODERN ERA Blaise Compaore is a consummate political survivor. Taking over from a popular hero and best friend in dubious circumstances hardly augurs well for a political career, yet almost 25 years later he is still in charge of the country. His administration has been rocked by scandal, yet he has weathered the storm, and no rival, political or military, has been able to capitalise.

Following the demise of Sankara, his first priority was to ensure the same fate did not befall him. Compaore immediately set about 'rectifying' Sankara's revolution, which in practice meant embracing free market reforms to bring desperately needed IMF and World Bank funds to the shattered economy, and to start moving towards democracy.

The latter occurred in fits and starts. For a brief period, a Government of National Unity existed, but this dissolved in enmity over the implementation of a new constitution. Opposition members withdrew first from the government and then from the 1991 election after political rallies were banned in the run-up. Compaore won easily and embarked on a period of consolidation.

Foreign policy came to the fore during the 1990s, as he played a lead role in resolving the Tuareg conflict in Mali and Niger. Compaore enjoyed stints in charge of the African Union and UEMOA (the West African Economic and Monetary Union). He has maintained close personal and political links with Muammar Gaddafi of Libya, who has invested personally in the country.

The election of Jacques Chirac as president in 1995 heralded closer ties with France, which sees Burkina as an important regional base and ally, particularly as Côte d'Ivoire, once the French *protégé* in the region, has become increasingly intransigent.

Other alliances were less illustrious. Burkina was a conduit for the trade of conflict diamonds during Sierra Leone's brutal civil war, for which it received censure from the United Nations. Blaise has enjoyed a long-standing association with Charles Taylor, the ex-leader of Liberia who made Ouagadougou his second home in the 1990s; during this update Taylor was still on trial in The Hague, charged with war crimes committed in Sierra Leone. It has been suggested that Taylor and Compaore have worked together to arm the northern rebels in Côte d'Ivoire (see page 32).

ZONGO AFFAIR AND AFTERMATH In 1998, Compaore was re-elected to a second term, with 88% of the vote. Turnout was 56% and the result was not contested. As with the previous poll, a coalition of opposition parties boycotted the election, and Compaore's two opponents were allegedly persuaded by the government to run, to create the perception of a contested election. Victory celebrations were short-lived, however, as Compaore became caught up in the biggest crisis of his political career.

In December of that year, four charred bodies were found in a 4x4 on a dirt road heading towards Leo. One of the dead men was Norbert Zongo, Burkina's most celebrated journalist and editor of *L'Indépendant* newspaper. He had been conducting an investigation into the death of the chauffeur of Compaore's brother François. The chauffeur, David Ouedraogo, was allegedly tortured by members of the Presidential Guard, the private army that reports to the president and is headed by François Compaore.

Zongo's death, and the apparent impunity of those behind the killing, sparked a wave of popular protest that threw the country into a political crisis. Opposition parties, activists, trade unions and media responded strongly to what they saw as a totally unwarranted act of political aggression. Even if the killing had not been sanctioned at the highest levels of power, it appeared as though the institutions that were supposed to ensure and protect the rights of Burkinabes were simply tools of obfuscation.

Initially, police responded violently to incendiary street protests in Ouagadougou and Zongo's hometown of Koudougou with mass arrests and a crackdown on opposition MPs and student leaders.

As the scale of the crisis grew, the presidency opted for a conciliatory tack, convening a special committee of traditional and religious leaders to try and create a new spirit of unity. The president and his council of wise men released doves as part of a ceremony at the national stadium, in which Compaore asked the nation to come together in a spirit of forgiveness to exorcise the ghosts of the past.

Eventually, four members of the Presidential Guard were jailed for Ouedraogo's death. A host of unanswered questions remains. For more, the documentary film *Borry Bana, le Destin Fatal de Nobert Zongo*, by Abdoulaye Diallo and Luc Damiba, looks into the affair in depth.

Pressure grew on the president for more general political reforms that would shore up democracy and transparency in Burkina's institutions.

The May 2002 legislative elections were the first fully contested multi-party elections to take place in Burkina and a change in the voting system ushered in proportional representation. In elections that international observers considered substantially free and fair. Compaore's party, the Congrès pour la Democratie et le Progres (CDP), saw its share of seats fall from 101 to 57, out of a total of 111.

In the mind of the people, however, the Zongo affair has never really gone away. Zongo's wife, Genevieve, has never given up hope of bringing the perpetrators to justice. In 2008, on the tenth anniversary of his killing, she took part in a demonstration in which activists posted stickers saying 'Avenue Norbert Zongo' along main streets in the capital. Pressure was stepped up for the reopening of the investigation into his death; a group of musicians including Sams'K le Jah (see page 105) released a tribute single entitled 'Artistes Unis pour Norbert Zongo', journalists gathered names on petitions, and even private TV stations broadcast infomercials along the same lines. But so far, their calls have fallen on deaf ears.

TROUBLE IN CÔTE D'IVOIRE The most important foreign policy issue in Burkina in recent times has been the crisis in neighbouring Côte d'Ivoire, which has been split between the Burkina-friendly north, and the south, where former president Laurent Gbagbo still receives widespread support. The northern rebels, many of whom have historic links to Burkina, have always claimed to be fighting against what they see as years of discrimination and neglect following the death of Houphouet-Boigny. A subsequent president made popular the idea of *Ivorité*, whereby anyone of mixed parentage is not considered a true Ivorian, and is denied ID papers and the right to vote.

An estimated three million Burkinabe live and work in Côte d'Ivoire, on both sides of the divide, and many have been there for years. An operation was mounted in 2003 to try and repatriate 300,000 Burkinabe fleeing the fighting; often they were seen by pro-government militias as rebel sympathisers and killed or mutilated. But after this, things settled down, as a long wrangle began over when the next presidential elections should take place. Originally mooted for 2005, the postponements went on for years.

The crisis reached a new peak when the elections finally took place in late 2010. Laurent Gbagbo, the incumbent president, narrowly won the first round ahead of his long-standing rival, rebel leader Alassane Ouattara, but neither achieved the 50% necessary for an outright victory. The run-off, held on 28 November 2010, led to an extraordinary situation. Results announced by the Electoral Commission on 2 December gave victory to Ouattara with 54% of the vote. However, this was overturned the next day by the Constitutional Council, led by a Gbagbo supporter, which claimed that certain northern results were invalid, disqualified 400,000 votes and said Gbagbo was the winner with 51%.

International uproar ensued, with most bodies and countries – including the UN, ECOWAS, the US, France and, of course, Burkina – backing Ouattara and calling for Gbagbo to step down. The African Union looked increasingly split, as pro-Gbagbo supporters sought to paint Ouattara as a foreign-backed imperial stooge. Gbagbo refused to budge; both sides gathered their own armies and both men were sworn in as president among their own supporters, despite the ongoing efforts of external negotiators. War seemed almost inevitable. Fighting broke out across the country, along with allegations of atrocities on both sides. By 11 March 2011, Ouattara had decided that all peaceful attempts at a solution were futile, and launched a full-scale offensive that pushed steadily towards Abidjan. Hampered by international financial sanctions, Gbagbo lost ground rapidly, but still refused to accept defeat. French and UN forces entered the fray on 4 April, backing Ouattara and launching air strikes against Gbagbo's fighters. The former president was eventually arrested at his official residence on 11 April 2011.

With Ouattara at last in power, Cote d'Ivoire looks set to regain some stability, though the underlying divisions still remain. Human rights organisations are calling for transparency about alleged atrocities on both sides of the conflict as the only basis for true peace and democracy in the country. It remains to be seen whether Ouattara will heed the call. Meanwhile, Burkinabe are largely happy with the outcome, but are still dealing with the economic fallout: price increases for basic commodities that most can ill afford. By early 2011, Blaise Compaore's own boat had begun to rock.

RE-ELECTION The November 2005 election was an important watershed, to see whether the encouraging democratic trends started in 2002 would continue, or slide back into less transparent days. It got off to an inauspicious start. The constitution had been amended in 2000 to limit the presidential term of office to five years, renewable once. But in an excellent sleight of political hand, Compaore argued that the provision was not retroactive and therefore should not apply to the two terms of office he had already served. The Constitutional Court, of which he is a member, interpreted the constitution in his favour, despite strident protest from opposition parties, clearing him to run for the next two elections.

At the polls, Compaore was re-elected with a massive majority of 80%. An estimated CFA983 million was spent on a slick, well-executed Compaore campaign full of glitzy self-promotion, involving flashy helicopter trips around the country, packed stadium rallies with top music acts, and thousands of free T-shirts, badges, earrings and water bottles distributed to the party faithful.

Turnout among the 3.9 million registered voters was a lowly 58%, but the election passed peacefully, and was declared free and fair by international observers. The overriding view was that Compaore did not need to cheat to win, since the opposition was so fractured and financially incapable of matching him. Even the leader of the main opposition party (the ADF-RDA), Gilbert Ouedraogo, tipped as one of the rising stars of Burkinabe politics, supported Compaore's bid in the interests of political stability, leaving a rag-tag bunch of 11 other candidates to scrap for electoral crumbs. Benewende Sankara (no relation to Thomas), was the next closest candidate, with 5% of the vote. Hermann Yameogo, an outspoken critic of the government and son of Burkina's first president, Maurice, withdrew from the race, but in a saga of political farce his face remained on ballot papers and polled more votes than two of the lesser-known contenders.

The election of 2010 was a case of déjà vu. More electioneering ('*Avançons ensemble*' exhorted a smiling Blaise from a thousand posters), a populace resigned to the result, an even more apathetic turnout of 54.9% and victory to the tune of 80.2% of ballots cast. The closest rival was Hama Arba Diallo, the Mayor of Dori, who with Fulani support managed to claw 8.2%. The day itself, 21 November, passed without incident; conversation between Burkinabe in coffee kiosks was dominated not by their own election, but by the goings-on in Côte d'Ivoire. 'Better the devil we know,' mumbled many, seemingly unwilling to sow the seeds of change.

But appearances were deceptive. In February 2011, the death of a student in custody led to widespread strikes and protests by schools and universities across the country. While police blamed meningitis, few doubted that police brutality was the real cause, and the protests provided an outlet for frustration with the top-heavy system as a whole. By March, the unrest had spread; soldiers in the capital mutinied, protesting against unpaid housing allowances. Ouagadougou was held to ransom as the soldiers fired into the air and went on the rampage, looting shops and businesses to the outrage of the population. The mood spread, with army protests breaking out in most of the larger towns across Burkina. Meanwhile, in Ouaga, traders protested at the losses incurred by the army, while the general population joined in with wider demonstrations about human rights abuses, corruption and the rising cost of living.

Blaise's initial response was to flee the capital, and it seemed that perhaps his time had come. But he soon returned to take control of the situation by dissolving the government, making a series of rapid reappointments and sacking both the army chief and the head of the presidential guard. Sporadic protests continued, but the possibility of regime change began to fade. In early June 2011, a protest by soldiers in Bobo-Dioulasso was quickly quelled. It remains to be seen whether Blaise will cling on to power until the 2015 elections, and if so, whether he will then at last bow out, in line with the terms of the constitution.

GOVERNMENT AND POLITICS

While political parties share a grant of CFA200 million per year depending on their performance at the ballot box, party politics in Burkina today is dominated by the CDP. In the latest round of National Assembly elections, held in May 2007, 73 out of a possible 111 seats were won by the CDP – an increase of 16 seats. Most appointed provincial officials and traditional chiefs are also CDP members. Membership confers advantages, particularly for businessmen and traders in competition for open bidding contracts.

Executive power is enacted by a cabinet of presidential appointees, headed by a prime minister, currently Luc-Adolphe Tiao, who was appointed following the unrest in April 2011. The President of the National Assembly, Roch Marc Kabore, is also the President of the CDP. Women have been able to vote and stand for election since 1958, although it was not until 1978 that a woman was elected to parliament. Women now hold six out of 40 ministerial posts. The judicial branch also consists of a Supreme Court and an Appeals Court.

ECONOMY

Burkina is among a select group of African countries experiencing decent annual economic growth, managing an average of more than 5% a year for the decade up until 2005, when it dropped to about 3.5%; it wobbled for a few years, affected by low cotton prices and the worldwide economic crisis, but rose again to 5.2% by 2010, boosted by growth in the mining industry. With a free market economy, the government hopes to shift resources to the education and health sectors as part of its anti-poverty strategy.

This is a priority. Take any indicator you like – infant deaths, life expectancy, literacy, yearly income, exports – and Burkina Faso tells a sorry story. Among the poorest countries in the world, it is ranked 161 out of 169 in the UN's latest Human Development Index. Average gross national income (GNI) is US$430 per person. In Burkina, 82% of the population is estimated to be living in poverty.

Wealth is parcelled out among the few. The richest 10% account for 32.2% of all income and spending, compared with 2.8% for the poorest 10%. One of the UN's eight Millennium Development Goals (MDGs), intended to bring an end to poverty by 2015, aims to halve the number of people surviving on US$1 a day. Yet so far, the percentage of Burkinabe in this category has barely shifted, moving from 44.5% in 1994 to 42.8% in 2008; unsurprisingly, the chances of meeting the target are deemed 'improbable'.

Life expectancy is 53.7 years, and the scale of malnutrition is hard to grasp. About 9% of the population is undernourished and nearly 17% of Burkinabe children under five die every year. Another UN MDG aims to reduce the number of child and infant death rates by two-thirds before 2015. In Burkina, the figure went from about 10.7% in 1993 to 9.1% in 2006, making it another goal to be labelled 'improbable'.

Over the last five years, debt service has reduced from 12.5% to 5.2% of the value of exports, and Burkina was one of the first countries to reach its target under the Highly Indebted Poor Countries debt reduction scheme. But to meet its MDGs, annual growth of 7% is required year-on-year until 2015, which it has consistently failed to reach; furthermore, rising inflation has mitigated the effects of growth in real terms. The country's GDP is still massively dominated by the twin pillars of many an African economy: international donor aid and customs duties. In 2003, Burkina received US$451.1 million in overseas development aid (ODA). That's US$37.30 for every person in the country and about 10% of the economy. The majority of funds come from France and the UN. Denmark, the Netherlands, Germany and the EU are also high-level contributors.

COTTONING ON Cotton has long been the mainstay of the Burkinabe economy. Introduced by the French in the early 20th century in an attempt to forge some large-scale industry, it earns about 30–50% of export earnings, providing 3.5 million people with some means of income. Almost all the cotton produced is exported, mostly to Turkey and Asia.

In 2004, more land than ever before (521,466ha) was cultivated, following a grain surplus and consequent drop in grain prices in 2003–04 that convinced many farmers to abandon cereal, particularly maize, in favour of 'white gold'.

Despite poor rains, the mass land-switch, aided by powerful industrial fertilisers, resulted in a record-breaking harvest of 535,367 tonnes in 2004–05. This made Burkina Africa's largest cotton producer. But the switch has not paid off. Despite hopes for ever-increasing harvests, production has continued to hover around the 500,000-tonne mark, up to and including 2010. At the end of 2004, the world price for cotton dropped by 30% in dollar terms, leaving Burkina and other west African cotton-producing countries clamouring for the kind of subsidy support the US gives to its own farmers, which in 2004 amounted to US$4.2 billion in subsidies, more than the entire GDP of Burkina. Oxfam estimates Burkina Faso lost 12% of potential export earnings because of US subsidies alone.

By contrast, Burkina's farmers rely on a dual funding support system: guaranteed minimum floor pricing at the beginning of the planting season, alongside a bonus the following harvest year if world crop prices are good.

The Société Burkinabe des Fibres Textiles (Sofitex), which transports and gins cotton grains, supplies inputs (fertilisers and seeds) to farmers and promotes textile production, terms the triple whammy of low world prices, a weak dollar and US cotton subsidies 'the monster with three heads'. And it was recently hit with another blow to its profits, thanks to Burkina's landlocked status. Traditionally, Côte d'Ivoire has provided the route for cotton exports; but with the new crisis and sanctions against Laurent Gbagbo's southern regime, 20,000 tonnes of Burkinabe cotton lay languishing in Abidjan, and Sofitex had to reroute the rest via Togo and Ghana at an estimated cost of CFA25 per kilo.

Faced with a lack of subsidies, Burkina's cotton industry has made sterling efforts to open up to a modicum of competition and greater efficiency. Part-privatisation of Sofitex in 2000 saw the state's share reduced to 35%, with a private French company, Dagris, holding 34%, the Burkinabe cotton union holding 30% and two Burkinabe banks, BIB and BICIA-B, taking the final 1%. Banks continue to play an important role in the future of the industry; in early 2011, Sofitex received a loan of CFA72 billion from local banks including Ecobank, SGBB, BIB and Bank of Africa. With this it hopes to boost output to reach the holy grail of 700,000 tonnes in 2011–12.

Another important, if controversial, factor has been the introduction of genetically modified seeds, undertaken by US firm Monsanto, which are resistant to some of the insect pests that plague Burkinabe crops. Burkina is only the third African country to accept biotechnology, the others being Egypt and South Africa. GM production began in 2009 and mushroomed in 2010, with up to 90% of farmers adopting the seeds. While optimism is running high, the long-term effects of the switch have yet to be assessed, and organic cotton farmers are already complaining about the contamination of their crop. In the meantime, market-distorting subsidies remain in place.

A NUGGET OF HOPE Until recently, Burkina was often dismissed as an unlucky country, because of its apparent dearth of mineral or energy wealth. Unlike neighbours Sierra Leone, Liberia, Equatorial Guinea and Nigeria, it has no diamonds and no oil. But things have changed: Burkina has, quite literally, struck gold. What was once considered a sliver has become a treasure trove, all thanks to a Mining Act in 2003 that ushered in a new era of exploration.

A number of major mining operations have opened across the country, and the numbers rise year on year: 383 research licences were granted in 2009 alone. While less than a single tonne would have been the average output a few years back, production mushroomed to 30 tonnes in 2009 – the year in which gold overtook cotton as the country's biggest export.

The shiny stuff is more or less everywhere. Major mining operations include the Etruscan mine in the department of Boulgou to the southeast; Semafo's operation at Bale in the western department of Mouhoun; and mines in the northern provinces of Yatenga, Soum and Namentenga. One of the largest is the Canadian Iamgold mine at Essakane, in the northernmost province of Oudalan. Here, the potential is estimated to be between 90 and 120 tonnes, and extraction is expected to take more than 12 years.

The Burkinabe government has stakes in most of these companies; at Essakane, for example, Iamgold owns 90%, the government 10%. And gold is not the only mineral to be swelling its coffers. Substantial deposits of zinc and manganese are being mined at Perkoa and Tamboa respectively, while prospectors are investigating deposits of copper, iron, phosphates and bauxite, among others. It remains to be seen how much of this new wealth will trickle down to the Burkinabe population.

AGRICULTURE AND CATTLE With a rural population of more than 80%, the economy is predominantly agricultural. Most farmers grow what they need to survive, relying on millet and sorghum. Production usually tops two billion tonnes, on around 3.5 million hectares of farming land.

Other crops include maize, rice, yams, sweet potatoes and *fonio* (a wild grass). After the harvesting season, these are stored in granaries to provide for the year ahead. Vegetables such as tomatoes and onions are often grown in small market gardens near reservoirs.

The areas of well-watered country around Banfora are the centre of the country's sugarcane industry, with production of around 40,000 tonnes annually. Most of this is for Sosuco, formerly state-run but now in the hands of the Aga Khan Development Network (AKDN), and not for export. Green beans, mangoes, *karite* (shea butter nuts), groundnuts and sesame seeds are also grown for a small export market. In the Sahelian zone, more than one million white gum trees were planted in 1996, to rekindle the production of Arabic gum in response to increased world demand.

Burkina is renowned as a livestock hub for the region, with an estimated 20 million animals, of which beef accounts for about a fifth. Burkina's beef industry has long supplied coastal neighbours Ghana and Côte d'Ivoire, where livestock is more susceptible to disease.

Life is far from easy for Burkinabe farmers, with mediocre soils, the prevalence of drought, and the more recent threat of floods that seems to have worsened over the last decade. Famine is a constant danger, with major crises during the droughts of 1930, 1970 and 1984–85. Some consider the word for 'drought' so bad it should not even be said aloud.

In 2004, a locust outbreak severely damaged the grain harvest in the northern provinces. Combined with a drastic shortage of rains, northern Burkina fell prey to the same food crisis that affected Niger in the summer of 2005. While 3.6 million people in Niger were perilously short of food, one million in Burkina needed food relief.

Prices for the staple food, millet, shot up, as market traders tried to make a buck from a hungry population. In Dori's daily grain market, a 100kg sack of millet cost 26,000f, compared with 10,500f the year before. In one town prices reached 38,000f, and even then traders mixed the grain with refuse and sand to bulk up bags.

At the same time, livestock prices collapsed as herders clamoured to sell their cows to raise cash for grain. Sorry-looking beasts that might have fetched 100,000f the previous year sold for 15,000f. In total, a quarter of all herds died from lack of food and water. Cattle herders were forced to sell a further 50% of what remained of their precious livestock.

Things improved briefly in 2005, but in 2007, disaster struck again. The rains arrived late, but came with lashing force, swamping the country with floodwater and killing about 50 people; and then, just as suddenly, they ended prematurely, and the spectre of drought rose again. It was estimated that 160,000 people in farming households were adversely affected. Then, 2009 brought the heaviest rains in almost a century, which again caused devastation; around Ouagadougou alone 25,000 people were made homeless and 300ha of crops were lost. The Food and Agriculture Organisation of the UN, with partners, launched an appeal to raise more than US$18 million to get the nation's agriculture back on its feet again.

TRADE IN THE REGION Burkina Faso benefits from a certain level of financial stability through its membership in the West African Economic and Monetary Union (UEMOA), the regional trading bloc that also includes Benin, Guinea-Bissau, Côte d'Ivoire, Mali, Niger, Senegal and Togo. The bloc uses a common currency, the CFA franc, and the free movement of labour and certain goods is unrestricted.

Following independence, the CFA franc was permanently pegged to the French franc at a rate of CFA100. At the beginning of 1994, a 50% currency devaluation saw the currency flop, obliterating many people's savings. At the same time as losing purchasing power, it made imported goods much more expensive, stimulated domestic production and increased exports.

With the currency now pegged to the euro (at a rate of CFA656), Burkina's foreign exchange risk is significantly reduced, stimulating external investment. Traditionally, close financial ties with France have constrained export potential, and French firms maintain a privileged position. This changed briefly under Thomas Sankara, whose defiant mood of self-reliance encouraged people to buy Burkinabe, with the slogan '*consommons Burkinabe*'.

In 1991, Burkina signed an agreement with the IMF. The onset of structural adjustment coincided with Blaise Compaore's new, breathy commitment to multi-party democracy, which was a condition of continued international financial support. Burkina undertook economic reforms to liberalise domestic markets, privatise productive and commercial enterprises, encourage private investment and reduce infrastructure costs. Strong economic management has brought significant progress in implementing market-oriented reforms. A number of previously state-owned industries have been partly or fully privatised, including Sofitex, the main cotton company. Inflation was fixed and the aim set on growth, averaging 3.9% in the period 1991–97.

Hopes for wide-ranging regional integration come in the form of UEMOA, the West African Economic and Monetary Union, whose head offices are in Ouagadougou. Since the devaluation, UEMOA members have worked to improve and deepen their economic and monetary union, bringing the promise of easier trading. Yet freer trade presents a problem for many members, including Burkina Faso – trade restrictions, particularly in the form of customs duties, are vital for swelling government coffers. According to UEMOA, customs taxes can account for half of member states' budgets.

The long-term effects on business are counter-productive. Days spent waiting for licences and customs clearance in west Africa cost companies millions of US dollars in lost revenue every year, and governments lose even more from businesses deterred from pursuing opportunities in the first instance. According to estimates from the UN, the average customs transaction in Africa involves 20–30 different parties, 40 documents, 200 data elements (30 of which are repeated at least 30 times) and the re-keying of up to 70% of all data at least once. The World Bank estimates that every day goods spend in customs is equivalent to an additional 1% tariff.

A wider regional organisation, the Economic Community of West African States (ECOWAS), with 15 members from both francophone and anglophone west Africa, has embarked on a free-trade area, although without much success to date. Despite four decades of integration efforts, intra-Africa trade accounts for only 10.5% of Africa's total trade. Intra-regional trade accounts for 11% of trade between ECOWAS members, compared with 18% within UEMOA. Plans to outdo the European Union at its own game seem, for the time being, misplaced.

PEOPLE

At the heart of west Africa, with its history of trans-African trade routes, invading peoples and borders made and remade over time, it is perhaps not surprising that more than 60 ethnic groups live in Burkina Faso, speaking a cacophony of individual languages and dialects. What is remarkable, given a recent history of brutal civil war among close neighbours Côte d'Ivoire, Sierra Leone, Liberia and Guinea, is that Burkina's people live in relative harmony, peace and stability.

One can make broad generalisations about the areas inhabited by different people, but migration is a fact of Burkinabe life. You can find a northern Fulani woman in a western village, and a southern Dagara man studying in Ouaga. Everyone goes everywhere. Yet there are still concentrations in certain places, and allegiances to different points of the country's compass remain long after individuals have migrated to the big towns, or further afield, to Côte d'Ivoire and Ghana.

One sign of Burkina's robust diversity is a strong sense of *plaisanterie* (teasing) between different groups. This is particularly strong between the Mossi and the Samo, and virtually everyone else of the Fulani. One frequent and friendly jibe is to accuse a pal of being a bandit. The response is more often than not: 'he's my slave', followed by much back slapping and laughter.

While on the surface this is all good clean fun, little currents of discontent run below. Argument persists today over whether the Mossi dominate to the detriment of others, and many campaigners follow the ethnic composition of cabinet and parliament, the judiciary, civil service and the world of academia closely. Such is the fear of Mossi dominance that it has been a struggle to convince some ethnic groups that the polio vaccine is not in fact a Mossi plot to wipe out their people.

MOSSI The Mossi make up about half the population, making them by far the biggest group. The Mossi have a tradition of never having been occupied, which means the lands in the central plateau have remained unquestionably their own for several centuries. Stability has long been considered a characteristic of Mossi culture, which is deliberately hierarchical, conservative and static.

Mossi leaders resisted Islam for years, suspicious of an external influence that might detract from existing power structures. Even after Moro Naba Dulugu was converted to Islam in 1785, Muslim extremists, including those within his own family, were frequently exiled. When the French arrived, rather than displacing or dismantling the ties that bind Mossi society, they found the ready-made centralised social structure very handy as a foundation for their own.

SCARIFICATION

For the Mossi, scarification is a kind of antiquated identity card. Lines gouged out of young faces with a hot knife reveal people's region of origin. The design indicates social rank, as well as a considerable ability to weather pain during initiation. It has pretty much stopped among Burkina's younger generation, along with circumcision and excision (a more dramatic form of female genital cutting), but still occurs occasionally. One popular and very obvious design is a semi-circle reaching from the nose to the lower left cheek, known as the *nintam tegre*, or shortish lines fanning out from the eyes, like cats' whiskers. Another looks like an elongated tear drop, from the inside corner of the right eye out towards the cheek. Much more prominent markings include a swirl over the entire face from the forehead, past the ear, towards the chin, known as *yeg-we*, as well as *dir-orbo*, a three-lined run around the entire face, bar short parallel incisions over the forehead, and nothing on the chin.

The Mossi are ruled by various kings, known as *nabas*. The top dog is the Moro Naba (king of all Mossi-controlled land), who lives in his palace in Ouagadougou. There are other *nabas* for different provinces and historic kingdoms, the most important of whom are located at Ouahigouya and Tenkodogo. The royal courts also contain minor *nabas* who in the past performed important individual roles, such as the Ouidi Naba, who was in charge of the king's cavalry, and the Larle Naba who was the king's principal advisor. Both positions still exist today, in the Ouidi and Larle districts of Ouagadougou.

Yet for all this stability, the system of succession, from brother to brother rather than father to son, has led to perpetual power struggles, and was eventually responsible for eating away at Mossi society from the inside. For this reason, many positions in the court were filled not by members of the ruling family, considered almost too close to be trusted, but often by ex-slaves and outsiders.

One reason the Mossi enjoyed their dominance in the region was that many indigenous peoples, who already occupied the land before they arrived, belonged to highly diffuse, autonomous groups not organised around a ruler, whereas Mossi society was cohesive. Yet the Mossi also left existing structures as they found them. Indigenous earth priests (*tengsoba* in Moore) were left in place among groups such as the Nyonyose and Gourounsi, to exercise their valid claim to the land and administer ancient customs and traditions, so long as the Mossi *nabas* retained political and organisational control.

Political leaders have tried to limit the power of traditional chiefs since independence. While their role in politics was officially disestablished as part of the 1983 revolution, unofficially their influence remains strong. It is widely thought that the president still consults the Moro Naba.

FULANI The Fulani (known as *Peulh* in French) form about 8% of the population, and are Burkina's second-largest group. Fulani women, who plait silver discs into their hair, are famed for their beauty. Historically nomadic cattle herders, they started to arrive in the Burkinabe Sahel in the 17th century, migrating from eastern Senegal in the search for grazing pasture. The Fulani took to Islam much earlier than many other populations, and established emirates at Dori and Djibo that were often in conflict with indigenous people. Certain Fulani leaders also allied early with the French on their raids down through Mali, and were paid to put down rebellions.

Although the Fulani are increasingly sedentary, the commitment to animals rather than crops has led to rivalry for patches of land and a sense of incursion among others. Some consider the Fulani too proud, and their nomadic lifestyle can give the impression that they have little respect for others. 'I'd trust a *Peulh* as much as I'd trust an Arab,' said one Burkinabe man. Whatever that may mean, tensions sometimes bubble up. In early 2005, the government sent in the army to calm ethnic clashes in Po between Gourounsi farmers and Fulani herders. Banditry on the route to Po has also been laid, without evidence, at the door of 'men with a Fulani look to them' in some more inflammatory newspaper articles. Other journalists have been quick to quell incendiary prejudice.

Modernity has not been altogether kind to the Fulani. When colonialists arrived in Fulani country, they wanted to recruit children to go to schools. The Fulani did not trust or respect the new education system enough to offer their own children. Instead, they tended to send along children of the Rimaibe, the Fulani's former captives and slaves. Now the 'slaves' are government officials and many Fulani feel their interests are not defended.

MY KINGDOM FOR A HORSE

The Burkinabe are the cowboys of west Africa. While they may prefer headscarves and swords to Stetsons and six-shooters, the tough-talking rhetoric remains pure John Wayne, particularly when it comes to horses: 'A horse is your wife, your car, your colleague, your best friend,' say the Fulani.

The horse was the medieval Ferrari, the ultimate form of transportation out of the reach of most ordinary mortals. Among the Fulani, such is the prestige associated with horses that families would surrender bags of millet to riders, without prompting. Today, a good horse can cost US$1,000 – a fair whack in a country where the annual per-capita income averages US$345.

The status remains today. A Tuareg would never dream of mounting a lowly donkey, for example, preferring the vantage point of a dromedary hump or horse. By contrast, the Bella, many of whom were in the past taken captive by the Tuareg, are perfectly at home on a stumpy ass.

The Mossi are not short on love for horses either, believing their country began as the result of a frantic horse ride from Ghana, carrying Princess Yennenga from her father's kingdom into the arms of the elephant hunter Riale. In memory of these mythical origins, the country's most popular surname is 'stallion' (Ouedraogo).

Horse health went on to determine the extent of Mossi domination. Chronic disease in the south of the country, beyond the confines of the central plateau, weakened and killed much of the cavalry and their steeds, allowing the Gourounsi farmers some respite from their mounted invaders.

Horses are still a common sight on busy Ouagadougou streets. There are at least three stables in the capital, the national football team is known as Les Etalons (the Stallions), and the grand prize at Fespaco, Burkina's internationally renowned pan-African film festival, is not a palm leaf or a little chap called Oscar, but a golden stallion.

OTHER GROUPS We give here only the briefest of overviews of Burkina's rich patchwork. For more, see the regional chapters.

The east is home to the Gourmanche. Closely related to the Mossi, they are also considered neo-Sudanic, with similar social structures. They make up about 7% of the population. Some of the poorest and least accessible villages in the country can be found here, and animist rites remain strong. The Bobo, found predominantly in the west of the country, also make up about 7% of Burkina's population.

The Bissa and Samo together number 6%. They are part of the large Mande grouping, which originated from the Niger Valley; this group also includes the Bwaba (sometimes called the Bobo-Oule), who make up 3%, and the Dioula and Marka, who together make up 2%.

In the south, the Gourounsi consist of closely related groups, including the Lela, Nuna, Kassena, Sisola, Winye, Puguli, making up 6% of the population.

Further south are the Birifor, Dan, Dagara and Lobi, grouped together under the umbrella name Lobi, who moved into Burkina from Ghana. In the far southwest, Senoufou country contains a number of closely related groups: the Karaboro, Tusya, Turka, Gwe and Wara, making up 2% of the population.

In addition to the Fulani, the groups in the north include the Songhay, kel-Tamashek (Tuareg, 'speakers of Tamashek') and Bella, the former slaves of the Tuareg.

Burkina is also home to a small but economically significant Lebanese and Syrian community of about 1,500, who run many of Burkina's businesses, and a small francophone expatriate population.

CASTE SYSTEMS In many groups, including the Mossi and Bwaba, traditional life is divided up according to a form of caste system. In addition to the ruling class (*nangsoba* in Moore) and the land-cultivating class, the two most specialised castes are *griots* and blacksmiths.

The *griot* is part-journalist, part-historian, with the power to bring the past back to life, recounting legends and songs of old, and so consolidating the power of the rulers. In the act, some of that power is conferred on the *griot* too. They are also skilled musicians, and something of a court jester figure. Today the tradition of rewarding popular *griots* for their efforts to entertain continues. You may see people stuffing notes into the hands or clothes of criers and musicians, if they are judged to be giving a particularly hot performance. For an entertaining introduction into the world of the *griot*, follow the work of Burkinabe film director Dani Kouyate, himself from a long line of *griots*. In addition to his 1995 film, *Keita! L'Heritage du Griot*, the *griot* in *Sia, La rêve du python* is a two-faced sycophant and political manipulator, one of the emperor's bunch of yes-men, adoring his master to his face and engineering his downfall behind his back.

The blacksmiths are another important caste. While they had no power over the land, they made the picks and hoes required to work it. They were also given responsibility for mask-making, and were feared because of the magical nature of their work. They are often seen as mediators in conflicts between families. So otherworldly were they that, even in the 20th century, a Yatenga noble could marry a slave-girl but not a blacksmith's daughter. In earlier times, it was the blacksmith who had the responsibility for cutting the umbilical cord on newborn babies.

Blacksmiths and *griots* often occupy the same quarter of a village or town, and intermarriage between these groups is allowed, although other castes are forbidden from marrying them. Some blacksmiths and *griots* maintain separate family lines.

LANGUAGE

French is the official language of government, of academia and of the media. It is universally spoken in urban areas. In the countryside it is not, and you may have some trouble making yourself understood. However, even the smallest of villages usually has a clutch of French speakers who can help out if you are having real difficulties.

There are three further national languages – Moore (pronounced '*more-ray*'), Dioula (pronounced '*Jula*'), and Fulfulde. Moore is spoken by the the Mossi. Dioula evolved as a Muslim trading language and is spoken throughout west Africa. In Burkina it is most widely used in the southwest and northwest areas of the country. Fulfulde is the language of the Fulani, spoken in the north.

In 1984, revolutionary president Thomas Sankara renamed the country Burkina Faso, employing all three languages. *Burkina* is a Moore word, meaning 'honour' or 'dignity'. *Faso* is a Dioula word, meaning 'fatherland'. Together they mean 'land of the honourable' (*pays des hommes intègres* in French). Fulfulde is not left out, however. A person from Burkina Faso is called *Burkinabe*. The *-be* ending is the Fulfulde plural term for children or people, hence the Burkinabe are the children of honour, the people of the country. The symbolism was clear: not only was the French colonial name of Haute-Volta (Upper Volta) cast out, but Burkina's new name was also an act of national unity.

ARABIC PHRASES

While little Arabic is spoken in Burkina, you can't go wrong among Muslims with a few choice phrases:

Insha'allah – 'God willing', suggesting hope or possibility for the future, as well as the chance something might not get done
Al hamdulillah (also ***hamdalaye***) – 'praise be to God', general expression of satisfaction and thanks
As-salamu 'alaikum – 'peace be upon you', standard greeting throughout the Islamic world, to which the reply is: ***wa 'aleykum assalaam*** – 'and upon you be peace'
Bismillah – 'in the name of God', said by some before eating or drinking, and so a fitting name for the odd snack bar

The country as a whole has as many languages as it has ethnic groups. Most are within the Gur or Voltaic group of the Niger-Congo family of languages and include Moore, Lobiri, Senoufou, Gourmanchema, Gourounsi, Dagara, Tusyan, Birifor and Bwamu. Dioula belongs to the Mande family of languages, which have traditionally been a common vehicle for the spread of Islam. The Samo, Bobo, Bissa and Marka are also within this group, and speak languages similar to Dioula. Fulfulde is known as a west Atlantic language. The Tuareg speak Tamashek, a Berber language derived from Arabic, and are properly known as kel-Tamashek (Tamashek-speaking people). We refer to them as kel-Tamashek throughout the book.

USE OF ACCENTS IN THIS BOOK A quick note about language in this book. We have not included accents on non-French words – this includes place names (such as Leo), other proper nouns (such as Ouedraogo) and other terms in all languages spoken in Burkina. It is unlikely you will see them written in the same way in Burkina, but for a non-French audience legibility is increased without accents. If words are Moore or Dioula, so long as you pronounce every vowel, especially at the end of words, you should be fine.

RELIGION

There is a fairly accurate saying in Burkina that the country is half Muslim, half Christian, and 100% animist. Religion of some sort is without doubt a cornerstone of society. Confess that you are atheist, agnostic, unbaptised or unconfirmed, and expect raised eyebrows, whether you're talking to a Christian or a Muslim. At the same time, religious coexistence, and the continuing strength of traditional beliefs and customs, tend to mean that zealotry and fundamentalism are rare.

ISLAM Islam dominates in the north of the country, particularly among the Fulani and kel-Tamashek, as well as among many urban Mossi. Mosques are found throughout the country and the call to prayer can be heard frequently. In rural areas, beware treading into a series of low-lying stones forming an enclosure – it could well be an impromptu, but nevertheless sacred, mosque. In the absence of a mosque, many Muslims will simply face east on prayer mats, which they carry with them at all times. You may come across lax Muslims who call themselves *Musulman* *à la gauche* (leftist Muslims), allow themselves the odd bottle of beer, and won't always been seen at Friday prayers.

Islamic festivals The most important festival is **Tabaski**, also known as the *fête du mouton*, commemorating the story of Abraham and his willingness to sacrifice his son Isaac to God. The day involves prayers, new clothes and a grand feast on sacrificed sheep. People visit one another and offer good wishes for the coming year. If you're in Burkina for Tabaski, head for Tenkodogo for an elaborate and bloody celebration that mixes Islam with Mossi heritage (see page 203).

Muslims also maintain a daytime fast during **Ramadan**, and celebrate **Mouloud**, the birthday of the Prophet Muhammad. A prayer service lasting up to 12 hours recounts all the passages of the Koran that talk of the Prophet's life. Gifts are given to children and the poor.

CHRISTIANITY Roman Catholicism has the edge on Protestantism across the country, although both are practised widely. Churches are found in most towns, and a local-language service, whether you are religious or not, is well worth seeing, particularly at Christmas or during one of the festivals following Easter Sunday. In the dry season, many local services take place outside the church in the grounds, and the hymns carry lightly in the warm, still air.

Midnight mass on Christmas Eve sees churches packed out and chorusing to the full. During Advent, many Christians put small nativity crèches made of brightly painted mud bricks outside their homes.

SETTING UP SHOP

Jean-Pierre Jacob

Shrines and sacrifices are important for many cultures in Burkina, none more so than the earliest settlers of the Gourounsi. Anthropologist Jean-Pierre Jacob, who has worked among the Winye group in central western Burkina for more than 20 years, explains the role and rites of the two main shrines in any village: the earth shrine and the bush shrine.

The earth shrine is superior to all other village cults, including the cults of the bush, water, hunting and masks. Not only does it purge villagers' impurities, it also brings fertility – of soil, of herds and of children.

Shortly after a group settles in an area, the founder will set up an earth shrine, so long as diviners have detected no opposition from local spirits. The founder becomes the earth priest. The newly appointed council of elders seals its solidarity by drinking a communal cocktail of millet beer, honey and the blood of sacrificed animals (a cock, and an ox or a goat), into which the earth priest adds three pinches of dirt. This must happen every time a new priest is initiated.

This also seals an alliance between the three different orders of beings – people, ancestors and spirits. The main spirit, *sen ñubo*, is an invisible priest-king, and reigns over all other water, fire, wind and earth spirits at large in the land. The shrine purges the land of the spirits, so that villagers can live in the area and go about their business without fear of disapproval. The installation of an earth shrine allows the cultivation of village fields, the plantation of fruit trees, sexual relationships, burial, or fire-building for cooking. As the result of this installation, human beings have strong property rights on the village land.

At least one year must pass before the earth priest can make an inaugural sacrifice to the uninhabited land around the village (the bush), a space that will

Fasting is still widely practised during Lent. The rest of the year any christening, marriage, funeral or festival provides an excuse to party. After Ascension in particular, there tend to be regular mass baptism fêtes, where families come together for lively Sunday services followed by much drinking of *dolo*.

TRADITIONAL BELIEFS AND ANIMISM Animism is basically a belief in spirits – both in the souls of ancestors that continue to hold an influence over the living world, and in natural forces such as the earth or air. Beliefs vary from group to group, but rituals tend to involve seeking benediction from the spirits who look after the earth, harvest and elements. These spirits can be angered by wrongdoing, including sins such as adultery, murder or suicide. They can be appeased by sacrifices, usually of chickens. For special festivals, goats, sheep, cows or even the odd camel can be put to the sword. The blood washes away the evil spilled on the earth, and the soil will remain fertile if the spirits who watch over it are happy.

A fetish is a sacred object dedicated to the worship of spirits. It can be a statue, a place of sacrifice or a shrine, usually made of wood or stone. These may be inside or outside the home, or hidden deep in fields or forests. Look out for remnants of feathers and blood.

A *féticheur* is someone who knows what to do when it comes to dealing with the spirit world. While they may command a relatively hefty fee for their advice, the role is sacred and revered. Earth priests bless the land before it can be worked to ensure a good harvest; bush priests deal with unknown spirits that can escape from forests to do harm.

henceforth be viewed as a special place for making offerings to a powerful bush spirit called Nyimbi.

In return for regular tributes, this spirit allows the farmers to carry out agricultural activities unmolested. Nyimbi prevents his 'slaves' (lions, snakes) from attacking these farmers, while using these same 'slaves' to thwart thievery, whether it be of tools or of the land itself. The spirit does not tolerate any form of disorder or dissolution in his dominion, especially murder or sexual relations. The earth priest is usually the bush priest although he can delegate the function to another person (his eldest son or the eldest of the second lineage to settle in the village).

Once an initial sacrifice has been offered to the bush shrine, land can be cleared for fields and the first proper houses can be built in the village. Up until this point the farmers have been living in huts made out of cut branches similar to those set up in the fields for sheltering workers from the rain. In contrast to the village land, bush territory cannot be completely conquered. Even when worked intensively it is never directly marked out with an iron tool and the farmers are not permitted to construct adobe houses or plant fruit trees. Indeed, it is often said that this patch of earth must be perpetually renegotiated with the spirits, its original owners.

The occupation and cultivation of this land can only be guaranteed through a combination of physical work (clearing, cultivation) and religious work (offerings, sacrifices, searching out 'medicines' for repelling evil spirits), with the latter being just as demanding as the former.

Jean-Pierre Jacob is based in Ouagadougou and is an associate professor at the Graduate Institute of Development Studies in Geneva, Switzerland.

WHY DID THE CHICKEN LAND ON ITS BACK?

Sacrificial rites differ from group to group, but generally involve cutting an animal's throat, a shared eating of the flesh and an offering of the blood to the spirits.

In cases where foul play is involved, such as theft, murder or suicide, the sacrificer cuts the throats of several chickens, but the chickens' role is far from over. The position in which a chicken dies (on its stomach or back or some other mangled position) allows those present gradually to answer whatever question they cannot agree on: who is responsible for this crime? Who is the owner of this land?

The last chicken to be sacrificed is black and its head is smashed against the ground. In contrast to normal sacrificial proceedings, the people present do not feast on the sacrificed animal. Instead it is buried in its entirety on its back. Its burial is accompanied by maledictions delivered by the officiating priest. The rite enables those present to call on the bush spirits to punish severely land stealers and murderers.

CUSTOMS All sorts of customs revolve around not only the traditional chief (*chef*), but also village life in general. For example, in some Mossi villages, only a chief may own a horse with five white markings (four white feet and a white stripe on the nose).

The Mossi also refuse to kill black animals as they believe this will release evil spirits. Butchers have *gris-gris* (special charms) from a *féticheur*, which give them special dispensation, and black goats and sheep sell for the cheapest prices. If someone hits a black animal on the road, people won't move it. Cars and *motos* have even been abandoned at the roadside because people are so scared that evil spirits will be released unless some sort of penance is made.

Other rules include banning Mossi women from whistling. This extends to everyone at night time, in case it attracts evil spirits. The number three tends to refer to man and the number four to women, which explains why stools for men have three legs and low chairs for women have four.

Older remnants of traditional beliefs among some groups include circumcision (of both boys and girls) and scarification (see box, page 39). Both these practices are now illegal, but continue in some parts.

EDUCATION

Education in Burkina is currently dominated by attempts to meet its Millennium Development Goals (MDGs): two of which are to achieve primary education for all, and to promote equality between the sexes. Until recently, literacy rates were some of the poorest in the world (24.8% in 2005); education has tended to favour males, and those in urban areas. Now, this is slowly changing, but there's a long, hard struggle ahead. The school day starts and ends early to avoid the pounding heat, with a long break in the summer time to help families working in the fields.

In the 1980s, the Sankara administration adopted a Cuban and Nicaraguan model by decreeing that the vernacular be used in primary schools in a bid to curb illiteracy. But teachers felt this did children no favours in the context of the wider world, and the experiment didn't last. Today's schooling is in French, with French qualifications at primary and secondary level, culminating in the *baccalauréat* (Bac).

PRIMARY AND SECONDARY SCHOOLS A glance at the figures for school enrolment in Burkina seems to suggest that the country is making good progress. According to a 2010 UN report, schools' net enrolment rate went from 34.9% in 1997 to 57.9% in 2008. But in fact, at this rate it will not reach the MDG of 70% by 2015; and while enrolment has greatly improved, keeping children in school is proving to be a much tougher challenge. By 2008, only 41.1% of pupils completed their primary education. Given that the goal was for 100% completion by 2015, it is far from likely to be achieved. The situation is proportionately worse in the north and east, where school can be viewed as a threat to traditional values, and where the figures for girls are lower across the board.

A US$12.9 million programme, funded by the US, has been supporting the development of education for girls in particular. The idea is to improve rates of primary school completion by constructing 132 new 'girl-friendly' primary schools with on-site canteens, separate bathrooms for boys and girls, and day-care centres to relieve school-age girls from looking after younger children. Schools also provide take-home food (to give parents an incentive for girls to maintain a 90%-plus attendance rate) as well as female mentors and teachers. But the percentage of girls completing their primary education by 2008 remained a lowly 37.8%.

Encouraging teachers to stay in villages has proved a problem. Many teachers train in order to reach the big cities, and are loath to work in villages far from either home or hoped-for urban destinations. In addition, female teachers have found they are sexually harassed in villages.

So the battle continues; in 2007, the government passed an act introducing compulsory free primary education in certain areas on an experimental basis; the act also extended the length of basic education from six to ten years. But Burkina still faces enormous problems in terms of the administration and organisation of its schools, and, importantly, in the quality of education that state schools can provide. Anyone with the means to do so avoids the system, and simply goes private.

UNIVERSITY Burkina has three state universities: Koudougou's focuses on training teachers and nurses, Bobo's is a polytechnic that specialises in management, and Ouagadougou's covers the full range of arts, sciences and social studies. Increasing demand has led to the recent creation of Université Ouaga II, about 20km east of the city. The courses themselves are free, but Burkinabe students must pay an annual 15,000f in enrolment fees. Students from neighbouring countries and further afield pay 250,000f. There are private universities too, including an Open University and various Catholic establishments.

The student voice has been a powerful and vocal component of civil society over the years, and the student union, ANEP, is powerful within student politics and in the country as a whole. Strikes and protests have regularly been met with police batons and teargas canisters. Before the 1966 and 1980 coups, intense student and trade-union activity and protest sparked the more widespread civil unrest that prefigured power seizures.

A period of heightened activism followed the death of investigative journalist Norbert Zongo, when student marches turned to riots. In the academic year 1999–2000, in continuing protest over government inaction, ANEP declared a strike at the University of Ouagadougou, taking the entire campus with it. The university closed down, was guarded by police, and no exams were taken that year.

In June 2008, cuts in facilities and difficult living conditions led to a series of clashes between police and student protesters, and once more, the University of

Ouagadougou closed down – this time for two months. A handful of students ended up in jail. Things simmered down again, only to erupt in February 2011, following the news that a student had died in police custody; apparently beaten to death. This time, the protests began in Koudougou (where the death occurred) and rapidly spread to Ouaga and beyond, lasting for several weeks. Clashes on the streets became violent, resulting in a number of deaths, before wider protests by the army and the population in general eclipsed the crisis.

CULTURE

MUSIC

Traditional instruments Musical traditions are particularly strong in Burkina. There is always a jam going on somewhere, whether under the shade of a tree, in a backstreet bar or in the national stadium. In Ouaga it can seem at times that everyone you meet on the streets plays the *djembe*, and wants to share the art. Many visitors take up the offer, if the summer planeloads of French students and teenagers crowding departure lounges with all manner of souvenir drums are anything to go by. To pick up some musical tips, the best place to enquire about organised tuition is at the French Institute or Cultural Centre (CCF), in Ouagadougou or Bobo.

In Burkinabe society, the function of musical instruments goes beyond the mere sound they make. The instrument and its notes carry deep spiritual and cultural significance. Music forms a backdrop to every important event in life: marriages, funerals, births, initiation ceremonies, prayers, celebrations. Combined with the oral input of *griots*, music weaves in a healthy dose of mythology and history.

Handmade instruments tend to differ according to region, made from local materials and according to local know-how. An excellent starting place for the enthusiast is the well-researched Museum of Music in Ouaga, but the place to buy instruments, particularly finely made *balafons*, is Bobo-Dioulasso.

Drums Percussion forms the basis of music-making in Burkina. Drums are used in daily life, to signal a journey or return from the fields, to accompany mask dances and to codify secret languages understood solely by initiates. The war drum, sacred in royal households, symbolises power, raising the alarm at a time of attack and announcing significant events.

Considered the king of drums among the Mossi, the *bendre* is also found in the royal household and made from an enormous round calabash, lopped off at the top and covered with a goatskin to make the drum head. It can perform the function of a *griot*, with a complex pattern of rhythms recounting in a tapestry of beats the complete history of Mossi kings, from the mythological Ouedraogo right up to the present day. The study of this function is known as bendrology. The *rabingo* drum is similar, but made from clay, giving a lower, more booming sound.

The *lunga* is a long, thin cylindrical drum, with a head at both ends. Normally slung over the shoulder and played with a beating stick, it is popular among the Gourounsi as an accompaniment to mask dances. The *tam-tam* is a much smaller drum, popular with *griots*, which can be tucked tight under the arm and is beaten vigorously with a curved stick to accompany verbal antics.

The largest drum is the *gangaogo*, a kind of cylindrical fat bass drum, covered at both ends. The *djembe* is a popular upright drum, originally from Guinea and popular in Burkinabe street stalls. Made from wood and covered with goatskin, it is usually played on the ground and carries a recognisable, fairly high-pitched sound.

Strings Stringed instruments can be fantastic-looking items, either plucked with the fingers, yielding a sound between a guitar and a harp, or played with a bow, often with the player resting the instrument in their lap. The range of notes is often played in repeating patterns. Strings are popular among travelling *griots* and hunters, and across the Mossi and Bwaba regions.

The *kora* looks a bit like a banjo. It is made from a goatskin-covered half-calabash, with a wooden neck, and is usually plucked. The *kunde* or *luth* is a similar three-stringed instrument of Fulani origin, used by *griots* to accompany popular songs as a kind of guitar. The *sokou* is a simple violin, with a soundbox that can be made from virtually anything to hand: a calabash, an empty tin, a coconut shell.

A simple variation combines wind and strings in the rather graceful form of the musical arc, played by the San (and called the *lolou*) and the Bissa (*guienguila*). Wood is bent into an arch, across which strings from horse hair or vegetable fibre are strung. The musician places one end in his mouth, to help it resonate, and plucks at the string with a wooden baton.

Keyed instruments and noisemakers The *balan*, known popularly as the *balafon*, is like a xylophone, and if there is one sound that will stay in the head long after leaving Burkina it is the percussive, hypnotic notes and rhythms of this instrument. Originating in the Mande countries of Mali and Guinea, the *balafon* is found predominantly in the southwest, notably in the cabarets and bars of Gaoua and Banfora. Each instrument consists of wooden 'keys' of varying lengths, positioned on a wooden frame. Below each key is a calabash, which acts as a resonator for the sound. The *balafon* can take different shapes: steeply curving among the Bwaba, flatter among the Dagara, Lobi and Senoufou, with 14–18 keys, while Mande and Dioula *balafons* tend to have 21.

Bwaba, Senoufo and Bobo are fond of bells and shakers that can be attached to the body to click or jangle, popular in initiation rites. The *sanza* is a small, round wooden board containing raised strips of metal flicked with a downward motion of the fingers.

Wind Adapted from cattle or antelope horns, *baorgo* are resonant horns, often beautifully painted and decorated, to accompany dances (*warba*) and agricultural ceremonies.

Whistles (*sifflets*), made from wood or clay, are popular among the Gourounsi, often as an accompaniment to mask dancers as they wend their way through town before starting the dance proper, when the drums take over. Whistles often contain two or four holes on either side, enabling the player to produce a range of notes by covering or uncovering them.

Long associated with wandering shepherds, flutes are popular with the nomads of the north, particularly the Fulani. Usually carved from wood, flutes are grouped into female–male pairs, and into larger orchestras of three to seven pairs. They are also used by bird hunters, enticing birds with mimicry of their calls.

Modern music Bobo-Dioulasso is the musical capital of Burkina, with many artists based there. Its most famous export, the traditional music group **Farafina**, now restrict themselves almost entirely to the European gig circuit. One of the founder members, Mahama Konate, went on to create an offshoot, **Farafina Lili**, for the next generation of musicians. That band has proved a training ground for a host of Burkinabe talent, including percussionist and *balafon* player Desire Ouattara, whose five-piece group, **Saramaya**, has toured internationally. **Les Frères**

Coulibaly are similar exponents of the sound and their *Senwie* album, released in 2001, serves as a good introduction. **Idak Basabe** and **Amity Meria** are both established Burkinabe names singing in Dioula, while two more up-and-coming traditional artists gaining national recognition are **Big de Sale** and **Kantala**. For something in a traditional vein, but from a younger generation, see if you can dig up a copy of *Sira Ba Kele*, from the group **Yirimassa**.

The Bissa *chanteuse* **Sami Rama**, blending old chants with an Afrobeat style, has recently reappeared on the scene after a promising career was interrupted by vocal chord surgery, and her last album, *Afriquii Bii*, is worth tracking down. **Aicha Kone** is another strong female vocalist.

American rap and French hip-hop have immense currency among Burkinabe youth, feeding into a lively homegrown scene that even has an awards ceremony. The name on everyone's lips going into 2011 was Florent Belemgnegre, **Floby**, who won the Golden Kunde gong for best Burkinabe musician in December 2010. In the running with him were two other greats of recent years, **Dez Altino** and **Alif Naba**. All sing in Moore. Hot on their heels is a female vocalist, **Wendy**, who burst onto the scene in 2008 and has brought out a hugely popular album, *Gal Yam*.

Housewives' favourite **Yeleen** is a four-strong boy band with a popular African twist on nu-soul and R&B, but their star is waning. **Bil Aka Kora** is a pop-friendly hero, whose guitar-led singalong anthems are immensely popular without ever really grabbing the heart. After years of plugging away, he's still going strong and brought out a new album, *Yaaba*, in 2010.

A recent surprise has been the success of **Victor Deme**, a musician who spent many years doing the rounds in the clubs and bars of Ouaga and Bobo with his guitar and rich soulful voice. In his mid forties, a chance encounter gave him the opportunity to make an album, *Victor Deme*, and start touring; he made an appearance at WOMAD in 2009.

Further afield, you can't walk down a Burkinabe street without hearing the distinctive *kada-kada, kada-kada* of Ivorian music, and likely as not it's **DJ Arafat** behind it. He is *the* man of the moment, and immensely prolific, having produced six albums between 2005 and 2010; the latest is called *Gladiator*. Ivorian reggae star **Alpha Blondie** is also adored in Burkina, particularly for his political lyrics treating the conflict in Côte d'Ivoire. Even more hip is **Tiken Jah Fakoly**, the other giant of Ivorian music, whose highly political, unpretentious Rasta style goes down well in the clubs and bars of Bobo and Ouaga. Two internationally known west African stars – Senegalese singer **Youssou N'Dour** and Malian **Salif Keita** – regularly visit Burkina for concerts and are keenly followed, as is the late Ali Farka Toure. The Malian star **Habib Koite** is another name worth looking out for if you are sizing up gig options in Ouagadougou.

CINEMA Ouagadougou is the undisputed capital of African cinema, hosting the international Fespaco festival (see box, opposite) in late February or early March every odd-numbered year. But Burkinabe big screens don't just flicker come Fespaco time. At a recent count, Burkina had 1.5 million cinemagoers and the industry picked up CFA5 billion a year.

The country's long and productive cinematic history dates back to the 1960s, when it was decided to nurture talented local filmmakers. What followed was a generation of competent directors, producers and technicians and, best of all, watchable, engaging films that formed the basis of an enduring cinematic tradition.

The enthusiasm and appetite of Burkinabe filmmakers continues today. As Gaston Kabore, godfather of Burkinabe film and a previous winner of the grand prize at Fespaco, says: 'Africa is a huge treasure of tales, legends, and myths. We have a responsibility to ourselves and the rest of the world to learn how to tell them.'

History of an industry Burkina Faso is relatively rare among African countries in supporting a film industry. Directors can draw on two battered, state-owned 35mm cameras and the government provides logistical support and locations to homegrown productions. Many technicians are state employees, so can be loaned to productions. The president, a keen cinephile, has in the past donated his own money to make sure films get finished.

Politics and film are never far away. Fespaco was born of a stand-off, not long after independence, between the Burkinabe government and the French companies that controlled the country's film distribution industry. When the French tried to hike ticket prices, the government decided to nationalise cinema. The first Fespaco in 1969 celebrated the attempt to forge a new post-colonial identity through film. Such was Burkina's success that the Congolese sent spies to find out how the country had managed to take on its old masters.

A national film school, Inafec, trained film greats Gaston Kabore and Idrissa Ouedraogo. Ouedraogo has previously won prizes at Cannes, with his films *Yaaba* and *Tilai*, while Kabore's films *Wend Kuuni* and *Buud Yam* have reached worldwide acclaim. Faced with a lack of funding, Inafec lasted only a decade, until 1986. For 18 years not a single film student was formally trained in Burkina Faso. The 'Cannes

FESPACO FUN

'Fespaco is the greatest film festival I know. Burkina digs film,' says Branwen Okpako, the half-Nigerian, half-Welsh director of *Valley of the Innocent*, one of 20 feature films that competed for the top gong at the 2005 edition of Fespaco.

The glitz and glamour of Africa's biggest film festival brings film buffs from all over the world. For eight days, dust-clogged corners of Ouagadougou throng with international stars, homegrown hopefuls and truanting schoolchildren, mobbing the city's cinemas for their glimpse of Africa on the big screen. In the cramped confines of the shared green taxis that splutter around the city, every passenger turns pundit. Vegetable sellers in the markets cackle with excitement at the prospect of the free nightly concerts that take over the centre of town.

While other star-studded opening ceremonies unfold inside the gilded ballrooms and cinemas, Fespaco kicks off in the national football stadium in front of 35,000 people. The exuberance of the 2005 ceremony was marred by tragedy, as a crowd stampede in the stadium caused two deaths and 15 injuries. In Fespaco's 36-year history, this is the first time that anyone has died, but it pays to be aware of the crowd if you decide to go. The same applies to smaller venues: in 2011, several people had to be treated for heatstroke after hundreds were kept waiting for hours outside the Institut Français.

The Gold Stallion of Yenenga, Fespaco's top gong, is awarded to the film that 'best portrays Africa's realities'. In 2011, it went to Moroccan film *Pegase*, directed by Mohamed Mouftakir – a disturbing portrayal of patriarchy in which a girl is raped by her father, who then tries to blame her pregnancy on the devil. In second place was a film from Chad, *Un Homme qui Crie*, by Mahamet-Saleh Haroun, which also won the Jury Prize at Cannes 2010.

SEVEN MUST-SEE BURKINABE FILMS

Wend Kuuni (Gaston Kabore, 1982)
Yaaba (Idrissa Ouedraogo, 1987)
Sia, le Rêve du Python (Dani Kouyate, 2001)
Tasuma, le feu (Daniel Kollo Sanou, 2004)
La Nuit de la Verité (Fanta Regina Nacro, 2005)
Une Femme Pas Comme Les Autres (Abdoulaye Dao, 2008)
Le Fauteuil (Missa Hebie, 2009)

of Africa' was haunted by a lost generation of cinematographers, editors, sound engineers and lighting designers.

Since 2005, two new film schools have begun to reverse the decline of film culture on the continent. Kabore has ploughed millions of francs of his own money into **Imagine** (*50 36 46 16; e imagine@fasonet.bf*), a Ouagadougou training school which welcomes students from around the world.

The second school is the **Institute Superieur de l'Image et du Son/Studio École (ISIS/SE)** (*50 34 03 01; e cilboudo@gmail.com; www.isis.gov.bf*), also based in Ouagadougou near the new, eye-catching Fespaco building. The Burkinabe state is funding the project, heralded as the future of training in the region, in conjunction with international donors. In 2010, the EU donated high-quality equipment, estimated at CFA311.6 million in value. Students from all over the world pay an annual fee of 600,000f to attend the three-year course.

Suffering cinema They may arrive just in the nick of time. While many African films are as scintillating as ever, the problem remains getting them onto cinema screens. Only 1% of film output in Burkina shows Burkina-made content: the rest is a stodgy diet of Hollywood blockbusters, Bollywood melodramas and Hong Kong kickathons.

Audiences have declined by half in recent years. Of 55 cinemas in Burkina Faso, only 11 now work. The industry battles nightclubs, *maquis* and television for public attention. And at between 200f and 1,500f a throw, entry rates can be a significant expense. Problems such as piracy, production and distribution need urgent attention. This grey market is one of the few sectors making money from film. On every street corner, vendors publicly hawk pirated copies of the latest films, both homegrown and international. At the last count, in mid 2002, there were 800 identified premises illegally distributing pirated copies in Burkina Faso.

Foreign money undoubtedly keeps the African film industry alive, with international grants coming mainly from France and the EU. Some think this is a problem, since whoever holds the purse strings can attach a few strings of their own. In the official feature film competition at Fespaco 2005, nine out of 14 sub-Saharan films were produced with EU support, of €130,000–300,000 each. French funding comes with the condition that post-production work takes place in France and that key personnel among the crew are French.

The cost of shooting on 35mm film is a considerable drawback to African directors. One fount of hope is an ongoing project to replace 35mm cinema projectors with digital projectors, so that films shot in popular, cheap digital formats can be easily shown to audiences. This plan would revolutionise the way films can be seen, and offer the possibility of African cinemas showing African films regularly. In the past, digital movies have been restricted to high-volume, low-quality markets such as the booming 'Nollywood' VHS and DVD market in Nigeria. Many believe that digital is the holy grail that African filmmakers have been waiting for.

THEATRE Burkinabe theatre is strong, and homegrown productions tend to be highly demonstrative, encouraging audience participation. The decade following independence saw the emergence of young playwrights such as **Moussa Savadogo**, **Ouamdegre Ouedraogo** and **Pierre Dabire**, who saw the theatre as a way of not only reaching the masses, but also helping people to find their own voices. In the eyes of pre-eminent Burkinabe theatre critic Prosper Kompaore, this kind of 'forum theatre' can challenge the notion of fatality, about individuals' roles and the possibilities open to them, that he believes is ingrained in much of African society. Kampaore's Atelier Théatre Burkinabe is one theatre company at the forefront of this movement, and regularly tours productions. A number of companies, mostly within Ouagadougou, Bobo-Dioulasso and Koudougou, perform both new work and established classics of African and world literature. There are also regular theatre festivals in Ouagadougou (see *Ouagadougou*, page 115).

LITERATURE Burkina's literary scene is small. The first novel published by a Burkinabe author was in 1962: *Crépuscule des temps anciens* (*The Dawn of Ancient Times*) written by **Nazi Boni**. Prior to this, one of the country's most significant works was *Maximes, pensées et devinettes mossi* (*Maxims, Thoughts and Riddles of the Mossi*) by **Dimdolobsom Ouedraogo**, published in 1934. In this meticulously collected tome of sayings he captured the living literary heritage of his countrymen. Burkinabe historian **Joseph Ki-Zerbo** is a doyen of African history, writing on both Burkina's early history and that of the continent as a whole.

As for fiction, names are few and far between, and many writers prefer the dramatic possibilities of theatre and film, which reach out to a wider audience. An exception is **Augustin-Sonde Coulibaly**, one of a new wave of writers who emerged in the 1970s. **Frederic Guirma** has taken traditional tales and written them down. **Bernadette Sanou**, an ex-culture minister and current director of the ONTB, Burkina's tourist board, is an award-winning author of both poetry and prose, including *La dernière épouse* (*The Last Wife*) in 1997. In recent years, another writer to come to the fore has been **Ansomwin Hien**, an economic advisor in Ouaga who hails from the small town of Dano. Two of his novels, *L'Enfer au Paradis* and *Une Flamme Dans Le Noir* are available in the Diacfa bookshop. The country's pre-eminent novelist is **Monique Ilboudu**.

SPORT

Football Like most of west Africa, Burkina Faso is obsessed by football, although supporting the national team, *Les Etalons*, is not an easy business. Despite hosting the African Cup of Nations in 1998, when the team reached the fourth round, Burkina has struggled to become a footballing force. Ever since then, it has either gone out in the first round or even failed to qualify, and dreams of World Cup qualification remain slim. Having managed to beat both Malawi and Guinea in the lead-up to the 2010 World Cup in South Africa, Côte d'Ivoire proved too strong and *Les Etalons* lost out. Hope may be around the corner, however, in the form of the junior team, *Les Etalons Cadets*. In January 2011, they came home as national heroes having actually *won* La Coupe des Cadets, the FIFA under-17 Africa Cup. The crowds in Ouaga went wild; trick riders on both horses and motorbikes performed ridiculous feats up and down Avenue Kwame N'Krumah, such was the nation's joy at a taste of success at last.

THE TOUR DU FASO

with thanks to Christoph Herby

Blink and you've missed it – such is the whirlwind speed at which the nation's cycling heroes zoom past, encased in lycra, chasing glory and the ultimate accolade: to come home first on the Tour's final day. In 2010, it was a Burkinabe who did just that, spurred on by the roaring crowds in central Ouaga. The Tour du Faso is a serious international competition, attracting teams from Europe and all over Africa. Africa's only 2.2 road race (as classified by the Union Cycliste Internationale/UCI), it's organised along the same lines as the Tour de France and was originally created by Francis Ducreux of the Amaury Sports Association (ASO).

Like the Tour de France, it's an annual team event, with individual winners wearing the yellow jersey from one day to the next. There are six riders in each team, and with around 13 teams taking part, the 70-odd riders create a worthy spectacle. The race usually takes place in late October, and covers 1,300–1,400km over ten days, following a route that changes from one year to the next. It sticks mostly to tar, but has exciting dusty sections of dirt track – 24km in 2010, sometimes more. Locals love to catch it as it whizzes through villages and towns, cheering wildly for the Burkinabe team.

The Tour du Faso is now organised by the Burkinabe government, and the nation is justly proud of it. In 2010, the total budget was CFA395 million, just over half of which came from the Ministry of Sport. European riders pay for their flights, but are thereafter well cared for on the ground, and stay in the Hotel Excellence when in Ouaga. In 2010, the final presentation was attended by Belgian cycling legend Eddie Merckx; with feathers like that in its cap, the Tour looks set to remain jaunty.

Most towns have a stadium where you can watch club teams play, including Ouagadougou's Stade Municipal, and the teams from the principal towns compete in a regular league. Ouaga's other stadium, Le Stade du 4 Août, hosts international matches.

Burkina state television regularly shows matches from the Champions League and a round-up of goings-on in England's Premiership. For European midweek games, men gather on street corners to cheer and howl at Manchester United, Liverpool, Chelsea and Arsenal on small outdoor TV screens blaring long into the night.

Other sports As one would expect from a bike-mad nation, there is an annual **cycling** competition, the Tour du Faso (see box, above), which takes place in late October or early November. It regularly attracts entrants from all over the world and, unlike the Tour de France (which captures viewers across Burkina), has some stages on uncovered roads. A new competition, known as La Boucle du Coton, went through Burkina in 2005.

Tennis is also popular. There are courts at some of the more upmarket hotels in Ouagadougou, including the Laico Ouaga 2000, the Silmande and the Azalai Hotel Independence.

With a reputation as the flattest country going, **golf** is one beneficiary. There is a course 15 minutes outside Ouaga, played on savanna scrub, with the occasional stand-in patch of astroturf for when the going gets too rough (see page 223).

Basketball and **volleyball** are also popular sports and there is a **rugby** team in Ouagadougou. If you're sticking around in Ouaga, you might consider attending an African **dance** lesson or two (check with the Institut Français).

Finally, Burkina's towns are filled with **table football** stands, and *le babyfoot* is almost as popular as the Beautiful Game itself. The tables are heavy, well greased and usually surrounded by an 11-a-side's-worth of children, scrambling to get their fingers to the handles. At 10f or 25f a game for five–ten balls, depending on the state of the table, quality entertainment comes cheap. Start playing and you'll make friends immediately. A no-spinning rule is fairly entrenched, as is a desperate desire to eke out the game by not actually scoring and thereby losing a ball's worth of play. If you pay for the first game, it sets a good precedent and someone should be gallant enough to shout you the next go. Winner stays on.

Basketball and volleyball are also popular sports and there is a rugby team in [illegible]. If you're keen on dancing around in Ghana, you might consider attending an African dance lesson or two (check with the Institut Français).

Finally, Ghanaian towns are filled with table football stands, and it seems to be almost as popular as the beautiful game itself. The tables are heavy, well greased and usually surrounded by a 10-metre-width of children scrambling to get their fingers to the handles. [illegible] It's a game for five to ten balls, depending on the state of the table; once a sufficient number comes along, start playing and you'll make friends instantly. Any playing rule is of secondary concern, with a desperate desire to keep the game going, not actually scoring and thereby losing a ball's worth of play. Paying for the first game makes a good precedent and someone should be [illegible] to shout out the next go. Winner stays on.

2

Practical Information

WHEN TO VISIT

Received wisdom is that you can only visit Burkina between October and February, and most recommend November and December as the best months of all. While the weather is at its most palatable then, there is no need to restrict oneself to such a small window. Whatever the season, Burkina has something to offer.

Any chance to tie in a trip with one of Burkina's numerous large-scale international festivals – the biennial pan-African cinema festival Fespaco, held every odd-numbered year in February, the arts and crafts extravaganza SIAO, held every even-numbered year in October, or Bobo-Dioulasso's culture week, held in March every even-numbered year – is worth taking.

MILD SEASON (OCTOBER–FEBRUARY) The weather is generally dry and no warmer than 35°C, with cool evenings, although you will battle the Harmattan after Christmas. This desert wind blows in from the Sahara, and can sometimes feel as if it is depositing half the desert on top of you. Some days the sky will appear cloudy, and you can look directly at a dull yellow ball of sun as though it is a second moon. It also means that every available surface, inside or out, will be covered in a fine film of reddish dust.

HOT SEASON (MARCH–MAY) The mercury starts to climb throughout March and April, and by May, just before the rains break, temperatures are uncomfortably hot across much of the country, regularly hitting 45°C in the Sahel region. This is the toughest time to visit but one good reason to brave the heat is the round of local celebrations. Villages hold marvellous mask festivals to celebrate the end of the harvest and to mark funerals. Towards the end of the hot season, as water sources become increasingly scarce and vegetation is low, game viewing is at its best.

RAINY SEASON (MAY–SEPTEMBER) Downpours are by no means daily and should not prevent you from getting around on Burkina's main highways, with coaches plying most of their usual routes. The temperatures, and the sunsets, are a big draw. So too are the lush fields and hills, heavy with tall crops and grass. Many traditional crafts usually practised in the villages, such as weaving and pottery-making, are suspended as the entire population goes out to the fields. Restaurants, and institutions such as the French Institute, tend to close for August–September. The rains bring increased risk of hassle from mosquitoes.

HIGHLIGHTS

THRILLING CULTURAL CELEBRATIONS Dramatic mask festivals in Dedougou, Hounde, Pouni and Boromo; heart-pounding Fulani horse-dancing in Barani; Fespaco, the pan-African film festival; and SIAO, the arts and crafts festival

THE ROMANCE OF THE SAHEL Desert markets, camel safaris and secret dune encampments

SOME OF WEST AFRICA'S BEST WILDLIFE Nose-to-trunk with elephants in Nazinga, lion-tracking in W National Park, sunsets with hippos in Lake Tengrela and close encounters with Bazoule's crocodiles

ACTION ADVENTURE ALONG THE GOBNANGOU ESCARPMENT Hiking, climbing and exploring caves

MAGIC AND MYSTICISM IN LOBI COUNTRY Animist rites are still performed in villages where traditional beliefs are as strong as the home-brewed millet beer.

ARCHITECTURE Stunning mud houses at Tiebele and Tangossoko

HIKING TRAILS Through the peaks of Sindou, abandoned cliffside houses and troglodyte houses of Senoufou country

EXCELLENT CUISINE AND NIGHT-TIME HIGHLIFE In Ouagadougou and Bobo-Dioulasso

STUNNING ARTISANSHIP Bronze forges, woodcarving, leatherwork, mask-making, fine jewellery, expert cloth-weaving and sculpture gardens

SUGGESTED ITINERARIES

There are three key areas of Burkina – the southwest, around Banfora and Bobo-Dioulasso; the far southeast, around Pama and south of Diapaga; and the Sahel in the north. If you have only seven–ten days it is worth choosing one region and sacrificing the others, depending on what sounds more appealing. There is too much travelling to visit them all, especially on public transport, and not enough time to settle.

The itineraries below (moving at the speed of a whirlwind tour) merely suggest what is on offer, and they can be mixed and matched if you have the time to linger. The more time you can give Burkina, the more it grows on you.

THREE DAYS

Wild west Ouagadougou – crocodiles at Bazoule – elephants at Boromo/Deux Bale – Bobo-Dioulasso (overnight) – hippos at Tengrela, domes at Fabedougou, falls at Karfiguela – Banfora (overnight)

Wildlife and culture Ouagadougou – elephants at Nazinga Game Ranch (overnight) – mud architecture at Tangossoko and Tiebele (overnight)

City vibes Live music and dancing in Ouagadougou (overnight) and Bobo-Dioulasso (overnight)

Herder's trail Ouagadougou (overnight) – artisan and leather market at Kaya – Friday cattle market at Dori (overnight)

FIVE TO SEVEN DAYS

Crocodiles, hippos and waterfalls Ouagadougou (overnight) – crocodiles at Sabou/Bazoule – elephants at Boromo (overnight) – mask-making in Hounde – Bobo-Dioulasso (two nights) – domes of Fabedougou, falls at Karfiguela – Banfora (overnight) – hippos at Tengrela (overnight)

Mossi Plateau Ouagadougou (overnight) – crocodiles at Sabou/Bazoule – elephants at Boromo/Deux Bale (overnight) – Koudougou (overnight) – Yako and goldmines – Ouahigouya (overnight)

Sahel escape Ouagadougou (overnight) – Loumbila Beach/goat farm – leatherworking village at Kaya (overnight) – mud mosques at Bani – Dori (overnight) – Gorom-Gorom (overnight) – camel rides, dunes and markets at Markoye/Tin-Akof (overnight) – museum at Oursi – hidden desert camp at Gandefabou (overnight) – rock carvings at Aribinda – Djibo – Ouagadougou

Magic and mysticism Ouagadougou (overnight) – Gaoua (two nights) – Loropeni ruins and Gan Kingdom – diviner's room at Kampti – women's gold market at Doudou – fortress Lobi housing – ruins at Sati – Leo – Po (overnight)

Senoufou country Ouagadougou (overnight) – Bobo-Dioulasso (overnight) – Banfora (overnight) – trekking at Sindou peaks (overnight) – troglodyte houses at Negueni/Niansogoni (overnight) – forgers at Noumassouba and Kankalaba (overnight)

Safari sortie Ouagadougou (overnight) – Fada N'Gourma – lakeside lodge at Pama (overnight) – game-viewing at Arly (overnight) – trekking along Gobnangou Escarpment (overnight) – game-viewing and Koudou Falls in W National Park (overnight) – Fada N'Gourma (overnight)

TWO WEEKS

Culture and scenery in the south and southwest Ouagadougou (overnight) – elephants at Deux Bale (overnight) – Bobo-Dioulasso and surrounds (overnight) – Orodara (overnight) – walking tour of Senoufou country (two nights) – Sindou peaks (overnight) – Banfora and surrounds (two nights) – Loropeni ruins, Kampti and Gaoua (two nights) – elephants at Nazinga Game Ranch (overnight) – Po – mud houses at Tangossoko and Tiebele (overnight) – Ouagadougou

Desert escape and safari adventure in the north and east Ouagadougou (overnight) – goat farm at Loumbila – honey-making at Fada N'Gourma (overnight) – lakeside retreats at Pama (overnight) – game-viewing in Arly (overnight) – hiking along Gobnangou Escarpment (overnight) – Diapaga and W National Park (overnight) – Ouaga (overnight) – leatherworkers at Kaya (overnight) – mud mosques at Bani – Dori (overnight) – Gorom-Gorom (overnight) – Markoye and Tin-Akof (overnight) – museum among the dunes at Oursi (overnight) – hidden desert camp at Gandafabou (overnight) – Ouagadougou

THREE WEEKS

Animists and animals Ouagadougou (overnight) – bees at Fada N'Gourma (overnight) – lakeside retreat at Pama (overnight) – game-viewing in Arly (overnight) – exploring Gobnangou Escarpment (two nights) – W National Park (overnight) – Ouaga – Tiebele and Tangassoko (overnight) – Nazinga Game Ranch (overnight) – Ouagadougou (overnight) – sacred crocs at Bazoule and Sabou (overnight) – elephants and artisans at Boromo/Deux Bales (overnight) – Bobo-Dioulasso and environs (three nights) – Banfora (overnight) – hippos at Tengrela – falls at Karfiguela – domes of Fabedougou – sacred baobab of Toumousseni – Sindou peaks (overnight) – cave dwellings Niansogoni/Negueni (overnight) – Gaoua (two nights) – Loropeni ruins and Gan Kingdom, Lobi villages, diviner's room at Kampti – Ouagadougou

Architecture and artisans Ouagadougou (two nights) – museums – artisans' village – craft workshops – Manega – rock sculptures at Laongo – leatherworkers at Kaya (overnight) – mosques at Bani (overnight) – Dori – market at Gorom-Gorom (overnight) – desert *campements* in Tin-Akof, Markoye (overnight) – ruins and museum at Oursi (overnight) – desert camp at Gandefabou (overnight) – mud architecture in Djibo (overnight) – Ouahigouya (overnight) – mud mosques of Gassan and Lanfiera – Tougan – Dedougou (overnight) – mosque, arts and crafts in Bobo-Dioulasso (two nights) – Banfora's weavers and potters, Tengrela, domes of Fabedougou, falls at Karfiguela (overnight) – mask-making in Hounde – mud architecture/artisans in Boromo (overnight) – lakeside crafts and crocs at Sabou (overnight) – Koudougou's artisans (overnight) – Ouagadougou (overnight) – Tiakane, Tiebele and Tangassoko (overnight) – Ouagadougou

ONE MONTH

Action adventure and wildlife Ouagadougou (overnight) – Bobo-Dioulasso (two nights) – swimming at La Guingette, exploration of Koro and Koumi – Banfora and environs (two nights) – hippos at Tengrela, falls at Karfiguela falls, hiking around the domes of Fabedougou – hike to caves at Douna (overnight) – Sindou peaks (overnight) – camping/hiking in Senoufou country, Niansogoni/Negueni, Mount Tenakourou (two nights) – Ouagadougou (overnight) – jet-ski at Loumbila Beach – leatherworking and lakes at Kaya (overnight) – exploring mosques at Bani (overnight) – Dori, Gorom-Gorom (overnight) – camel trek to Oursi via Menegou (two nights) – birdwatching around Mare d'Oursi (overnight) – desert camp at Gandefabou (overnight) – Ouagadougou (overnight) – lakeside retreat at Pama or Diapaga (two nights) – Arly National Park (overnight) – climbing, hiking, exploring caves along Gobnangou Escarpment (two nights) – W National Park and Koudou Falls (overnight) – Ouagadougou (overnight) – quad bikes/mountain bikes at Koubri – cycling in Kassena country (two nights) – Nazinga Game Ranch (overnight) – Ouagadougou

Culture, arts and mysteries Ouagadougou (three nights) – nightlife and fine dining – museums, Village Artisanal, *ateliers* – Manega, Loumbila, rock sculptures at Laongo – leatherworkers at Kaya (overnight) – mosques at Bani (overnight) – cattle market at Dori (overnight) – museum, ruins and dunes at Oursi – Ouagadougou (overnight) – *ateliers* in Koudougou (overnight) – crocs and crafts at Sabou (overnight) – palace of Kokologho – Boromo/Deux Bale elephants (overnight) – masks at Hounde – village retreat in Gombele-dougou (overnight) – Bobo-Dioulasso (three nights) – nightlife and music – old town and artisans – Koro and Koumi – Banfora and environs (two nights) – weavers and potters – Tengrela, Toumousseni, Karfiguela and Fabedougou – Sindou peaks (overnight) – cave dwellings at Niansogoni (overnight) – Gaoua (three nights) – Loropeni ruins, Gan King, Kampti and Lobi villages – Leo (overnight) – ruins at Sati – Nazinga Game Ranch (overnight) – Tiebele, Tangassoko and surrounds (two nights) – retreat at Koubri (overnight) – Ouagadougou

TOURIST INFORMATION

According to official statistics, Burkina received 226,000 tourists in 2008 (although it is not clear how many of these combined sightseeing with business), bringing an estimated CFA30 billion into the country. The real number of holidaymakers is apparently closer to 15,000–20,000 a year. So if you pick Burkina, you are likely to have much of it to yourself, which is half the attraction.

There are two branches of Burkina's national tourist office (the ONTB), in Ouaga and Bobo. Both can help with hotel options, travel agencies and opening hours. Many shops, offices and banks close for a long lunch break, from 12.00 to 15.30.

TOUR OPERATORS

IN THE UK For many anglophone Western tour operators, Burkina Faso only crops up on transcontinental overland tours as a bridge between Mali and Ghana and is generally passed through quickly. If you want to mix getting around under your own steam with some short tours, buy your plane ticket first and then co-ordinate with one of the Burkina-based tour operators once in-country. If you want a more organised tour, either around Burkina or including neighbouring countries, contact a Burkina-based tour operator in advance and request they organise flights as well. International tour companies are listed below. For local tour operators, see page 62.

Dragoman Overland Camp Green, Debenham, Stowmarket, Suffolk IP14 6LA, UK; 01728 861133; e info@dragoman.co.uk; www.dragoman.co.uk. Both its Dakar to Accra & Dakar to Douala overland trips pass through Burkina Faso.

Oasis Overland The Marsh, Henstridge, Somerset BA8 0TF; 01963 363400; e info@oasisoverland.co.uk; www.oasisoverland.co.uk. Oasis Overland's 9-week UK to Accra trip passes through Burkina.

Responsible Travel Pavilion Hse, 6 Old Steine, Brighton BN1 1EJ; 01273 600030; e amelia@responsibletravel.com; www.responsibletravel.com. This company runs a 2-week trip specifically around Burkina, taking in the Sahel, Kassena country, Nazinga, Banfora area, Sindou & Lobi country, as well as Ouaga & Bobo.

WORLDWIDE

Adventures Abroad Based in the US; 0114 247 3400 (UK), 1-800-665-3998 (US); e info@adventures-abroad.co.uk; www.adventures-abroad.com. Offers 2 different tours that take in surrounding countries, as well as Burkina.

Mandinka Tours Rue 250, Porte 731, Hippodrome, Bamako, Mali; 00 223 2072 9084; f 00 223 2022 6657; e info@mandinkatours.com; www.mandinkatours.com. Based in Mali but offering many tours across West Africa.

TransAfrica Rue Moyama 66, BP 265, Lome, Togo; + 228 221 68 23; e transafrica@transafrica.biz; www.transafrica.biz. This tour company is based in Togo, & run by an Italian with 20 years' experience of west Africa. He is an expert in African art & knows the whole region well, including Burkina Faso.

IN BURKINA FASO In our experience, most of Burkina is welcoming and accessible enough to be explored on one's own. But for those tight on time, in search of less hassle, greater comfort, or seeking out the harder-to-reach parts of the country, organising a trip with a local tour operator may be best. You can organise a tour once you arrive, of either short overnight trips, or longer visits, including neighbouring countries. Some tour operators can offer English-speaking guides. The list of tour operators below is not exhaustive. These tour operators are all in Ouagadougou.

Africa Evasion (in conjunction with **Meycom Voyages**) 50 33 09 83; www.africa-evasion.com. The result of collaboration between Noufou Compaore, a well-respected Burkinabe tour operator, & a French couple who now also run Le Grand Baobab hunting lodge near Arly. Can offer tours around the country; good for eastern safaris.

Couleurs d'Afrique Opposite Stade du 4 Août; 50 34 19 56; m 78 81 11 48; e cdafrique@yahoo.fr; www.couleurs-afrique.com. Highly thought of, this agency, run by an enthusiastic Frenchman with good experience of Burkina, enjoys good links with many of the best budget hotels in both Ouaga & Bobo, & can organise trekking, tours, or transport with 4x4s & motorbikes. Tours can include Mali, Benin, Togo & Ghana.

L'Agence Tourisme Rue Joseph Badoua; 50 31 84 43; e contact@agence-tourisme.com; www.agence-tourisme.com. An excellent tour agency, run by a French couple & based at the stylish Les Palmiers Hotel in Ouaga. They run the full gamut of trips from west African expeditions in 4x4s, camels, canoes & on foot, to day trips within Burkina. They can offer English-speaking guides.

STMB Tours Av Kwame N'Krumah; 50 30 20 44, 50 30 35 50; e contact@stmb.bf; www.stmbtours.com. STMB is a Burkina-wide phenomenon, offering coach travel as well as tours. They know their tourism, & can offer everything from flight-inclusive packages to local trips.

Tourisme et Développement Solidaires 50 31 25 94; e contact@tourisme-dev-solidaires.org; www.tourisme-dev-solidaires.org. This French-based organisation has pioneered responsible tourism packages that involve staying in traditional accommodation in specially constructed traditional compounds & learning local arts & crafts. The 4 camps are in different parts of the country – Doudou, 35km from Koudougou, in Gourounsi country; Koirezena, a Songhay village between Dori & Gorom-Gorom in the north; Zigla Koupele, near Garango in Bissa country; & Boala, near Kaya, in the Mossi Plateau. To organise a stay in advance, a 12-day trip, with flights all-inclusive from Paris, costs from €1,690; 16 days from €1,835. Alternatively, the tourist village has an office in Ouagadougou, which can organise weekend visits at considerably cheaper prices for people already in the country.

Vacances OK Raids 91 Rue Bitto, Patte d'Oie; 50 38 88 63/96; e okraids@okraids.bf; www.okraid.com. Efficient & friendly operator, with English-version website. Can organise a variety of trips within the country & flights.

Wango Aventures Office in Pissi, but also runs Le Baobab Hostel, Secteur 1; 50 50 25 04; m 78 62 91 47; e info@wango-aventures.com; www.wango-aventures.com. Ouaga-based agency with an emphasis on responsible tourism; supports a number of local projects. Offers a good range of 1-, 2- & 3-day trips around Ouaga as well as longer excursions. Rates go down for larger groups; eg: a 2-day trip to Tiebele & Nazinga costs 151,000f each for 2, 90,000f each for 4.

Yenenga Travel Service Secteur 30; 50 37 75 44; m 78 00 98 00, 76 62 42 94; e yenenga@yenenga.com; www.yenenga.com. Since it specialises in weekly departures, it can afford to put people together in groups, & do tours within Burkina for as little as 100,000f, offering guides in all languages.

LOCAL GUIDES In a country where rites and rituals are many, local knowledge is an invaluable aid to understanding some of what you see. Where relevant we have listed throughout the book people we have met and consider worthwhile guides. Few have official tourist badges of accreditation, but they know their regions extremely well, and will give strangers a great welcome. Discuss a fee up front. In general, budget about 5,000–10,000f per day for guiding. This depends on your programme and, obviously, what you think of the guide.

RED TAPE

If you are not a citizen of ECOWAS (the Economic Community of West African States), you will need a visa. In 2010, there was a massive price hike, especially for visas on arrival; so if you fail to get one in advance, you will have to pay a whopping 94,000f at the airport (it would appear that the same applies at borders), which is roughly double what you would pay back home. This can then be converted to a three-month single-entry visa at the **Service des Passeports** in Gounghin, a process that takes at least two days (leave it in the morning one day, collect it at 16.00 the next; no service over the weekend). Should you wish to stay for longer, or need multiple entry, there will be further expensive charges. So, the message is clear: get one before coming. They're still not cheap as African visas go, but you will save time as well as money. All visas require two passport photos.

REGIONAL VISA The Visa Touristique Entente (VTE) is a one-off regional visa that allows free movement within Benin, Burkina, Côte d'Ivoire, Niger and Togo. For those planning on travel throughout francophone west Africa this would considerably cut down on visa costs: valid for 60 days, it costs €40. However, it is notoriously difficult to get hold of, and it's unclear how it would play out with the new Burkinabe visa requirements. The Togolese embassy in Brussels (*264 Av de Tervuren, Brussels; +32 02 770 17 91; ambassadetogo@ambassadetogo.be; www.ambassadetogo.be*) is the best bet in Europe; you could, however, try the Togolese embassy in Paris (*8 Rue Alfred-Roll 75017 Paris; +33 01 43 80 12 13; http://consulatogo.org*). Once in west Africa, try any Togolese embassy.

OTHER DOCUMENTS Make sure your **passport** is valid for more than six months. Carry it or a photocopy on you at all times; you are especially likely to be checked by police while on public transport or on a moped. You also need a **yellow fever vaccination certificate.**

If you plan on hiring or driving a vehicle in Burkina, sort out an **international driving licence** in advance: both the AA (*www.theaa.com*) and RAC (*www.rac.co.uk*) can issue them in the UK. The licence is valid for one year, but carry your home driving licence as well: technically an international licence is not valid without it. The licence can also be a useful form of picture identification in case of a lost or stolen passport.

Make sure your **travel insurance** is up to date, for protection against loss, theft and medical emergencies. The current travel advice from some countries' governments (including France and the UK) is against travel to certain areas (see pages 153 and 223), and many people believe that to ignore such advice invalidates their insurance. This actually depends on the insurance company: while many high-street insurers have a blanket policy, others continue to insure against all but the specified danger. So, with regard to the threat in the north, if you fall off a bike and break your wrist, you may be covered; if you're kidnapped, you're not. Best to check before you leave, and think very carefully before going against the advice in the first place.

Photocopies of all vital documents are essential, and having two sets means one can be left at home and faxed anywhere if necessary, while the other set should be stowed somewhere safe but out of the way, in case anything goes missing.

EMBASSIES

Burkina Faso has full diplomatic representation in the following countries, and also in Côte d'Ivoire, Ghana, Mali, Morocco, Nigeria and Senegal.

ABROAD

Austria Prinz Eugen Strasse, 18/3AA 1040 Vienna; +431 503 8264; e s.p@abfvienne.at. Also provides consular representation for Hungary, the Czech Republic, Slovakia & Slovenia.

Belgium Pl Guy d'Arezzo 16, 1180 Brussels; +322 345 9912; f +322 345 0612; e ambassade.burkina@skynet.be; www.ambassadeduburkina.be. Download the form from the website; take 3 filled-out copies, 3 passport photos & the fee to the embassy in person.

Canada 48 Range Rd, Ottawa; +1 613 238 4796; f +1 613 238 3812; e burkina.faso@sympatico.ca; www.ambaburkina-canada.org

Denmark Svanemollevej 20, 2100 Copenhagen; +45 3918 4022; e amba@ambaburkina.dk

France 159 Bd Hausmann, 75008 Paris; +33 01 43 59 90 63; e amba.burkina.faso@wanadoo.fr. There are honorary consuls in Marseilles, Lyon, Rouen Cedex, Avanton (Poitiers) & Nice.

Germany Karolinger Platz 10/11, 14052 Berlin; +49 30 3010 5990; f +49 30 3010 5992; e embassy_burkina_faso@t-online.de; www.embassy.bf.org

India P 3/1 Vassant Vihar, New Delhi 110057; +91 11 2614 0641/42; f +91 11 2614 0630; e cmd@embassyburkindia.com; www.embassyburkina.com

Italy Via Venti Senttembre, 86-00187 Rome; +39 06 4201 3355/0611; e ambabf.roma@tin.it

Japan 3-1-17 Hiroo Glisten Hills, 3F Shibuya-ku, Tokyo 150-0012; +81 3 3400 7919; f +81 3 3400 6945

Netherlands Ministerie van Buitenlandse Zaken, Postbus 20061, 2500 EB The Hague; www.dfait-maeci.gc.ca/burkina_faso/menu-en.asp

Switzerland Chemin Louis-Durant 7-9, Case Postale 119 1211, Geneva 20; +41 22 734 6330; f +41 22 734 6361; e mission.burkina@ties.itu.int

Taiwan 6G, No 9-1, Lane 62, Tien Mou West Rd, Taipei; +886 22 2873 3096; e abftap94@ms17.hinet.net

UK Mr Colin Seelig, Honorary Consul of Burkina Faso, The Lilacs, Stane St, Ockley, Surrey RH5 5LU; +44 1306 627 225; e consul@colinseelig.co.uk; www.burkinafasovisa.co.uk. Not an embassy, but an honorary consul who can issue visas. 3-month single entry costs £65. Download the online application form from the website, fill it in & send 2 copies with 2 passport photos, your passport, a registered stamped addressed envelope & the fee to the above address. A normal tourist visa should be processed within 3 working days.

US 2340 Massachusetts Av NW, Washington DC; +1 202 332 5577; e ambawdc@rcn.com; www.burkinaembassy-usa.org

IN BURKINA FASO Contact your own embassy if you have troubles in Burkina, such as loss or theft of passports. For onward travel to other countries in the region, contact the embassies of destination countries to arrange visas. In some cases you can buy a short-stay visa at the border (for Benin; Dogon country in Mali via Ouahigouya; Niger; and Togo), usually for 10,000f, which you can extend once you reach the capital. Nearly all embassies have half days on Friday, and many take a long lunch (12.00–15.00 Monday–Thursday).

For **visa extensions within Burkina**, visit the Services des Passeports on Avenue Kadiogo, Ouagadougou, a bit further down from Fespaco on the left (*50 34 39 28, 50 34 26 43*). Take two passport-sized photos. These embassies are all in Ouagadougou.

Canada 316 Av Professeur Joseph Kizerbo; 50 31 18 94; f 50 31 19 00; e ouaga@dfait-maeci.gc.ca; www.burkinafaso.gc.ca. The embassy also looks after citizens of Commonwealth countries such as Australia, New Zealand & South Africa.

Denmark Av Professeur Joseph Kizerbo; 50 32 85 40; f 50 32 85 77; e ouaamb@um.dk; www.ambouagadougou.um.dk

France Rue du Tresor; 50 49 66 66; f 50 49 66 09; e ambassade@ambafrance-bf.org;

www.ambafrance-bf.org. Visas for **Gabon, Mauritania, Senegal** & **Togo** are available here.
Germany 399 Av Joseph Badoua; t 50 30 67 31/32; f 50 31 39 91; e amb.allemagne@fasonet.bf
Ghana Av President Sankara; t 50 30 76 35; f 50 30 69 60. During the course of this update, the embassy inexplicably stopped issuing visas to all but Burkinabe residents. You can't get one at the border either: you must obtain one in your own country of residence.
Mali Av Bassawarga; t 50 38 19 22, 50 30 05 35; f 50 38 19 21; e amba.mali.ouaga@fasonet.bf. Visas cost 20,000f for 3 months (take 2 passport photos).
Netherlands Av Kwame N'Krumah; t 50 30 61 34/35/36; f 50 30 76 95; e oua@minbuza.nl
Nigeria Av President Sankara; t 50 30 66 67/68, 50 36 10 87
Senegal Off Av Yennenga; t 50 31 28 11; e spe@fasonet.bf
Taiwan 994 Rue Agostino Neto; t 50 31 61 95; f 50 31 61 97; e ambachine@fasonet.bf
UK t 50 30 88 60; f 50 31 25 43; e delalande.ici@fasonet.bf. There is no British embassy in Burkina Faso but there is an honorary consul, Patrick de Lalande, who should be contacted in the first instance.
US Av Sembene Ousmane, Ouagadougou 2000; t 50 49 53 00; f 50 49 56 28; e amembouaga@state.gov; http://ouagadougou.usembassy.gov

GETTING THERE AND AWAY

BY AIR Getting to Burkina is likely to be the single biggest cost. Most connections go through Paris, and Air France has the best and most frequent service. Cheaper options include Point Afrique, Royal Air Maroc and Afriqiyah Airways.

Afriqiyah Airways (*www.afriqiyah.aero*), a Libyan airline, was a decent and cheap option before the recent unrest in Libya, flying between Ouaga and London Gatwick twice a week using Tripoli as a hub. All flights were suspended at the time of writing; its fate hangs in the balance.

Air Burkina (*www.air-burkina.com*) flies from Paris twice a week, stopping off at Marseilles. It also flies to Bobo-Dioulasso twice a week, and to neighbouring countries in the region.

Air France (*www.airfrance.net*) has the most regular service between Paris and Ouaga. It can also get you all over the world with trouble-free links to London Heathrow and the US. It's undoubtedly the most comfortable (and expensive) way into and out of Burkina.

Brussels Airlines (*www.brusselsairlines.com*) has arrived relatively recently in Ouaga and has two flights a week to and from Brussels, on Monday and Friday, with connections from there. Look out for promotional fares.

Ethiopian Airlines (*www.ethiopianairlines.com*) flies to and from Addis Ababa four times a week, with connections around the continent and to London. It specialises in flights to Asia.

Point Afrique (*www.point-afrique.com*) has flights only during the French high season. During the low season, flights are those of Air Burkina. There are some bargains to be had if you can be flexible about dates – flights go from Paris for as little as €141 (one-way). It can also arrange tours and visas.

Royal Air Maroc (*www.royalairmaroc.com*) has good deals, linking up to various cities worldwide via Casablanca. It flies to Ouaga five times a week.

From Ouagadougou there are good links to a number of regional hubs, including Accra, Dakar, Abidjan and, across the Sahara, Casablanca, Tripoli and Algiers. These provide ways into other parts of Africa, and open up routes to European and international destinations. The following airlines, listed alphabetically, have good regional connections to and from Burkina. You can contact Ouagadougou Airport

(✆ *50 30 65 20, 50 31 15 02*) for weekly flight schedules, but here are details at the time of writing:

Afriqiyah Airways Av Kwame N'Krumah; ✆ 50 30 16 52; e aawoua@afriqiyah.aero; www.afriqiyah.aero
Air Algerie Av Kwame N'Krumah; ✆ 50 31 23 01; e airalgerie.bf@fasonet.bf; www.airalgerie.dz. Flies once a week to Algiers, via Bamako.
Air Burkina Av de la Nation; ✆ 50 49 23 45/46/47; e resa@airburkina.bf; www.air-burkina.com. For phone reservations only. Also acts on behalf of Air Mali. Their office on Av Kwame N'Krumah is the place to come to pick up tickets in person.
Air France Av de la Nation; ✆ 50 30 63 65/66/67; www.airfrance.net
Air Ivoire Hotel Palm Beach, Av Kwame N'Krumah; ✆ 50 30 04 50/51; e airivoireoua@airivoire.com; www.airivoire.com. Has 4 flights a week to Abidjan, 1 via Niamey; possible to connect to Dakar, Bamako, Conakry, Niamey, Accra, Lome, Cotonou, Douala & Libreville. Owing to the unrest in Côte d'Ivoire, all had been suspended at the time of writing.
Brussels Airlines Av John F Kennedy, Koulouba; ✆ 50 33 14 44/45/46; e ouagadougou@brusselsairlines.com; www.brusselsairlines.com
Ethiopian Airlines Av Kwame N'Krumah; ✆ 50 30 10 24/25; www.ethiopianairlines.com
Point Afrique Opposite SIAO; ✆ 50 33 16 20, 50 30 00 42; www.point-afrique.fr
Royal Air Maroc Av Kwame N'Krumah; ✆ 50 30 50 81; www.royalairmaroc.com. Flies to Casablanca 5 times a week, with connections to London.

OVERLAND Crossing into Burkina from neighbouring countries now seems to be subject to the same massive 94,000f fee as at the airport (see page 63). If you have a visa already, you should have no problem.

If you are coming from Mali, the main tourist crossing point is close to Dogon country, between Koro in Mali, and Thiou in Burkina. The main entry point from Niger is between Makalondi and Kantchari; from Benin it is between Dassari and Tindangou; from Togo between Senkanse and Bitou; and from Ghana at Paga.

✚ HEALTH *with Dr Felicity Nicholson*

People new to exotic travel often worry about tropical diseases, but it is accidents that are the biggest danger. Road accidents are very common in many parts of Burkina Faso so be aware and do what you can to reduce risks: try to travel during daylight hours, always wear a seatbelt and refuse to be driven by anyone who has been drinking. Listen to local advice about areas where violent crime is rife too.

BEFORE YOU LEAVE Preparations to ensure a healthy trip to Burkina Faso require checks on your immunisation status: it is wise to be up to date on tetanus, polio and diphtheria (now given as an all-in-one vaccine, Revaxis, that lasts for ten years), and hepatitis A. Immunisations against cholera, meningococcus and rabies may also be recommended. Proof of vaccination against yellow fever is needed for entry into Burkina Faso if you are coming from another yellow fever endemic area. The World Health Organisation (WHO) recommends that this vaccine should be taken for Burkina Faso by those over nine months of age, although proof of entry is only officially required for those over one year of age. If the vaccine is not suitable for you then obtain an exemption certificate from your GP or a travel clinic. This does mean that you will not be protected against the disease, which puts you at risk. Yellow fever is transmitted by day-biting mosquitoes, so if the trip is imperative then wear loose long-sleeved clothing and protect exposed skins with insect repellents.

Hepatitis A vaccine (Havrix Monodose or Avaxim) comprises two injections given about a year apart. The course costs about £100, but may be available on the NHS; protects for 25 years and can be administered even close to the time of departure. Hepatitis B vaccination should be considered for longer trips (two months or more) or for those working with children or in situations where contact with blood is likely. Three injections are needed for the best protection and can be given over a three-week period if time is short for those aged 16 or over. Longer schedules give more sustained protection and are therefore preferred if time allows. Hepatitis A vaccine can also be given as a combination with hepatitis B as 'Twinrix', though two doses are needed at least seven days apart to be effective for the hepatitis A component, and three doses are needed for the hepatitis B. Again this schedule is only suitable for those aged 16 or over.

The newer injectable typhoid vaccines (eg: Typhim Vi) last for three years and are about 85% effective. Oral capsules (Vivotif) may also be available for those aged six and over. Three capsules over five days lasts for approximately three years but may be less effective than the injectable forms. They should be encouraged unless the traveller is leaving within a few days for a trip of a week or less, when the vaccine would not be effective in time. Meningitis vaccine containing strains A, C, W and Y, is ideally recommended for all travellers, especially for trips of more than four weeks (see page 77). Vaccinations for rabies are ideally advised for everyone, but are especially important for travellers visiting more remote areas, especially if you are more than 24 hours from medical help and definitely if you will be working with animals (see pages 77–8).

Experts differ over whether a BCG vaccination against tuberculosis (TB) is useful in adults: discuss this with your travel clinic.

In addition to the various vaccinations recommended above, it is important that travellers should be properly protected against malaria. For detailed advice, see below.

Protection from the sun Give some thought to packing suncream. The incidence of skin cancer is rocketing as Caucasians are travelling more and spending more time exposing themselves to the sun. Keep out of the sun during the middle of the day and, if you must expose yourself to the sun, build up gradually from 20 minutes per day. Be especially careful of exposure in the middle of the day and of sun reflected off water, and wear a T-shirt and lots of waterproof suncream (at least SPF15) when swimming. Sun exposure ages the skin, makes people prematurely wrinkly; and increases the risk of skin cancer. Cover up with long, loose clothes and wear a hat when you can. The glare and the dust can be hard on the eyes, too, so bring UV-protecting sunglasses and, perhaps, a soothing eyebath.

Malaria Along with road accidents, malaria poses the single biggest serious threat to the health of travellers in most parts of tropical Africa, Burkina Faso included. It is unwise to travel in malarial parts of Africa whilst pregnant or with children: the risk of malaria in many parts is considerable and these travellers are likely to succumb rapidly to the disease. The risk of malaria at altitudes of 1,800m or more above sea level is less, but may still be present.

The *Anopheles* mosquito that transmits the parasite is found throughout Burkina Faso, therefore it is wise to take precautions. There are six strains of malaria but the most common is *Plasmodium falciparum*, which is invariably fatal if untreated.

Malaria prevention There is not yet a vaccine against malaria that gives enough protection to be useful for travellers, but there are other ways to avoid it; since most of Africa is very high risk for malaria, travellers must plan their malaria protection properly. Seek current advice on the best antimalarials to take: usually mefloquine, Malarone or doxycycline. If mefloquine (Lariam) is suggested, start this two-and-a-half weeks (three doses) before departure to check that it suits you; stop it immediately if it seems to cause depression or anxiety, visual or hearing disturbances, severe headaches, fits or changes in heart rhythm. Side effects such as nightmares or dizziness are not medical reasons for stopping unless they are sufficiently debilitating or annoying. Anyone who has been treated for depression or psychiatric problems, has diabetes controlled by oral therapy or who is epileptic (or who has suffered fits in the past) or has a close blood relative who is epileptic, should probably avoid mefloquine.

In the past doctors were nervous about prescribing mefloquine to pregnant women, but experience has shown that it is relatively safe and certainly safer than the risk of malaria. That said, there are other issues, so if you are travelling to Burkina Faso whilst pregnant, seek expert advice before departure.

Malarone (proguanil and atovaquone) is as effective as mefloquine. It has the advantage of having few side effects and need only be continued for one week after returning. However, it is expensive and because of this tends to be reserved for shorter trips. Malarone may not be suitable for everybody, so advice should be taken from a doctor. The licence in the UK has been extended for up to three months' use and a paediatric form of tablet is also available, prescribed on a weight basis.

Another alternative is the antibiotic doxycycline (100mg daily). Like Malarone it can be started one day before arrival. Unlike mefloquine, it may also be used in travellers with epilepsy, although certain anti-epileptic medication may make it less effective. In perhaps 1–3% of people there is the possibility of allergic skin reactions developing in sunlight; the drug should be stopped if this happens. Women using the oral contraceptive should use an additional method of protection for the first four weeks when using doxycycline. It is also unsuitable in pregnancy or for children under 12 years.

Chloroquine and proguanil are no longer considered to be effective enough for Burkina Faso, but may be considered as a last resort if nothing else is deemed suitable.

All tablets should be taken with or after the evening meal, washed down with plenty of fluid and, with the exception of Malarone (see above), continued for four weeks after leaving.

Despite all these precautions, it is important to be aware that no antimalarial drug is 100% protective, although those on prophylactics who are unlucky enough to catch malaria are less likely to get rapidly into serious trouble. In addition to taking antimalarials, it is therefore important to avoid mosquito bites between dusk and dawn (see box, page 76).

There is unfortunately the occasional traveller who prefers to 'acquire resistance' to malaria rather than take preventive tablets, or who takes homeopathic prophylactics thinking these are effective against killer disease. Homeopathy theory dictates treating like with like so there is no place for prophylaxis or immunisation in a well person; bona fide homoeopathists do not advocate it. It takes at least 18 months residing in a holoendemic area for someone to get some immunity to malaria, so travellers to Africa will not acquire any effective resistance. The best way is to prevent mosquito bites in the first place and to take a suitable prophylactic agent.

Malaria diagnosis and treatment Even those who take their malaria tablets meticulously and do everything possible to avoid mosquito bites may contract a strain of malaria that is resistant to prophylactic drugs. Untreated malaria is likely to be fatal, but even strains resistant to prophylaxis respond well to prompt treatment. Because of this, your immediate priority upon displaying possible malaria symptoms – including a rapid rise in temperature (over 38°C), and any combination of a headache, flu-like aches and pains, a general sense of disorientation, and possibly even nausea and diarrhoea – is to establish whether you have malaria, ideally by visiting a clinic.

Diagnosing malaria is not easy, which is why consulting a doctor is sensible: there are other dangerous causes of fever in Africa, which require different treatments. Even if you test negative, it would be wise to stay within reach of a laboratory until the symptoms clear up, and to test again after a day or two if they don't. It's worth noting that if you have a fever and the malaria test is negative, you may have typhoid or paratyphoid, which should also receive immediate treatment.

Travellers to remote parts of Burkina Faso would be wise to carry a course of treatment to cure malaria, and a rapid test kit. With malaria, it is normal enough to go from feeling healthy to having a high fever in the space of a few hours (and it is possible to die from falciparum malaria within 24 hours of the first symptoms). In such circumstances, assume that you have malaria and act accordingly – whatever risks are attached to taking an unnecessary cure are outweighed by the dangers of untreated malaria. Experts differ on the costs and benefits of self-treatment, but agree that it leads to overtreatment and to many people taking drugs they do not need; yet treatment may save your life. There is also some division about the best treatment for malaria, but either Malarone or Coarthemeter are the current treatments of choice. Discuss your trip with a specialist either at home or in Burkina Faso.

Travel clinics and health information A full list of current travel clinic websites worldwide is available on www.istm.org/. For other journey preparation information, consult www.nathnac.org/ds/map_world.aspx. Information about various medications may be found on www.netdoctor.co.uk/travel.

In the UK

Berkeley Travel Clinic 32 Berkeley St, London W1J 8EL (near Green Park tube station); ☎ 020 7629 6233; ⊕ 10.00–18.00 Mon–Fri, 10.00–15.00 Sat

Edinburgh Travel Health Clinic 14 East Preston St, Newington, Edinburgh EH8 9QA; ☎ 0131 667 1030; www.edinburghtravelhealthclinic.co.uk; ⊕ 09.00–19.00 Mon–Wed, 09.00–18.00 Thu–Fri. Travel vaccinations & advice on all aspects of malaria prevention. All current UK prescribed antimalarial tablets in stock.

Fleet Street Travel Clinic 29 Fleet St, London EC4Y 1AA; ☎ 020 7353 5678; e info@fleetstreetclinic.com; www.fleetstreetclinic.com; ⊕ 08.45–17.30 Mon–Fri. Injections, travel products & latest advice.

Hospital for Tropical Diseases Travel Clinic Mortimer Market Bldg, Capper St (off Tottenham Ct Rd), London WC1E 6AU; ☎ 020 7387 4411; www.thehtd.org; ⊕ 13.00–17.00 Wed, 09.00–13.00 Fri. Consultations are by appointment only & are only offered to those with more complex problems. Check the website for inclusions. Runs a Travellers' Healthline Advisory Service (☎ *020 7950 7799*) for country-specific information & health hazards. Also stocks nets, water purification equipment & personal protection measures. Travellers who have returned from the tropics & are unwell, with fever or bloody diarrhoea, can attend the walk-in emergency clinic at the hospital without an appointment.

InterHealth Travel Clinic 111 Westminster Bridge Rd, London SE1 7HR; ☎ 020 7902 9000; e info@interhealth.org.uk; www.interhealth.org.uk; ⊕ 08.30–17.30 Mon–Fri. Competitively priced, one-stop travel health service by appointment only.

MASTA (Medical Advisory Service for Travellers Abroad) At the London School of Hygiene & Tropical Medicine, Keppel St, London WC1E 7HT; ☎ 0906 822 4100 (this is a premium-line number, charged at 60p per min); e enquiries@masta.org; www.masta-travel-health.com. For a fee, they will provide an individually tailored health brief, with up-to-date information on how to stay healthy, inoculations & what to take.

MASTA pre-travel clinics ☎ 01276 685040; http://www.masta-travel-health.com/travel-clinic.aspx. Call or check the website for the nearest; there are currently 50 in Britain. They also sell malaria prophylaxis, memory cards, treatment kits, bednets, net treatment kits, etc.

NHS travel websites www.fitfortravel.nhs.uk or www.fitfortravel.scot.nhs.uk. Provide country-by-country advice on immunisation & malaria prevention, plus details of recent developments, & a list of relevant health organisations.

Nomad Travel Clinics Flagship store: 3–4 Wellington Terrace, Turnpike Lane, London N8 0PX; ☎ 020 8889 7014; e turnpike@nomadtravel.co.uk; www.nomadtravel.co.uk; walk in or appointments ⊕ 09.15–17.00 daily with late night Thu. Also has clinics in west & central London, Bristol, Southampton & Manchester – see website for further information. As well as dispensing health advice, Nomad stocks mosquito nets & other anti-bug devices, & an excellent range of adventure travel gear. Runs a Travel Health Advice line on ☎ 0906 863 3414.

The Travel Clinic Ltd, Cambridge 41 Hills Rd, Cambridge CB2 1NT; ☎ 01223 367362; e enquiries@travelclinic.ltd.uk; www.travelcliniccambridge.co.uk; ⊕ 10.00–16.00 Mon, Tue & Sat, 12.00–19.00 Wed & Thu, 11.00–18.00 Fri

The Travel Clinic Ltd, Ipswich Gilmour Piper, 10 Fonnereau Rd, Ipswich IP1 3JP; ☎ 01223 367362; ⊕ 09.00–19.00 Wed, 09.00–13.00 Sat

Trailfinders Immunisation Centre 194 Kensington High St, London W8 7RG; ☎ 020 7938 3999; www.trailfinders.com/travelessentials/travelclinic.htm; ⊕ 09.00–17.00 Mon, Tue, Wed & Fri, 09.00–18.00 Thu, 10.00–17.15 Sat. No appointment necessary.

Travelpharm www.travelpharm.com. The Travelpharm website offers up-to-date guidance on travel-related health & has a range of medications available through their online mini pharmacy.

In Ireland

Tropical Medical Bureau 54 Grafton St, Dublin 2; ☎ 1 271 5200; e graftonstreet@tmb.ie; www.tmb.ie; ⊕ until 20.00 Mon–Fri & Sat mornings. For other clinic locations & useful information specific to tropical destinations, check their website.

In the USA

Centers for Disease Control 1600 Clifton Rd, Atlanta, GA 30333; ☎ 800 232 4636/6348; e cdcinfo@cdc.gov; www.cdc.gov/travel. The central source of travel information in the USA. Each summer they publish the invaluable *Health Information for International Travel*.

IAMAT (International Association for Medical Assistance to Travelers) 1623 Military Rd, #279 Niagara Falls, NY 14304-1745; ☎ 716 754 4883; e info@iamat.org; www.iamat.org. A non-profit organisation with free membership that provides lists of English-speaking doctors abroad.

In Canada

IAMAT (International Association for Medical Assistance to Travellers) Suite 10, 1287 St Clair Street West, Toronto, Ontario M6E 1B8; ☎ 416 652 0137; www.iamat.org

TMVC Suite 314, 1030 W Georgia St, Vancouver, BC V6E 2Y3; ☎ 604 681 5656; e vancouver@tmvc.com; www.tmvc.com. One-stop medical clinic for all your international travel health & vaccination needs.

In Australia and New Zealand

IAMAT (International Association for Medical Assistance to Travellers) 206 Papanui Rd, Christchurch 5, New Zealand; www.iamat.org

TMVC (Travel Doctors Group) ☎ 1300 65 88 44; www.tmvc.com.au. 30 clinics in Australia & New Zealand, including: *Auckland* Canterbury Arcade, 174 Queen St, Auckland 1010; ☎ 9 373 3531; e auckland@traveldoctor.co.nz; *Brisbane* 75a Astor Terrace, Spring Hill, Brisbane, QLD 4000; ☎ 07 3815 6900; e brisbane@traveldoctor.com.au; *Melbourne* 393 Little Bourke St, Melbourne, Vic 3000; ☎ 03 9935 8100; e melbourne@traveldoctor.com.au; *Sydney* 428 George St, Sydney, NSW 2000; ☎ 2 9221 7133; e sydney@traveldoctor.com.au

In South Africa

SAA-Netcare Travel Clinics ☎ 011 802 0059; e travelinfo@netcare.co.za; www.travelclinic.co.za. 11 clinics throughout South Africa.

TMVC NHC Health Centre, Cnr Beyers Naude & Waugh Northcliff; ☎ 0861 300 911; e info@traveldoctor.co.za; www.traveldoctor.co.za. Consult the website for clinic locations.

LONG-HAUL FLIGHTS, CLOTS AND DVT

Any prolonged immobility, including travel by land or air, can result in deep-vein thrombosis (DVT) with the risk of embolus to the lungs. Certain factors can increase the risk and these include:

- Previous clot or a close relative with a history
- Being over 40, with increased risk over 80 years old
- Recent major operation or varicose veins surgery
- Cancer
- Stroke
- Heart disease
- Obesity
- Pregnancy
- Hormone therapy
- Heavy smoking
- Severe varicose veins
- Being very tall (over 6ft/1.8m) or short (under 5ft/1.5m)

A deep-vein thrombosis causes painful swelling and redness of the calf or sometimes the thigh. It is only dangerous if a clot travels to the lungs (pulmonary embolus). Symptoms of a pulmonary embolus (PE) – which commonly start three to ten days after a long flight – include chest pain, shortness of breath, and sometimes coughing up small amounts of blood. Anyone who thinks that they might have a DVT needs to see a doctor immediately.

PREVENTION OF DVT

- Keep mobile before and during the flight; move around every couple of hours
- Drink plenty of fluids during the flight
- Avoid taking sleeping pills and excessive tea, coffee and alcohol
- Consider wearing flight socks or support stockings (see *www.legshealth.com*)

If you think you are at increased risk of a clot, ask your doctor if it is safe to travel before you do so.

Personal first-aid kit A minimal kit:

- A good drying antiseptic, eg: iodine or potassium permanganate (don't take antiseptic cream)
- A few small dressings
- Suncream
- Insect repellent; antimalarial tablets; impregnated bednet or permethrin spray
- Aspirin or paracetamol
- Antifungal cream (eg: Canesten)
- Ciprofloxacin or norfloxacin, for severe diarrhoea
- Tinidazole for giardia or amoebic dysentery (see below for regime)
- Antibiotic eye drops, for sore, 'gritty', stuck-together eyes (conjunctivitis)
- A pair of fine-pointed tweezers (to remove hairy caterpillar hairs, thorns, splinters, coral, etc)
- Alcohol-based hand rub or bar of soap in plastic box
- Condoms or femidoms

IN BURKINA FASO

Medical facilities There are several reliable options in Ouaga and Bobo. Pharmacies throughout the country are often well stocked and you do not need a prescription to buy many of the drugs.

Hospital and medical centres

Centre Medical de l'Ambassade de France (CMI) 50 30 66 07; m 70 20 00 00 (in emergency); e cmi.ouaga@gmail.com; closed Sat afternoon & Sun. By far the best option for travellers, with quick & efficient diagnosis, although the waiting room gets busy. A consultation costs 15,000f & a malaria blood test 12,000f; out-of-hours consultations cost 25,000f, or 40,000f after 20.00. Any medicines prescribed cost extra, & you can get them from a pharmacy.

Centre National Hospitalier Universitaire Yalgado, Av Oubritenga; 50 31 16 55/57, 50 31 59 90. For hospital ambulance 50 30 66 44/45.

Pharmacies In Ouagadougou, you don't have to go far to find a pharmacy. They generally close for lunch but stay open until 19.00. There are also several that stay open 24 hours a day, and stock a wide range of drugs. The 24-hour pharmacy (*50 30 66 41*) at Hospital Yalgado is always open. Consult page two of *Sidwaya*, the state daily paper, for the 24-hour *pharmacie de garde* for any given day.

Common medical problems

Travellers' diarrhoea Travelling in Burkina Faso carries a fairly high risk of getting a dose of travellers' diarrhoea; perhaps half of all visitors will suffer and the newer you are to exotic travel, the more likely you will be to suffer. By taking precautions against travellers' diarrhoea you will also avoid typhoid, paratyphoid, cholera, hepatitis, dysentery, worms, etc. Travellers' diarrhoea and the other faecal-oral diseases come from getting other people's faeces in your mouth. This most often happens from cooks not washing their hands after a trip to the toilet, but even if the restaurant cook does not understand basic hygiene you will be safe if your food has been properly cooked and arrives piping hot. The most important prevention strategy is to wash your hands before eating anything. You can pick up salmonella and shigella from toilet door handles, and, possibly, banknotes. The maxim to remind you what you can safely eat is:

PEEL IT, BOIL IT, COOK IT OR FORGET IT.

TREATING TRAVELLERS' DIARRHOEA

Dr Jane Wilson-Howarth

It is dehydration that makes you feel awful during a bout of diarrhoea and the most important part of treatment is drinking lots of clear fluids. Sachets of oral rehydration salts give the perfect biochemical mix to replace all that is pouring out of your bottom but other recipes taste nicer. Any dilute mixture of sugar and salt in water will do you good: try Coke or orange squash with a three-finger pinch of salt added to each glass (if you are salt-depleted you won't taste the salt). Otherwise make a solution of a four-finger scoop of sugar with a three-finger pinch of salt in a 500ml glass. Or add eight level teaspoons of sugar (18g) and one level teaspoon of salt (3g) to one litre (five cups) of safe water. A squeeze of lemon or orange juice improves the taste and adds potassium, which is also lost in diarrhoea. Drink two large glasses after every bowel action, and more if you are thirsty. These solutions are still absorbed well if you are vomiting, but you will need to take sips at a time. If you are not eating you need to drink three litres a day plus whatever is pouring into the toilet. If you feel like eating, take a bland, high carbohydrate diet. Heavy greasy foods will probably give you cramps.

If the diarrhoea is bad, or you are passing blood or slime, or you have a fever, you will probably need antibiotics in addition to fluid replacement. A dose of norfloxacin or ciprofloxacin repeated twice a day until better may be appropriate (if you are planning to take an antibiotic with you, note that both norfloxacin and ciprofloxacin are available only on prescription in the UK). Ciprofloxacin is considered to be less effective in Burkina Faso. If the diarrhoea is greasy and bulky and is accompanied by sulphurous (eggy) burps, one likely cause is giardia. This is best treated with tinidazole (four x 500mg in one dose, repeated seven days later if symptoms persist).

This means that fruit you have washed and peeled yourself, and hot foods, should be safe, but raw foods, cold cooked foods, salads, fruit salads that have been prepared by others, ice cream and ice are all risky; and foods kept lukewarm in hotel buffets are often dangerous. That said, plenty of travellers and expatriates enjoy fruit and vegetables, so do keep a sense of perspective: food served in a fairly decent hotel in a large town or a place regularly frequented by expatriates is likely to be safe. If you are struck, see box, above, for treatment.

Eye problems Bacterial conjunctivitis (pink eye) is a common infection in Africa; people who wear contact lenses are most open to this irritating problem. The eyes feel sore and gritty and they will often be stuck together in the mornings. They will need treatment with antibiotic drops or ointment. Lesser eye irritation should settle with bathing in salt water and keeping the eyes shaded. If an insect flies into your eye, extract it with great care, ensuring you do not crush or damage it otherwise you may get a nastily inflamed eye from toxins secreted by the creature. Small elongated red-and-black blister beetles carry warning colouration to tell you not to crush them anywhere against your skin.

Prickly heat A fine pimply rash on the trunk is likely to be heat rash; cool showers, dabbing dry, and talc will help. Treat the problem by slowing down to a relaxed schedule, wearing only loose, baggy, 100%-cotton clothes and sleeping naked under a fan; if it's bad you may need to check into an air-conditioned hotel room for a while.

Skin infections Any mosquito bite or small nick in the skin gives an opportunity for bacteria to foil the body's usually excellent defences; it will surprise many travellers how quickly skin infections start in warm humid climates and it is essential to clean and cover even the slightest wound. Creams are not as effective as a good drying antiseptic such as dilute iodine, potassium permanganate (a few crystals in half a cup of water), or crystal (or gentian) violet. One of these should be available in most towns. If the wound starts to throb, or becomes red and the redness starts to spread, or the wound oozes, and especially if you develop a fever, antibiotics will probably be needed: flucloxacillin (250mg four times a day) or cloxacillin (500mg four times a day). For those allergic to penicillin, erythromycin (500mg twice a day) for five days should help. See a doctor if the symptoms do not start to improve within 48 hours.

Fungal infections also get a hold easily in hot, moist climates so wear 100%-cotton socks and underwear and shower frequently. An itchy rash in the groin or flaking between the toes is likely to be a fungal infection. This needs treatment with an antifungal cream such as Canesten (clotrimazole); if this is not available try Whitfield's ointment (compound benzoic acid ointment) or crystal violet (although this will turn you purple!).

Other insect-borne diseases Malaria is by no means the only insect-borne disease to which the traveller may succumb. Others include sleeping sickness and river blindness (see box, page 76). Dengue fever is less common in Burkina Faso than say Asia or the Caribbean, but there are many other similar arboviruses. These mosquito-borne diseases may mimic malaria but there is no prophylactic medication against them. The mosquitoes that carry arboviruses bite during the day, so it is worth applying repellent if you see any mosquitoes around. Symptoms include strong headaches, rashes and excruciating joint and muscle pains and high fever. Viral fevers usually last about a week or so and are not usually fatal. Complete rest and paracetamol are the usual treatment; plenty of fluids also help. Some patients are given an intravenous drip to keep them from dehydrating. It is especially important to protect yourself if you have had dengue fever before, since a second infection with a different strain can result in the potentially fatal dengue haemorrhagic fever.

Sleeping sickness African trypanosomiasis, or sleeping sickness, is a parasitic infection caused by *Trypanosoma brucei*, transmitted by the tsetse fly. There are two sub-species: one predominates in east Africa and usually causes an acute infection, whereas the other predominates in central and west Africa and causes a slower, progressive, chronic infection.

The parasite is transmitted by the bite of an infected tsetse fly. Tsetse flies are around the size of a honey bee. In west Africa, the main reservoir for the parasite is humans. The tsetse flies responsible tend to inhabit damp river areas. In east Africa, the main reservoirs for the parasites are domestic and wild animals such as antelope and cattle. The tsetse flies here tend to inhabit savanna and woodland areas. One bite from an infected tsetse fly is enough for a human to become infected. Trypanosomiasis cannot be spread directly from person to person.

For west African trypanosomiasis, symptoms (skin lesions around the bite with lymphadenopathy) may not present for some weeks after the infective bite. East

African trypanosomiasis is a much faster-progressing disease than the west African form, which can progress over a number of years.

There is no vaccine or drug to prevent sleeping sickness. The only way to prevent it is to avoid tsetse-fly bites and be aware of the risk. Tsetse flies are attracted by movement and dark colours, particularly blue. They have been known to follow moving vehicles, therefore windows should remain closed when driving through endemic areas. Travellers are advised to wear insecticide-treated close-weave and loose-fitting clothing and use a good repellent containing N, N-diethylmetatoluamide (DEET) on exposed skin. If sunscreen is also being used, repellent must be applied after this. More information about the disease is available from the NaTHNaC website (*www.nathnac.org*).

Bilharzia or schistosomiasis

With thanks to Dr Vaughan Southgate of the Natural History Museum, London, and Dr Dick Stockley, The Surgery, Kampala

Bilharzia or schistosomiasis is a disease that commonly afflicts the rural poor of the tropics. Two types exist in sub-Saharan Africa – *Schistosoma mansoni* and *Schistosoma haematobium*. It is an unpleasant problem that is worth avoiding, though can be treated if you do get it. This parasite is common in almost all water sources in Burkina Faso, even places advertised as 'bilharzia free'. The most risky shores will be close to places where infected people use water, wash clothes, etc.

It is easier to understand how to diagnose it, treat it and prevent it if you know a little about the life cycle. Contaminated faeces are washed into the lake, the eggs hatch and the larva infects certain species of snail. The snails then produce about 10,000 cercariae a day for the rest of their lives. The parasites can digest their way through your skin when you wade, or bathe in infested fresh water.

Winds disperse the snails and cercariae. The snails in particular can drift a long way, especially on windblown weed, so nowhere is really safe. However, deep water and running water are safer, while shallow water presents the greatest risk. The cercariae penetrate intact skin, and find their way to the liver. There male and female meet and spend the rest of their lives in permanent copulation. No wonder you feel tired! Most finish up in the wall of the lower bowel, but others can get lost and can cause damage to many different organs. *Schistosoma haematobium* goes mostly to the bladder.

Although the adults do not cause any harm in themselves, after about four–six weeks they start to lay eggs, which cause an intense but usually ineffective immune reaction, including fever, cough, abdominal pain, and a fleeting, itching rash called 'safari itch'. The absence of early symptoms does not necessarily mean there is no infection. Later symptoms can be more localised and more severe, but the general symptoms settle down fairly quickly and eventually you are just tired. 'Tired all the time' is one of the most common symptoms among expats in Africa, and bilharzia, giardia, amoeba and intestinal yeast are the most common culprits.

Although bilharzia is difficult to diagnose, it can be tested at specialist travel clinics. Ideally tests need to be done at least six weeks after likely exposure and will determine whether you need treatment. Fortunately it is easy to treat at present.

Avoiding bilharzia

- If you are bathing, swimming, paddling or wading in fresh water which you think may carry a bilharzia risk, try to get out of the water within ten minutes
- Avoid bathing or paddling on shores within 200m of villages or places where people use the water a great deal, especially reedy shores or where there is lots of water weed

AVOIDING INSECT BITES

As the sun is going down, don long clothes and apply repellent on any exposed flesh. Pack a DEET-based insect repellent (roll-ons or stick are the least messy preparations for travelling). You also need either a permethrin-impregnated bednet or a permethrin spray so that you can 'treat' bednets in hotels. Permethrin treatment makes even very tatty nets protective and prevents mosquitoes from biting through the impregnated net when you roll against it; it also deters other biters. Otherwise retire to an air-conditioned room, burn mosquito coils or sleep under a fan. Coils and fans reduce rather than eliminate bites. Travel clinics usually sell a good range of nets, treatment kits and repellents.

Mosquitoes and many other insects are attracted to light. If you are camping, never put a lamp near the opening of your tent, or you will have a swarm of biters waiting to join you when you retire. In hotel rooms, be aware that the longer your light is on, the greater the number of insects will be sharing your accommodation.

Aside from avoiding mosquito bites between dusk and dawn, which will protect you from elephantiasis and a range of nasty insect-borne viruses, as well as malaria (see page 67), it is important to take precautions against other insect bites. During the day it is wise to wear long, loose (preferably 100%-cotton) clothes if you are pushing through scrubby country; this will keep off ticks and also tsetse flies and day-biting *Aedes* mosquitoes, which may spread viral fevers, including yellow fever.

Tsetse flies hurt when they bite and it is said that they are attracted to the colour blue; locals will advise on where they are a problem and where they transmit sleeping sickness.

Minute pestilential biting **blackflies** spread river blindness in some parts of Africa between 19°N and 17°S; the disease is caught close to fast-flowing rivers since flies breed there and the larvae live in rapids. The flies bite during the day, but long trousers tucked into socks will help keep them off. Citronella-based natural repellents (eg: Mosi-guard) do not work against them.

Tumbu flies or *putsi*, often called mango flies in Burkina Faso, are a problem where the climate is hot and humid. The adult fly lays her eggs on the soil or on drying laundry and when the eggs come into contact with human flesh (when you put on clothes or lie on a bed) they hatch and bury themselves under the skin. Here they form a crop of 'boils' each with a maggot inside. Smear a little Vaseline over the hole, and they will push their noses out to breathe. It may be possible to squeeze them out but it depends if they are ready to do so as the larvae have spines that help them to hold on.

In *putsi* areas either dry your clothes and sheets within a screened house, or dry them in direct sunshine until they are crisp, or iron them.

Jiggers or **sandfleas** are another flesh-feaster, which can be best avoided by wearing shoes. They latch on if you walk barefoot in contaminated places, and set up home under the skin of the foot, usually at the side of a toenail where they cause a painful, boil-like swelling. They need picking out by a local expert.

- Dry off thoroughly with a towel; rub vigorously
- If your bathing water comes from a risky source, try to ensure that the water is taken from the lake in the early morning and stored snail-free, otherwise it should be filtered or Dettol or Cresol added
- Bathing early in the morning is safer than bathing in the last half of the day
- Cover yourself with DEET insect repellent before swimming: it may offer some protection.

HIV/AIDS The risks of sexually transmitted infection are extremely high in Burkina Faso, whether you sleep with fellow travellers or locals. About 80% of HIV infections in British heterosexuals are acquired abroad. If you must indulge, use condoms or femidoms, which help reduce the risk of transmission. If you notice any genital ulcers or discharge, get treatment promptly since these increase the risk of acquiring HIV. If you do have unprotected sex, visit a clinic as soon as possible; this should be within 24 hours, or no later than 72 hours, for post-exposure prophylaxis.

Burkina Faso was thought to have the highest HIV rates in west Africa; though this may no longer be true, the rate among women aged 15–24 is around 9.7%, while condom use among women aged 15–49 is less than 14%. 'If you ask a man to wear a condom he thinks you're accusing him of being unfaithful,' said one woman. Condoms are readily available from corner shops, supermarkets and pharmacies, though you would be wise to bring some from home where the quality can be guaranteed.

Several health workers suggest infection rates have dropped only because reporting is so low, or because prevalence rates always drop once people start dying of AIDS. Few people go for tests and there is widespread fear of the stigma of being found positive.

Opportunistic prostitution is common, and incidence rates tend to be higher at transport nodes such as main towns and trucking stopovers. In cities there are professional prostitutes, but such is the potential earning that many women will sleep with a man in return for money. If you are going to indulge then do so safely.

Meningitis This is a particularly nasty disease as it can kill within hours of the first symptoms appearing. The tell-tale symptoms are a combination of a blinding headache (light sensitivity), a blotchy rash and a high fever. Immunisation protects against the most serious bacterial form of meningitis and the tetravalent conjugate vaccine ACWY (Menveo) is recommended for Burkina Faso by British travel clinics. The less effective polysaccharide meningitis ACWY is still preferable to no vaccine. Although other forms of meningitis exist (usually viral), there are no vaccines for these. Local papers normally report localised outbreaks. A severe headache and fever should make you run to a doctor immediately. There are also other causes of headache and fever; one of which is typhoid, which occurs in travellers to Burkina Faso. Seek medical help if you are ill for more than a few days.

Rabies Rabies is carried by all mammals (beware the village dogs and small monkeys that are used to being fed in the parks) and is passed on to man through a bite, scratch or a lick of an open wound. You must always assume any animal is rabid, and seek medical help as soon as possible. Meanwhile scrub the wound with soap under a running tap or while pouring water from a jug. Find a reasonably clear-looking source of water (but at this stage the quality of the water is not important), then pour on a strong iodine or alcohol solution of gin, whisky or rum.

This helps stop the rabies virus entering the body and will guard against wound infections, including tetanus.

Pre-exposure vaccinations for rabies is ideally advised for everyone, but is particularly important if you intend to have contact with animals and/or are likely to be more than 24 hours away from medical help. Ideally three doses should be taken over a minimum of 21 days to make a difference to treatment. Contrary to popular belief these vaccinations are relatively painless.

If you are bitten, scratched or licked over an open wound by a sick animal, then post-exposure prophylaxis should be given as soon as possible, though it is never too late to seek help, as the incubation period for rabies can be very long. Those who have not been immunised will need a blood product called rabies immunoglobulin (RIG) and five doses of vaccine over 28 days. RIG is expensive (around US$800) and is often hard to come by – another reason why pre-exposure vaccinations should be encouraged.

Tell the doctor if you have had three pre-exposure vaccines, as this will change the treatment you receive in that you will no longer need the RIG but just two further doses of vaccine given three days apart. And remember that, if you do contract rabies, mortality is 100% and death from rabies is probably one of the worst ways to go.

Tickbite fever African ticks are not the rampant disease transmitters they are in the Americas, but they may spread tickbite fever and a few dangerous rarities in Burkina Faso. Tickbite fever is a flu-like illness that can easily be treated with doxycycline, but as there can be some serious complications it is important to visit a doctor.

Ticks should ideally be removed as soon as possible as leaving them on the body increases the chance of infection. They should be removed with special tick tweezers that can be bought in good travel shops. Failing that you can use your fingernails: grasp the tick as close to your body as possible and pull steadily and firmly away at right angles to your skin. The tick will then come away complete, as long as you do not jerk or twist. If possible douse the wound with alcohol (any spirit will do) or iodine. Irritants (eg: Olbas oil) or lit cigarettes are to be discouraged since they can cause the ticks to regurgitate and therefore increase the risk of disease. It is best to get a travelling companion to check you for ticks; if you are travelling with small children, remember to check their heads, and particularly behind the ears.

Spreading redness around the bite and/or fever and/or aching joints after a tick bite imply that you have an infection that requires antibiotic treatment, so seek advice.

Snakebite Snakes rarely attack unless provoked, and bites in travellers are unusual. You are less likely to get bitten if you wear stout shoes and long trousers when in the bush. Most snakes are harmless and even venomous species will dispense venom in only about half of their bites. If bitten, then, you are unlikely to have received venom; keeping this fact in mind may help you to stay calm. Many so-called first-aid techniques do more harm than good: cutting into the wound is harmful; tourniquets are dangerous; suction and electrical inactivation devices do not work. The only treatment is antivenom. In case of a bite that you fear may have been from a venomous snake:

- Try to keep calm – it is likely that no venom has been dispensed
- Prevent movement of the bitten limb by applying a splint

- Keep the bitten limb BELOW heart height to slow the spread of any venom
- If you have a crêpe bandage, wrap it around the whole limb (eg: all the way from the toes to the thigh), as tight as you would for a sprained ankle or a muscle pull
- Evacuate to a hospital that has antivenom

And remember:

- NEVER give aspirin; you may take paracetamol, which is safe
- NEVER cut or suck the wound
- DO NOT apply ice packs
- DO NOT apply potassium permanganate

If the offending snake can be captured without risk of someone else being bitten, take this to show the doctor – but beware, even a decapitated head is able to bite.

Blister beetle The blister beetle is a bright insect that secretes an acid when disturbed. If affected, the area may become red, itch, burn and blister painfully. The beetle tends to squirt the face and neck area in particular, and the secretion can be fatal if swallowed. Do not squeeze or scratch the blisters, but keep them clean and dry. Do not use greasy creams, since this will spread the toxin.

Scorpion stings These are rarely fatal, although the injected poison from the tail may tingle and burn, and may affect the central nervous system, bringing on dizziness, sweating, chills, nausea and vomiting, slurring of speech and abdominal cramps. Antihistamines will help reduce the swelling.

Water sterilisation Tap water is treated in cities and large towns, although drinking it is probably not worth the risk if you are visiting for a short while. Anyone staying longer should be able to drink the tap water in Ouaga and Bobo without too many problems. Some water sold in clear plastic sachets is simply regular tap water cooled down in a fridge – avoid it. Outside city centres, local water may have viruses, bacteria, parasites and worms. To be absolutely safe, buy branded bottled water with the seal intact, and avoid ice cubes. If you ask for bottled water in a restaurant, check it's unopened when it arrives at your table.

If you are away from shops and your bottled water runs out, make tea, pour the remaining boiled water into a clean container and use it for drinking. Alternatively, water should be passed through a good bacteriological filter or purified with iodine or the less-effective chlorine tablets (eg: Puritabs).

SAFETY

ROAD SAFETY With their overlapping traffic of bicycles, mopeds, cars and enormous trucks, Ouaga's roads can be a terrifying experience. Throw in the odd donkey cart, crazed coach drivers and wheeled trolleys carrying such hazards as long steel rods, it is a wonder the instance of accidents in Burkina Faso is not higher. When driving in the two main cities, constant vigilance is absolutely vital. Cars drive on the right. At roundabouts, traffic coming onto the roundabout has right of way, so vehicles on the roundabout must stop to let oncoming traffic pass.

Two wheels Two-wheeled riders in particular often seem to be under the misapprehension they are driving a pick-up truck, piling on ladders, improbable numbers of chickens, iron rods, paint pots, cows' heads, chairs, and any combination of lover, baby and child, often with a basketful of vegetables perched high on heads.

Hiring a bicycle or moped is likely to pose the single greatest threat to your health, after malaria. Although few people wear them, crash helmets are now a legal requirement, and can be bought in the market. Many of the busier roads in the capital have bike and cycle lanes, although the area around markets can be a free-for-all. In theory there is a 30km/h speed limit for *motos* in cities, and it is wise to stick to it.

CRIME It is difficult to think of a safer country than Burkina Faso. Certainly, downtown New York, London or Sydney pose more problems for strangers late at night than Ouagadougou, which at no stage felt threatening. Burkina Faso has the lowest murder rate in the world, although whether that's down to under-reporting is hard to say. Despite gun shops adorning what can sometimes feel like every urban street corner, armed violence is rare.

Awareness As a traveller, you will be on show at all times. You are bound to get attention, and while it is most likely to be nothing more than some good-natured attempts to sell you things, it helps to have your wits about you. If you are enjoying a drink or two, people will know. If you are overindulging in a drink or ten, people will also know. Don't flash the cash, and only take with you what you need for an evening. Most ATMs are located inside walk-in booths, rather than directly on the street, which helps discretion. Use ATMs on busy streets, decreasing the risk of an attack, and don't be put off by the hordes of sellers hanging around, mostly selling mobile-phone credits or belts – they are rarely a danger.

Bag-snatchers are few and far between in general, but can strike in Ouaga, speeding past on mopeds. You are particularly vulnerable on a bike or moped. Keep car doors locked, especially when stationary, and keep belongings close when walking down streets. Never leave your bag unattended, even for a moment; they are easily swiped from bars and cinema halls.

One would be hard-pushed to call anywhere in Ouaga off-limits, although at night it pays to be vigilant, especially around the market and the town centre near Avenue Kwame N'Krumah. Locals also advise against walking alone at night in the Zaca area, south of Avenue de la Cathedrale. Thieves sometimes take advantage of the Ouaga 2000 suburb's deserted streets at night, as well as the area at the *barrage*. In the past there have been muggings in the area southeast of the mosque. There have been occasional hold-ups at knifepoint. If in any doubt whatsoever about walking somewhere in Ouaga, hail a taxi and pay for a *déplacement*.

Deux droits A hard-to-spot danger is pickpocketing, known as *deux droits* (two fingers) because of the light, dextrous digits behind the crime. Don't keep valuables, such as a passport, in back pockets or gaping pockets of the combat-trouser variety.

The risk of a *deux droits* tends to be highest in the shared green taxis of Ouaga, Bobo and a few other towns. Beware passengers making a show of getting out of the cab to let you in first, or anyone who makes a massive play of not being able to shut the car door. Any fumbling with doors, seats or bags may be a big show to divert your attention while going for your pockets.

In case of loss or theft If your passport, money or anything else is stolen, you need to register the crime at the central police station (*commissariat central*). You will receive a receipt (*récépissé*, for which you pay only a small stamp tax), which you need to present to your embassy to get a replacement passport, or to your insurance

DRIVING TIPS

Sheep, cows and goats tend to respond to horn honking, donkeys do not. Truckers tend to be polite and remarkably road-aware given their enormous towering loads and the frequency of out-of-action wing and rear-view mirrors. Drivers will usually move over to let you overtake, often indicating right towards the kerb to give you the go-ahead. If you see a lorry indicating left without a road turning in sight, this means there is oncoming traffic ahead and is a cue not to overtake. Likewise, if an oncoming lorry is indicating to its left, it is not about to career across your lane, but is signalling your presence to traffic behind it. Vehicles flash headlights if they think you have not seen them (for example if you are pulling out to pass a group of motorcycles or donkey carts). An oncoming driver putting his thumb to the windscreen is less likely to be giving you the thumbs-up than making sure any stones kicked up by your passing vehicle do not crack his glass.

Branches on the road at regular intervals are the equivalent of a red hazard triangle, and mean that a broken-down vehicle lies ahead, taking up most of the lane.

If you are caught up in an accident, assuming there is no immediate danger to your person, the general rule is to stay at the scene, and to move nothing until the traffic police arrive, although circumstances may dictate this is not possible. Carry two spare tyres and assume you'll always have a flat tyre on every trip.

On secondary roads and dirt tracks slow down when you see pedestrians or other traffic, as your speed kicks up dust that can be unpleasant and obscure the road.

Never drive at night. Upturned lorries and burnt-out shells on the roadside testify to the folly of this. Trucks, cars, motorbikes and bicycles frequently travel without lights. There is also the occasional chance of night-time road bandits.

company if you are applying for compensation. A common piece of advice is to offer an informal reward for the return of your passport (or any other item, perhaps around 10,000f) at the police station, since sometimes criminal networks get to hear about this sort of thing and the goods mysteriously show up.

Road attack In recent years, there has been an increase in the number of armed bandit attacks on vehicles. Notorious trouble spots are the Po road, heading south from Ouaga to Ghana, the road between Dori and Gorom-Gorom, and the route east to Niger via Fada N'Gourma. The last named now has a convoy system in place between Fada and Kantchari, which acts as effective protection for vehicles. Attacks on foreigners are extremely rare.

In 2005, there was some evidence that unrest in neighbouring Côte d'Ivoire may have had an effect on security in Burkina Faso. On the Po road a well-armed gang held up and robbed an army colonel during daylight hours.

While the risk of attack is low, vigilance and instinct are always the best bets. Never travel at night. Don't tell strangers your route or your final destination if you can help it, particularly if you'll be in a town for long enough for people to get onto the road ahead of you.

If you see a roadblock far in advance – such as trees, branches or vehicles barring the route – it may be best to turn around and head back. If you leave it too late to make this decision, bandits have been known to shoot if you're within range. Co-operate if caught.

POLICE PROTOCOL Always carry a passport or some other form of photo ID at all times, particularly if you are on a motorbike or coach. Police spot checks are common and you will have to pay a fine of several thousand CFA francs if you cannot produce identification.

TERRORISM Foreign governments have recently reassessed the north of Burkina as posing a high threat of terrorism, with white foreigners being a principal target. Current advice is therefore to avoid the region. The off-limits area varies from country to country – check your own government's advice before travelling – but areas close to the borders with Mali and Niger are considered the most dangerous. For more details, see the introduction to *The North*, page 153.

WOMEN TRAVELLERS

Women travelling in the company of men are unlikely to find much bother, other than being asked how their husband is doing and, if they've not got either a husband or children, why not and hadn't they'd better hurry up and get on with it.

For women travelling alone, it is a different matter. Claiming you have a boyfriend, girlfriend or husband is unlikely to cut much mustard. 'Yes, I have a girlfriend too, now let's go and get it on' is as likely as not to be the reply.

Most women say they don't feel in danger, but are worn down by persistent and unpleasant advances. There is the occasional stereotyped view that travellers and tourists are easy, and some men are quick to try their luck. It pays to be aware and exercise caution. Be on your guard at rowdy nightclubs, meeting places for touts on the streets, and bus and coach stations. If you feel uncomfortable in a taxi, ask to be let out before you reach your ultimate destination, or choose a suitably important person's home as your destination – the local chief's or *naba*'s palace, for example.

Don't expose unnecessary flesh. While girls in gold shiny singlets whooshing round on bikes are *de rigueur* for Ouaga, it's best to reassess outside the capital. In Burkina, legs are considered sexually attractive. Short skirts and shorts court controversy. On the other hand, wearing a piece of colourful local cotton, no matter how badly or self-consciously, acts as an ice-breaker. Women will notice the effort, love the idea and even give tips on how to tie it properly.

GAY TRAVELLERS

Homosexuality is legal in Burkina Faso; the legal age of consent for same-sex activity is 21 (it's 13 for heterosexuals). However, bear in mind that society is very conservative and that homosexuality goes against most people's religious and traditional beliefs; so it's best to be discreet.

DISABLED TRAVELLERS

The chaos of Burkinabe streets is not ideally suited to the needs of disabled travellers, and specialist facilities of any kind are hard to find. Most hotels, for instance, do not provide wheelchair access; and you can forget adapted bathrooms and the like. That said, the Burkinabe are endlessly resourceful about getting from A to B. This is combined with immense good cheer and helpfulness, with the result that the improbable can, and often does, happen. If you can risk throwing yourself upon this fount of goodwill, you may find that you achieve more than you would have thought possible.

TRAVELLING WITH CHILDREN

The average Burkinabe woman gives birth to 6.2 children. This may not always be an active choice, but nevertheless it's safe to say that children are viewed as a blessing, and are generally adored. Moreover, with the gradual emergence of a middle class, the number of child-oriented locations is increasing. Some hotels and parks have playgrounds with swings, rocking horses and so forth; Loumbila Beach, outside Ouaga, even has a Disney-esque inflatable slide.

In general, the problems that families have to face are the heat, and the risk of diseases such as malaria. It would be wise to consult a travel health clinic before setting out (see page 69). A paediatric version of Malarone is available, and common-sense measures should be practised: avoiding the heat of the day; ensuring they wear suncream and a hat; and giving plenty of cool drinks.

WHAT TO TAKE

CLOTHES Since it is so hot, lightweight cotton clothing is best. For women, strappy tops are fine, but long-sleeved tops to keep you safe from the sun and evening mosquitoes also come in handy. For men, a couple of T-shirts are the most obvious items, although a light long-sleeved shirt is also worth considering. Shorts and skirts revealing women's legs are ill-advised. Men should know that in Burkina it is usually only young boys who wear shorts. Despite being landlocked, the number of swimming pools makes a costume or trunks a must. A lightweight anorak and a light sweater are good for the rainy season. Take a towel, as cheaper hotels often do not provide one. Some hotels have decidedly grubby sheets, and silk sleeping-bag liners (available in singles and doubles) that pack down to minute sizes are a boon; or sew up a cotton sheet. If you're planning on going to the Sahel, take a light sleeping bag as well.

Comfortable sandals are good, although you can pick up popular plastic pairs for less than 1,000f on the streets. Decent trainers are worth packing, especially if you plan on doing much walking, but there is no real need for hiking boots. In the larger towns, there are plenty of places to go out dancing, so something fancy for the evenings will hardly go amiss. A wide-brimmed hat or headscarf to keep the sun off is also worth thinking about.

KIT Travel as light as possible. Sunglasses, suncream and aftersun are essential, as are matches and a torch, a multi-purpose tool such as a Swiss Army knife or Leatherman, a compass, a whistle, mosquito net (they come in singles and doubles) and insect spray. A camera, and binoculars for safaris or birdwatching, the odd book, a short-wave radio and some sort of device for playing music are all optional extras.

A medical kit should have at a minimum a healthy supply of painkillers; a thermometer (doctors in Burkina use the Celsius system, not Fahrenheit, so one with both readings is good); antiseptic creams and antihistamines; sterile needles and syringes; and bandages. See page 72 for more details of what to take in a first-aid kit. Puritabs are an idea if you want to drink tap water, although they are not essential as bottled water is easily found. Plug adaptors will also be useful if you need to charge anything, since Burkina relies on the standard French two-pin system.

Unless you are a committed camper, there is little need for a tent, as even the smallest of towns has some kind of accommodation. Likewise, unless you plan on spending a lot of time in the bush, it is difficult to recommend any cooking equipment, seeing as good, fresh food is available virtually everywhere.

Taking a mobile phone is an excellent idea. You can enable international roaming to make and receive calls, or make sure the handset accepts other SIM cards (which you can pick up very cheaply on the ground) and set up with one of three local mobile networks (see page 106).

MAPS **International Travel Maps** (*530 West Broadway, Vancouver, BC V5Z 1E9, Canada; ☎ +1 604 879 3621; www.itmb.com*) publishes a recent map of Burkina Faso (1:1,000,000), which has been used to produce some of the maps in this guide. The French **Institut Geographique National** map 3615 of *Burkina Faso* (1:1,000,000) is excellent. If you're venturing further afield than Burkina, the **Michelin Motoring & Touring** map (1:4,000,000) of north and west Africa is a good bet too. If you're in the UK, an easy option is to go to Stanfords map shop in London's Covent Garden (*12–14 Long Acre, London WC23 9LP; ☎ 0207 836 1321; e sales@stanfords.co.uk; www.stanfords.co.uk*). It stocks all three and also does online ordering.

Many towns in Burkina have never been mapped, and we have tried to help out here. Be warned that they are hand-drawn sketch maps, which should put you on the right track, but won't win any Ordnance Survey awards.

The **Institut Geographique du Burkina** (IGB) has an office in Ouagadougou (see page 119), where it sells a range of maps covering all parts of the country. It produces an excellent 1:1,000,000 tourist map of Burkina (*Burkina Faso: Carte touristique et routière*), as well as in-depth city plans of Ouagadougou and Bobo-Dioulasso. For the longer-term resident, there are also detailed 1:50,000 maps of local areas.

RUDIMENTARY FRENCH A working knowledge of French will be the most useful thing you can take with you. Very few Burkinabe speak English, so even reanimating scraps of ancient, rusty school French will help, and you will no doubt feel the need to improve rapidly. See *Appendix 1*, page 305.

$ MONEY

Burkina's currency is the franc of the *Communauté Financière d'Afrique* (CFA), which it shares with the other members of the West African Economic and Monetary Union (UEMOA) – Benin, Guinea-Bissau, Côte d'Ivoire, Mali, Niger, Senegal and Togo.

Throughout the book we have given prices in CFA (pronounced 'seffa') francs, denoted by 'f' or 'CFA'. As an easy but oversimplified exchange guide, €1 is reliably pegged at about 656f; £1 is much less reliably about 750f and a US dollar about 450f.

Notes are available in denominations of 10,000f, 5,000f, 2,000f and 1,000f. Coins come in 500f, 250f, 200f, 100f, 50f and 25f. Rarely, you will see 10f and 5f coins too. Finding change can feel like an Olympian quest at times, particularly in taxis, at street stalls and in small restaurants, so always ask for the smallest possible denominations, and guard coins jealously. A pocketful of change may be ungainly, but it will save bags of time, not to mention goodwill in transactions.

CASH If you want to bring hard currency to Burkina, you can bring pounds sterling or US dollars, but don't expect to change them outside Ouaga or Bobo. You can change them for CFA francs in some banks and, in Ouaga, foreign-exchange bureaux. Euros offer more flexibility, as you can change them in a wider range of banks across the country, some hotels, foreign-exchange bureaux and also in branches of Marina Market supermarket. Generally, banks give the best rates, though some bureaux are excellent and offer a quicker service. One we can recommend is **Business Change** (*50 50 00 78; m 78 89 84 82, 70 69 05 82*) on the north side of the Zabre-Daaga market in Ouaga, which offers good rates for pounds and you're in and out in a jiffy. Don't be tempted to turn to the black market; there are too many tales of swindles. The only other currencies you'll be able to change – again, in Ouaga or Bobo only – are Canadian dollars and Swiss francs.

The simplest advice is to keep your money in as many different places and as many different forms as possible, to guard against loss or theft.

A shirt pocket is a useful place in which to keep loose change, as it's difficult for anyone else to get to without you noticing. Money belts are useful for storing cash, but not if you want to take money from them in public – they're cumbersome, they give the game away and you'll likely as not feel awkward. Keep day-to-day money in a thin purse, not in your back pocket. Consider sewing a pocket inside your trousers for easy and secure access to folded notes. It will keep you safe from pickpockets, who, while not omnipresent, act quickly, lightly and before you have a chance to react.

CREDIT AND DEBIT CARDS For the traveller, by far the most convenient way of drawing out money is with a Visa credit or debit card, although charges will be higher with a credit card. For either, you'll save money by taking out a larger sum, as there's usually a charge per transaction. In recent years, the number of ATMs has burgeoned so that even if one isn't working, you'll find another that is; smaller towns generally have a couple, though these can be less reliable. The arrival of Banque Atlantique has brought with it a network of MasterCard/Maestro ATMs to add to the Visa options.

For Visa machines, BICIA-B, BIB and Ecobank are the most widespread, with Bank of Africa and SGBB popping up occasionally. All are guarded around the clock, have always been perfectly safe to use in our experience, and generally function properly.

Plusher hotels accept payment with a Visa card, as do a very few of the pricier restaurants and some supermarkets, such as Marina Market in Ouaga and Bobo. American Express and MasterCard are occasionally accepted at hotels and banks.

TRAVELLERS' CHEQUES While travellers' cheques offer greater security, it's often hard to find somewhere to change them and a hassle when you do. Several banks operate rather unfathomable policies, which can involve tedious waits for clearance from the top brass upstairs, or changing only before lunch. Euro travellers' cheques are by far the best option and when changing travellers' cheques to cash, you'll receive local currency. US-dollar travellers' cheques are much harder to change, and you can forget sterling. Always keep a copy of the serial numbers separate along with contact numbers in case of theft, and leave a copy for people at home.

BICIA-B bank (*50 31 19 55; e info@bicia.bf; www.biciab.bf*) is one of the most helpful for the foreign visitor, with foreign exchange, Visa machines and travellers' cheque services. Other decent banks are Banque Atlantique (*50 49 24 46, www.banqueatlantique.net*), BIB (*50 30 00 00*), Ecobank (*e ecobankbf@ecobank.com; www.ecobank.com*) and SGBB (*50 32 32 32; www.sgbb.bf*). Watch out for opening hours, as BICIA-B bank, for example, opens early (07.15) but closes 11.45–15.00, not reopening until 17.00, Monday–Friday.

WIRE TRANSFERS There are plenty of Western Union branches, handy if you're in a fix and need someone to wire you money. Even in the smaller towns, you can find them at branches of Sonapost (the postal service), BICIA-B and other banks. Branches of Moneygram are beginning to pop up here and there too.

BUDGETING

Compared with the West, life in Burkina is seriously cheap. Compared with other countries in the region, it is somewhere in the middle. Food and lodging is cheaper than Mali, for example, but more expensive than Ghana.

On a shoestring, you can find dingy rooms for 3,000f a night and meals for less than 500f a go. Big bottles of local beer cost 600–800f, depending on where you are.

A much more pleasant and sustainable accommodation budget is 7,000–15,000f a night in towns and perhaps 5,000–8,000f in small towns and villages. You can get by on *brochettes* and chips or other local dishes for 500–2,500f, or go on a minor splurge for 4,000–10,000f.

If money is less of a concern, allow 30,000–50,000f a night for good hotels and safari camps (although you'd be hard pushed to find anywhere that expensive in smaller towns), and 7,000–30,000f for each meal.

As for travel, allow about 1,500f for every 100km or so by coach. Moped hire is about 4,000f a day and the best means for short trips. If you take a trip to the more inaccessible parts of the country, such as Arly, you'll need a car or 4x4, which will add up to 50,000f a day. It may be cheaper to go through a local tour operator, to arrange an all-inclusive price for short trips.

GETTING AROUND

There are an increasing number of good tarmac roads in Burkina; once the Koudougou–Dedougou stretch is finished (scheduled for 2013), all the main arteries heading out from Ouaga and Bobo will be covered. The quality of unpaved roads varies enormously, depending on volume of traffic and time of year.

There is a good network of coach companies, many of which run decent services and leave on time. Moped is the favoured vehicle for locals in town and for short spurts between towns as well, and it is easy to hire them wherever you find yourself. For some destinations, car or 4x4 will be the only option, however, and even then some smaller roads will be ropey if not impassable, especially in the rainy season. Only train enthusiasts should try the rail network.

If none of the above applies, there will always be a bush taxi, or local vehicle passing between towns on market days or delivering the post. As an old hand said to us: 'Any day you want to leave you can. You can always find transport.'

BY BUS Burkina is brimming with coach companies, and Ouaga is the central departure point. There is competition on all routes, with daily departures; and although companies tend to co-operate on setting prices, fares have dropped a little over the last five years. Budget on about 1,500f for every 100km. Nearly all *aller-retour* (return) tickets are cheaper than the price of two singles. Timetables are generally adhered to, and it pays to arrive at least half an hour before the allotted departure time.

Local opinion tends to vary about which lines are flavour of the month. Companies operate their very worst vehicles on specific routes, though with more tar roads being completed and coaches abandoning those that aren't, this is less of an issue these days. There are five companies – TCV, STAF, Rakieta, TSR and STMB – that will meet most travellers' needs; they all pride themselves on reliability and punctuality, and generally achieve both. Overall, STAF has a reputation for fast drivers and loud music, while STMB's buses, once the best, are now the most run-down.

There will be a supplement for extra luggage, such as a bicycle (250f) or moped (500–1,000f) on the roof.

In addition to main depots, buses have secondary garages, so it's worth checking the departure point in advance. Tickets are usually valid for one month, so buy them in advance on busy routes if you want to be sure of getting a seat.

If you're a little perplexed by the range of companies on offer, work out where you want to get to and stop someone to ask which company you need and where to go. There is always an answer.

Burkinabe coach companies Below is a summary of the main companies (in alphabetical order), along with Ouaga telephone numbers, main routes plied and any particular features that mark the company out. In each case, see individual entries in the *Getting there and away* sections in the regional chapters for details on stops, timings, local station numbers and prices. The *Bobo–Dioulasso* section on coaches is also packed with timings and prices (see pages 274–5). Timings are referred to below only when routes are not listed elsewhere.

CTI Gounghin & Dapoya; m 75 90 76 31. Heads to Abidjan Mon, Tue, Fri & Sat.

Gare Air Namende Near the *gendarmerie* in Paspanga; ☎ 50 33 12 11. Departs daily at 10.00 to Boulsa, via Pouytenga, with a second service at 15.00 on Fri & Sat. One-way tickets for 3,000f.

Gare de Leo Near the *grand mosquée*; m 70 25 38 78, 76 43 10 70, 78 18 01 11. Not a company as such, but a station that sends out roughly 4 minibuses daily to Leo.

LTI Also known as Liza, near Ouagainter; ☎ 50 38 74 10. Daily service to Dedougou & Nouna.

DISTANCES FROM OUAGA, IN KILOMETRES

Destination	km	Destination	km
Abidjan (Côte d'Ivoire)	1,200	Koudougou	97
Accra (Ghana)	900	Kongoussi	110
Bamako (Mali)	800	Koupela	138
Banfora	441	Leo	169
Batie (Ivorian and Ghanaian borders)	400	Lome (Togo)	1,000
Bobo-Dioulasso	356	Markoye (towards Nigerien border)	358
Boromo	176	Niamey (Niger)	527
Cotonou (Benin)	1,100	Nouna	282
Dedougou	225	Orodara	429
Diapaga	432	Ouahigouya (towards Malian border)	182
Djibo	205	Oursi	358
Dori	268	Pama (towards Benin border)	345
Fada N'Gourma	225	Po (towards Ghanaian border)	160
Gaoua	434	Sindou	504
Gorom-Gorom	321	Tenkodogo	180
Ivorian border (via Niangoloko)	500	Togolese border (via Bitou)	264
Kantchari (towards Nigerien border)	376	Tougan (via Ouahigouya)	276
Kaya	98	Yako	110

OA Rue des Douanes; ☎ 50 31 32 10. Runs a regular shuttle between Ouaga & Kaya, stopping at Loumbila & Ziniare.

Ouagainter Near SIAO on the route to Po. The place to come if you're heading to Ghana; various services leave at around 08.00 daily bar Sat. Services to Po pull in here; also a range of minibuses for southern destinations leave when ready. One minibus can take you all the way to Tiebele.

COACH PRICE GUIDE TO NEIGHBOURING COUNTRIES

Prices for coaches from Ouaga to Burkina's neighbours are fairly fixed, and listed below. Price bears some relation to the level of comfort, distance and time. International coaches will stop at domestic towns on the way, so a Togo coach is a good bet for Tenkodogo; Niger for Fada N'Gourma; Ghana for Po. See *Burkinabe coach companies*, page 87, for contact details.

Abidjan, Côte d'Ivoire One-way for 27,000–35,000f: CTI charges only 27,000f for trips at 08.00 on Monday, Tuesday, Friday and Saturday; Sito Transport leaves at 16.00 daily for 32,000; STP-KZA leaves at 16.00 on Tuesday (35,000f). There are many more services to the northern town of **Bouake**, usually for 16,000–17,000f (TCV, Rakieta, TSR all go).
NB: At the time of writing it was not safe to visit Côte d'Ivoire, and travel advice from foreign offices caution against going; many coach services had been suspended.

Accra, Ghana One-way for 16,000f: both STKF and Imperial Express leave at 08.30 daily bar Saturday; NTI leaves at 08.30 Sunday, Tuesday and Thursday.

Bamako, Mali One-way for 15,000–17,000f: SKV leaves at 22.00 Wednesday and Saturday; TCV (air conditioned) leaves at 23.00 daily (17,000f); Rakieta leaves at 22.45 daily; Rimbo Transport leaves at 13.00 daily.

Cotonou, Benin One-way for 16,000–20,000f: TCV leaves at 05.00 Sunday (20,000f); TSR leaves at 06.00 Thursday and Sunday (16,000f); SKV leaves at 05.00 Tuesday and Sunday (17,000f).

Dakar, Senegal One-way for 40,000f: Rimbo Transport's service to Bamako leaves at 13.00 daily and has a connection for Dakar.

Kumasi, Ghana One-way for 9,000–12,000f: SKV leaves at 07.00 Tuesday and Sunday (9,000f); STKF and Imperial Express leave at 08.30 daily bar Saturday (12,000f); NTI leaves at 08.30 Sunday, Tuesday and Thursday (12,000f).

Lagos, Nigeria One-way for 28,000f: TCV leaves at 05.00 Sunday.

Lome, Togo One-way for 12,500–17,500f: STMB leaves at 06.00 Sunday (12,500f); SKV leaves at 13.00 Tuesday, 07.00 Thursday and Sunday (15,000f); TSR leaves at 06.00 Thursday and Sunday (14,000f); TCV's air-conditioned service leaves at 06.00 Sunday (17,500f).

Niamey, Niger One-way for 10,000–11,500f: STMB leaves at 06.00 daily bar Monday; Rimbo Transport leaves at 05.30 daily (10,000f, but air-conditioned service 11,500f).

Rakieta Av Larle Naba Agba; ☎ 50 31 40 56; m 70 74 14 66. Offers tough competition to TCV, operating another express AC service to Bobo (stops only in Boromo); 5 departures daily. Change in Bobo for onward services to Banfora. Also 1 daily departure for Bamako & Bouake. Also at Rue du Commerce (m *70 32 81 24*). 3 departures daily for Zorgho, Koupela & Fada-N'Gourma, & at Rue Emile Damiba (☎ *50 30 62 84*). 3 departures daily for Po, & 2 for Manga at 10.30 & 17.00 (1,500f).

Rimbo Transport Dapoya; m 78 00 87 11, 78 12 00 77. International services – 05.30 daily to Niamey (sometimes AC), 13.00 daily to Bamako, with onward service to Dakar, Senegal (40,000f).

Sito Transport Dapoya; m 72 00 11 88. Services to Côte d'Ivoire; daily to Bouake & Abidjan, thrice-weekly to San Pedro.

SKV Av du Mogho; ☎ 50 30 01 01. Bobo & on to Bamako twice a week. Also goes twice-weekly to Cotonou & Kumasi, thrice-weekly to Lome.

Sogebaf Gounghin & Dapoya. Since the death of its owner in 2009, this firm has been slowly falling apart. The only service worth considering is the twice-weekly coach to Markoye. Don't count on it, & don't bother trying to find it in Ouaga; it's better to pick it up in Dori or Gorom-Gorom.

Sotradyf Rue des Douanes; ☎ 50 33 37 03. 4-times daily between Ouaga & Zorgho, Koupela & Tenkodogo.

STAF Near the *grand marché*; ☎ 50 30 19 21. 7 departures daily between Ouaga & Koudougou. Also at Av Larle Naba Agba (m *70 28 17 96*). Rules many routes these days, & particularly good for the north, with 12 daily services to Yako & Ouahigouya, 2 to Tougan, 2 to Dori, 2 to Kongoussi, & 1 to Djibo; also 7 to Bobo, 2 to Gaoua, 1 to Kampti & 2 to Fada.

STMB Cité An III; ☎ 50 31 34 34, 50 31 13 63. One of the largest fleets in the country, if no longer the best; 2 daily departures to Po & Paga, 2 to Dori, 5 to Koupela & Fada, 2 to Sinkassé via Tenkodogo, 3 to Yako & Ouahigouya, & 4 stopping services to Bobo. Also has once-weekly service to Lome, & to Niamey daily bar Mon.

STP-KZA Behind Rood Wooko market; ☎ 50 30 03 47, 50 44 05 98. Heads to Koudougou every 2hrs. Also has a daily service to Bobo, & weekly to Abidjan on Tue. Also at Gounghin (☎ *50 30 03 47*). Another stop; if you want to load luggage, use the central garage.

TCV Near Hotel Oubri; ☎ 50 30 14 12. Pretty smart (the 'c' stands for comfort) & its express AC service to Bobo is much in demand (book in advance if possible). Leaves for Bobo 7 times a day (stops only at Boromo), including a night journey. Also runs to Bamako & Bouake daily & Cotonou, Lome & Lagos once a week.

TRS Also known as Rayi's, near the grand marché; ☎ 50 33 27 13. Runs between Ouaga & Koudougou every 2hrs until 18.00.

TSR Rue de la Culture; m 70 14 86 13, 70 46 13 49. Another of the big companies. Hourly service to Kaya 06.00–18.00, 8 daily runs to Koudougou, 2 to Dori & 3 to Fada. Also next to Total station, Gounghin (☎ *50 34 25 24;* m *70 25 31 38*). Second station, with hourly stopping service to Bobo 06.00–22.00 (some are AC); also 3 daily services to Gaoua, 4 to Leo, 6 to Ouahigouya. Daily services to Bamako & Bouake; heads to Lome & Cotonou on Thu & Sun.

TZJ-TPW Behind the *grand mosquée* & Gounghin; ☎ 50 44 02 25, 50 31 23 26, 50 34 70 08. Has 8 departures daily for Koudougou; the first of the day continues to Bobo. Devout Christian owner: no Sun service.

ZST Gounghin; ☎ 50 34 41 69. Runs to Abidjan Thu & Mon.

BY BUSH TAXI Bush taxis are a great option when coaches don't dare service a particular destination, or for local hops from market day to market day.

It's easiest to pick up a bush taxi at a town's local *gare routière*, where you will spot Toyota minibuses and Peugeot 504s. If not, try the *poste de police* at the end of town since all cars and trucks have to stop here. It's wise to approach the police officers, shake hands and explain your presence. Then just sit and wait. Prices depend on distance and state of the road, usually about 1,500f for a 100km stretch on tarmac. Count on paying up to twice as much for dilapidated dusty roads. Hiring an entire bush taxi means you get to choose the destination (known as a *déplacement*), but you pay for all the seats.

BY MOPEDS AND MOTORBIKES The motorbike (commonly called a *moto*, whatever its size) has replaced the horse as a Burkinabe's pride and joy. They are everywhere, from put-put *mobylettes* that are part-bicycle, part-moped, to heavy-revving Yamaha beasts. They are vulnerable to road accidents, particularly in Ouaga.

Outside Ouaga, Bobo and Banfora, there are few official moped-hire outlets. Ask at your hotel, however, and invariably a battered machine will turn up within minutes, exhaust on the verge of falling off, petrol tank relying on fumes only. You may have to bargain, since owners are occasionally loath to lend their only means of transport to strangers. Expect to pay 2,500–5,000f per day (excluding petrol) for a P50, the dinky little 50cc models that are easy to use and most commonly seen around town, and more for bikes with gears and clutches. Prices are cheaper if you want to hire something for a longer period of time. A litre of fuel costs about 690f at the time of writing.

When hiring, ask for the bike papers, as you may need to produce these if stopped by the police to prove the vehicle is not stolen. Failure to produce valid documents may lead to a fine or to the bike being impounded.

BY CAR It will certainly make life easier to have a 4x4, but it's not your only ticket for getting around. In the wet season, however, many roads become impassable, especially to the north and in the far southwest.

Car hire If you're hiring a car, check it well. Make sure you have all the proper paperwork – international driving licence, registration, MOT, insurance – or risk paying fines several times if you are stopped by police. Agree price and terms in advance, especially in case of damage, and sort out whether you will be reimbursed for any repairs you pay for on the road. If you want to drive outside Ouagadougou or Bobo, many companies will rent out a car only on condition that it comes with a chauffeur – which has both advantages and disadvantages. Cars tend to cost around 20,000–30,000f a day, 4x4s 40,000–70,000f. Prices often include chauffeur but exclude fuel. For details of local car-hire options, consult the regional chapters.

Péages A series of road tolls helps maintain the pot-holes nationwide and a checkpoint (*péage*) is generally found on every main road leaving and entering a sizeable town or city. You can buy singles or returns. Make sure you have some coins, as change may not be forthcoming. Mopeds do not have to pay.

Example rates (one-way): Ouaga–Sabou 200f; Fada–Kantchari 200f; Ouaga–Fada 400f; Ouaga–Nazinga 400f; Ouaga–Gaoua 600f; Ouaga–Bobo 800f; Ouaga–Banfora 1,000f.

BY TRAIN Despite the war in neighbouring Côte d'Ivoire, SITARAIL trains go regularly between Ouaga and Abidjan. Services leave Ouaga on Tuesday, Thursday and Saturday at 07.30 for Abidjan, stopping at Koudougou (1,500f), Bobo (5,000f) and Banfora (8,000f). The return journey from Abidjan should pass through on Wednesday, Friday and Sunday in the evening. There was no working telephone at the time of writing, but it may be worth trying ☎ 50 31 07 35/38/39/42 or 50 30 60 52.

BY AIR For the wealthy or those in a hurry, Air Burkina (☎ *50 49 23 45/46/47*) has internal flights to Bobo. You can also hire a small Cessna and pilot for trips from Ouagadougou to tiny airfields in far-flung corners of Burkina and beyond. Richard, at Hotel Ricardo (☎ *50 30 70 72*), is your man, with prices from 160,000f an hour (petrol price permitting).

BY BICYCLE This is the preferred method of transport for millions of Burkinabe. In Ouagadougou, bikes of all shapes and sizes throng the streets, sometimes five or six abreast at rush hour. You can always find someone prepared to hire out a bike for a day or two if you want cheap transport to explore dusty streets or surrounding countryside. The quality varies enormously, but don't expect anything flash.

Planning a tour of the country by bike is a different matter, but equally feasible. Topographically, Burkina won't leave you gasping to get to the top of mountains. It is on the whole quite flat, with the odd undulation, which makes daily distances of more than 100km possible on tarmac. Off-road excursions can be much more pleasant. In particular, the forested regions of the southwest, criss-crossed by smooth red-earth roads, make great cycling country. You may even enjoy some shade from overhanging trees, as well as respite from fast traffic. Much of the following advice comes from Anna Heywood and Luke Skinner, who toured Burkina in spring 2005 (see box, pages 92–3).

Equipment If you plan to stay on tarmac and travel light, it's feasible to make it around Burkina on a standard tourer. If you plan on going off-road but keeping distances down, a decent mountain bike will do the job. Much better, and giving greater flexibility, is a hybrid touring bike.

Spare parts are tough to come by locally. For a trip of two to three weeks, a thorough pre-trip check of your bike and replacement of worn-out parts might be sufficient. If your trip is longer or you don't mind the extra weight, it is well worth taking a range of spares. Spare inners are pretty obvious, but tyres are probably a bit bulky. Get decent ones fitted new before you go – Schwalbe's Marathon XRs are hard to beat – and remember you can pick up some sort of tyre in absolutely any village throughout west Africa to get you to the next large town. Take brake blocks, chain links, brake and gear cables, a puncture-repair kit and know how to fix a puncture. A range of Allen keys and ring spanners, a chain tool, standard and Phillips screwdrivers and a spoke key are also worth packing. In addition, a Leatherman multi-tool is handy for the pliers, wire cutters and knife. If you aren't a crack bike mechanic then Richards's *Bicycle Repair Manual* is easy to follow and not too heavy.

On the road there will be a workshop in every town that can patch your machine up and get you going, but service your bike before you go. Don't load yourself down with too much gear – it will seriously diminish your enjoyment.

Ouagadougou has an excellent cycle market, just south of the centre (see map, pages 116–17) and it's probably the best place in west Africa to buy a bike (or moped). Not only does it have the best selection of spare parts going, it also has some skilled mechanics who know what they are doing when it comes to servicing and repairs. The patron, Adama Zongo, is highly recommended.

Health On the road, drink lots of water, even when you don't feel thirsty. There are pumps and wells in virtually every village for filling up, although you may want to treat it first. Sticking to bottled water can work out expensive, and creates a whole load of plastic waste. For a simple but effective refrigerator, slip a black sock over one of your bottles and douse it with water. As the water in the sock evaporates it cools the water in the bottle. Sprinkle more salt than usual on your food to make up for salts lost through sweating, and add a pinch to soft drinks, which provide a

BURKINA BY BIKE *Anna Heywood and Luke Skinner*

Cycling through Burkina may not be up there with lounging on a Caribbean beach when it comes to popular dream holidays, but take the plunge and you might just love it.

Our time in Burkina was part of a longer trip from London to Cape Town, but even if you've never cycled in Africa before, Burkina is a good place to start. We cycled on expedition models hand-built by Thorn in Bridgwater, UK, and had very few really serious problems.

For us, highlights included the hospitality of local people, the juicy feast of the mango harvest, seeing hippos and elephants at close quarters in little-visited wildlife reserves and sampling millet beer in the midst of a Gourounsi village festival.

We coped with the heat by getting up in the dark each morning, and departing just after dawn to take advantage of the coolest hours of the day. This can be a lovely time to be on the road. In the quietude and clear light of early morning, little grey donkeys patiently wait to be loaded up, women bear bundles of kindling home for the breakfast fire, children blearily wander to school in much-darned uniforms and men are already bent low in the fields, wielding hoes and tending their millet and cassava. By 10.00 the heat is mounting, the asphalt is shimmering and sticky and the donkeys have wisely sought out what little shade is available under the eaves. We intended to do the same – cycle from 06.00 to 11.00, have a long lunch break and a sleep, then continue cycling in the less ferocious heat of late afternoon.

We found this impractical mainly because rural Burkina is home to despicable little insects called (we think) sweat bees, although we called them plenty of other things besides. They seek out any moisture on your body – in ears, up noses, behind knees. On the bike, the breeze keeps them off but once you stop, they descend in seconds. We found we couldn't stop for more than ten minutes. So we pushed on through the hottest part of the day, or simply finished early.

We camped throughout Burkina without any problems and wouldn't consider sleeping in the bush as intrinsically dangerous. In general, we filled up with water in a village and then continued for about 5km before camping at least 100m off the road. Exercise common sense – camping on land that is obviously planted with

welcome sugar hit. Build in plenty of rest days to stop yourself getting overtired. If you are cycling with another person or a group allow for differing appetites, abilities and weaknesses.

 ACCOMMODATION

Burkina's hotel industry is dominated by well-equipped but slightly bland hotels that pick up a healthy trade from the endless conferences that criss-cross Burkina.

That said, there is some excellent budget and not-so-budget accommodation across the country that combines comfort, ambience and service. Plush lodges, lush courtyards, cosy traditional huts, roof terraces or desert beds under the stars offer lovely variety.

In recent years, it seems that everyone with a few savings tucked away has decided to build a *campement* or a little *auberge*; the top end of the market is expanding at a similar rate. The result is that Burkina is awash with accommodation, perhaps too much. You'll rarely find anywhere fully booked, and older establishments with

crops may anger a farmer, and stopping close to a village may lead to unwelcome attention. Avoid cattle trails and beware of semi-controlled bush fires at the end of the harvest season.

Pick a spot hidden from view. In Burkina this is not so much for security as to avoid a huge crowd of local kids coming to watch you as you cook, wash and go to the loo. Many guidebooks and individuals will suggest approaching a village leader before pitching your tent but to be honest we didn't feel this was necessary or always practicable.

Heat aside, we found the biggest challenge to be the constant attention you attract. Being under such intense scrutiny can be wearing. It's hard to get used to being stared at and to the lack of privacy. Burkina is, though, less exhausting in this regard than some other west African regions. In Senegal and The Gambia we were shouted at aggressively, in Ghana everyone demanded rather than enquired 'where are you going', in Morocco rag-tag bands of kids occasionally threw stones at us in the countryside and in Nigeria we were overwhelmed by the sheer volume of people crowding round us in each village – sometimes 200. The attention you will get in Burkina is sometimes frustrating, occasionally intrusive but nearly always friendly. Sometimes it is sheer magic.

A few kilometres out of Bobo-Dioulasso a man passed on a moped with his two small children, who smiled and waved. The little girl reached out a small hand and handed Anna a tiny bunch of beautiful vermilion-coloured flowers. The moped sped off but must have stopped somewhere down the road as it overtook us again half an hour later, and this time the boy had a posy ready to hand to Luke – obviously he was not to be upstaged by his sister. The sun was warm but not too hot, the water in our bottles not yet tepid, the villages picturesque and the trees dotted with weaver birds, hornbills and Abyssinian rollers.

At times like this you whistle as the wheels spin round, and think you are possibly the happiest person in the world.

Anna Heywood and Luke Skinner began a two-year trans-Africa cycle trip from London to Cape Town in 2004 in aid of Link Africa.

maintenance issues are languishing in the shade of newer ventures. Even the most obscure of towns is likely to have several options, although they can be aimed at the NGO or company budget rather than the independent traveller. Many towns have cheap *maisons de passage* that take visitors. Bars with budget rooms attached often double as makeshift brothels.

In general, décor is not always tasteful, but the basics of a comfortable bed, a shower that works, and a mosquito-free night are usually possible.

A fan or air conditioning is normally the dividing factor in price. With a bit of acclimatisation, it is usually possible to sleep in a room with a powerful ceiling fan (smaller standing fans are often a poor substitute), although air conditioning is more comfortable. Some towns cut the electricity at night, so the debate may prove pointless. Hot water is not usually available in budget and some mid-range accommodation. In the hot months, this is almost a boon; less so in the cooler months between November and February.

Breakfast is often an overpriced disappointment. A bit of stale bread, a cup of Nescafé and an omelette is delicious when bought at a buzzing breakfast kiosk;

ACCOMMODATION PRICE CODES

Accommodation listings are laid out in decreasing price order, under the following categories: Luxury, Upmarket, Comfortable, Mid range, Budget and Shoestring. The following key (also on the inside front cover) gives an indication of prices. Prices are based on a double room per night in high season and generally include taxes.

Luxury	**$$$$$$**	45,000f+
Upmarket	**$$$$$**	30,000–45,000f
Comfortable	**$$$$**	20,000–30,000f
Mid range	**$$$**	12,000–20,000f
Budget	**$$**	5,000–12,000f
Shoestring	**$**	< 5,000f

paying ten times the price for it in a hotel is not. So, generally, avoid breakfast in your hotel and grab something on the street.

A NOTE ON HOTEL BEDS Some hotels charge by the head, some by the room. When sizing up rooms, bear in mind that 'single' rooms usually contain a double bed. A 'double' room usually contains a larger double bed for more money. A 'twin' room will contain two separate beds. In rare cases, however, a single room really does contain a single bed, and many double rooms contain two separate beds. Clear? Best to see the room first.

TAXES There are usually two taxes to bear in mind. The first is a tourist tax, calculated at a daily rate and paid per person. It is graded according to the standard of accommodation – 300f for one-star, 700f two-star, 1,000f three-star and 1,500f four-star. There is little standardisation about whether hotels include this in their advertised prices or not, although as a rule of thumb the more expensive hotels will do so. There is also a one-off community tax, at 1,000f per stay.

LAUNDRY Most hotels can wash clothes, and many have a rule that forbids doing it yourself in the room. In cheaper places, the system is often informal, and paying a member of staff to do your laundry can be a valuable way to bump up a pitiful salary. Otherwise, there are places in towns, which charge 100–300f per item; prices

HOME FROM HOME

A new phenomenon in Ouaga and Bobo is that of *maisons d'hôtes* – private homes with rooms for visitors, rather like bed and breakfasts in Europe. Many, but not all, are French- or French/Burkinabe-run. They are generally great value and very comfortable; many have lovely living areas and offer additional services such as airport pick-up and bike/car hire or excursions; some have swimming pools. Meals are usually available; for some, the evening *table d'hôte* is an important part of the hospitality, offering an opportunity for exchange and relaxation at the end of a long day. The only possible downside, depending on how you like to travel, is the sense of being in someone else's home; this varies from house to house.

can stack up if you have a big load, but they will come back beautifully pressed and folded. Look out for signs saying *blanchissage* or *repassage*.

EATING AND DRINKING

AFRICAN DISHES The national staple is *tô* (*sagbo* in Moore), a white, starchy mountain made from pounded millet and water. Tasteless and filling, it's often combined with a fairly tasty green sauce (*sauce feuille*) made of baobab leaves, rich in calcium.

A more adventurous alternative is *foutou*, from neighbouring Côte d'Ivoire. It has a similar texture to *tô* but is made from yams. *Foutou banane* has plantain added and is delicious.

Classic dishes are *riz gras* and *riz sauce*, available at resto-bars across the country. *Riz gras* is rice covered with cabbage and bits of bitter African aubergine, with a few morsels of meat in a tomato sauce. *Riz sauce* consists of plain white rice with one of two sauces – *sauce tomate* is the most common, but you'll also find *sauce arachide*, a thick reddish-brown groundnut sauce; a Burkinabe satay. Vegetarians take note: both have chunks of meat thrown in. Prices vary (150–1,500f a plate), depending on how smart the restaurant, and how much sauce you get. Fish and chicken soup are readily available. They can look unappetising, but generally slurp down well.

Chicken is easy to come by in the smallest of bars, often killed the moment it is ordered and taking some time to arrive as a result. Be warned that nothing is wasted by locals – head, neck, eyes and all – although a *maquis* may take squeamish foreign sensibilities into account. Several tasty preparations mask the often poor quality of meat, including lime juice, mustard and onions, garlic, tomato and green peppers. Two chicken stews, *poulet yassa*, strong on onions and lemon and from Senegal, and *poulet kedjenou*, from Côte d'Ivoire, are popular in Burkina. *Poulet bicyclette* is a classic, local take on rôtisserie chicken and when done well, with lashings of garlic, is difficult to beat. *Poulet rabilet* makes good use of *soumbala*, in a pungent, slightly sweet, nutty sauce.

Another Burkinabe classic is *pintade* – domesticated guineafowl; their raucous cackling is commonly heard across the country. You'll find them roasting alongside chicken at countless roadside chop stalls; they tend to cost a bit more. They also feature on numerous restaurant menus.

With so much cattle in the country, there is also plenty of beef on offer. Small chunks, skewered and grilled, are called *brochettes*, and available for as little as 100f, sometimes served with onions, tomatoes, green peppers and plenty of garlic. You can also find *merguez* sausage.

RESTAURANT PRICE CODES

Restaurant listings are laid out in decreasing price order, under the following categories: Expensive, Above average, Mid range, and Cheap and cheerful. The following key (also on the inside front cover) gives an indication of prices. Prices are based on the cost of a main course per person, including taxes.

Expensive	$$$$	6,000f+
Above average	$$$	3,000–6,000f
Mid range	$$	1,000–3,000f
Cheap and cheerful	$	<1,000f

AGOUTI OR NOT? *Janice Booth*

If the 'agouti' that you see on menus in Burkina Faso were truly agouti (*Dasyprocta leporina*), it would have strayed a very long distance from its South American homeland! The rodent colloquially called 'agouti' in Burkina Faso (and other west African countries) is in fact a grasscutter or cane rat (*Thryonomys swinderianus* or *gregorianus*) and is a very popular part of the local diet. It's Africa's second-largest rodent after the porcupine; the average weight for an adult male is 4.5kg and for a female 3kg.

In several places grasscutters are farmed for food, as the quality of the meat is good and it's a valuable (and easily available) source of protein. For example the UK-based charity Send a Cow (*www.sendacow.org.uk*) has a project to provide grasscutters for breeding purposes to poor families in Cameroon, working in conjunction with Heifer Cameroon (*www.heifer.org*).

In the wild, grasscutters can live just about anywhere – among the tall grasses of the savanna, on rocky ground, in cultivated forest, in sugarcane plantations, and in cultivated fields of crops such as groundnuts, maize, rice and cassava.

Just don't try asking for grasscutter in your best French in a Burkina Faso restaurant – you'll be better understood if you stick to the more familiar misnomer of 'agouti'.

Pork is popular in animist/Christian districts. A favourite way to cook it is in a little mud-brick oven, when it's known as *porc au four* (oven-cooked pork). Some *maquis* make it their speciality and are justly famous as a result; good *porc au four* is heavenly. It's more of an option for late morning/lunchtime than for evenings. Not to miss out on a treat, Muslims have their own variation – oven-cooked mutton, or *mouton au four*.

Agouti is a gamey, rich meat that could easily pass for rabbit when you don't know what it is. When you learn that it is cane rat by another name it quickly becomes a little harder to swallow. Dogs and cats are also eaten in Burkinabe villages.

If you see anyone with food in front of them, wish them *bon appétit*. This is often met with the response *vous êtes invité* (you are invited) – not an actual request to share the meal so much as a warm expression of hospitality.

Accompaniments *Alloco* is chopped, fried plantain, popular in Côte d'Ivoire, which complements any dish as a sweeter alternative to chips. *Attieke* is shaved cassava, looks a bit like couscous and goes well with any casserole-type dish, particularly *poulet yassa*. Yam and sweet potato chips are great alternatives to French fries. Couscous, spaghetti, chips and baguettes are also widely available. Green beans, fried in garlic and butter, sometimes with small tomatoes or bacon thrown in, is another delicious side order, best in season when the beans are fresh. There are some interesting European-style culinary takes on other common ingredients. The best is perhaps shea butter ice cream, which tastes a little like frozen hand cream. It's also a disarming fluorescent green.

In the markets A wander around any town market will offer several eye-openers, along with a good selection of tomatoes, onions, peppers, aubergines and garlic.

Soumbala smells, and tastes, of dirty socks. It is a bundle of tightly packed soft black balls made from fermented *nere* seed, high in protein. It's pretty much the original African stock cube, and is used to add flavour to dishes, although it's something of an acquired taste. Children are also particularly fond of the sweet yellow powder found inside *nere* pods. *Kurakura* is the equivalent of the Burkinabe pretzel, made of dried peanut butter. Dried fish, flat and angry-looking, can be underestimated. One poor traveller once combined the dried offering from the marketplace with lettuce and cucumber in a sandwich. Suffice to say he didn't get much beyond a bite. His error was to eat it raw; it is another pungent seasoner used as a stock cube, dispersed in giant pots of liquid with stewed vegetables and sometimes meat, to accompany starchy *tô*, or rice for special occasions.

You may even see women selling pieces of calcium-rich cement, which expectant mothers are advised to chomp on for the sake of junior.

Street food Watching the preparations for Burkina's endless night-time meat barbecues can be fascinating, if a little off-putting. Men bring razor-sharp machetes down onto a wooden chopping block, splicing all manner of meat cuts into small chunks. You can't help but shut your eyes in an involuntary wince every time the knife comes down. Portions are parcelled out in brown paper over grills, and a powerful orange spice, called *can-can-can* and made from groundnuts and chillis, is added. It makes anything taste edible, and has a local reputation for aphrodisiac properties. Day and night, women fry up plantain and maize on the streets, sell mangoes and groundnuts and fry up starchy snacks. *Samsa* (*beignets* in French) is made from black-eyed beans (*benga*), pounded until their starchy skin comes off. The remaining powder is added to water, fashioned into rounds and fried in shea butter. Eaten hot, ensuring flies have no time to settle, they're pretty good. You can also pick up sesame-seed biscuits – shaped like hearts come Valentine's Day – in every street-side shop and petrol station.

DRINKS

Water The two main brands of bottled water are Lafi and Jirma. The largest bottles (1.5l) cost 350–500f, much more in restaurants and bars. There is also a host of sachet brands, usually in clear plastic bags of 50ml, such as Cascade and Jirma, which cost 50f each. Unmarked sachets, for 10f, contain tap water, although chilled.

Soft drinks With so much fruit in Burkina, delicious juices are available, often sold on the street in 50f plastic sachets. *Bissap* juice is a bit like a cross between

KOLA NUTS

Kola nuts are conker-sized, but more ragged in shape. Once broken along the seam, they reveal a perfect mauve inside, smooth and undulating. Biting into one is a bitter experience; as though you've just picked up a plant stalk and started chomping into it. It might seem strange why something so tart is such a special offering – kola nuts are given as a sign of respect to chiefs and elders, and being invited to share one is an important sign of recognition. But wait. After you swallow, the aftertaste gives your mouth a moreish little buzz. It is a mild stimulant and takes away hunger pains, and for anyone not allowed to drink alcohol, it comes in pretty handy. You can find kola nuts in villages, but also on the streets of Ouaga. They cost about 25f each. If you are visiting a village, it is good to have some to hand. While younger villagers may prefer a beer, kola nuts are likely to go down a treat as a way of thanking older men and women for their hospitality.

elderberry, cranberry and blackberry, made from deep purple petals of the bissap flower. Tamarind juice looks like light-coloured Coca-Cola, but tastes entirely different: sweet, rich and slightly spicy. *Limburghi*, or *gingembre* (ginger juice), can really pack a punch and, served ice-cold, is delicious.

Brakina, the nation's brewer, also makes a range of soft drinks. Flavours such as mango, cola, pineapple and fruit cocktail can become a bit sickly after a while, but their main advantage is that they come in plastic bottles, so you can take them on the road with you. They can be bought from street-side kiosks from 300f. The canned, non-alcoholic version of Guinness, called Malta, is also available.

Sharing Chinese tea, often several servings from the same pot, is a much-enjoyed social activity. The preparation process has a laborious, ritualistic element to it that, rigorously observed, can take half an hour, providing the opportunity for a good gossip. A small iron stand is swirled around to introduce as much air as possible to the coals, and a small teapot placed on top to cook slowly. When finally ready, the dark tea is poured into small thimble-like glasses, with a fine froth on the top. This ensures the tea is not too hot when it touches the lips. The more froth you're offered, the greater the honour.

Beer Burkina's two main beers are Brakina and So.b.bra (pronounced 'So-bay-bra'), sold in big 650ml bottles (about 600–800f). Both have a delicious wheaty taste and the latter is slightly stronger. The slightly more upmarket favourite is

MILLET BEER

Dolo or *chapalo* is the alcoholic beverage of choice in villages. A potent homegrown beer, it is brewed from fermented red millet. It's drunk mostly by men, but made by women on a three-day rotation and then taken to the nearest market for sale. It's one of the few money-making schemes available to women and therefore of great economic importance to family life. In many societies, such as the Winye, women give their husbands a first taste for free, but after that even they have to pay.

Preparation In enormous earthenware pots, ground millet mixed with water is boiled over hot coals. The resulting paste is mixed with yeast at the end of the second day and left to ferment overnight. From the following morning the *dolo* is ready to drink, but in the heat of the day the fermentation process continues, making the brew stronger and less sweet as the day goes on.

Protocol When offered a bowl, form dictates that you offer it back so that the brewer can have the honour of the first sip. If in Mossi country, say *you*, which means 'drink', as you give it back. When it's your turn, hold the calabash in your right hand only, and never smell it before tasting. Unlike Western traditions, where inhaling deeply and making nice noises about your food in advance is a compliment to the chef, sniffing perishables in Burkina implies you don't trust the maker enough to go right ahead and eat or drink.

You may be offered a *goût de voir* first – an entire calabash filled to the brim, for free. This is in theory to decide whether the batch is sufficiently to your liking, but nobody ever drains the *goût de voir* and says it's not. It does mean that you should drink at least one more calabash-worth (or offer it around), usually costing 50–100f.

Flag, brewed in Burkina but hailing from Senegal. It is available in a smaller 330ml bottle (known as a *flagette*) and is slightly heavier. Castel is another option. Locally brewed beer (*dolo* or *chapalo*) is widely available in villages and towns (see box, opposite). Palm wine (*banji*) is popular in the south, as is an extremely strong sugarcane liquor known as *qui m'a poussé* ('who's pushed me?').

PUBLIC HOLIDAYS

1 January	New Year
3 January	Soulèvement Populaire, also known as SOUL POP, celebrating the 1966 popular uprising against Upper Volta's first president, Maurice Yameogo
8 March	Women's Day
March/April	Easter Monday
1 May	Worker's Day
May	Ascension Thursday
5 August	Proclamation of Independence/National Day
15 August	Assumption
1 November	All Saints' Day
11 December	Proclamation of the Republic
25 December	Christmas Day

Muslim festivals such as Ramadan, the end of Ramadan (Aid el Segheir), Tabaski (70 days after the end of Ramadan, also known as Aid el Kebir or feast of the sacrifice), El am Hejir (New Year) and Mouloud (birthday of the Prophet) are also celebrated, but have no fixed calendar dates since timings are determined by the lunar year. If any holiday falls on a Sunday, it is carried over to the following Monday.

SHOPPING

There's no danger that you'll spend your last moments in Burkina on a frantic hunt for the desultory airport souvenir. Burkina Faso has a thriving crafts sector, reaching back centuries and across several disciplines.

COLLECTORS' ITEMS The Western market for west African art is growing. Once located in Abidjan, it has since flown to the US and to Paris, where many experts are located.

The real finds are those considered 'pre-contact' – pre-colonial, and thus in some way 'naïve'. A replica statue can sell for 3,000f on the tourist trail, 30,000f if it's halfway decent, and 300,000f if it's the real thing. It is not always easy to spot the real thing, and Burkina's thriving crafts sector knocks out masks, statues and fetishes regularly.

It is worth thinking long and hard about buying such 'authentic' art, even that dating from the post-colonial period. It may well have been stolen from a village or family by a relative keen to make some money, leaving a gaping spiritual hole in the community. There are several examples of anthropologists who have heard villagers mourn the disappearance of a statue or fetish, only to see it turn up in a prestigious international art exhibition, a stolen and sacred artefact.

In the 1990s, one German collector discovered that he had exactly such a totemic item. He has returned it to Burkina, where there are plans to install it in a small museum in the north of the country, in Pobe Mengao.

The fact that something is not an antique museum piece, or sacred, does not mean that it is not genuine, however. Master craftsmen whose skills have been passed down over generations can be enlisted to make stunning masks, in a variety of traditional styles, at generous prices. Not only does this provide someone with a living, it will ensure that somewhere, in a village far, far away, a sacred mask can still be taken down once or twice a year and worn on special occasions, rather than get stolen and sold to feed Western appetites.

MASKS Masks tend to represent ancestors, animals and spirits. The act of putting on a mask is loaded with significance, as the wearer (only male) is no longer responsible for his actions. Masks can act as spiritual telephones, as a way of communicating with each other or directly with the ancestors. Sometimes the mask hands control over to the spirits completely, and masked dancers, transported by the music of the dance, have been known to hurl themselves into terrified audiences, breaking a few spectators' bones along the way.

Masks are also a powerful way of reminding people of their creation myths, in which masked men take on the characters of the totemic founding fathers. Some fetish masks have particular jobs, such as warding off leprosy or encouraging fertility. Others are used by young chaps who dance and flounce about on market day to woo the ladies, and are anything but sacred.

Almost all groups in Burkina, bar the Lobi and Gourmanche, revel in mask culture. The Bwaba, in particular, are renowned master craftsmen. Their mask-making skills are so expertly passed down through generations that many other cultures drafted them into their communities when their own mask-making abilities died out.

Many masks take on the stylised form of animals such as the crocodile, hawk, ram, antelope or hornbill. Young men receive an animal identity during their bush initiation, and learn the dance for that animal.

Most masks are made of wood, sometimes leaves or tissue. The face mask is part of a larger costume, usually a full bodysuit of *rafia* fibres or woven leaves stitched together so no part of the body shows. Some masks, known as *bayiri* to the Bwaba, stretch high above the wearer's face, plank-like, towards the sky. Others stretch out wide, like elongated butterfly wings. The colours, mostly red, black and white, come either from modern paints or more traditional sources – lizard and sacred snake excrement, or chalk, for the white; pounded, iron-rich soil for the red; and powdered charcoal or boiled *nere* seeds for the black. The design may then be glazed with egg or gum Arabic from acacia trees.

Public mask festivals take place after the harvest is gathered and before the new planting season. This is during the hottest months, from about February until April or May, when there is the time to give thanks and to start asking for benediction for the rains to come. For more information, see page 271.

WOODCARVING AND STATUES Wood sculpting and carving is popular in forms other than masks. Like masks, statues are not solely for decorative purposes. They also communicate with spirits, and are something to keep close to home, or in areas where both the spirit world and villagers might need a bit of reassurance, such as forests and fields. The Lobi in particular are known for their statues, and it is not hard to find 50- to 80-year-old examples.

Poupies are crudely carved wooden dolls. They do not have a sacred function, but are companions for young girls, to practise the basics of motherhood as they watch their own mother with younger children.

TAKING ART OUT OF THE COUNTRY

If you do buy works of art, ask for and keep all your receipts. You may be asked for these at the airport when attempting to take artwork out of the country.

All export of objects of old and traditional art is subject to approval by the Ministry of Culture, Arts and Tourism. The ministry is especially concerned about masks and dance ornaments, statues, puppets, doors, locks and sculpted pillars, traditional furniture, ancient weapons such as clubs, bows, arrows, lances, swords, knives, rifles, sceptres, textiles and leather and musical instruments such as drums, flutes and *balafons*.

Anything for export requires a typed declaration. You can get this from the directorate of the National Culture and Patrimony in Ouagadougou, at 800f per piece of art. Visit www.artcultureburkina.bf for more details, or contact the Ministry of Culture, Arts and Tourism (*+226 50 33 09 63*).

BRONZE From the gleam of neatly aligned objects on show at tourist stands, you might think bronze-making in Burkina was a distinctly mass-market and soulless affair. Not so once you have seen the workers in action, employing age-old methods to make every single piece (see box, pages 262–3). The Mossi in particular have earned a well-deserved reputation for their excellent bronzework.

In large bronze workshops, such as the one in Koudougou, workers have different roles, including artists who shape the initial model out of wax, mould-makers who create a cast of the wax image and *bronziers*, who melt the metal and cast the object. Finally, workers smooth and shine the finish on each item.

You can visit workshops in the Niogsin and Ouidi quarters of Ouagadougou, as well as the Village Artisanal, the Vitrine du Bronze and several craft shops around town (see page 145). If you don't like anything you see, feel free to ask for a commission.

When visiting a village, it is worth asking to visit the forge, which often consists of a small earthen chamber topped by bellows, traditionally made of goatskin, more often with spare bicycle parts to pump in air. Forgers make the farm tools that sustain the village, as well as occasional sacred objects.

WEAVING The Marka are particularly keen on weaving, and Marka women are reputed to be the most skilled dyers in central Burkina. While women look after pigment, men tend to work the looms, turning out blue- and white-banded cloth from local silk.

In the Mossi region, look out for *bogolan* woven cloth. The word means 'soil' in Moore, and the blankets and robes have a dusky ochre hue and earthy feel to them. The Yarse, Muslim traders who arrived in the Mossi region from Guinea in the 15th century, are also expert weavers.

Beautifully patterned cotton fabrics adorn markets all over the country, although much of the material is imported from Asia and dyed in Nigeria, while the thinner sheets that shimmer with golden thread hail from India. Indigo cloth is also available. Dori, in the north, is a centre for woven blankets. In the southwest, basket-weaving is popular. The greater humidity prevents stalks and leaves from the palm-like *ronier* tree from drying out too quickly and cracking.

LEATHERWORK With so many cows around, nomads have had a long time to develop their leatherware skills. Goats, sheep and camels all lose their hides to Burkina's expert *maroquiniers* in the service of gorgeous leatherwork boxes, handmade satchels or pokerwork purses, all made the traditional way. There are tanning centres all over the country – look out for the Tan-Aliz factories that do so on an industrial scale. There are also plenty of local tanneries you can visit. For a really good idea of the process, head for Kaya (see page 172).

JEWELLERY With so many gold mines, large and small scale, there is a lot of 18-carat gold around, and plenty of window shopping on offer. The Mossi have always had an eye for a bit of jewellery. When the French captain Binger arrived in the 19th century, he found them 'loaded with copper armlets and leg-guards – some of them carry over 20lb of copper on their arms'.

Today, you may see people, particularly men, wearing rather crude copper and twisted iron bracelets and rings. These are a form of protection, to ward off evil spirits and disease. Women tend to wear similar versions above their elbows, as well as anklets. Brass and copper is also used in combination. They may be intended to encourage fertility, or bring a good harvest.

As a result of roaring trans-African trade, many European and Indian beads found their way into much-vaunted Mossi necklaces. Look out too for Fulani girls decked out in the most marvellous hairdos, earrings and necklaces, even on the most mundane of days. Amber is particularly popular in old Fulani hair ornaments, while both Fulani and Mossi make necklaces of carnelian, a translucent orange/red stone prized for its healing properties, thought to stop bleeding and cure diseases of the blood.

MODERN ART Burkina's contemporary art scene is thriving. Inspiration and invention tends to come from the everyday, in form as well as subject matter: abandoned scrap metal is reincarnated as witty and wonderful bird-sculpture, old newspaper headlines end up in enormous collages. It is possible to pick up original work, neither twee nor aimed at a tourist market, at excellent prices.

One of the most talented and best known of Burkinabe artists in recent years is Saidou Soungrana 'Beybson', who was born near Accra in 1966 and sadly died in 2004

POTS OF POTS

Ceramic pots come in all shapes and sizes. For women, they are a considerable sign of status, piled up in columns around the walls of the kitchen.

Voluminous and earthen, the largest of the family, known as the *canari*, is the fridge of rural Burkina, keeping water cool and undisturbed. Pots and jars are also used to store and cook grain and millet beer. Where brewing is concerned, women – who rule the roost in this activity – say beer from a metal tin tastes nothing like as good as beer brewed in earthenware pots.

Among the Mossi, both men and women make pots. To the west, on the way to Dedougou, and in Lobi country in the south, this is the work of women. In one single day, a woman can make two or three jars, ten cooking pots or five or six *canaris*.

Pots are made from clay and either coiled, moulded or, among the Lobi, Samo and Marka, fashioned by hand and pulled into shape. Before firing in what is often an open wood fire, repeating patterns are impressed into the clay, using twisted cord. Others add a clay relief to the walls of pots meant for special occasions. They are usually glazed with a sort of dark-brown vegetable stew, which has thickened as it has reduced during cooking.

of cancer. An exhibition of his work at the French Institute in Ouaga showcased his meticulous, playful, cartoon-like style, depicting in bright colours detailed portraits of Ouaga life – motorcyclists carrying improbable numbers of chickens on their mopeds, women with babies on their backs and fruit piled high on their heads, hectic nightlife and street scenes. His paintings sell for around 200,000f, but this is likely to increase. A member of the same workshop, 'Babs' has a similar style.

'Kely' is another local Ouaga artist who has made many a *maquis* seriously funky, producing trees, tables and chairs out of bits of old bicycles, cars and odds and ends. For an idea of his work, head for the Fondation Olorun, a workshop for Ouagalais creatives who have exhibited in Europe and New York, many of whom are masters of amusing oil-drum sculpture. Others among them are painters. For an idea of some of the work that has emerged from the Foundation, visit www.modern-african-art.com.

Otherwise, an excellent first stop is the French Institute in either Ouaga or Bobo to find out about the latest exhibitions. Look out also for *Artistes Plasticiens de Ouagadougou*, a handy guide to the hip and happening names in Burkinabe contemporary art that is compiled by the Ministry of Culture, Arts and Tourism and the French embassy. Some shops and restaurants, such as the K-Lala boutique in Ouagadougou, may have a copy. Otherwise, try asking officials, or visiting www.culture.gov.bf.

PHOTOGRAPHY

In general people love being snapped. Children in particular follow the first appearance of a camera as if it were the Pied Piper, determinedly positioning themselves along the bottom of every shot you frame. A few stagey group shots can assuage young prima donnas, leaving you free to snap what you had originally seen, although chances are it's no longer the image you wanted.

It's always nicer to ask permission of your subjects. You risk being told no of course, or asked for money. However, people tend to lose natural smiles and poses and act immediately self-conscious, as if at a police line-up. The key is to establish a rapport first – perhaps by buying something from a stallholder before asking for a shot, or taking the time to get to know someone before asking if you can photograph them. Paying directly for a shot almost always voids the chance, although sometimes making an offering to village elders can be a fair exchange.

FREE PHOTOGRAPHY PERMIT Get a free photography permit from the ONTB tourist office in Ouaga on your arrival in Burkina. It's quite possible you will never be checked, but this slip of paper is always worth having around if you want to avoid a fine or, worse, confiscation or destruction of your images. The airport, government buildings and installations, communications facilities and systems, water-treatment plants, military installations and military personnel are off-limits, even with a permit. Why most travellers would be seen near any of these, let alone want to photograph them, is difficult to fathom. The only building that may be a problem is the attractive presidential residence.

MEDIA AND COMMUNICATIONS

While the Burkinabe media are stronger than many others in Africa, and free of the kind of rabid bias that surfaces elsewhere, it is worth bearing in mind the continuing involvement of the state. Public media include the Burkina Information Agency,

National Television, National Broadcasting Corporation, Rural Radio, six local radio stations and two radio stations broadcasting on FM. Private media include three daily papers, eight weeklies, 15 FM radio stations and two TV channels. Independent newspapers and media outlets, which have grown rapidly since 1990, receive a state subsidy. In 1997, this was CFA100 million, offered in the form of material aid, tax and customs relief. This subsidy was 'to enable the private press to develop and play its role in the strengthening of democracy'.

NEWSPAPERS Burkina is home to a vibrant selection of newspapers, and freedom of the press, on the surface at least, is in rude health. While sales are low, all the papers have a high read-on value for friends and family members. However, given literacy rates, they reach only a fraction of the population. Generally, poor distribution networks and absence of regional printing presses mean it is difficult to find papers, even out-of-date ones, outside Ouaga and Bobo. Some speculate that the licence given to independent publishers on what they write has little effect for exactly this reason, and that the state keeps much tighter control of radio, which reaches out to many more people, especially since there are local-language as well as French broadcasts.

Newspaper culture has a fascinating recent history. The killing in December 1998 of a prominent journalist, Norbert Zongo, a campaigning investigative reporter who also edited his own weekly newspaper, *L'Indépendant*, almost led to the downfall of the recently re-elected government, and the story rumbles on even now. For more information, see *History*, page 31.

The country's most-read daily newspaper, *Sidwaya*, is state-run. While professionally produced and a good read, both it and its Sunday counterpart, *Sidwaya Hebdo*, will certainly exhibit pro-government bias, although more in choice of stories than in style of coverage.

In addition to *L'Indépendant*, local opinion tends to rate *L'Observateur* and *Le Pays* as trusted dailies. *L'Evénement* is a fortnightly paper that frequently takes a critical line against the government, without strongly aligning itself with any opposition figures, and its strident views are often worth reading. The fortnightly satirical paper *JiJi* (*Journal de Jeudi*) is a must-read for information-hungry Ouagalais, keen to see the spotlight turned on state supremos. *L'Express du Faso* (daily) and *L'Opinion* (weekly) are also popular for their critical approach.

There is a widespread culture of paying for stories to appear in newspapers, including by government, certain NGOs and foreign embassies keen to publicise their good works on behalf of the Burkinabe people. For NGOs in particular, press coverage is a good way of securing a funding increase from donor countries for the year ahead, but international organisations that demand corruption-free practices on the one hand, while paying journalists to attend press conferences and write stories on the other, put themselves in an illogical position.

RADIO The national broadcaster RTB (88.5FM and 99.9FM) is a solid bet for national news, while Pulsar (94.8FM) has good coverage. The BBC World Service can be found on 99.2FM, with much daily output by its French-language service, BBC Afrique. Count your blessings: listening to the BBC in French West Africa was banned by Vichy France during World War II. The BBC is also available on a range of short-wave stations. In the morning, try band 16 (17830); during the daytime band 16 (17830), band 19 (15400), band 25 (11835), band 41 (7160) or band 49 (6005); in the evening try band 16 (17830), band 19 (15400) or band 25 (11835). Voice of America broadcasts a mix of news, documentary reportage and music on

102.4FM. Another English-language station is Radio Canada International (RCI), which broadcasts on short wave to Burkina Faso. For a schedule of times and frequency of broadcasts, check the RCI website (*www.rcinet.ca*).

Radio France International (RFI) has excellent coverage of pan-African news on 94.0FM, complemented by a mixture of news and cultural documentaries and reportage, and Africa Numero Un (90.3FM), the francophone African broadcaster, is a good bet for news, analysis and the continent's big sporting fixtures. Arc en Ciel (96.6FM), sponsored by the French broadcaster Canal, is music-focused, playing French and US hip-hop, as well as the latest sounds coming out of Africa.

Ouaga radio stations include Horizon FM (104.4FM), which has a highly entertaining late-night agony-uncle phone-in show. Nostalgie (94.4FM) plays mostly Western power ballads, while Radio Salankoloto (97.3FM) pumps out a good range of African music, from traditional styles to modern hip-hop. Radio Savane (103.4FM) is also worth a listen for music and news.

One station that has courted controversy in recent years is Ouaga FM (105.2FM), in particular for Karim Sama, a reggae host (also a reggae singer, going by the name of Sams'K le Jah) whose outspoken criticisms of the government are followed eagerly by young Ouagalais. Friday night, 20.00 to 22.00, is the best time to tune in. In 2007, he received death threats, which were followed by the torching of his car outside the Ouaga FM building. Undeterred, he has continued to broadcast, and remains at the forefront of protests about Norbert Zongo and other contentious issues.

TELEVISION The channels most easily available are the national broadcaster Radio Television Burkinabe (RTB); Canal 3, which is privately owned; and Sport-Music TV (SMTV). RTB has two channels and is concerned with local and regional news and Burkinabe culture; Canal 3 is also a general interest channel. Both show the odd film in the evenings; SMTV's name speaks for itself. Also widely available, but based in Bamako rather than Burkina, is Africable – a francophone pan-African channel based in Bamako that offers good coverage of news stories across the continent. A new arrival, launched in August 2010 and available only around Ouaga, is BF1. It has styled itself as *la chaine qui ose* (the channel that dares), and aims, at least, to hold up a mirror to Burkinabe society.

For anything else a satellite connection is required, and you may find CNN on the channel menu of some of the more upmarket hotels. Hotel Splendid also has BBC News, which you can watch in the restaurant. More widespread is Euronews, which covers European news in French. French sports channels, if you can find them, are a broad church, extending to Champions League football coverage, the FA Cup, NBA basketball and NFL American football.

TELEPHONE

Numbers Telephone numbers in Burkina have eight digits. Very occasionally, you'll see a restaurant sign or hotel card with six only, from the former system. In the west, numbers have the prefix 20; in the centre, the prefix 50; in the north and east, the prefix 40.

For mobiles, Telmob numbers have the prefix 70, 71, 72 or 73; Airtel numbers the prefix 74, 75 or 76; Telecel numbers the prefix 78 or 79.

Land lines Land line charges for the national provider, Onatel, vary according to destination, and there's a slight difference between pre-paid and post-paid charges. Local calls are about 45f for the first minute, 22f thereafter; national calls about 80f for the first minute, 40f thereafter; calls to Burkinabe mobiles about 130f for the first minute, 65f thereafter. Charges for international calls have been slashed recently; prices used to vary substantially from one international zone to another, but now the three zones cost much the same. Calls cost about 180f for the first minute, 90f thereafter.

Mobile phones Since 2002, the number of mobile phones throughout Africa has outstripped the number of land lines. With pay as you go the preferred method, and mobiles offering a more reliable service, it makes sense both financially and practically to use a mobile.

If you want your own Burkinabe mobile number while you are in the country – and it's an excellent idea – take your mobile phone with you (as long as it is configured to handle other SIM cards), or pick one up at a street stall. An old Nokia should cost 10,000–20,000f, a new one 20,000–30,000f. Then buy a SIM card; you shouldn't pay more than 2,000f, and some come effectively free; you pay for the pre-installed credit. Airtel, Telecel and Telmob are the three mobile operators in Burkina. Airtel has changed hands a number of times (former incarnations are Celtel and Zain). Zain scratchcards still work. Coverage tends to vary around the country, so many Burkinabe have SIM cards for at least two and often all three companies, hence the proliferation of numbers that you'll find in this book. Call charges tend to be the same across the board; around 1.5f per second. Airtel may be slightly cheaper for international calls. Scratchcards are sold by hawkers on street corners everywhere in 500f, 1,000f, 2,500f, 5,000f and 10,000f denominations.

POST AND INTERNET Sonapost (postal service) bureaux are found in nearly all mid-sized towns. In general, the service is slow, but things tend to arrive eventually. Allow three weeks for delivery from Europe; perhaps a month from the US. Stamps for a letter bound for the US, for example, cost 830f.

DHL has an office in Ouaga (*50 31 19 47*) on Rue Sangoule Lamizana, next to the ONTB office, but sending items this way is expensive (at least 50,000f) for even the smallest of packages to Europe.

Internet access is widely available and prices are not expensive, although connections can be slow and unpredictable in smaller towns. There are some excellent and reliable options in Ouaga (see page 149 for details). In recent years, many mid-range to upmarket hotels in larger towns (and some budget options, especially *maisons d'hôtes*) have installed a Wi-Fi service, generally free of charge to guests.

CULTURAL ETIQUETTE

In a country where illiteracy is widespread, conversation ranks high. Enthusiastic and involved greetings are a prelude to discussion, enquiring after someone's day, their health, their family, their work and wellbeing. The chance to break out of the stereotype of the uptight Westerner is one that, if embraced, will enthuse many people you meet, as will a few words in a local language (see *Appendix 1*, page 305).

BODY LANGUAGE One of the nicest things about Burkina is that everyone – no matter what position they inhabit in society – offers, and deserves, a handshake. It may take time, but there's a dignity to it that's hard to beat. Small children, transfixed by ogling a foreigner, are likely to recover their wits, walk up to you and extend a hand formally and dutifully, without saying anything. If they are particularly keen to show deference they will support their right hand with their left as they shake hands, or put their left hand behind their back.

From time to time, someone may offer you their right wrist, rather than hand. Shake it as you would a hand. It's either because their right hand doesn't work, or because their hand is dirty, or wet. Likewise, if you've just eaten, or washed, or have a cut, offer your right forearm at greeting times.

Among young people a variety of handshakes exists. The most common is to end a normal handshake with a click of each other's middle fingers. The first couple of times this click-shake may be embarrassingly silent, but it's easily picked up. Sometimes the greeting is finished by drawing a right hand or fist to your heart – to signal thanks and respect. Others follow the finger click by touching both right fists against each other, before reaching for the heart. It's best to think of your partner as taking the lead in a dance, and follow quickly. Hands clasped together in front of you, with a slight bow, is another way of showing respect in greetings, particularly for older people.

A lovely tradition at New Year, or after a long absence, is the first greeting with friends. As if exhausted by a long drawn-out boxing match, each will nuzzle their head against the other's and swap places four times, air kissing for foreheads.

As for kissing on the cheek, Britain has one, France has two, Switzerland has three, and Burkina has four. It's lovely to see people take so long over being friends.

Hand-waving can be surprisingly disarming – and immediately met with a warm wave and bright smiles in response. A low hand wave, especially when accompanied by smiles, can be deceptive – it's often a request for a car to stop and offer the road-weary a lift.

In public, your right hand is for eating, shaking hands, passing an item to someone and for any other public role. Not doing so may well cause offence, particularly in rural settings. Your left hand is for the loo.

If offered a gift, take it in both hands, for fear of suggesting the gift is insubstantial or unimportant if accepted with one hand only.

Thumbs up is generally universally understood, although rarely practised. Pointing at people is – as always – considered rude and is best avoided. In restaurants or on roadsides, Burkinabe tend to beckon waiting staff and street traders with a cupped hand, back of the hand upward, in a sort of downward burrowing action. It is often accompanied by loud and persistent hissing to attract attention. This can feel strangely disrespectful and demanding, and there's no need to follow suit if you don't feel comfortable with it.

Burkinabe wearing sunglasses will frequently take them off when speaking to you if they are keen to put you at your ease. It's thoughtful to do the same. In Burkina casting your eyes downward is considered a sign of humility and respect, not of sulking or dishonesty.

Not long ago, it might have been unheard of for a Burkinabe couple to walk down the street hand-in-hand or arm-in-arm. In town, these conventions have now been overtaken by something a little more relaxed and visitors need not feel too stiff around their partners.

Only men working in the fields tend to wear shorts. For visitors, it might be more in keeping with the local atmosphere to wear trousers.

Finally, if you have the chance to go into a mosque, take off your shoes first.

BARGAINING No-one will be offended if you bargain; everyone does. You might feel decidedly taken for a ride if you don't. It's always best to try and have an idea of the price of an object before you ask. This comes only with trial and error, but it is worth bearing in mind that while negotiation over a price is usually a given, not all starting points are as grossly inflated as you might think. Another tip is to set the initial price you're prepared to pay, as you'll generally get a better deal by working up from your starting point, than by from working down from the vendor's high starting price.

TIPPING There are no rules. In a *maquis*, or a taxi, people might think it odd if you tipped. In the more well-to-do restaurants, most people tip. Anyone asking for a *cadeau* is certainly asking for a tip. It's often heartening to reward those who don't ask and assess more carefully whether those that do have earned it.

BEGGING Giving money to beggars is a personal decision. Many Burkinabe, even young children, give small change to beggars, both men and women.

However, many make the fair observation that children especially tend to beg only in areas popular with tourists, rather than according to need. A sophisticated form of begging is asking for a *correspondent* back home; generally not a penpal but a rich donor. English-speaking Africans in Ouagadougou may say they are Liberian refugees trying to get home, and ask for help in this.

NO SUBSTITUTE FOR LOCAL KNOWLEDGE

Burkina Faso is home to thousands of sacred spaces, and their sanctity is to be respected. The most innocent of rocks or copses can in fact be important shrines to ancient spirits, and the penalty for any non-initiate who enters is grave. If you are exploring the bush, it is always good to listen to local advice about where not to go, unlike Captain Louis-Parfait Monteil, who passed through Burkina Faso in 1891 as part of his epic expedition, from Saint-Louis to Tripoli via Lake Chad. While no-one can doubt his derring-do, these edited diary extracts show that an insensitivity to local customs and shrines frequently got his expedition into hot water.

MARCH 1891, SOURO

I arrived at the outskirts of the village without seeing my men and, spotting a rocky outcrop covered with superb trees, dismounted and took to the shade. I gave the order to unload and sent to the village for word of Makoura and the guide, Abdoulaye.

I gave the order to make camp and to sweep the thick carpet of dry leaves from under the trees. A quarter of an hour later, a little surprised that still no-one had arrived, at last the guide and Makoura appeared, accompanied by a man from the village. They told me he was the chief.

I tried in vain to calm this man who appeared to be terrified. Eventually he told me that I had to leave this place, which was the sacred wood of the village. I wanted to move the camp about 200m further away, beyond a huge gallery to trees next to a stream, but this too was sacred.

Passing inspection of the camp, I noticed the absence of my rifle. I called Abdoulaye and asked him what he had done with it and sent to the place where he had left it. Nothing. We searched again without success. So I sent Makoura and him to the village chief to make enquiries.

They spoke for a long time. Finally, at night, they told me that the arm could not be recovered. An evil spirit, unhappy at the violation of the sacred wood that morning, had taken the rifle as punishment.

I was not disposed to hear these stories, so I insisted menacingly that I would inform Tieba (who held sway in these parts) of this matter. He already had various griefs against the village and would happily come to raze it to the ground.

HASSLES Compared with many other African countries, there are remarkably few hassles in Burkina. You can walk down the street without feeling hounded, and officials are courteous and polite. Watch out for pickpockets (see page 80).

Street hawkers You will encounter street hawkers and 'tour guides' soliciting custom. In the cities, street hawkers sell a range of goods at street-side tables. Jewellery, international magazines, DVDs, cigarettes and tissues are all on offer, as are mobile-phone top-up cards, immaculately arranged for different denominations and networks on little wooden boards. Particularly enthusiastic hawkers may attempt to flog you distinctly domestic goods, such as plastic toys, torches, batteries, calculators, shoes, pots, pans or prayer mats. Guides and artisans will be much more conversational. There may often be a lengthy prelude of greetings and questions before you are asked into a shop or about possible travel plans.

Feel free to buy something, but if you don't want to, a simple *ça va* with a smile and a shake of the head (along with an enthusing *bon marché*, *bonne journée* or

Throughout the night the village was full of rumours; processions went from door to door through the inside and outside of the compounds, accompanied by tamtams, bells and torches, the magicians performed exorcisms to persuade the spirit to reveal who had stolen it. All in vain, the night passed without the return of the rifle. That devil, they told me, was inflexible.

APRIL 1891, YAKO

Having seen the previous day some impressive hills towards the south, I made it my goal to get a better view of the surrounding countryside. Arriving at the summit, I found some rocks and a bit of matting that I sat down on. I was there for five minutes, totally absorbed, when, without being aware of his approach, a man with a menacing air came towards me. In a raised tone he talked of things that I did not understand, he even put his hand on his sabre. He made a sign at me and left…The reflection came to me that perhaps I was profaning one of the many forms of sacred place.

At that moment, I heard a lively altercation; approaching I found the *diatike* and Baba in animated discussion with some overexcited men. The subject was my trespass of the morning, because I had well and truly profaned a sacred place where the sorcerers mixed their poisons and medicines.

The custom is that any non-initiate who enters that place is beaten to death. Baba hotly took up my cause and showed that I was ignorant about this place being sacred. After lots of shouting things seemed to calm down, until one of my porters came running and crying from the same hill, bleeding profusely from a double blow on the nape of the neck.

The individual who of that morning had not dared to hit me had no hesitation in hitting an unarmed black man. I saw the man striding along, and told the *diatike* to stop him. When he refused, I told him I wanted to see the Naba.

At the audience, the sorcerers were present, but already Baba and the *diatike* had pleaded my cause, which had won out. The Naba voiced his discontent at the sorcerers and retired in high anger. A half-hour afterwards, he sent to my camp to apologise for what had happened and presented his excuses. At the same time, he sent me some *dolo*.

All was finished well and I was on my way in the afternoon.

merci) will usually do. Ignoring people is usually not the best policy as, quite rightly, they would prefer to elicit a reaction than for you to pretend they do not exist. So long as you remain polite you are unlikely to feel hassled.

Police Burkina's officials are numerous: there are national and local police, customs officers and *gendarmes*. Generally all are polite and friendly and it always helps to wave and show deference when passing checkpoints. If problems occur, never lose your cool.

There are occasional tales of arbitrary requests for payment of a 'tourist tax' to enter certain towns, such as Gorom-Gorom. This is certainly not official policy, and you should manage to refuse politely.

Identification papers Keep your passport, or a photocopy, on you when travelling, as spot checks are common, particularly on coaches. If you do not have some form of identification on you, there will be a fine in the region of 3,000f. You will also hold up the bus, which will not endear you to the driver or your fellow passengers.

Traffic offences Moped riders and other road users beware: Burkinabe police are in the habit of setting up hidden checks at traffic lights, often late at night. Even the

LEARNING FOR ALL

In a country where even the most able child stands a low chance of completing his or her education, opportunities for a child with learning difficulties are virtually nil. Parents of children with anything from Down's syndrome to autism struggle to find understanding in the wider community, and often end up simply hiding the child away in the family home. In 1991, a remarkable group of such parents decided to change the situation by setting up APEE (*Association des Parents et Amis d'Enfants Encephalopathes*).

The big achievement of the association has been the creation of a school, which has gone from humble beginnings to a roll of 86 pupils. And the parents have come up with an ingenious way of providing integration for their children: they have created a 'normal' school around the special-needs one, which 242 children now attend.

The school has NGO status, but running it is far from cheap. Although the government will pay staff in the 'normal' section, no funding is available for the specialist teachers, and the fees to keep it all going are way beyond the means of average Ouagalais parents. One of the big expenses is a minibus that drives around Ouaga in the morning, collecting pupils who would be otherwise incapable of getting to school by themselves. Many pupils rely on private sponsorship.

Ria Butcher is an English volunteer who spends several months every year helping the school. She takes on a class of a dozen or so teenage boys with a wide range of learning difficulties; together, they make papier-mâché bowls, cover them in fabric and varnish them. One boy sits solemnly snipping up bits of paper, others painstakingly paste and stick. Ria is constantly looking for ways to market the bowls, the sale of which can give the boys a small income and something infinitely more valuable: a sense of worth, and respect from their families.

You can visit the school, or buy bowls at Galerie Nuances. To find out more, contact Ria at e riabutcher@yahoo.co.uk, or the school at e apee@liptinfor.bf.

HELPING YOUNGSTERS FIND THEIR FEET

This initiative, set up by an ex-volunteer in Burkina, is one example of the kind of grass-roots project that puts something back into the community.

Tanwalbougou is a village in the east of Burkina Faso, one of the poorest regions of the country. Primary-school enrolment is much lower than average and children are failing to complete their primary education because of the cost of books.

The primary school consists of one old but well-maintained building with three classrooms and a newer unfinished building with no floor and no roof, which houses another three classrooms. The community lacks the funds to complete the construction.

Children who complete primary education in Tanwalbougou must travel 50km to the secondary school in the provincial capital Fada N'Gourma, but public transport is sparse and expensive. In addition, secondary-school fees are much higher than primary-school fees, and parents lack the means to pay for fees and lodging.

Since 1999, FEET (*Fondation pour l'Education des Enfants de Tanwalbougou*) has rewarded the best pupils of the primary school with a scholarship to continue their education in Fada N'Gourma. The students share a simple house in Fada built by FEET's volunteers.

FEET also provides school books and other teaching materials to Tanwalbougou's primary school and helps the village maintain the old school building. Primary-school attendance rates have seen a sharp rise. In 1999, the primary school had 156 pupils. Today more than 370 boys and girls attend.

For more about FEET's work, e feet@muchomail.com

slightest infringement of traffic laws – running an amber light, or failing to touch your foot to the ground at a stop sign, for example – can result in an on-the-spot fine to avoid the bike being impounded. Receipts are usually issued for fines in the region of 1,000–6,000f. If you have hired a moped, make sure you are carrying the vehicle's papers.

TRAVELLING POSITIVELY

Burkina Faso ranks among the poorest countries in the world – assessed as 161st out of 169 countries in the UN's latest survey of human development.

Fewer than 40% of those aged 15–24 can read. Nearly 17% of children under five die every year. About 82% of Burkina's 16.7 million population survives on less than US$2 a day. Although nearly 60% of children start primary school, only about 40% manage to complete their basic studies.

The statistics tell a sorry story, and hundreds of international development organisations and local associations are on the ground trying to make a difference. All the big international charities, such as Oxfam, Plan, Save the Children, Water Aid and others, have programmes in Burkina.

It is hard to recommend one organisation or action. The first thing to do is to keep your respect for the country uppermost in your mind. Beyond that, as you travel, look out for grass-roots organisations you feel may be making a difference.

STUFF YOUR RUCKSACK – AND MAKE A DIFFERENCE

www.stuffyourrucksack.com is a website set up by TV's Kate Humble that enables travellers to give direct help to small charities, schools or other organisations in the country they are visiting. Maybe a local school needs books, a map or pencils, or an orphanage needs children's clothes or toys – all things that can easily be 'stuffed in a rucksack' before departure. The charities get exactly what they need and travellers have the chance to meet local people and see how and where their gifts will be used.

The website describes organisations that need your help and lists the items they most need. Check what's needed in Burkina Faso, contact the organisation to say you're coming and bring not only the much-needed goods but an extra dimension to your travels and the knowledge that in a small way you have made a difference.

One couple, for example, was so moved by a visit to a Burkinabe orphanage that they offered to pay the monthly electricity bill. If you feel you've found something you can trust, then by all means set up something on a similarly local scale, or fund-raise back at home. If you see an international organisation managing a project you like, such as one in education, health, agriculture or local business, for example, you might also consider a monthly direct debit to the charity.

Development itself can be something of an industry, with agencies seeking funding from international donors at any cost, no matter what may be happening on the ground. Burkina is considered a good aid destination because management tends to be good and the need is great. That doesn't stop corruption by any means, nor debates about the best way to implement aid.

One argument goes that the best contribution you can make is to spend your money wisely and spur the economy, avoiding aid dependency and stimulating enterprise. Your presence as a spending tourist, investing in arts, crafts, hotel stays, food and transport, will certainly have its impact. The news and views are endless, and the decision will remain personal.

Part Two

THE GUIDE

Ouagadougou

It's not just the spectacular name that makes Burkina's capital so enticing. There might not be much in the way of sightseeing or architectural marvels, but as far as people-watching, eating and dancing goes, its dust-choked streets and endless selection of gardens and outdoor bars offer a brilliant bazaar of modern west African life – all in a city small enough to get across in about half an hour, and so safe it puts Western capitals to shame.

Ouaga also bills itself as a global arts capital, on a par with New York, London and Paris, and the wealth of culture on offer is not to be missed. There are festivals throughout the year – dance, theatre, poetry, film, modern art, jazz, masks, hip-hop, puppetry – and cutting-edge craftsmanship on offer.

Burkina's capital has changed a lot since it became the place of permanent residence of the Mossi top dog, the Moro Naba, in 1681. One of the first European visitors to Ouaga, Captain Binger, could not hide his disappointment, finding the Moro Naba's palace 'no more than a cluster of wretched buildings surrounded by heaps of rubbish and straw structures'. It was only with the reconstitution of Upper Volta in 1947 that Ouagadougou wrested capital-city status from Bobo-Dioulasso. The city took shape rapidly under Thomas Sankara, as mud-brick dwellings in the middle of town were replaced with government ministries, and affordable modern housing for civic workers went up in surrounding areas. Today, to the south of the city centre, the futuristic Ouaga 2000 district draws embassies, government ministries and the ultra-rich towards an exclusive new suburb. Meanwhile, a mass of buildings in the middle of town torn down to make way for the fabled Project Zaca urban regeneration programme remains largely undeveloped. Building work has started in places, and a few brave businesses and restaurants have staked their claim there; but the skyline remains for the most part undisturbed.

Although the capital is home to 1.5 million people, civic pride is nonetheless strong – a small army of dedicated street-sweepers patrols central roads picking

NOTE ON THIS CHAPTER

Shortly after the completion of this update, the capital experienced a wave of protests and unrest (see page 34), which led to the looting of a large number of shops and businesses in central Ouaga. Avenue Yennenga and Avenue Kwame N'Krumah were hit particularly hard, with few establishments left untouched. The protests simmered down, and at the time of going to press, the capital was calm once more. However, bear in mind that some of the listings on the main avenues may not have resumed normal trading by the time you read this.

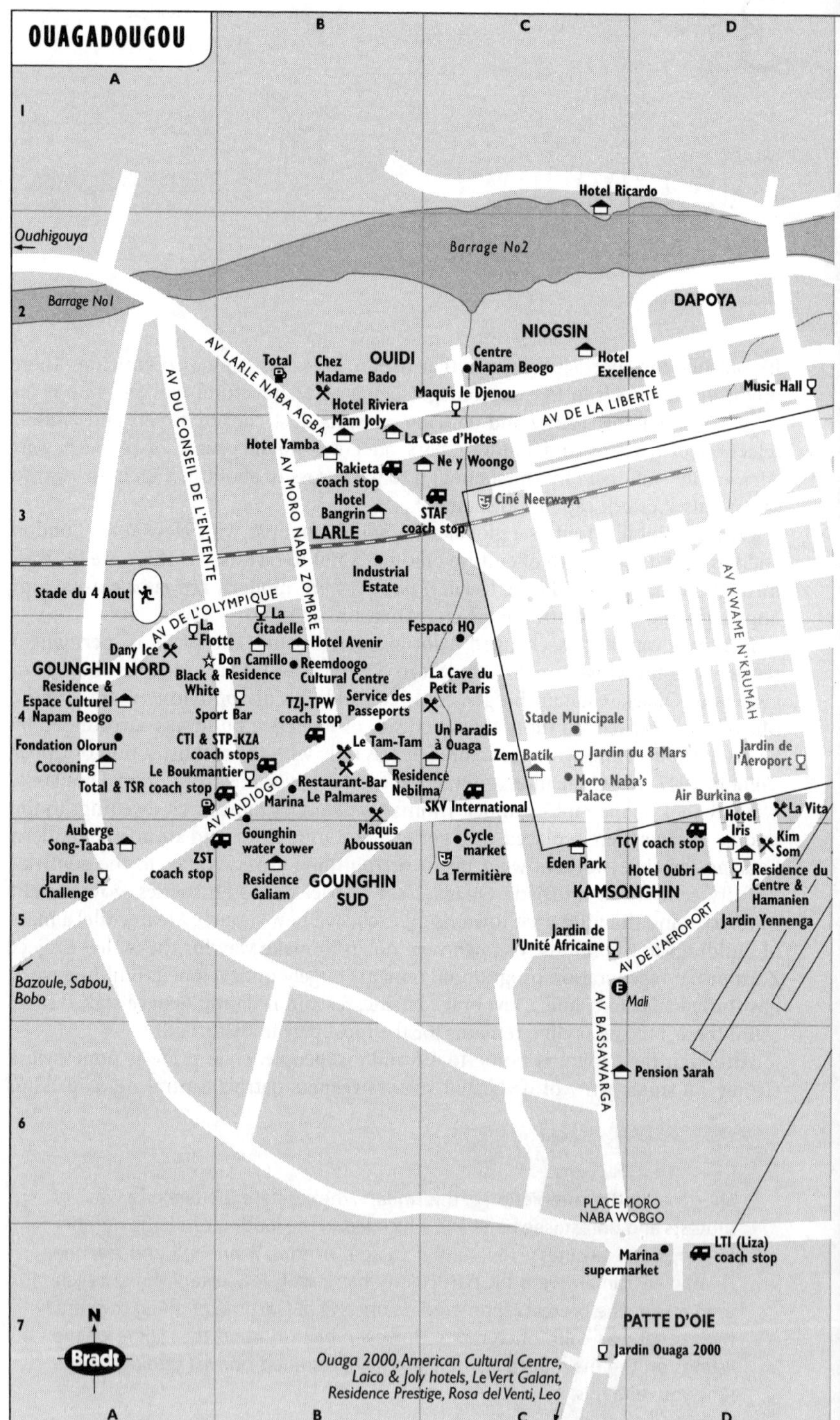

OUAGADOUGOU
A
B
C
D
1
2
3
5
6
7
Hotel Ricardo
Ouahigouya
Barrage No2
Barrage No1
DAPOYA
NIOGSIN
AV LARLE NABA AGBA
Total
Chez Madame Bado
OUIDI
Centre Napam Beogo
Hotel Excellence
Music Hall
AV DU CONSEIL DE L'ENTENTE
Hotel Riviera
Maquis le Djenou
AV DE LA LIBERTÉ
Mam Joly
La Case d'Hotes
Hotel Yamba
Rakieta coach stop
Ne y Woongo
AV MORO NABA ZOMBRE
Hotel Bangrin
STAF coach stop
Ciné Neerwaya
LARLE
Industrial Estate
AV KWAME N'KRUMAH
Stade du 4 Aout
AV DE L'OLYMPIQUE
La Flotte
La Citadelle
Hotel Avenir
Fespaco HQ
Dany Ice
Don Camillo
Reemdoogo Cultural Centre
La Cave du Petit Paris
GOUNGHIN NORD
Black & White
Residence
Residence & Espace Culturel 4 Napam Beogo
Sport Bar
TZJ-TPW coach stop
Service des Passeports
Stade Municipale
Fondation Olorun
CTI & STP-KZA coach stops
Le Tam-Tam
Un Paradis à Ouaga
Zem
Batik
Jardin du 8 Mars
Jardin de l'Aeroport
Cocooning
Le Boukmantier
Total & TSR coach stop
Restaurant-Bar Le Palmares
Residence Nebilma
Moro Naba's Palace
Air Burkina
AV KADIOGO
Marina
SKV International
Hotel Iris
La Vita
Auberge Song-Taaba
Gounghin water tower
Maquis Aboussouan
Cycle market
TCV coach stop
Kim Som
ZST coach stop
Eden Park
Jardin le Challenge
Residence Galiam
GOUNGHIN SUD
La Termitière
Hotel Oubri
Residence du Centre & Hamanien
KAMSONGHIN
Jardin de l'Unité Africaine
AV DE L'AEROPORT
Jardin Yennenga
Bazoule, Sabou, Bobo
Mali
AV BASSAWARGA
Pension Sarah
PLACE MORO NABA WOBGO
Marina supermarket
LTI (Liza) coach stop
N
Bradt
PATTE D'OIE
Jardin Ouaga 2000
Ouaga 2000, American Cultural Centre, Laico & Joly hotels, Le Vert Galant, Residence Prestige, Rosa del Venti, Leo

Loumbila, Ziniare, Kaya, Dori
Gare de l'Est, La Consolatrice, Fada N'Gourma
La Case de la Sculpture
Dragon Hotel
Hotel Silmande
Parc Urbain Bangr-Weoogo
Barrage No3
Yalgado Hospital & 24hr Pharmacy
AV PRESIDENT SANKARA
Le Karité Bleu
ZONE DU BOIS
Theatre Espace Culturel Gambidi
L'Orient
Restaurant Gondwana
Hamburger House
PASPANGA
Ghana
Club de l'Etrier
Issaabi Dimas
Auberge Le Zephir
Chez Tess
Gare Air Namende
La Rose du Desert
Le Paradisio
National Museum
Galerie Lafon
University
BD DU GENERAL DE GAULLE
French medical centre
French ambassador's residence
WEMTENGA
Museum of music (temporary site)
Ciné Wemtenga
KOULOUBA
Chez Giuliana
Thomas Sankara's grave
see pages 124–5
Ouagadougou International Airport
SIAO
Village artisanal de Ouagadougou
Point Afrique
BD CIRCULAIRE
Auberge Le Lion Dort
Gigot à la Ficelle
Hotel OK Inn
Ouagainter coach & bush taxi stop
Residence Alice
Village Nong Taaba
0 500m
0 500yds
Ouaga 2000
Golf course, Koubri, Po

up rubbish, and the competition among taxi drivers for fresh blood arriving off the plane is positively courteous, while many young urban Ouagalais have never left the city except via the airport.

The centre of town is a busy mixture of old and new. In the morning rush hour, it's hard work just crossing the roads. Moped culture exploded in the 1980s, and boys pushing donkey carts compete with chic, sunglasses-sporting girls in sexy vests on the latest two-wheelers, along with bicycles, taxis and gleaming 4x4s with darkened windows.

As far as diversion goes, there are plenty of daytime trips on offer: to artisanal treasure troves, nearby museums, sacred crocodile lakes and homemade goat's-cheese farms. You can cool off with swimming pools and ice cream, and spend your nights enjoying superb food, cinema, cultural spectaculars, pavement cafés and dancing.

GETTING THERE AND AWAY

BY AIR Ouagadougou International Airport (*50 30 65 20, 50 31 15 02 for information on flight times*) has to be one of the most centrally located in the world. From the centre of town, you can practically smell the rubber coming off the runway, and if you like to travel light, walking to check-in from a centrally located hotel is certainly not out of the question.

Most international flights arrive in the evening. Unless you have a firm idea of the layout of the city and fancy a stroll, there is little choice but to hop in a taxi. It should not cost more than 2,000f for a centrally located hotel, although €5 or 3,000f is a common starting point for new arrivals. If you are booking a hotel in advance, ask if they do an airport pick-up.

If you are leaving Ouagadougou by air, departure tax is 7,000f. This is usually included in the price of intercontinental flights, but not always for local or regional ones.

For airline options, see pages 65–6.

BY TRAIN The railway line arrived in Ouaga in 1954, 20 years after it started up in Bobo. Trains leave at 07.30 on Tuesday, Thursday and Saturday for Abidjan, stopping at Koudougou (1,500f), Bobo (5,000f) and Banfora (8,000f) *en route*. The return journey from Abidjan passes through on Wednesday, Friday and Sunday evenings. It takes an astonishing nine hours to travel between Ouaga and Bobo. The ongoing problems in Côte d'Ivoire tend to disrupt the service, too, so check in advance that your chosen train is running on time.

BY COACH Coach is the cheapest, most efficient and comfortable way of exploring Burkina; the price of tickets on many routes has actually dropped over the last five years. There is no central bus station in Ouagadougou (with the exception of coaches bound for Ghana from Ouagainter; see below). Coach companies have individual depots. Buying tickets in advance is easy, and coach drivers are in general admirably serious about departure times. See *Getting around*, pages 86–92, or refer to the regional chapters for more information.

Ouagainter [116–17 E6] There are only two good reasons to come to this sprawling dusty station for bush taxis and coaches to the south of the city: if you're heading to Ghana, or if you want to travel direct to Tiebele without stopping first in Po. Otherwise, you can and should avoid it: it's hectic and has few fixed timetables, mostly sending off minibuses once they fill up. It can be unsavoury at night.

There are plenty of coach departures for Ghana every day other than Saturday. They include STKF (m *76 09 95 32*), which leaves at 08.30 Sunday–Friday; Imperial Express (m *78 46 64 47*), which leaves at 09.00 Sunday–Friday; and NTI (m *76 45 89 81*), which leaves at 08.30 on Sunday, Tuesday and Thursday. All go to Kumasi (12,000f) and Accra (16,000f).

A minibus leaves for Tiebele at around 08.00 every day bar Saturday. Tickets cost 3,000f.

Gare de l'Est This is the equivalent of Ouagainter but for the route east to Fada and, eventually, Niamey in Niger. It is on the main road about 15 minutes east out of town.

ORIENTATION AND MAPS

Ouagadougou city centre is pretty compact. The main axes to bear in mind are Avenue Kwame N'Krumah (running north–south with the airport at the lower end) and Avenue de la Nation (running east–west), once called Avenue Nelson Mandela. They form, roughly, the eastern and northern boundaries of the city centre, meeting at the city's main roundabout – Le rondpoint des Nations Unies to anyone you're asking directions of, and so-called for the big steel globe engulfed by the blue UN logo that rests atop it. These two roads are home to many of the city's more upmarket hotels, and Avenue Kwame N'Krumah also hosts nightlife, restaurants and airline offices. To the west of N'Krumah lie the market, the main mosque and many of the budget hotels. To the east lies Koulouba, home to many high-quality restaurants and trendy bars. The cathedral and the palace of the Moro Naba are on the west side of the city centre, near the municipal stadium.

Most of the city is laid out on a grid system, so orientating yourself is usually no trouble, except after dark when the jumble of *maquis*, telecentres, late-night bakeries and petrol stations have a tendency to merge into one.

Beyond the city centre, Ouaga's more lively districts are spread out in all directions around the city's hub. These include **Dapoya, Gounghin** and **Cité An III**, a leafy suburb commissioned by revolutionary president Sankara to house the state's civil servants, and home to the Ciné Neerwaya.

When out and about, it helps to think in terms of landmarks (petrol stations, water towers, key hotels) rather than street names. While the maps in this guide refer to the most recent street names there is no guarantee that these are widely known among Ouagalais.

MAPS The **Institut Geographique du Burkina** [124–5 G2] (*IGB; 651 Av Independence,* ☎ *50 32 48 23/24;* e *institute.geog@fasonet.bf; www.igb.bf*) has a good selection of regional maps. It has an excellent tourist map of Burkina with principal sites of interest marked that has recently been updated and costs 5,000f. It also has town plans for Ouaga (1:20,000) and Bobo (1:15,000) at 2,500f each, but these are pretty out of date. If you are staying put in one place for a while, local maps produced for certain parts of the country at 1:50,000 are a good guide to the surrounding area. There are route maps, from Yako to Mali or Bobo to Dedougou, for example. It can also produce black-and-white aerial shots of any part of the country to order, at 5,000f for every 1:20,000 image.

ONTB produced a good city plan of Ouaga in 2007. Parts of it – such as the ever-changing Ouaga 2000 – are already out of date, but on the whole it's extremely useful. It includes street numbers as well as names, which can be a boon when you're ferreting around backstreets. Go to the ONTB office to pick one up, or buy one from the many street hawkers who tout it.

Good city and country maps are also available from Diacfa bookshop, on Rue de l'Hotel de Ville, opposite the market.

GETTING AROUND

While Burkina's national transport system provides a shining example for other countries in the region, the same cannot be said for its capital. Ouaga's public transport system is relatively poor, perhaps because so many Ouagalais travel independently on two wheels; buses are sporadic, and for anything other than set routes, taxi fares can soon mount up. If you have the cash, fine; if you don't, your best bet, if you're able, is to plan on getting yourself two wheels from the outset.

ON FOOT Central Ouagadougou is certainly manageable on foot, but the city is sprawling, and even a walk around the covered central market will be hot and sticky any time between 11.00 and 15.30. Thankfully, Ouaga is full of great cafés and patisseries to duck into for a snack or cold drink.

BY BICYCLE Hiring or buying a bike in the capital makes excellent sense. Cycling makes the city seem very compact, with interesting outlying areas – Gounghin, Dapoya, Zone du Bois – all well under 30 minutes from the centre. Many major arteries have bike lanes (which, admittedly, you share with a fleet of *motos*). Bike theft is rare in Ouaga, perhaps thanks to the guarded parking system that exists outside most buildings (a fee, if there is one, is no more than 50f).

Avoid cycling at night. If you must, stick to well-lit, busy routes, and don't carry a bag over your shoulder; unfortunately, it's relatively common for guys on *motos* to whizz up behind you, snatch your bag and zoom off. If you're lucky, the strap breaks; if you're not, you're pulled right off the bike and risk being injured. This happens to Ouagalais too, but if you're white, you're an obvious target.

BY MOTORBIKE You can get around faster, and go further than on a bike, with a wide range of day trips opening up, but the same advice applies as above. If you're inexperienced and feel that the chaos of Ouaga is not the best place to learn, bear in mind that there are many guides – or just friendly Ouagalais – who will be happy for you to ride pillion. Accidents are common.

BY TAXI Fleets of green Mercedes and Peugeots (*taxis verts*) throng the city, tooting for custom like angry greenflies. You share them with whichever customer happens to be in there already and hope you can negotiate getting dropped off along the way. These shared taxis can perform marvellous contortions with time and space, squeezing up to seven people into their battered interiors. Competition between drivers can seem less for custom than for the state of disrepair the car can be reduced to and still function. While lights, windows, door handles and even brakes are sometimes considered a luxury, the stereo can usually be relied upon to work at full volume.

A short daytime trip in the town centre along usual taxi routes should be 200f per person. At night, expect to pay twice as much. If you ever need to get somewhere in a hurry, they can be a nightmare as the taxi rolls to a halt to reverse back up the road for a customer who wants to take on board bicycles, sacks of rice and the odd mattress in addition to people. You can commandeer a *taxi vert* solely for yourself, as long as no-one is in it already – simply make that clear before hopping in, and pay more. If you're deviating from its usual route, it's called a *déplacement*. Drivers will generally ask for at least 1,000f, this being the sum that they would earn if they had a full complement of passengers; they may take less with a bit of haggling. Or you can hire one for about 3,000f per hour.

Hailing a *taxi vert* after dark should not lead to any problems, although several agencies (such as US Peace Corps) recommend their workers don't do so. If you are going to get pickpocketed in Burkina, the most likely place it will happen is in a green taxi (see page 80).

BY URBAN BUS SOTRACO [124–5 C1] (*2257 Av du Sanmatenga;* ☎ *50 35 48 68 for bus information, 50 35 67 87, 50 35 77 01;* e *sotraco@fasonet.bf; www.sotraco.bf*) is a city bus service with 55 shiny green vehicles plying about ten lines. Unfortunately, almost half the buses can be out of service at any given time. As a result, if you play 'spot the green bus', anyone who gets up to three in a day deserves a big prize. There's talk of another 100 being injected into the system, but there's no sign of them yet.

For what it's worth, every journey costs 100f, no matter how far you go, or 5,000f for a monthly pass. Buses run 05.30–21.30 Monday–Saturday and 07.00–20.30 Sundays. Key routes are below.

Line 1 Runs from Place Naba Koom in front of the train station to the UN roundabout & out east past the university & National Museum, ending up at SIAO
Line 2 Starts and finishes in the same place as line 1, but goes south through the city, passing Ciné Burkina, Cité An II & the Ouagainter bush taxi & coach stop
Line 3 Runs northwest from the centre, on the route to Ouahigouya, via Tampouy & Larle
Line 4 Runs through the popular suburb of Gounghin, on the route southwest to Bobo
Line 5 Runs from the train station out east past Bangr Weoogo, the urban park
Line 6B Heads northeast from the train station past the Silmande Hotel
Line 7 Runs from the train station east, good for restaurants in the affluent Zone du Bois, the cathedral & the Moro Naba's palace
Line 9 A short run through Kadiogo, passing the diplomatic quarter & the airport

VEHICLE HIRE

Bikes and mopeds

EKAF Motos Location [124–5 D3] Opposite Pharmacie Rood Wooko, central market; ☎ 50 33 62 83; m 71 33 22 68, 78 62 87 01. A one-stop shop for everything from bikes to off-road motorbikes. Also does sales. Daily hire rates are 1,500f for a bike; 2,500f for a P50; 4,000f for a standard *moto* with gears; 6,000f for an off-road version.

Nouf m 78 02 38 35. Often found outside the Institut Français, can rent P50 mopeds for 2,500f a day or 2,000f if you're taking it for a month or more. Comes recommended from a reader.

Cars and 4x4s In addition to official vehicle-hire companies, many hotels in the capital offer car rental. These may be cheaper, but in all cases inspect the vehicle first and check papers. Try the following:

🚗 **Centre Napam Beogo** Ouidi or Gounghin; ☎ 50 35 35 14, 50 34 66 26; m 70 23 84 86; e asso_napambeogo@yahoo.fr; www.napam-beogo.org. An informal option with a wide range of vehicles. Daily prices, all including driver, are: 5-seat saloon 20,000f; 7-seat saloon 30,000f; 9-seat 4x4 45,000f; 15-seat minibus 70,000f. Also does P50s for 2,000f & motos for 3,000f.

🚗 **Dez Auto Location** Secteur 6; ☎ 50 39 81 64. Has 4x4s from 45,000f per day.

🚗 **Leopan Auto Location** Secteur 23; ☎ 50 47 80 60; m 70 27 20 12. Run by a friendly guy who also works at Hotel Silmande. Daily rates are 35,000f for saloons, 45,000f for 4x4. Has a travel agency too.

National Location By the airport; 50 31 65 80. Expensive, but may offer more guarantees than most.

Thierry Gilat Dapoya; m 75 35 65 47, 70 31 05 25. Another informal option; has 4x4s for as little as 25,000f per day. Check vehicles thoroughly first.

TOURIST INFORMATION

TOURIST OFFICE

Office National Tourism de Burkina (ONTB) [124–5 F4] CGP Bld, Av Sangoule Lamizana; 50 31 19 59/60; e ontb@cenatrin.bf; www.ontb.bf. This is the place to ask for a photography permit (free) & to request the ONTB's selection of leaflets on excursions & tour agencies in the country.

GUIDES There are several guides who can take you round Ouaga. You can ask for a list from ONTB, or contact **Association Songtaaba des Guides du Burkina** (*50 45 26 83*; e *tourisme.songtaaba@yahoo.fr*), who donate 15% of their fee to vulnerable or orphaned children. Another option is a young independent guide called Amadou Dicko (m *71 46 33 48*), who's friendly, reliable and can whizz you around Ouaga on his motorbike, or organise trips beyond. He's used to backpackers and can also sort out seriously cheap accommodation with Burkinabe families in the Dapoya area. For an able talker and good-humoured guide, try Idrissa Compaore (m *70 25 51 90, 78 18 63 83*). He has an old brown Mercedes, and confesses to knowing Ouaga like the back of his hand. He can take you round for a fairly expensive fee of 10,000f per hour. He can also do day trips from Ouaga; discuss a fee in advance.

WHERE TO STAY

Many of Ouagadougou's hotels are located in a compact area in the centre of town and cover a wide range of styles and budgets. However, there are an increasing number of budget options in the outlying districts, especially *maisons d'hôtes* (see box, page 94). As a well-known conference magnet, Ouaga has a high number of soulless business hotels, with several overpriced for the levels of service and ambience that they offer. Others happily punch above their weight. In the hotter months, a hotel with a pool makes an enormous difference. We've tried to find the more intimate options at both higher and budget ends as well as listing the usual suspects. It is not exhaustive, so if there's a great find we've missed, let us know.

IN THE CITY CENTRE

Luxury

Azalai Hotel Independence [124–5 F2] (176 rooms) Av Pdt Sangoule Lamizana; 50 30 60 60/64, 50 30 84 44; e independence@azalaihotels.com. Opened in 1961 to usher in a new post-colonial era, but you wouldn't guess it now: a complete overhaul has turned this into Ouaga's swishest central hotel. It boasts 4 stars, & is also the unofficial headquarters of Fespaco every 2 years. Rooms have all the mod cons you'd expect; tennis courts, a fitness centre & the capital's only Olympic-sized pool complete a luxurious ensemble. Takes Visa & Amex. Pool 3,000f to non-guests Mon–Fri; a whopping 4,500f at weekends. **$$$$$$**

Faso Hotel [124–5 G4] (32 rooms) 50 33 07 89/90; e info@fasohotel.bf; www.fasohotel.bf. New 3-star hotel in central Ouaga, sporting scalloped sinks, ornate bedheads & floral bedding. Get beyond that to all the usual mod cons, including Wi-Fi, room service, TV & minibar. **$$$$$$**

Hotel Splendid [124–5 E6] (146 rooms) Av Kwame N'Krumah; 50 31 72 78/79/82; e sph@fasonet.bf; www.splendid-hotel.bf. A swanky 4-star option, & a favourite with corporate types. Choose between Splendid I (a bit cheaper), & Splendid II – slightly plusher with more modern bathrooms. All have minibar & Wi-Fi. You can have a pleasant drink & a daytime meal at the poolside, but you'll be hard pushed to have a decent swim in the semicircular pool (2,000f for non-guests). Decent bar, La Cruche, & restaurant, Les Délices. **$$$$$$**

La Palmeraie [124–5 E3] (23 rooms) Av Agostino Neto; 50 30 48 90; e reservation@lapalmeraie.biz, lapalmeraieouaga@fasonet.bf; www.lapalmeraie.biz. Under newish management & has dropped from 3 stars to 2, but still a lovely place to stay with classy rooms, pool & lush gardens. Attractive terrace restaurant does good-value 3-course buffet for 7,500f Mon–Fri. **$$$$$$**

Princess' Yenenga Lodge [124–5 G2] (14 rooms) Av de la Grande Chancellerie; 50 30 63.16; m 70 21 63 15/16; e princesseyenenga@yahoo.fr; www.princessyenengalodge.com. Created by French couple Sebastian & Lucile, this classy lodge combines modern comfort with beautiful traditional features, & prides itself on its service. An extraordinary layered-straw *togona* forms the reception area, complete with Dogon door, while some rooms are housed in Tiebele-style buildings; inside, rooms have all mod cons, spacious bathrooms & Wi-Fi, & there's a sparkling pool in the centre of the neatly kept gardens. Also home to one of Ouaga's best restaurants. **$$$$$$**

Upmarket

Hotel Amiso [124–5 B3] (47 rooms) 198 Av Mgr Thevenoud; 50 30 86 74/77, 50 31 51 80/81; e amiso@fasonet.bf. This friendly hotel offers better taste than many in the city, with AC rooms that are light, airy & classily designed. No pool, but the pool nearby at La Forêt Restaurant is free to Amiso guests. **$$$$$**

Hotel Central [124–5 C3] (48 rooms) Av du Grand Lyon; 50 47 60 26, 50 30 89 24; m 78 87 18 63; e centralhotel17@yahoo.fr. Formerly part of the Hotinter chain, the Central is under new management. Right opposite the central market, the location's great, but ochre yellow walls give it a dated feel. Rooms are fine: clean, with AC, TV, Wi-Fi & hot water. Some have fridges & balconies. **$$$$$**

Hotel Nazemse [124–5 E4] (80 rooms) Av Leo Frobenius; 50 33 53 28; m 70 20 43 23; e hotel_nazemse@yahoo.fr. With a lobby like a used-furniture warehouse & a pool area that feels like an army barracks, this is not Ouaga's most inspiring option. Rooms are spacious though, with fridges, TV & AC. Some even have baths. **$$$$$**

Hotel Palm Beach [124–5 E5] (101 rooms) Av Kwame N'Krumah; 50 31 09 91, 50 31 68 29; e palmbeach@fasonet.bf; www.palmbeachburkina.com. A good, central choice that does business travel well. Warm service, with nicely decorated rooms, all AC, with TV, radio, phone, minibar, Wi-Fi & windows that block out the noise. Sizeable rectangular pool popular with travellers; non-guests pay 2,000f for a dip. The Baraka Restaurant & Cascade Bar are both fine but quiet & it's more fun to eat at numerous nearby bars & restaurants. Takes Visa & Amex. B/fast 5,000f; prices negotiable. **$$$$$**

Hotel Palm Beach Annexe [124–5 D4] (61 rooms) 902 Av Yennenga; 50 30 87 74; e palmbeach@fasonet.bf. More of the same, except without the pool (although free use of the pool at Palm Beach). **$$$$$**

Hotel Relax [124–5 D2] (75 rooms) Av de la Nation; 50 31 32 31/33; e relax.hotel@fasonet.bf; www.groupe-soyaf.com. Decent lobby & pool area (2,000f to non-guests) are not matched by the rooms, which are depressingly poky for the price. Still, there's AC, Wi-Fi, fridges & an attempt at ambience with wooden doors & mood lighting. B/fast 3,500f. **$$$$$**

Hotel Soritel [124–5 E3] (44 rooms) 370 Av Kwame N'Krumah; 50 33 04 78, 50 33 05 79; e soritel@fasonet.bf; www.soritelfaso.bf. Manages to feel almost cosy despite its central location. Tasteful rooms with plenty of locally made furniture on show & a swimming pool make this one of the better executive-style hotels in town. Prices higher than most in this section, but have dropped in recent years, & you can negotiate further in the off-season. **$$$$$**

Hotel Yibi [124–5 E6] (26 rooms) Av Kwame N'Krumah; 50 30 73 23/70/71; e yibi.hotel@fasonet.bf; www.yibihotel.com. One of

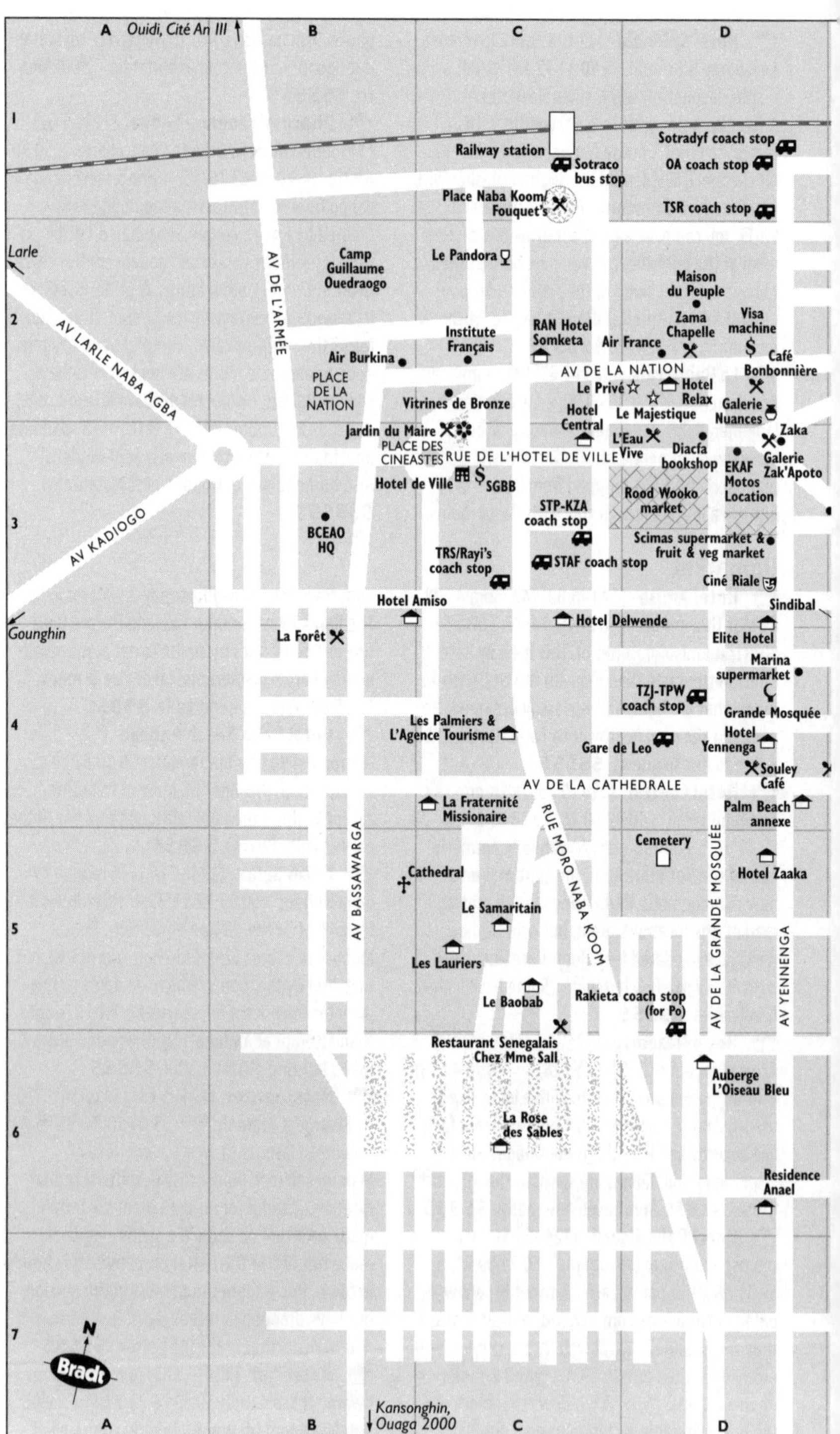

A
B
C
D
Ouidi, Cité An III
1
2
3
4
5
6
7
Railway station
Sotradyf coach stop
OA coach stop
Sotraco bus stop
Place Naba Koom/ Fouquet's
TSR coach stop
Larle
AV DE L'ARMÉE
Camp Guillaume Ouedraogo
Le Pandora
Maison du Peuple
AV LARLE NABA AGBA
Zama Chapelle
Visa machine
Institute Français
RAN Hotel Somketa
Air France
Café Bonbonnière
Air Burkina
AV DE LA NATION
PLACE DE LA NATION
Le Privé
Hotel Relax
Vitrines de Bronze
Hotel Central
Le Majestique
Galerie Nuances
Jardin du Maire
L'Eau Vive
Diacfa bookshop
Zaka
PLACE DES CINEASTES
RUE DE L'HOTEL DE VILLE
EKAF Motos Location
Galerie Zak'Apoto
Hotel de Ville
SGBB
Rood Wooko market
AV KADIOGO
BCEAO HQ
STP-KZA coach stop
Scimas supermarket & fruit & veg market
TRS/Rayi's coach stop
STAF coach stop
Ciné Riale
Hotel Amiso
Sindibal
Gounghin
La Forêt
Hotel Delwende
Elite Hotel
Marina supermarket
TZJ-TPW coach stop
Grande Mosquée
Les Palmiers & L'Agence Tourisme
Hotel Yennenga
Gare de Leo
Souley Café
AV DE LA CATHEDRALE
La Fraternité Missionaire
RUE MORO NABA KOOM
Palm Beach annexe
AV BASSAWARGA
Cemetery
AV DE LA GRANDE MOSQUÉE
Cathedral
Hotel Zaaka
Le Samaritain
AV YENNENGA
Les Lauriers
Le Baobab
Rakieta coach stop (for Po)
Restaurant Senegalais Chez Mme Sall
Auberge L'Oiseau Bleu
La Rose des Sables
Residence Anael
N
Bradt
Kansonghin, Ouaga 2000

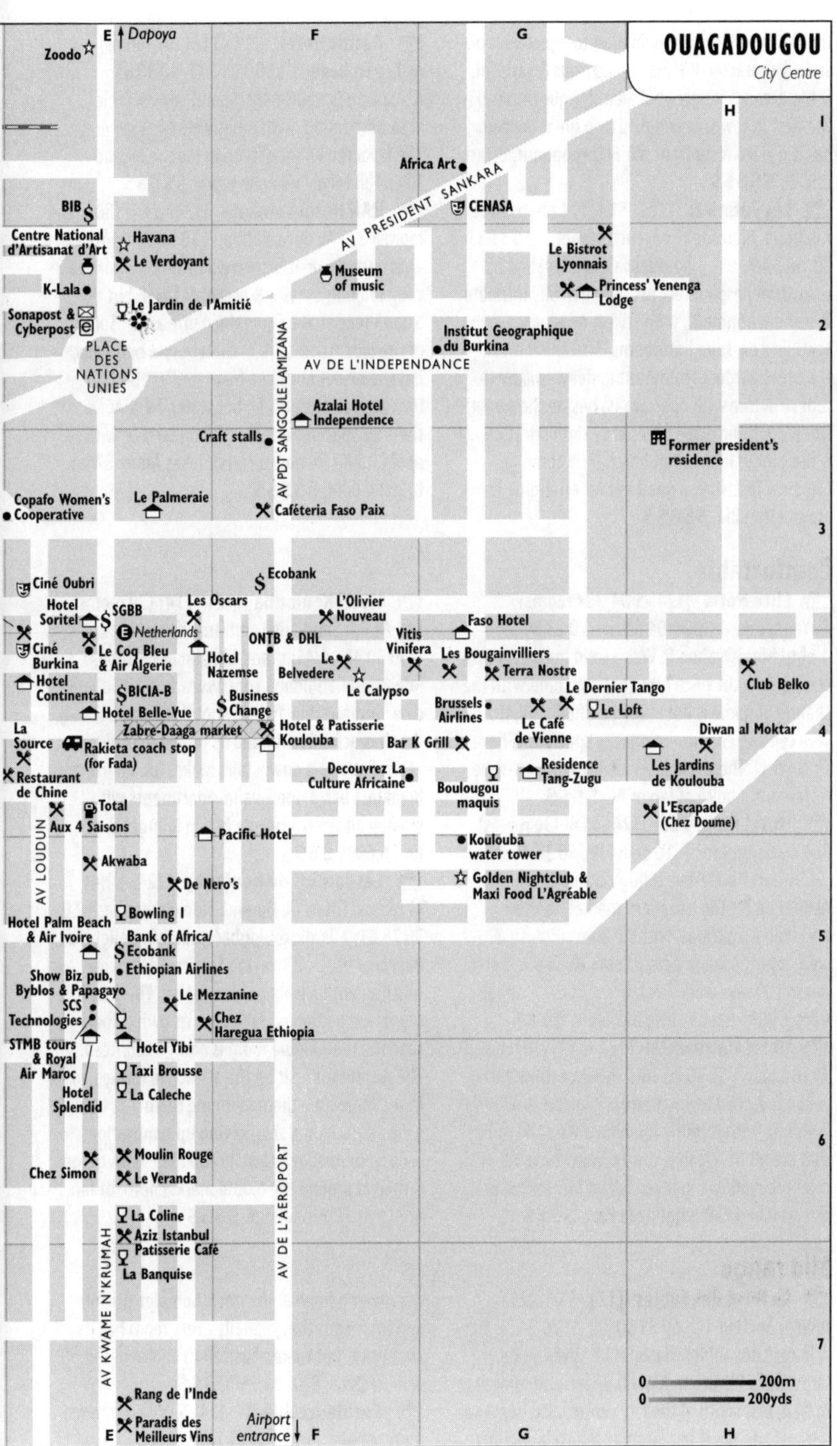

Ouagadougou WHERE TO STAY 3

the few hotels on the main drag to inject a bit of style & character. Rooms are spacious & tasteful, & the green & jungly pool area (for guests only) is the best in town, overlooked by a great outdoor bar & terrace restaurant. Wi-Fi throughout. B/fast 2,500f. **$$$$$**

Les Palmiers [124–5 C4] (14 rooms) Rue J Badoua, opposite the French school; 50 33 33 30, 50 39 91 91; e hotellespalmiers@yahoo.fr; www.hotellespalmiers.net. Wonderfully intimate 2-star environment, with stylish AC rooms, sparkling en-suite bathrooms, African statues & a great outdoor restaurant under a *paillote* (a roof structure with open walls) beside the sweet, small pool. The place oozes easy sophistication, & feels more lodge than hotel. Also home to L'Agence Tourisme, a good bet for arranging tours around Burkina. **$$$$$**

Pacific Hotel [124–5 E5] (97 rooms) Av Leo Frobenius; 50 31 30 37, 50 30 65 42. Spacious, spotlessly clean & comfortable accommodation, with quietly efficient service. The favoured haunt of Ivorian reggae legend Tiken Jah Fakoly when in town. **$$$$$**

RAN Hotel Somketa [124–5 C2] (80 rooms) 323 Av de la Nation; 50 30 61 06/07/08; e hotran@fasonet.bf; www.ran-hotel-somkeita.com. Friendly service & eccentric foyer, but the 5 conference rooms give the game away. Some of the older rooms are in chalet-style buildings, but the newer ones in a huge soulless block. However, all have Wi-Fi, hot water, TV & AC, & there's a spacious outdoor dining terrace with pool (1,500f for non-guests). Takes Amex & Visa. B/fast 4,000f. **$$$$$**

Comfortable

Elite Hotel [124–5 D4] (34 rooms) Av Yennenga; 50 31 04 63; m 70 23 80 59; e elite.hotel@yahoo.fr. Was a solid budget option (ex Sigri), & the price hike that has come with the change of name is not really justified. Still, it's very central; en-suite rooms are spacious & have TV & Wi-Fi. There is also a café & a canteen-style restaurant. Choice of fan or AC. **$$$$**

Hotel Belle-Vue [124–5 E4] (30 rooms) Rue du Commerce; 50 30 84 98, 50 31 10 32; e hbv.hotel-belle-vue2000@caramail.com. Geared up for the travellers' market, rooms are clean & spacious, with AC & en suite, TV & well-kept mosquito nets. There's Wi-Fi too, but it doesn't always work. Restaurant does set meals from 1,500f. Car hire also available. **$$$$**

Hotel Continental [124–5 E4] (30 rooms) Av Loudun; 50 30 86 36; e hotelcontinental1@yahoo.fr. A solid town-centre option, set in a lovely building, with recently renovated en-suite rooms that are all AC, clean & comfy. Some have Wi-Fi; internet available in foyer. B/fast inc, served in the attached Cafeteriat de la Paix. **$$$$**

Hotel Koulouba [124–5 F4] (29 rooms) 844 Av Pdt Sangoule Lamizana, Koulouba; 50 30 40 44/45; e hotel.koulouba@yahoo.fr, info@hotel-koulouba.com; www.hotel-koulouba.com. Comfortable, friendly hotel (AC throughout) that has actually dropped its prices in recent years. Patisserie downstairs makes for a perfect breakfast bar. 4 good-value apartments with kitchen all sleep 3 (single bed in lounge) & go for 36,600f. **$$$$**

Les Jardins de Koulouba [124–5 H4] (4 rooms) Off Av de Burkina Faso, Koulouba; 50 30 25 81; e jardinkoulouba@yahoo.fr. Delightful *maison d'hôte*, all swaying fabrics & Moroccan touches, with a leafy garden & pool. The 3 double rooms are gorgeous, each with its own colour scheme; the 1 single room is oddly overpriced. The restaurant – sit on the attractive terrace, or in the Moroccan-themed dining room – is worth a visit in its own right, serving up temptations such as *tournedos Rossini* or *capitaine* with ginger & lime at around the 6,000f mark. Choice of fan or AC; Wi-Fi throughout. **$$$$**

Mid range

La Rose des Sables [124–5 C6] (25 rooms) Secteur 1; 50 31 30 14; m 70 24 78 80; e la.rose.des.sables@fasonet.bf; www.hotel-larosedessables.com. A good upper-end budget option, just south of the city centre, also home to a travel agency. It has large, comfortable rooms & a green garden at the back. Complex pricing system means that virtually every room has its own price, but there's basically a choice of fan, AC & more beds. B/fast 1,250f. **$$$**

Residence Anael [124–5 D6] (20 rooms) Av Yennenga; 50 30 13 71/72;

m 78 87 93 16; e tangzugu@yahoo.fr; www.residencetangzugu.c.la. Stuck out in the Zaca wastelands, but feels fresh & lively if a bit on the corporate side. All rooms have AC, hot water, TV & Wi-Fi; there's a bar & restaurant. Also 4 apartments with kitchen for 29,500f. **$$$**

Residence Tang-Zugu [124–5 G4] (10 rooms, 4 flats) Av de Koulouba; 50 33 05 36/58; m 78 88 57 34/36; e tangzugu@yahoo.fr; www.residencetangzugu.c.la. Near all the nocturnal delights that Koulouba has to offer, smallish but comfy rooms have AC, TV, fridge, hot water & Wi-Fi. Paintings & the odd artefact inject a bit of character, & the bar-restaurant, bedecked in blue with blue lighting, has a cosy feel. B/fast 1,500f. **$$$**

Hotel Delwende [124–5 C3] (14 rooms) Rue Patrice Lumumba; 50 30 87 57; e hoteldelwende@yahoo.fr. With a balcony overhanging the busy street below, it is well placed, clean & comes with a restaurant attached. Unfortunately we've had reports of dishonesty & bad service recently. Choice of en-suite fan or AC. **$$–$$$**

Hotel Yennenga [124–5 D4] (24 rooms) Av Yennenga; 50 30 73 37. The lobby may look a little dingy, & the rooms may be battered too; but this is a Ouaga institution, right in the centre of town, with a sense of community & helpful, hard-working staff who keep it spotless. There's a café for breakfast & simple meals out back, both much frequented by locals. Choice of AC, or fan with inside/outside loo. **$$–$$$**

Hotel Zaaka [124–5 D3] (18 rooms) Av Yennenga; 50 39 87 32. Under the same management as the Yennenga up the road, with the same friendly welcome & pricing system. Rooms vary in standard, so take a look around; most have lost their mosquito nets. The tiny restaurant next door, Chez Tantie Koro, serves *riz gras* & other simple dishes. Choice of fan (with/without loo) or AC. **$$–$$$**

La Fraternité Missionaire [124–5 C4] (37 rooms) Cathedral, Secteur 1; 50 31 02 36. Just inside the cathedral gates & a great budget option, managed by the jovial Gerard. Some fan rooms a bit dustier & noisier than tranquil Les Lauriers, but still secure with mozzie nets; en-suite AC options are well positioned & good value. B/fast on site 1,000f, but head to Les Lauriers for meals. **$$–$$$**

Zem Batik [116–17 C4] (22 rooms) Behind the Moro Naba's palace, Secteur 1; 50 31 56 24. Behind the extraordinary towering façade – the peppermint-green ironwork has something Art Deco about it – lies a marvellous budget option, with simple fan or AC rooms, a tranquil garden restaurant out back & Wi-Fi throughout. Zem himself is a fine batik worker; climb a dizzying spiral staircase to his *atelier* at the top of the building, with great views all around & solar panels to heat the water; or browse in the on-site shop. Car & bike hire available. B/fast 1,200f. **$$–$$$**

Budget

Auberge L'Oiseau Bleu [124–5 D6] (15 rooms) Rue Emile Damiba; 50 30 86 02; e yamdama_ezanno@yahoo.fr. A great new venture by the owners of Fondation Charles Dufour, a nearby orphanage, which the *auberge* helps to support. Good-value en-suite rooms are spotless with mozzie nets & choice of fan/AC. There's a nice little roof terrace too. B/fast 1,500f. **$$**

Le Samaritain [124–5 C5] (11 rooms) Quartier St-Léon; 50 33 20 23; e auberge_le_samaritain@yahoo.fr. Within the narrow streets of Ouaga's old quarter, near the cathedral, this is a nice, basic hostel. Bedrooms are clean, with mosquito nets, lined around a leafy garden with restaurant. Only downside is the hike to the loos; only 1 AC has en suite, the others (fan or AC) have showers only. B/fast 800f. **$$**

Les Lauriers [124–5 C5] (26 rooms) Cathedral, Secteur 1; 50 30 64 90; e camleslauriers@fasonet.bf. A firm favourite, with no-nonsense basic fan rooms (most with single beds), each one spotless, with internal shower but no loo. Set in the pretty cathedral grounds & run by nuns, it is secure & quiet. Set mealtimes are at 12.00 & 19.00, & the food, at 2,300f, is well received. B/fast 1,000f. **$$**

Shoestring

Le Baobab [124–5 C5] (16-bed dorm; 2 rooms) Rue Song le Magre (Rue 1.36), Secteur 1; m 78 50 93 85, 70 66 90 61; e arsenecompaore@hotmail.com. Perhaps the only true backpacker-style hostel in central Ouaga, with an immaculate bunk-bed dorm – each bed has a net & a funky little bedside cabinet, some of which actually lock – great little yard out back (camping possible), self-catering kitchen, communal fridge & groovy wall artwork signalling you've found the right place. 2 double rooms, 1 with shower, the other without, go for 6,000–7,000f. Home to Wango Aventures tour agency, so a good place to set up trips. **$**

OUT OF THE CITY CENTRE

Luxury

Hotel Silmande [116–17 F1] (165 rooms) Route de Kaya, just over *barrage* no 3; 50 35 60 05; e info@silmande-hotel.com; www.silmande-hotel.com. Set in lovely surroundings, with plenty of amenities (including swimming pool & tennis courts) & once Burkina's best. Rooms have dropped in price recently; they have lumpy pebbledash walling & alarming scarlet sinks, but marvellous views. Wi-Fi throughout, 2 bars & 2 restaurants. About to switch ownership again, so things may change. Visa & Amex accepted. **$$$$$$**

Joly Hotel (79 rooms) Ouaga 2000; 50 37 62 57/58; e jolyhotel.ouaga2000@yahoo.fr, jolyhotel.ouaga2000@fasonet.bf; www.jolyhotel.bf. A new addition to Ouaga's crop of 4-stars. Everything here is aimed at the business visitor, but with a fresh touch, from the airy bar/restaurant to the rooms' soft, light colour scheme. Rooms come with minibar, safe, Wi-Fi & – a nice addition – hairdryers. Some have baths. Set over 2 adjacent sites, 1 has the pool & a massage room, the other a shop. **$$$$$$**

Laico Ouaga 2000 (231 rooms) Ouaga 2000; 50 49 98 00; m 76 44 12 00; e resa.ouaga@laicohotels.com; www.laicohotels.com. The only 5-star hotel in the country. Built by Gaddafi with Libyan financing (locals still call it 'Libya hotel'), it's changed hands a few times since. Rooms are chic, full of dark wood & understated luxury, with balconies & crisp bathrooms. 2 restaurants serve excellent French cuisine; there's jazz every night, & nightclub The Mask at weekends. A pool, gym & tennis courts complete the mod cons. The price tag goes way beyond that of any other hotel in Burkina – doubles start at 110,000f. Visa accepted. **$$$$$$**

Residence Alice [116–17 F6] (8 flats, 2 bedrooms each) Southern ring road; 50 37 23 81; e residal@fasonet.bf, residal3@yahoo.fr. Enormous apartments with kitchens, lounge, dining area & en-suite rooms (2 doubles per flat). There's secure parking, a restaurant, bar & attractive pool. Pricey if you want only 1 bedroom, but starts to look reasonable if you can fill a flat, & there are reductions for longer stays. There's a sneaky non-refundable 15,000f charge for kitchen kit. **$$$$$$**

Residence Nebilma [116–17 B4] (9 flats) Behind Service des Passeports, Gounghin; 50 34 00 39; e residencenebilma@fasonet.bf; www.residencehotel.nebilma.bf. For those who like to self-cater in style. These are fully equipped flats, finished to a high standard; the lounges are a bit small & furnished in dubious taste, but the kitchens are a joy: spanking new oven/stove, fridge/freezer, coffee machine, microwave plus full complement of crockery. Sparkling communal pool. Prices negotiable for longer periods. **$$$$$$**

Upmarket

Don Camillo Résidence [116–17 B4] (21 rooms) Gounghin; 50 34 27 82/83; m 76 57 91 07; e karambirif@yahoo.com. If you like to swing your luggage around, this is the place for you: some of the rooms are enormous. All are comfy with good beds, AC, TV & phone. Wi-Fi allegedly on the way. **$$$$$**

Dragon Hotel [116–17 E1] (42 rooms) North of *barrage* 3; 50 31 07 88; e dragonhotel@yahoo.fr. Nothing wrong with the rooms per se; all neat & clean with king-size beds, AC, fridge, TV & Wi-Fi, but the building's like something from the former Eastern bloc. Chinese restaurant & 25m pool (1,500f to non-guests). Twin rooms cheaper to appeal to conference guests. **$$$$$**

Hotel Avenir [116–17 B4] (36 rooms) 1538 Av Moro Naba Zombre, Gounghin; 50 34 06 21/22; e avenir@fasonet.bf. Decent 2-star hotel, close to Ouaga's industrial estate. Rooms are of a good standard, with AC, en suite, hot water, TV, telephone, 50s dressing table, balcony & mosaic floor tiling. Takes Visa. **$$$$$**

Hotel Excellence [116–17 C2] (50 rooms) 339 Rue Mariame Derme, Dapoya; 50 30 00 84/85, 50 33 13 67; e excellence.hotel@fasonet.bf, infos@excellence-hotel.net; www.excellence-hotel.net. A massive expansion has left this former oasis feeling a bit functional & cramped, with the small pool overshadowed by a towering block; but rooms have TV, fridge, Wi-Fi & aren't badly priced. Its claim to fame is that it gets taken over by the Tour du Faso when it's in town. Takes Visa & can pick-up from airport. **$$$$$**

Hotel OK Inn [116–17 E6] (28 rooms) Bd de la Jeunesse, Patte d'Oie, behind Ouagainter; 50 37 00 20, 50 37 24 51; e hotelok_inn@yahoo.fr, hotelok-inn@mail-bf.com; www.hotelokinn.com. Lovely hotel in shady grounds, it feels like a ranch in the middle of a city. Perfect for travellers, it has personality & charisma, with nice boutiques & ambience, a good pool & restaurant. The only drawback is that you have to get there by going through Ouagainter, the truck stop, but after current roadworks, this may change. Camping & parking of mobile homes possible in the grounds. Takes Visa. Villa for 5 people good value at 55,000f. **$$$$$**

Hotel Ricardo [116–17 C1] (20 rooms) North of *barrage* no 2; 50 31 17 17; e hotel.ricardo@hotmail.fr; http://ricardotel.ifrance.com. On the far side of one of the city's reservoirs, Hotel Ricardo is a Ouagadougou legend. Hunting trophies adorn the walls, the pool is a great hangout (for non-guests too), with good poolside dining & a nightclub at the weekends. The rooms are simple but tasteful, perfectly reflecting the country's colours with warm browns & yellows, & have excellent bathrooms. The patroness speaks English. **$$$$$**

Residence Prestige (10 rooms) Ouaga 2000, near Joly Hotel; 50 37 43 20, 50 50 08 09; e residenceprestiqe@yahoo.fr; www.hotelresidenceprestige .com. Set in what seems like a large house rather than a hotel, the en-suite AC rooms here offer comfort at a much lower price tag than most in Ouaga 2000. They're bright, fresh & tasteful with big beds & Wi-Fi. B/fast inc. **$$$$$**

Hotel Iris [116–17 D5] (34 rooms) Av Yennenga; 50 30 00 53; e iris@fasonet.bf; www.hotel-iris-burkina.com. Near the airport & a solid choice for travellers. Decked out in fabulous wood-panelled kitsch, but about to be refurbished, so this may go. Rooms are clean & comfortable, with big beds & pillows; some have balconies. All have AC, TV & en-suite bathrooms with hot water. **$$$$–$$$$$**

Le Karité Bleu [116–17 F2] (8 rooms) Gate 214, Onatel Bd, Zone du Bois; 50 36 90 46. Now managed by a former director of the École Française, this gorgeous boutique hotel is now sublime, possibly the best that Burkina has to offer. Set in tranquil gardens, it's warm, comfortable & stunningly beautiful throughout, with high-quality *artisanat* everywhere & fairytale lighting in the evenings. Each room is themed (Mossi, Fulani, Mauritanian, etc), with exquisite attention to detail. Book in advance; longer bookings preferred, so for anything less than a few days, you may have trouble getting in. B/fast inc. **$$$$–$$$$$**

Comfortable

Hotel Eden Park [116–17 C5] (110 rooms) Av Bassawarga; 50 31 14 91. Once an upmarket option, but sliding downhill. Reception staff are remarkably candid. 'It's supposed to be 4-star, but it's more like 3. Or even 2,' they say. 'We'll usually negotiate down to 25,000f.' At prices like that, the rooms are fine, & the bonuses are a restaurant, swimming pool, hot water & AC. Officially **$$$$$$**

Chez Tess [116–17 F2] (5 rooms) Zone du Bois; m 76 03 06 06; e tess@tessagadez.com; www.tess.eklablog.com. Run by a Swedish woman who speaks fluent English, this is a homely, lively *maison d'hôte*, full of light & beautiful objects. Rooms are all AC with Wi-Fi, each with its own ethnic theme; choice between en-suite/shared bathroom. All the *artisanat* around the house is for sale & a crafts shop bursts with lovingly selected items. Car hire, laundry service & meals available. B/fast inc. **$$$–$$$$**

Hotel Bangrin [116–17 B3] (33 rooms) Larle; 50 30 89 80; m 78 73 11 35; e rasoued10@yahoo.fr. All rooms with AC, TV & hot water. Nothing special, but spacious & comfortable enough, & the pool (1,000f to non-guests) is a bonus. Restaurant & bar frequented by guests & non-guests alike. **$$$–$$$$**

🏠 **Un Paradis à Ouaga** [116–17 C4] (5 rooms) Off Av du Mogho, Gounghin; ☎ 50 34 02 57; m 70 97 57 52; e http://unparadisaouaga.free.fr. A *maison d'hôte* that lives up to its name with billowing bougainvillea, tranquil gardens with pool, & stylish, comfortable lounge & terrace. Artisanal touches are everywhere. The prettiest option is an AC thatched hut with delicate paintings on the walls, but all are excellent & there's 1 cheaper fan room. Wi-Fi & washing machine. Excursions can be organised. **$$$–$$$$**

🏠 **Village Nong-Taaba** (14 rooms) On the Po road; ☎ 50 46 00 92; m 71 37 66 97, 70 18 27 01; e info@hotelnongtaaba.com; www.hotelnongtaaba.com. Not to be confused with the simpler Song-Taaba (see below), this is a mid-market pleasuredome with a glorious pool (free to diners & guests; otherwise 2,000f), dining in shady *paillotes*, *pétanque* & children's play area. The baked-mud huts & *voûte nubienne* rooms are all en suite with great beds, AC, TVs & lovely features such as alcoves or arched windows. The 4 junior suites are the nation's poshest huts, with enormous beds, fitted circular seating, fridge & TV; a funky glass-roofed corridor leads to stylish bathrooms with kidney-shaped baths. On the right after the southern flyover. **$$$–$$$$**

🏠 **Residence Galiam** [116–17 B5] (16 rooms) Off Rue Gunge, Gounghin Sud; ☎ 50 46 16 94; m 70 02 75 54; e contact@residence-galiamouaga.com; www.residence-galiamouaga.com. Run by a charming Burkinabe woman, this welcoming place has good-value fan rooms, rather pricier AC ones, bar-restaurant & a small pool. Bike, *moto* & car hire can all be arranged. B/fast 1,500f. **$$–$$$$**

Mid range

🏠 **Auberge Le Lion Dort** [116–17 F6] (21 rooms) Off southern ring road; ☎ 50 37 70 49. The only real reason to stay here is its proximity to SIAO & the Village Artisanal. Rooms have AC, TV & Wi-Fi; they're a bit shabby but clean enough. **$$$**

🏠 **Auberge Le Zephir** [116–17 F2] (10 rooms) Zone du Bois; ☎ 50 50 61 06; m 78 54 28 29. A distinct lack of character here, but rooms better than you might expect – all AC, en suite with TV & Wi-Fi, light, airy & spotless with crisp white sheets. **$$$**

🏠 **La Case d'Hôtes** [116–17 B3] (6 rooms) Opposite Maternite de Pogbi, Ouidi; ☎ 50 31 03 61; m 78 00 86 16; e casehotes@yahoo.fr; www.case-hotes.com. A classic *maison d'hôte* in the heart of Ouidi, where friendly host Alain prides himself on his *table d'hôte* – the evening meal where guests can exchange their daily news. There's a range of comfy rooms with AC or fan, a shady terrace for chilling, & a rescued patas monkey. Wi-Fi throughout. 3-course evening meal 4,000f. B/fast inc. **$$$**

🏠 **Les Manguiers** [139 E2] (13 rooms) Av de la Liberte, Dapoya; ☎ 50 30 03 70; e jacksonhotel@yahoo.fr; www.jacksonhotel.frgd. Under new management, & not quite what it was; many of the artisanal touches have gone, & it's overshadowed by ongoing extension work. But the garden's still lovely, & the round huts nice to stay in; simple AC & fan rooms do the job too. All are en suite, with mosquito nets. Decent restaurant & a well-stocked spirits bar. **$$$**

🏠 **Ne y Woongo** [116–17 C3] (4 rooms) Rue 11.56, Larle; m 72 75 27 99; e neywoongo@gmail.com; http://neywoongo.com. A cosy, welcoming *maison d'hôte* run by a French–Burkinabe couple. The rooms, sweetly decorated in matching fabrics, are arranged around a neat courtyard & are either fan or AC. There's a good evening *table d'hôte* (3 courses for 4,000f); services such as washing, bike hire, excursions & an aromatherapy masseuse can all be arranged. **$$$**

🏠 **Auberge Song-Taaba** [116–17 A5] (10 rooms) Rue Toagba, Gounghin; ☎ 50 34 65 70; m 70 23 32 85; e salif_asso7@yahoo.com. Budget travellers will love this place, which supports local women & disadvantaged children. Most rooms are built in traditional banco, *voûte nubienne* style, with cute arches leading into the bathrooms & over the windows. There's 1 AC room in the main building & Wi-Fi throughout. Bargain bike hire (750f per day); car & *moto* hire also available. B/fast inc. **$$–$$$**

🏠 **Chez Giuliana** [116–17 F3] (5 rooms) Rue Lamine Gueye, 1200 Logements; ☎ 50 36 33 97; m 71 00 55 05; e dacasto@fasonet.bf; www.chezgiuliana.com. A fun-filled *maison d'hôte,* full of surprising nooks & crannies that overflow with Giuliana's love of colour & fabrics. A women's sewing workshop is on site; there's a library, roof terrace with fabulous views & self-catering kitchen for guests. Fan only in 2 rooms, AC in others; Wi-Fi throughout. Separate villa available for longer stays. **$$–$$$**

Cocooning [116–17 A4] (5 rooms) Off main road to Stade 4 Août, Gounghin; 50 34 28 14; m 76 17 02 38; e cocooning.faso@yahoo.fr; www.cocooning.faso.com. The simplest of all the new *maison d'hôtes*; there's a pleasant lounge with TV, internet access & a small *paillote* in the back yard. All rooms are en suite; 3 have fans, 2 are AC. 1 is a triple, with bunk-bed. A 2-course meal can be ordered for 4,000f. B/fast 1,500f. **$$–$$$**

Hotel Dapoore [139 E3] (18 rooms) Dapoya; 50 31 33 31. The attached restaurant, Le Chalet Suisse (see page 136), is much nicer than the dingy rooms, which have lost their mozzie nets but are otherwise functional. Choice of en-suite fan or AC. **$$–$$$**

Hotel Oubri [116–17 D5] (14 rooms) Kamsonghin, Secteur 6; m 78 05 64 29, 71 35 25 05. Dingy rooms that don't feel clean; now that there's no functioning restaurant, neglect is closing in. However, close to both airport & TCV garage. Fan or en-suite AC. **$$–$$$**

Hotel Pavillon Vert [139 D2] (20 rooms) Av de la Liberte, Dapoya; 50 31 06 11; m 76 22 88 50; e hotelpavillonvert@yahoo.fr; www.hotel-pavillonvert.com. A travellers' favourite with all the extras you might expect: craft shop, travel agency, Wi-Fi & car/bike hire. Set in lovely gardens, with a pretty outdoor restaurant set under a *paillote* roof, worth the trek even if you're not a guest. Delightfully decorated en-suite fan or AC doubles; even the simple fan rooms with outside loo are nicely done, with mosquito nets & bamboo-lined walls. **$$–$$$**

Hotel Riviera Mam Joly [116–17 B3] (24 rooms) Av Larle Naba Agba; m 74 60 34 41. An old budget option that has long passed its peak. Round en-suite bungalows are dotted around a courtyard & garden, but the beds sag like hammocks & the mozzie nets are no more. Still, the staff are friendly & helpful, & there's a decent laundry service. Choice of fan or AC. **$$–$$$**

Hotel Yamba [116–17 B3] (14 rooms) Av Larle Naba Agba; 50 31 25 26, 50 30 08 06. The cramped reception area belies the rooms, which are clean & bright with en suite. On-site restaurant & bar. Vehicle hire available. Choice of fan or AC. **$$–$$$**

Pension Sarah [116–17 C6] (34 rooms) Av Bassawarga, Cité An II; 50 38 14 49, 50 38 08 30; e pensionsarah@hotmail.com. Popular travellers' hole-up, perfect for exploring the quarter's nearby market. Basic but lovely, with wonderful attention to detail – decorated walls, mosaic tiled floors, & *paillotes* overflowing with greenery. All rooms with en suite; Wi-Fi throughout. Lovely shaded garden restaurant has meals for around 1,000f. B/fast 800f. **$$–$$$**

Residence du Centre [116–17 D5] (4 rooms) Off Av Kwame N'Krumah; 50 47 90 56; m 71 19 70 24. Clean, new, uninspiring rooms, 1 en suite, with choice of fan or AC. Proximity to airport – 5mins' walk – the only real selling point. **$$–$$$**

Budget

Residence Napam Beogo [116–17 C2] (10 rooms) 50 34 42 29; m 70 23 84 86; e espacenapambeogo@yahoo.fr; www.espacenapambeogo.com. The brainchild of an enterprising craftsman, who saw a need for artists' accommodation. Now stretching over 3 venues (Espace Culturel Napam Beogo is just around the corner; the *atelier* is in Ouidi), this one has the most rooms, which are simple en suites with fan & Wi-Fi. Ideal for those with specific cultural interests. Car & *moto* hire. Meals available. B/fast 750f. **$$**

WHERE TO EAT AND DRINK

Wherever you are in Ouagadougou, you can eat spectacularly well. The range of nosh on offer, let alone the quality, is impressive. You can try French, Italian, Swiss, Austrian, Lebanese, Chinese, Vietnamese, Moroccan, Indian, Senegalese, Ivorian or Togolese cuisine, as well as tasty US-style fast food and the odd local Burkinabe speciality. For this reason, the following restaurant listing is long, but, if you like your food, worth scanning. Think nothing of turning up on Avenue Kwame N'Krumah after 23.00 and hoping for a meal: there always is one.

IN THE CITY CENTRE New restaurants open all the time. Ask around with young Ouagalais if you want to know what's hot. For the moment, Koulouba is the place that's bursting with exciting eateries; there's a new crop at the bottom of Avenue Kwame N'Krumah too.

Expensive

✕ **Le Bistrot Lyonnais** [124–5 G2] Av du 11 Decembre; ☎ 50 33 01 65; ⏰ Tue–Sat. The setting is stylishly understated, indoors or out; the eloquent chef from Lyon nevertheless lets his food do the talking, with a menu that shows loving attention to detail. A must-try is any of the fluffy *quenelles*, a Lyonnais speciality, but classic French cuisine backs them up. For those with deep pockets, there are *grand vins* such as Château Haut Marbuzet or Gevrey Chambertin; a 3,500f *fillette* (25cl) offers solace to the struggling. $$$$

✕ **Le Coq Bleu** [124–5 E4] 406 Av Kwame N'Krumah; ☎ 50 30 01 93; ⏰ Wed–Mon. One of Ouaga's most established lunch & dinner destinations, but a bit of a fusty atmosphere. Green beans with lardons & garlic are a delight, while *poulet coq bleu* is a solid example of French-style cooking. The Austrian owner also runs the Tam Tam. $$$$

✕ **L'Olivier Nouveau** [124–5 F3] Rue Maurice Yameogo; ☎ 50 33 58 71; m 76 11 32 46; ⏰ Tue–Sun. French cuisine in what is arguably the stuffiest restaurant in town, but with starters such as traditional fish soup with garlic croutons & *rouille*, followed by *filet de boeuf tartare*, foodies should leave with a smile. Dining is indoors, mostly in a slightly cramped dining area of starchy tables, but a private room is available. Service is attentive without being intrusive. $$$$

✕ **Princess' Yenenga** Av de la Grande Chancellerie; ☎ 50 30 63 16; m 70 21 63 15. This hotel's restaurant is a highly rated destination in its own right. With features such as a waterfall at the back & twinkling lights above, it manages to ooze warm & easy luxury rather than kitsch. The menu is short & sweet, changing regularly to keep a loyal clientele on their toes; everything is scrupulously sourced, local produce featuring as far as possible. Basic meals on Sun, the chef's day off. $$$$

✕ **Le Dernier Tango** [124–5 G4] Av John F Kennedy, Koulouba; ☎ 50 50 45 70; m 78 90 41 40. Has a series of enticing nooks & crannies, from relaxing terrace, comfy indoor dining room to snug, well-stocked bar, where you might catch the Belgian owner playing chess with a regular. As well as excellent pizzas, there's a range of dishes done in the wood-fired oven, such as *gratin de capitaine aux epinards*, or *saucisses de Toulouse*. $$$–$$$$

✕ **Vitis Vinifera** [124–5 F4] Av President Blaise Compaore; ☎ 50 33 15 35; m 78 76 21 20. Has all the eagerness of a new place fresh out of the starting blocks. The wine cellar entrance looks classy, as does the terrace, tables separated by burgundy drapes; but the bar's wonderfully tacky, all red cushions & heart-shaped tables suffused in a pink glow. Both menu & wine list short & sweet. $$$–$$$$

Above average

✕ **Akwaba** [124–5 E5] Av Kwame N'Krumah; ☎ 50 31 23 76; ⏰ Mon–Sat. Ivorian chef, friendly service, terrible music, odd décor. If you are feeling adventurous, try the surprisingly rich taste of agouti (bush rat) with *sauce feille*, along with regulars such as *foutou igname* & *attiéké*, *alloco* & several chicken options. $$$

✕ **Chez Haregua Ethiopia** [124–5 E5] Av l'UEMOA; ☎ 50 50 52 38. Very new, trying to find its niche in the Zaca area. Ethiopian specialities are dished up with rice or *injera*, the country's distinctive spongy flatbread. It's nicest to sit on the terrace, where there's attractive low seating. $$$

✕ **Club Belko** [124–5 H4] Av du Burkina Faso, Koulouba; ☎ 50 30 75 80. Popular with well-heeled Ouagalais, this offers a classy garden environment & a good-looking menu of meat & fish dishes, plus African specialities. $$$

✕ **La Forêt** [124–5 B4] Av Bassawarga; ☎ 50 30 72 96. Set back from the road in pretty gardens, with intimate tables in leafy corners. The popular pool is free to Hotel Amiso guests, otherwise 1,500f, & the menu includes both French & African specialities. $$$

✕ **L'Eau Vive** [124–5 D3] Rue de l'Hotel de Ville; ☎ 50 30 63 03; ⏰ 12.00–14.15 & 19.30–

22.00 Mon–Sat. One of the most pleasant nights out in Ouaga. Set in a lush garden, tables are ranged round a tinkling fountain & statue of the Virgin Mary. Every night, the Carmelite nuns who double as waitresses sing the Ave Maria at around 21.45. Everything stops after that, including diners & kitchen staff, so get your order in early. It serves up good European & African food: *medaillons* of beef are particularly good, as are wonderful & inventive ice cream desserts. $$$

✕ **L'Escapade (Chez Doume)** [124–5 H4] Near L'Archeveché, Koulouba; 50 31 19 61. With terrace seating set around a romantically lit pool (free to diners), this is another good addition to the Koulouba list. The owner is Corse, & flies in a few specialities: cheese & *charcuterie*, & serves up 'Aziminu' (bouillabaise) on Fri. Otherwise, good

MAQUIS MAGIC

The *maquis* is the cornerstone of Burkinabe outdoor living and a great place to eat and drink on the cheap. Below are some favourites, but rock up anywhere and you should find a beer and *brochettes*.

Many Burkinabe are inveterate daytime drinkers, and some haunts have built their reputation on this. Head for the inaptly named **One Night** [139 F3] in Dapoya at 09.00 of a weekend and you'll find the regular crowd already tucking in; they'll still be there, much the worse for wear, at around 17.00 when the whole thing winds down. For those who feel the need for sustenance, don't miss **Chez Madame Bado** in Ouidi [116–17 B2] (*Rue 11.41; find the Ouidi Naba's palace, then ask*), famous across Ouaga for her *porc au four*. Order a 500f portion and you'll get a pile of juicy chunks interspersed with crispy crackling; you'll immediately order more, which is why it's usually all gone by about 15.30. Likewise, **Zama Chapelle** [124–5 D2], within a corner of the Maison du People, is a marvellous lunchtime haunt for meat-lovers. Pick out your tender chunk of steak, chicken or any sort of offal, and it'll arrive at your table deliciously sautéed with onions and tomatoes. Mop up the juices with hunks of fresh bread, wash it down with a Brakina and watch the parade of non-touristy hawkers, who do brisk business in everything from nail-clippers to underpants.

When night falls, the bright-yellow **Boulougou** [124–5 G4] in Koulouba becomes popular with a slightly older Burkinabe crowd, especially for a post-work drink. It used to do great spit-roast chicken but it's gone all modern; the birds now appear mysteriously from a kitchen, and aren't as good. However, you can still get marvellous chicken at the stalls outside the Stade Municipal, which is also a tranquil place to down a beer or three. Some whisper that the best garlic chicken of all is to be had at **Fouquet's** (see box, page 135).

On Boulevard Charles de Gaulle heading east, **La Rose du Desert** [116–17 G3] is a firm local favourite. It isn't much to look at, but the music goes on until 04.00 and the fish, especially the carp, is good. Kids may come round and ask for your reject bones, to turn into soup later.

More upmarket options include the **Maquis Aboussouan** [116–17 B4] (*50 34 27 20; m 73 32 30 96*), which is so posh it calls itself a restaurant these days. Its name means 'family' in Ashanti, although it models itself along Ivorian lines as far as food goes. Most dishes are around the 4,000–5,000f mark, but you can get the best *brochettes* in the country for 2,500f apiece. There's even a wine list. It's in Gounghin Sud; most taxi drivers know it. Or try **La Consolatrice**, some way out of Ouaga on the Fada road, a Sunday-lunch favourite for local families.

pizza & mains do the job, & there's a well-stocked bar. $$$

Le Verdoyant [124–5 E2] Av Dimdolobson 50 31 54 07; Thu–Tue. A Ouaga classic, right on the town's central roundabout, & always busy. Well-deserved reputation based on its fantastic pizzas & wickedly tempting dessert menu in a comfortable garden ambience. Deliveries possible for 1,000–2,000f, depending on distance. $$$

Moulin Rouge [124–5 E6] Av Kwame N'Krumah; 50 30 46 53. A popular fixture on the main drag, with tables inside & out. Menu includes grills, salads, pizzas with great toppings (eg: goat's cheese, squid), plus tapas. Portions are enormous, & genial host Alain is omnipresent, checking everyone's happy. $$$

Paradis des Meilleurs Vins [124–5 E7] Av Kwame N'Krumah; m 78 04 08 24/12. With raised table centres & a tempting wine list, this place has a certain laid-back panache. The menu is very French – *cotelettes d'agneau*, *steak au poivre* or a plate of *charcuterie* – but you can get cheap plonk as well as classier options, & it's popular with Ouagalais. $$$

Rang de l'Inde [124–5 E7] Av Kwame N'Krumah; m 70 27 00 00, 70 39 97 43. Ouaga's only Indian restaurant is distinctly unspicy. Rushed, over-attentive service makes you feel like the only customer in months; bland sauces are a lame disguise for the rough cuts of meat. Best avoided unless you're desperate for a curry. $$$

Restaurant les Bougainvilliers [124–5 G4] 313 Av John Kennedy; 50 31 48 81; m 76 68 00 01; Mon–Sat. Pizzas (including calzone), pasta & European dishes in pleasant tree-clad garden. Over-attentive but friendly service. Also have a take-away service. $$$

Terra Nostre [124–5 E4] Av John F Kennedy; 50 33 03 06. A popular addition to Ouaga's pizza-pasta crop, with good-quality meat & fish dishes too. For the delicate of stomach, all veg is washed in permanganate. Choose between a pleasant outdoor terrace or AC dining room. $$$

Aux 4 Saisons [124–5 E4] Av de la Cathedrale; 50 30 06 24. Decked out in scarlet with red-rose ceiling balls, it's perhaps stuck on 1 season, but the effect is warm & jolly. The food, ranging from cheerful burgers & *chawarmas* to good salads, pizza & mains, is fine & reasonably priced. $$–$$$

Belvedere [124–5 F4] Rue Raoul Follereau; 50 33 64 21; Wed–Mon, closed lunchtimes. Specialises in Lebanese & Italian food, with lovely covered garden seating & bar. Good pizza, *meze* & salads. $$–$$$

Café de Vienne [124–5 G4] Av John F Kennedy; 50 39 82 45; Fri–Wed. Brightly lit, so feels more caff than restaurant, but with a scrumptious menu that includes everything from Viennese cakes & pastries (*strudel*, *sachertorte*) to full English breakfasts & – vegetarians take note – the best range of veggie dishes in Ouaga. There's also free Wi-Fi. $$–$$$

Chez Simon [124–5 E6] 1266 Av Kwame N'Krumah; 50 33 21 46, 50 30 26 92. Another great street-side location makes this Lebanese café a lunchtime & Sun morning favourite. Good selection of fruit juices, pastries & salads, *chawarma* & sandwiches, as well as more pricey pizza & mains. $$–$$$

Diwan al Moktar [124–5 H4] Koulouba; 50 33 57 75; m 70 24 45 13; e saficom@fasonet.bf; Tue–Sun. The most extensive Lebanese menu in town, including excellent *tabouleh*, *charwarma* & sweet folded pizzas. $$–$$$

Le Veranda [124–5 E6] Av Kwame N'Krumah; 50 50 77 77. Big menu features all the usual suspects from cheaper sandwiches to steaks, salads & pizzas, but there's not much of a buzz here. There's an AC dining room as well as the large veranda. $$–$$$

Restaurant de Chine [124–5 E4] Av Loudun; 50 31 18 60; m 76 62 48 98; Wed–Mon. Enormous 1st-floor dining area, packed with red lanterns & starchy tablecloths, gives views onto the streets below & delicious garlic beef & pork dishes pack a punch. $$–$$$

Zaka [124–5 D3] Av Yennenga; m 76 22 88 46. Built in the style of a traditional Mossi courtyard, Zaka is an old travellers' favourite & an attractive place to while away an hour or two. It's under new management, however; the food's pretty average & overpriced. Free Wi-Fi is a bonus, & live music may start up again. $$–$$$

Mid range/Cheap and cheerful

De Nero's [124–5 E5] Av Leo Frobenius; 70 26 68 18; m 70 24 78 18; Mon–Sat, closed lunchtimes. Pleasantly divey pool bar & veranda with a range of salads named after the big man's movies, as well as a wide choice of fish, omelettes, crêpes & ice cream, & truly excellent cheap steak. Closed for lunch & on Sun. $$

Le Mezzanine [124–5 E5] Av l'UEMOA; 50 50 97 57. A brave new venture in Zaca-land, serving up African specialities, mostly from Côte d'Ivoire: maize & millet *tô*, *foutou*, *attiéké*, *kedjenou* & the like. On a 1st-floor terrace, hence the name. $$

Sindibal [124–5 E4] Av Loudun; 50 30 58 74. Quiet hangout with fast-food section outside, dishing up *chawarma* & burgers on the roadside terrace; inside it's brightly lit but does a good range of cheap nosh with an emphasis on Lebanese. The spaghetti bolognese is excellent. $$

Aziz Istanbul Patisserie Café [124–5 E6] Av Kwame N'Krumah; 50 30 81 86. Great range of cakes & biscuits, mouth-watering ice creams & pastries, along with *borek* & Turkish pizzas. $–$$

Café Bonbonnière [124–5 D2] Av de la Nation; 50 30 63 52; from 06.00. Pastries,

OUTDOOR GARDENS

With strings of lights hanging from trees, and the smell of garlic grills on the air, a city garden is perfect for taking the evening slowly. Tables for two or four, set a courteous distance from each other, often with the entertainment of live music, and waiters bringing steaming *brochettes*, pancakes and ice-cold beer, create a setting that is tranquil and lovely. Usually situated in some of the busiest intersections in town, each one offers immediate respite from the racket outside.

Le Jardin de l'Amitié [124–5 E2] (*50 33 72 38*) on Avenue Dimdolobsom, is hidden behind a hedge on the central roundabout. The garden contains plenty of hidden nooks and crannies so you never feel crowded. Rising popularity has seen prices go up, standards of service fall, and a profusion of guides and artisans touting for business on the way in; but it's still the spot for nightly live music (traditional during the week; bands at weekends), which makes it worth the hassle and an extra 500f or so.

Place Naba Koom [124–5 C1], opposite the train station, is in the shadow of an enormous sculpture of a woman offering a calabash of water, representing Burkinabe hospitality to new arrivals. It's home to restaurant **Fouquet's**, which is justly famous for its garlic chicken; there's often live music too. Go with company, as the square's pretty big, and tables are tucked in secluded corners.

Jardin du Maire [124–5 C3] (*50 30 43 05*), overlooking Burkina's monument to cinema, is set behind pretty hedgerows but feels a bit neglected. It's not a bad stop for a tasty African dish, though – good poultry classics, such as *poulet yassa* and *pintade au rabilet*.

Jardin du 8 Mars [116–17 C4], opposite the Moro Naba's palace, is open every day.

Jardin de l'Unite Africaine [116–17 C5], near the Malian embassy, attracts a younger, fun-loving crowd, particularly on weekends. Keep going south on Avenue Bassawarga, and you'll reach **Jardin Ouaga 2000** [116–17 C7] (*50 38 62 56*).

Jardin de l'Aéroport [116–17 D4] (*50 31 71 38*) makes another good stop, with a nice terrace. Also close to the airport, **Jardin Yennenga** [116–17 D5], beautifully maintained and decorated, is popular for a post-work beer. **Jardin le Challenge** [116–17 A5], tucked behind the Bobo flyover in Gounghin, has a series of large concrete gazebos within a profusion of greenery, but it's a bit run-down these days.

shortbreads & cakes, & caramelised onion pizza make this an excellent breakfast hangout; under the same management as the Patisserie Koulouba. $–$$

Cafeteria Faso Paix [124–5 F3] Av Pdt Sangoule Lamizana; 50 47 92 94; part of the café 24hrs. Corner caff serving up cheap grub at no-nonsense prices. Good for a burger, salad or a kebab & chips; also does pastries, yoghurt & African rice dishes. Sit on stools at the bar, at plastic tables inside makeshift surrounds or on the pavement terrace. $–$$

La Patisserie Koulouba [124–5 F4] Av Pdt Sangoule Lamizana; 50 30 77 17. Renowned breakfast option, the range of sweet delicacies here makes it a suitably sticky place to start a day's exploration of the city. $–$$

La Source [124–5 E4] Av Loudoun; 50 50 56 57. Tranquil 1st-floor restaurant with balcony terrace overlooking the street below. Good, cheap salads, solid staples & tasty juices. $–$$

Les Oscars [124–5 E3] Av l'UEMOA; 50 31 06 01. Right next door to the Hotel Nazemse, this is one of Ouaga's famed ice cream joints, but it's also good for lunch & does nice salads. $–$$

Restaurant Senegalais Chez Mme Sall [124–5 C5] Rue Emile Damiba. Wonderful Senegalese family atmosphere; the extended family all gather to eat on the floor, but there are plenty of tables too. Good home cooking, with salads & chicken to back up the rice options. $–$$

Souley Café [124–5 D4] Av de la Cathedrale. Always buzzing, with locals perched on stools at its street-side bar day & night. Great for cheap staples (*riz sauce*, *riz gras*), but there are yoghurt & omelettes too, plus ice-cold bottles of *bissap*. $

You can't beat street food in Ouaga, whether it's meat cuts sizzling away outside a *maquis*, women char-grilling stalks of maize or serving enormous plates of rice and sauce. All are delicious, and available for a few hundred CFA francs. Come dusk, you won't be able to walk down a street without seeing someone cooking something.

OUT OF THE CITY CENTRE

Expensive

Le Vert Galant Opposite Joly Hotel, Ouaga 2000; 50 39 67 60. Having moved from the centre of town, this restaurant has seamlessly maintained its décor – from the fresh green & white garden effect with plants & green trellises – & its excellent food. The cuisine is French, the prices surprisingly reasonable. Takes Amex & Visa. $$$$

L'Orient [116–17 F2] Av Babanguida; 50 36 15 09. Opposite the Algerian embassy in Zone du Bois. Looking a bit run-down these days, but serves good Chinese food at reasonable prices. Diners have the option of a slightly drab interior, complete with dog wandering into & out of the kitchen, or a beautifully lit garden. $$$$

Restaurant Gondwana [116–17 F2] Zone du Bois; 50 36 11 24; Tue–Sun. In the middle of Ouaga's poshest residential quarter, Gondwana is a treat, for the eye as much as the taste buds. Themed areas include a Mauritanian salon, a Tuareg tent, a Gourounsi house & a garden, with plenty of traditional & modern art on show for sale. An extensive & tempting menu includes delights such as *boulettes de boeuf aux épices et à la menthe*, but there are some surprises, such as cheeseburger & chips for 4,500f. Favoured by diplomats & Burkina's *glitterati*, including cineaste Gaston Kabore. $$$$

Restaurant Le Chalet Suisse [139 E3] Av Dapoya; 50 31 33 31. Just when you thought you couldn't possibly get cheese fondue in Burkina Faso... This is pure Alpine chalet, with chequered tablecloths, tacky wooden beams, & wooden African animal masks hanging on the wall where there would normally be ancient snow boots. A steaming side of *raclette* arrives alongside potatoes, cornichons, cold meat, or beef to fondue yourself. A real find – but was just changing hands at the time of writing, so its fate hangs in the balance. $$$$

Above average

Gigot à la Ficelle [116–17 F6] Southern ring road; m 70 15 34 34, 76 78 78 14. A quirky destination featuring regular live music & sketches, staff who whizz around on rollerskates,

&, of course, *gigot à la ficelle*: leg of lamb cooked hanging from string. Portions are enormous; a 3-course meal costs 8,500f. $$$

Hamanien [116–17 D5] Av Kwame N'Krumah; 50 50 98 35. A reincarnation of an established restaurant, serving up mostly Ivorian cuisine. All very new & spacious, it manages to seem fresh & cosy at the same time. European dishes available too. $$$

Kim Som [116–17 D5] Av Kwame N'Krumah; 50 30 88 31; e lmnguyenbf@yahoo.fr; Tue–Sun. A great oriental restaurant near the airport, in rather delicate surroundings, with tasty ginger dishes & good noodles. Also does take-away. $$$

Restaurant-Bar le Palmares [116–17 B4] Rue Nakom-Suga, Gounghin; 50 34 17 17. Fairly pricey, standard European & African menu in a homely garden setting. Has a good reputation locally. $$$

Rosa Del Venti Ouaga 2000; 50 37 59 53. If you're down this end of town, stop by for Italian classics such as gnocchi, polenta & fresh pasta; plus pizza of course. Sit on the terrace & take a dip in the pool while you wait, or hide away, Godfather-style, in a private room with buzzer. There's a wine list, or a *pichet* of plonk for 1,500f. $$$

La Cave du Petit Paris [116–17 C4] Off Av Kadiago; 50 34 02 34; m 70 27 19 38. Tucked down a little side-road in Gounghin, this is an Aladdin's cave for wine lovers; no beer or soft drinks in sight. A classy cellar stuffed with French wines (from 4,000f the bottle) fronts a delightful, intimate courtyard restaurant with a short but delicious menu. As one reader put it, it's like going to France for the evening. $$–$$$

Le Paradisio [116–17 F3] Just before Petrofa station, Zone du Bois; 50 36 81 12. Restau-bar much patronised by expats. The great range of food includes good pizzas & *merguez*. The owner combines the restaurant with a modern art gallery, while the on-site tailor's makes shirts from African print cloth & can take your order while you eat. $$–$$$

Le Tam-Tam [116–17 B4] 1647 Av Kadiogo; 50 34 71 03; Wed–Mon. The only place in the country for pigs' trotters & sauerkraut – the house speciality, served up at the weekend. The Austrian owner serves up all manner of sausage meat, in a pleasant garden at decent prices. You can also get more usual fare, including steak & chips. $$–$$$

Restaurant La Vita [116–17 D4] Av Kwame N'Krumah; 50 30 18 28. One of a new crop of restaurants at the bottom end of the drag, with a menu a mile long. Well-priced pizzas & Lebanese snacks stand out. $$–$$$

Mid range/Cheap and cheerful

Bar-restaurant Le Festival [139 A3] Av de l'Armée, Cité An III. Pavement restaurant serving up superb braised garlic chicken, chips, *brochettes*, hamburgers & cheeseburgers. If the music outside is too much, a good *jardin* houses a few *paillotes* & the occasional guitarist if you want something quieter. $$

Hamburger House [116–17 G2] Behind the Red Cross, Zone du Bois; 50 50 48 19; m 78 87 65 76. With a Togolese chef who spent 6 years in the American school up the road, & a loyal following of Peace Corps volunteers around the corner, this is the place for a taste of the US. Hash browns, waffles & syrup, & double bacon cheeseburgers all feature. $$

Resto Art Café Pyramides [139 F2] Dapoya; m 76 94 69 56. Chilled-out place with arty atmosphere; offers a bit of respite from the throbbing joints nearby. Great for a quiet beer & simple nosh such as spaghetti bolognese, couscous, chips & *ragout*. $$

Issaabi Dimas [116–17 F2] Near the market, Zone du Bois; m 76 24 60 28. A different take on African cuisine: the name means 'It's delicious' in the Portuguese Creole of Guinea-Bissau, the owner's country of origin. There's fish & beef cooked Bissau-style, plenty of goat, & the tasty little pasties & croquettes that the women of Bissau rustle up for parties. $–$$

ENTERTAINMENT AND NIGHTLIFE

Ouaga likes to think of itself as a city that never sleeps, and its inhabitants make a darn good attempt at living up to that status. Street-side bars stay open into the wee hours on weeknights and weekends alike, and kitchens stay active way after midnight. Prostitutes, both professional and occasional, are part of the territory and many bars double as pick-up joints, so be prepared for attention, particularly if you're on your own.

BARS AND CLUBS

In the centre

☐ **Bar K Grill** [124–5 G4] Across from Brussels Airlines, Koulouba. Funky little place that specialises in grilled meat, but is more notable for its enormous curved wooden bar & mock-vinyl record decorations. Plans for live music on the terrace.

☐ **Bowling 1** [124–5 E5] Av Kwame N'Krumah; m 78 86 86 01. Finding ten-pin bowling lanes in central Ouaga comes as a bit of a surprise, but here they are, & you can even knock back draught beer as you play. A game costs 3,000f. There's also pool (500f). Another 4 lanes can be found at **Le Pandora** [124–5 C2], on Rue Mogho-Naba. It's under the same management but a bit quieter, with more pool tables.

☐ **Le Loft** [124–5 G4] Off Av John F Kennedy, Koulouba; ☎ 50 31 20 21; m 76 62 48 93. Sophisticated lounge-bar with UV lighting, snug seating & a small but enticing dance floor. Join expats & well-heeled Ouagalais for a cocktail & catch live jazz, R&B or traditional music every Fri from 22.00. Live reggae on Sat in the pipeline.

☐ **Show Biz Pub** [124–5 E5] Av Kwame N'Krumah; ☎ 50 30 53 63. Delightfully tacky terrasse café & a Ouaga classic, though its popularity has waned of late. It's a bit of a pick-up joint, & ideal for watching Ouaga's nightlife strut by. Styling itself as an American bar, it does a great range of cheap & tasty food, including burgers, salads & *chawarma* wraps. The Lebanese owner, Omar, is very friendly, speaks English, & his spirit measures are super-generous. There's a cocktail happy hour from 18.00 to 21.00, & the *mojitos* really pack a punch.

☐ **Taxi Brousse** [124–5 E6] Av Kwame N'Krumah. The first in a line of drinking holes running down the main drag, where you can pick up a cold beer, chicken & *brochettes*. Open till the small hours, & popular with ladies of the night & street hawkers, so best to go with company. A bit further down, you'll find **La Caleche** [124–5 E6], **La Coline** [124–5 E6], & the big street-side terrace of **La Banquise** [124–5 E7] if you fancy something quieter.

☐ **Zaka** [124–5 D3] Av Yennenga. Worth an enquiry: it's under new management, & used to host regular live music, which may start up again.

As for dance spots, **Le Calypso** [124–5 F4] is firmly on every clubber's agenda, just down from Les Bougainvilliers Restaurant. Entry is free, and it rocks the whole week through. **Byblos** [124–5 E5] (formerly Jimmy's) midway along Avenue Kwame N'Krumah, is an established haunt. The relatively stiff entry fee (3,000f) keeps it popular with the well heeled. Also check out **Papagayo**, just above. Newish, and swankier, is **Golden Nightclub** [124–5 G5] behind Koulouba water tower – a three-storey extravaganza, comprising all-comers on the first floor, a VIP-only second floor and Piste Gabana on the third, which spins Afro-American music. It's open Friday and Saturday; entry is 5,000f, an eye-popping 10,000f for the VIP lounge, and there's a dress code, so dig deep. If you're in need of refreshment, head no further than **Maxi Food L'Agréable** [124–5 G5] next door. Decked out in cheerful primary colours, matched by an equally colourful menu, it's an upmarket fast-food joint designed with flagging clubbers in mind; it's open until dawn on club nights. Just up from the Verdoyant, the **Havana** club [124–5 E2] was about to burst on to the scene, sporting mirrors, massive air-conditioning units and distressed burgundy paintwork. There'll be a garden restaurant out the back too. **Zoodo** disco [124–5 E1], further up the same road beyond the *douane*, has mixed music and fancy decorations in a nice garden with no entry fee. Head west and you'll find **Le Privé** [124–5 D2] next door to the Relax Hotel. As the name suggests, it's not for

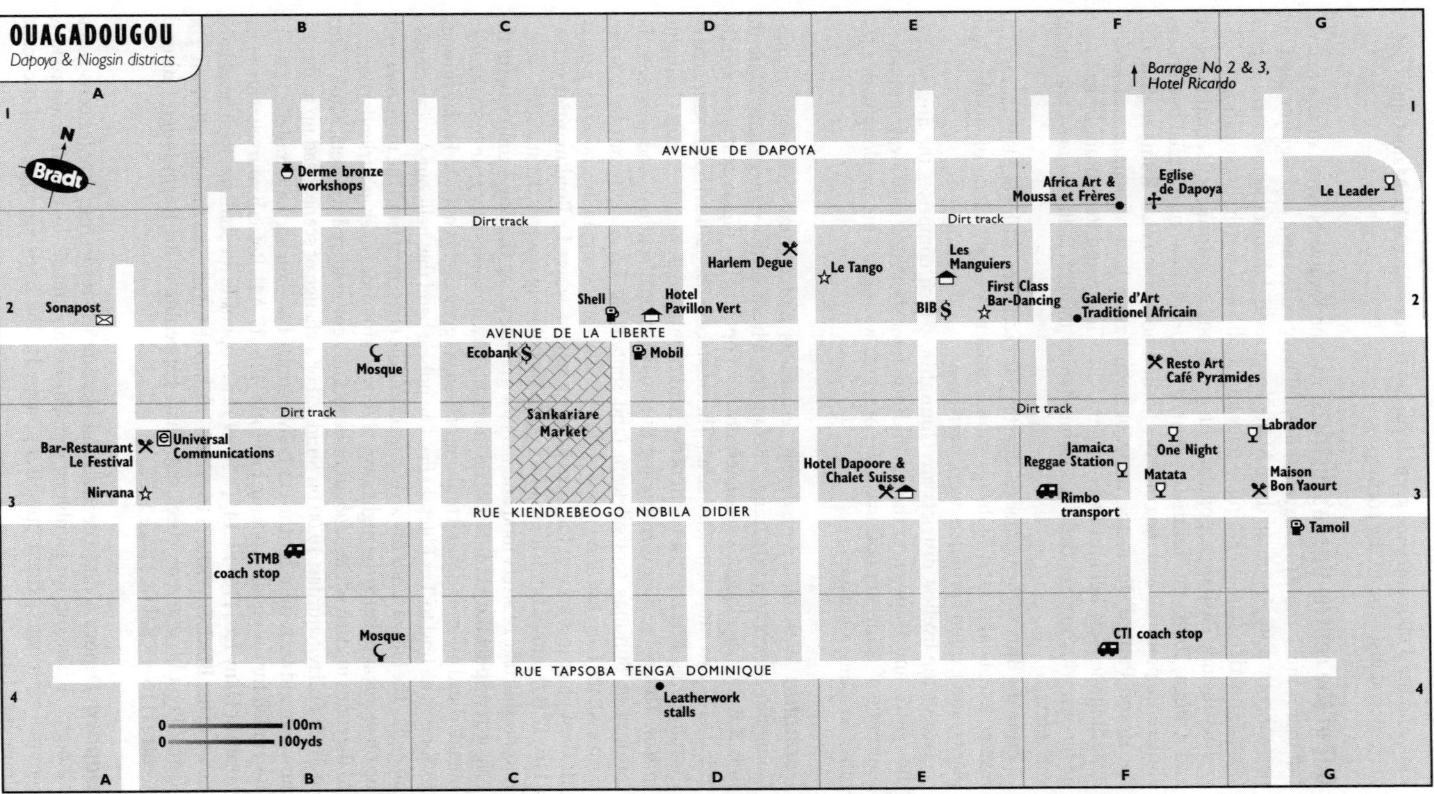
OUAGADOUGOU
Dapoya & Niogsin districts
Bradt
N
Barrage No 2 & 3, Hotel Ricardo
AVENUE DE DAPOYA
Derme bronze workshops
Africa Art & Moussa et Frères
Eglise de Dapoya
Le Leader
Dirt track
Dirt track
Harlem Degue
Le Tango
Les Manguiers
First Class Bar-Dancing
Sonapost
Shell
Hotel Pavillon Vert
BIB
Galerie d'Art Traditionel Africain
AVENUE DE LA LIBERTE
Ecobank
Mobil
Mosque
Resto Art Café Pyramides
Dirt track
Sankariare Market
Dirt track
Labrador
Bar-Restaurant Le Festival
Universal Communications
Jamaica Reggae Station
One Night
Hotel Dapoore & Chalet Suisse
Matata
Maison Bon Yaourt
Nirvana
Rimbo transport
RUE KIENDREBEOGO NOBILA DIDIER
Tamoil
STMB coach stop
Mosque
CTI coach stop
RUE TAPSOBA TENGA DOMINIQUE
Leatherwork stalls
0 100m
0 100yds

kids, and the 3,000f entry fee keeps it so; but there's solace at **Le Majestique** [124–5 D2], tucked just around the corner.

Out of the centre: Ouaga's districts Avenue Kwame N'Krumah is a marvel. But there's much more to Ouaga culture, culinary excitement and nightlife than this permanently pumping main drag. Made up of several distinctive *quartiers*, each of Ouaga's districts has something to offer and a vibe well worth investigating.

They include **Paspanga**, popular with artists and *dolo* drinkers in equal measure, and **Ouaga 2000**, the futuristic cement jungle of new ministerial residences, conference premises and the country's flashest hotel, the Laico. **Kamsonghin, Cité An II** and **Patte d'Oie** to the south of town have a host of *maquis* and *jardins*, including the New Rejouissance, L'Opera, Club Tokyo and Restaurant Jabez (m *76 58 06 50*), which serves delicious Cameroonian food including braised fish, *ndole* and *mbongo*.

Zone du Bois is the upmarket quarter *par excellence*, with smart restaurants to match. Expats and local high-ups mingle under the leafy shade of suitably lush plants, and garden sprinklers work overtime.

Two of the liveliest districts are **Gounghin**, which comprises the area west of the centre, and **Dapoya**, to the north. Both are a short taxi ride away, and offer a multitude of going-out options, some of which we suggest below, along with a few other far-flung nightspots.

Gounghin With plenty of decent restaurants and cultural diversion on offer, Gounghin teeters towards trendy. Before the advent of the rather stuffy Zone du Bois, it was Ouagadougou's swankiest district, populated by diplomatic types and the grandest of government functionaries. The elegance of its southern half is tempered by the fun-loving streets to the north of the road running to Bobo, which cuts Gounghin in half. This is the area surrounding Burkina's national stadium, and whatever the fortunes of Burkina's football team (and supporting *Les Etalons* can be a trying business), the bars, fast-food joints and street stalls are always in the mood for a party. The best place to start is at the Total garage junction, where **Le Boukmantier** *maquis* [116–17 B4] pumps out Ivorian tunes. Keep on going up towards the stadium – you'll find no shortage of street food and bars for grazing along the way – until you hit the bright-red **Sport Bar** [116–17 B4] on the right. Pick up some tasty grub from the stalls outside, head on in, and you'll find one of Ouaga's great nights out. On Friday through to Sunday, it's host to 'Les Elites du Faso', an upbeat band that belts out African classics all night. The crowd tends towards genteel middle class; men from the ministries rock up on *motos* and dance the night away with wives (or more likely girlfriends) done up to the nines in crisp white *boubous* or beautifully embroidered two-sets. Music starts at 21.00 Friday/Saturday, 19.00 on Sunday. For a change of scene, head up to the top junction and turn right for the eternally popular bar-dancing **La Citadelle** [116–17 B4], or left for the equally rocking **La Flotte** [116–17 A4]. Refresh yourself with an ice cream at **Dany Ice** [116–17 A4] (*50 39 19 62*) opposite the stadium, then head back down to the **Black & White** [116–17 A4] nightclub to take you through till dawn. For something a bit different, check out what's happening at the **Reemdoogo Cultural Centre** [116–17 B4] (see page 142).

Dapoya Dapoya is disco central, and like any self-respecting dive it keeps going all night. A hangout for gamblers, womanisers and music-lovers, its main road is jammed with neatly lined-up shining mopeds. The heels are high, and the jeans drainpipe-tight.

No night-owl should miss **Matata** [139 F3]. It was once a great live-music venue; those days have gone, but it's still a hugely popular nightspot, and not entirely *pour les bandits*, as some older Ouagalais would have you believe. Sink a few beers here, then head around the corner to **Jamaica Reggae Station** [139 F3], which plays host to live reggae from 22.00 on Friday, Saturday and Sunday. There's sometimes a small cover charge. If reggae's not your bag, wend your way up to **Le Tango** [139 E2] (locals say 'Tango-Tango', which means 'a bit drunk' in Moore), where they've rammed in umpteen tables around the glitterball dance floor; work up an appetite, then graze at the food stalls outside, or refresh yourself at **Harlem Degue** [139 D2] across the road. *Degue* is a delicious Mossi yoghurt and millet mix, not a million miles away from Fulani *gappal*. When it all gets too hot, try out **First Class Bar-Dancing** [139 E2], where the seating's all red velvet under glowing red lights, but the air conditioning keeps things cool.

Nearby, **Maison Bon Yaourt** [139 G3] is the Bar Italia of Ouagadougou, offering much-needed all-night refreshment to weary revellers. During the day, it is quite the refined patisserie and espresso house. Come 02.00, it contains shells of men taking brief respite before ploughing back into the music and beer pits. You can buy pastries, real coffee from Italian machines, cold soft drinks and excellent fresh yoghurt. Up around the corner you'll find **Labrador** [139 G3], a real men's talking shop, where groups of friends wave their arms around, putting the world to rights and yelling to have the music turned down if they can't hear each other speak. Follow the road up, take a right and then a left to find **Le Leader** [139 G1], an unmissable *maquis* where the music thumps night and day; **Music Hall** [116–17 D2] has lively outdoor dancing with a laid-back atmosphere, with a 500f entry ticket on Saturdays. With your back to Matata, head left for a three-minute drive until the asphalt stops, turn right and it's on your right.

Towards Cité An III, **Nirvana** nightclub [139 A3] is a dazzling, mirrored place that's free on Fridays, but charges 4,000f entry on Saturdays. Don't dream of turning up before midnight.

Others out of the centre For anyone in search of further nightclub vibes, **La Tapoa** is still going strong on weekends at the Hotel Silmande and attracts a high-class crowd, as does **The Mask**, down in the Laico Hotel in Ouaga 2000.

CULTURAL CENTRES

Institut Français (former CCF)

(*Av de la Nation; Mediathèque* ☎ *50 30 60 97/98;* e *ccfgm@ccfouaga.com; www.ccfouaga.com;* ⊕ *09.00–12.00 Tue, Thu & Sat, 15.00–18.30 Tue–Sat; tickets from 1,000f*) Comprising an exhibition space, cinema, bar and restaurant, theatre, concert hall and library, the Institut is a hive for the best of culture in the capital, and plays a part in every major festival in Ouagadougou, whether screening top films at Fespaco or red-hot jazz concerts. A new *mediathèque* was opened in January 2011, adding sizeable press, youth/children's and sound/image sections to the ensemble. You can pick up a neat monthly guide to what's on from the bar, free of charge. Night-time shows and courses include pop concerts, traditional and modern drumming sessions, monthly hip-hop contests, African and European films, art exhibitions and dance lessons. The bar/restaurant cooks up a good range of quick dishes and salads, and is Ouaga's Left Bank – full of young artists plugging paintings, deconstructing culture, and looking for like-minded souls.

Espace Culturel Napam Beogo

[116–17 C2] (*Rue Niandjila, Gounghin;* ☎ *50 34 66 26;* m *70 23 84 86;* e *espacenapambeogo@yahoo.fr; www.espacenapambeogo.*

com) Less focused on performances and more on exhibitions, training of artisans and artists, and development. There's a rehearsal studio and exhibition space; meals and some accommodation are available (more around the corner at the Residence Napam Beogo). This is also the headquarters for Fair Trade in Burkina.

Le Reemdoogo cultural centre [116–17 B4] (*Rue de Grenoble, Gounghin;* ☏ *50 34 61 18/19*) Comprising music practice studios, a concert space and music café-restaurant, it's well worth giving the centre a call to find out what's going on.

American Cultural Center (*Ouaga 2000;* ☏ *50 49 53 00*) This good anglophone resource has upped sticks from the centre, along with the American embassy, so is now a fair hike for the average traveller, but worth it if you're around for a while. The **Martin Luther King Library** is also nearby.

THEATRE AND DANCE The **Theatre Espace Culturel Gambidi** [116–17 H2] (*Bd Charles de Gaulle;* ☏ *50 30 59 42*) is a lively centre near the National Archives and National Museum, housing both Radio Gambidi and Theatre Gambidi with a nice outdoor snack area, showcasing local scriptwriting and performing talent.

FESTIVALS IN OUAGA

In addition to the biennial treats of **Fespaco** (see page 51) and **SIAO** (see page 146), Ouaga hosts plenty of other festivals.

JAZZ À OUAGA (*Institut Français & Maison du Peuple;* m *70 25 85 08, 70 26 28 03;* e *jazz_ouaga@yahoo.fr; http://jazz.zcp.bf*) It's not always strictly jazz, but Burkina is proud of hosting a celebration of what former culture minister Mahmoudou Ouedraogo called 'one of the greatest recognised and accepted contributions of the black man to the edification of universal civilisation'. Previous performers include Burkina's Bil Aka Kora, Mali's Ali Farka Toure, Dutch group Fra Fra Sound and the French Florin Niculescu quartet. After every official evening concert, all musicians are welcome for an impromptu late-night jamming session. In 2010 and 2011, it was at the Azalai Hotel Independence, but it's supposed to move regularly. The ten-day festival is held every April.

FESTIVAL OUAGA HIP-HOP (m *70 23 73 89,* e *umaneculture@yahoo.fr*) Takes over the coolest city hangouts every October and November. There are hip-hop dance lessons, graffiti workshops and sound-technician and management guidance. Venues include Ciné Neerwaya for the national finals of the Ouaga Rap Awards, and the Institut Français.

INTERNATIONAL FESTIVAL OF THEATRE FOR DEVELOPMENT Organised by the famed Atelier Theatre Burkinabe, this festival takes place every February in even-numbered years, with numerous theatre workshops and powerful performances bringing alive themes such as sexual health and justice.

FITMO (☏ *50 36 59 42;* m *70 25 07 32*) One of the most visually arresting of Burkina's festivals, the International Festival of Theatre and Marionettes of Ouagadougou sees 10m-high puppets parade around Ouaga's main streets. Held every even-numbered year in October.

OPEN-AIR CINEMA

No cinephile should leave Burkina without visiting an open-air cinema. *Ouaga Saga*, a film by Burkinabe director Dani Kouyaté, captures perfectly the romance of outdoor movie-going, with its depiction of a group of young Ouagalais at the flicks, their wide, transfixed eyes reflecting the images of the big screen as they perch on concrete pews under the stars. You can have the same experience at **Ciné Wemtenga** [116–17 G3] (*behind Bd Charles de Gaulle*), where it was filmed. Seats are 200–400f; some include a covered section with metal chairs, but all deliver the magic of cinema under a starry African sky. In the town centre, head for **Ciné Oubri** [124–5 E3] (*50 31 14 79*) on Rue Patrice Lumumba, the road running south of the market.

CENASA (*Av Oubritenga; 50 31 78 54; e cenasa@cenasa.bf; www.cenasa.bf*) is a lovely theatre with regular productions. **La Termitiere** [116–17 C5] (*50 30 51 60*) is a centre for choreography and dance south of the Stade Municipal. The **Maison du Peuple** [124–5 D2] (*Av de la Nation*) is a concert and theatre venue, regularly hosting national and international artists, while the **Institut Français** also regularly puts on African and touring plays.

CINEMA Don't miss out on movie-watching in the capital of African cinema. A visit is likely to be an experience in itself, no matter what is showing. Audiences tend to be mightily involved in the action, and don't hold back, cheering every punch and plot twist; hissing at the nefarious machinations of onscreen villains; and laughing at gloriously inappropriate killing-spree moments. The spell may be broken by frequent trilling of mobile phones, loud and lengthy conversations and audience members shuffling in and out with every frame.

Where to watch

Ciné Burkina Av Loudun; 50 31 72 72; m 78 85 79 52. Another upmarket choice in the centre of town, with a patisserie & coffee bar for matinée showings & an outdoor terrace that gets pumping on première nights. The interior is all dark-wood panels, with a section of ultra-posh seating. Tickets cost 1,000–2,000f, depending on the film & where you sit.

Ciné Neerwaya [116–17 C3] Cité An III; 50 31 72 72. A large, indoor hall, assisted by powerful AC, Dolby stereo & comfortable seats, makes for the country's finest screen. It doubles as a concert hall for events such as the annual Burkina Hip-Hop Awards & has a lively outdoor bar & eaterie serving *brochettes*. Tickets cost from 1,000f.

The **George Méliès Cinema** at the **Institut Français** has themed cinema seasons.

SHOPPING

Ouaga is home to some of the best arts and crafts in Africa. There are endless opportunities for browsing stalls and shops that house workmanship of exceptional quality. Alongside this, there is also more pedestrian work that is aimed at an undiscerning tourist market.

MARKETS

Marché Rood Wooko [124–5 D3] Having been destroyed by fire in May 2003, the Rood Wooko market was slowly rebuilt and finally reopened in 2009. Its airy, orderly rows of stalls are a far cry from its former incarnation; the thousands of kiosks that were jumbled together across all floors and corners had become too hectic, and too difficult to regulate. The fire provided a welcome excuse to close it down and start again from scratch.

The new market is not without its controversies. Many of the merchants who used to ply their trade here have now returned – but many, also, have not. Disputes over rights to shops and kiosks still rage, with the result that many remained locked and unused; for others, the new regulated rental system is too expensive, and they continue to trade elsewhere.

A wander around will bring endless calls and appeals from traders, mostly good-humoured. The ground floor belongs to fresh produce and meat, kitchenware and the like, while upstairs is the preserve of clothes and fabrics and a substantial artisanal section, on the southern side. Traders complain here that business is very slow, so you will be made very welcome, and it may well be a good spot for a bargain.

Other markets The destruction of the main market helped business in outlying districts, and even with its reopening, these areas continue to thrive. **Sankariaré**, in Dapoya, is one of the largest markets in Ouagadougou. **Pissi** is popular on Thursdays and **Gounghin** on Fridays. **Zabre-Daaga market** [124–5 E4], with stationery and electrical goods, runs east from Avenue Kwame N'Krumah and its narrow stalls make a nice detour.

FOOD Several supermarkets stock imported goods and fresh meat at correspondingly high prices. **Marina supermarket** is the best known, with three branches in town: opposite the *grande mosquée* on Avenue Yennenga ([124–5 D4] *50 31 09 65*); in Gounghin (*50 34 09 96*); and by the Patte d'Oie roundabout ([116–17 D7] *50 38 27 38*). Women sell a decent selection of fruit and veg outside each. **Scimas** [124–5 D3] (*50 30 62 80*) is a smaller supermarket, also on Avenue Yennenga.

Marché des Fruits There is fruit and vegetable action all over Ouaga, at markets where women who speak only Moore sell their wares under wooden frames. But for unrivalled craziness, head for the road beside Scimas supermarket on Avenue Yennenga.

Here, even a momentary stop to investigate a couple of squishy mangoes will bring hordes of persistent young women running. Any intention to purchase confirms you as their prey, and fights frequently break out between the women over customers. To keep you away from competitors, fruity deals may be done in secret far from the market, with a go-between rushing backwards and forwards to find the products you want. Any return trip – if you can take another one following such an experience – will find you greeted as a long-lost friend and you will have to buy from your original saleswoman or risk starting another punch-up, so choose wisely.

A smaller, more civilised collection of fruit and veg sellers can be found behind the bus stop outside Patisserie Bonbonnière on Avenue de la Nation. If you want an easier, although more expensive experience, head for the stalls outside supermarkets, or find a veg market in a little-frequented district unused to foreign visitors. Perhaps the nicest way to buy is from one of the many female street vendors who walk alone, piling – depending on season – delicious fresh strawberries, carrots, tomatoes, peppers, green beans, bananas, pineapples, papayas or avocadoes into baskets on their heads.

BOOKS Tiny metal stalls hung with the word *Librarie* can be a wonderful source of secondhand books. Try the area behind Jardin de l'Amitié, at the UN roundabout, or the bookshops opposite the Culture Ministry. Scour carefully and you may find literary classics from Nigeria and Ghana, in English. **Diacfa** bookshop [124–5 D3], Rue de l'Hotel de Ville, opposite the market, is an excellent source of maps, current-affairs magazines, culture and history titles and some local-language books.

MUSIC You won't go far in the centre of town, day or night, without being approached by someone selling CDs. Numerous *discothèques*, many with sound systems to try-before-you-buy, also sell CDs for around 1,000f each, less if you buy in bulk. The stall on Avenue Lumumba, opposite Photoluxe, is one good starting point. The stalls outside the Ciné Burkina are another good bet.

ARTS AND CRAFTS If you buy something, get a receipt and keep it. You may need it at customs when you leave the country.

Craft centres There is no shortage of talented Burkinabe making objects from wood, leather, cotton, clay, iron and bronze across the land, and several craft centres in the capital offer excellent viewing and buying opportunities. Alongside galleries where you can look at and purchase a range of goods, you can often see artisans at work as well. Below we list a few craft centres where works are made on site, but plenty of their wares are also available at the gift shops in the next section.

Village Artisanal de Ouagadougou [116–17 F5] (*Av Tansoba Kiema;* ☎ *50 37 14 83;* e *village.artisanal@fasonet.bf*) More than 300 artists and master craftsmen exhibit at this arts and crafts centre and the quality of work is outstanding. A stroll around the workshops – turning out one-off bronze and wooden sculptures, jewellery, leatherware, fabrics and cloth and musical instruments – is the epitome of non-stressful shopping. A particular find is the stall making animal-horn cutlery, necklaces and hair accessories. Bobo-based Gafreh (see page 286) have a workshop here, as do Papiers du Sahel (see page 148). Prices in the workshops are negotiable, while the air-conditioned boutique, which takes Visa, displays selected artisanal work at fixed and slightly higher prices. You can recover at the Café des Pros coffee shop, which also does decent food; there's also a bureau de change and cybercafé.

Le Centre National d'Artisanat d'Art [124–5 E2] (*Av Dimdolobsom;* ☎ *50 30 68 35, 50 30 22 30;* e *cnaa@mcc.gov.bf*) A smaller, more central option. Prices are fixed, so a fairly hassle-free visit can give you a sense of what to pay, especially if you're keen to bargain hard with the street traders plying their sometimes pretty decent wares on the road outside. You can visit workshops behind the small showroom.

Vitrines de Bronze [124 C2] (*Av de la Nation*) This is the public-friendly locus of bronzework in the city, with clean-cut kiosks displaying a range of work. You can see the bronzers at work in the square behind the kiosks. Xavier Bougma (m *70 30 79 18*) will be happy to explain his work to you.

Atelier de Fonderie de Bronze Derme [139 B1] Niogsin is the city's bronze-making quarter, where children learn their grandparents' craft. The Derme family is one of Ouaga's best-known exponents, with *ateliers* in Ouidi, Niogsin and Dapoya. At the **Atelier Derme Daouda et Fils** (*Av de Dapoya*) you can see artisans at work, all expert in the lost-wax technique, and choose from a range of statues, bracelets,

SIAO

Every even-numbered year in late October, Burkina hosts a continent-wide artisanal extravaganza. Batik, paintings, handmade drums, bronzes, baskets, sculpture, furniture, textiles, shoes, pottery, jewellery, ceramics, leatherwork and clothing from all four corners of Africa are on show.

The first Salon International de l'Artisanat de Ouagadougou (SIAO) took shape in 1988, developing an earlier idea, Handicraft '84, which saw Burkina's craftsmen from different spheres coming together to compete. These days, SIAO opens its doors to more than 300 exhibitors from dozens of nations, housed in a specially constructed building next to the Village Artisanal, selling in a hassle-free environment and attracting a quarter of a million international buyers and visitors.

The informal sale of arts and crafts is a huge money-making sector for Burkina. More than half a million Burkinabe are artisans, generating 25% of GDP, second only to agriculture. It's hard to turn this into an export success, however. That's why the market is accompanied by eight days of discussion and addresses from the president and other dignitaries. Recent talking points include encouraging exports, stemming the drop in prices, the role of e-commerce, and advice from craftsmen, trainers and specialists on maintaining standards. Perhaps a victim of its own success, local artisans complain the price of a stall at SIAO has become prohibitively high, favouring other better-established African markets rather than Burkina's own fledgling industry.

Despite the discussion of the bottom line, there is plenty for the casual viewer – rather than the bulk buyer – eager to find a unique piece that calls out to be bought. Showrooms open at 09.30 to professionals, and at 12.30 for the public; tickets cost 1,000f to enter all areas, or 500f excluding air-conditioned pavilions.

village scenes and the odd ashtray. If you don't like what's on show, you can request a design – allow a week for a chunky bronze bracelet.

Centre de Formation Feminine et Artisanale (*Gounghin;* ☎ *50 34 28 90, 50 34 31 41;* ⌚ *Mon–Fri, Sat mornings*) You can visit this state-funded rug-making school for young women and see the work close-up. They dye the cotton, weave it on a loom and finish it all by hand. Alongside the usual tablecloths and placemats are deliciously thick and well-made pile rugs in red-brown, black and white – typical Ouaga colours. Have your money at the ready, as the rugs can be suitably expensive (130,000f for large designs).

Fondation Olorun [116–17 A4] (*Rue Toagba, Gounghin*) A cutting-edge workshop that turns out contemporary art and furniture, much of it made from reclaimed oil barrels, wood and anything else the talented bunch of young artisans and ex-street kids can salvage. It also hosts exhibitions of painters. Turn right at the big yellow *immeuble* just before the Bobo flyover.

La Case de la Sculpture [116–17 E1] (*Behind Silmande Hotel;* m *78 81 71 00*) An excellent *atelier* that works mainly in ebony, teak, cedar and hippo's tooth (an ivory substitute). Well worth a visit to see the carvers at work, spilling out from the small boutique all over the street. There are examples of their work across the city

– look out for carved trees in public spaces. Speak to the patron, Monsieur Konate, to discuss bespoke orders.

FM (*Zone du Bois;* *50 36 14 92;* *Mon–Fri, Sat mornings*) Women's co-operative making handmade embroidered and tie-dye tablecloths, placemats, aprons and children's clothes.

Centre Napam Beogo [116–17 C2] (*Rue 11.39, Ouidi;* *50 35 35 14;* m *70 23 84 86;* e *asso_napambeogo@yahoo.fr; www.napam-beogo.org*) Artisanal centre specialising in musical instruments, bronze and batik; the *atelier* of the cultural centre and residence of the same name in Gounghin. Also offers workshops and training.

Gift shops and artefacts

Copafo [124–5 E3] 50 50 47 91; Mon–Fri, Sat mornings. This women's co-operative in the centre of town turns out a great selection of tasteful shirts, dresses, fabrics, bags & earthy necklaces.

Decouvrez La Culture Africaine [124–5 F4] Av de Koulouba, just after the Radio Nostalgie bdg, Koulouba; 50 31 61 43; m 78 81 88 20. This cluttered shop has an impressive range of artefacts, new & old, from across west & central Africa, in wood, bronze & iron. Statues & masks are particularly strong, & the owner, Osseini knows his stuff.

Galerie Lafon [116–17 E3] Rue Raoul Follereau, off Bd Charles de Gaulle; 50 33 43 40; e mathiaslafon@africartisanat.com; www.africartisanat.com. Galerie Lafon makes for a wonderful visit, even if you don't wish to buy. There are wood sculptures, masks, benches & brass from all over west & central Africa, at fairly fixed prices. Elegant Mauritanian chests vie for space with square, blue-moon representations from Côte d'Ivoire, & enormous Guinean totems. It is an easy shopping environment, with no pressure to purchase, though with items starting from as little as 1,500f it's hard to leave empty handed. If you're uncomfortable buying anything that may rightly belong in someone else's home, ask the owners about the provenance of the artefacts. Next to Radio Burkina; go through the military post & it's on the left (white gates).

Galerie Nuances [124–5 D2] Av Yennenga; 50 31 72 74; e nuancebf@yahoo.fr; early closing Sun, & for the 3 months of the year that the owner spends in Europe. A good one-stop shop before you hit the plane back home if you're looking for hassle-free shopping, housing Tuareg & other jewellery, recycled paper, shea-butter soap, wooden frames & a delightful collection of cotton & leather bags. Earthenware bowls & mugs are exceptionally reasonably priced. The owner takes a supportive interest in small *ateliers*, & is a good person to ask if you're interested in arranging visits.

Galerie Zak'Apoto [124–5 D5] Av Yennenga; 50 45 99 54; e apoto50@yahoo.fr. This shop, within the Zaka complex, sells a good range of paintings & fabrics (including *bogolans*), along with clothes & jewellery.

K-Lala [124–5 E2] Av Dimdolobson; 50 31 76 09; m 70 20 55 81; e k-lala@liptinfor.net; www.k-lala.net. Run by a Franco-Spanish woman who is a dab hand at interior decoration, adapting traditional African art to Western tastes with unabashed panache. Tasteful designs go down well with expats setting up home in the capital, although smaller items & jewellery would make good gifts.

Other places include **Galerie D'Art Traditionel Africain** [139 F2] (m *78 56 00 79, 70 12 81 13*) in Dapoya, which has a good selection of Dogon doors, and an even better one of masks from right across the region. **Africa Art** and **Moussa et Frères** [139 F2] (m *78 82 50 15*) opposite Dapoya church are also worth a look for masks, statues, benches and bronzes. Africa Art has two other branches, one in Larle and the other opposite CENASA near the Lycée Nelson Mandela. There is also a great **jewellery shop** at the Stade Municipale [116–17 C4], especially highly

PAPIERS DU SAHEL

Papiers du Sahel is a papermaking project that was started in 2001 by Beth Jacob, an American archaeologist, with the aim of sustaining the lives of poor Ouagalais women, many of whom used to rely on heavy and ill-paid labour such as sorting gravel for their living. In the early days, it was in a tiny workshop in Wemtenga, with no electricity or running water. The women did not know how to hold a pair of scissors, or follow a design. With Beth's guidance, they soon learned, and the project went from strength to strength.

The papermaking process is a lengthy one. Various organisations, including the French embassy, tip off shredded scrap paper every month, and the women add water to turn it into a pulp. Depending on the style of the paper, boiled grasses and dyes are added, and pounded in the same way as millet. Still moist, the paste is added to two bathtubs of water. The women pan the water for pulp with a muslin screen, and press out the sludge onto fabric squares, which are piled up and compacted in a press.

The next stage is to peg the fabric, like rows of brilliant-coloured clothes, to a washing line, until the sheets dry out in the sun. After peeling the sheets from the fabric backing and giving each a final iron, the paper is ready to be cut, folded and stuck with local glue made from yam starch. Then it's fashioned into eminently purchasable items: handmade envelopes, scrapbooks, memo blocks, photo albums, printer paper, boxes and greeting cards.

The idea was for all profits to go to the women and to the running of the centre; the aim was to take enough orders for each woman to earn 2,000f a day. The women worked long hours on painstakingly fiddly orders to realise that aim – until Beth left in 2008. Before doing so, she tried to assure the women's future by securing a site at the Village Artisanal. The 18 women moved, and have been based there ever since. A happy ending? Sadly, no. The rent for the site is a crippling 40,000f a month, with 2,500f for electricity on top. The women struggle to make any profit for themselves; without Beth's input and contacts, the wider market has dried up, and the Village is their only outlet. When we visited, they were understandably depressed and discouraged.

This tale illustrates how hard it can be to sustain a living as an artisan. Visitors can help enormously by buying the products, or by providing sustained support in some other way (see *Travelling positively*, page 111).

recommended for its made-to-order beaded necklaces, design flair and quality. It can combine new and old, *avant garde* and any other style you care to mention.

Street sellers The road alongside Hotel Independence has an enviable selection of mostly recently made but pretty good wooden masks, seats, statues and bronzes. The hard sell can be a bit *too* hard, but it's real bargaining territory, so if you see something you like see what price you can get. There are similar stalls opposite the Centre Artisanal on Avenue Dimdolobsom.

OTHER PRACTICALITIES

MONEY It's hard to walk around central Ouaga without passing a bank, and most of them have ATMs. **BIB**, **BICIA-B**, **SGBB**, **Bank of Africa**, **Ecobank** and **Banque Atlantique** are the most visible; BIB and BICIA-B have probably the most reliable

Visa ATMs, and may also be able to change travellers' cheques. Head for branches of Banque Atlantique for MasterCard ATMs. Avenue Kwame N'Krumah has branches of all the main banks. Other cash machines can be found along Avenue de la Liberté in Dapoya; on Avenue de la Nation opposite the Bonbonnière patisserie; at the SGBB bank next to the town hall; and opposite the Tam-Tam restaurant in Gounghin, and in many other locations. Marina supermarket can also change euros.

COMMUNICATIONS Ouaga is full of internet cafés, of varying quality. Most of them will let you use USB keys to upload or download files, but check first. **SCS Technologies** [124–5 E5] on Avenue Kwame N'Krumah (*50 30 12 71; e scs_sarl@yahoo.fr; 24hrs*) has a fast but expensive connection, at 750f an hour. It has a kiosk for digital camera memory cards (of all types), enabling customers to burn pictures to CD-ROM. At the UN roundabout, the post office, **Sonapost** [139 A2], has a good, reliable service for 500f an hour. For a cheap central option, go to La Toile (*Av Loudoun; 50 31 58 91*), which has a pretty good connection for only 300f an hour.

If you're up in Dapoya, head for **Universal Communication** [139 A3] (*white building that forms the corner of Le Festival bar; 50 30 50 50, 50 30 40 40; until 21.30 daily*), an IT centre and training school a little out of the way by the Shell station. Fast and reliable connections are excellent value (300f an hour). It also has a printer, photocopier and fax. Abdou Ouedraogo, the friendly owner, speaks good English.

EMERGENCIES

Ambulance 50 30 66 44/45	**Police** 17 or 50 30 63 83, 50 30 71 00
Fire service 18 or 50 30 69 47/48	**Police distress calls** 80 00 11 45
Gendarmerie 50 31 33 39/40	

French medical centre [116–17 E3] The **Centre Medical de l'Ambassade de France (CMI)** (*50 30 66 07; m 70 20 00 00 in emergency; e cmi.ouaga@gmail.com*) is by far the best option for travellers, with quick and efficient diagnosis, although the waiting room gets busy. A consultation costs 15,000f and a malaria blood test 12,000f; out-of-hours consultations cost 25,000f, or 40,000f after 20.00. Any medicines prescribed cost extra, and you can get them from a pharmacy.

Pharmacies Many pharmacies operate a rotation system to ensure there is always 24-hour access in the centre of town. Consult page two of *Sidwaya*, the state daily paper, for that day's *pharmacie de garde*, or head for the **Centre National Hospitalier Universitaire Yalgado** [116–17 E2] (*Av Oubritenga; 50 31 16 55/57*), where the pharmacy is always open.

WHAT TO SEE AND DO

MORO NABA'S PALACE AND CEREMONY [116–17 C4] (*Av Bassawarga*) A visit to Ouagadougou without paying appropriate respects to the Mossi emperor, whose seat of power has rested here since 1681, would be a little churlish. The perfect time to do it is on a Friday morning at about 07.00, in time for the short weekly ceremony of the False Departure.

Local Mossi dignitaries and loyal Ouagalais arrive from 06.30 in cars, buses, bicycles and motorbikes. Nobles sit on the ground in order of seniority, while onlookers gather in the scrub area by the trees. Courtiers ready the Moro Naba's horse with saddle and decorative riding regalia. The Moro Naba emerges, dressed in warrior red, to the beat of a solitary drum, ready to sally forth from his kingdom.

Following frantic exhortations from his most senior advisors, he undergoes a change of heart, his horse is unsaddled and he goes back into his palace. He returns dressed in white, to show his commitment to his people and to peace. Watch out for the rather surprising, and noisy, cannon shots that accompany all this.

As far as the legendary significance of the False Departure goes, there are several explanations. One of them is that back in the early 18th century, the Naba Warga's favourite wife ran off with palace fetishes for the village of La. The Moro Naba, on waking to find both missing, was furious and prepared to set off and bring them back. As he saddled his horse and chose his warriors, his ministers argued his duty lay in Ouagadougou. Happily for the kingdom, the Moro Naba was persuaded and stayed put.

More romantic versions have it that the favourite wife had merely gone to visit her family, and the Moro Naba was sick with worry when she didn't return. Whatever the story, the weekly re-enaction is still an important show of unity, and a reminder of a Mossi leader's commitment to his people rather than his pride.

MUSÉE NATIONAL DU BURKINA FASO [116–17 H3] (*Bd Charles de Gaulle; 50 39 19 34; musee-national.burkinafaso@yahoo.fr; Tue–Sat; entry 1,000f*) Following extensive French-funded renovation, re-cataloguing and rebranding to the tune of more than CFA150 million, the National Museum is up and running again. The collection contains 7,500 exhibits, including jewellery, archaeological remains, Bobo masks, Lobi and Senoufou wooden statues, musical instruments, arms and farming tools. It has also launched a travelling exhibition about the history, practice and dangers of excision, which tours rural villages every year. In 2011, it was about to launch a new programme of activities and exhibitions; first up will be 'A comme Afrique', an A–Z of 26 modules. B will be for bronze, C for cuisine, D for diaspora, E for exploitation, and so on. It's set to run until February 2012.

MUSÉE DE LA MUSIQUE (*Av Oubritenga; 50 32 40 60; www.museemusique.com; Tue–Sat; 1,000f*) The museum's marvellous fairytale building has been undergoing extensive renovations to improve its ventilation and expand the exhibition space. When it reopens, there will be a cybercafé, café-restaurant and music studio to boot. Should there be a delay, you can still find a temporary version not far from the National Museum along Boulevard Charles de Gaulle.

The museum houses an array of traditional instruments, some of which you're free to touch and try to get a sound out of. A good guide can take you round several rooms, each dedicated to a different type of instrument – drums, keys, wind and strings. In the course of equipping the museum, researchers found that many chiefs refused to let go of sacred instruments for fear of offending the spirits and the ancestors, while others demanded too hefty a fee, such as a cow for sacrifice. Other chiefs, however, were delighted to help and the collection is excellent and worth supporting.

PARC URBAIN BANGR-WEOOGO (*100f; photo permit 1,000f*) Ouaga's urban park, with crocodile lagoons, a mini zoo and well-tended gardens, is home to some lovely wooden sculpture from local artists. Try to go as early or as late as possible to escape the sun. An amiable café along Boulevard Charles de Gaulle offers some respite, serving up stock meals such as *riz gras* and chips.

CATHEDRAL OF THE IMMACULATE CONCEPTION [124–5 B5] (*Av Bassawarga; 50 31 13 39; Mass takes place in Moore at 05.45 Mon–Fri, 06.00 & 07.30 Sun. French mass is sung at 18.30 on Sat/Sun*) This distinctive red-brick cathedral was first conceived in 1926 by Monseigneur Thévenoud, although the first stone was not laid until 1934. The benediction of the cathedral took place in 1936, and the building has served as the centre of the Christian community ever since. Services are worth a look, especially at momentous moments in the Catholic calendar.

MAISON DU PEUPLE (*Av de la Nation*) Right in the middle of town, this concert hall hosts all manner of dance, musical and theatrical acts. Look out for signs posted on trees around town for news of the next one. Past shows have included an ace performance by Malian blues legend Ali Farka Toure, during the ten-day Ouaga Jazz festival, and a rather unlikely beer-fest every April with only west African beers on offer. Still, at marginally cheaper-than-bar prices, it was very popular.

THOMAS SANKARA'S GRAVE [116–17 G4] (*Cimetière Dagmounouna, Zogona*) Easily reached from the Rue Tansoba Kiema that goes past the Village Artisanal, this overgrown cemetery includes the revolutionary president's distinctly low-key tombstone. The grave itself is decorated with gaudy writing like the side of a soap box and with a *boubou* design on the top of the sarcophagus. His wife is buried next to him (she died in 1992) and 12 lieutenants are lined up behind. It still draws pilgrims from across Africa, and fresh flowers are still regularly placed on the grave.

Sankara's father, Joseph Sambo Sankara, an ex-*gendarme*, still lives near the *gendarmerie* in Paspanga. His house, should you want to pay homage to it, is just down the road from the small Carmelia resto on none other than Rue Sankara Sambo Joseph.

HORSERIDING As befits a country with the equestrian heritage of Burkina, the capital hosts some good stables. There are three riding schools in town (see below), with competitions and cultural shows a frequent feature. You can also organise a spot of horseriding with the self-styled *chevaliers* who hang out in places such as the Institut Français, Ouaga Jungle and Zaca. While competent guides and riders, their horses might not be as well broken-in as those at official stables, and can be more difficult to control. **Elsa** (m *76 62 79 96*) has eight horses to the west of Ouaga and comes highly recommended from a reader, but despite persistent efforts we have been unable to contact her on the number we have, shown above: it is worth a try, nonetheless.

The **Club de l'Etrier** [116–17 E2] (m *78 86 38 38*), just off the Fada road in Zone du Bois, is the most central option. It's beautifully kept, with full-size schools, and is registered with the FFE (*Federation Française de l'Equitation*). There's a wide range of mounts to suit all abilities. It offers lessons, or hacks in the nearby Parque Urbaine for 10,000f an hour.

The **Oasis du Cheval** (m *78 20 63 67, 70 20 63 67;* e *oasisducheval@yahoo.fr; www.oasisducheval.com*) is at the eastern edge of town, on the Fada road. Turn right at the big OTAM petrol station, head towards Saaba and it is further on the left. It is run by Modibo Traore, one of Burkina's most proficient horsemen. An hour's hack costs 12,500f, two hours 20,000f, or you can do trail rides into the bush, visit surrounding villages and camp overnight. The team goes out ahead to prepare a campfire and food. All you need to do is arrive, feast on *brochettes* and baked potato, and ride back in the cool of the morning. Camping trips cost about 30,000f per person for six, going up to 45,000f if there are only two of you. Modibo can hire out tents and mattresses.

The stables at **Club du Cheval Mandingue** (*50 43 60 76;* m *76 61 43 56;* e *chevalmandingue@gmail.com*) in Pissi regularly puts on horse spectaculars to celebrate Burkina's heritage. From the Bobo road, take a right at the Yampoutin Restaurant (if you see the Boulmiougou reservoir on your left you've gone too far). After about 800m take a left and it's past a patch of waste ground and the Lycée Jeanne d'Arc. An hour's ride costs 5,000f; two hours, 8,000f.

SPECTATOR SPORTS The main stadium in the country is **Stade du 4 Août,** running alongside Rue Wintoog Kieeda in Gounghin, where you can see international football matches and Burkinabe club matches. If you decide to attend, be on your guard for pickpockets and get to the stadium with enough time to pick decent seats. Tickets sell for 300f, 500f and 1,000f.

The **Stade Municipal**, near the Moro Naba's palace, also hosts Burkinabe club football matches, and occasionally comes alive as a venue for music concerts.

A word of caution: crowd control is not always what it should be. It is very rare that anything goes wrong, but at the opening ceremony of Fespaco in 2005, two girls were killed in a crush. For this reason it may be worth avoiding Block 18 in the Stade du 4 Août. It's popular because it's near the most expensive seats and offers shade from the sun, but people tend to overfill it, even when other blocks are half empty.

SWIMMING Non-guests can swim in many of Ouaga's hotel pools for a fee. Most charge 1,500–2,000f. For the cheapest swim in town, head to **Hotel Bangrin** in Larle, which has a clean, decent-sized pool without much atmosphere for 1,000f. The only Olympic-size pool in Ouaga is to be found at the **Azalai Hotel Independence**, but at 3,000f (4,500f at weekends) it's more pricey than most. On Avenue Kwame N'Krumah, **Hotel Palm Beach** is your best bet for a decent swim, and **Hotel Splendid** down the road is a good option for lounging around with a drink. The pools at **Hotel Relax** and **RAN Hotel Somketa** are both fine too.

A number of restaurants have pools: **La Forêt**, **L'Escapade** and **Les Jardins de Koulouba** are the most central. In Ouaga 2000, the **Rosa del Venti** has a pool for diners too.

Out of the centre, there are a couple of places that are really worth the trek for an afternoon of fun and frolics. Head north of *barrage* 3 for the pretty surroundings of **Hotel Ricardo**, with dining tables all around the pool, a raised terrace (tempting to dive from) and diving board. At the opposite end of town, on the road to Po, the **Village Nong Taaba** [116–17 F7] has a lovely pool surrounded by shady *paillotes*; it's free if you dine for 4,000f or more.

AROUND OUAGA

There are some lovely excursions within easy reach of the city centre. In the north, the Mossi museum at **Manega**, rock carvings at **Laongo**, the president's zoo at **Ziniare**, the holiday camp and goat's-cheese farm in **Loumbila** are all good options (see *Near Ouaga*, page 155). You can make an action-packed and tasty day of it by sandwiching lunch and a swim at Loumbila within a circuit that takes in all four.

To the south, try a swing on the **golf course**, or head for the wilderness hotel with pool at **Koubri** (see *Heading for Po*, page 223). Towards the west, sacred *caiman* lakes at **Bazoule** and **Sabou** offer plenty of arts and crafts diversion besides docile crocs (see *Near Ouaga*, page 253).

4

The North

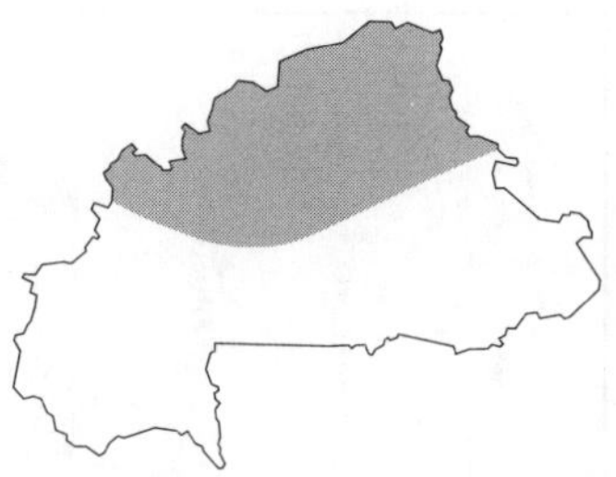

Sadly, tourism in the north of Burkina has taken a major hit recently in the form of negative travel advice from foreign governments. The UK advises against all travel in a big arc north of Boulsa, 25km from Ouaga, which effectively eliminates most of this chapter; the French advice is against travel north of Dori and into the Sahel proper. This is due to the perceived threat of terrorism from al-Qaeda in the Islamic Maghreb (AQIM), which is active across the Sahel in Mali, Mauritania and Niger. Kidnappings have been the main activity, often leading to the death of hostages; white foreigners are a principal target.

Debate rages in Burkina as to whether the advice is justified. As of mid-2011, there had been no such terrorist attacks on Burkinabe soil. Many locals, seeing tourist numbers dwindle, argue that 'their' Sahel is too small, its population too interconnected, for the threat to apply in Burkina; moreover, security measures have been stepped up, with increased police checks, and patrols along the borders. Others say, uneasily, that there is always a first time, and that the threat is, by its very nature, difficult to quantify.

The level of advice seems unlikely to change in the near future. To go is undeniably a risk, and will remain a personal decision; travel insurance is not necessarily invalidated, as many believe (see page 63). If you do decide to go, you will discover a region that has history and romance in spades.

The north's major attraction is the vast expanse of semi-desert that makes up the Burkinabe Sahel. Home to kel-Tamashek traders and Fulani cattle-herders, the ambience is totally different from the rest of the country. The town of Dori signals the change, and Gorom-Gorom, more isolated, has always enjoyed a reputation as the essential Sahelian market town. But it is trips beyond here that really delve into the magic of the sand-swept region. The dunes of Oursi hide some of the most significant archaeological ruins in west Africa, and the rainy season brings delight for the bird-spotter at its seasonal lakes. Far-flung camps at Gandefabou and Tin-Akof, where you can sleep outside under the stars in absolute stillness, capture perfectly the desert ambience.

Also in the north is the great Mossi kingdom of Yatenga, which rivalled that of Oubritenga for power and wealth. Nowadays its once-fiery capital Ouahigouya is likely to engulf you in low-slung living, and its reputation as a nonchalant party town is well deserved. Kaya is the centre of leathermakers countrywide, and anyone who likes a bag or three would be mad to miss it.

The north is also home to Burkina's old-style, and dangerous, gold-mining industry. While it may not be everyone's cup of tea, a visit to one of the settlements to see the work required in recovering just a few tiny grains of dust is fascinating.

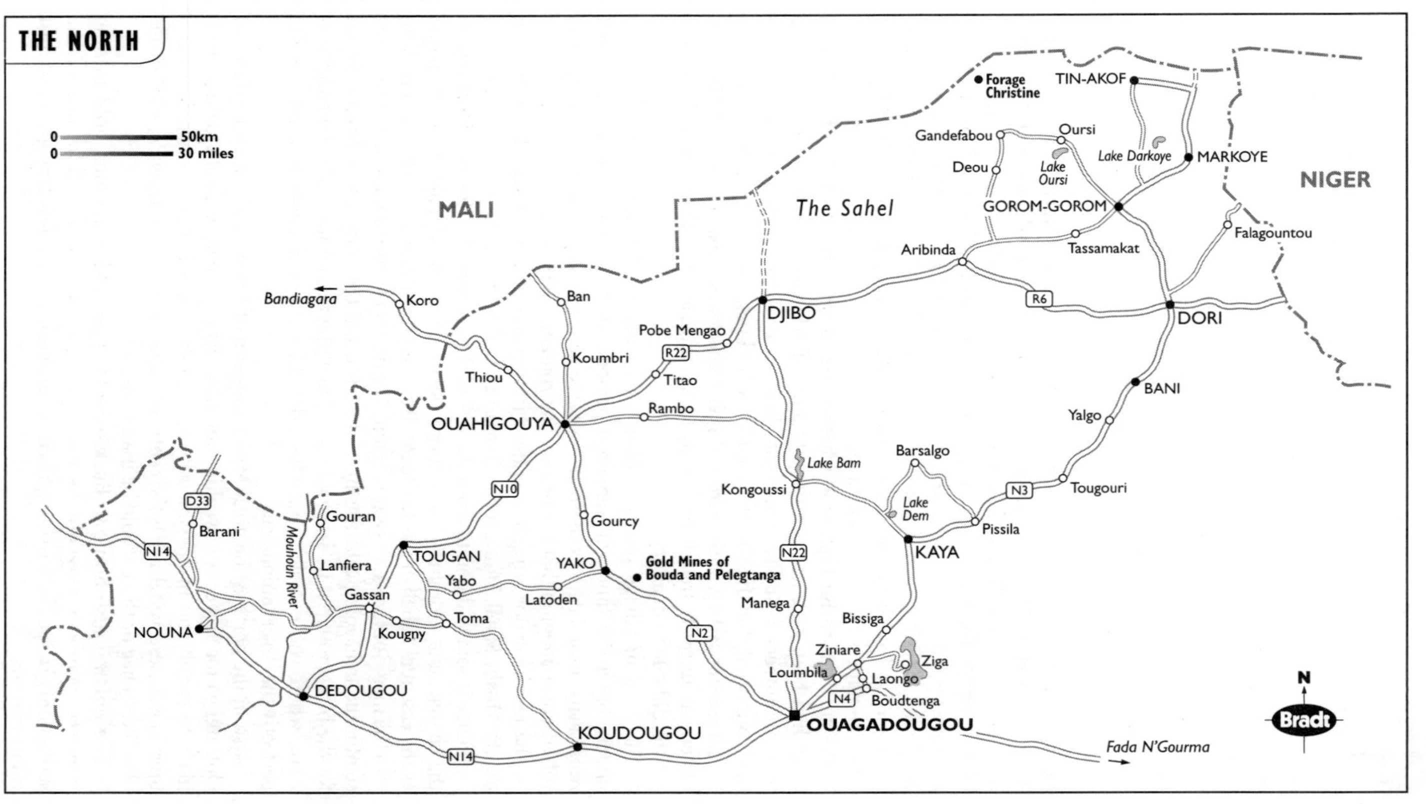
THE NORTH
0 50km
0 30 miles
MALI
The Sahel
NIGER
Forage Christine
TIN-AKOF
Gandefabou
Oursi
Lake Darkoye
MARKOYE
Deou
Lake Oursi
GOROM-GOROM
Falagountou
Aribinda
Tassamakat
Bandiagara
Koro
Ban
DJIBO
R6
DORI
Pobe Mengao
R22
Koumbri
Thiou
Titao
BANI
Rambo
OUAHIGOUYA
Yalgo
Barsalgo
Lake Bam
Kongoussi
N3
Tougouri
Lake Dem
D33
Gouran
N10
Gourcy
Pissila
Barani
Mouhoun River
N22
KAYA
N14
TOUGAN
YAKO
Gold Mines of Bouda and Pelegtanga
Lanfiera
Yabo
Latoden
Gassan
Manega
Toma
Bissiga
NOUNA
Kougny
N2
Ziniare
Ziga
Loumbila
Laongo
N4
Boudtenga
DEDOUGOU
N
Bradt
OUAGADOUGOU
KOUDOUGOU
N14
Fada N'Gourma

HEADING NORTH FROM OUAGA

There are three routes north from Ouagadougou. The most travelled is the highway to Ouahigouya, which continues to Dogon country in Mali. Ouahigouya can be reached via a good tarmac road in a couple of hours from the capital. On the way, the town of Yako (see page 157) makes a good stopping-off point, with local gold mines easily accessible.

There are two routes into Burkina's not-to-be-missed Sahel. One takes you to Djibo, via either Ouahigouya or Kongoussi. The more popular route is through Dori, via the good tarmac road that takes in Kaya, Loumbila and the presidential hometown of Ziniare.

NEAR OUAGA

Most of the following destinations can be managed by moped from Ouaga, with the exception of Kongoussi.

MUSEUM OF MANEGA (*Road to Kongoussi;* m *76 43 30 24, 76 47 42 78;* ⊕ *08.30–17.30 daily; entry 2,000f*) This is a museum highlight of Burkina, around 60km north of the capital on the road to Kongoussi. The turning is on the right, and it's a 4km drive on a dirt track after that. It began life as the private collection of celebrated Burkinabe barrister, academic and man of letters, Frederick Pacere Titinga, who had managed to amass an impressive collection of African artefacts in his home town. Titinga was also the author of the seminal book *Bendrology*, which explores the language of Mossi drumming, analysing its patterns and rhythms to illustrate how the *griots* can recount the histories of the *nabas* through their percussion skills.

The collection provides a great window on to the life and traditions of the Mossi and other groups, and although there is now a tragic lack of money to ensure the museum's upkeep, efforts are constantly being made to improve it. A new building opened in 2008, housing all the site's military artefacts; it's a bit bare, but a row of ancient rifles is impressive, along with mock-ups of soldiers on horseback in various kinds of traditional uniform.

The building housing items related to death and death rituals is of particular interest. Owing to the sacred nature of these artefacts, visitors are required to take off their shoes and step inside backwards, out of respect.

In the courtyard are examples of traditional Burkinabe architecture, including Senoufou and Fulani housing. A very smartly painted replica of a Kassena house from Tiebele was opened in 2010.

KONGOUSSI Situated on the shores of Lake Bam, Burkina's largest lake, Kongoussi makes for a pretty stopover on the way up to Djibo. The proximity to water explains the town's importance as a market-garden centre, and has earned it a reputation for its green beans, which can be found in the supermarkets of Europe – one of Burkina's few international exports.

Getting there and away Kongoussi lies on the N22 to Djibo, 112km north of Ouaga. It's smooth tar all the way. STAF leaves daily from its Larle stop at 07.30 and 15.30. Tickets cost 2,000f, 3,500f return. Coming back, departure times are 07.00 and 16.00.

Where to stay

Hotel du Lac Bam (14 rooms) 40 45 90 75. Pleasantly situated on the edge of Lake Bam, & the prettiest option in town. Smallish rooms are all AC & en suite. Was in the process of being taken over by the Pacific chain; the restaurant/bar was closed, but is likely to reopen. There are another 5 enormous rooms on the main drag towards Djibo, but they lack atmosphere. **$$$**

Hotel Wend Kuuni (19 rooms) m 70 40 02 48. On the left heading towards Djibo. Not much to look at from the street, but AC & fan en-suite rooms are arranged around a nice enough courtyard with a *paillote* out the back. Poky but clean; some have nets. **$$**

Centre St Martial (approx 15 rooms) m 70 30 64 92. Run by nuns; set in spacious leafy grounds on the other side of the lake. Restful, spotless rooms (AC or fan), most en suite but some with outside loo. 3 good meals a day available. About 3km from town – turn right when coming from Ouaga, & follow the road around. **$–$$**

Hotel Major (18 rooms) 40 45 92 86; m 70 14 79 04. Seriously cheap option, signposted on the right before the roundabout. Simple rooms have external facilities; some have fans. **$**

Where to eat and drink **Restaurant Le Mont Blanc**, a couple of doors up from Hotel Wend Kuuni, has good salads, chips and spaghetti as well as the usuals, served up in a well-kept courtyard garden under *paillotes* and shady booths. **Restaurant Le Rond Point**, just off the roundabout, has billowing curtains and a good menu that includes local green beans. **L'Ambiance** just across the road is a lively corner *maquis* with some dodgy rooms out the back.

LOUMBILA

Loumbila Beach (m *78 08 01 93, 70 37 06 59; www.loumbila-beach.com*) Set on the shores of a lake, this jaunty holiday camp offers family fun. While adults dine in the spacious bar-restaurant, kids can head for the sizeable playground, inflatable slide and bouncy-castle 'ball house' or large swimming pool. On the lake are jet-skis (*10,000f for 10mins, 25,000f for 30mins*), pedalos (*2,000–5,000f an hour, depending on size of boat*) and outboard motorboats (*7,500f for a circuit of the lake*). All lake activities are at weekends only unless by prior arrangement with Marcel (m *71 89 24 10*) or Eric (m *78 02 60 24, 70 20 45 41*).

Le Cabri de Loumbila (m *70 21 35 45*) Just along the track from Loumbila Beach and popular with Ouagalais and expats, especially at Sunday lunchtimes, this delightful goat farm and restaurant serves excellent warm, fresh goat's cheese salad, as well as goat *brochettes* and slices of stuffed pig. Hidden from the main road in calm surrounds, seating is in a shaded wooden area, with animals and children roaming free. You can take away little *crottins* of the light fresh cheese (700f each, 800f with garlic or herbs), or take a tour to see goats and tortoises, go camel riding and see how the cheese is made.

Getting there and away Take the Kaya road northeast from Ouaga; Loumbila is shortly after the toll booths. The jaunt is most pleasant by moped, or take one of several coaches (OA, STAF, STMB or TSR) headed daily for Ziniare and Kaya. From the main road, take a signposted turning on the left and keep going into the scrub, following signs all the way.

Where to stay

Loumbila Beach (12 rooms) Within the grounds, but set slightly apart from all the fun, AC bungalows are neat & clean with matching fabrics & TVs. Some rooms, on the 1st floor up winding iron stairs, have king-size beds & balcony views of the lake. **$$$$**

ZINIARE President Blaise Compaore was born here, which is why you may occasionally hear his supporters referred to as Ziniarists, in opposition to those who support his predecessor, the Sankarists. As a result, Ziniaire has the feel of a town going places.

A number of developments, both buildings and agricultural projects, seem to have found their way here. The most auspicious, if it comes off, will be the relocation of Ouagadougou Airport. For now, the town's main attraction is a small wildlife park, located in the expansive grounds of a presidential ranch retreat.

Getting there and away Several daily coaches (OA, STAF, STMB and TSR) headed for Kaya stop at Ziniare.

What to see

Presidential zoo (*entry 1,500f*) More like a private reserve than a conventional urban zoo with cages, it is possible to see lion, giraffe, ostrich and a host of antelope. Gaining entry is done via the mayor's office in Ziniare. In practice, if you show up at the weekend when the *mairie* is closed, you can pay at the gates.

LAONGO (m *76 45 99 76, 70 43 33 36, 79 18 31 47; entry 2,500f*) This remarkable outdoor gallery of rock sculptures is a tribute to creative spirit across the globe. In 1989, artists from all over the world descended on the granite formations at the village to carve out their niche in history. The 18 sculptors, from 13 countries including Canada, Iran, Mali, Switzerland and the UK, have since been joined by other artists' contributions; there are now about 180 sculptures dotted around the site. At the gate, you can find four suggested circuits. To do them justice, allow a couple of hours. Guides (not obligatory) are available to give explanations along the way – there is no fee, but a tip is usually expected. A second site down the road is home to another 60-odd sculptures.

LE VILLAGE OPERA Near the Laongo sites lies a shattered dream. The brainchild of Christoph Schlingenseif, a German opera director, the ambitious aim of the project was to create a wondrous snail-shaped concert hall, a cultural studies centre, a school, a clinic and accommodation for artists and visitors. The first stone was laid in February 2010, but then tragedy struck: Christoph was killed in an accident in August 2010. His dying wish was that his friends should see his project through to completion, but for now, it has ground to a halt.

Getting there and away After Ziniare, take a right and keep going for about 6km along what is perhaps the finest tar road in Burkina; there are even white lines. Alternatively, head east on the Fada road (N4), swing left at Boudtenga and keep going, also for about 6km.

NORTH TO YATENGA KINGDOM

YAKO Sandwiched between the Mossi empires of Oubritenga and Yatenga country, about 100km from Ouagadougou, Yako has been involved in a tug-of-war between the two rivals throughout its history and, politically, has learnt how to court the approval of both without incurring the wrath of either. More recently, it was the birthplace of revolutionary president Thomas Sankara.

Yako has the feel of a large village rather than a town. Part of its appeal is the utter lack of tourist savvy, making it a good place to hole up for the night and then head

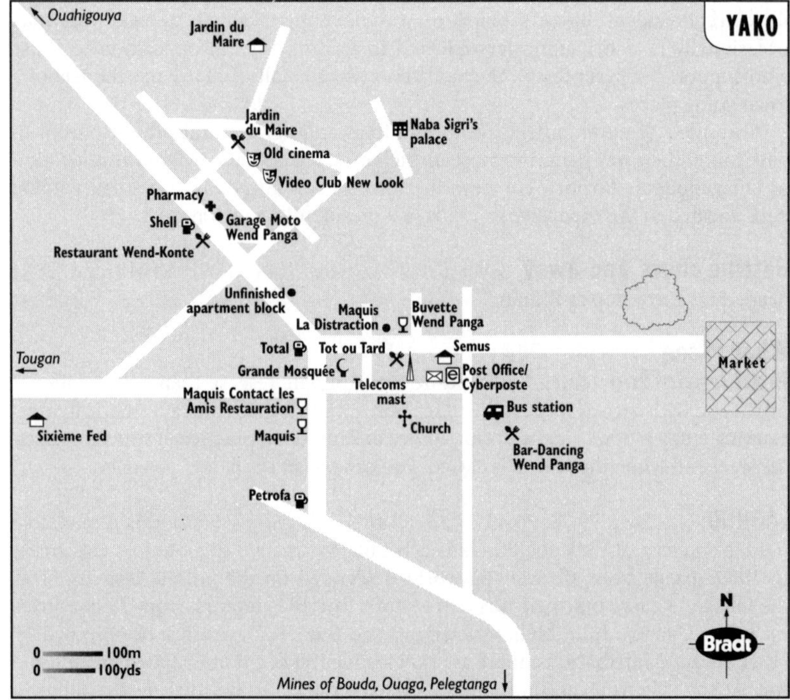

for the gold mines nearby. A wander around is likely to yield something interesting – kids melting scrap metal in makeshift forges to fashion soup spoons to sell at market, a World War II veteran happy to talk about his service on behalf of France and still regularly fathering children well into his eighties (his courtyard is by the Jardin du Maire), outdoor hair salons full of immaculately coiffed and made-up girls, and an eye-popping market. Semus (see below) has an internet café, **Cyber@ Semus** (⌚ *Mon–Fri, Sat mornings*), which charges 500f an hour. The post office also has an internet service.

Getting there and away A straight run up the N2 from Ouaga, Yako is about 90 minutes by car on good surfaces. The great triumvirate of STAF, STMB and TSR all have regular coach services; STAF (m *70 28 17 96*) has the most frequent, leaving from its stop in Larle almost hourly from 06.00 until 18.30 (1,500f). STMB (☎ *50 31 13 63*) leaves from Cité An III at 06.45, 13.00 and 17.15 and is cheaper (1,000f). TSR (☎ *50 34 25 24*) leaves from its Gounghin stop at 06.00, 08.00, 11.00, 13.00, 16.00 and 18.00; tickets cost 2,500f.

From the main bus station, all three companies head on to Ouahigouya (1,000f), or back to Ouaga; STAF also has a service to Tougan, which leaves at 10.30 and 16.00 (2,500f). The best thing may be to turn up at the bus station, ask which company will hit your destination next, and wait – with so many departures, you won't have to wait around for long.

Where to stay

Semus (11 rooms) ☎ 40 54 01 78; e semus@fasonet.bf. By far the best & most central option is run by the Sahelian development association Semus (Association

Solidarité et Entraide Mutuelle au Sahel). Semus acts as an umbrella for a number of NGOs, & chatting to their workers can give a fascinating insight into the area. Rooms are spacious & clean with en suite; communal hangout areas give a friendly, homely atmosphere. Choice of fan or AC. Fan single 4,000f. **$$**

Jardin du Maire (4 rooms) There is a basic, mosquito-heavy accommodation block near the restaurant of the same name, with ceiling fans & shared showers, and flush loo (no door) for the 4 rooms. You'd have to be desperate to stay here. **$**

Sixième Fed (6 rooms) 40 54 00 98; m 76 30 40 07. There are 3 sets of 2 double fan rooms, each set sharing a bathroom, in an unappealing block out on the Tougan road. However, it's better once you're inside, & there's a self-catering kitchen with functioning fridge & sink. The friendly manager can arrange for guests to hire a small gas cooker. **$**

Where to eat and drink The **Jardin du Maire** (m *78 82 36 45*) is a real oasis, with shrubs and pink petals surrounding shaded bandstands, and alfresco tables and chairs perfect for night-time eating. Food is substantial, with chicken and steak on offer and good-value *brochettes* in the gardens for 100f a stick. There's *porc au four* in the mornings and dancing at the weekends, but it can be eerily quiet on weeknights, when a better bet is just along from Semus. Here, three places work in synchronicity: **Tot ou Tard** (Chez Helen la Togolaise) dishes up healthy portions of *riz sauce* and *riz gras*, **Buvette Wend-Panga** has a good chicken stall just outside (2,000f per chicken), and **Maquis La Distraction** provides everything you might desire to wash it all down. You can sit at any of them and be served by all three.

On the main drag, rows of grills will keep carnivores happy, while **Restaurant Wend-Konte** dishes up the usuals; wander down the road towards Ouaga and you'll find a cold Brakina at **Maquis Contact les Amis Restauration**.

Much the most popular place in town, however, is the new **Bar-Dancing Restaurant Wend-Panga** behind the bus station, with dancing at the weekends and music all week. Its restaurant opens at 11.00 and serves up things you'd expect, and a few you might not – cows' feet, for instance, and *ragout de nyam*.

What to see

Market At the edges it is all secondhand clothes and plastic sandals. But plunge further in. There are pottery stalls, shacks selling African cotton prints and indigo cloth, metal spoons, and a surprising amount of strong rope on sale. If you visit the gold mines nearby, with 60m-deep shafts, it begins to make sense.

Deep in the market are several fetish stalls, selling ingredients for all variants of luck, good and bad. You may find one selling elephant skin – tough, hairy and incredibly smelly. The thick black hairs on the rutted hide are almost plastic to the touch. A piece the size of, and as smelly as, a big toe (human) sells for 100f; a larger hunk costs 300f. Local farmers use the smaller portions in conjunction with other ingredients as a charm to stave off the heat and keep going in the fields. Other medicine men offer up various dried bits of animal. You can find bundles of long elegant porcupine needles, the entire skin of a python (used to do bad to someone), a lizard skin with matching head, and aardvark paws. The market is held every three days.

Grande mosquée Perfectly placed at a kink in the main road, its four minarets, each with a star and crescent on top, dominate the town skyline. Decked out in white and green, it catches the evening light with lustre.

Visit the naba The local Mossi chieftain, Naba Sigri, is perfectly happy to welcome visitors to his palace, and is a good person to speak to, particularly about power struggles between the rulers of Ouagadougou and Yatenga that focused on the town.

Video Club New Look As with so many of Burkina's imposing concrete cinemas, Yako's doesn't work. Next door, locals have set up a video club and it's almost as good as the real thing, only on a smaller screen. There are two showings every night, at 19.15 and 21.15, at 50f a throw, with a different DVD each time. The room is regularly packed out with more than 100 film-goers and the noise of the telly can be heard for several blocks in every direction.

GOLD MINES OF BOUDA AND PELEGTANGA It has been said that Burkina is blissfully free of the resource curse. With mining operations growing year on year, this is gradually changing, and it has long been true that thousands of Burkinabe risk their livelihoods, and sometimes their lives, to strike it rich. The north of the country is dotted with mining operations, some official, some not. Like the Wild West more than a century ago, impromptu settlements spring up the moment there is evidence of gold in the area – this is the situation at Bouda and Pelegtanga. Without high-tech, large-scale interests of state enterprise or foreign investors, this is gold the cottage-industry way. To visit larger (commercial) mining operations in Burkina, it will help to have written permission from the Ministry of Mines, Quarries and Energy in Ouagadougou (*50 31 84 29*).

High on the sun-baked, pock-marked hills, golden-hued mud spills out across the land as men, women and small children work in whatever way they can to coax out enough tiny specks of gold to make their labour count. A few years back, the villagers staged something of a revolt, throwing out the state agency that previously weighed all the gold and set payment rates for mine workers. The local state *comptoir* (payment office) paid 3,500f per gram of gold. Now administered by villagers, prices have gone up steadily to reach 7,000f per gram. The collected gold is passed up the chain to officials from the CBMP, the Burkinabe Office for Precious Metals, whose prices vary according to the world market rate.

Getting there and away A 20-minute *moto* ride from Yako, you may need to rely on asking directions to get to the mines, and the track to the village is too narrow for a car. Issa Dianda, who owns Garage Moto Wend Panga opposite the Wend-Konte Restaurant in Yako, can rent out a P50 moped (2,500f) or a Yamaha (3,500f) for the day; he also has bikes for 1,000f. From town, head south on the Ouaga road past the Petrofa station and keep going past fields, trees and the reservoir. After ten minutes, you should see some concrete benches shaded under trees on your right. After another ten minutes, you should cross a bridge. Wriggle along a red dirt track forking off to the left, and you'll eventually reach the village of Bouda.

It is not a tourist site and there is no infrastructure or entry fee. Ask politely if it might be possible to talk to the council of village elders who look after the mines. If you haven't arrived with a guide, the *vieux* may suggest a villager who can show you around. It would be nice to offer something at the end. Having someone who speaks French (as well as Moore) to show you around is a boon.

YATENGA COUNTRY

PRINCELY BEGINNINGS Steeped in history, the Mossi Kingdom of Yatenga, which begins beyond Yako, has an oral tradition as carefully preserved as anything in

Ouaga. It was originally born of a conflict between two princes competing for control of the newly formed Mossi state – Kumdumye and Yadega. They may have been brothers, they may have been cousins, but, most importantly, both were grandsons of Naba Oubri, the first Mossi ruler based at the royal capital of La. After losing out to Kumdumye in the struggle for power, Yadega, angry and disillusioned, left La for the nearby settlement of Gourcy. He had the consolation of leaving with

THE POT AT THE END OF THE RAINBOW

The area around Yako is renowned for its gold content. Several different – often difficult and dangerous – techniques are used in the hunt for the shiny stuff.

MINING Small shafts, which can go 100m deep, dot the white crests of the gravelly land. Pits are reinforced with sandbags and wood. Workers descend barefoot, using a combination of foot-holes and ropes. At any one time there can be as many as 40 men working underground on the same mine pit. The number of shoes left at the mouth of the shaft is the only evidence of how many men are beneath the surface.

DIGGING Women and young girls – old enough to go to school but caught up in the gold rush – make little headway with axes on the surface and gather rocks and mud by hand and in buckets. It takes five house-sized trucks full of rocks just to have enough gold to make one wedding ring, so excavating by hand is pretty unforgiving work.

POUNDING As you approach the hill-top quarry town the air is alive with what first seems like a rhythmical beating and musical tinkling from a distance. It is the noise of women pounding rocks into powder with furious regularity. The more energetic pounders compete for how high they can raise their metal baton, about the size of a rounders bat, letting go at the top of its arc to clap before catching it and bringing it back down with crushing force. Many do this with babies bundled on their backs or at their breasts. It's not easy work, requiring concentration, rhythm, speed, strength and tremendous stamina.

PANNING Whether miners or pounders, every group will have a panner – someone who can actually sift the gold from the best efforts of the earth to keep it secret. Only one woman per group, of two-dozen or so per tent, has the know-how. She takes the pounded powder, mixes it with muddy water in a huge bowl and swills it round and round until the shreds of gold appear at the edges.

PAYMENT Among the teams of pounding women, lone men sit in huts, kings of their miniature castles, to weigh out the gold and pay the workers for their morsels. The fine powder is deftly measured out on hand-held scales. For every matchstick's-worth of gold (equivalent to one-twelfth of a gram), villagers receive 600f. Coins are used for other weights: a 25f coin for 6g (42,000f); a 1 French franc coin for 1g (7,000f) and a crude half version for half a gram (3,500f). Often the gold arrives still mingled with earth, and a heavy magnetic disc held behind a sheet of paper attracts the dirt and leaves behind the inert shreds of gold. The middlemen collect about four cylindrical tubes per week to sell on to CBMP agents.

the royal amulets of power, which had been stolen for him by his eldest sister, Pabre, who obviously wasn't sticking around either.

GUILE OF YADEGA Oral history recounts Yadega's guile in conquering Gourcy, prefiguring the wily resourcefulness frequently attributed to Yatenga's rulers. Hearing that the existing chief of Gourcy was an excellent tailor, Yadega invited him to his palace for a robe fitting. A rug was laid over a pit at the entrance to the court, into which Gourcy's unsuspecting chief promptly fell on arrival. Having taken out the opposition, Yadega occupied the village with ease.

Yadega's second son, Naba Geda, went on to break links with Oubritenga at the end of the 16th century. Henceforth the two dynasties, representing the two poles of Mossi power and influence in the region, were entirely separate. Following the infamous reign of Naba Kango (1747–87) (see box, page 167), in which the capital was moved from Gourcy to Ouahigouya, the Yatenga Kingdom was riven by internecine conflict and incursions by raiders, and began its decline. Competing *nabas* tended to recruit Samo archers and Fulani cavalry to settle their quarrels by force. Beset by fratricidal struggles, Naba Baongo (1885–94), turned to the French for assistance towards the end of the 19th century.

FRENCH INFLUENCE Under Captain Desteneves, a French expeditionary force had already captured Bandiagara, in Mali, and was hungrily eyeing the borders of Yatenga country. Desteneves initially preferred to watch from the sidelines to see who among Yatenga's rulers would emerge victorious from the palaver. Baongo pressed ahead with his campaign to subdue the prince Bangrey, but was killed in the ensuing battle. Bangrey (who became Naba Bully) immediately asked for a French treaty of protection, knowing all too well how greatly the throne was coveted.

Rather than shoring up his position, however, this move sparked a popular uprising among the Yatenga, who saw Bully's alliance with the French as an act of betrayal. Long after Bully's death in 1899, the rebellion continued.

The kingdom only returned to order in 1912. In 1932, the region became part of the Western Sudan (Mali), as a result of the dissolution of Upper Volta, until 1949 when the colony was reconstituted.

OUAHIGOUYA

Nowadays, Ouahigouya's violent past is well behind it and there are few outward signs of a capital that once rivalled Ouagadougou for power and status. Indeed, on a lazy Saturday afternoon it is a struggle to think that much happens here at all; even the market trades with languor. Come evening time, the town likes to party with a passion. Perhaps the lack of distractions is one reason the weekends are so highly prized.

Despite being the largest town in the north, with a population of over 70,000, there is no industry in Ouahigouya. Its reservoir is a plentiful source of fish, and the town is also known for its onions, tomatoes and, in particular, potatoes, so much so that in season, an 'Ouahigouya salad' is always sure to contain them.

The other distinctive feature of Ouahigouya is its vultures. They haunt the town – its treetops, streets, telegraph poles and rooftops – perhaps in memory of the bloodthirsty appetites of its rulers.

GETTING THERE AND AWAY The N3 that links to the capital is one of the best roads in the country. Expect the journey to take two hours. Of the bus companies

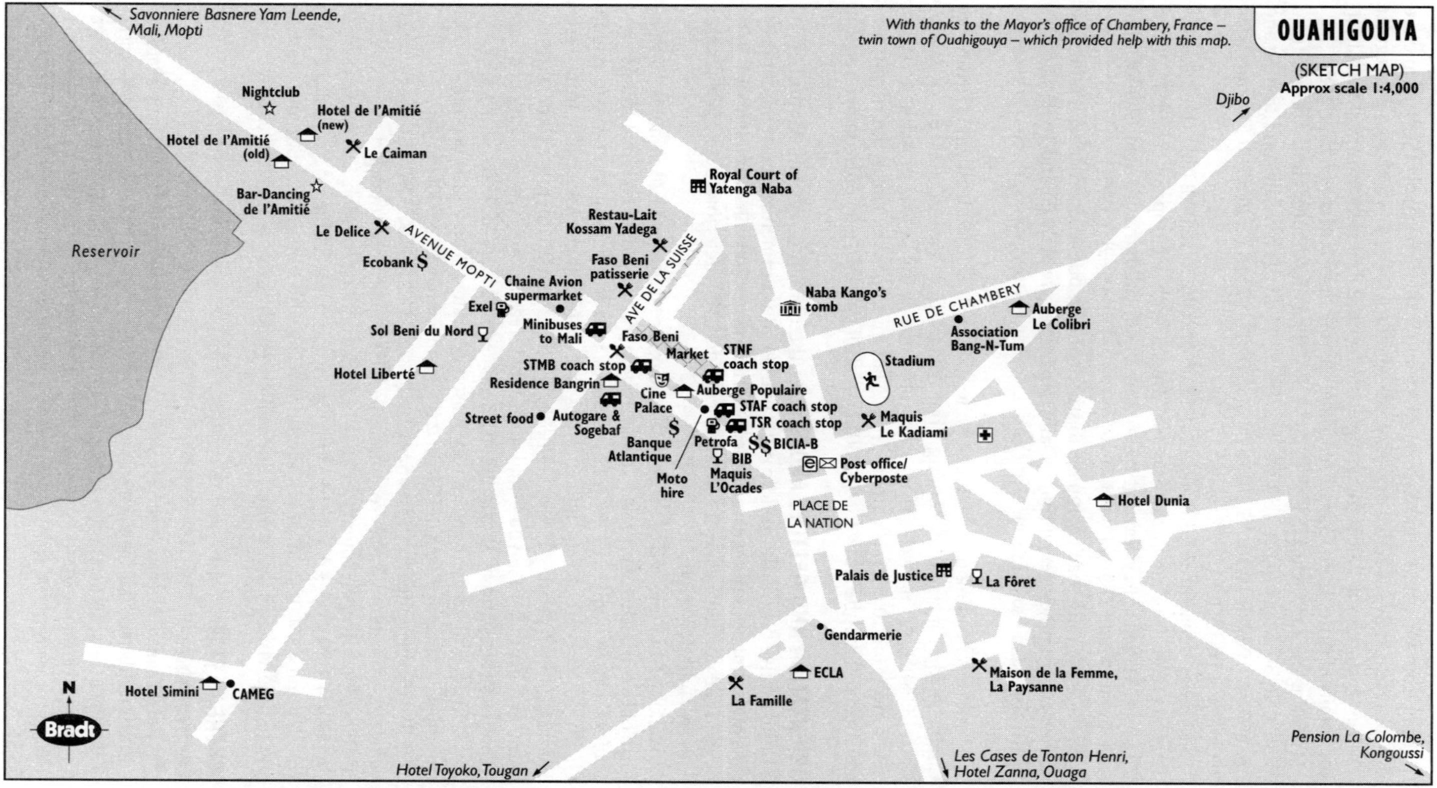
OUAHIGOUYA
(SKETCH MAP)
Approx scale 1:4,000
With thanks to the Mayor's office of Chambery, France – twin town of Ouahigouya – which provided help with this map.
Savonniere Basnere Yam Leende, Mali, Mopti
Djibo
Reservoir
Nightclub
Hotel de l'Amitié (new)
Hotel de l'Amitié (old)
Le Caiman
Bar-Dancing de l'Amitié
Le Delice
AVENUE MOPTI
Ecobank
Royal Court of Yatenga Naba
Restau-Lait Kossam Yadega
AVE DE LA SUISSE
Faso Beni patisserie
Chaine Avion supermarket
Exel
Sol Beni du Nord
Minibuses to Mali
Faso Beni
Market
STNF coach stop
STMB coach stop
Hotel Liberté
Residence Bangrin
Cine Palace
Auberge Populaire
Street food
Autogare & Sogebaf
STAF coach stop
TSR coach stop
Banque Atlantique
Petrofa
BICIA-B
BIB
Maquis L'Ocades
Moto hire
Naba Kango's tomb
RUE DE CHAMBERY
Association Bang-N-Tum
Auberge Le Colibri
Stadium
Maquis Le Kadiami
Post office/ Cyberposte
PLACE DE LA NATION
Hotel Dunia
Palais de Justice
La Fôret
Gendarmerie
ECLA
La Famille
Maison de la Femme, La Paysanne
Hotel Simini
CAMEG
Bradt
N
Hotel Toyoko, Tougan
Les Cases de Tonton Henri, Hotel Zanna, Ouaga
Pension La Colombe, Kongoussi

running from Ouaga to Ouahigouya, STAF and TSR are probably the best, and are also more expensive at 2,500f one-way, 4,000f return. STMB, which also has regular services, is cheaper at 2,000f for a single, but some of its coaches are past their best. For details of times from Ouaga, see *Yako, Getting there and away*, page 158.

Heading back to Ouaga, STAF (*40 55 30 75*) has departures almost hourly from 05.30 to 18.30. Many of the TSR services (m *72 11 42 01*) have air conditioning and run at 06.00, 08.00, 10.30, 13.00, 16.00 and 18.00. STMB (*40 55 00 59*) runs back to Ouaga at 06.15, 09.15, 13.15 and 17.15.

STAF has departures for Tougan at 12.00 and 16.00 (2,000f). At the *autogare*, there are also minibus departures for Tougan with a company called TDM, or Djjgouya Magna. They leave at 07.00 and 11.00, calling at Tougan (2,000f) and Dedougou (3,000f) before heading on to Bobo-Dioulasso (6,000f).

STNF is the only coach company to still do the Djibo run, its coaches a reflection of the battering they get *en route*. Daily departures are at 09.00 and 16.00 (2,000f). STNF also has a Ouaga service, but with so many better options, there's little reason to use it.

Minibuses heading into Mali can be found down a little turning just before the Chaine Avion supermarket coming from Ouaga. They leave at 09.00 every day for Koro (3,000f). A one-week visa can be obtained at the border crossing in Thiou, 36km away, for 10,000f. If coming from Mali into Burkina, check the situation in advance: you may be stung for 94,000f, so if at all possible, get your visa beforehand.

ORIENTATION AND GETTING AROUND At the bottom of Avenue Mopti lies the administrative centre, the middle is the market and commercial centre, and most of the entertainment options are at the top. The town's reservoir, located about 300m beyond the northern edge of town as the road to Mali deteriorates to gravel, makes a lovely sundown stroll.

Walking from one end of the town to the other takes a good 20 minutes, so some form of two-wheeled transport is a boon. There are a few town taxis that charge up to 500f for a town hop (m *74 26 74 06*). Bicycles are a particularly good way to explore Ouahigouya's quiet streets, and it is possible to hire them informally from Hotel Dunia for 1,000f per day. In town opposite the STAF station, there are some big metal gates, and behind these you'll find a veritable treasure-trove of bikes, mopeds and *motos* of all ages and in all conditions. Ali Ouedraogo (m *76 06 69 21, 78 42 05 72, 71 47 50 26*) will let them out at very reasonable rates. With a little negotiation, you should get a bike for 1,000f, a P50 for 2,500f and a *moto* for 3,500f per day.

A 4x4 can be rented from **Issa Sangare** (m *78 86 41 71, 76 53 84 80;* e *sangissabil@yahoo.fr*), who comes highly recommended. He can arrange transport by private car to Djibo, Dori, Dogon country or anywhere else difficult to reach. His rates are (with no driver) 35,000f per day for the Ouahigouya area, 40,000f per day up into Dogon country and 45,000f for the rest of Burkina. He is also a qualified guide and can take you to little-visited sites nearby. His chauffeur/guiding rate is 17,500f per day.

WHERE TO STAY

Comfortable

Hotel Zanna (26 rooms) 40 55 36 36; e hotelzanna@hotmail.live. The pink monstrosity on the left on the way in from Ouaga. A spacious foyer done out in chrome & black leather leads to the sort of nondescript AC rooms you'd expect. **$$$$**

Hotel de l'Amitié I (90 rooms in total) Av Mopti; 40 55 05 21/22; e amitie@fasonet.bf. Ouahigouya's largest hotel consists of 2 large buildings opposite each other at the northern edge of town. The newer hotel offers plenty of comfort without enormous amounts of character, although its swimming pool (1,500f for non-guests, including those in l'Amitié II) & garden greenery are welcome. **$$$–$$$$**

Hotel Toyoko (11 rooms) 40 55 35 33; e hoteltoyoko@yahoo.fr. At the end of the tarmac on the Tougan road, the semi-rural setting belies the liveliest place in town. Rooms are wisely set apart from the popular restaurant & nightclub; all are AC & in splendid bad taste with big beds, TV, fridge & Wi-Fi. **$$$–$$$$**

Residence Bangrin (24 rooms) 40 55 05 81; m 78 35 31 58. Bang in the centre of town, this place should have been great, but its design means it misses the mark. Standard AC doubles are nothing special; the next level up features enormous but soulless rooms. **$$$–$$$$**

Mid range

Hotel de l'Amitié II The cheaper, older hotel is steeped in a combination of 1970s pink & brown kitsch & traditional wall paintings of nabas throughout history. There are some cheap fan rooms here, but they're pretty dingy. **$$–$$$**

Hotel Dunia (15 rooms) 40 55 05 95; e mbachourf@yahoo.fr. Run by a Syrian family, this has the feel of a family home that welcomes guests. Warm & familiar, the friendly landlady is a constant fixture in the ivy-clad courtyard, which also contains a swing bench, tiny swimming pool, & serves the best meals in town. A delicious breakfast of homemade cheese, mango and bissap jams is served. Choice of fan or AC. B/fast 1,000f. **$$–$$$**

Hotel Liberté (20 rooms, 2 dorms) 40 55 05 72. A nice enough option, set around a shaded courtyard, though it's looking a little tired. Choice of en-suite AC or fan, or fan with outside loo. There's a 9-person dorm at 15,800f, & a 4-person dorm for 12,500f. **$$–$$$**

Hotel Simini (12 rooms) 40 55 00 88. It's hard to fathom why anyone would construct a nightclub in the middle of an *auberge* (where the courtyard used to be); but such is the case here. It's also a long trek from town, but at least the rooms are bright & clean. Choice of fan or AC. **$$–$$$**

Budget/Shoestring

Être Comme Les Autres (ECLA) (27 rooms) m 76 61 44 89, 78 47 27 33, 76 89 97 02; e ecla@fasonet.bf; http://ecla.free.fr. Possibly the best budget option within easy reach of town (coming from Ouaga, ask to be dropped at the *gendarmerie*). It's actually a training centre for disabled people, but there's usually plenty of room. A leafy garden leads past a pleasant dining/TV area, with walkways to accommodation beyond. Spotless en-suite fan rooms with several beds go on a per-person basis (single 4,000f); AC doubles are per room. Simple meals served. B/fast 750f. **$$**

Les Cases de Tonton Henri (4 rooms) 40 55 33 69; m 70 03 67 38. On the left on the way in from Ouaga, these brick huts are beautifully built, with matching brick floors & thatched roofs, & are set in a profusion of greenery. No AC, but hot water & towels. A little way out of town, but there's a good-value P50 (2,000f per day) & Yamaha (3,000f) for hire. B/fast 2,000f. **$$**

Auberge Le Colibri (13 rooms) 40 55 07 87. A good budget option, with simple AC or fan rooms set around a pleasant paillote & courtyard. All have mozzie nets & en suite. **$–$$**

Pension La Colombe (11 rooms) 40 55 34 12. About 2km out of the centre off the Kongoussi road, this place is tricky to find, but offers a warm welcome in a village setting & some great-value en-suite rooms. All have TVs; AC rooms have fridges too. Taxis from town about 500f. **$–$$**

Auberge Populaire (6 rooms) Av Mopti; 40 55 06 40. Not an appealing accommodation option, with grotty rooms & a noisy bar. It is better for a bit of down-n-dirty nightlife though. **$**

WHERE TO EAT

Mid range The more upmarket hotels all have restaurants. Of these, **Hotel Dunia** stands out, offering a fine three-course set dinner for 5,000f. If you are not staying at the hotel, phone about three–four hours in advance to reserve your place at the communal table. The restaurant at **Hotel Toyoko** ($$) is also worth a look, if you can handle chrome and black leather: mains such as chicken or steak include a side so are good value, and as this is the top-spot in town, there's a bit of a buzz.

With a pretty little terrace & soft lighting, **Le Delice** (m *70 39 60 38, 76 57 21 14;* $–$$) is a laid-back place. Owner/cook Beatrice offers a warm welcome and tasty home cooking.

CHEAP AND CHEERFUL The centre of town abounds in cheap street-food options. Avenue de la Suisse is a good place to start. Outside **Sol Beni du Nord**, two friendly youngsters run their own excellent grill, serving up tasty roasted garlic chicken, guinea fowl and *brochettes*. On the main drag, the **Maquis l'Ocades** opposite Petrofa plays host to a number of chicken and brochette grills; there's also a woman frying up fish, plantain and chips. Close to the *autogare* is a popular **take-away joint**, serving tasty, filling portions of *attiéké* with fried mackerel. **Faso Beni** next to the STMB coach station passes the wait with local dishes for little money, and cold drinks.

Avenue Mopti and around

✕ **Le Caiman** Situated behind the annexe of Hotel de l'Amitié, Le Caiman has outdoor garden tables & serves excellent *brochettes*, grilled garlic chicken, chips, steak, rice & spaghetti. It's perhaps a victim of its own success, as it's swarming with hawkers. $

✕ **Restau-Lait Kossam Yadega** Av de la Suisse; m 78 15 51 91. A co-operative of Fulani herdsmen (*kossam* means 'milk' in Fulfulde), facing the vegetable market. Perfect breakfast spot, serving espresso coffee, yoghurt, cakes, sandwiches & the Fulani speciality *bassi* – millet soaked in milk with sugar. Hachim Diallo, the manager, is happy to chat about Fulani culture. $

Further afield

✕ **La Famille** Just down from ECLA on the Tougan road, this place is deservedly popular, serving all the usuals plus great salads & *brochettes* in a pleasant garden setting. $

✕ **La Paysanne** A well-organised restaurant managed by the local women's co-operative at the Maison de la Femme, indicated by a sign on the main road close to the water tower. It serves particularly well-made & reliable *riz gras* & *riz sauce*, beef or chicken soup, *tô*, salad & beans at rock-bottom prices. $

✕ **Maquis Le Kadiami** Just after the stadium. This place has large concrete *paillotes* & used to be a good bet, but its food isn't really up to much these days. $

ENTERTAINMENT AND NIGHTLIFE **Sol Beni du Nord** is a popular local bar, and on weekends at the beginning of the month, when salaries have just been paid, it can be very lively. The **Auberge Populaire** is also a lively nightspot. **La Fôret** is a lovely quiet drinking spot favoured by locals, with shady booths partitioned by cane mats. It's just opposite the Palace de Justice off the Kongoussi road.

For dancing, there's a **nightclub** up from the **Hotel de l'Amitié** on Saturday nights. The stiff 2,000f entry includes one drink. This is not to be confused with the **Bar-Dancing de l'Amitié**, closer to town, which also hosts occasional events for those with lighter pockets. The place to be, though, is the nightclub at **Hotel Toyoko**, which revs up on Friday, Saturday and Sunday. Entrance is free, but bottled drinks are all 1,000f thereafter.

If you fancy catching a film, head to the **Cine Palace** on the main road. Tickets cost 200/300f.

SHOPPING For groceries, tinned goods, alcoholic beverages and mineral water, try the small grocery store attached to the Shell station, or the **Chaine Avion**

supermarket about halfway along Avenue Mopti. The shops at the east side of the market facing the vegetable section are also reasonably stocked.

For arts and crafts, check out the gallery at **Association Bang-N-Tum** (*40 55 44 60; zanboukari@yahoo.fr*) on Rue de Chambery. This organisation of disabled people sells calabashes, leather boxes, hammocks and lovely dyed fabrics. The **Savonnerie Basnere Yam Leende** (*40 55 08 55; cfpb@fasonet.bf*) sells homemade soap, made from shea butter, neem and other medicinal oils. The shop is on the main street, about 100m after Hotel de l'Amitié, on the premises of Groupement Naam. The **Maison de la Femme** sells hand-dyed fabrics made by local women. Hand-woven fabrics are also on sale at the market for between 1,250f and 6,000f a *pagne* (sheet).

OTHER PRACTICALITIES **BIB**, next to Mobil, and **BICIA-B** banks may change travellers' cheques as well as foreign currency, and have Visa cash machines. **Banque Atlantique** has a machine that accepts MasterCard/Maestro too. For internet, head to the **cyberposte** (*Mon–Sat, Sun mornings*), located at the bottom of town near BICIA-B, where an hour costs 500f. The **post office** next door includes express mail and Western Union money transfer services. Staff are friendly and helpful.

NABA KANGO'S GHASTLY RULE

While in exile in Mali, he killed and quartered one of his opponents, before cooking him in a pot. The mortar of his fortress walls was mixed with the blood of his many victims. He took the most beautiful young girls of his village and encased them alive in earth as the pillars of his palace. He ordered that all the young boys of Yatenga be killed.

These are just a few of the tales that surround Naba Kango, one of the most fearsome and feared Mossi leaders. Unravelling the reality from the myth of this 25th ruler of Yatenga is no easy business.

What is known is that he came to the throne in 1754, but was almost immediately ousted. He spent three years in exile in Mali, recruiting troops for a mission to retake the empire. In 1757, Kango returned to Yatenga, backed by Samo, Bwaba and Bambara mercenaries, who were trained in the use of firearms. Ruthless in victory, he had his own Bambara troops executed to remove any future threat to his power.

Determined to make his mark, and further isolate himself from the rival Mossi Kingdom based at Ouagadougou, he relocated his capital from Gourcy to Ouahigouya, built a new palace, and summoned all the Yatenga chiefs to the new settlement. The name 'Ouahigouya' means literally 'come and pay homage' in Moore – a not-so-subtle reminder to any potential rival of his status as top dog.

For the next 30 years he ruled as despot, putting villages to the sword in his struggle to maintain the security of the kingdom against organised crime, an aristocracy out to get him, and mercenary soldiers.

Again, local legend injects a colourful portion of just desserts into his 1787 death. On passing through a village, he discovered that a mother pounding millet had hidden her male child from one of his pogroms and demanded that she pound the boy to death. When she refused, he unsheathed his sword and went to finish the job himself. The desperate mother turned on him with her millet pounder, and brought a bloody end to the bloodiest of rules.

WHAT TO SEE AND DO

Naba Kango's tomb The tomb is a rather forlorn white pillar surrounded by a garden of straggly plants and a rickety fence. There is usually a youngster guarding the entrance, who will run off and get the local custodian if you are interested in entering and hearing a little history. Although there is no official ticket office, you will be asked for a small entrance fee. Donations are discretionary for the guide, but 500f might be considered appropriate. Apparently, any chief who walks around the tomb will come to a sticky end.

Royal court of Yatenga Naba For anyone wanting to see how the modern Yatenga court operates it is also possible to meet with the current *naba*, who is generally welcoming to visitors. In this technological age, you may receive a mobile-phone number for one of his courtiers from the young bucks lounging around outside his palace. A better approach may be to lay the groundwork in advance by approaching the Rassam Naba – the First Minister of the Yatenga Naba and also the best local source of Yatenga heritage and history. His compound is very close to Naba Kango's tomb, and if you ask around in the square you will be directed.

EXCURSIONS FROM OUAHIGOUYA The village of **Ramatoulaye** is 25km east of Ouahigouya on the road to Rambo. For Mouloud (the birthday of the Prophet Muhammad), an impressive pilgrimage to the village mosque takes place and it is easy to find public transport.

It is also possible to visit **Gourcy**, 42km south of Ouahigouya on the Ouaga road, to see where the kings of Yatenga are enthroned. Alternatively, **Somniaga**, site of the tombs of many of the other Yatenga *nabas*, is a 7km jaunt from Ouahigouya on the Ouaga road.

About 25km north of Ouahigouya, the waterfalls at **Koumbri**, on the way to Ban, make a great day trip.

DOGON COUNTRY, BURKINA STYLE

With thanks to Bernadette Kuijpers

While it may seem odd to recommend a country for its proximity to tourist attractions that lay beyond its borders, Burkina is an ideal launchpad for a visit to the famous Dogon country of neighbouring Mali.

Ouagadougou is closer to the Bandiagara Escarpment than is the Malian capital, Bamako, 691km away. The road from Ouagadougou is surfaced and in good condition until Ouahigouya; the final 143km to Bankass, in Mali, is on a dirt road, and the entire journey is possible on public transport for 7,000f.

To avoid being hassled by local guides in Bankass or Bandiagara, it is often easier to make arrangements in advance with a good Dogon guide by telephone or email. One recommended option is Ogomono Saye (*+223 243 06 00; e ogosaye@hotmail.com*) who speaks local languages as well as English and French. You can also ask for the *guerisseur* (traditional healer) (*+223 503 43 10*), well known locally, who charges 25,000f for two days of guiding.

For an all-inclusive package (camping, food, luggage transport, taxes and guiding) prices vary from 10,000f to 20,000f per person per day depending on the size of the group, the number of days and the trekking route. Once in Dogon country, prices for everything go right up, so stock up on soft drinks, beer and even kola nuts at the market in Ouahigouya.

KAYA Within easy reach of Ouagadougou, Kaya is in the heart of Burkina's lake district, offering some great hiking and wildlife opportunities among gently rolling hills that surround the town. These sprout into life with the arrival of the rains. It is also the capital of Burkina's leather industry. Local villagers are expert in turning out supremely stylish leather goods in all shapes, colours and sizes. The low-key market, held every three days, is a pleasure and prices are reasonable.

History The story goes that the town was founded in the 15th century by Sanboundo, a Mossi prince sent by his father, Moro Naba Oubri, to quell frequent raiding. He gave rise to the town's original name, Sanmatenga ('land of Sanboundo', in Moore), and this is still the name of the province. As for Kaya, what's pretty much agreed is that it comes from the Moore for millet, *kaye*. The confusion may have arisen when a Frenchman turned up at the end of the 19th century and asked a local woman where he was. She thought he was asking what she was drying out in the sun, and answered *kaye*.

Getting there and away

By bus Located 98km from Ouaga, the road is tarmac all the way, leaving by the road out past the Silmande Hotel.

OA (*Rue des Douanes;* ☎ *50 31 32 10*) specialises in transport to Kaya. From central Ouaga, coaches head off every hour or so, the first at 06.00 and then on the half-hour from 07.30 to 19.30. Singles are 1,500f. There's stiff competition from TSR down the road (*Rue de la Culture;* m *70 46 13 49, 70 14 86 13*), which also leaves at 06.00 and then on the hour until 18.00 for the same price. Both stop *en route* at Loumbila and Ziniare, and have stations in central Kaya (*OA,* ☎ *40 45 31 74; TSR,* m *70 26 00 36*). It's much the same on the way back, except that OA starts earlier with a 05.30 service. The journey takes about two hours.

Any coach headed for Bani (2,500f) and Dori (3,000f) stops on the main road at Kaya; each company has its own makeshift stop near the northern junction into town. STAF's super-fast services (m *72 82 46 12*) leave Ouaga from Larle at 05.30/06.00 and 12.30/13.00, passing through Kaya at about 07.30/08.00 and 14.30/15.00; STMB (☎ *40 45 00 58*) in Cité An III has departures at 07.00 and 13.00, passing through at 09.00 and 15.00; TSR has additional Dori services that don't go into Kaya town, leaving Ouaga at 07.00 and 13.00. Then there's STN, which has a single service to Dori at 07.00. All these head back to Ouaga in the mornings and afternoons, but with such a plethora of services from central Kaya, you're unlikely to need them.

By train Don't be fooled by the train tracks. Sankara's bid to make Kaya Burkina's manganese export hub by extending the railway has not worked out, and, with the tracks having fallen into disrepair, trains no longer serve the town from Ouaga. The bedraggled monument to Burkina's railway workers is all that is left.

Getting around If you're keen to explore the cattle market, tannery and nearby lakes, a moped is perfect. Souleyman (m *70 22 51 84*), in the market, has bicycles (1,500f a day) and *motos* (4,000f a day) for hire. If he's not around you should be able to hire *motos* at 4,000–5,000f a day from another trader. Adama Sawadogo (m *76 54 06 21, 71 57 28 96;* e *manadams@yahoo.fr*), the self-appointed president of the local guides association, can help with trips around town. He's earnest and knowledgeable, and can organise trips to visit weavers, blacksmiths or overnight

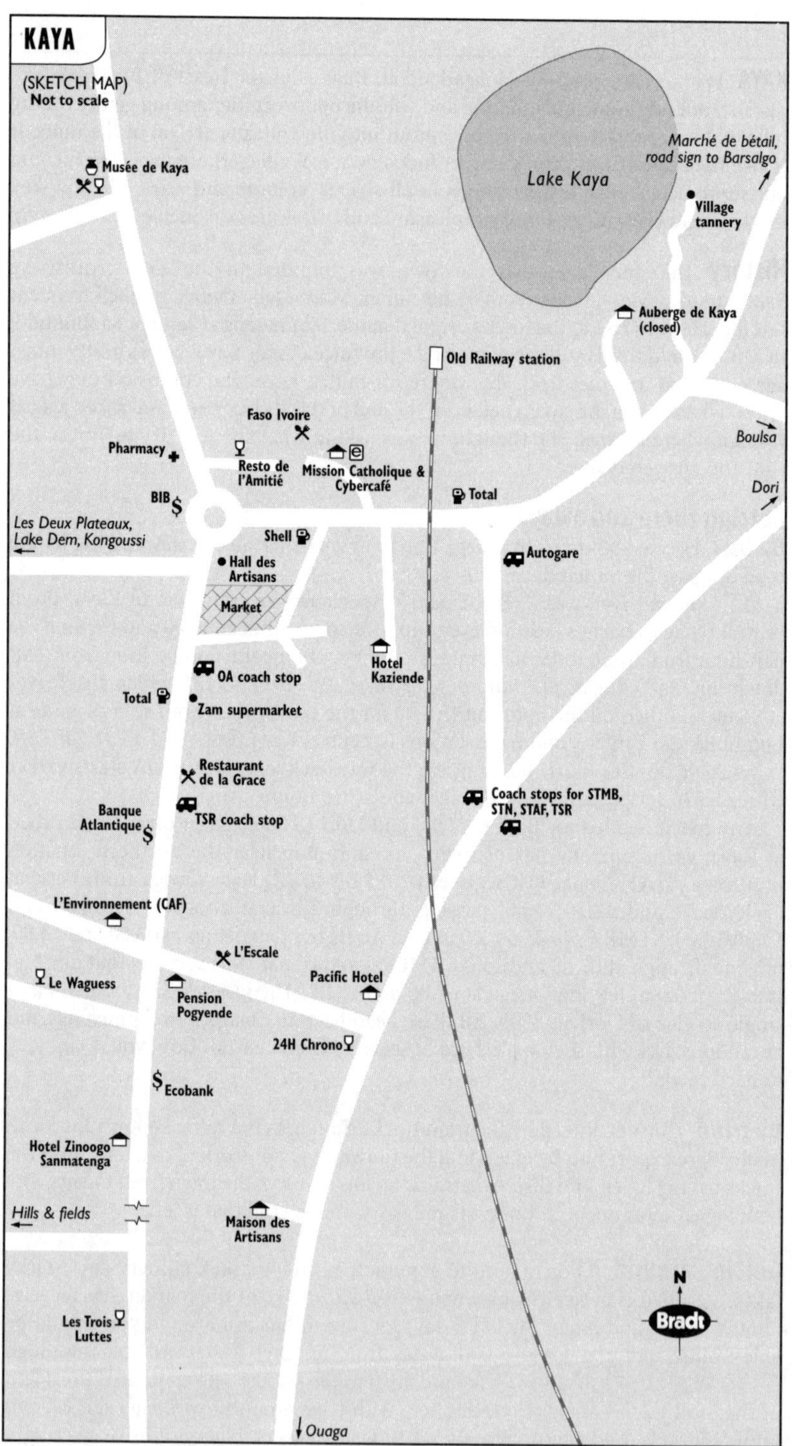
KAYA
(SKETCH MAP)
Not to scale
Musée de Kaya
Lake Kaya
Marché de bétail, road sign to Barsalgo
Village tannery
Auberge de Kaya (closed)
Old Railway station
Faso Ivoire
Pharmacy
Resto de l'Amitié
Mission Catholique & Cybercafé
Boulsa
Total
Dori
BIB
Les Deux Plateaux, Lake Dem, Kongoussi
Shell
Hall des Artisans
Autogare
Market
Hotel Kaziende
OA coach stop
Total
Zam supermarket
Restaurant de la Grace
Coach stops for STMB, STN, STAF, TSR
Banque Atlantique
TSR coach stop
L'Environnement (CAF)
L'Escale
Le Waguess
Pension Pogyende
Pacific Hotel
24H Chrono
Ecobank
Hotel Zinoogo Sanmatenga
Hills & fields
Maison des Artisans
N
Bradt
Les Trois Luttes
Ouaga

stays in local Fulani villages. He's also the person to ask about Kaya's Wedbinde festival, which is held every two years (next in 2012).

Where to stay

Upmarket/Comfortable

Pacific Hotel (27 rooms) 40 45 12 12. The pink monstrosity with reflective blue windows near the turning into town, & part of the Pacific's new chain. Rooms (all AC) have enormous beds, TVs, fridges, hot water; some have baths. Wi-Fi on the way, there's a pool, but it's all a bit soulless – & pricey; but you can negotiate. **$$$$$**

Hotel Kaziende (30 rooms) 40 45 35 35; e kaziende@fasonet.bf. Decent central hotel, with hot water, well-maintained gardens, occasionally catering for conferences, without feeling too businesslike. Excellent bar area & good restaurant. Fan rooms aren't great value, however. **$$–$$$$**

Mid range/Budget/Shoestring

Mission Catholique (17 rooms) 40 45 08 87. Clean rooms in a quiet setting next to the rather splendid church, with evening services in French on Sat & in Moore on Sun. Simple fan or AC rooms have inside shower, outside loo & are mostly singles, though some fan rooms have 2 beds. More expensive than your average mission. **$$–$$$**

Hotel Zinoogo Sanmatenga (48 rooms) 40 45 32 54; e hotel.zinoogo@fasonet.bf. The crisp gravel driveway holds promise, but it's all downhill from there; the gloomy reception leads on to fusty AC rooms with trailing wires & damp patches creeping up the walls. Fan rooms with shower but outside loo aren't too bad. **$–$$$**

Pension Pogyende (36 rooms) 40 45 31 36. Great-value en-suite fan or AC rooms are pleasant, clean, with blankets, mozzie nets & fabulous shower heads. Beds a bit lumpy. **$–$$**

L'Environnement (9 rooms) 40 45 32 34. This Ministry of Environment training centre (also known as CAF) has basic, cheap rooms. They're a bit grim, but you can get a beer, a plate of rice & watch the football, & there's even a bargain AC room up for grabs. **$**

Maison des Artisans (1 room) 40 45 31 16. This is a seriously budget option, with no shower & outside loo, & they'll look a bit startled to see you. Still, there's a tap & a bucket, & it's for an excellent cause, as all funds go to the association to plough back into training for budding artists. The room is 2,000f, or camp in the spacious courtyard for 1,000f. **$**

Auberge de Kaya A real shame: the best-located hotel in Kaya, on top of a little hill overlooking the lake, has closed. Ask around to find out if it's opened under new management.

Where to eat and drink, entertainment and nightlife

Thanks to its leather industry, Kaya has its own culinary speciality. 'Brochettes de Kaya' are not your standard beef, but a mixture of goat and mutton with a tasty peanut coating, and go for 50f a throw. You'll find them all over town, in restaurants and on the street; they're so highly rated that people passing through buy ten or so, wrap them up and take them home as foodie gifts. A word of advice: the peanut coating can burn before the meat's cooked, so check before tucking in if you're concerned about eating it rare.

For top-notch food, head for the restaurant at **Hotel Kaziende**, where there's a three-course set menu for 5,500f, but you may find yourself eating alone. Otherwise, your best bet is the *maquis* at the **Musée de Kaya**, which has a huge jaunty *paillote* and extensive menu that includes chips and *pintade* as well as the usuals. **Faso Ivoire** near the Catholic Mission dishes up huge portions of tasty *alloco* and salads to go with *brochettes* and chicken; there are Ivorian dishes on the go too. **Restaurant de la Grace** on the main drag is good for rice and couscous.

L'Escale is fine for a plate of rice, but better for booze and dancing, especially at the weekends; another good dance spot is **Les Deux Plateaux** on the Kongoussi road, where fairy lights encircle the good-sized dance floor and the music throbs into the night. The younger crowd rate **24H Chrono**, out on the Dori road, and **Le Waguess**, tucked up a side road near Hotel Zinoogo. **Resto de l'Amitié** is a bit past it, but fine for a quiet beer, while **Les Trois Luttes** is a nicely lit *maquis* at the other end of town.

Shopping Kaya's small market near the OA bus station kicks off every three days, in a close-knit series of criss-crossing streets. It is good for leather, Dori blankets, batik and indigo cloth. Look out too for the odd wood and bronze sculpture, and pottery. Market day also hosts the ***marché de betail***, an outdoor cattle market held at the other end of town, past the *auberge* and down the winding dirt track signposted towards Barsalogo. It is just after a U-bend, on the right.

The **Hall des Artisans** is satchel-and-sandal heaven, and excellent for browsing Kaya's leatherwear. Nothing is made on site, but it's all locally produced and orders are taken. It is open daily, and on market day vendors arrive from all over the region.

Maison des Artisans (☏ *40 45 31 16*) is a dynamic artisanal training centre started by local volunteers. Men and women practise a range of crafts, including weaving with four-pedal looms (one of only three sites in the country), soap-making, carpentry and *maroquinerie*. You can visit on weekdays and see people at work up close. Look out for the 'Espace Artisanal' sign on the road as you enter Kaya from Ouaga.

Other practicalities There are several **cybercafé** options. One is near the Catholic Mission (🕘 *mornings only*), charging 400f per hour. **Zam** is an excellent **general store**, almost as well stocked as the supermarkets in Ouaga and Bobo, offering cheese, yoghurt, tins and televisions. There are a few banks: **BIB** and **Ecobank** have Visa machines, while **Banque Atlantique** has a MasterCard option. There's a **pharmacy** next door to BIB. The cinema no longer works, but plenty of **street-side televisions** and the occasional DVD showing make up for it. Just follow the blare.

FROM HIDE TO HANDBAG

Kaya's leatherworkers, known as *maroquiners*, take the skins of camel, cow, sheep and goat and work them dexterously. Goat skins cost 500–2,000f, depending on size, from the town abattoir. The skin is first soaked so that the hair can be scraped and beaten off, and the hide is then left to dry like clothes on a washing line. Meanwhile, women prepare peanut oil to rub into the finished skins to give them a suppleness and a deep sheen when the leather is polished up. While many leatherworkers skip this stage, Kaya's village tanners are convinced this is why their objects are so good. After that, the hides are either left raw, or dyed black, brown or red. Both black and brown pigments come from a mixture of black rock, rusted iron and starchy *tô* water, which is left to stew until suitably pungent. The red comes from crushed millet stalks. Next, the dyed leather is shined up with wooden blocks against a wooden board. It is then ready to be cut according to a given design, stitched and sewed. Some *maroquiners* weave strips of different-coloured skins from different animals, coming up with innovative designs. Others keep it simple and stylish.

What to see and do

Tannery Tucked behind the lake, experts on the outskirts of Kaya prepare animal hides in family courtyards. They turn them into bags, purses, briefcases and much else besides.

Boureima Ouedraogo (m *70 23 29 51*) is the grand old man and expert tanner of the village, while his brother Mahamado (m *71 17 29 48*) is the head of the workshops, but there are more than ten others who work tirelessly every day, and set their standards high. Visitors are welcome to watch, and you can buy on site, although there is a remarkable lack of pressure to do so. Products are cheaper than they would be in Ouaga or even Kaya market, with perfectly finished and stylish wallets going for 1,500f; handbags and shoulder bags for 6,000–8,000f; and some lovely old-school satchels for 10,000f. You can also put in personal orders: take any plastic, material or paper bag you like, and they can turn it into a leather wonder. Stop off on your way to the Sahel, place your order, and pick it up on your way back to Ouaga.

From the cattle market, keep going on the circular track, veer left and then take a minute path on the right until you end up in the courtyard. Best to call Boureima or Mahamado – they'll happily send someone to pick you up – or take a guide.

Kaya Museum (*40 45 00 89; 08.00–12.30 & 15.00–17.30 Tue–Fri, 08.00–13.00 Sat; 1,000f*) The Musée de Kaya displays a range of Mossi statues, traditional objects, mats and Fulani straw mattresses. Another draw is the popular *maquis* on the site, offering a cheap lunch.

Kaya's lake district Lake Kaya is about 2km north out of town, by the defunct *auberge*. It's easy walking, through millet fields and market gardens. Lake Dem is 16km along a dirt road that begins in the town centre. The route is a joy, and if you're into hiking, camping or picnics, the grassy hills make for perfect excursions.

Take the small unpaved road heading northwest for Kongoussi from the main roundabout, out past the BIB bank. The going is fairly straight, bar a diversion when the road turns into a series of troughs. At a gathering of huts, venture right down a winding donkey track. It's best to go with a guide, or ask at the huts: the trip takes around half an hour.

You can rent a *pirogue* for about 2,000f per person, depending on how long you go; take it out on the lake and fish for your lunch. A little further on from the lake itself, a flat-topped hill is ripe for a quick-ish climb (beware the heat).

If you get bitten by the lakes-in-a-landlocked-country bug, then there a couple at Tougouri and Yalgo to explore; much closer to Ouaga is the enormous Ziga *barrage*. To get there you can head out east from Ouaga towards Koupela and stop at Linoghin, or on the Kaya road, stop at Bissiga, a little after Ziniare.

BANI To some visitors, Bani is one of the most memorable villages in the country, with its stunning collection of hilltop mud mosques. Others feel the entire town is reaching out for the tourist ticket in the most crass of ways.

While it's true that on arrival you are likely to be somewhat swamped by children asking for *cadeaux*, the story behind the mosques that ring the town is fascinating.

In a break with Islamic norms, six mosques fan out on the hills around the town. They snub Mecca, facing in towards Bani's central mosque rather than facing east. The local *imam*, El Hadj Hama Mohamadou Ibn Hamadou, turned away from prevailing Islamic dogma in the 1970s and created his own breakaway sect, which saw him come into conflict with the authorities and be accused of all sorts of grisly acts, including cutting off dead men's penises. His son is now *imam* and effectively acts as head of the village.

Stepping over the chunky, fallen wooden beams inside the main prayer hall, you'd be hard pushed to believe it was constructed less than 30 years ago. Built of crumbling sand, the mosques feel hundreds of years old, and a lack of proper maintenance has weathered them prematurely; only one of the hilltop mosques still has its minaret. The geometric patterns, towers and hillside arrangement are nevertheless impressive, and the villagers, led by the *imam*, are trying to organise themselves to rescue and reconstruct what's left. As a result, there may soon be a structured guide system for visiting the *grande mosquée*, along with an official entry fee.

Getting there and away All the buses heading for Dori (STMB, STAF, TSR, STN) stop at Bani (3,500f from Ouaga).

Guides You may soon find a Bureau des Guides at the *grande mosquée*, and be allocated an official guide to show you around. The fees involved will go some small way to the upkeep of the crumbling buildings. Otherwise, head for Nomade II, where either owner Nouhoume Cisse or one of the boys working there can organise a meeting to discuss the *imam*'s take on Islam; camel safaris and sleeping out under the stars among nearby sand dunes; or a visit to the gold mines at Tchagel by moped or in shared taxis. Proceeds go in part to Nouhoume's association Pamtiral M'Jamu, which supports numerous activities from children's education and women's issues to the conservation of the mosques.

Where to stay

Hotel Fofo (6 rooms) m 76 44 63 84; e csouaibou@yahoo.fr. Less of a welcome than Le Nomade (see below), & the simple rooms with mozzie nets are not quite as attractive, but it's well placed on the main road. It's run by the *imam's* brother, who is also in the process of setting up the Bureau des Guides. **$**

Le Nomade I and II (3 rooms, 8 huts) 40 46 72 08; m 76 00 40 18; e noumcisse@yahoo.fr; nomadebani@yahoo.fr. The rooms at Nomade I were being redone when we visited; the pretty huts at Nomade II are nicer anyway, set in a tranquil yard in the depths of the village & well tended by the posse of young guys who run the place. There are external facilities, mozzie nets, simple meals & lots of friendly faces. **$**

THE SAHEL

Mention the north to anyone who knows Burkina well and a misty look may come into their eyes. 'Ah,' they'll whisper, barely audible in their reverence: 'I love the north.' Even the fierce desert heat can't drive them away.

Travellers lose themselves to the Sahel. They traverse the dunes, sleep beneath its enormous canopy of stars, and a part of them never comes back. Couples love the romance so much they marry there.

A threshold region, the Sahel is fascinating for its very in-between-ness. Barren desert and lush fertility compete constantly, governing the movement of kel-Tamashek and Fulani nomads. It is a battle the desert seems to be winning, encroaching by 5cm every year.

Despite its beauty, surviving in the Sahel is a constant challenge. Life is lived at the mercy of the rains and the food crisis that swept across west Africa in 2005 hit the Burkinabe Sahel hard. A lethal combination of drought and locust invasion saw some villages' crop for the year entirely ruined, leaving one million people in need of food aid. Poor harvests continued for the next few years, until at last in 2010, decent rains brought some relief.

HISTORY The battle for control of the Sahel has been as varied as its shifting sands. The original inhabitants were the Kurumba. Mossi colonisation in the 14th century was repulsed within 100 years by expansion of the mighty Songhay Empire of Askia Mohammed, based in what is now Mali. This in turn fell to north African Berber armies under the control of Morocco in 1591. Towards the end of the 17th century, they too abandoned the Sahel, not having found the riches for which they hoped.

Since the 15th century, Fulani migrants settled in the region, stopping wherever the pasture and water was good enough for their cattle to flourish. This included Dori and the surrounding emirate Liptako (meaning 'place where we cannot be defeated' in Fulfulde). Another wave of immigration followed in the 18th century, emanating from Massina, in present-day Mali, and a second Fulani emirate, Jelgodji, based at Djibo, emerged. Initially the Fulani came to an uneasy accord with Gourma farmers already there, whereby the latter retained control over the land and its inhabitants, and had the right to choose Fulani chiefs to administer the territory. The fragile compromise ended up satisfying neither side and the Sahel rapidly slid into civil war. Stoked by Muslim fanaticism emanating from the influential Kingdom of Sokoto, in Nigeria, the Fulani declared a *jihad* on Gourma animists, pushing them southwards.

kel-Tamashek (Tuareg) Unique among the groups of Burkina Faso, the kel-Tamashek are a Berber people, originally from north Africa. Their pursuit of cross-Saharan trade brought them southwards from the 10th century. With the fall of the Songhay Empire, the kel-Tamashek reached the banks of the Beli River, at the northernmost edge of Burkina. Warlike and proud, the Udalan kel-Tamashek clan, whose ancestors originated in Algeria, launched a number of offensives into the Burkinabe Sahel, forcing Liptako to cede the northern part of its kingdom. Today the kel-Tamashek word Oudalan survives as the name of Burkina's northernmost region.

European visitors Heinreich Barth was the first *kefir* (infidel, in Arabic) to enter Dori in 1853, staying for eight days. He was not its happiest visitor, writing that 'I was very disappointed on seeing not the clean and pretty little town that I had dreamed of, but a confluence of all the elements of decadence and misery.' His lack of cowrie shells to pay for items was a real problem for local merchants. He also complained about the drought that was taking place at the time, and what he saw as 'anarchy' in the town as a result of the factionalism between the rival Fulani groups seeking to control it.

Yet his account of the market, with Arabs bringing salt from the Saharan mines of Taoudenni, Songhay merchants unloading wheat and shea butter, Ouangara traders from Guinea bringing white kola nuts and *kourdi* from the west coast, and Mossi selling their sturdy donkeys, sheets of cotton, and copper and bronze, gives a flavour of Dori's importance as part of the trans-Saharan trading economy. Even today, the weekly Friday market is the highpoint of the town.

GETTING THERE AND AWAY The north requires patience and a certain spirit of adventure to explore properly. A good tar road runs as far as Dori, but after that it's dirt roads, or just rough tracks in the sand. Many of the best spots are remote.

On leaving Dori for Gorom-Gorom, the landscape begins to change. The dunes of the Sahel begin to replace flat Sudanic plains. As you hit the trough between

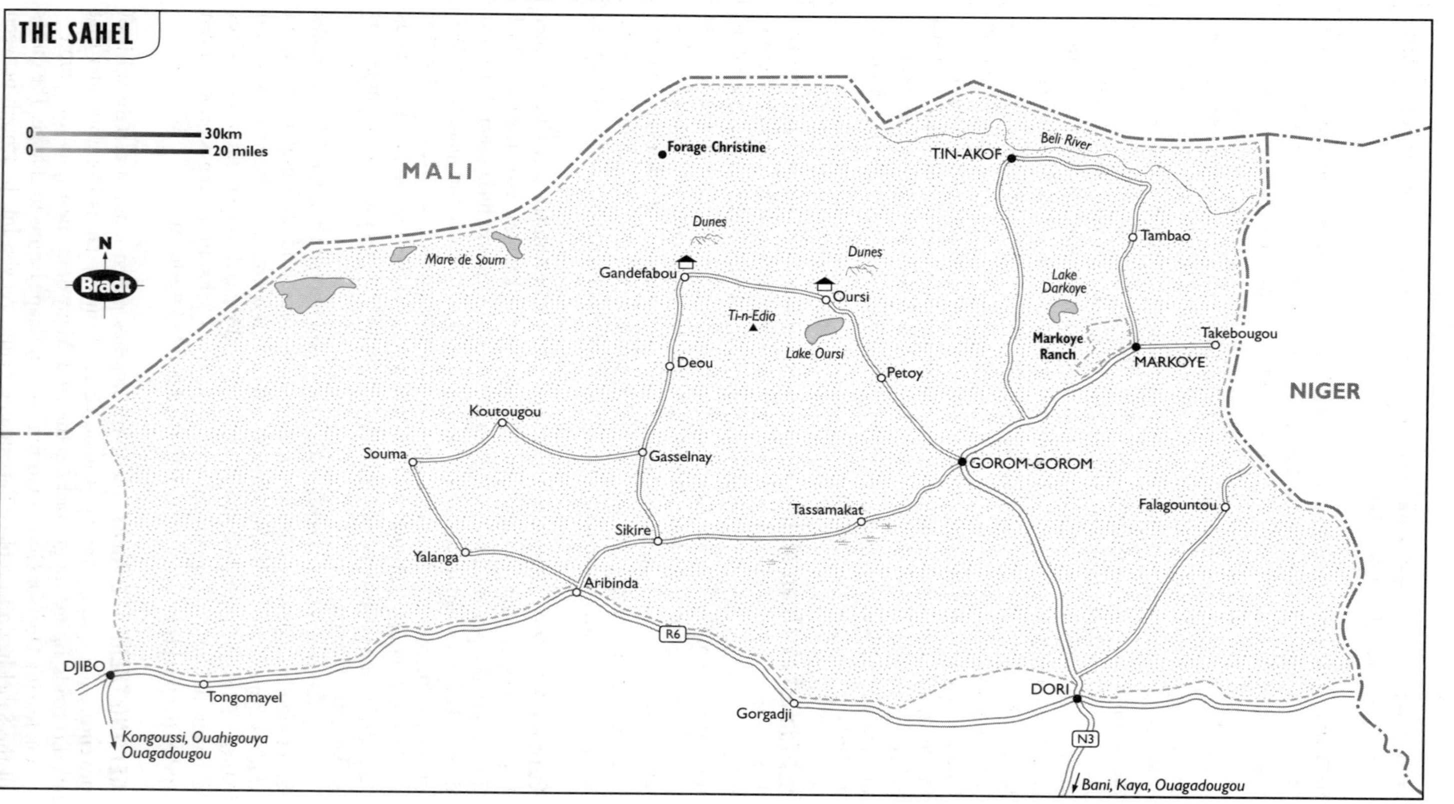
THE SAHEL
0 30km
0 20 miles
N
Bradt
MALI
Forage Christine
TIN-AKOF
Beli River
Mare de Soum
Dunes
Dunes
Tambao
Gandefabou
Oursi
Lake Darkoye
Ti-n-Edia
Lake Oursi
Markoye Ranch
Takebougou
MARKOYE
Deou
Petoy
NIGER
Koutougou
Souma
Gasselnay
GOROM-GOROM
Falagountou
Tassamakat
Sikire
Yalanga
Aribinda
R6
DJIBO
Tongomayel
Gorgadji
DORI
N3
Kongoussi, Ouahigouya
Ouagadougou
Bani, Kaya, Ouagadougou

each dune, the vegetation of palm and scrub thickens, and in the rainy season the normally dry riverbeds spring to life. As you reach the top of each dune you should have good views of the surrounding country. Note that we're generally talking *dunes mortes* here (dead dunes), which, paradoxically, means they're covered in vegetation. *Dunes vivantes*, which consist of 'live' shifting sands, are found only in pockets, the most accessible being at Oursi.

Flash flooding in the rainy season means you may have to wait a day or two in the far north, until swollen seasonal rivers have subsided. Even in a 4x4, it's not worth the risk: two people drowned in 2005, when their cars were washed away trying to cross rivers.

GUIDES There are numerous local guides who can arrange excursions throughout the Sahel, including camel treks and visits to local markets. They can even meet you at Ouaga and travel north with you and many will be hanging around the bus stations looking for customers. They tend to be young one-man bands with a bit of patter, but nevertheless know the terrain and are used to travellers. Unfortunately, not all are terribly scrupulous, and we've had very bad reports of some; some travellers have, for instance, advised us that it's best to avoid Diallo Hama and Marga Issa, should they cross your path. Guide rates tend to be about 7,500f for the day; or 17,500f per person per day for a camel safari, including tent.

For an excellent, well-connected kel-Tamashek guide, based in Dori, contact Mohamed ag Alhatab Dicko (m *78 82 25 61*). He is not a guide by profession, but offers a calm, intelligent and dedicated insight into the Sahel and has the connections to arrange all kinds of adventures in its hidden reaches. He speaks Fulfulde, Dioula and Tamashek, in addition to French. The best thing is probably to arrange your own transport and meet him in Dori.

DORI Dori signals the start of the Sahel proper, with sandy streets and tranquil night-time ambience hinting at the stillness of the dunes beyond. Famed for its thick woven blankets, you can still pick them up in the market, which is the focal point of the town.

Getting there and away STMB, STAF, TSR and STN all ply the good tar road from Ouaga to Dori (4,000f). The journey takes about 4½ hours, though that may be more like four hours with STAF, which has a reputation for speed to the point of recklessness. See *Kaya*, page 169, for departure times. On the way back to Ouaga, STMB (m *78 85 35 52*) leaves at 07.00 and 13.00; STAF has four departures, at 05.30/06.00 and 11.30/12.00; TSR (m *70 99 49 25*) goes at 06.30 and 13.00. STN has the last service, at 15.00, but it's also the most rickety, so check it's still running.

SAHEL MARKET DAYS

Monday	Markoye, Tassamakat
Tuesday	Sawga
Wednesday	Djibo, Tin-Akof
Thursday	Gorom-Gorom
Friday	Dori
Saturday	Deou, Aribinda
Sunday	Oursi, Essakane

YOGHURT

Yoghurt is an important feature of the culinary landscape of Burkina and much of it hails from the Sahel. It might seem strange that so much store is set by a few bacteria when a dodgy electricity supply makes refrigeration such a nightmare. Yet a rummage around even the unlikeliest of fridges will usually reveal yoghurt in sachets, in bottles, in pots.

It all comes down to a combination of Burkina's cattle-rearing heritage and a climate too hot to handle fresh milk before it goes off. Although yields are relatively poor – a Burkinabe cow produces on average a litre of milk a day compared with 35 litres a day in Europe – numerous collectives and cottage outfits have sprung up to produce delicious milk and yoghurt that is found all over the country.

Lait caillé is essentially soured milk, and forms an important part of a cattle-herder's diet. *Gappal* is another popular brew, although an acquired taste. The chewy bits that resemble muesli flakes or porridge are millet grains, thrown in virtually raw after a bit of pounding, giving the mixture the consistency of Polyfilla. In people's homes, *gappal* is made using soured milk and is fairly runny. Order it in a local restaurant and you will probably be treated to a thick yoghurt version. Often it'll be served without spoons – just take the bowl to your lips and slurp it down. It's sweet, fibrous and delicious.

For onward travel north up the dirt road, the only coach company still running is Sogebaf (see *Gorom-Gorom*, page 181). More reliable are the minibuses that go to Gorom at around 07.00 or 08.00 daily, and again at around 11.00 or 12.00, leaving from the *autogare*.

Orientation and practicalities The Total station makes a great meeting point, right at the centre of the town. Off to the east, past the Liptako Hotel, lie some good accommodation and nightspots, while across the road is the *gare routière* for taxis to outlying destinations; the tar road twists its way through town before coming to a halt about 1km on the other side. The **cyberposte** in the centre of town has internet for 500f an hour, as does **Sahel Informatique** (m 70 13 45 83), towards the east. The **BIB** bank has a Visa ATM, Western Union facility and can change euros; **Ecobank** also has a Visa machine.

Where to stay

Mid range

Hebergement Dintal (21 rooms) 40 46 05 48; m 70 25 52 76, 76 68 00 10; e fdiagous@yahoo.fr. A work in progress so a bit of a building site, but en-suite rooms are comfortable with choice of fan or AC, & there may be a garden to sit in before long. **$$–$$$**

Hotel Liptako (11 rooms) 40 46 01 70; m 78 21 55 42; e adamatoure69@yahoo.fr. A good central option. Complicated apartment structure, 1 with fans only, means sharing bathrooms in all but 3 AC rooms (which have TV & hot water) – but in practice, you'll probably get a lounge & bathroom to yourself, plus a balcony for watching donkey/*moto* action below. **$$–$$$**

Hotel Oasis du Sahel (10 rooms) 40 46 06 00. Run by the proprietor of the Hotel de l'Amitié in Ouahigouya, but with nowhere near the same care. A row of white faux leather sofas (with gold studs) adorns the foyer; beyond are echoey, desolate rooms with bare concrete floors. Choice of fan or AC, the latter with TV & hot water. **$$–$$$**

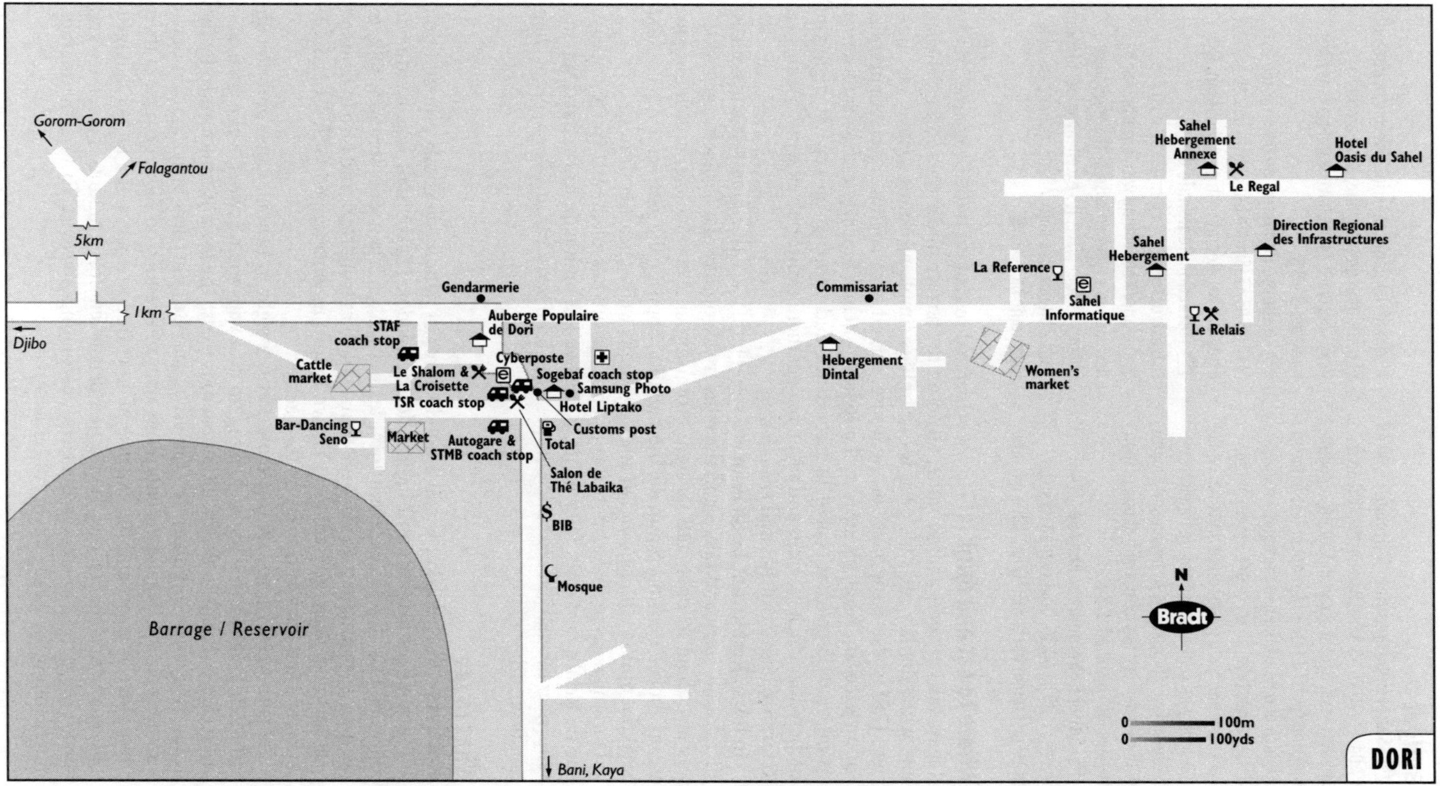

DORI

Gorom-Gorom
Falagantou
5km
1km
Djibo
Gendarmerie
Auberge Populaire de Dori
STAF coach stop
Cattle market
Le Shalom & La Croisette
Cyberposte
Sogebaf coach stop
Samsung Photo
Hotel Liptako
TSR coach stop
Customs post
Bar-Dancing Seno
Market
Autogare & STMB coach stop
Total
Salon de Thé Labaika
BIB
Mosque
Bani, Kaya
Barrage / Reservoir
Commissariat
Hebergement Dintal
La Reference
Sahel Informatique
Women's market
Sahel Hebergement
Le Relais
Direction Regional des Infrastructures
Sahel Hebergement Annexe
Le Regal
Hotel Oasis du Sahel
N
Bradt
0 100m
0 100yds

Budget

Sahel Hebergement (40 rooms) 40 46 07 04; m 70 75 58 85; e nadejustin@yahoo.fr. Friendly staff, decent accommodation, a popular meeting spot/TV venue, & more or less home to a bunch of guys working in the nearby mines. Noise carries here, so try to get a room at the back. Veranda good for roadside drinking, while the courtyard restaurant serves up omelettes for breakfast. Choice of AC or fan en-suite rooms with mozzie nets; fan rooms with showers soon to have loos installed. **$$**

Sahel Hebergement Annexe (14 rooms) 40 46 00 36. Quieter than its sister hotel just round the corner. Good value en-suite AC or fan rooms are cheerful blue-green instead of institution grey & white, & set around a leafy courtyard. Some have standing fans only, however. **$–$$**

Auberge Populaire de Dori (8 rooms) 40 46 05 55. Simple but central hostel, next to a popular bar. Rooms with or without fan. **$**

Direction Regionale des Infrastructures (7 rooms) 40 46 02 99. If you fancy hobnobbing with government or development types *en mission* this *maison de passage* is your place. It's excellent value, though feels a bit out on a limb. All rooms have en-suite loos; some have AC. **$**

Where to eat and drink The most celebrated restaurant is the Sengalese-run **Le Regal**. Tasty *riz gras* and *riz sauce*, taken on the terrace under the setting Sahelian sun, while donkey carts file past, is one of life's simple pleasures. *Gappal* (see box, page 178) is also a speciality of the house, served with yoghurt rather than milk. For an excellent meat fix, head to **Le Relais**, where a lunchtime chop stall serves up delicious *brochettes* coated in tasty sauce and chopped-up veg. At night the kitchen does chicken, chips and salad, but get there early or it's all gone. Maquis **La Reference** has rice dishes and *grillades*.

In town, **Restaurant Le Shalom** is a sweet little place that does teas and coffees, juices, soup, steak and salads and the regular rice options; **La Croisette**, next door, was just about to open and its sign, promising an extensive menu including ice cream, looked exciting. **Salon de Thé Labaika**, opposite the *gare routière*, is a good breakfast option with *café au lait* and yoghurt as well as heartier dishes.

Dori manages to shake off its torpor once the sun has relented. If you're out east, **Bar Le Relais**, decked in fairy lights, is the liveliest option; in town, **Bar-Dancing Seno**, near the market, announces its presence loud and clear, and has a row of chop stands outside.

What to see

Markets Dori's **market** is still a good source of handmade goods – in addition to the range of blankets and indigo cloth, Amadou Dicko's stall sells handmade cotton tablecloths. An excellent local leather-maker, Mamadou Ibrahim, sells to boutiques. He lives in the village of Mamassiol, 4km from Dori, and is so in demand that Burkinabe couples have been known to turn up on a moped, pick up a couple of poufs and return with them on the back.

Friday's weekly open-air **cattle market** is a sight to behold. Cows gore the air with their long twisting horns, kicking up dust with their hooves, while goats and sheep change hands in the shade of generous trees. The town is transformed by the steady procession of Fulani, kel-Tamashek and Bella herders arriving from dawn with their beasts. Despite the enormous array of livestock on show, because of their importance as assets and the expense of cows in particular, not a lot actually gets sold on a typical market day. The furious debate, endless drinking of green tea and intense inspection of udders is utterly fascinating however. To find the market, simply follow the steady lowing of cattle.

GOROM-GOROM Hailed as the crowning glory of the north, Gorom-Gorom's market day is an impressive riot of colour and activity. Every Thursday morning before daybreak, arrivals from across the region set off on moped, bicycle, donkey and camel, to lay out their stalls. In the evenings, Gorom residents who have completed a good day's business give the town's bars a lively feel. Fulani cattle herders mingle with Songhay farmers, kel-Tamashek barter with Mossi merchants; there are even Moors, originally from north Africa, selling dates and rock salt on the fringes of the market square.

Sadly, the market has suffered in recent years. It is as colourful as ever, but many of the traditional handicraft stalls have been replaced by imported Chinese products: plastic shoes, kettles and buckets take pride of place. You need to look hard to find jewellery, carvings and leather goods for which the market gained its reputation, although they are certainly still there. It is a great place to soak up Sahelian vibes, and a good staging post for treks to hamlets and villages deep in the dunes that make for some of the most beautiful locations in Burkina.

Getting there and away Sogebaf runs buses to Gorom from Ouaga twice a week, on Wednesdays and Sundays, which carry on to Markoye. However, since the death of its owner, the company is falling into disarray. The garage in Ouaga is now lost, unmarked, in the backstreets of Dapoya and is a nightmare to find; better to get a reliable service to Dori and take it from there. Minibuses to Gorom leave Dori *gare routière* at around 07.00 or 08.00 daily and again at about 11.00 or 12.00 (2,000f); both then leave Gorom early in the morning to coincide with lunchtime coach departures to Ouaga from Dori. The Sogebaf service, if it continues, leaves for Ouaga on Thursday and Monday.

Orientation, getting around and practicalities While town life revolves around the market square, most of the town's accommodation and nightlife are dispersed elsewhere. Walking is a great way of exploring the town, although you could enquire about bicycle hire in the market or at your hotel if you want get around quickly. You're best taking out money or changing travellers' cheques in Ouagadougou, as Gorom is not well served by banks.

There are three internet cafés, all central, where an hour costs 500f – **Cybercafé Informatique** is near the Catholic Mission; **Hakime Cyber** is just off to the left before the police post, and the third is on the main road in from Dori.

Guides As a result of the slump in tourism, many guides in Gorom have been forced to look for other work, which means that stepping off the bus is not the hassle it used to be. However, if you want to arrange a camel trek, or an excursion to outlying villages, some form of accompaniment is a good idea and there are still plenty of people to call on. Of the hotels, the Campement Wouroutou and Relais du Campement Edjef are your best bet. The rates at the Edjef are pretty good, and give you a guideline – 15,000f for a full day's camel trip; 9,000f for a half day; 7,500f for a couple of hours; guiding 5,000f a day. In town, try **La Maison du Sahel Suudu-Baaba** (m *70 72 55 97, 70 38 23 46;* e *lamaisondusahel@yahoo.fr*), which provides an umbrella for ONTB-recognised guides. At 15,000f per day they're not cheap, however. Alternatively, Moussa Kadri (m *70 42 26 85*), who has motorbikes for hire, can also arrange overnight camel trips to Menegou for 15,000f.

Where to stay There have been some good additions to the Gorom accommodation list in recent years; unfortunately, they're mostly out of the centre, so ring ahead if you want to avoid a long trudge.

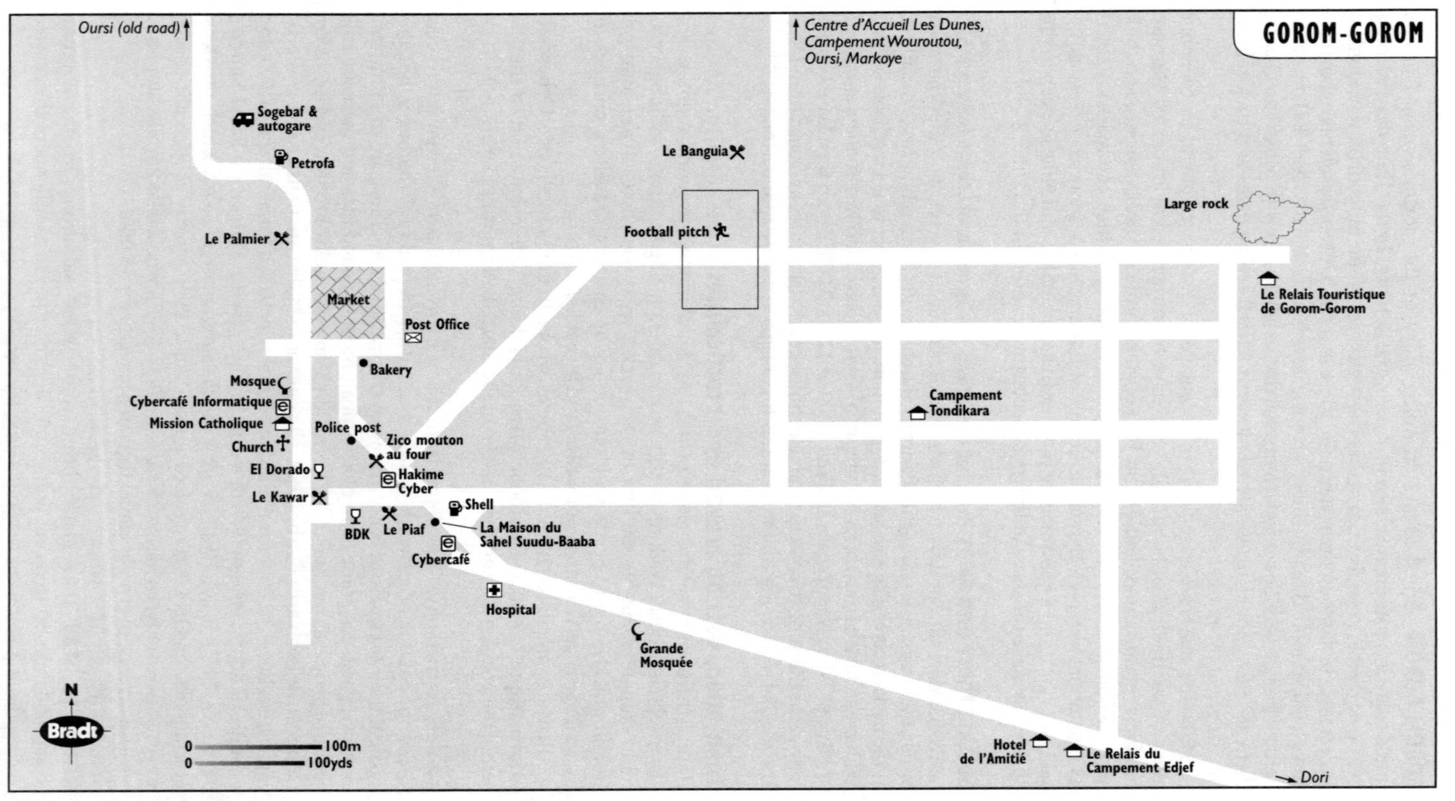
GOROM-GOROM
Oursi (old road)
Centre d'Accueil Les Dunes, Campement Wouroutou, Oursi, Markoye
Sogebaf & autogare
Petrofa
Le Banguia
Large rock
Football pitch
Le Palmier
Market
Post Office
Le Relais Touristique de Gorom-Gorom
Bakery
Mosque
Cybercafé Informatique
Mission Catholique
Church
Police post
Zico mouton au four
Campement Tondikara
El Dorado
Hakime Cyber
Le Kawar
Shell
BDK
Le Piaf
La Maison du Sahel Suudu-Baaba
Cybercafé
Hospital
Grande Mosquée
N
Bradt
0
100m
0
100yds
Hotel de l'Amitié
Le Relais du Campement Edjef
Dori

Mid range

Campement Tondikara (20 rooms) 40 46 90 29. A good 15mins from town. Pretty stencilling on the walls goes some way to make up for the air of neglect. All en suite, the AC rooms are a bit overpriced; the fan options aren't bad. **$$–$$$**

Hotel de l'Amitié (20 rooms) 40 46 94 40; m 70 55 84 19. Reasonably convenient location on the road in from Dori doesn't make up for bare concrete floors & mean-looking beds. AC option the most expensive in town, & not worth it. Fan option reasonable. **$$–$$$**

Budget/Shoestring

Campement Wouroutou (4 rooms) m 76 43 44 59, 76 08 74 73; e wouroutou@yahoo.com. One of the very few places in Burkina set up by an Englishman, out on the Markoye road. The dinky banco rooms are built in *voute nubienne* style, so are refreshingly cool; they're neatly painted, & have finishing touches such as arched windows & little mirrors. Meals & drinks available, also 4x4 hire & excursions. A word of caution: Diallo Hama was working here when we visited (see page 177). **$$**

Centre D'Acceuil Les Dunes (10 rooms) 40 46 91 17/18. Run by nuns (the proceeds go towards an orphanage), these neat en-suite AC rooms, set around a tranquil indoor courtyard, offer both comfort & excellent value. You can get breakfast & meals in the pleasant but canteen-esque restaurant. Off to the left up the new Markoye road. B/fast 750f; meals 2,000f. **$$**

Le Relais du Campement Edjef (4 rooms) 40 46 93 96; m 70 32 66 46, 79 03 86 37; www.gandefabou.org. The first of the trio of Gandefabou camps, this is a basic stopping-off point for visitors rather than a place that you might want to spend a few days. About 1.5km from the centre, simple huts have a bucket shower area & solid concrete beds with mattress on top. Rates that seem fine out in Gandefabou appear a bit steep here: simple meals are 2,500–3,500f, & per-person pricing (5,000f) makes the huts poor value too. However, this is an excellent place for arranging excursions & onward travel to Oursi/Gandefabou. **$$**

Le Relais Touristique de Gorom-Gorom (11 rooms) 40 46 94 44. Creaking slowly towards completion, it's to be hoped that this ONTB project will finally open by the time of publication. About 1km from town, the tranquil location is presided over by a solitary rock outcrop perfect for sunset scrambles, & the building, in solid red brick, contains attractive en-suite rooms, some of which will have AC. Phone to check if it's open & for prices.

Mission Catholique (7 rooms) 40 46 92 57. The slightly complicated rooming system consists of 3 rooms each containing 2 single beds, & then an apartment-style arrangement with 3 double rooms (without doors) off a corridor containing 2 single beds. Everything from rooms to external toilet & showers is pretty dilapidated, but there are mozzie nets, & it's cheap. **$**

Where to eat and drink **Le Kawar**, near the Catholic Mission, has shady seating, a simple tasty menu and bottles of fresh juice. Just before the police post coming into town, there's a great *mouton au four* place (oven-cooked mutton) that gets going at around 10.00; there's no sign, so ask for 'Zico'. They do chicken and *pintade* in the evenings, which you can pick up and take to one of the *maquis* nearby – **BDK**, or **El Dorado**. In the same area, **Café Resto Le Piaf** is a good breakfast spot.

Around the market, you can find *café au lait* in the morning and chicken in the evenings, while kiosk **Le Palmier**, just to the north, dishes up standard rice fare.

Le Banguia, with its large bar and dancing area, used to be the centre of Gorom nightlife, drawing visiting civil servants, local traders and occasional expats. It's not quite what it was, but the garlic chicken is still worth waiting an age for, and the beer is always ice-cold. When it first opened, the restaurant at **Hotel de l'Amitié** had delicious couscous with chickpeas; it's worth seeing if they've kept it up.

BEAUTY CONTEST WITH A DIFFERENCE

Fulani women, with their immaculately coiffed hair, and decorated with eye-catching silver coins, bright fabrics and striking facial tattoos, have a reputation for beauty. It is also said that while beauty is highly prized in Fulani culture, women are not always terribly well treated. The *kalala* is a traditional game played on the last day of any feast that does not exactly do wonders for womankind. In the afternoon, Fulani elders go round the party as a kind of quality control, weeding out any girl considered too ugly for the gathering. The unfortunate guest is then left to languish in a makeshift enclosure, unseen, where she cannot spoil anyone's enjoyment of the party. It is up to her friends to buy her out of this prison if she wants to rejoin the evening's fun.

NORTH OF GOROM

Markoye The town's splendid Monday market is its highlight, with extensive cattle trading, and a wonderful selection of traditional arts and crafts including decorated saddle bags and traditional sandals (*samaras*). This is real camel-trekking territory, with excursions to nearby Lake Darkoye a good option.

Markoye also has importance as an archaeological site. Researchers at the University of Ouagadougou have discovered a Neolithic settlement that is the oldest recorded evidence of human habitation in Burkina Faso. At the time of writing, the Ministry of Culture, Arts and Tourism was looking at ways of preserving the site and opening it up to visits. A local association has been set up, and a museum is under consideration.

The village of Takebougou, 10km east of Markoye, is famed for its rock paintings.

Getting there and away The Sogebaf bus that stops at Gorom continues on to Markoye; departure times from Gorom are at roughly 19.00 on Sundays and Wednesdays, if it makes it at all. From Markoye, departures are 14.00 on Mondays and 13.30 on Thursdays. Bush taxis from Gorom leave early on Monday mornings and cost 1,000f.

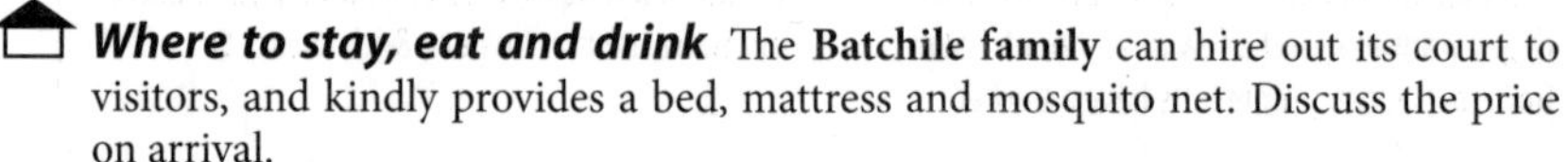

Where to stay, eat and drink The **Batchile family** can hire out its court to visitors, and kindly provides a bed, mattress and mosquito net. Discuss the price on arrival.

Sahel Espace Zigberi; 50 30 18 02 (Ouaga); http://sahel.espace.free.fr. A hunting lodge some distance from Markoye towards Darkoye & the village of Zigberi. Well-decorated rooms cost 20,000f a night. **$$$**

Gite de l'Oudalan (6 rooms) 40 46 99 13. A delightful *campement* in the centre of town with simple huts, or en-suite rooms. Meals available. **$**

Tin-Akof The tiny town of Tin-Akof, 75km north of Gorom, is situated on a bend of the Beli River, a tributary of the Niger that forms the last natural border before Mali. Nestled among the dunes, it is one of the most picturesque Sahelian villages, and an ornithologist's dream.

Perhaps due to its inaccessibility, Tin-Akof has retained a genuine kel-Tamashek market, where nomads arrive from Burkina, Mali and Niger every Wednesday to trade camels. Expect to see locally made guitars, leather sandals, silver jewellery and camel whips too. Tin-Akof is also great for launching a trip to Gao and Menaka, in

above **Barren desert and lush fertility compete constantly in the Sahel, governing the movement of kel-Tamashek camel caravans** (DF/P) page 174

below **Villages around Koudougou rely on subsistence agriculture, including rice-planting** (KM/JK) page 265

left Sindou Peaks are a series of monumental sculptures formed by the age-old movement of oceans, and the beating of the rain and the wind (GH) page 299

below The lakeside village of Tengrela is known for its hippopotami, but is also a great hang-out for anyone in search of an introduction to rural Burkina (GH) page 297

above Niansogoni is notable for its dramatic collection of abandoned cave dwellings built into the stunning escarpment that looms over the village (GH) page 302

right One of more than 200 sculptures at Laongo sculpture park (GH) page 157

below Scramble around, swim or sunbathe at Karfiguela falls (GH) page 296

above Daily prayers at Bobo-Dioulasso's *grande mosquée*, the largest in Burkina Faso (L/P) page 288

left The Bobo-Dioulasso market was renovated in 2001, but many of its older features have been left intact (SS) page 287

below Capital city Ouagadougou offers a brilliant bazaar of modern west African life (SS) page 115

bottom Mud-bricked buildings in the hilltop village of Koro, overlooking the plain to Banfora (KM/JK) page 289

above The Lobi build with slabs of mud, not bricks (GH) page 240

right The striking sculpture in Place Naba Koom, home to some of Ouagadougou's best garlic chicken (BR) page 135

below Bani's *grande mosquée.* Controversially, six mosques face towards it on the surrounding hillside, instead of facing Mecca (GH) page 173

above **The Tour du Faso hits a dirt road section** (CH) page 54

left **Burkina hosts a continent-wide artisanal extravaganza, called SIAO, every even-numbered year** (GH) page 146

below left **The Marka are particularly keen on weaving, and while women look after pigment and dying, men tend to work the looms** (FOR/R/C) page 101

below right **Raindancer tribal mask, Ouagadougou** (SS) page 100

above right Turka granaries in Toumousseni (GH) page 298

right Dori's weekly open-air cattle market is a sight to behold (GH) page 180

below A bronze vendor takes a break from selling his work (BR) page 101

above Sacred reptiles – crocodiles and humans are thought to share the same spirit (GH) page 256

left The gnarled baobab tree is a constant sight in Burkina; one of the most striking is at Toumousseni (L/P) page 298

below Tortoises are a sign of virtue, happiness, fertility and longevity, linking men and the spirits (GH) page 255

Mali, and further on to Hombori, Djenne, the Dogon land and Timbuktu. There are also interesting routes across Gourma country to the northeast via Tessit or Tillit, with the possibility of crossing the Niger at Gourma Rharous.

Getting there and away During winter months you can reach Tin-Akof in one day from Ouaga. It is also possible to reach Tin-Akof from Ouahigouya, via Djibo, although if you do this by public transport count on three to four days. Bush taxis leave from the centre of Gorom every Tuesday evening, to arrive in Tin-Akof about three hours later in time for Wednesday market day. It costs 2,000f one-way. Taxis return on Wednesday evening, after the market. For car or *moto* hire options, see section on getting to Oursi (below).

Local trips and guides When arriving in Tin-Akof ask for Ayad, a friendly kel-Tamashek with excellent knowledge of the region. He is the local representative of Abis (Association Burkinabe Idi du Sahel), an organisation protecting and promoting kel-Tamashek sites and culture.

A travel programme organised by him can include camel trekking to Bella, Fulani and kel-Tamashek camps; *pirogue* trips on the Beli River; visiting typical Sahel markets, mines and goldfields; wildlife-spotting around Lake Darkoye; music and dance performances; visits to local artisans; and occasional marriage feasts and sacred ceremonies.

Where to stay

Campement Abis Basic, but a Tuareg tent provides enough shade & there are acceptable toilet & washing facilities & water supplies. **$**

Campement Assilim Namane (3 huts) m 70 67 27 29, 70 30 82 87. The name means 'by the water' in Tamashek, giving an idea of the *campement's* setting, close to the river. 3 simple Tuareg tents each have 2 beds; meals can be rustled up with a bit of notice. It's on the way out of town on the left. **$**

WEST OF GOROM

Oursi Oursi is one of Burkina's undiscovered pearls – a spectacular natural setting on an enormous lake, the Mare d'Oursi. Nearby dunes imbue it with a suitable Saharan feel, significant archaeological remains give the area historical interest and an international project has created the opportunity for some great birdwatching. Sadly, due to current concerns about security in the region, tourists are no longer allowed to sleep out in the open if there's a *campement* nearby – in other words, among the dunes at Oursi. The logic is a little odd, as you can still camp in more remote locations such as Menegou or Tasmakate.

A new *mairie* in Oursi has introduced a 1,000f tourist tax to be paid by all visitors to the village. In practice, the *campements* may get you out of it, their argument being that they already pay a nightly tax for you.

Getting there and away A few years back the Dutch financed an excellent dirt road, complete with shiny roadsigns, from Gorom to Oursi. Those with their own vehicle in search of a little old-fashioned romance can pick up the old road to Oursi, which starts behind the new cattle market – 'a little bit more Paris–Dakar' as one well-seasoned visitor put it. The rough, rutted track meets up with the new Oursi road after about 10km.

Neither the Gandefabou or Oursi camps offers a pick-up service as such; they will come, but on the basis that you're hiring the vehicle or motorbikes – rates are 45,000f per day for a 4x4, or 15,000f for *motos* (both excluding fuel; can include driver). Other options in Gorom include the Wouroutou camp, which can arrange 4x4 hire; Moussa Kadri (m *70 42 26 85*), who has motorbikes for hire at 15,000f a day, notably *including* fuel; and guys in the market, who charge similar rates. *Moto* hire is more expensive than elsewhere in the country because they're generally high-suspension off-road beasts that nevertheless take a battering in the sand. If you do find a moped, you'll be fine as far as Oursi, but don't hope to take it any further.

Plenty of transport leaves for Oursi early on a Sunday morning, coming back in the evening or on Monday, and sporadically at other times too. Tickets cost around 1,000f. Another possibility is to ask around the market for 'Cowboy', who has a Land Rover that he drives up and down between Gorom and Deo, passing through Oursi *en route*.

Where to stay

Campement Aounaf (variable number of huts/tents) 40 46 90 64, 40 46 70 12. Fantastically atmospheric camp of open-sided Tuareg tents, sweeping, low-roofed Fulani shelters (often remade, so numbers change), *voute nubienne* mud & armadillo-like Songhay huts, all overlooking the lake. Or simply take your bed & net outside & sleep out under the stars. The friendly manager is a kel-Tamashek ex-nurse who speaks a smattering of English. The restaurant serves good food, including excellent mechoui, although you must order in advance. There is even an open-air dancefloor if you want to hire the camp for a party (100,000f). **$$**

Relais du Campement Edjef (3 huts) 40 46 70 15; m 72 42 28 74. Another simple stopping-off point for the Gandefabou camp; big mud huts house mattresses & bucket showers among the *dune mortes* at the far end of Oursi. Meals available. **$$**

What to see and do

Camel treks From Campement Aounaf and the nearby ruins, you can trek out to Ganadaouri Lake. It's about a 45-minute camel ride, and the shade of lakeside trees makes for a good picnic lunch spot as Fulani herdsmen bring their flocks down to drink. Treks cost 15,000f per person.

Oursi dunes These are within walking distance of Oursi – they are also about a day's camel ride from Gorom – and make a wonderful spot to watch the sun go down. From here you have magnificent views across the Sahel to the Mare d'Oursi.

Oursi ruins and museum Well preserved because the settlement was sacked in a raid around 1,000 years ago, the Oursi **ruins** are 'one of the most important archaeological sites in west Africa', according to Christoph Pelzer, a German historian who first discovered them in 1996 and has devoted much of the last 15 years to protecting and developing the site (see box, opposite). It's very much an ongoing project, in that digging will recommence if or when funding is found. The fascinating excavations are now shielded from the Sahel wind and sand by a big barn-like structure.

The adjacent **Hu-beero Museum** (*40 46 70 25;* m *70 36 76 33, 70 60 87 84; www.oursi-hubeero.com; entry 2,000f, covers both ruins & museum*) is beautifully laid out in a mud *voute nubienne* building, the work of the Development Workshop in Djibo (see page 191). It gives clear explanations (in French) of the dig and its aftermath, along with the history of the region, and includes some great photography. The two guides on site, Mero and Aly, are friendly, helpful and are learning English.

Camel treks up to the museum from Campement Aounaf cost 10,000f. The journey takes around 30 minutes.

Birdwatching The Mare d'Oursi is home to roughly 20,000 aquatic birds, comprising 150 species (of which 50 are palearctic). It's been designated a ZICO site (Zone Important pour la Conservation des Oiseaux), and an international partnership, which includes BirdLife International and RSPB, is working on its protection. A vital aspect of this consists of planting grasses around the shores of the lake to slow down its gradual silting up with sand, while surveys and ringing programmes monitor the bird populations and awareness programmes create understanding among local people.

MIDDLE AGES HIDDEN BEHIND SAND DUNES

Christoph Pelzer

If you want to see how the history of the Sahel has changed in the last millennium, Oursi offers a hands-on archaeological site. In 2000/2001, a team of archaeologists from the universities of Frankfurt/Main (Germany) and Ouagadougou excavated a site that they had discovered some years earlier. They named it, together with the villagers, Oursi *hu-beero*, meaning 'the big house of Oursi' in Songhay, the language spoken in the village.

This complex structure, dating from the 10th century, is a rare example of preserved mud-brick architecture ruins. Normally, such ruins are completely destroyed by wind and weather shortly after the inhabitants have left. Here, an unhappy event for the medieval population turned *hu-beero* into a sensational archaeological find: because the house had been attacked and burnt down by raiders its basic structures were hardened by the fire and preserved intact. The collapse of a massive roof structure further protected the basic structure for the next millennium.

After the research project had ended, I stayed on in Burkina Faso as a member of the archaeological team to develop the site as a pilot project for cultural preservation and tourist development in the Sahel. Co-operating with the Burkina Ministry of Culture, Arts and Tourism, we raised funds from international donors and worked with the population to preserve the site from its immediate destruction by erosion. The project is now run by locals, but remains under national authority.

The result is an entirely covered and protected site, complemented by a beautiful little mud-brick museum, aesthetically designed to fit the landscape and ecologically built in woodless construction.

Inside the museum, the fine white sand of the dunes covers the floor, exactly as in the settlement a millennium ago. The exhibition tells the story of the project, displays replicas of objects recovered from the site, gives information on what was discovered in the excavations and explains the historic changes over the last centuries that have turned the Sahel into the area it is now.

From the museum you can visit the site next door to experience history at first hand. Structures remain in place to a height of 1.5m, most notably the large pillars that would have once supported the heavy roof on top of which people lived and worked. Different parts of the house are clearly visible, with some objects still in place. Of special interest is the kitchen area, which contains storage jars and grinding stones.

Situated at the top of a whole series of settlement mounds, you get a nice view over a typical Sahelian landscape to the north. It is just possible to imagine the sight of medieval horsemen riding up to you from the far distance.

For more information, e christoph.pelzer@oursi-hubeero.de, or visit www.oursi-hubeero.com.

'Le groupe de soutien au site' has an office (m *70 47 08 51, 70 36 76 33*) next to Campement Aounaf. Local guides have been well trained, and know of a series of natural hides around the lake. Binoculars (1,000f a day) and telescopes (3,000f a day) are available for hire, along with copies of Borrow & Demey's *Birds of Western Africa* (1,000f a day). There are a further 11 lakes in the surrounding region, which can also be visited. Guiding fees are 10,000f per site.

Gandefabou One of Burkina's most remote outposts, this kel-Tamashek village is a haven amid the dunes. Soaking up the serenity of the location can be enough for many visitors; with only the odd glass of steaming green tea or the jingle of cattle bells to disturb the scene. The more actively minded can organise a visit to the village on the other side of the *wadi*; trek to nearby nature reserve Forage Christine; explore a local burial site on foot; visit the hills around the town of Deo; or take camel rides on the dunes. Rissa, who runs the local camp, is a great source of local knowledge and information.

Where to stay

Campement Edjef (variable number of huts) 40 46 68 54; m 70 61 21 30. Edjef means 'dune' in Tamashek, giving an idea of the camp's idyllic setting alongside a seasonal riverbed. Each traditional Tuareg or Fulani shelter has a kerosene lamp & double bed, or you can sleep outside. The idea is to drink in the local way of life; if you want luxuries such as soft drinks or beers, bring them with you, or order in advance. If you don't have wheels, a transfer here involves car or *moto* hire (see Oursi, above); meals cost 2,500–3,500f pp, more for *mechoui*, for which you'll need to give notice. **$$**

Aribinda On the approach to Aribinda the countryside begins to change significantly, as large granite outcrops, seemingly dropped from the sky and spaced at wide intervals, dominate the countryside.

You can explore the rocks that loom over the town, which are also home to rock paintings depicting animals and hunters. Don't expect too much in the way of explanation, however, as remarkably little is known about who made them and when. The paucity of historical information about these daubings is perhaps a reason simply to enjoy the gentle 20-minute exertion of a climb to the top, which gives a good panorama of the plain below. Whether you take a guide or not, a band of curious, excited children will most likely accompany you.

Djibo Much less visited than Dori, the small, sleepy outpost of Djibo makes a convenient alternative entry point into the Sahel for anyone coming via Ouahigouya or Kongoussi.

Like Dori, Djibo was also the headquarters of a Fulani emirate, Jelgodji, which came under the influence of the theocratic state of Massina, in Mali. On passing through Jelgodji in 1853, Heinrich Barth noted an independent spirit – Djibo detested the strict authoritarianism of the Massina Empire, and was regularly in revolt. On the streets, men smoked openly, and the women wore jewellery – both of which were outlawed in Massina.

The highlight of Djibo is its lively cattle market, every Wednesday, and its local jewellery industry is still strong. Djibo's architecture is also worth observing. In addition to some fancy mud-brick dwellings, it is also the headquarters of a new initiative to promote woodless construction (see box, page 191).

The town is also a good staging post for trips up into Dogon country in Mali, and there are a number of independent guides hanging around the bus stations who can organise a trip.

Getting there and away STAF (m *70 28 17 96*) has a daily departure for Djibo from Ouagadougou, via Kongoussi, which leaves at 07.30. Tickets cost 4,000f/7,000f return. There's another departure at 15.30 for Kongoussi; you could try to get a bush taxi from there.

If you are already in Ouahigouya, the back route to Djibo is a great way into the Sahel, taking in notable mud-brick mosques at the villages of You and Toulfe and the museum at Pobe Mengao. If you have a couple of days, take your time in the back of a bush taxi, stopping off along the way at anywhere that takes your fancy.

The only coach company to do the Ouahigouya–Djibo run is STNF. Departures from Ouahigouya are at 09.00 and 16.00 (2,000f); they also stop at Titao and Pobe Mengao.

There is no regular public transport to continue from Djibo to either Dori or Gorom-Gorom, but you can often find trucks or *bachées* heading towards local markets in the region. To get a lift go to the police post and wait.

Where to stay and eat

Auberge La Savane 40 56 06 02; m 70 38 55 05. On the right on the way in from Ouaga – look out for the sign. Pleasant AC bungalows offer the most upmarket accommodation in town. **$$$**

Hotel Massa m 76 03 04 71. Well equipped for *brochettes* & simple meals; rooms not so appealing, but functional & central. Choice of fan with outside loo, or en-suite AC. **$–$$**

Auberge de Djibo (12 rooms) m 76 50 94 14. On the way in from Ouaga. Has basic, fairly grim rooms with outside facilities. **$**

Around the market there is the usual selection of tasty meat grills.

POBE MENGAO Pobe Mengao, 27km southwest of Djibo and 82km northeast from Ouahigouya, represents the spiritual centre of Kurumba country. The Kurumba have their origins in the region of Say and Niamey in present-day Niger, but moved westwards to settle on the fertile plains bordering the Sahel and establish the Kingdom of Lurum, centred at Pobe Mengao.

When the Mossi arrived centuries later, they took control of the region through integration rather than subjugation, grafting their own socio-political system onto what already existed.

In a pattern repeated with other indigenous peoples, the Mossi assumed what they saw as their rightful position as political masters, while recognising that power over the earth resided with the Kurumba, who were there first. So alongside a *naba* to adjudicate on matters of law and order, the earth priest of each Kurumba town was left in place to preside over all matters relating to agriculture and the all-important rituals associated with harvest and the rains.

Nowadays, the Kurumba are almost totally assimilated with the Mossi. Along with Pobe Mengao, where the pre-eminent Kurumba earth priest is still based, Aribinda and Djibo are both important Kurumba towns.

You can visit the village chief, an authority on village history and the Kurumba, although he does not speak French, so it is best to go with a translator. Arm yourself with an appropriate gift, of either money or kola nuts.

Pobe Mengao is also home to an important fertility statue, known as Mamyo. This disappeared in the mid 1990s, and eventually turned up in the collection of a private German collector, who was successfully persuaded to repatriate the stolen object. There are plans to create a museum at Pobe to explain the significance of Mamyo and other local treasures, although at the time of writing this project was still ongoing.

SAMO AND MARKA COUNTRY

The region west of Yako and southwest of Ouahigouya brings you into the heart of Marka and Samo country. The Marka, or Dafing, are distant cousins of the Samo, and related to the Mande people in Mali. Both have a long history of struggle, whether against the Mossi of Yatenga, the Fulani of Barani, the empire of Massina, or the French. The rebellion against forced conscription of Burkinabe soldiers to the killing fields of the Western Front during World War I first began here.

Famed for their fighting prowess, the Samo have a reputation as excellent soldiers, having seen off Djerma invaders near Tougan in 1893. They have traditionally hired themselves out to various overlords, and even today army service is a popular calling for many young men. It can even prove a route into politics: two Burkinabe presidents were Samo, both of them army men who seized power via coups – chief of staff Sangoule Lamizana, who managed to stay in charge for 15 years, and Colonel Saye Zerbo, whose tenure was nearly two years.

The countryside changes significantly in the region of the Sourou River, which is a haven for birdlife. The pretty 'sugar-loaf' mud mosques that dot the villages are testament to the influence of the powerful Islamic empires of the Songhay, and the Tukulur state of Al-Hajj Omar.

A trek round these parts also forms a great prelude to an alternative entry into Mali via the border towns of Djibasso and Madouba. Tougan and Nouna are pleasant stop-off towns, while reaching the remote village of Barani for its annual horse festival makes for a serious adventure. For anyone whose spirit leaps at a strike into the unknown, this is a great corner of Burkina to explore.

GETTING THERE AND AWAY West from Ouaga, the N1 and N14 pass through Koudougou and Dedougou *en route* to Nouna. Tougan is reached from Ouahigouya, Yako, Koudougou or Bobo by bus. Access is slowly improving, with tar having now reached Dedougou from the south; until the tar road between Koudougou and Dedougou is completed, your best bet is to approach from either Bobo or Ouahigouya, unless you're particularly fond of rough dirt washboards that keep drivers on their guard and bus passengers' teeth on edge.

WEST FROM YAKO **Latoden** can get very busy on its lively market days. Towards Yabo, the brush and trees become thicker as you head west, and granaries change from man-size egg-shaped straw baskets nestled on wooden trestles to mud constructions a little like raised phone boxes that come to a four-sided pyramidal peak at the top. *Karite* and kola-nut trees line the roads. **Kawara** has a big well, 10m across, with water said to have healing properties. Rituals take place at the well, which is covered with tree trunks. Moving the logs takes place in a ceremony that happens every three years.

Tougan Spiritual home to the Samo, Tougan has a low-key, friendly feel, with accommodation right in the centre. The middle of town forms a rough triangle shape, with *maquis* and street food ranged around it. There is also a petrol station, numerous telecentres and an internet café.

Getting there and away STAF (✆ *40 55 30 75 in Tougan*) goes to Tougan from its Ouaga stop in Larle, at 09.00 and 14.00 twice daily, for 4,000f (7,000f return). You can pick these services up in Ouahigouya at 12.00 and 16.00 (2,000f). TDM, aka Djigouya-Magni, also runs daily minibuses from the Ouahigouya *autogare* at 07.00 and 11.00 (2,000f) that head down to Bobo. Its departure times from Bobo (4,000f to Tougan) are the same in reverse, services that you can pick up in Dedougou at roughly 12.00 and 16.00 (1,500f). Fasowcar (m *76 79 15 26*) also runs to Tougan from Bobo, (4,000f), leaving at 09.00 daily, returning from Tougan at 07.30 daily. TKF has an 07.00 daily coach departure from Tougan to Koudougou (3,000f).

Where to stay

Mid range

L'Auberge SMAK (10 rooms) 20 53 41 40; m 70 25 05 03; e smak.inter@yahoo.fr; http://smak-hotel.com. An ambitious project to bring something a little more elegant to town. New, spotless rooms in a setting that tries hard: imported tropical plants, mini lawn & elaborate brickwork bar & restaurant. Choice of fan or AC. **$$$**

Hotel de l'Amitié (10 rooms) 20 53 42 23, 20 53 50 01. Lovely budget hotel, with balcony & disco courtyard, about 1km from the centre off the Bobo road. Range of rooms from en-suite AC with TV to fan with outside loo. Popular bar, noisy at the weekends. **$$–$$$**

Hotel Zeela (17 rooms) 20 53 50 10. Nondescript en-suite fan or AC rooms are set in spacious grounds on the Yako road, close to the town centre. Overpriced, but you can negotiate. Restaurant under construction. **$$–$$$**

WOODLESS CONSTRUCTION

Wood has always been used in the construction of houses in Burkina and across the region. With chronic deforestation, efforts are being made to look at other methods.

From an engineering point of view, wood is not always the best option. It rots over time, ravaged by a lethal combination of heavy rains and persistent termites, reducing the life expectancy of the mud walls it supports. If you visit the mosques at Bani, you'll see this wasting away in action.

As an alternative to wood, corrugated iron or aluminium sheeting is often employed for roofing and seen as an aspirational symbol of modernity. Although weather resistant, it has the unpleasant effect of turning homes into saunas, is expensive and is no better for the environment.

One solution lies with the land itself. The idea of constructing a building entirely from mud may sound a bit *Three Little Pigs*, yet it is possible, and construction methods are becoming increasingly sophisticated. Because the earth is one resource that is never going to be in short supply, using it benefits the environment and saves money.

Djibo is the Burkinabe headquarters of Development Workshop (DW), an NGO specialising in woodless construction that is trying to circulate architectural and engineering know-how to roll it out on a larger scale. The headquarters in Djibo practises exactly what it preaches. It is a gloriously high-ceilinged affair; light, airy and, most important, immeasurably cooler inside than other buildings. Windows tend to be small and high, but to counter the lack of light the interior is painted brilliant white. Simply ask for *Construction sans Bois* and someone should be able to direct you. Similar architecture is found at the Oursi ruins museum (see box, pages 186–7). Another French organisation doing similar work in Burkina is La Voute Nubienne (*www.lavoutenubienne.org*), based in Boromo (see page 269), where you can stay in an attractive *auberge*. They can also point you in the direction of further examples of their work, which is dotted all around Burkina.

Development Workshop (Construction sans Bois) (50 38 70 90, 40 56 01 96; m 78 85 52 62; e dwbf@dwf.org; www.dwf.org).

Budget/Shoestring

Hotel Neerwaya Annexe (6 rooms) A 10min tramp away from the main square through quiet backstreets, these are well-kept en-suite AC rooms in a pleasant building. Enquire at Hotel Neerwaya (see below). **$$**

Residence Bandalou (8 rooms) m 72 66 89 63, 78 84 99 23. More basic rooms on a quiet street close to the centre, with either fan or AC, inside shower & outside squat loo. **$–$$**

Auberge Toa-Turu (7 rooms) m 72 67 00 86. Cheap, basic rooms with internal shower, external loo in an unappealing accommodation block. **$**

Hotel Neerwaya (5 rooms) 20 53 41 35. Located in the main town square, with spotless white-tiled rooms & basic en-suite loo & standing fans. Good value, but a bit noisy – the back garden has a disco. At the front you can indulge in street-side drinking & simple meals. **$**

Where to eat and drink The restaurant at **L'Auberge SMAK** ($$$) is one of the most ambitious in rural Burkina. The young Togolese chef was tricked into the job, believing he was going 'somewhere near Ouaga'. He can certainly cook, but whether he'll last is another matter. Ingredients are shipped in from Ouaga for the menu that covers everything from pizza to *gigot d'agneau* and *lapin sauté au vin blanc*. Rather down the scale, you can eat simply and well at any of the joints around the main square, including the **Hotel Neerwaya**'s street-side bar. **Restaurant Togolais le Sahel** dishes up hearty portions of *riz sauce* and *ragout de nyam*.

Gassan Travelling 32km southwest from Tougan, the pretty town of **Gassan** is the site of a distinctive mud mosque. Nearby **Kougny**, 10km east, has a similar structure, and is also the site of indigo dye-pits where cloth is coloured.

Safari Shortly after Gassan, on the road west to Nouna, is the start of a 35,000ha private wildlife reserve and lodge, **Express Safari du Sourou** (*50 31 11 72, 50 31 47 32; http://safaridusourou.com*). Because the reserve is primarily used for hunting, visits are usually pre-booked and pre-paid by French tour groups, but it is possible to turn up and stay, or better still, to ring the office in Ouagadougou in advance to check there will be space, and ask for an empty room to be cleaned before you arrive. Simple villas, with en-suite bathroom, cost 30,000f. The restaurant is staffed by an avuncular chef with a will to please, who can cook up tuna and tomato salad and decent grilled chicken at short notice. There is also a swimming pool. The surrounding area is full of plant life and birds (partridge, guinea fowl, ducks and bustards); warthog, hippo and antelope can also be spotted, and you can take a canoe out to fish on the Sourou River. Daily rates for guides will vary. Look out for the wood sculpture in the grounds by Mamadi Doumbia, an excellent young Ouaga-based artist.

Lanfiera This was once an important seat of Islamic learning and culture, because of an enlightened *marabout*, Karamoko Ba ('great knower of things') who was revered as an important and moderate source of religious leadership in the region.

The village's beautiful mud mosque, built by Ba and his followers, eschews simple flat walls, and is instead constructed from a series of cylinders, with the walls ballooning outwards in graceful curves, each tapering to a cone at the top. The French explorer and colonist Captain Monteil was prompted to call the mosque 'the most artistic of all those I have seen in the Sudan'.

Ba warmly welcomed the French, who in turn thought a great deal both of him and Lanfiera. 'By the sole influence of his character and his talent, [he] has succeeded in making the small village of Lanfiera the veritable political capital of all Dafina [Marka country],' wrote Monteil.

Gouran At the most northerly point of the Sourou River in Burkina, on the border with Mali, is a hidden village. At the last count, there were 589 inhabitants on tiny **Toma Isle** in the middle of the river, which has been occupied for the past 500 years and is only accessible by canoe.

Getting there and away From Tougan, head west past Bassan and Kassoum on the D25, join the N10 trunk road at Lanfiera and hang a right up along the river. It is just southwest of Di, on the way to Mali. Without your own transport the best bet is a bush taxi from Tougan or Gassan to Gouran. Don't confuse Toma Isle with the town of Toma, which is east of Gassan.

Nouna For anyone taking the less-travelled route up to the town of San in Mali, Nouna is a worthwhile stopping point. It is a pretty, open town, with some lovely mud-brick architecture, and is home to the Marka people.

Getting there and away LTI, or Liza Transport (*50 38 74 10*), leaves Ouaga at 08.00 daily, from its station near Ouagainter for Nouna (5,500f) via Koudougou and Dedougou (pick it up here at about 14.00, for 1,500f). It leaves Nouna for Ouaga at 08.00 daily. STT has a service for Bobo that leaves at 07.00 daily, also via Dedougou. Rickety minibuses leave for Dedougou throughout the day, the last one at about 18.00.

 ***Where to stay***

Le Jardin du Maire (10 rooms) m 71 99 04 23, 78 59 10 17. Set in an unappealing, wind-blown 'garden', clean, simple rooms have mozzie nets & do the job. Choice of en-suite AC, or fan with inside shower, outside loo. Bar-restaurant on site. **$–$$$**

Auberge Populaire de Nouna (6 rooms) 20 53 70 86. Double fan rooms have shower inside, loo outside, & mozzie nets. Better for its bar, which is indeed popular. **$**

Les Cailloux Sauvages (5 rooms) m 71 06 02 60, 70 12 33 20. The nicest place in town. Spotless en-suite fan rooms have 2 single beds each & are set around a lovely bougainvillea-lined courtyard. From the bus station, turn left at the Mobil sign; after CFB, head right, & ask. Good meals, including omelettes & salads, available on order. B/fast 500f. **$**

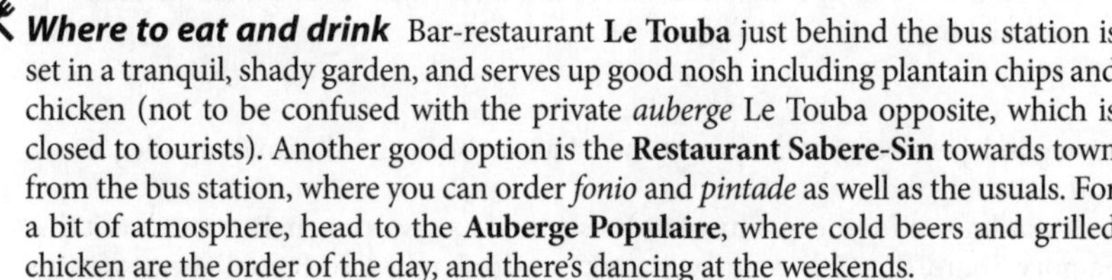

Where to eat and drink Bar-restaurant **Le Touba** just behind the bus station is set in a tranquil, shady garden, and serves up good nosh including plantain chips and chicken (not to be confused with the private *auberge* Le Touba opposite, which is closed to tourists). Another good option is the **Restaurant Sabere-Sin** towards town from the bus station, where you can order *fonio* and *pintade* as well as the usuals. For a bit of atmosphere, head to the **Auberge Populaire**, where cold beers and grilled chicken are the order of the day, and there's dancing at the weekends.

Shopping **Souvenir d'Afrique** (*chez Kinda Abdoulaye; 20 53 70 41*), the town's only artefact and curio shop, is on the way in from Tougan. The friendly owner has a selection of Bwaba, Senoufou and Kong masks, some painted, others plain wood. He also has Dogon statuettes and doors, bows, quivers and arrows and ancient shackles. Prices start at 7,500–15,000f for a reproduction mask, rising to 50,000–300,000f for original pieces.

Barani Barani played a key role in the French colonial mission to control the region at the end of the 19th century. A Fulani village, it has sought to foster a

WEST AFRICAN COWBOYS

Barani's Fechiba festival is a lifeline for the village, which in recent years has suffered: no phone line, no electricity, no secondary school, jagged dirt roads impassable in the rainy season and hardly a horse to its name. Twenty years ago there were 600 people in the town.

Barani's diaspora has tried to reinvigorate its equine heritage, to turn the eyes of the state towards the village's development needs. In short, horses mean houses. Several village protégés, from the worlds of business, academia and public service, have formed Adeba – the Association for the Economic Development of Barani – to raise the profile of their home town.

In days gone by, Barani hosted a festival to celebrate the skill of their riders, who could make their horses dance to the rhythms of deftly handled drums, and kneel before the chief, all amid a cacophony of wailing, singing and thunderous gunfire. The day would culminate with the *haaro* ('horserace' in Fulfulde), a frantic course with up to 200 horses taking part.

This has been reincarnated as the Festival Culturel et Hippique de Barani (Fechiba). The first hosting, in 2000, attracted 20 horses and a few villagers, but it has grown enormously since; now, extended family members from the great clans of Barani arrive from as far afield as Mali, Guinea, Senegal and Nigeria. Cultures from all over Burkina dance their hearts out and *griots* compete with one another to regale the village with the lineage of the visiting chiefs; indeed, visitors in recent years have said that speech-making has seemed almost as important as the horses. That said, it is the horses and riders, resplendent, wild, proud, that really steal the show.

The handful of foreigners who attend receive an extraordinary welcome, as villagers, already inundated with extended family and friends, make extra space for unexpected guests: sleeping in mud-brick houses, or pitching tents under the baobabs, or taking mats out under the stars. Meals are shared with families that take a shine to you.

As one of the organisers has said, 'We can give people a good meal. It's our custom. If you go to Barani and don't get anything you will think people don't like you.'

And the young children of Barani are once again asking their parents about horses.

strong independence; at the same time it has not been afraid of making allegiances, and switching them to survive.

It was known for the quality of its horses, and its cavalrymen. Rumour has it that Samory Toure, the 19th-century Malinke warlord, relied on Barani's beasts for his ferocious and prolonged attacks into the west African interior.

To commemorate the value of horses in the life of the village, the annual festival Fechiba is a grand affair, with stallions in the hands of ancient *chevaliers* dancing and bowing before the village chief, as well as frantic horseracing in the afternoon heat (see box, above). It is one of the most exciting and arresting spectacles in the country and if you are in Burkina around the end of January or beginning of February it is seriously worth making the trek. Look out for posters in Ouagadougou, or contact Douramane Sidibe (m *76 60 08 42*), Mamadou Sidibe (m *70 28 51 91*), Moussa Sidibe (m *70 26 53 06*) or Abdallah Sidibe (✆ *20 97 63 83;* m *70 25 54 45*).

Getting there and away Barani is about 90 minutes north of Nouna on a bumpy, sandy road frequently impassable in the rainy season. In the dry season, a 4x4 is preferable. Ask around in the centre of Nouna for any transport that is Barani-bound. There should be daily departures of *bachées* for about 500f.

Where to stay, eat and drink There is currently nowhere to stay in Barani. The chief's court is located on the far side of the mosque. Upon arriving, ask politely if it is possible to pitch a tent somewhere on the outskirts of town. One picturesque spot is out past the *forage* (well) on the eastern side of town. Plans to construct simple huts where you can shelter for the night have not yet borne fruit, for the simple reason that such an investment makes little sense for a few days each year. Food and drink options are thin on the ground, but there is a small restaurant serving *riz sauce* and *riz gras* around the market. On the other side of the market, near the mosque, there is a breakfast *buvette* that does hot drinks. You can also find women frying up *beignets* on the streets.

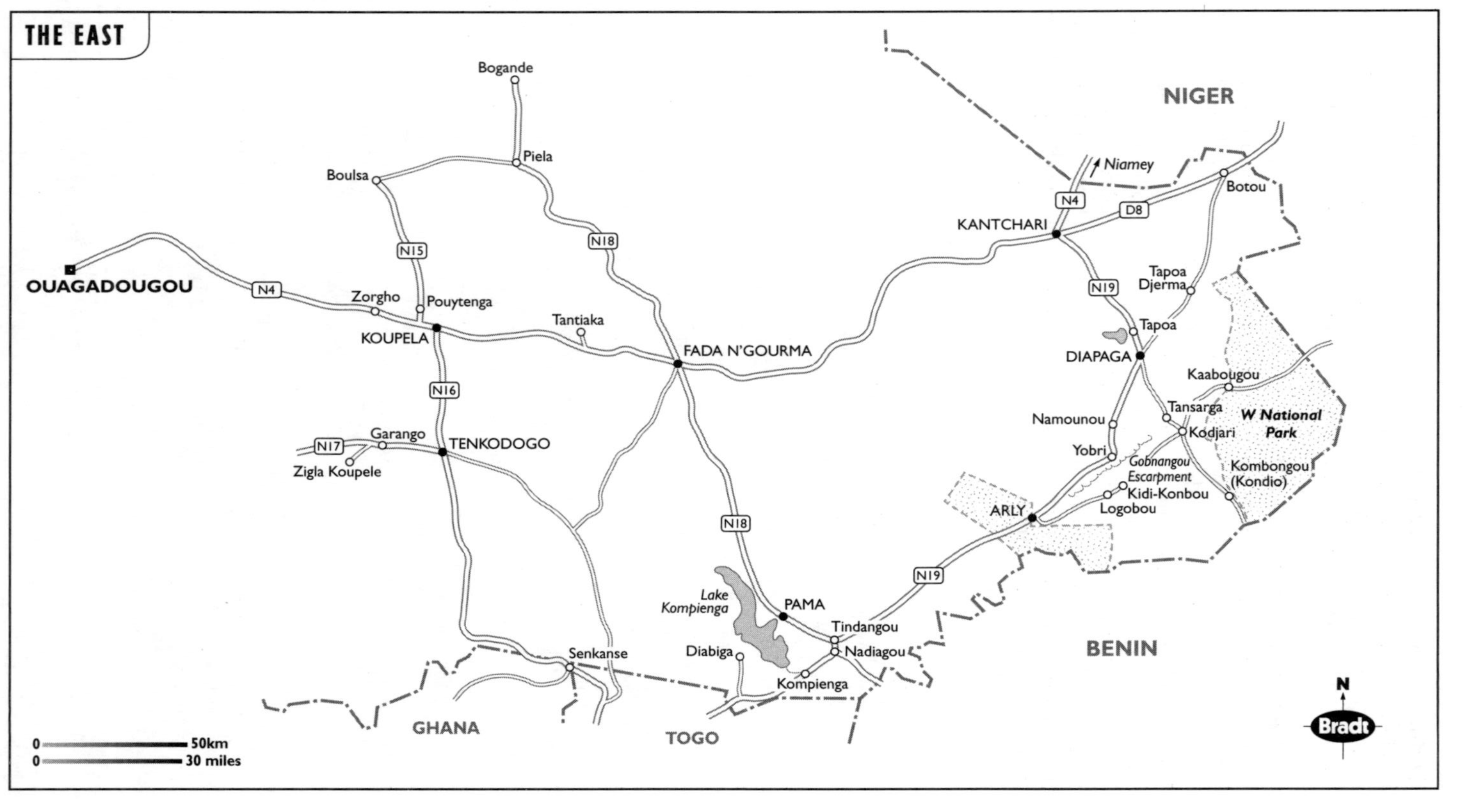
THE EAST
Bogande
NIGER
Piela
Niamey
Boulsa
N4
Botou
D8
KANTCHARI
N18
N15
OUAGADOUGOU
N4
Tapoa Djerma
N19
Zorgho
Pouytenga
Tantiaka
Tapoa
KOUPELA
FADA N'GOURMA
DIAPAGA
Kaabougou
N16
Tansarga
W National Park
Namounou
Kodjari
Garango
N17
TENKODOGO
Yobri
Gobnangou Escarpment
Kombongou (Kondio)
Zigla Koupele
Kidi-Konbou
Logobou
ARLY
N18
N19
Lake Kompienga
PAMA
Tindangou
BENIN
Senkanse
Diabiga
Nadiagou
Kompienga
N
Bradt
GHANA
TOGO
0 50km
0 30 miles

5

The East

The sweeping, sparsely populated plains of eastern Burkina are its wildlife highlight. This is lion, elephant and antelope country, set among vast national parks and private concessions that offer some of the best game-viewing in west Africa. Some 35 species of large mammals indigenous to the region can be found here. With EU money continuing to trickle into the parks, slowly improving the infrastructure, along with fairytale lakeside retreats near Pama and new tourism initiatives along the stunning Gobnangou Escarpment, the east is set to become a must on any traveller's agenda.

It's hidden and hard to get to, which, for the adventurous, makes it all the more appealing. Secluded game lodges may not be in the same class as the luxury retreats of eastern or southern Africa, but many are stunningly situated, and jealously guarded secrets.

The east is home to the Gourmanche and richly imbued with significant sites, ruins and legends. The capital, Fada N'Gourma, is a beautiful, sleepy town where even the hard sell is relaxing, while the ancient capital Tenkodogo is revered as the starting point of Mossi civilisation.

Heading towards the border with Togo and Benin, the Gobnangou Escarpment, a huge slab of granite rising out of the flat plains below, is a hiker's and climber's dream. It is sandwiched between the country's biggest game parks, Arly to the south, and W to the east and new village *campements* are making it possible to stay here and explore the area for the first time.

While coach routes do not cover every destination, smooth paved roads run east to Niger's Niamey, and south from Koupela. Further south the rutted dirt tracks of game parks drenched in mud call out for 4x4 adventure. Numerous companies and tour operators in Ouagadougou can arrange safari trips, while a new association in Diapaga can organise a wide range of activities on the ground.

KOUPELA

The main town between Ouaga and Fada, Koupela is a popular stop-off town for truckers headed east to Niger and south to Togo. It is short on attractions, but for anyone keen to leave the smog and bustle of Ouaga behind, it is a good staging post and offers plenty of sleepy small-town vibes.

Koupela was founded as the principal town of the Kouritenga region by Naba Yelwegtim, the fifth *naba*. Famed for his skill as a stock-breeder, he initially installed himself at Tulgu, and then acted on the advice of shepherds to settle near a natural well surrounded by white stones (*kug peela* in Moore, which later became Koupela).

At the start of the 20th century, Naba Zanre began developing the large and successful vegetable gardens that have earned Koupela the nickname 'town of guavas'. The daily market is fairly lively to this day, although the main event is only every three days. The town is also famed for its pottery, done by men rather than women, with line designs in white kaolin.

GETTING THERE AND AWAY

By bus STMB, STAF, Rakieta, Sotradyf and TSR all ply the route. From Ouaga, Rakieta (m *70 32 81 24*) is the cheapest, its single fare to Koupela 1,500f (all the others charge 2,000f). Happily, its station just off Avenue Kwame N'Krumah is also the most central, and has departures at 07.00, 13.00 and 17.30. However, STMB has the most departures, leaving from Cité An III at 06.45, 09.30, 13.00, 15.30 and 17.30; STAF leaves from its Larle station at 06.30 and 12.00; Sotradyf from Rue des Douanes at 08.00, 10.30, 13.30 and 15.30, and TSR from Rue de la Culture at 07.00, 12.00 and 17.00. Heading on to Fada, all charge 1,000f apart from TSR, which charges 1,500f. Sotradyf heads not to Fada but to Tenkodogo; STMB also has services to Tenkodogo (1,000f).

In Koupela, the STMB station (*40 85 35 40*) is down a side road just past the Calypso Bar, on the right. Coaches for Ouaga leave at 08.00, 10.30, 14.00, 16.30, 17.30 and 18.30 daily. Departures for Fada are at 09.00, 12.00, 15.00, 18.00 and 20.00. There are just two departures for Tenkodogo, at 09.30 and 15.30 daily (07.00 and 13.30 from Ouaga), which continue on Sinkassé on the Togolese border. STMB also has coaches for Niamey three times a week, at 08.00 on Tuesday, Thursday and Saturday (7,500f), and Lome once a week, at 08.00 on Sunday (10,000f).

The other three stations are all on the left-hand side of the Fada road, just after the turning for STMB. First is STAF (m *70 03 40 26*), with daily departures for Ouaga at 07.30 and 13.00 and for Fada at 08.30 and 14.00. Next is Rakieta (m *70 43 01 05*) which has a daily service to Ouaga at 08.00 (06.30 on Fridays), 14.00 and 19.00. For Fada, there are departures at 09.00, 15.00 and 20.00. TSR (m *71 46 98 51, 76 69 36 34*), the last in the line, has departures for Ouaga at 07.30, 13.30 and 18.30; for Fada at 09.00, 14.45 and 19.00. Its departures for Cotonou and Lome (06.00 every Thursday and Sunday from Ouaga) also stop in Koupela.

By taxi At the *autogare* on the Togo road, you can pick up a *taxi brousse* for Pouytenga (400f), Tenkodogo (750f), Fada (1,250f), Kantchari (3,500f) or Ouaga (2,000f), but there are no fixed departure times. Coaches also leave the *autogare* bound for Abidjan at 12.00 on Mondays and Thursdays (28,000f).

ORIENTATION AND PRACTICALITIES After coming the 137km from Ouaga, the road continues straight towards Fada (88km), or turns right towards Tenkodogo (46km) and Togo. The BICIA-B bank has a Visa machine at this junction, and the Banque Atlantique (on the left towards Fada) has a MasterCard/Maestro option. The town's post office is just along from there.

There are several decent internet points in town. The **Foyer des Elèves** (*40 70 09 87*), just on the Togo junction, charges 250f an hour, while the **Cyber Café Hotel.Net** is tacked on to the side of the Hotel de la Gare and charges 300f an hour. **Madiule Informatique Services** (*40 70 00 09;* m *70 28 14 54*) is just past the mayor's office, on the opposite side of the Fada road.

A couple of supermarkets in town are good for stocking up on drinks and snacks for a long journey. **Zoungrana et Frères** is opposite the Rakieta station; the Oubda supermarket is just after the hospital on the left.

WHERE TO STAY

Pacific Hotel (12 rooms) 40 70 07 67; e hotel.pacific@fasonet.bf; www.pacific-hotel.bf. Just off the Togo road beyond the autogare, 50m down a dirt track. This is Koupela's shiniest new venture, managed by the Red Cross. Spotless, spacious en-suite AC or fan doubles are arranged around a tranquil courtyard & sport enormous beds. Also 2 3-bed dorms & 1 twin room. B/fast & other simple meals available. B/fast 1,000f. Dorms 3,000f pp. **$$–$$$**

Hotel de la Gare (32 rooms) 40 70 03 52. Right opposite Koupela's autogare. 'New' AC rooms seem older than the originals & are overpriced, perhaps to pay for the bathroom overkill: urinal, bidet, shower, basin & toilet; some even have baths. The 'old' en-suite AC rooms are much better value at 10,000f. Fan rooms (choice of en suite or externals) come cheap. **$–$$$**

Hotel Le Calypso (12 rooms) 40 70 03 50. Rooms here are better than the reputation of the bar next door might suggest, but still somehow unappealing. Choice of en-suite AC, en-suite fan or fan with outside loo. **$–$$$**

Le Remblais (20 rooms) 40 70 07 50. Pleasant option about 1.5km out of town on the Fada road. Clean, simple en-suite fan or AC rooms all come with TV; AC rooms have hot water. There's a cheap restaurant & a club at weekends. Can pick up from coach stations in town. **$$**

Mission Catholique (40 rooms) 70 17 60 05. The clear winner for nice, clean rooms, which are hidden from the road amid rambling gardens. You can eat here – speak to the chef to see what's on offer. Coming from Ouaga, it is just before the Tenkodogo turning, behind the Catholic church. Choice of AC or fan. Dorms 2,500f pp. **$–$$**

Campement Hotel Le Kourita (4 rooms) 40 70 01 33. Has fallen into disrepair to the extent that a number of rooms are now unusable. The ones that are left (all fan with en suite & TV) aren't great either. **$**

Hotel Wend Wooga (13 rooms) 40 70 01 64. Just past BICIA-B bank *en route* south to Togo, this place is cheap, but not exactly tranquil: all rooms are set around the popular bar/restaurant. 1 outside toilet is reserved for hotel guests, but doesn't smell any better than the others. Rooms have internal showers & nets. **$**

WHERE TO EAT AND DRINK

Akwaba au Restaurant Kourita m 70 41 79 01. One of the best joints in town, which is doing rather better than its neighbour the Campement Kourita. The friendly, enterprising Flora serves up a robust menu including steak, chicken & good salads, & has a loyal clientele of weekday *fonctionnaires* who return to Ouaga at the w/ends. She has also just opened **La Fourchette D'Or** across the road from the water tower – bound to be worth a look. $–$$

Restaurant Club Sonapost m 70 22 74 74. Another newish venture on the main road, serving up the usual staples under pleasant *paillotes*. $–$$

Restaurant le Bon Samaritain 40 70 01 18; m 70 25 90 81. Located on the Tenkodogo road, the restaurant has a great, leafy courtyard, complete with DJ booth, & is a pleasant place to take in simple but tasty dishes. $–$$

Koupela does a fine job of answering the question 'Why did the chicken cross the road?' The pens of squawking fowl get to hear their mates sizzling over the tarmac every evening, when a row of stalls outside the market comes to life. A whole chicken goes for 2,000f. The **Wend Wooga**, near the bank, is better for eating than staying, both for beers and simple nosh. Next door, **Café Restau Le Routier** is another local favourite, where *riz sauce* goes for 250f. Offal-lovers can indulge here too: intestine soup, anyone?

ENTERTAINMENT AND NIGHTLIFE **Calypso** is the biggest, rowdiest bar in town, with a reputation for ice-cold beers and a slightly more aggressive atmosphere. For nightlife, **Bar Dancing NZ**, also known as the **Wend Dabo**, opposite le Bon Samaritain and behind the truck stop, is well thought of locally. The **Climat**, down the first turning on the right after the market towards Fada, is another good *bar-dancing* that caters for a slightly older crowd. **Le Soir au Calypso**, down on the Togo road, sometimes hosts live bands.

AROUND KOUPELA

Bagre Lake This enormous lake lies close to Koupela. Ask a local fisherman to take you out on a *pirogue*. The huge hydro-electric dam was built with Taiwanese and EU development assistance, and feeds Koupela and Ouaga with electricity, as well as watering 100ha of nearby rice fields. Much closer, on the outskirts of town going towards Ouaga, the **Barrage d'Itienga** reservoir has beautiful market-gardening projects that make a lush and leafy evening stroll.

Pouytenga Pouytenga has an excellent open-air cattle market every three days, following the Koupela market day. Amid total chaos, herders come south to sell their goats, sheep and cows. If driving, turn north on the road to Boulsa about 8km west of Koupela on the Ouaga road and continue for 7km; otherwise pick up a *taxi brousse* at the *gare routière* in Koupela (400f). You can stay at **Hotel Pouya** (*12 rooms;* ☎ *40 70 69 07;* **$–$$**). It is simple, with a bar and restaurant on site, with a choice of en-suite fan or air-conditioned rooms, or fan with outside shower.

TENKODOGO

Nowhere in Burkina will you hear the word *coutume* (custom) said as often as in Tenkodogo. It is the birthplace of the Mossi Empire – even the town's name backs up its status, combining the Moore words *tenga*, meaning 'land', and *kodogo*, meaning 'old'.

The story goes that Ouedraogo, legendary founder of the Mossi Empire (son of Ghanaian princess Yennenga and her stallion-riding hunk Riale), landed up here. Of his three sons, Rawa went northwards to found the Kingdom of Zandoma, Diaba Lompo headed east to lay the foundations of Gourmanche society, and Zoungrana, his youngest, stayed put to assume the mantle of Tenkodogo. According to oral tradition, three stones at a triple fork in the road at Ouargaye (a small village about 50km southeast of Tenkodogo) symbolise the diverging of the three princely paths.

The Tenkodogo Naba is considered, symbolically, the most important of the Mossi kings, and takes pride of place within official circles.

COLONIAL COMPETITION While Tenkodogo's political status has declined ever since the early reign of Zoungrana, at the end of the 19th century it was thrust back into the limelight, as a meeting of foreign powers took place here to decide Burkina's French-speaking fate.

After ousting the Moro Naba from Ouagadougou, the French had designs on Tenkodogo. But they had competition. To the south, British captain Donald Stewart was in charge of a military column that had travelled up from Kumasi in present-day Ghana, fully expecting to take part of the Mossi Kingdom for the British. He was even arriving by invitation, since Naba Wobgo, the ousted king who had fled the French in Ouagadougou, had sent an appeal to Stewart, requesting he come at once to stave off the French, 'for protection in virtue of the treaty concluded with Mr Fergusson [an English negotiator] in 1894.' Talks between the British and the French followed, on 7 February 1897, in rather salubrious surroundings. 'The representative of England received us with great courtesy and luxury, a comfort of which we had lost all idea since our leaving France,' gushed the French lieutenant Chanoine, writing in October 1897.

Stewart eventually agreed to take a step or 300 back, retreating to the Mamprusi Kingdom 120km further south in the Gold Coast – but only on condition that the French do pretty much the same, leaving Tenkodogo out of bounds for everyone. The French concurred. 'We agreed that the two missions will leave Tenkodogo on the same day at the same hour,' said Lieutenant Chanoine, 'to safeguard the dignity of both nations.'

It was ultimately a triumph for the French, however, who saw the retreat as only temporary. Meanwhile the British were out of Burkina for good. 'Our freedom of action remains therefore intact and the English mission returns… abandoning any idea of penetrating to the Mossi,' said Chanoine. With the British out of the picture, the French embarked on a rapid return.

'We've done it,' gloated Chanoine. 'The English were immobile at Kumasi, waiting for winter to pass to take occupation of Mossi and Gourounsi lands already taken by Binger, Crozat and Monteil. We have faith in our civilising mission, the certainty of working for the good of the land, and for the future of France.' Much later, the French used their control of the area to recruit Mossi fighters in Tenkodogo during World War I, and sent them to fight in German-controlled Togo.

GETTING THERE AND AWAY The coach trip from Ouaga takes about three hours. STMB departs from Cité An III at 07.00 and 13.30 (2,500f), continuing on to Sinkassé on the Togolese border. The station in Tenkodogo (*40 71 05 58*) is just before Hotel Djamou down a turning on the right; coaches pass through at 10.00 and 16.00. Sotradyf departs from Rue des Douanes in Ouaga (*50 33 37 03*) at 08.00, 10.30, 13.30 and 15.30; tickets are 2,500f, 4,000f return. The station in Tenkodogo (*40 71 02 60*) is opposite the tarmac turning for Garango, with departures for Ouaga at 05.00, 08.30, 11.00, and 15.00. At the *autogare* (first turning on the right after Hotel Laafi) you'll find TST, which offers the cheapest service to Ouaga (2,000f), leaving at 05.00, 08.30, 10.30 and 15.30.

ORIENTATION Tenkodogo, 183km from Ouaga (800f for a return ticket at the *péage* if you're driving) and 46km south of Koupela, is simply arranged, with most important buildings strung along the two roads coming from Koupela and from Garango, to the west. Both are tarmac, and converge at the market and church in the heart of town. From here, the road continues south to Togo and Ghana. The road towards Garango, which turns to a dirt track beyond Garango and eventually links up with the Ouaga–Po trunk road, goes through Bissa country.

WHERE TO STAY

Hotel Djamou (80 rooms) 40 71 00 80; e hotel_djamou@yahoo.fr. Plushest hotel in town, with marvellous garden (complete with porcupines & peacocks), considerable menu & Wi-Fi throughout; also a pool, though this was dried out after a client drowned in it. With options ranging from kitsch 70s-style suites to simple fan rooms, even those on a budget can enjoy the atmosphere, but the rooms themselves can be a bit dingy. Popular with conferences, so book ahead. **$$–$$$**

Hotel Djamou Annexe 1 (15 rooms) m 70 74 10 34. Run-down, with no food on offer, & overpriced. There's quite a range of rooms though, from fan with external facilities through to a stand-alone bungalow with big TV, fridge & garish bathroom. It's on the right on the road to Garango. **$$–$$$**

Hotel Laafi (30 rooms) 40 71 04 14. One of the town's best options, with well-kept rooms around an attractive courtyard. Look out for the decorative painted ceilings. Rooms range from en-suite fan with towels to 'luxury' AC with TVs & hot water. The restaurant has an ambitious menu & gives the option to eat inside or alfresco. A 4x4 is available for hire. It's the first hotel you come to (on the right) if arriving from Koupela. **$$–$$$**

Auberge Leina (23 rooms) 40 71 02 02. Well situated just behind the STMB garage, this place feels unfinished, but is a work in progress with an enthusiastic owner. Rooms are fine, mostly fan with a few AC options. **$–$$$**

Auberge Riale Annexe (14 rooms) 40 71 07 96. Tucked behind the gouvernorat on the Garango road. Pretty gardens & tranquil setting, but tricky to find so ring ahead for a pick-up. New, spotless rooms offer choice of en-suite AC, or good-value fan rooms either with or without loo. **$–$$$**

Hotel Djamou Annexe 2 (42 rooms) 40 71 03 53. Tucked away on a back road, this has the same neglected feel as its sister annexe. However, it's slightly more intimate than its namesake, & the prices are a bit lower. To get there, take a left at the dirt road signposted for the Maison des Artisans as you are heading for Garango on the tarmac road. Take the next left & the hotel is on your left. **$–$$$**

Auberge Riale (12 rooms) 40 71 00 40. There used to be a grand baobab tree behind the *auberge*, thought to be the place where Riale, father of Mossi leader Ouedraogo, hid himself. Ideally situated in the centre of town; shame the money that's gone on the annexe wasn't invested here. Huts & rooms are pretty miserable inside, but cheap at least, with mozzie nets. The simple restaurant dishes up the staples. Turn left before the church at the centre of town & it's on the right. A bed in a grim 7-bed dorm is 1,500f. **$**

WHERE TO EAT AND DRINK Despite the name, there is much more to **Restaurant Patisserie Salon du Thé** than tea, although its selection of yoghurt and pastries is a wonderful way to start the day. Garlic chicken, *riz soupe* and *riz gras* are all delicious and cheap. Chips are excellent. It is about 20m down a dirt track to the right off the main road when coming from Koupela. Look for the signpost. **Restaurant Gracias**, next door to the Auberge Leina near STMB, also serves up the usuals and is very popular with the locals – always a good sign. Down the road from Djamou Annexe 2, **La Paillote** lives up to its name with lofty *paillotes*; it's in a nice setting, but has slightly overpriced grub. **Hotel Djamou** has a comprehensive menu offering well-made dishes, with prices to match the lovely surroundings. The restaurant of **Hotel Laafi** offers good competition with a menu that includes pasta, pizzas and paninis.

OTHER PRACTICALITIES The main **market** takes place every three days, at which time you can hire a *moto* at excellent rates. If in doubt, call Ousseini Bidiga (m *70 72 23 46*), a local entrepreneur and guide who runs a telecentre in town. He is happy to hire out P50 *motos* for 2,000f a day, or *motos* with gears for 3,500f; he also speaks English.

The Oubda **supermarket** is on the Garango road opposite the **pharmacy**. If you take this tarmac road, there is a **craft centre** on the left after the *gendarmerie*.

There is an arts and music festival, Fesmar, which is usually held every two years in early December.

WHAT TO SEE AND DO

Naba's court Unlike many other Mossi rulers, the current *naba* of Tenkodogo, Naba Saaga, is not keen to welcome tourists for an audience on an ad hoc basis. Visitors are, however, welcome to watch the weekly Friday meeting of the *naba* and his traditional chiefs in the palace courtyard. The last Friday of every month is celebrated with more gusto than the others.

Look out for the *zande* enclosure inside the *naba*'s court. It might seem a ramshackle collection of upstanding branches under a straw roof, but it is reserved for royalty, and each visiting chief has a wooden pillar of his own among the closely stacked posts.

Palace protocol is extremely formal. For example, it is forbidden to ask the *naba* how many wives or children he has – it's not clear whether that's for modesty's sake or to avoid some other embarrassment.

As well as being a guardian of ancient tradition, the current *naba* is also a thoroughly modern man. Schooled in Europe and Japan (where he learned English to a pretty good standard), he is a doctor of pharmacology, consultant to the World Bank and ex-MP.

One hopes he will put his expertise to good use to bring Tenkodogo's rich cultural history to an international audience. The royal family at Tenkodogo has a fine and varied collection of Mossi heritage yet, for now, it remains unshared. There are rumours he plans to mount a permanent photographic display of Mossi *nabas* throughout the ages. If it comes off, it would make a fascinating exhibition. In the meantime, the Tabaski festival, a key date in the Muslim calendar, doubles as an enormous show of strength and power (see box, below).

To get to the *naba*'s court, take the dirt road opposite the church, heading left past the *auberge*, then the track that veers right towards the walled compound housing a grand yellow bungalow – that's the palace.

TABASKI IN TENKODOGO

In memory of the Old Testament story in which Abraham was asked to sacrifice his son to God as a test of faith and then, at the last minute, allowed to substitute a sheep, one would not expect Tabaski to be a festival for animal lovers.

In Tenkodogo, Tabaski is bloodier than a Quentin Tarantino movie, combining one of the most important Muslim festivals with an extended and highly complex celebration of the *naba's* own power.

The whole thing lasts three days, and begins before dawn on the first morning, when the genealogy of the Mossi kings is recounted by the griots. Village chiefs who claim affiliation with Zoungrana, the youngest son of Ouedraogo, arrive in Tenkodogo throughout the morning, each bringing a chicken and a sheep to be sacrificed in honour of his ancestors. On the first morning, three large cattle are beheaded under the skilful hand and razor-sharp blade of the sacrificing team, who are in for quite a busy day. The *naba* then tastes the innards, and ululating fills the air.

The *zande* enclosure inside the *naba's* court is filled with visiting dignitaries. Under a straw roof each chief sits by his own allotted wooden pillar amid the closely stacked, seemingly arbitrary collection of posts. The party drinks *dolo* in the *zande*, accompanied by more praise-singing from the *griots*.

On the eve of the second day of celebrations, the chief leaves his compound before dawn. Swathed in white robes, and red saddle-dressing, he goes to the mosque on horseback, leading an enormous procession from his compound to take part in an open-air prayer session. After this, the most difficult sacrifice yet: the chief caresses a rather nervous camel, before its throat is slit by courtiers, with nothing more sophisticated than a knife to the jugular. The *naba* returns to his court, where traditional hunters come to dance, playing Waa thumb-whistles, and a generous meal of rice and meat follows.

In Tenkodogo, Tabaski goes not the whole hog, but the whole herd.

BISSA COUNTRY

Bissa country, west of Tenkodogo and south of Koupela, is as strong on its cultural traditions as the Mossi capital it neighbours. Don't dream of asking a question of your guest before you've greeted, sat down, shared some water and greeted each other and your families again. In response to '*nyasi*' – the all-purpose greeting for arrivals – women should reply '*argay*' and men '*nambaa*'. Any local chief is known as *kiri*, forfeiting his two birth names to be honoured by that title alone.

Legend has it the Bissa are cousins of the Samo, after a family dispute resulted in a split that sent the Samo north and the Bissa south. More academic studies disagree over whether their origins are from the Marka or the Gourounsi. During conflict with the Mossi, many Bissa slaves were recruited into the Mossi army as archers, sent into domestic duties in the royal court, or sold abroad.

Living by farming and hunting, the Bissa have no formal central structure. Rather, local chiefs and earth priests take charge. Trees symbolise a claim to ownership of the land around them and represent the soul of the original ancestor who planted them. Only hunters, blacksmiths and diviners can marshal the forces of the bush, making sacrifices and performing rites to please them.

The Bissa are known for their fine artisanship, including pottery, forging, weaving and basketwork. Weavers dry out flattened millet stalks and weave them in geometric patterns, the occasional stalk dyed a bright pink or green and threaded through a sun-baked beige mesh. Basket rims are covered in leather, or decorated with cowrie shells.

For the dedicated cultural visitor, the highlight of Bissa country is a stay in the specially created tourist village of Zigla Koupele. It's basic mud-hut living, but well worth it if you are curious about local life.

GARANGO This small town is the capital of Bissa country. You can buy examples of local craftsmanship here, such as pottery, baskets and weaving. Between Garango and Tenkodogo, the **Tropicana maquis** enjoys a lovely setting beside a lake, with rice paddies and tall trees shimmering in the evening sun, and is a great place for a beer.

Every even-numbered year, the town hosts the Djerka festival, and a peanut festival every odd-numbered year. Contact Rosalie Bance (*50 43 67 99; m 70 23 89 25*) for more information. A bush taxi to Garango costs 600f from Tenkodogo. There is a cybercafé, **Espace Gargan**, at the end of town.

ZIGLA KOUPELE This village is home to a delightful guest compound, one of four in the country run by TDS (Tourisme et Développement Solidaires) (*www.tourisme-dev-solidaires.org*), a French tour operator committed to cultural exchange and responsible tourism. The idea is that people get as close as possible to genuine Burkinabe village life, and learn local skills and crafts. Depending on the time of year, visitors can participate in basket-weaving, pottery-making, shea butter and peanut oil extraction, and traditional dancing. The camp at Zigla Koupele was built in 2003, in the same style as local village housing. Nine straw-roofed round huts, each with two beds, mosquito nets and oil lamps, are ranged round a circular compound. Not only are the rooms clean, cool and lovingly simple, there is also a kitchen for preparing meals, as well as laundry facilities, and the local activities on offer are all thoughtfully presented and overseen by the staff of 23 local villagers. A small boutique sells dark red glazed pottery, dried bissap flowers for making the sweet red juice, locally woven textiles and shea butter, all at too-good-to-miss prices.

At the time of writing, it was not normal for the camp to accommodate visitors who turned up unannounced. In reality, it should be possible to work something out. Speak to Naba Salamgar (m 70 26 78 26), the clued-up village chief (*kiri*). Expect to pay around 20,000f a day, for board and activities. To organise a stay in advance, a 12-day all-inclusive trip, with flights from Paris, costs from €1,690. A 16-day trip costs from €1,835. The village receives 15,500f per day per person. The tourist village also has an office in Ouagadougou (☎ 50 31 25 94), which can organise weekend visits for people who are already in the country.

If you are getting there under your own steam, continue west on the tarmac road for about 5km after Garango and head down a dirt track to the left – it is almost impossible to find without a guide. Better to contact the Ouaga office first.

GOURMANCHE COUNTRY

Shrouded in mystery (even its origins are disputed) the Gourmanche land retains a great sense of spirit and traditional animism. It also has a feeling of being slightly cut off from the rest of Burkina, and has the unenviable privilege of hosting the poorest town in the country (Boulsa).

For the visitor, Pama is a historic town supplanted long ago by Fada N'Gourma as the Gourmanche capital. Further towards Niger, wildlife parks (Arly and W) and private reserves offer safaris with the chance to spot lion, hippo, elephant and a marvellous range of antelope.

HISTORY The Mossi like to think of the Gourmanche as cousins, descended from Diaba Lompo, one of the three sons of their first patriarch, Ouedraogo. He left Tenkodogo to found a new dynasty in the east. Over time the kingdom lost its ties with the Mossi and became a totally separate entity, while retaining certain similarities in language and ritual.

There is no cast-iron historical evidence for this, and some historians have seen this as a case of ideological imperialism on the part of the Mossi. The Gourmanche have a slightly different take on things, claiming that Diaba Lompo flew down from the sky, mounted on his steed, to found their state. Gourma's kings became famous for their magical capabilities, taking their cue from Diaba Lompo. Rocks outside Pama, the ancient seat of the region, are said to carry traces of his footprints, and were sundered in two by a blow of his spear.

Pama, at the southern edge of the kingdom, was the first capital, founded around the 14th century. It didn't last, however, due to hostile Tomba warriors in what is now Togo. In the 17th century, they razed it to the ground, burying the town under corpses.

In the wake of the massacre at Pama, Yendabri (1709–36), 14th king of Gourmanche, launched a counter-offensive, driving the Tomba back into Togo, where they stayed. To guard against any further attacks, he took the precaution of moving the Gourmanche capital north to Fada N'Gourma.

Like King Arthur in reverse, Yendabri is said to have thrust his stone into a rock in Bassar, in Togo, on his return from war, defying anyone to draw it out. It is still supposed to be stuck there, so eagle-eyed travellers should stay on the lookout.

INITIATION Initiation ceremonies are particularly closely guarded, and it is forbidden for any initiate to talk of them. Various neighbourhoods take their eligible men off to different bush camps, some held only every nine years. Initiates live wild for three months, speaking a secret language, hunting, and wearing loincloths, covered in earth coloured red, white or black. 'It's like training for the army,' whispered one initiate when asked. Outsiders risk a severe beating if they try to attend a camp, unless already initiated.

For Gourmanche women, the equivalent initiation tradition was excision. Although illegal since 1996, this practice still occasionally takes place in parts of the east, usually carried out by elderly women who lack medical training, proper tools or sanitary conditions. It can lead to short-term heavy bleeding, sometimes resulting in death; and infection, pain and difficulty during childbirth if scar tissue does not allow the birth canal to heal.

ECONOMY The districts of the east are among the poorest in a very poor country. There is no industry to speak of, and the soils are less fertile than on the central Mossi Plateau. The Piela and Bilanga *departements* are particularly impoverished, with low education rates and little understanding of HIV/AIDS and birth control. A local theatre group was so moved by the situation it made a film, *My Daughter Will Go To School*, in the local language, Gourmanchebe, to be shown to families to show them the benefits of education for their children.

In the absence of large-scale farming, animal husbandry (*élevage*) is much more popular. Fada is also the centre of Burkina's honey industry, and *miel du Gourma* is on sale throughout the country. Although processed in town, it is made in the outlying villages around Fada. Look out too for pottery from this region, which tends to be either engraved or painted, rather than employing the raised patterns popular in the north.

The Gourmanche are also known as skilled hunters and trackers, and Burkina's hunting industry is an important source of employment for the villages that border the hunting reserves. Much of the meat is handed over to villagers following a successful kill. The high-powered rifles brought in by European clients to bag their skins are a far cry from traditional Gourmanche methods, which involved hunting lion with nothing more than a quiverful of poisoned arrows and a stomach full of protective magic potions.

FADA N'GOURMA

Twinned with the French champagne capital, Epernay, Fada positively fizzes with low-slung charm.

A favourite hangout with development workers seeking to escape the occasional strain of Ouaga, the early sunset over the barrage washes away any tension. Yet it is not all sleepy: Fada is the main town on the route between Ouaga and Niger's capital Niamey, as lorries thundering past its roadside *maquis* let you know. There's plenty going on, with the old cinema now an open-air square for concerts and the town a centre for frequent celebrations of Gourmanche heritage and culture. Famligo (*40 77 03 53; m 76 66 06 41*) is another celebration, a festival for Burkina, Mali and Niger – the countries of the ancient Gourmanche kingdom of Liptako.

GETTING THERE AND AWAY

By bus STMB, Rakieta, STAF and TSR all run from Ouaga to Fada, stopping at Koupela *en route*. Tickets are 3,000f one-way, 5,000f return. For times from Ouaga, see *Koupela*, page 198.

STMB (*40 77 06 94*) has Ouaga services at 07.00, 09.30, 13.00, 15.30 and 17.45. Rakieta (*40 77 10 09*) leaves at 07.00 (05.00 on Friday), 13.00 and 18.00 daily. TSR leaves at 07.00, 13.00 and 17.30.

Heading east, banditry on the road towards Niger has led to the creation of a convoy system between Fada and Kantchari. Four times a day – at 06.00, 08.00, 12.00 and 16.00 – all vehicles queue up at the eastern police post to leave only on military say-so. Departures are prompt, and there's some form of military escort up front and behind. Once *en route*, however, bush taxis get up to all their usual antics and can arrive in Kantchari an hour apart.

Laangande Transport (☎ *40 77 17 84*) has a daily service for Kantchari (2,500f) and Diapaga (4,000f), which passes through Fada from its base near Eden Park in Ouaga to pick up the 12.00 convoy. It has its own station on the Niger road.

For an express coach to Niamey (Niger), your best bet is to head to the police post for the 06.00 or 08.00 convoy; they all have to wait there. Otherwise, you can pick up small coaches or minibuses from the *autogare*, where you can also find daily departures for Kantchari (2,000f), Diapaga (4,000f), and coaches that stop *en route* to Cotonou. There are also regular departures for Pama (1,500–2,000f), which head due south and are not affected by the convoys.

By taxi Villages such as Piela or Bogande to the north are easily reached by bush taxi on market days (every three days).

GETTING AROUND Fada is an ideal size for cycling. A bike should cost no more than 1,500f a day, and you'll find one easily enough in the market. A fleet of *taxi-motos* here is ideal for hops around town or to get you to an outlying hotel. Short town trips are 200f, longer ones up to 500f. You can negotiate a daily rate if you fancy being whizzed around. Fada is also in the happy position of hosting about five town taxis, based at the *autogare*. A couple of these are likely to hang around the Rakieta/STMB stations when coaches arrive.

WHERE TO STAY Accommodation options have burgeoned in Fada in recent years, and competition is keeping the prices down. In addition to cheap accommodation in Fada itself, there are a number of safari lodges nearby that offer classy, and expensive, alternatives.

In town

Comfortable

Campement de la Sirba (11 rooms) m 70 24 50 63, 78 11 18 51. On the way into Fada from Ouaga, on the right, this is designed with hunters & safari-goers in mind. The pool's fine (2,000f to non-guests), the shady *paillotes* perfectly pleasant, there's bushmeat in season in the restaurant, but the rooms (all AC) are gloomy with fluorescent strip lighting. However, this is a good place to organise a safari in Namoungou, 90km away, & beyond. **$$$$**

Hotel 11 Decembre (36 rooms) ☎ 40 77 71 85/6; e auberge11dfada@yahoo.fr. The spacious, well-finished AC bungalows should lift this enormous complex above conference terrain, yet don't quite manage to do so. Still, there's a positive vibe & a good-looking, reasonably priced restaurant. Choose between double or suite. **$$$–$$$$**

Hotel Panache (43 rooms, inc annexe) ☎ 40 77 03 73; e panachehotel_2003bf@hotmail.com; www.panachehotel.com. Well named, with lots of white marble & an extraordinary salt-water swimming pool complete with waterfall. Given this is 2,500f for non-guests, the fan rooms at 10,000f (with towels, soap & TVs) start to look excellent value. Otherwise, kitsch spiral staircases & deserted dining areas may have you looking elsewhere. **$$–$$$$**

Mid range

Auberge Bilimpo (9 rooms) ☎ 40 77 13 02; m 70 39 78 15. One of the best of the new crop. Centrally situated, it has sparkling, spacious en-suite rooms, all with TV, set around a slightly messy courtyard. Good cheap restaurant just outside. Fan or AC. **$$–$$$**

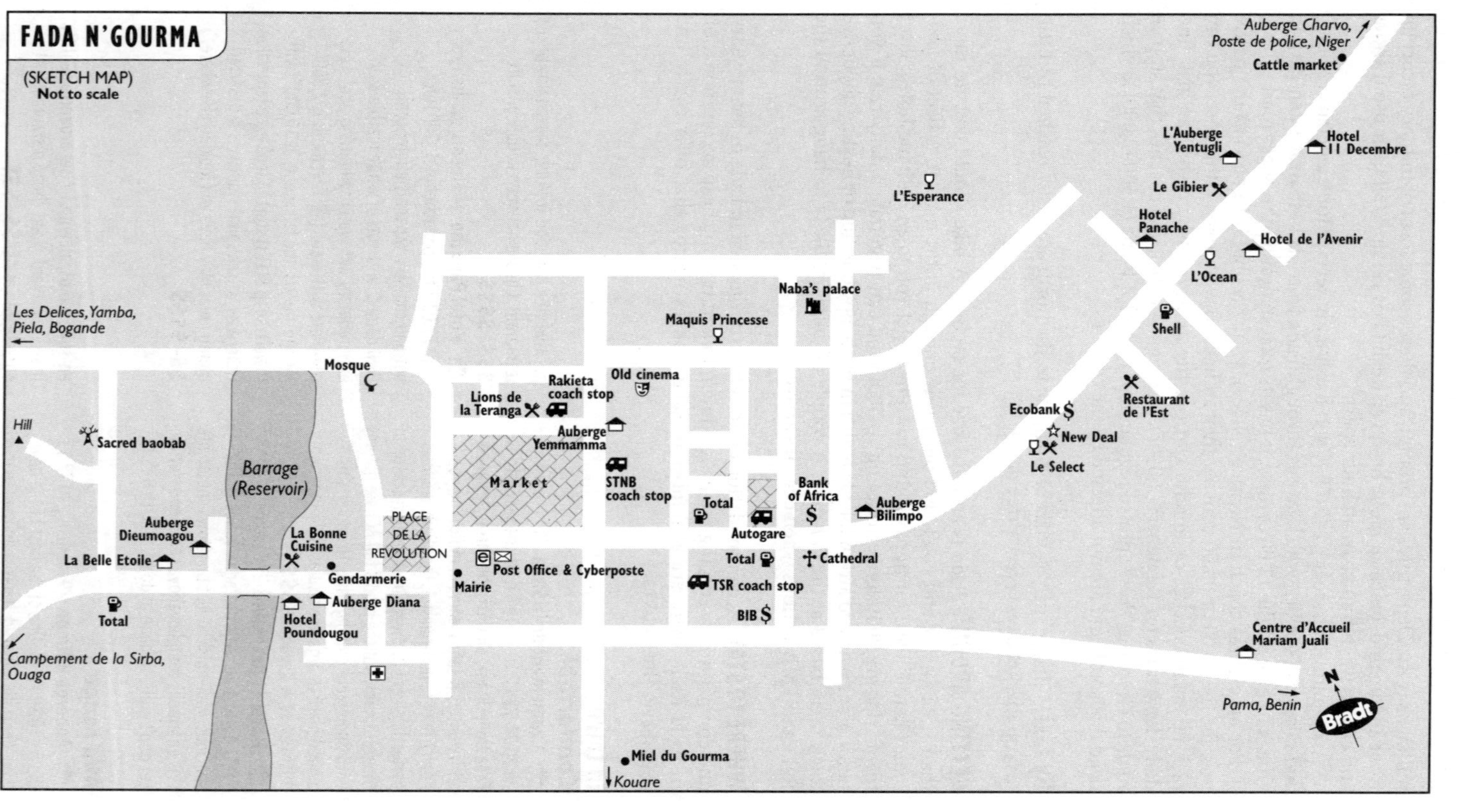

FADA N'GOURMA
(SKETCH MAP)
Not to scale
Auberge Charvo, Poste de police, Niger
Cattle market
L'Auberge Yentugli
Hotel 11 Decembre
L'Esperance
Le Gibier
Hotel Panache
Hotel de l'Avenir
L'Ocean
Naba's palace
Les Delices, Yamba, Piela, Bogande
Maquis Princesse
Shell
Mosque
Old cinema
Rakieta coach stop
Lions de la Teranga
Restaurant de l'Est
Ecobank
Hill
Sacred baobab
Auberge Yemmamma
New Deal
Le Select
Barrage (Reservoir)
Market
STNB coach stop
Bank of Africa
Total
Auberge Bilimpo
Auberge Dieumoagou
La Bonne Cuisine
PLACE DE LA REVOLUTION
Autogare
La Belle Etoile
Post Office & Cyberposte
Total
Cathedral
Gendarmerie
Mairie
TSR coach stop
Auberge Diana
Total
Hotel Poundougou
BIB
Centre d'Accueil Mariam Juali
Campement de la Sirba, Ouaga
N
Pama, Benin
Bradt
Miel du Gourma
Kouare

Auberge Diana (8 rooms) 40 77 01 40; e aubergediana@yahoo.fr. The little place that's thought of everything: TVs, towels, blankets for the cold season, & Wi-Fi on the way. Great location too. Rooms are small, though, & there's no restaurant. En-suite fan or AC. **$$–$$$**

Auberge Yemmamma (6 rooms) 40 77 00 39. Established place, very central, just down from STMB. Its shady courtyard has lovely wrought-iron seating, painted white. The rooms are simple but clean, all en suite, with fan or AC options. Sadly, the restaurant has closed for the time being. **$$–$$$**

Centre d'Accueil Mariam Juali (31 rooms, 3 dorms) On the road to Benin; 40 77 01 60. Catholic mission with a resthouse, comfortable beds & clean rooms. The gates close at about 23.00, so talk to the nightwatchman if you want to come back late. Wide choice here – AC with en suite; AC with shower only; fan double, or single. There are 2 6-bed dorms for 16,000f & 1 5-bed for 15,000f. **$$–$$$**

Hotel Poundougou (28 rooms) 40 77 17 44; e apoundougou@gmail.com. Open, but still unfinished at the time of writing, this new venture offers distinctly average fan or AC rooms with TV; some with hot water. **$$–$$$**

Budget/Shoestring

Auberge Chervo (8 rooms) 40 77 11 38; m 71 72 08 72. Right at the Niger end of town; walking distance to the far police post & waiting convoys. Clean, good-value AC or fan rooms come down in price if you're on your own or a couple. There's free secure parking for mobile homes. **$$**

Auberge Dieumoagou (4 rooms) 40 77 12 31; m 70 70 99 92. This tiny jewel has 4 gorgeously painted huts huddled around an intimate *paillote* decorated with calabashes & masks. Even the external showers are a riot of creative colour. Huts are clean & simple with bamboo beds & standing fans. Coming from Ouaga, turn left at the unmissable Iles de Paix sign before the barrage; it's on the left. **$$**

La Belle Etoile (7 rooms) 40 77 08 09; m 70 62 40 94; e belleetoile.info@yahoo.fr; www.burkinatours.com. Lovely basic *auberge*, run with a personal, idiosyncratic touch. All rooms have fan & outdoor showers/loo; choice of twin or double. Good meals served for 500f; a pizza oven on the way. Alfred Modibo, the owner, is dedicated to his local area & the place is a hive of activity. You can find out about local festivals here (see box, page 210), or organise a tour with professional guides. 4-bed dorm 2,500f per bed. **$$**

Hotel de l'Avenir (10 rooms) 40 77 04 09. Well past its best, but all rooms – fan or AC – have en-suite bathrooms & are set around a pretty courtyard. It has a unique selling point: the cheapest AC rooms in town. Staff are friendly & welcoming. **$–$$**

L'Auberge Yentugli (7 rooms) m 70 37 70 54; e auberyen09@yahoo.fr. Small friendly place that often caters for French students. Twin fan rooms shortly to be joined by 2 AC huts. **$**

Out of town

Campement Yentangou, Namoungou Safari (19 rooms) m 78 35 99 99; e contact@yentangou.com; www.yentangou.com. Heading east from Fada for about 30km, a sign on the right takes you 2.5km down a sandy track to a delightful camp, overflowing with bougainvillea, well-spaced, elegant huts & a swimming pool. For tourists as well as hunters, the camp can organise safari trips to the Namoungou private reserve, 26km further south. The camp is also close to Nagre market, which is held every Thu. Ring for prices.

Neerwaya Safaris 50 31 82 82 (Ouaga); m 70 10 30 30; e neersaf@fasonet.bf; ⌚ Dec–May. Another hunting camp, known as the *Campement du lion*, this is located east towards Kantachari just after Ougarou village, a few kilometres along a dirt track. Ring for prices.

WHERE TO EAT AND DRINK

Le Select Part of the chain of *maquis* on the Niger road rather than a restaurant, but with a fabulous range of grills, from chicken & *pintade* to *brochettes* & *emballées* (chunks of meat rolled up & cooked in cement paper). Rice & spaghetti dishes bubble away inside, while a salad girl sits next to the grills. $–$$

✕ **Lions de la Teranga** m 72 18 50 14. Spacious, with several *paillotes*, this nevertheless feels like stepping into a Senegalese family home, with a twist on the usuals: *yassa pintade*, for example, or *riz gras* that is actually *ceebu djen*. $–$$

✕ **Restaurant de l'Est** 40 77 01 28. At the Niger end of town. Set inside a walled courtyard, it serves good European & African food at decent prices. If you order in advance they can cook up a storm. $–$$

✕ **Les Delice** m 76 59 01 86. A great place serving healthy, hearty dishes, including liver & yoghurt. Owned & run by the charismatic Amina Nana, it is on the left of the dust road that runs from the reservoir towards Bogande. $

✕ **Restaurant La Bonne Cuisine** 40 77 74 10. The simple dishes here are nothing to write home about, but the beer's cold & the location, right by the barrage, can't be beaten. $

✕ **Restaurant Le Gibier** m 70 23 25 85. Shady courtyard, friendly management & a good reputation make this worth a look. Tasty *brochettes* for 100f. $

ENTERTAINMENT AND NIGHTLIFE As far as hotspots in town go, they change with the wind. The best thing is to ask around, as students frequently put on disco nights with DJs once a term or so, but the venue changes. At the time of writing, two places were vying for supremacy, both out on the Niger road. First up is **New Deal** just before Ecobank, with four turntables, ice-cold beer and a slightly older clientele. It's open Friday and Saturday (cover charge 1,000f). Further out is **L'Ocean**, which kicks off the weekend earlier, on Thursday, and is also open Friday and Saturday (cover charge 1,000f).

In town, the **Salle de Ciné**, now defunct, is occasionally good for concerts and hosts Festou (see box, below). **L'Esperance** also plays host to the occasional DJ. **Maquis Princesse** often has live music and dancing, under *paillotes*.

FESDIG AND FESTOU

For anyone wishing to gain an insight into the culture and traditions of the Gourmanche, it is worth co-ordinating a visit to the east with Fesdig – Festival Dilembu au Gulmu. For three days, the tiny village of Tantiaka, about 30km west of Fada, is a magnet for Gourmanche of the region, coming together to celebrate both traditional and modern life. Demonstrations of ancient activities such as forging metal, the histories of the *griots*, and lashings of homemade *dolo* fill the town, while Gourmanche hip-hop, which appals the village elders, is a sight to behold. Visitors are expected to camp, although it may be possible to find accommodation in a courtyard somewhere if you are lucky. It is customary to give a donation towards the cost of the festival, and bring a gift with you (kola nuts or Chinese tea for example) for the chief or elders of the village. Despite funding from NGOs, the bulk of the festival costs are shouldered by the organisers. For more details, contact the organiser of the festival, Alfred Modibo (*40 77 08 09*).

From the same stable but with a different emphasis, Festou – Festival des Oubliées (Festival of the Forgotten) – offers four nights of music and drama at the end of October. It's held in the old cinema in Fada itself; the music ranges from traditional to modern, and the drama sketches are in French. The Belle Étoile *auberge* is the place to find out more, though they may not be able to explain the festival's name. 'Come back next year,' they said. 'We might have an explanation by then.' Perhaps they just forgot.

OTHER PRACTICALITIES **BIB**, **Bank of Africa** and **Ecobank** all have Visa machines. The best internet option is the **cyberposte** (*until 21.30 Mon–Sat, until 12.00 Sun*) near the **market**, which charges 500f an hour.

WHAT TO SEE Mamadou Thiombiano (*40 77 00 11*) can give a good guided tour.

Honey in action You can visit **Miel du Gourma**, famous for its honey, just beyond the Lycée Diaba Lompo on the left. It also sells beeswax and a range of products that are nicely made and packaged – candles, pomades and so on. Much of the honey comes from the shea tree (*karite*), and has a dark colour and a strong taste. The friendly owners can show you around and explain how apiculture is practised in the region.

Cattle market Every Sunday, Fada hosts one of the biggest cattle markets in the country. Herders, including Fulani from all over the region, come to sell their animals.

Sacred mountain This holy hill, between the Yamba and Ouaga roads and about 30 minutes' walk from town, has either a dragon or a snake living beneath it, according to whom you ask. So tread carefully. Traditional sacrifices for the protection of Fada still take place up here, to appease its resident; there are rumours it was used as an altar to sacrifice disabled town-dwellers in the past. More recently, a man was sent to prison for taking the blood of a young albino resident up there to use in his magic potions. A spookily atmospheric place to watch the sun go down.

Sacred baobab Look out for the sacred baobab, supposedly 1,000 years old, rutted with horseshoe-shaped marks. Local myth runs that these belong to the steed of the most famous of Fada's rulers, Yendabri. He went up this tree to hide out until hostilities with an invader were over. Take the first right after the reservoir on the Yamba road.

Naba's court You can also make visits to the royal family. The *naba* is always happy to receive guests, although do leave something (2,000f is a decent amount).

Piela About 100km north of town, Piela is a friendly village with a small but lively market once every three days. If you have your own wheels you can visit the local gold mines in this region (ask around for directions). The association ADDESP (*40 77 95 08*) has *chambres de passage*. You can also visit Walambi, a few kilometres from Piela in the direction of Pouytenga; its women's co-operative grows vegetables close to a lake during the dry season.

PAMA

Once capital of the region, Pama now languishes under a gentle haze of quiet and reverence. A selection of elegant resthouses nearby makes for a tranquil retreat, and it's also a great staging post for trips into Benin's Pendjari National Park. Visas can be bought on the border for 10,000f, and travel agencies in Ouagadougou, as well as hotels in the region, can organise the trip.

You can hire *motos* in Pama from Ounpoungla (m *70 42 70 21*), at around 5,000f a day. He can also arrange transfers to the lakeside (Tagou or Thialy) for 2,000f per person.

GETTING THERE AND AWAY Pama is 100km south from Fada. You can ask any coach heading for Cotonou (Benin) via Fada to stop at Pama, but they don't stop as a matter of course. You'll have more choice of departure times if you take one of the many coaches to Fada, then hop on a minibus from there. Tickets are 1,500–2,000f. They leave from the *autogare* throughout the day, and cover the tarmac road quickly enough.

WHERE TO STAY

Hotel Bonanza (7 rooms) m 70 14 36 82. Originally run by an Italian proprietor, the main building is filled with a nostalgic embrace of his & his wife's glamorous past. On the wall are framed black-&-white photographs of the pair with 1940s haircuts, locked in love. Lovely, simple *rondavels* are set in a spacious courtyard, with iron bedsteads & en-suite shower & loo set behind a divider, or AC rooms within a side building. The small swimming pool might remain empty, but the place flows with care. Good meals are available, though are fairly pricey for the setting. On the left at the southern end of town, with green gates. **$$–$$$**

Auberge de l'Amitié/Hotel Albert (10 rooms) 40 77 60 11. Down a dirt track on the right just before the police checkpoint heading south, this resthouse – known by either name – arranges its round huts around a courtyard, with mango trees in the middle. Slightly run-down *rondavels* have twin beds with en-suite shower & loo; rooms have double beds. No meals. **$$**

Le Jardin du Maire (8 rooms) 40 77 60 70. Set in a grove of luxuriant mango trees, the well-maintained rooms are good value, all en-suite with a choice of fan or AC. A spacious *bar-restau* among the trees is a popular destination for a cold beer & simple meals. Look for the sign on the left at the southern end of town; it's about 100m down a winding track. **$–$$**

Around Pama Spending a few days at one or two of the lovely retreats around Pama is definitely worth a splurge. All offer comfortable accommodation in stunning settings, either by the lake or in the bush, and can organise excursions and safaris. Reckon on at least 30,000f each a day for accommodation and food (more at Yeryanga); trips, drinks and so on are extra.

Lakeside hotels

Campement de Tagou, Burkina Safari Club (10 rooms) Lake Kompienga; m 70 16 61 04, 78 58 27 78; e burkinasafariclub@yahoo.fr. Take a right on the approach to Pama from Fada, 500m before the checkpoint. A winding 14km of red dust track later you hit the edge of Tagou Lake to find a wonder of a hideaway. Once an island – until the dam created in 1994 lowered its water levels – the lodge sits high up on a rock formation reminiscent of the finale of the legendary Hitchcock film *North by Northwest*, with huts hidden among the boulders. There's a platform sitting over the glistening water. A small swimming pool is set below a large bar & restaurant area. Guides can arrange excursions on the lake (15,000f) as well as safaris, which take you to the Singou sister camp (see opposite). 4x4 hire costs 60,000f per day; entry fees to the reserve are extra (5,500f pp), as is a guiding fee (4,000f per day). There's a choice of fan or AC; prices include 3 meals a day. **$$$$$$**

Campement de Thialy (8 rooms) m 78 47 61 60; e thialyburkina@yahoo.fr. The mere sight of this hotel, shimmering across the water like the Isle of Avalon rising through the mist, is enough to set romantic hearts fluttering. It seems to be on an island, & tourist access is mostly by a short *pinasse* trip across the lake, but in fact there's a long way round via Kompienbiga (before Pama) if you have wheels. Set atop a hill – higher than the one at Tagou; it's a fairly stiff climb from the boat – the whole place is built in mud using *voute nubienne* techniques; rooms are simple, stylish & painted in yellow ochre. There's a restaurant, bar & swimming pool. Excursions on the lake & to fishing villages can be arranged. Prices include 3 meals a day & the boat transfer. **$$$$$$**

Safari lodges

Campement de Singou, Burkina Safari Club (10 rooms) 50 33 24 41 (Ouaga); m 70 12 91 79; e dermenz@yahoo.fr; 1 Dec–15 May. The sister camp of the Campement de Tagou, it is set about 25km along the N19 in the private 65,000ha Konkombouri reserve on the way to Arly from Pama, via Tindangou; you can't miss it. Pictures of big game adorn the walls of thatched-roof semi-detached bungalows, which cater for safari-viewers as well as hunters. At the latest count, there were over 60 lions & 650 elephants in the reserve, & the guides are expert at tracking them down in any of 6 4x4s, or in on-foot safaris. An enticing additional option is a night-time hide in the bush, kitted out with a couple of beds. Prices include 3 meals a day. **$$$$$$**

Yeryanga Safari, Campement du Buffle (12 bungalows) 40 77 60 17; e maurice.bardet@yahoo.fr; www.ysafari.com. Comes highly recommended, with bar, restaurant, salon & terrace with sunbeds beside the pool. You can hire a guide, a car, take a boat out or go fishing on nearby Lake Kompienga, & visit local Gourmanche villages – for a price (half a day on the lake costs 50,000f, plus 30,000f to get there). Turn left as you enter Pama (before the checkpoint) from Fada, & follow the track. Look out for signs on the road, which are better marked as you leave Pama for Fada. Prices drop slightly in low season. **$$$$$$**

KOMPIENGA

With the bush hotel falling into disrepair, Kompienga is less of a draw than it used to be, but still worth a visit if you're particularly interested in the dam.

GETTING THERE AND AWAY From Pama, head south to Nadiagou, the last customs post before Benin and Togo. The right turn towards the Togolese border is barred, so you must take a detour through the customs post full of parked lorries. Kompienga is 16km away. When you have passed through the town, turn right at the *gendarme* post on the gravel road leading towards the dam. When you reach an overhead banner for Onea, Burkina's water company, turn right again. Look for the sign at the end of the road, and then turn left. Kompienga is tricky to reach without your own wheels.

WHERE TO STAY

La Kompienga, Hotel de Brousse (11 rooms) m 70 12 25 01, 75 65 61 04. A real tragedy. Once a glorious holiday playpen, visitors are now greeted with tumbledown *paillotes*, a reception area cluttered with abandoned AC units & the sense that the whole place is defunct. 1 of only 3 ONTB staff will appear, however, to show you what's left: four 4-bedroom villas, 6 AC rooms & a single suite. Meals are still available, along with overpriced beer. Fortunes may be reversed if a private investor can be found; enquire with ONTB. **$$$$**

WHAT TO SEE AND DO

Hill walking It's well worth an early morning climb up the steep hill that towers over the hotel grounds. Not only are the views fantastic, but you may also spot some of the rock's sizeable baboon population. An hour and a half should see you up to the top and down again. Take water and aim to be back before 09.30. Or ask for directions to the nearby reservoir, which is hidden behind the hills; the return trip should take about three hours on foot.

Kompienga Dam Visiting a large hydro-electric dam may not be a priority, but the Burkinabe are remarkably proud of this enormous facility, the country's first hydro-electric station, responsible for supplying most of Ouagadougou's electricity

> **POWER TO THE PEOPLE**
>
> OK, so you probably didn't buy this guidebook for a lesson on electricity, but seeing as the authorities that run the enormous dam at Kompienga are so keen for visitors, you should at least know some background. Despite a wealth of natural resources, west Africa lays claim to the dubious title of world's least-reliable electricity supply. It is the region with the lowest rate of electricity generation in the world, with total regional electricity consumption at about 32,000 gigawatt hours (GWh), 46% of which is in Nigeria. Only a fifth of west Africa's population has access to electricity, while rural electrification in the region can fall to as low as 2%. Based on an existing generating capacity of about 10,000 megawatts (MW), west Africa must increase its generating capacity by about 17,000MW by 2023 to meet minimum development targets. It is certainly possible. Electricity in the region is currently generated by thermal (58.8%) or hydro (41.2%) sources. West Africa boasts vast untapped hydro resources with the mighty Niger and Volta rivers, and huge proven crude oil and natural gas reserves in the Gulf of Guinea. There is substantial hydro-power potential (estimated at 24GW), but estimates suggest only 4% of this potential is currently tapped. Lesson over.

(see box, above). For a visit to the control room, it is necessary to get authority from the state electricity parastatal, Sonabel (☎ *50 30 61 00*).

KANTCHARI

The last outpost before Niger on the road east, Kantchari has an out-of-the-way feel, perhaps because the town is set back from the busy highway that arrows towards Niamey. But head to the area around the police post, and you'll get a lively whiff of people on the move. It is easily reached from Fada, around 150km away on a good road, and 46km from Diapaga on regulation washboard dirt track. It is a good springboard for onward travel to W National Park, Arly and the Gobnangou Escarpment.

A young guide here, Ludovic Ouoba (m *70 28 71 67*) can organise trips to local Fulani villages. Another happy chappy with a motorbike is Ouoba Ounteni (m *70 14 28 36, 78 74 07 57*). He'll hire it out or ferry you around, and generally make himself useful.

GETTING THERE AND AWAY

By bus The only national coach service to leave Ouaga for Kantchari is Laangande Transport, which departs at 06.00 to catch the 12.00 convoy from Fada. It then continues on to Diapaga. From Fada, you can head to the police post to pick up coaches for Niamey (best bet is early morning), or get a bush taxi from the *autogare*. They fill up in town, then head to the police post to await the green flag. From Kantchari, the convoy system works in reverse, with the same departure times for Fada.

By taxi A model football on a pillar forms a roundabout in the centre of town – the best place to pick up a *taxi brousse* headed to Diapaga, for 2,000f. The last of these leaves Fada with the 16.00 convoy, passing through Kantchari around 18.00.

WHERE TO STAY

Auberge Delwende de Kantchari (7 rooms) m 79 25 68 54, 70 68 31 85. On the tarmac road, just down the hill from the customs post on the Niger side of town. Tucked behind a high-walled courtyard are simple, spacious fan rooms with en-suite showers & outside loos. Light sleepers will be happy to hear that the outdoor dancefloor is defunct, but still serves as a bar/restaurant. There's good *porc au four* on Sat. **$**

Ask around at the police post for the inexplicably named Hong Kong (say 'Onkong'), and you'll be led to a toothless, smiley old man who has ten very basic *chambres de passage* with inside shower and outside loo (**$**).

WHERE TO EAT, DRINK AND SHOP Football and beer seem to make Kantchari tick. The smell of *dolo* often hangs on the air and even on a Sunday morning, the **Buvette Jiirifuo**, looking out over the football-monument roundabout, hosts guests nursing their first of the day. Next door is a handy breakfast bar, the **Carrefour des Amis**, serving up yoghurt, fresh bread and coffee, while round the corner **La Solution** provides solace for many.

The area around the eastern police post is surprisingly happening. You may get no further than **La Causette**, a popular *maquis* where you'll find good grub (including *pintade* and grilled fish) and dancing at the weekends. Its rival **Le Trou** is tucked away nearby. **Restaurant MiYemanma** serves up simple fare as well, but for the biggest plates, nay trays of food in Burkina, head for **Chez Adama** on the tarmac truck park.

About 500m out of town towards Diapaga, the **Buvette de l'Amitie** is another shady drinking corner.

The market has lovely printed cotton fabrics at decent prices and no-hassle shopping.

AROUND KANTCHARI About halfway down the road to Diapaga, you pass a lake at a village called Boudieri. A village *campement* is under construction here.

Only 11km from the Nigerien border, **Botou** is the site of traditional weaving, where homespun cotton is worked into beautiful patterns on hand looms. It makes a good day trip from Kantchari, 70km away. For those without the time or inclination to get there, examples of Botou weaving can also be found at the market in Fada, and throughout the region.

DIAPAGA

The last main stop before Arly Reserve, W National Park and the Gobnangou Escarpment, Diapaga has a laid-back charm. Moreover, this is the place to find everything you need to know about onward travel; it's the headquarters for the new tourist initiatives to the south. It's also the best place to fill up with petrol if you're heading into the wilderness.

GETTING THERE AND AWAY The only practical option direct from Ouaga is Laangande Transport, which leaves at 06.00 daily from its stop near Eden Park Hotel. Otherwise, head to Fada and pick up transport from there (4,000f to Diapaga). A minibus bound for Namounou leaves with the 06.00 convoy on Wednesday and Saturday. Another daily minibus leaves for Diapaga with the 16.00 convoy. Ask around either in Fada or Kantchari for other transport passing through.

On the way back, the Laangarde departure for Ouaga is at 06.00. Otherwise, head to the roundabout for minibus departures. The Namounou minibus passes through Diapaga on Monday and Thursday mornings, bound for Ouaga. The daily Fada minibus also leaves early, but if you're lucky you may find a departure as late as noon, especially on Mondays.

WHERE TO STAY

In town

Hotel Oagapo (16 rooms) 40 79 10 88; m 70 28 84 97. Shiny new rooms are the most comfy that Diapaga can offer; all are en suite, most have TV & you choose between fan or AC. There's a nice *paillote* at the back, but for the time being the place lacks atmosphere. It's just near the main roundabout in town. **$$–$$$**

Bahanma Bar-Resto (10 rooms) 40 79 10 18; m 70 29 17 10. Also called the Gacilien, this is the best-known place in town, also not far from the roundabout. En-suite rooms are slightly run-down but fine, with nets & choice of fan or AC; 6 cheap fan huts are grubby, depressing & come with or without shower. There's always a bit of a buzz here, with a decent *restau-maquis* & a leafy garden drawing in plenty of locals for cheap grub, cold beer & TV. A new annexe of 4 new huts is under construction nearby. **$–$$**

Auberge Ougapo (10 rooms) 40 79 11 37. From the same stable as the hotel, & the best budget option, with clean, bright fan rooms. En-suite bathrooms no longer have running water so you get a bucket instead, but the price takes this into account. Coming from Kantchari, turn left after the police post, head across the footie pitch & it's the block within the big walled enclosure. There's also a small *maquis* here that serves up decent food. **$**

Campement Taamba (9 rooms) 40 79 10 41. Shabby bungalows are the grimmest in town, but also the cheapest. Turn left at the roundabout; on the right after about 200m. **$**

Out of town Wildlife lovers might consider accommodation outside Diapaga, particularly around the beautiful Lake Tapoa (Barrage de Tapoa), 4km along the Kantchari road, which boasts lovely scenery and a host of birdlife.

Tapoa Djerma Safari 50 31 44 19; m 70 21 35 05; fax: 50 30 13 99; e tapoasafari@fasonet.bf. Near W National Park & the northern hunting zone that borders it, this establishment rarely deals with anyone other than hunters on all-inclusive packages, including flights from abroad & 4x4 transfers from Ouaga. However, if you do turn up on the hoof on your way through to W (perfectly feasible), you can probably sort something out for around 30,000f each. The extensive publicity on show – posters explaining how you can bag a lion, a buffalo, a kob & an antelope in 12 days – make for morbidly fascinating reading. **$$$$$$**

La Palmeraie Libaboundi (16 rooms) 40 79 10 80; m 70 26 76 71, 70 35 12 21; e palmerairlib@yahoo.fr. Universally known as Chez Marie, after the owner, this is a delightful lodge popular with both hunters & sightseers, with a range of bungalows & a beautiful pool. Veg & herbs for the excellent restaurant are grown in an extensive lakeside garden; an orchard produces fruit. It can arrange *pirogue* trips (1,500f pp per hr), & 4x4 safaris. Pretty en-suite fan huts are great value; the AC options aren't bad either. Some have lake views. **$$$–$$$$**

WHERE TO EAT AND DRINK Now, Bernard is the chef at Chez Marie out of town, and he has two wives. Wife Number 1 has gone into business and runs **Chez Bernard**, by the Department of the Environment on the main drag; Bernard pops in when he has time. Meanwhile, Bernard's employer, the enterprising Marie, has employed Wife Number 2 to run **Café-Restau Poissonerie** (Chez Tantie Marie) just off the roundabout. Got that? How all this culinary competition plays out at home is anyone's guess, but either place is a good bet for cheap nosh and cold beers. The *poissonerie* dishes up healthy portions of ragout, couscous, spaghetti and rice on roadside tables; Bernard's has a series of pretty cane shelters out back, and serves up breakfast as well. Stroll along from Marie's place to find a lively sports bar, with the football playing full blast, and a *babyfoot* table for acting it out in person.

OTHER PRACTICALITIES The daily **market** peaks every Saturday with a larger-scale affair. There are numerous **telecentres**, and an **internet café** behind the Bahanma Bar-Resto.

WHAT TO SEE AND DO

Tourism project and museum An exciting new development is under way in Diapaga, spearheaded by Italian NGO ACRA (Association de Cooperation Rurale en Afrique). The green-roofed buildings opposite Chez Bernard now house the **Centre Populaire de Loisir**, comprising a museum (which focuses on the natural history of the area) and a crafts centre. This is also where you can find the **Biala Association** (m *72 98 13 00, 75 48 82 88;* e *ecobiala@yahoo.fr*), designed to promote tourism locally. It provides five qualified guides who know everything on offer in the region and how to organise it, including all the new hiking and climbing opportunities along the Gobnangou Escarpment, networks of caves to explore, waterfalls to splash in, villages, crocodile pools and ancient grainstores to visit. There are bikes for hire, and tents for camping trips. The guide we met, Miyemba Lombo (m *70 41 64 80*) was friendly and articulate.

THE GOBNANGOU ESCARPMENT

The Gobnangou massif (Falaise de Gobnangou) extends from the Arly Reserve to Niger, looming over the plains of Gourmanche country in great fissured cliffs and descending slowly to a low rise further east. The cliffs shelter vulture colonies and are good for other raptors (including fox kestrel), swifts and swallows. Villages nestle beneath it, comfortable in the protection it provides; waterfalls tumble down it, caves lie hidden in its depths and climbers can find an increasing number of routes to inch their way up it, thanks to the efforts of La Federation de l'Escalade Italienne (FASI). They have already opened several climbs and are aiming to create about 100.

Entry to the cliff area costs 3,000f per person per day, with a reduction for longer stays. Activities include hiking trips – either from the *campements*, or with tents hired from Biala; cycling trips and local visits. Climbing costs 2,000f per day or per climbing route. The fee is to enable local villagers to maintain the routes.

GETTING THERE AND AWAY

By bus Getting as far as Namounou, the first sizeable town on leaving Diapaga, is fairly easy; minibuses leave from Diapaga more or less daily (1,000f). Market day is Sunday, when you'll have no trouble finding something. A minibus heads to and from Ouaga twice a week (see *Diapaga*, page 215), and the town is also a popular truck stop.

Beyond Namounou, transport is sporadic. You can certainly find it – you can even find a ride through Arly and beyond, towards Togo and Pama – but you'll need to get lucky, or wait. You're better off talking to the Biala Association in Diapaga, which will sort out a 4x4 or *motos*, according to your budget.

By car If you have wheels, head south to Namounou. From there, you can take a left to Tambaga and follow the road down to the bottom of the cliff. It then runs along through the villages of Kidi-Konbou, Moredeni and Logobou *en route* to

Arly. Alternatively, carry on along the N19 from Namounou, which runs along the top of the *falaise*, passing through Yobri and Yereni.

If you're coming from Arly, you have the same choice in reverse. Take a right turn off the N19, and then a left, to follow the road less travelled along the bottom of the *falaise*, or carry straight up the N19 towards Diapaga.

WHERE TO STAY

Campement de Kindi Konbou (6 huts). Part of the same project, with the same methods & objectives, but this time at the bottom of the cliff. **$$**

Campement de Yobri (6 huts) via Biala Association, Diapaga (for contact information, see page 217). Built with local materials & with villagers' participation, this is a community project that has been developed with help from ACRA, who will be providing support for a year or so after opening. It has 6 en-suite huts, a bar/restaurant & a crafts shop. The idea is to co-ordinate the efforts of craftspeople along the *falaise* so that they can benefit from tourism. **$$**

Safari de la Gobnangou Moredeni. Just down from Kidi-Konbou, this is for hunters rather than tourists, but may provide more luxury than the *campements*. Ask the Biala guides for more information and for prices.

TANSARGA The sculptors of Tansarga, at the end of the Gobnangou Escarpment, 24km from Diapaga, are in such demand they are furniture-makers to the Gourmanche royal family. Working with local wood, they fashion pieces representing men and animals and their *ateliers* make for a great rummage if you are looking for some examples of quality contemporary workmanship.

ARLY RESERVE

Arly has suffered from bad press in recent years compared with neighbouring Benin's Pendjari Park, with some good reason. The *pistes* have been in bad shape, the scrub sometimes dismally scraggly, the accommodation run-down and it's generally harder to spot the prize game (lion and elephant). This should all be about to change with an injection of EU money; this is the second phase of the funding that has already vastly improved W, and comprises another €17 million to be spent in the WAP parks (W, Arly and Pendjari). Even as it is, in the driest of the dry season you're likely to see many animals, and relative inaccessibility makes it a rewarding adventure. The reserve is a vast area that includes the state-run Arly National Park, along with various private reserves and concessions, primarily for hunters. These private areas have the pick of the accommodation and better game-viewing than elsewhere.

GETTING THERE AND AWAY There are two ways to get to Arly. The quicker, more trouble-free route is on tarmac roads from Ouaga via Fada to Kantchari, and then 75km south to Diapaga, which acts as a springboard to either W National Park or Arly. See *Diapaga*, page 215, and *The Gobnangou Escarpment*, page 217, for transport options.

The alternative route, east via Pama, is an adventure. The turning for Arly is at the small village of Tindangou, 16km south of Pama. Look out for the Burkina Safari Club sign, and turn left. You'll pass the Campement de Singou *en route* to the park, 85km away. The western entry point to the park itself is unmanned, but well signposted. Very much first- and second-gear territory, it can sometimes feel more like an empty riverbed than a road, despite cotton lorries leaving telltale signs of their passing with soft white fibres hanging from the undergrowth. The track is particularly bad from Tanbarga to Arly itself, with lots of soft sand. You'll need your own 4x4, and you may get stuck (we did). Take plenty of water, something to eat and a strong rope in case you do need pulling out.

WHERE TO STAY

La Paix d'Arly – Le Grand Baobab (28 rooms) 50 33 09 83 (Ouaga); www.africa-evasion.com. A lovely option for safari-goers as well as hunters, not far outside the park, about 2km before the entry on your right. Accommodation is in en-suite painted huts; there's a pool, bar & restaurant – non-guest diners welcome. The French couple who now run the place took over from a well-known Burkinabe tour operator, Noufou Campaore, with whom they now run a tour agency. **$$$$–$$$$$**

Hotel Safari Arly (4 rooms) 40 79 15 78 (Arly park office); Dec–Apr. Set beside a seasonal riverbed & the only accommodation in Arly itself. It's severely run-down, to the extent that only 4 rooms of a former 18 are now functional. There's no running water & no food. However, the staff at the park office are helpful & friendly; the arrival of EU funding may turn the place around. If you have camping equipment, you can set up beside the hotel. **$**

ARLY NATIONAL PARK The 76,000ha park is home to about 200 elephants, 200 hippos and 100 lions. There are also buffalo, baboons, red and green monkeys, warthog, boars and several types of antelope: Western hartebeest, roan antelope, Buffon's kob, bushbucks, duikers, sable and waterbuck.

The best time to go out is from 05.00 (especially if you want to catch landside hippos) until 09.00, and 15.00 until 18.00. Lions are hardest to spot, only coming out of the scrub in the dry season and not keeping to fixed land areas. Guides can follow tracks, and seek them out near waterholes such as Tounga pool.

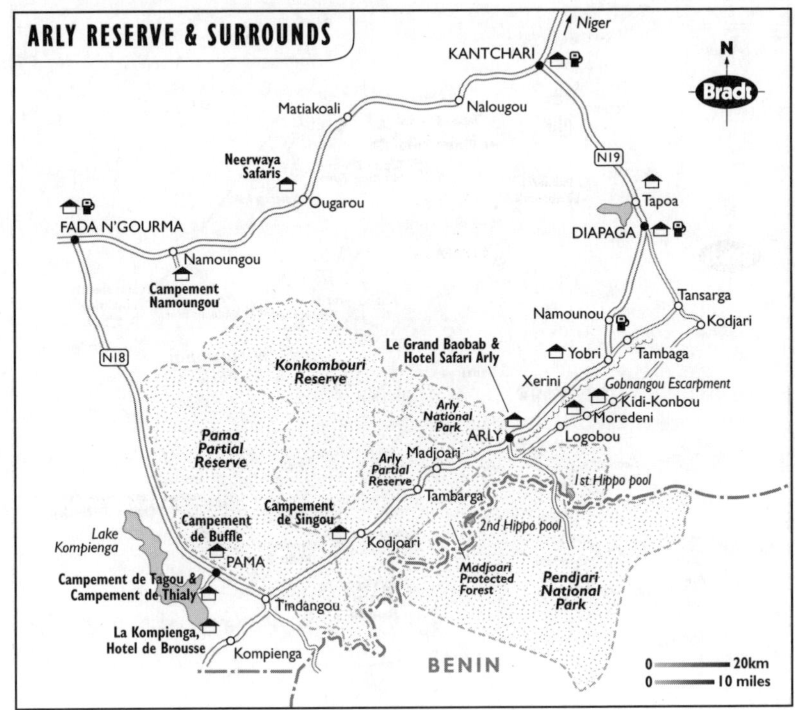

You can drive to one of two hippo pools, often filled with groups of 20. From 07.00 to 18.00 they're happiest in the water, so you'll have to be up pretty early to see them. Your guide will lead you on an intrepid foot safari through semi-dense undergrowth to the pool's edge. With a strong clearing of the throat, a bunch of the most dangerous animals on the continent will move to his command, rearing up in alarm at the sound.

Entry details A permit to enter the park, on any piste other than the N19 that cuts through it, costs 10,000f per person. A (compulsory) armed guide to accompany you game-viewing costs 6,000f per day. The office is on the N19 within the park itself.

W NATIONAL PARK

First created in 1954, the W National Park, covering more than 1m ha (14,000km^2) across three countries (Benin, Burkina Faso and Niger), is one of Africa's premier conservation areas. Its peculiar name (pronounced *double-v* in French) derives from the shape made by the Niger River that borders its northeastern side, looking like an upturned W.

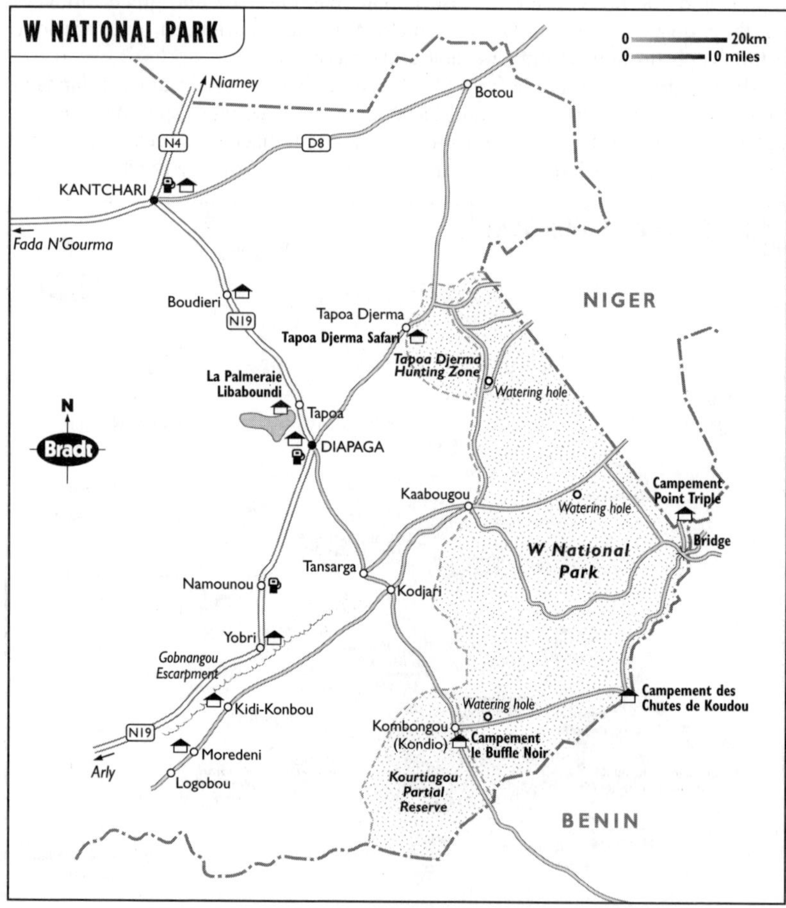

HUNTING

These days, the stereotypical big-game hunter is more Elmer Fudd than Ernest Hemingway. Large, louche and loaded, with a gung-ho appetite for beer, women and ammunition, neither the manners nor the motivations of hunters are kindly looked upon.

Yet for all those who scoff or scorn, hunting provides a lifeline for the communities that live alongside the wildlife of the African savanna.

In Burkina, hunting is big business. There are 23 hunting zones in the country, across an area of 1.4m ha, compared with five in Benin. Hunting permits worth CFA75 million were sold in 2010; the total revenue from hunting is estimated at CFA3–4 billion annually. It can cost more than £10,000 to hunt a lion, making it a much more lucrative industry than budget-orientated sightseeing safaris. In 2010, 1,401 hunters, 629 of them Burkinabe, went off in search of their prize kill in Burkina. The eastern region brings in by far the most money – more than half of all hunting receipts. If organised responsibly and properly, it can also make a positive contribution to the environment and can help stamp out poaching.

In the past, villagers turned to poaching simply as a way of feeding their families. Where the struggle for food, firewood and grazing land is paramount, wild animals are not seen through the rose-tinted spectacles worn by visitors, who don't have to share the land with them.

Hunting provides the financial incentive to abandon poaching. It provides employment to guides, porters and safari-ranch workers. Local committees become involved in running the reserves, and receive a share of the profits, as well as the meat from hunting kills.

As for the conservation aspects, hunters and those who run lodges also say their main concern in the long run is to maintain animal life, so that there will always be something to hunt. The number of licences issued for species such as lion and buffalo is tightly controlled each year, and breeding programmes ensure the continued existence of big game. The hunting of elephants, however, is not permitted in Burkina.

For visitors, it is worth bearing in mind that the private ranches, set up primarily for hunters, also tend to be better organised and maintained than areas used simply for vision safari. While there are none of the luxuries of east African encampments, clean air-conditioned rooms, bars, swimming pools and decent food soften the edges of bush living. You may even have the chance to find out more about the most misunderstood of all animals inhabiting the African savanna: the hunter.

'One of the great places of the planet,' says wildlife expert Roger Wilson of the park, where he has worked as researcher. 'The great feature of W is not what is special but what is characteristic in a fully functioning ecosystem on a grand scale, a rarity in itself in these times.'

The savanna woodland of W is home to 32 species of mammals, including 1,300 elephants, 200 lions, 3,300 buffalo, 2,350 roan antelope and 450 hartebeest. Five species – cheetah, hunting dog, manatee, elephant and topi – are considered highly endangered. There are also 350 species of birds. Despite being a semi-arid environment, three rivers – the Tapoa, the Alibori and the Mekrou – flow through the park and into the Niger. On the Burkina side, the Kourtiagou and the Pendjo rivers flow westwards into the Pendjari.

The turnaround in the park's fortunes has been remarkable. Following years of mismanagement and neglect, park routes were non-existent, animals heavily poached and there was little co-operation among the three countries. An ambitious €20 million venture to bring the park back from the brink started the process of turning it into one of the continent's most exciting game parks. The EU-funded project has improved park infrastructure, with major roads built through the park that are passable all year round to allow traffic between countries. A number of watering holes have been established to attract wildlife, creating important viewing points for visitors.

ENTRY DETAILS Entry to the park on the Burkina side is 5,000f per person. A plan to create a single pass, valid in all three countries, enabling visitors to criss-cross the park without additional payments, has not quite worked out in that you can't exit in Benin or Niger without incurring further costs. As long as you both enter and exit in Burkina, however, you should be fine. There are a number of entry points to the park, all via Diapaga. Tapoa Djerma is to the north, Kaabougou in the middle and Kondio in the south. All have forestry posts where you pick up your pass and also your obligatory guide (10,000f per day plus meals) and armed guard (4,000f per day). You will need your own transport, and bear in mind that you'll need to make room for two extra men.

WHERE TO STAY

Campement des Chutes de Koudou (5 rooms) Overlooking the spectacular Falls of Koudou, at the meeting point between Burkina, Benin & Niger, this camp is in Benin, but easily accessible from the Burkina side. It is a deliberate attempt to invoke the 'luxury camping'-style ambience of south & east African safaris, but at a fraction of the price. 5 separate teak huts, suspended above the ground on stilts, offer privacy & comfort, with en-suite bathrooms, & mosquito nets. The restaurant is perched on a rocky outcrop overlooking the falls, & the swimming pool avoids the temptation of bathing with the crocs in the nearby river. The tour agent is based in Cotonou, Benin (*+229 23 63 02 43, 22 43 00 47;* e *voyageur@internet.bj; www.hotels-benin.com*), & Kandi Lodge in Benin (*+229 23 63 02 43*) handles Koudou bookings. **$$$**

Campement Le Buffle Noir Kondio. This was always very much a hunting lodge, but we've heard that it has recently changed hands, & there may have been a change in emphasis too. Ask at the Biala Association in Diapaga for information and for prices.

Campement Point Triple (10 rooms) m 70 22 49 23. A new initiative, set at the point where the 3 countries (Burkina, Benin & Niger) meet. En-suite bungalows have tin roofs, but covered with straw so that they blend in better; there's also a restaurant. Call for prices.

Those in possession of a tent may be able to camp at one of the three forestry posts, which should be able to provide water but no other facilities. Alternatively, stay at one of the lodges around Diapaga.

6

The South

The south is a region of secrets. For a start, the most exciting elephant-viewing in west Africa is on Burkina's southern savanna. Further southwest, around Gaoua, powerful wooden fetishes and secret rituals, steeped in ancestral significance, take their place among the guarded Lobi. You can spend the night on flat mud roofs under the stars in Kassena country, and admire its remarkable cocoon-like fortress homes sculpted from the earth.

The south is a good bet if you have only a couple of days to spare. Nazinga Ranch and Kassena country, with good links to Ouagadougou, can be combined in a two-day trip. Alternatively, if you have your own wheels and are aiming for Banfora and Bobo-Dioulasso in the west, sweeping south through Kassena and Lobi country makes for an adventurous and interesting alternative to the main highway from the capital.

HEADING FOR PO

The tarmac road to Po has been a mess of roadworks for some distance out of Ouaga recently, but otherwise it's good and continues to Accra. However, it has been known to suffer from occasional attacks by armed bandits. The road narrows to cross the Nazinon River about 10km after Nobere, and robbers have struck at this bottleneck by barring the route with a truck. One attack in the summer of 2005 – on vehicles carrying a top lawyer, a Burkinabe colonel and a CNN award-winning journalist – put banditry back on the political agenda, and the government promised to deal with it. Patrols increased, and the French government has now lifted its warnings against the route, but in mid-2011, the British FCO still advised against it. Check before you go, take local advice, and stay vigilant.

GOLF CLUB There is a golf course, popular with expats, about 15 minutes from Ouaga, before the checkpoint (*péage*), marked by a sign on the right. It's a much-loved getaway, with a good view of Ouaga from the third tee. There's little grass, so you carry around a piece of astroturf, which you can use if your ball lands on the fairway. If it doesn't, you play off the rocks. There is a covered driving range and practice 'green'. Lessons are available and there are tournaments every year (January–June). Green fees are 10,000f for non-members. Tip the caddies too. Pay at the *buvette*, where you can get a cool beer.

KOUBRI AND KOMBISSIRI The little town of Koubri, lying on the fringes of a lake, offers respite from the capital, with plenty of village vibes and a sizeable fish market along the roadside. It has more than its fair share of great and original places

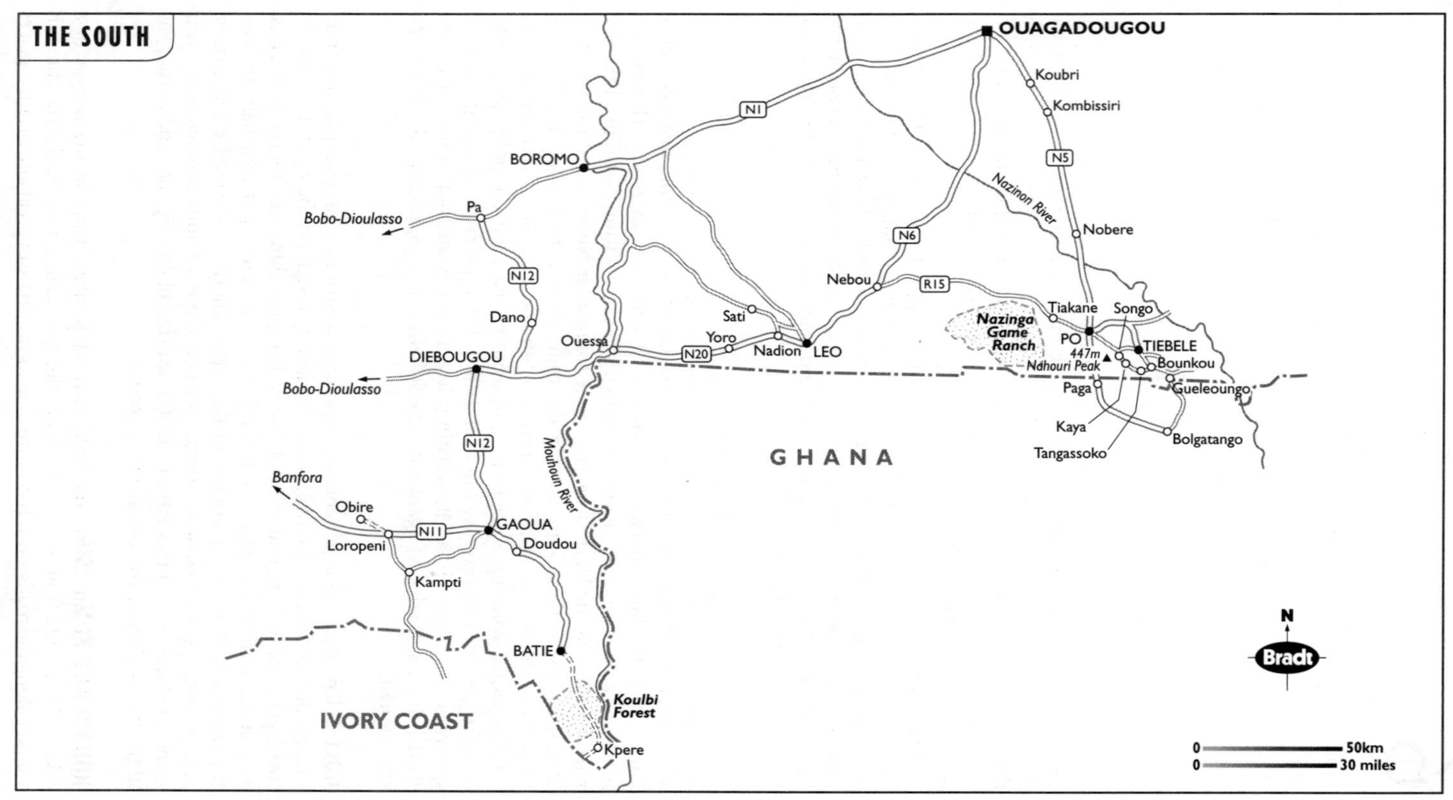
THE SOUTH
OUAGADOUGOU
Koubri
Kombissiri
N5
N1
BOROMO
Nazinon River
Nobere
Pa
Bobo-Dioulasso
N6
N12
Nebou
R15
Tiakane
Songo
Nazinga Game Ranch
Dano
Sati
PO
TIEBELE
Ouessa
Yoro
447m
Nadhouri Peak
Bounkou
Nadion
LEO
N20
DIEBOUGOU
Paga
Gueleoungo
Bobo-Dioulasso
Kaya
Bolgatango
N12
Tangassoko
GHANA
Mouhoun River
Banfora
Obire
GAOUA
N11
Loropeni
Doudou
Kampti
N
Bradt
BATIE
Koulbi Forest
IVORY COAST
Kpere
0 50km
0 30 miles

to stay, while the sprawling little town of Kombissiri, further on, can also offer a comfortable night's sleep.

Getting there and away For Koubri and Kombissiri, take any coach service headed for Po (see below). For Les Bougainvilliers and the monastery, you'll need wheels, or call ahead for a pick-up from Koubri. Take a left turn in Koubri at the sign for the *auberge* and follow the track for about 5km. When the road forks, take the left fork. There's a maternity hospital just ahead; another 200m on, a cement-sided cattle grid on the right is the monastery entrance. Head on over and turn sharp right. At a fork, veer left for the monastery and right for the convent. For Les Bougainvilliers, ignore the cattle grid, keep straight on and follow the signs. It's about 12km in total.

Where to stay

Auberge Les Bougainvilliers (18 rooms) m 70 09 00 69, 78 42 80 34; e nadinelietar@gmail.com; www.bougainvilliers-bf.com. Buried even deeper than the monastery, this is a fantastic wilderness hotel set amid a wealth of lakes, bumping tracks & trees. The emphasis is on natural living; power is provided as far as possible by solar panels, & owners Nadine & Pierre grow much of their own veg. There's oodles of fun on offer – lakeside fishing; cross-country cycling; swimming in a neat clean pool; ping-pong; *pétanque*; volleyball; plenty of good food & drink under *paillotes*; & the *pièce de résistance*: quad-biking. Set among orchards sprouting oranges & lemons, grapefruit, mango & papaya, square huts & round huts (much nicer) dot the compound, & are being converted from AC to fan to save power. Cycle hire is free on site, 1,000f per hr outside the camp; an introduction to quad biking costs 3,500f & 15,000f per hr (150cc) or 20,000f per hr (250cc) thereafter. B/fast inc. **$$$**

Escale de Koubri (4 huts) m 78 90 04 33, 78 02 38 78. In Koubri itself near the lake, & tucked well behind the popular *maquis*, are surprisingly high-quality AC huts, complete with en suite & towels. **$$$**

Hotel Mitibkeita Kombissiri (42 rooms) 50 40 51 41; m 70 97 85 91. More neat, clean comfort on the main drag. All rooms have AC, TV & en suite with hot water. There's also an AC restaurant/bar. **$$$**

Benedictine monastery (14 rooms) m 78 18 63 84, 72 71 81 96. Hidden deep within the forest, this quiet retreat started up in 1963. There's a sister **Benedictine convent** where you can also stay (m *70 33 06 24, 78 01 66 27*) & between them they run a significant dairy farm. Milk, cheese, honey, jams, syrups & eggs are all produced at the farm itself, while the sisters also produce yoghurt sold in Ouaga. The day is organised around mass & several prayer services, but you don't have to attend; sanctuary and tranquillity are prized above all else. Rooms are simple, with external facilities; beds, mostly single, have nets. You can eat 3 good meals a day. **$$**

Auberge Bananerie de Koubri (5 rooms) m 78 70 95 97. Follow the sign on the right to find a lush banana grove, with simple huts hidden in the thick of it. Winding pathways through the grove reveal secluded seating areas; a swimming pool & fish pond are on the way. The huts have bucket showers & nets, & are so close to the trees you can almost pick the fruit from them. Bananas for breakfast, anyone? **$**

PO

Po is the main gateway on the road south to Ghana, 20km away, and it's a good place to stop before onward travel to Tiebele, or west for Tiakane and Nazinga Ranch. From here, there is a circular route along much-improved pistes that takes you to Tiebele, Boungou, Tangassoko, Kaya and Songo, ending up back in Po. If you're pushed for time, this can be done in a day by either *moto* or car.

Home to Burkinabe army commandos, Po was once the country's revolutionary hotbed. Thomas Sankara launched his attack from here to install

Jean-Baptiste Ouedraogo as president in 1982. Less than a year later, Blaise Campaore did the same, this time marching against Ouedraogo to demand Sankara's release from prison. Since his own takeover of power, Blaise has dispersed much of the town's military focus. However, his bunker remains. Look out for the military roadblock to the left as the tarmac road leading to Tiebele comes to an end. Don't try to go in.

GETTING THERE AND AWAY By car, the 147km from Ouaga to Po takes about two hours. Coach journeys take longer.

By bus Single fares are 2,500f; returns 5,000f. From Ouaga, take your pick from either STMB in Cité An III or Rakieta's Po garage not far from the cathedral. STMB (*50 31 13 63, 50 31 34 34*) has two departures, at 07.30 and 15.30 daily; Rakieta (*50 30 62 84*) has three, at 07.00, 12.30 and 16.30 daily. Coaches and bush taxis heading for Ghana from Ouagainter also stop at Po.

On the way back, STMB has two departures, at 07.30 and 13.30 daily, while Rakieta departs at 07.15 (08.00 Sunday), 12.30 and 17.30 daily.

From Po you can take a bus 18km to Paga, the final stop on the Burkina side of the Ghanaian border. Tickets are 500f with STMB. From here you can find a bush taxi to Bolgatanga, in Ghana, or buses heading all the way to Accra.

GOUROUNSI HISTORY

'The appearance of the land is as wild as its residents, who never go to the fields without their rifles to hand,' said the French lieutenant Chanoine of his first foray into Gourounsi country.

The word 'Gourounsi', sometimes Grusi, was originally used by the Mossi and the French imperial invaders to describe those living to the south and west of the Mossi Plateau and descended from many of the land's earliest settlers.

But it is not the integrated state the French imperialisers held it to be – with neither king nor centralised social and political structure. Today, Gourounsi remains an umbrella term commonly used by anthropologists for several distinct groups, including the Kassena, Winye, Lela, Nuna, Puguli and Sisala, all of whom speak variants of the vast Gur family of languages and make up about 6% of Burkina's population.

You will rarely find anyone identifying themselves as Gourounsi. It's worth respecting this. People generally identify themselves by their immediate grouping, and speak a local variant of the language (eg: Kassena people speak Kassem).

The Gourounsi were the original inhabitants of Burkina Faso, predating Mossi arrival, but their lack of social organisation made them prey to frequent attacks. By the time of the French arrival, the Gourounsi had been subjected to repeated forays by mobile and skilled Muslim raiders (known variously as the Djerma, Djermabe and Zabermabe), who swept down from east of the Niger River.

The Mossi were also partial to the odd 'expedition' to round up Gourounsi men, women and children for the lucrative transatlantic slave trade. They sent them on to slave markets in Gao, Djenne, Segou and southern Ashanti (Ghana), ready for shipping to Brazil, where descendants speak a version of the Gourounsi language today.

When the Djerma and Mossi weren't attacking, Malinke warlord Samory Toure, who had set himself up further to the south, was giving the Gourounsi cause for concern.

By taxi For other destinations, such as Tiebele or Tiakane, find a bush taxi in Po. Tickets cost 500f.

GETTING AROUND Being hounded the second you descend from a bus is a rare experience in Burkina; unfortunately, it can happen in Po. The gaggle of young guys can be very tenacious, because they're after a bit of commission for 'leading' you to your hotel. You can go along with it, ignore them (difficult), or call ahead for someone to come and meet you.

For moped hire ask at the market, or call Diarra Paul Cassinnohiré (m *76 59 80 74, 70 09 15 29*) who has Yamahas for 5,000f a day. They're in good nick, as he's a mechanic. Abdoulaye 'Pasteur' Ouedraogo (m *75 09 72 37;* e *rastaalin@yahoo.fr*), who works at the Hotel Esperance Tiandora, can arrange *moto* hire and also makes for a very amiable guide; if you're on your own and would like to be whizzed around riding pillion, he's your man. For vehicle hire, Nabarwe Dieudonne (m *70 33 52 41, 78 54 40 54;* e *awelana2010dieud@yahoo.fr*) comes highly recommended. For the Po/Tiebele circuit, a saloon car with (obligatory) driver is 30,000f a day including petrol, or 15,000f a day without fuel; for Nazinga, a 4x4 or 15-seater minibus with driver is 60,000f a day including petrol, 35,000f without fuel. For further afield within Burkina, prices for 4x4/minibus and saloon car are 35,000f and 25,000f a day respectively, without fuel.

The population had benefited from roaring north–south trade, with local merchants taking Lobi gold, as well as kola nuts, gunpowder and rifles to the north, and returning with Timbuktu salt, Mossi horses and cattle, cotton, rice, indigo and ivory.

But the wild invasions of the Djermas burnt many a local village to a crisp, and turned the region into a no-go zone, ruining all commerce with it. Merchants no longer passed through Gourounsi country, preferring to travel via Ghana. 'For 17 years, they had the run of Gourounsi country,' said Chanoine of the Djerma, 'destroying everything in their path.'

The Gourounsi were nevertheless fierce fighters, and one Gourounsi arrow found its way to the gullet of the Djerma warlord Madugu. Despite an ad hoc alliance, several Gourounsi leaders and Muslim converts revolted against their fleeting Djerma partners. One Djerma, the famed Hamaria, even switched sides to lead the Gourounsi. But it was not enough to see off the Djerma for good.

The Gourounsi turned to the French for protection from enemy chief Baba-To in 1896. He had a fearsome reputation for setting fire to all sorts of things, including the French flag, which peeved the colonial conquerors, who rushed to help Hamaria.

On 14 March 1897, Chanoine went into battle against the Djerma, taking 800 rifles and 300 cavalrymen with him. Fierce fighting on both sides saw the Djerma lose six chiefs and the French emerge victorious.

'Now that the land is pacified and the savage populations that neighbour the Volta are submissive,' said Chanoine a few months later, 'we want to re-establish the great commercial run from Ivory Coast to Timbuktu, using the course of the Black Volta [now the Mouhoun], navigable at all times, passing through Lobi country, the land of gold, and fertile, populated lands… France will keep its flag flying high in every place that we pitch it.'

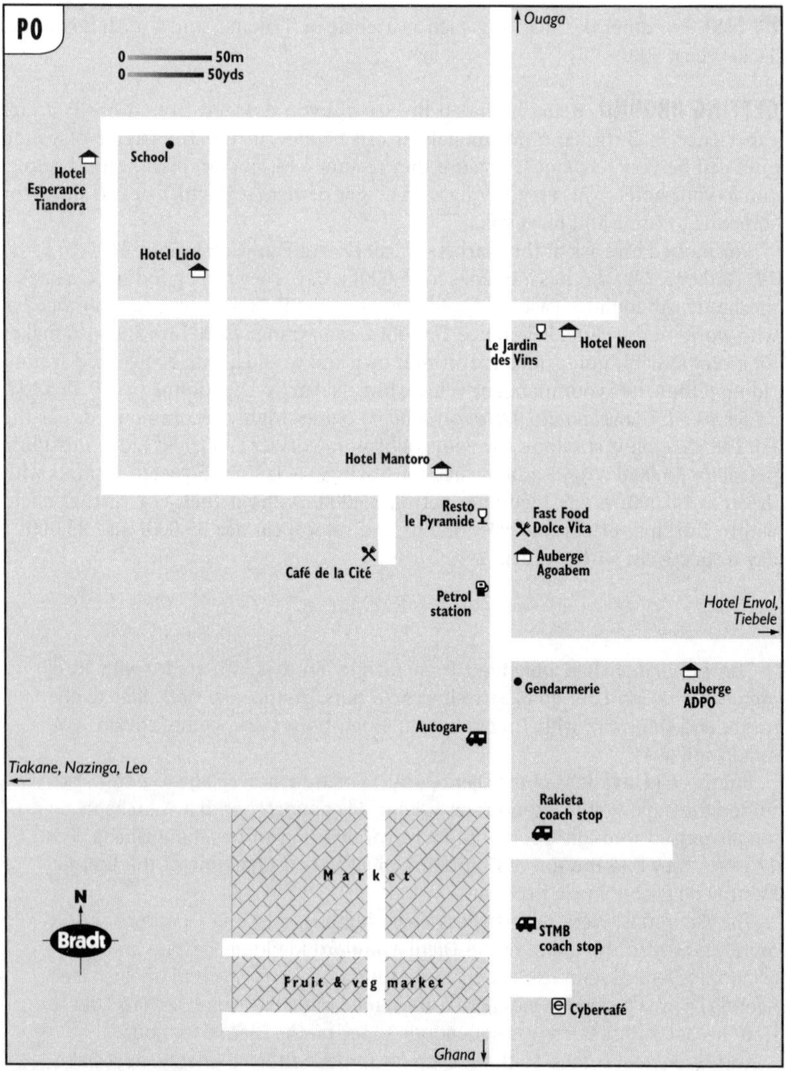

WHERE TO STAY

Hotel Envol (10 rooms) 50 40 36 08; m 71 17 97 76. Po's newest, shiniest hotel has sadly misjudged its own value. Rooms are spotless, fresh & amply tiled, but there's nothing here to justify the high prices. Choice of en-suite fan or AC; all have TVs. **$$$**

Hotel Esperance Tiandora (12 rooms) 50 40 34 39; e tiandorahotel@yahoo.fr. Get past the building-site entrance (extensions & renovations have been going on for years) & you'll find the nicest place in town, complete with a painted Kassena-style hut to sleep either in or on top of, under the stars. Choice of good-quality en-suite fan or AC rooms. AC with king-size bed 12,500f. **$$**

Hotel Lido (16 rooms) 50 40 32 41, 50 40 30 39; m 70 74 00 69. Popular with tour operators, the hotel is an old hand at providing an efficient service for travellers. Cloistered around a pleasant, arched courtyard, fan or AC rooms are clean, simple, all en suite &, given that prices haven't changed in years, good value. **$$**

Auberge Agoabem (10 rooms) 50 40 31 42. Beyond the popular *bar-restau* & reception area lie great-value fan rooms with shady porches, set around an open courtyard decorated with elephant murals. Choose between en suite or outside loo. **$–$$**

Auberge ADPO (9 rooms) Simple en-suite fan rooms on the Tiebele road, some with mozzie nets. The bathrooms have seen better days. **$**

Hotel Mantoro (11 rooms) 40 40 30 25. The oldest hotel in town, whose pleasant courtyard shaded by enormous trees is surrounded by fan rooms with tiled terraces & outside loos. It's limping along these days; the restaurant has closed (they'll direct you to Café de la Cité – see below). **$**

Hotel Neon (7 rooms) m 70 66 84 15. No sign from the road, & no neon in sight, which is lucky, as it would be a shame to divert too many tourists here. On 2 recent visits, the guardian failed to produce any keys; what were the roughest rooms in town have probably remained so. Cheap, though. **$**

WHERE TO EAT AND DRINK Hotel restaurants, such as the standalone **Restaurant Zounn-die** at Hotel Lido or the **Tiandora**, are plentiful. The kitchen at **Auberge Agoabem** serves up robust grub, piling on the rice; its *riz sauce* is still only 300f, and you can pick up great *brochettes* and chicken just outside too. **Fast Food Dolce Vita** next door is good for breakfast, serving *café au lait* and omelettes all day. **Resto le Pyramid** is the biggest place in town. You can't miss it, or fail to hear its night-time sound system. However, it's been somewhat knocked off its perch by **Le Jardin des Vins** (*50 40 34 28*), which is the place to be these days. It offers the decadence of French wines by the bottle, or cheerful Spanish plonk at a bargain 300f per (large) glass, good cheap nosh, and a dance floor that rocks at the weekend. For a bar crawl, head along the Tiebele road, which is thronged with good-looking *maquis*; for something a bit quieter, *maquis* **Café de la Cité** offers cheap eats in a pleasant courtyard.

OTHER PRACTICALITIES An extensive daily **market** sits off the main road at the southern end of town. **Ecobank**, just north of the Rakieta station, has a Visa ATM, but don't count on it working. There is a small **cybercafé** on the little road just south of the STMB bus station, and another on the right on the way in from Ouaga.

KASSENA COUNTRY

The perfect destination for a Dinky (double income no kids yet) couple's dream pastime, Kassena is all about house-viewing. In a country where mud architecture is arresting and varied throughout, the small group of villages east of Po inhabited by the Kassena – one of the sub-groups comprising the Gourounsi – is a unique marvel.

The houses are variously circular, square or figure-of-eight-shaped depending on the status of the occupants. They are beautifully decorated with geometric, repeating patterns on the walls.

The best-known and most visited examples of this style are at **Tiebele**, where a relatively established tourist structure can sometimes feel a little showy or cloying. Still, it's exactly what the guides say it is – a living museum – and makes a fascinating visit. At **Tangassoko**, the houses feel more cared for, the atmosphere quieter, and it was much our favourite.

KASSENA SOCIETY Numbering about 100,000 inhabitants, Kassena country straddles the Burkina/Ghanaian border, in the southeastern pocket of Gourounsi country. Society is based around the village chief, who is in theory descended from the first settler (from around 1600) and whose personal plot of land takes on some rather unusual functions. Outside his yard there is a sacred mound of dirt, known as the *pourrou*, which is scaled by messengers and *griots* announcing important news to the village. This mound also has the unlikely honour of hosting the placentas of every child born inside the chief's compound.

Just as the beginning of life is celebrated in strange and wonderful ways, so is the end. When someone in the village dies, the body of the deceased is placed in the

KASSENA CODE

CALABASH The walls of Kassena houses are painted with a repetition of coded geometric signs. The most popular symbol is the calabash – not that you would necessarily recognise it by looking at the paintwork. It is the mainstay of Kassena culture and breaking one is considered a minor catastrophe. It is a jack of all trades: drinking goblet, paint-pot, tombstone, receptacle for sacrifices. The calabash is entwined in particular with the life, and death, of a woman. A lifelong kitchen companion, it is the only object she is said to take with her after death, and the only object authorised for worship. By tradition, a calabash will be broken on the fourth day after a woman dies, on the path that leads to her parents' house. All this is represented in the repeated rows of diamond and triangular geometric shapes – fragments of the calabash.

BATS The Kassena think well of mosquito-eating bats, believing that a house without a bat is an evil one. They endeavour to protect them, and honour a stylised image of bat wings on their walls.

SPARROWHAWK WINGS Sparrowhawks are feared because they hunt poultry and, the Kassena believe, eat human flesh. Only priests and pallbearers may eat the birds of prey, since only they can avoid serious disease.

BOA CONSTRICTOR Look out for these, sculpted in bas-relief onto the sides of houses. They are sacred, thought to hold the spirits of grandmothers, and so never killed, unlike the common fate befalling the viper.

CROSSES Scarification – cutting people's faces so that healed scars remain in geometric patterns – was much more widespread among the Mossi, mainly for reasons of recognition. But Kassena medicine men believed in scarification to protect against disease. It was practised on children up to the age of three.

TORTOISE This is the sacred totem of the royal family. Should a courtier come across a tortoise in the wild and bring it back to the royal court, he will soon be married, or, if he is already married, he will shortly have a child of the same sex as the tortoise.

OTHER POPULAR SIGNS Look out for **sun and moon** designs, representing the universe; various **zig-zags** show the footprints of both chickens, used extensively in sacrifices, and birds of prey; fish skin, drums, bat-wings and poisoned arrows, used in hunting and in battle; **lizards**, required to 'christen' a house by running across it before it can be lived in; the **quiver**, a reminder that every person is a hunter and warrior; and the **pipe** and **sack**, essential accoutrements of old age.

maternal household, sometimes for two or three days. During this time there is a festival of drinking and ritual dancing, with the family sleeping near the tomb for three days. On the evening of the third day, the women of the family present three big calabashes full of *tô*, which they serve up to the children of the family with a range of sauces, to represent continuity from one generation to the next.

The next morning is the most important, as it is the final goodbye (*yitechega*). If the deceased is a man, the mask he wore during his war-dancing days is broken. If it's a woman, old women break calabashes filled with shea butter on the path leading to her parents' house.

HOME SWEET NOTHING Given repeated violent and vicious attack from all sides (see box, pages 226–7), many Gourounsi lived with a perpetual siege mentality. Even a home could function as a weapon. Moulded out of mud, without windows, and hollowed low into the ground, the contrast from blazing sunlight to abject darkness on entering is striking, and takes some time to adjust to – giving inhabitants vital seconds to defend themselves.

Low, child-sized entrances are blocked almost immediately by interior walls of a similar height, protecting those inside from any arrows fired outside, or from marauding wild animals.

The low entry forced incoming aggressors to stoop and come in head first, giving residents poised over the doorway the perfect opportunity to chop off their heads. The wall provided a second hiding place, so occupants could deliver sharp upper thrusts as adversaries tried to clamber over.

CONSTRUCTION RITES Dwellings are constructed from a mixture of mud and dung. Small, stand-alone round huts (*draa*) with straw roofs reinforced with branches are for bachelors aged 15 and up. Rectangular houses (*mangolo*) are for newly married couples. Figure-of-eight dwellings shaped like smooth-sided egg-timers (*dinian*) are for grandparents and grandchildren, with connecting circular chambers. These mother huts are built first as they are believed to shelter the spirits. The roof is flat and used for sleeping in the hot months. It can also be used to store crops and dry vegetables safe from animals. The larger chamber tends to be a communal room for sleeping, while the inner room is for cooking. Low mud shelves running around the outside of the dwelling act as benches and have holes built into them, so chickens can roost.

PAINTING LADIES The bulk of hut-painting is done by women, at the beginning of the dry season. First they sand down the mud surface with flat stones. Then they apply a wall coating, made from a mixture of earth, cow dung and ash. The final base layer involves a sticky red-brown glaze, made from pounded laterite (Burkina's prominent, reddish topsoil), water and boiled seeds of the *nere* tree. Red paint comes from kaolin, black from a mix of pounded graphite and volcanic rock, and white from calcium. Brushes are fashioned from the feathers of guinea fowl. At Tiebele, more hard-wearing materials such as bitumen have been introduced, allowing the painting to take place every three years instead of annually.

The result of this work is the most arresting set of houses and fortress compounds you are likely to come across (see box, opposite).

TIEBELE This small market town, close to the Ghanaian border, is the best place to see well-preserved Kassena houses, and you can even stay the night on the rooftop of the chief. The friendly daily vegetable market is set in the twinkling shade of enormous trees, and filled with a sea of bright headscarves. The town is used to visitors, and provides a lovely retreat for a couple of days. Around mid-February the end of the harvest (*faa can dia* in Kassem) is celebrated with the Tiebele arts and culture festival, Fescat, which features displays of archery, painting, music, *djongo* (the local dance), theatre, stories and riddle-telling.

Getting there and away

By bus From Ouagainter you can pick up a minibus every day bar Saturday that goes direct to Tiebele (3,000f). It leaves at around 08.00. Otherwise, take a coach to Po and hire a moped for the remaining 31km, or pick up a bush taxi. The least you'll pay is 500f.

By car Tiebele is easily reached by car or *moto*, even in the rainy season. After Po the tarmac peters out, but the tree-lined dirt track is wide and drives well, against a pleasant hilly backdrop. Passing villages contain the first hints of the painted diamond-pattern huts to come.

By taxi There is a daily bush taxi departure for Po from Tiebele that leaves not long after midday.

Getting around There is no official outlet, but it's pretty easy to hire a bike or moped for visits to neighbouring villages. A good place to start is with one of the 12 official development association guides (✆ *40 32 83 93;* e *assodjawolim@yahoo.fr*), as they are used to dealing with people keen to explore beyond Tiebele. At the time of writing, there were no car-hire options in the village; this had to be arranged from Po – a situation that could easily change, so ask around. *Moto* hire costs about 5,000f per day, which should include a litre of petrol. Hiring a bicycle for the day is great for the local Tiebele area. Energetic and hardy bikers can also get to Tangassoko, about 12km away. Auberge Kunkolo has bikes for hire, at 1,000f per day.

Where to stay Tiebele has followed the national trend with burgeoning accommodation options. There are now four *campements* as well as the royal court itself, and they are all delightful, offering well-made traditional-style huts with external facilities. If you're visiting in the hot season, ignore the hut – take your bedding up on to the roof and sleep under the moon. The fresh breeze will keep the mosquitoes off and you can often hear village drumming late into the night.

Village D'Acceuil Jean Viars (12 rooms) ✆ 50 40 42 09. Just opposite the entrance to the royal court, the most central option is also the most expensive. Prettily painted Kassena-style huts come with or without fan; 2 en-suite AC rooms were nearing completion. Meals available. **$$**

Auberge Kunkolo (8 rooms) m 76 53 44 55; e kunkolo_tiebele@yahoo.fr. The oldest & most established place was set up by a youthful Frenchman who arrived in Burkina more than a decade ago. It's now very ably managed by Pierre Guidan, a Kassena local & mine of information. Kassena-style huts are set around a courtyard with a big *paillote* for late-night chilling. It's not far beyond the royal court, on the left on the road to Boungou. Meals available. B/fast 1,000f. **$**

Auberge La Tranquilité (4 rooms) m 76 59 00 13, 70 76 35 36. On the road out of Tiebele towards Gueleoungo, this place lives up to its name. Work was still ongoing when we visited, but the completed huts were very nicely done & a *paillote* was under construction. No electricity, so little lamps provided instead. Meals also available (owner also runs the Titanic in town). **$**

Campement Eco-Solidaire Le Manguier (6 rooms) m 76 61 72 71. This lovely place just pips the others to the prize for prettiest *campement*. The huts are exquisitely painted & set in a leafy walled garden with *paillote*. It's on the right on the road in from Po; other Kassena houses nearby are worth a visit. Meals available. **$**

Royal court When there are no rooms elsewhere, or if you ask nicely, you may be able to sleep on a roof in the chief's compound. It's certainly not a hotel, so there's no menu, the mattress is thin and everything else, including the African loos, you'll be sharing. But, somehow, it's a treat. The only fixed charge is 500f to put the mattress on a roof. Beyond that, it's up to you what you offer, but 2,000f per person will avoid insult.

Where to eat and drink All four *campements* can provide meals, if given a little notice. In town, **Chez Madeline** cooks a mean chicken and *riz sauce*, although only at lunchtimes. In the evenings, choose between the large open courtyard housing several sacred bamboo shoots at **Miou Bar**, or **Kiosque Le Titanic** (m *76 59 00 13*). This serves up all the regular dishes, well spiced. The sign outside makes the bar's priorities clear: there is an elephant balancing a bottle of Ghanaian Star lager atop his trunk, while the Titanic ship sinks unnoticed in the background. You can also get a good game of table football on the street, just along from Le Titanic, for 25f a throw.

What to see and do

Royal court of Tiebele (*entry 2,000f – you need a guide*) This is one of the few officially 'touristy' activities you can undertake in Burkina. The local development association, the Association Djawolim de Développement (e *assodjawolim@yahoo.fr*), has 12 official guides, all of whom give a good account of Kassena beliefs and practices described above. The tour of the court, which is home to about 300 people, takes roughly 45 minutes. The association ensures the entrance fee is split equally between the royal court and the village; it goes towards the houses' maintenance, villagers' medical and school fees, and has also resulted in a library. Some of the guides can be pushy and grasping; you could try Abdou 'Rasta' (m *76 94 69 47, 78 77 09 02*), who lives within the court itself and takes his work very seriously. Guides charge groups a fixed fee of 5,000f, but for individuals a tip is discretionary. Unless you feel otherwise, 1,000–2,000f is reasonable. Be prepared for the naff and slightly depressing flock of traders, and assorted requests for money as you leave the compound. Photographs are allowed, except of certain sacred sites, such as the big fig tree and sacrificial altar outside the chief's compound.

AROUND TIEBELE For many visitors, Tiebele used to be as off the beaten track as they were likely to get *en route* to Ghana. Now, with the tracks to outlying villages much improved, many manage to see what's known as the 'circuit', but to do them justice it's worth resisting the temptation to whizz around in a single day. An extra day or two also allows for **Nahouri Peak** (Pic de Nahouri), which, at 447m, is worth an early morning ramble before the sun reaches its zenith.

Boungou This small village is famed for its skilled pottery workers. Old women make the pots, deciding just how big and what shape depending on intended use. Huge round clay *canaris* keep water cool despite the heat. They also store huge vats of *dolo*. Smaller pots house cooking implements, along with sauces and flavourings. There is also a sacred crocodile lake, where children lure out the caimans with frogs and songs.

LOCAL MARKETS

Many market days are on a three-day rotation.

Po	daily, fixed open-air and covered market
Tangassoko	every three days
Boungou, Kaya	the day after Tangassoko
Tiebele, Gueleoungo	the day after Bounkou and Kaya

Local markets often trade in Ghanaian cedis alongside the CFA franc. Much produce also comes from Ghana. Popular favourites are luminous yellow abrasive soap sold in 75cm-long bars; sweet Ghanaian bread and bags of sugar from across the border. Petrol, which is much cheaper, is smuggled over the frontier at night by bicycle, in tottering plastic jerry cans. As well as imported bottles of Ghanaian Star Beer, expect to see an invasion of Pepsi, 7-Up and Miranda to challenge Burkina's hegemony of Coca-Cola, Sprite and Fanta.

The markets are a great place to indulge in a bowl of *dolo*; locals (especially the old men) will love you for ever if you treat them to a litre or so, which at 100f is unlikely to break the bank. Look out for groups of men huddled over a tray of meat away from the main throng – they're probably eating dog. Munching its salty flesh is a purely male preserve, forbidden to women.

It's a 20-minute drive from Tiebele and forms part of the circuit. Head out of the village past the royal court and Auberge Kunkolo, then carry straight on.

Tangassoko While the highlight of a trip to this small village is a visit to its beautiful Kassena court, the lively market day is full of Ghanaian produce and frenzied social activity (look out for the outdoor hairdressers, washing hair over the gutter and preening with pride on the street). If you tire you can pick up a beer, bottled drinks or *dolo* from the compound opposite the market – a women's meeting place. To get there, take a very sharp right in Boungou – blink and you'll miss it, so check locally that you're on the right track. Look out for examples of more Kassena housing along the way.

Forge Several villagers wear heavy iron bangles around their wrists, made at the village forge. The blacksmith, Yarpanga Koubouga, who doesn't know how old he is, works under a tree, and guards his craft and sacred rock with dignity.

Royal court (*entry 2,000f – photos are permitted*) The chief's compound (*chefferie*) here is arguably more spectacular than the compound at Tiebele on account of its wonderful setting among fields and mango trees. The compound is smaller, with about 100 inhabitants. It has a much less touristy feel, and the welcome is incredibly warm, perhaps because the chief and his immediate family are happy to meet and greet visitors (unlike at Tiebele, where the chief remains largely hidden from view, even from the villagers themselves). There is no formalised structure of guides. The old chief Allou Sana died in 2009 and has not been officially replaced; in the meantime one of his younger sons, Allou Nabili (m *70 49 36 44*), takes care of the tourism side of things, and does so with a beaming smile. Unlike Tiebele, livestock are allowed inside the central area of the compound, so it's worth keeping your eyes on the ground as well as the magnificent buildings, as everything from large zebu to tiny chickens are likely to be running about or ruminating. The immaculately cared-for buildings are sculpted and smooth, in contrast to the chaos of the courtyard, and have a more organic feel than Tiebele's. The villagers stick to painting with traditional materials, so they repaint every year.

The royal compound lies about 1km from the town proper, just beyond the forge. You can spend the night on the rooftops here for another 1,000f, and meals can be prepared for you here or back towards the village. Allou Nabili and the villagers also have an association, Association pour la Sauvegarde du Patrimoine Culturel et le Développement Communautaire Diin-Lama (e *diinlama@yahoo.fr*).

Gueleoungo Gueleoungo is good to visit on market day – it is large and busy with none of the quiet, sedate shade of Tiebele's daily affair. Look out for the fetish stalls selling horn, leather, wood and feathers for use in traditional medicine and appeals to the ancestors. From here you can walk into Ghana – simply follow the road south.

Kaya and Songo If you are looping back to Po, you will pass through these villages *en route*. Kaya is nestled among pretty hills, while Songo's market is a joy to visit, laid out in a grove of shady trees. Visitors who stop by are a rare sight here: wander around and you'll be given a rapturous welcome.

Nahouri peak (*count on paying 2,000f each to the village as an entrance fee & for a guide*) The climb takes at most a couple of hours. Owing to its inaccessibility, take a sleeping bag and camp overnight by the peak if you want to climb it for sunrise. You will be down again before the sun is too hot. Situated a few kilometres west of Tiebele, the best way to reach it is with an ADT guide from the village. Take water for the fairly heavy walk to the top.

ON THE WAY TO NAZINGA Nazinga Ranch is clearly signposted from Po. It is about 30km from the dirt track that heads west to Leo and the only passing traffic is likely to be safari-goers in 4x4s. You can try hitching a lift at the turn-off (which does not offer much shade), organise transport in Po, or organise a trip from Ouagadougou.

Tiakane The village prides itself on having hidden French explorer Captain Louis-Gustave Binger, who sought shelter in 1888, during his three-year journey from the Gulf of Niger to Guinea. Villagers say his life was saved by the hospitality of the chief. While on the run from Djerma raiders, he stayed in a house at the heart of the chief's compound, which exists today only as ruins, but is well worth the crawl down memory lane, under low wood-supported roofs. Binger's journals back some of this up, revealing that he thought the chief about 30 years old and 'most kind to me'.

Things got a little sticky once Binger wanted to head to the next town, however. The chief's 'attitude changed and he tried to intimidate me'. The chief wanted recompense for the time he'd put Binger up, relying on delaying tactics that infuriated the Alsatian, who in turn became 'immediately hostile'. The tricksy Frenchman wanted to fool the chief into thinking he and his men were more of a threat than they really were. 'As we cleaned my revolver it appeared first from the holster, then from a bag or from the pockets of one of my men, making him think all my men were armed to the teeth.'

It worked. The chief kept a low profile on the journey to the next town, until he started to harry Binger with demands for presents of 'two fine *boubous*' as an informal sort of road tax along the way. Binger was having none of it.

In the end, they argued over the gift the whole way, and it took the French captain four hours to travel 5km.

Getting there and away From Po, negotiate a bush taxi to take you the 7km east to Tiakane, on the Leo and Nazinga road, or take a moped. It is also, at an early morning push, walkable. The village is nowadays pretty spread out, and an unlikelier-looking royal residence is hard to find, so you may need to ask directions to the *chefferie*. It's a walled compound set back from the road on the right.

The compound A tour around the subterranean chambers of the chief's crumbling old compound would not receive an endorsement from health and safety; it is falling further and further into disrepair. The old chief died in 1997, and has been replaced by his son who shows little sign of grasping the maintenance nettle, although plans are allegedly under way. Unless action is taken fairly soon, a visit here may be disappointing.

The mud fortress, said to have started up sometime in the 16th century, is still part-inhabited today. Beneath the low-joisted roofs are ritualistic sacrificial animal skulls, calabash gourds and hunting gear. The maze of dark cavernous rooms forces you to hunch almost double to pass through precariously supported chambers, parts of which have caved in. As you progress towards the sacred heart of the complex – the twilit cooking chambers are still used by the women of the village on special occasions – dive-bombing bats criss-cross your path, skimming hair and eyes. If the Kassena are right about these animals bringing good luck, these are the most blessed houses going.

There is no fixed fee, but your (compulsory) guide will expect something for the tour. In addition, there is a *canari* in one of the subterranean kitchens, and in a rather decent gesture you can leave a contribution inside for the women of the village towards the next meal.

NAZINGA GAME RANCH

With 800 elephants in this smallish park, an encounter is basically assured. During the height of the dry season, when water elsewhere is hard to come by, you simply need to turn up at the lakeside camp at around noon for a spectacular bathing show.

The observation area on the lake's edge puts you right at the heart of the action. Young bulls, absorbed in the minutiae of their daily routine, stop and slowly look up, within touching distance. You can see the crevices and cracks of the caked mud on heffalump sides, the layer of stubbly hair covering trunks, and feel their elephantine breath on you. Elephants regularly wander through the camp to chow down on the well-watered shoots and leaves. If staying the night, take a torch if you're prowling the campsite, to avoid bumping into one of the hairy monsters.

There's more to the ranch than elephants. Nazinga's 94,000ha contain more than 20,000 animals, including 39 species of mammal, and a number of beautiful hornbills, hawks, herons, and bee-eaters, among 275 bird species. There are more than 500 buffalo, thousands of antelope, including roan antelope, waterbuck, oribi, reedbuck and Buffon's kob, 5,000 warthog, crocodile, more than 10,000 primates (including red monkeys and baboons) and hyenas. No-one has ever seen lion, although sightings of tracks are occasionally reported.

ENTRY DETAILS The ranch is open all year round. The best time to visit is at the end of the dry season (late March–late May) when animals will come out to find the few remaining water sources. In November and December grasses are high and hide the game; park rangers burn some sections to improve visibility and to tempt grazers with fresh green shoots, but plentiful water still tends to keep animals deep in the scrub. By February it's drier and the heat is not as onerous as March to May time. The early morning (06.30–09.00) and early evening (16.00–18.00) are prime viewing times. You can see elephants in the lake next to the Akwazena camp throughout the day, including the afternoon. Entry costs 10,000f per adult and 2,000f per child; guides cost 5,000f; a photo permit 2,000f; a video permit 5,000f; car entry 1,000f; *moto* or bicycle 500f; arrival by aeroplane (there is a landing strip) is charged at 50,000f.

HISTORY Begun in 1979, the ranch was the brainchild of Clark Lungren, a Canadian who grew up in Burkina. Widespread poaching had killed off most of the animals in the area, and what little was left was unlikely to return, as water entirely dried up in the hot months. Together with his wife Carol, brother Rob and a committed few, they set about a conservation project to encourage local people to look after animals and environment, urging them to see both as a long-term source of income.

With local labour and materials, they constructed huts, dams and 600km of roads; hired poachers and turned them into patrol keepers; and invited volunteer researchers to survey the land. The turnaround was magnificent, and sustained. Eight Buffon's kob were reintroduced into the park in 1988 – there are now more than 300. Lungren is no longer at Nazinga, having handed the park over to the government. Since then standards have fallen slightly. The easiest way to help maintain them is to visit.

GETTING THERE AND AWAY Nazinga is within three hours of Ouaga, although not easy to reach without your own wheels. You can take a coach to Po and then try and arrange a bush taxi to the gates, but from there it's another 35km or so before you get to the central camp and you'd be unlikely to find a taxi willing to take you round like a safari bus. Camp literature says you can rent a vehicle for 35,000f a day, but in practice there is never one available.

This leaves you with the hair-raising option of safari by motorbike, moped or bicycle, any of which, quite remarkably, is permitted. The best options are to go on an organised tour, or hire a car in Ouaga or Po – ideally a 4x4; the track to the main camp is just about passable by saloon car, but owners won't be too chuffed if you try it. From Po, take the road west past Tiakane towards Leo and then take a left turn after 20km, at the Nazinga sign. The control post at Waleme handles entrance fees, with a further 35km through park scrub to the camp.

WHERE TO STAY AND EAT

Le Campement de l'Elephant (12 rooms) 50 42 82 00; m 70 17 34 34, 70 29 78 78; e contact@nahourisafari.com; www.nahourisafari.com. Outside the ranch itself, just on the left before the Waleme control post, a bougainvillea-lined driveway leads to a delightful camp. The richly decorated reception area may be a bit Baroque for some, but rooms (all AC, en suite) are tasteful with great beds, towels & even shampoo. Some have 2 massive king-size beds, offering good value for groups of friends. The swimming pool was dry, but about to be filled. Prices negotiable. **$$$$**

Campement Akwazena, Ranch de Nazinga (26 rooms) 50 35 64 15 (Ouaga office), 50 41 36 17 (on-site reception & reservations); e ranchnazinga@yahoo.fr; www.nazingasafari.com. Past its peak, dingy in fact, but more than good enough if you can handle no-frills & functional. For early morning & late-afternoon wildlife viewing, the location can't be beaten. Choice is between pretty en-suite twin fan huts or en-suite twin fan rooms ('apartments'). There's also an 18-bed dorm. Dorm 5,000f a bed. **$$–$$$**

If you're more into food than fauna, this may decide where you stay. The restaurant at the Campement de L'Elephant prides itself on high-quality cuisine and can rustle up a good meal at short notice ($$–$$$); bread for the mornings is baked on site every day. The Akwazena's restaurant ($–$$) has a variable reputation and generally offers a short and uninspiring list of dishes such as couscous with veg sauce. During the hunting season, both places can sometimes serve up game won during the hunts – rich buttery antelope meat, for example, or warthog and hartebeest. If you're staying at the Akwazena or just out for the day, taking a picnic from Po or Ouaga is never a bad idea, and a cool box an even better one; the price of a Brakina at either bar is eye-watering. Carry drinking water in your car.

SOUTH TOWARDS LEO

About 10km south of Ouaga on the Leo road, there's a nice rural *campement*. The emphasis is on cultural exchange, local education and development, so it's an interesting place to hang out if you have a few days to spare. Luili Yiila (m *78 18 39 28, 71 51 46 01;* e *info@luiliyiila.com; www.luiliyiila.com;* **$$–$$$**) has a couple of en-suite doubles, a twin and a four-bed dorm.

LEO

The small town of Leo is a good base for exploring the nearby ruins, all wreckage from the relentless Djerma invasions of the late 19th century. If you're planning a trip that joins up the wildlife and architecture of the Gourounsi with the cultural

BURKINA FOR THE BRITISH

Leo has seen its fair share of power struggles over the years, not only between the Djerma and the Gourounsi, but also between the French and the British who, from their base in the Gold Coast (Ghana), nurtured colonial designs on the region.

Chanoine, the French lieutenant sent to quell the Gourounsi, first got to Leo on 27 March 1897, and recalls in his journals being 'a bit amazed to see six British soldiers who came to greet me'.

Chanoine considered the Gourounsi country French turf. The presence of armed British soldiers on his patch was an insult. The British told Chanoine that their commander, while passing through Leo, had ordered them to stay until told otherwise.

The British were looking for the Gourounsi leader Hamaria, fully intending to woo him for themselves. Not finding him in Leo, they showered the local chief with gifts, including paper (not the hardest of hard-sells). Leo's chief quite rightly said he could do nothing without the consent of Hamaria, who had already made an alliance with the French some six months earlier.

The British continued the search for Hamaria, leaving a small detachment of soldiers at Leo on the pretext that they were ill, saying they would fetch them on their return. When Hamaria refused the British overtures the Brits went on their merry way, completely forgetting the six armed men in Leo. Off they went to woo Djerma chief Baba-To, by now a renowned enemy of France and an almost universally acknowledged brigand.

After waiting politely for a bit, the villagers of Leo asked the British soldiers to leave. They refused, saying they were awaiting marching orders, which of course never came.

heritage of Lobi country further southwest, it makes a decent stopover. To do this, you'll need plenty of time or your own wheels, as transport from anywhere other than Ouaga is sporadic at best. Market day is Sunday, which raises the odds for picking up transport.

GETTING THERE AND AWAY Leo is 165km south of Ouagadougou on the N6. From Ouaga, TSR in Gounghin has four departures, at 07.00, 09.00, 12.30 and 16.00 daily (3,000f). You can also pick up minibuses at the Gare de Leo near the *grande mosquée*. There are at least three departures daily (2,500f). From Po, Leo is 95km west along the R15 and a further 35km south after it joins with the N6 at Nebou. For this route you will need to get very lucky, or have your own transport; there are no regular bush taxis. From Diebougou, Leo is 133km east, and there's a sporadic bush taxi service – Tuesdays and Saturdays are your best bet.

WHERE TO STAY

Auberge Bethel de la Sissili (21 rooms) 50 41 32 32; m 78 25 77 12. On the road in from Ouaga. Rooms range from fan doubles with shared loo, to AC doubles with en suite. **$$–$$$$$**

Auberge Natou (18 rooms) 50 41 30 19. A fairly simple, cheap option near the marketplace, with both fan & AC rooms, restaurant & bar. **$–$$$**

AROUND LEO

SISSILI SAFARI (*50 41 37 45; m 76 64 04 20*) This is a 44,000ha private reserve created by Burkina's most famous journalist, Norbert Zongo, who was murdered in

Chanoine sent the soldiers packing to the British top dog nearby, with a letter that 'registered my surprise at seeing armed soldiers on land under the protection of the French'.

A few months later, the British were back in Leo, seeking refuge rather than conquest. On 11 April, a note was received by the French from a frantic Captain Cramer, scribbled in crayon on the back of a packet of cartridges, describing a disastrous defeat by the Malinke warlord Samory Toure and Cramer's 'anxious desire' to take shelter.

The French magnanimously sent cavalrymen to escort the British column into Leo, and the next day welcomed two captains, a doctor and 57 soldiers, exhausted, injured and out of ammo. After providing food, water and horses, they were again sent packing.

A week later, Chanoine met Captain Donald Stewart at Yarba. After pleasantries, the two men drew up provisional frontiers between their occupied territories and then turned to the thorny issue of Baba-To, now under British protection.

'We presented certain objections to this,' wrote Chanoine. 'In the first place, he [Stewart] could not shelter this man who burnt the French flag and is the enemy of France.'

Having defeated the Djerma the previous month, and routed Baba-To, Chanoine did not want him to mount a counter-offensive. Sporting as ever, the British 'saw the justice of this', and said they would keep Baba-To off French territory and take responsibility for any new aggressions against the French. With that, Stewart went back to the Gold Coast. And back the French went to Leo.

1998 (see page 31). Now run by his son and brother, the reserve contains antelope, warthog and buffalo. While the emphasis is on hunting, sightseers are welcome. Accommodation is in round, mock-traditional huts, 30km from Leo (**$$**). You can simply rock up and stay, or organise the whole thing – including flights, Ouaga pick-up and the stay – by telephone in advance.

SATI Perhaps because it was the spiritual heart of Gourounsi country, Djerma invaders decided to annex Sati as one of their city-states at the end of the 19th century.

Initially the relationship was collaborative. The Djerma brokered alliances between warring Gourounsi groups in 1860 and 1872. They made alliances with Gourounsi chiefs and converted them to Islam.

Yet when the Djerma settled at Sati in 1893, they turned against the Gourounsi. Led by chief Kazare, they held them to ransom and raided. Gourounsi Muslim leaders revolted. One Djerma, the famed Hamaria, went with them. Sarantye Mori, son of the Malinke warlord Samory Toure, offered his skills as negotiator to reconcile the chiefs of the Gourounsi and Djerma, but Hamaria discovered that Sarantye Mori was secretly nursing ambitions to take over himself. Finding himself caught between a rock and a hard place, Hamaria turned to the French and in September 1896, signed an agreement with French Captain Paul Voulet at Sati.

Getting there and away Sati is 22km northwest of Leo. Head west towards Ouessa and Diebougou along the N20. After 12km, look out for a blue signpost to Sati at Nadion, and take a right.

Ruins The town's ruins consist of a few short sections of mud-brick battlements and crumbled, overgrown foundations. The joy, and burden, of a tour is the hand-holding given by villagers. They are a wonderful source of local history: accounts are colourful and orientated to impressing visitors, but nevertheless worth hearing. Look out too for the chief's personal mosque and compound.

HEADING WEST FROM LEO West of Leo, on the N20 towards Ouessa and Diebougou, **Yoro** has a selection of ruins, comprising a long stretch of wall, thought to have once been a Djerma holding place for slaves and booty acquired in raids on the Gourounsi. **Ouessa** is 81km further west from Leo along the N20. From there, you can keep going west to Diebougou, where you brave a bumping tertiary road to Bobo-Dioulasso, or head down south to Gaoua on the N12 (and then west to Banfora). West of Ouessa, hills, river crossings and greener surroundings start to appear.

LOBI COUNTRY

'The Lobi is a farmer, a hunter, and a herder, but above all he is a warrior,' says Gaoua's museum of the country's most reclusive people and some of its earliest settlers.

Victims of slave raids, rival clans and internal disputes, the Lobi have long lived in a permanent state of high alert. Among the fiercest, proudest inhabitants of Burkina, they were constantly subjected to attacks from the Guiriko and Kenedougou empires throughout the 19th century. Bakary Ouattara, brother of the founder of the Guiriko Empire, led campaigns against the Lobi in 1815. Despite torching numerous villages he never fully gained control of the territory, and was eventually killed with a poisoned arrow from a Lobi bow. His successor, Karakara, continued the attacks, launching a devastating offensive in 1850. Despite heavy losses and numerous defeats, the Lobi were never completely vanquished.

The French and the British decided in June 1898 that the Lobi would fall under French jurisdiction, but unlike other territories – such as the Mossi or Gourounsi country – the Lobi had never asked for either of them to be there. Following problems controlling the population, the onset of World War I saw the French come down hard. The colonial administration of Gaoua, the Lobi capital, conducted a merciless repression in 1914. So great was the trauma that village elders banned anyone from following in the ways of the white man.

This has wed the Lobi to tradition almost as a form of defiance, long after other groups have been wooed by modernity. They remain fierce guardians of animist traditions still practised today. Given as a gift by their ancestors, the *balafon*, or *yolon* in Lobin, the local tongue) – a kind of xylophone – is the musical mainstay of the region, used on special occasions. The Lobi also spend a lot of time in their version of the pub: the *cabaret*, which acts as a gathering place for drinking home-brewed beer and music-making. In towns such as Gaoua and Batie, they are mud-brick bars. Further afield, they are simply regular spots under the shade of a mango tree where, late at night after the last calabash of *dolo* is drained, the only guide home will be the thud of a distant drum-beat.

Many Lobi have shared some of their beliefs and traditions with visitors, and there is a nascent cultural tourism circuit around Gaoua.

LOBI SOCIETY Individuality and independence are highly prized qualities among the Lobi. With the exception of the Gan sub-group (see box, pages 251–2), who have a king, Lobi societies have no central political structure, and individual families operate as autonomous units. Each of these is run by the chief of the compound (*tekan-sob* in Dagara and Birifor, and *dithildaar* in Lobiri). On rare occasions, a council of elders can be called together to act as an informal arbitration panel in the case of a dispute, but collaboration on social matters is more exception than rule.

Children take family names from their mother. There are four principal Lobi family names, known as matriclans, or *caar*: Hien (Hienbe for the Dagara), Da,

CHILDREN OF THE FOREST

'Lobi' is an umbrella term for several closely related ethnic groups that comprise about 7% of Burkina's population: the Lobi proper, Birifor, Dagara, Dorossy, Dyan, Gan and Teguessy.

The word comes from two Lobiri words – *lou* (forest) and *bi* (children). These 'children of the forest' settled initially on the left bank of the Mouhoun River, which slices Burkina and Ghana in two, before moving further into the interior in a search for fertile land. Language, codes and traditions vary, but the Lobi are united by a number of similarities. Families are determined by female lineage; they live in distinctive defensive mud compounds; share initiation rites and a reverence for bows and poisoned arrows; maintain animist beliefs and safeguard the spirit world with vigour; and craft distinctive wooden statues, which they worship as fetishes.

For the Lobi, the Mouhoun is equivalent to the river Styx of ancient Roman myth, the dividing line between this world and the next. Centuries ago, the Lobi crossed the Mouhoun from east to west to settle in their present lands, and the spirits of the deceased must cross back to rejoin the great ancestors in the spirit world, loaded with cowrie shells to pay death's ferryman. Its banks are used in initiation rites and its fish and animals are sacred.

BOW AND ARROWS

Famed as excellent hunters and warriors, the bow is the Lobi weapon of choice. A young Lobi boy's most precious gift is a bow given by his father, and it kicks off a lifelong relationship. Carrying a bow embodies masculinity, nobility, courage, soundness of body and spirit, privilege and virility, inalienable freedom and dignity.

Through their fearsome reputation, Lobi archers have for centuries blocked the route of numerous invaders, and held up colonial penetration.

With this honour comes responsibility. In the past, the Lobi have meted out justice and revenge with the use of the arrow shot. Poisoned arrows are a particular speciality, and a good hunter must be capable of completely mastering his weapon.

There are many rules surrounding its use. Village codes dictate a number of things that cannot be hunted: animals, plants, objects and above all the totem animal of the clan. If a man harms one of these forbidden elements by mistake, he must atone by certain rites and sacrifices.

Maximum precautions must be taken with poisoned arrows, including abstention from sex the day before preparing the poison. At his death, a man's bow is hung outside his hut, facing towards it.

Kambou (Kambire for the Dagara and Birifor), and Some (Palenfo for the Birifor). Given names come from the father's side, and show the order of birth. For each matriclan, people worship the same sacred animal, which it is forbidden to kill or eat; and respect the same type of tree, which it is forbidden to burn. Land rights, houses and fetishes are passed down from father to son, but pretty much everything else (wealth, wives, animals) are passed through the maternal line, to the closest male relative. At initiation, the Lobi also receive a new name, from the father's line.

ANIMISM The Lobi are profoundly animist. In the absence of organisation along class lines or obedience to a king or elders, they take their cues from a wholly otherworldly authority. The worship of spirit ancestors and the use of fetishes – which has given rise to distinctive and highly sought Lobi sculpture – remains strong. Fetish houses outside mud compounds are part of everyday life, and their influence is intensely felt.

Christian missionaries working in the area have heard tell of one elderly villager who renounced the spirits in favour of Christianity by throwing his fetishes into a nearby lake. As he turned his back on the lake and his animist traditions, the fetishes leapt out of the lake and onto his back to reclaim him.

The Lobi have little contact with Thagba, the creator of all things, instead relying on nature spirits (*thila*) as intermediaries. These invisible beings can harness their supernatural powers for both good and evil. Like the ancient Greek and Roman gods, the *thila* are subject to mortal virtues and vices – wisdom, jealousy, and rage. They set the rules, known as *zoser*, by which people live. The *zoser* are far-reaching, governing what people should wear or eat, what and when they should sacrifice and whether or not they should have sex. Failure to follow them invariably results in punishment.

It falls to the village diviner (*thildar*) to act as a spiritual secretary, taking down and interpreting the rules dictated to him by the spirits. Considered extremely powerful, they are said to have a hotline to as many as 50 *thila* at a time. They can, for a fee, hire out access to them for villagers in need.

They are also pretty nimble. Invested with supernatural powers, a diviner is said to be able to turn into an animal and become human again, transform someone else or eat the soul of another person.

Villages have several priests, each in the service of a particular spirit. The priest has to keep his spirit happy (through sacrifice) and look after anyone who has got on its wrong side. For a glimpse inside the literally shadowy world of this communicator with the spirit world, visit the diviner's house at Kampti (see pages 247–8).

LOBI FIGURES

Lobi statues are among the most famed in Africa. Known as *bouthiba*, meaning 'medicine (*thi*) that speaks obscure words (*bour*)', the statues are the children of *thila* nature spirits.

Made mostly from wood, but also from brass, clay or ivory, the *bouthiba* are considered living, sacred beings, placed on shrines to make the *thila* visible and to act as intermediaries between earth and the beyond.

Popular in museum showcases all over the world (including that of Gaoua), and among European private collections, the proper place of the Lobi statue is in the *thilduu* – the room of powers in every Lobi home. Even today, you can find statues standing outside walls, a profusion of feathers and blood marking them out as places of sacrifice. Deep in the bush, you can also find older statues under trees and in caves.

Their design – squat, heavy and imbued with a stern dignity – seems to embody the Lobi reputation for a refusal to submit. They are prized for their significance much more than for the quality of workmanship. In fact, many specimens can be positively ropey looking, but that's half the point: anyone can make a Lobi statue. It's the *thila* that decide on the creation of a new statue, not a master craftsman.

Common features make the statues recognisably Lobi. The head is disproportionately large, taking up about a fifth of the total size. Figures tend to be human-derived, standing rigid and upright. Features on the head are stylised, with eyes cut as simple incisions, demonstrating a traditional Lobi aversion to curiosity, which is thought thoroughly impudent. The nose tends to be short and angular, with lips and ears cut in relief. From the head down things are less focused, with the legs and base paid the least attention of all. The arms and hands are stuck stiff to the sides and the body is short.

The shape and pose of the *bouthiba* depend on the mission assigned to it. A figure with bowed head and hands clasped behind its back is mourning the death of a loved one, so that the keeper of the shrine will not have to. A figure with one arm stretched out sideways blocks the entrance of malevolent spirits into the family home. A figure looking left is invoking the matriclan, right for the patriclan.

The less human the *bouthiba*, the more powerful the *thila* it represents. Two heads and multiple limbs are all good news in the *bouthiba* potency stakes. Once placed on a shrine, the *bouthiba* can become animated by the *thila* it represents, coming to life to take action, by beating up witches, for example. *Bouthiba* can also be asked to pick out a husband or wife, help women conceive, cure impotency or guard against illness.

LOBI HOUSES

Dotted throughout the region, each large rectangular or polygonal Lobi compound, known as a *maison soukala*, resembles a mini-fortress.

Spaced far from one another (at least an arrow shot's distance away), everything about the design protests protection and isolation, reflecting the long history of Lobi conflict. Composed of a single vast mud *banco* wall, raw and cracked, there is only one small entrance. Sometimes, if the walls have not received a final covering, you can see how they are built up with slabs of mud, giving an attractive beehive effect. In the past, there was no door at all; instead, ladders, cut from notched, forked branches, went up to the roof, where small holes would allow entry into the *soukala*. The flat terrace roof was once a lookout post for spotting arriving assailants, but is now a place to sleep and dry grain. The all-important cereal granaries sit inside, but their entrance is also through a hole in the roof, and only the chief of the household can give permission to enter. In the past the *soukala* would have contained a well for water and enough space for all the domestic animals. Nothing was left vulnerable outside.

The rooms inside are shrouded in almost perpetual darkness, housing up to 15 people. Each wife has a room for herself and her children, where meals are prepared. Stacked *canaris* – large, earthenware jars used for holding water or *dolo* – piled up against kitchen walls denote the rank of a Lobi woman.

INITIATION The *djoro*, the prinicipal Lobi initiation, is a powerful affair. Boys and girls from Burkina and Côte d'Ivoire head for a long ordeal on the banks of the Mouhoun, in memory of the ancestors who crossed it.

Some claim the trials are so unforgiving that some initiates, wounded by sacrificial rites and abandoned in forests, have bled or starved to death.

Each clan heads for a special far-off site and lives naked, save for a few cowrie shells for women, and loincloths for men. They learn a secret language, an initiation dance, undergo trials of endurance, drink a powerful potion (called 'milk', after mother's milk) that makes them forget about their past life, and learn how to summon the rains and have a successful hunt.

The initiation ceremony takes place every seven years over several months, for first-timers aged seven to 15 years old. Some keep coming back for more, to further their understanding and courage, creating a sort of hierarchy defined by the number of initiations. When initiates emerge, villages hold grand rejoicing ceremonies for those returning to the world.

GAOUA Settled deep among the red earth, green hills and fast-flowing streams of southwestern Burkina, Gaoua is the capital of Poni province and gateway into the world of fetishes, sacred rites and bush lore of Lobi country.

Locals say Gaoua was created when Lobis came up from northern Ghana, where they found similar Gan people already in place. As a result, Lobis called their trek north 'the route of the Gan people' (*Gan-houo*), which over time contracted down to Gaoua.

Getting there and away You can get to Gaoua from Ouaga (381km) in a day. It may be easier to break up the journey by stopping at Boromo. From Ouaga, the turn-off for Gaoua is at the small town of Pa, 48km after Boromo on the route to

Bobo. From here head south to Dano and Diebougou, and then on to Gaoua. It's tarmac all the way, and should take about six hours from Ouaga if you don't stop.

STAF and TSR both have daily departures from Ouaga. Tickets cost 6,000f one-way, 11,000f return. TSR (*50 34 25 24*) leaves from Gounghin at 07.30, 14.00 and 15.30; STAF (m *70 28 17 96*) leaves from Larle at 07.00, 14.30 and 15.00. The final service continues on to Kampti.

In Gaoua, the coach terminus is inconveniently situated 3km out of town on the Ouaga road; a couple of taxis may be hanging around when you arrive (500f into town), otherwise call a hotel for a pick-up. STAF leaves for Ouaga at 07.00, 08.00 and 14.00, TSR at 07.00, 08.00 and 15.00. All are stopping services, which you can take to Diebougou (1,000f), Dano (2,000f), Pa (2,500f), Boromo (3,000f) or Sabou (5,000f).

There are three alternative routes, less direct, taking in cultural highlights in the south and west. The first is via Banfora, in the far southwest. A wide, Canadian-built compacted dirt road, the N11, links Banfora to Gaoua; however, it has not been well maintained and all the coach services have given up on it. There are still daily bush taxi departures from Banfora *autogare*, but be prepared for countless loadings and unloadings of man, beast and bicycle; a 197km journey that should take three hours can take the best part of a day. The (small) compensation is that you will arrive at the little *autogare* in the centre of Gaoua.

The second route is from Bobo, via Pa along the tarmac road. TSR leaves at 08.00 and 15.00, and at the same times back from Gaoua. Singles cost 5,000f.

The third option is to arrive from Gourounsi country, and the scenery between Leo and Gaoua is lovely and little travelled by foreign visitors. One tourist caused three passers-by to fall off their bicycles in dumbfounded shock, one of whom pitched into a flooded rice paddy and was unable to extricate himself because his leg was caught between the bicycle frame and the handlebar. The tourist stopped to go back and help him up, and the man was still speechless. For this, you ideally need your own wheels, though there is a sporadic bush taxi service between Leo and Diebougou.

Getting around and guides Gaoua has a small taxi service comprising about five cars. You should pay no more than 500f for a daytime hop, 1,000f at night. You can hire mopeds from the market, but make sure you take a good look at them first. A better bet is Aboubacar 'Papa' Kambou (m *76 47 72 48, 78 31 92 41;* e *kambouboubacar@yahoo.fr*), a well-respected local guide who offers both car hire (20,000f per day) and *moto* hire (5,000f per day). He runs a small travel agency, Lobi Decouvertes (*www.lobidecouvertes.wifeo.com*) and can organise anything from day trips riding pillion to trips throughout the region and into Mali. Local trips can include overnight stays in villages, Loropeni and an audience with the Gan king. If he is not available, he will recommend someone who is. Alternatively, try the hotels: you can arrange vehicle hire at Hotel Hala, which can likewise put visitors in touch with top-notch guides; the Auberge Donsamby has a seven-seater 4x4 (30,000f per day including driver, excluding fuel) and one *moto* (5,000f per day).

Where to stay

Comfortable/Mid range

Hotel Hala (22 rooms) 20 90 01 21. Set back from the main road, with spacious lobby, restaurant & bar area, the rooms are arranged in tiers behind a pleasant garden. Run by a Lebanese family since 1981, service is excellent & portions at mealtimes are generous. The front porch is perfect for drinks at sundown & the back patio for breakfast. The rooms, however, are nothing special & somewhat overpriced. About 1.5km from the centre, it is on the way into town

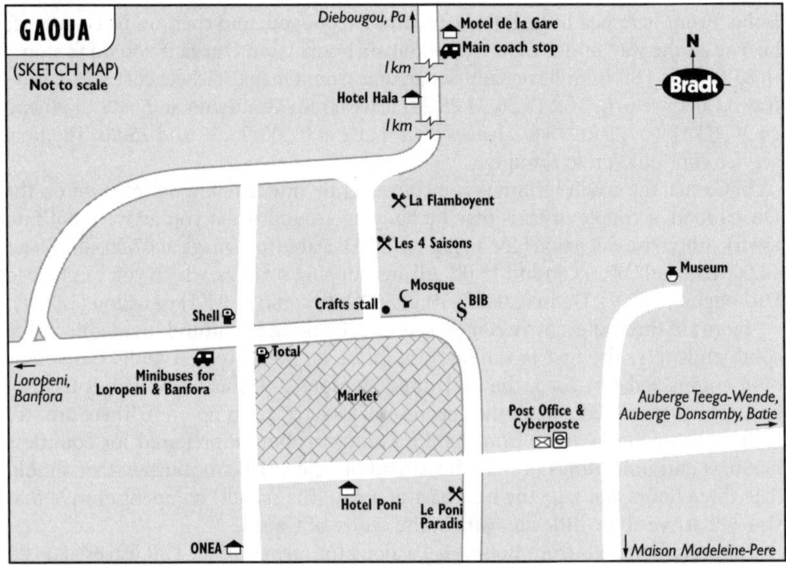

coming in from Diebougou. Choice of en-suite fan or AC. **$$$–$$$$**

Auberge Teega-Wende (8 rooms) 20 90 08 41/37. Everything new & shiny, with better-value AC rooms than at the Hala, but it's short on outside space for chilling. Indoor restaurant lacks atmosphere. About 1km out of town on the Batie road. Choice of en-suite fan or AC. **$$$**

Budget/Shoestring

ONEA (3 rooms) m 70 43 03 64. Cheap en-suite rooms meant for waterboard staff (who take priority) are the best that central Gaoua can offer. Clean sheets, mozzie nets & an AC option for just 1,000f more. Fan single 4,000f. **$$**

Auberge Donsamby (8 rooms) m 79 12 66 19, 71 26 93 39; e auberge.donsamby@yahoo.fr. About 2km out of town on the Batie road, this welcoming place has basic rooms with external facilities & no electricity (but solar lighting), set around a pretty, slightly untidy courtyard. There's the odd luxury, such as espresso coffee, & car/*moto* hire. Meals can be ordered. B/fast 500f. **$**

Hotel Poni (9 rooms) 20 90 02 00. Opposite the daily market, dilapidated fan rooms with grim external facilities have beds that resemble hammocks. Better for its bar, which can serve up simple food. **$**

Maison Madeleine-Pere (4 rooms) 20 90 03 26. Simple twin rooms, well cared for by nuns, have either inside or outside loo. It's a little far out, in Secteur 4, but everyone knows it so it's easily found by asking. No meals available. **$**

Motel de la Gare (8 rooms) 20 90 00 14. Gloomy but just about functional fan rooms out at the coach station. **$**

Where to eat and drink The best option is **Hotel Hala** ($$$), where you can enjoy good Lebanese food in secluded surrounds. The set menu includes *labneh*, houmous and *baba khanoush* (grilled aubergine). Beer costs 1,000f and chips a staggering 2,000f. For something cheaper, and frequented by locals rather than tour groups, try the central **Les 4 Saisons** (*20 90 04 57; $–$$*), which has a street-side terrace for watching the world go by or a pleasant garden out the back. There are the usual suspects – *riz sauce*, spaghetti – plus a range of meat and fish. **La Flamboyent** (also known as **La Grotte**) ($–$$), a popular *maquis* set back from the road towards the market in a small square, is another good option with an attractive central *paillote*. **Le Poni Paradis** ($) serves simple dishes out the back, and is a popular bar with a club, open Saturday night (500f entry). Gaoua is also at the heart of *dolo*-making country, so it's a good place to knock back a bowl or three; *dolo* dens are known as *cabarets*. All you need to do is ask locals to point you in the right direction and you'll be made very welcome.

Shopping The market is a daily affair in Gaoua, but it's the Sunday market that draws people from around the region. Earthenware pots, fetishes, rings, bracelets, chains and leatherware can all be seen. There's also a stall near the mosque that sells crafts, mostly leather goods.

Other practicalities In addition to the **museum** the town boasts a few decent accommodation options, an arresting mosque set on high ground near the town centre, a **BIB** bank next door with a Visa ATM (no exchange service, but you can change euros at Hotel Hala), and **internet** at the **post office** (**cyberposte**, 500f an hour). Most important, it is a pleasant base for exploring the villages of Lobi country. Because of the strength of local beliefs and customs, a guide here is more important than perhaps anywhere else in the country. Without one, Lobi country will be closed to you. Gaoua is a good place to pick up such a guide, arrange transport, and set off.

What to see

Museum (*20 90 01 69; 08.00–12.30 & 15.00–18.00 Tue–Sun, 15.00–18.00 Mon; entry 2,000f, 300f for Burkinabes*) Madeleine Père, who lived among the Lobi from 1961 until her death in 2002, set up the museum in 1990. Housed in a handsome 1920s colonial building, the museum includes separate rooms dedicated to women, men and culture. They are packed full of artefacts, including hunting tools, fetishes and statues, cowrie shells and strings of beads, musical instruments and bronze casts. There are also models of traditional housing, specially constructed within the museum grounds. Don't miss the remarkable black-and-white photographs taken by French colonial commander Henri Labouret between 1914 and 1924, and those by Arnold Hein in 1934. Two books written by Père are also available for borrowing – scholarly, full of information about the social structure of Lobi, but in French.

Church With such a strong animist current, Christian missionaries have flocked to the region. The church in Gaoua is run by Lobi Protestants, with a strong social commitment to local education. There is also a Lobi translation of the Bible that is worth a look.

AROUND GAOUA A trip through the surrounding countryside is good for seeing the remarkable fortress houses (see box, page 244), but it's advisable to take a good and well-connected guide. The area is also famed for its craftwork. If you time it right and visit in the fallow period following the harvest (January–April), you can visit villages such as **Bouroum-Bouroum**, deep at work on fetish sculpture, basketwork and pottery. Towns will also give you a flavour of the different groups making up the Lobi: Dano for the Daguera, Batie for the Birifor and Loropeni for the Gan.

Kampti Kampti is home to a diviner, and a visit to this house of the ancestors is quite an experience. Inside, nestled in the darkness, Lobi wooden statues are sat neck-high in cowrie shells and the diviner sits awaiting his next visitor. Crouching low, he throws cowries to consult the spirits on questions of fertility, the coming rains, the harvest or the chance of success.

Getting there and away The town is 42km southwest of Gaoua, along a dirt road, and makes for an excellent ride through Lobi country. Alternatively, head west to Loropeni (39km) along the N11 and drop down south for 21km. STAF's last service of the day from Ouaga to Gaoua, at 15.00, continues on to Kampti.

Doudou Lobi country is famed for its gold deposits. As early as the 14th century, Mande merchants were active in the region, moving gold north to Djenne in Mali. In an interesting division of labour, Lobi women have traditionally traded gold, while men have mined it. Women were banned from wearing gold, presumably in an attempt to limit the temptation to skim off merchandise. As a modern example of the gold business, the women's gold market, held in Doudou every five days, is fascinating stuff. Doudou is 14km southeast of Gaoua, on the Batie road.

Sansana Further on along the Batie road, off to the right about 25km from Gaoua, Sansana makes for a rewarding visit. Most Lobi villages have a speciality, such weaving or making pottery; here, it's making *dolo*. From early in the morning the women stoke fires under enormous vats. It's a great place to see countless fetish huts, and the attractive beehive effect that results from Lobi building methods. You may also see women painstakingly pounding rocks to extract the gold, beating cow dung into their rooftop terraces, or men mixing *banco* to repair a wall. It's a deeply traditional place: go with a guide, and make sure you leave a gift.

Batie Set among pretty green hills, the capital of the Birifor is a slightly down-at-heel town of 10,000 people. The market is well known for its pottery, tablecloths and yams, the last a highly prized ingredient of the popular Ivorian dishes, *foutou* and *ragout igname*.

Jules Dah (*20 90 40 28*) is a highly knowledgeable local guide, who works at the town hall. He can arrange visits to blacksmiths, village pottery makers, Birifor homes and sacred sites.

Further south, **Koimoteon** and **Zindo** villages both have sacred hippo and *caiman* pools. Legend has it that armed Lobi rode hippo-back to cross the river in wartime, and that singing to them at the lakeside will bring them out of the water. Whether you have any luck or not, it is a lovely spot for a walk or a picnic, and Jules can arrange a visit by *moto*-taxi, as well as a trip out on the lake with local fishermen.

The **Koulbi Forest**, wedged between Côte d'Ivoire and Ghana, is not at all developed, but contains monkeys and wild boar. A 55km trip to the village of **Kpere** will take you through the forest and to the intersection of the three bordering countries, but you will need your own wheels, and a visa if you cross the border into Ghana.

Getting there and away Batie is an hour south of Gaoua (60km). A TRANSMIF bus leaves Ouaga for Batie at 09.00 daily (7,500f), but the station in Gounghin is tricky to find; it may be easier to pick up the service at the coach station in Gaoua at about 15.00 (1,500f). Alternatively, you can take a bush taxi from the *autogare* in central Gaoua.

Bouroum-Bouroum The traditional market here is good for wooden sculpture, basketwork and pottery. Take the N12, 25km north of Gaoua on the route to Diebougou.

Diebougou This Birifor town has a range of crafts on offer, including pottery and basketwork, as well as some intriguing caves, known locally as *les grottes*. They were built under French colonial command using local labour, and form a network of defensive tunnels to the west of town. You can combine a visit here with a wander through a little section of forest, and to the *barrage* – a little lake that's atmospheric at sunset.

Association No-biel (m *70 30 52 18, 72 58 87 91*) is a group of friendly, earnest young guys who run training and awareness courses in local villages on issues such as AIDS, excision and violence towards women. Every year, European (mostly French) volunteers pitch up to help them renovate village schools. They can put on dance and drama performances, and also act as guides for trips to the caves, the *barrage* and to visit potters and weavers.

Getting there and away

By bus Diebougou is 74km north of Gaoua and 133km west of Leo. TSR, STAF and TRANS-MIF all have daily services passing though Diebougou (5,000f) *en route* for Gaoua. TSR also has two daily services from Bobo (4,000f) (for services, see *Gaoua*, page 244).

By taxi You can pick up bush taxis for Leo in Diebougou, but not every day – Tuesday and Saturday are your best bet.

Where to stay

Le Relais (7 rooms) 20 90 52 80. Years as the town's only hotel have resulted in sloppy service & dingy rooms that are vastly overpriced. Decent restaurant menu, but half of it unavailable. Behind the BIB bank near the Dano–Gaoua junction. Fan or AC rooms. **$$$–$$$$**

Auberge Dapago (7 rooms) m 70 64 27 77. Fresh, clean en-suite fan or AC rooms, small but sparkling, & a friendly welcome. Turn left just before Shell garage coming from Ouaga; it's about 500m on the left. A bar & restaurant were just about to open. **$$–$$$**

La Gare (6 rooms) m 70 64 38 14. Basic rooms with mozzie nets within the coach station itself; you may feel a bit exposed stepping out to use the loos & showers. **$$**

Maison des Ordres (3 rooms) m 70 71 60 50. The cheapest option is also the most difficult to find, tucked away near a school named Ecole B. Best to ring for help. Spacious fan rooms have en suite or bathroom just next door. Quiet courtyard & terrace where you can get cold drinks or simple meals. **$**

Where to eat and drink Apart from the various hotel options, you could try **Le Bon Gout**, which is the most popular *maquis* in town. It's central, signposted on the left coming from Ouaga, and has simple meals, cold beers and dancing at the weekends. Another good *maquis* is **Chez Flo** – take a left before the Shell garage, pass the Auberge Dapago and head left across the wide open space; it's just ahead.

Dano This small town, whose market is good for pottery and weaving, is home to the Dagara. They embraced Christianity with much greater zeal than most in the region. Perhaps this had something to do with a wish to do away with their funeral rites. In the past, the deceased was left outside his court on a makeshift covered throne, dressed in all his finery, until the family arrived to mourn. If grieving relatives were slow off the mark, or had a long way to come, the dead body could spend up to a week in the sun – not the greatest for nearby family members maintaining a constant vigil.

Getting there and away From Diebougou, the tarmac road heads towards Leo for 14km before turning left onto the N12 towards Pa; continue for 25km to reach Dano. Take any of the coach services heading for Gaoua, Ouaga or Bobo (for services, see *Gaoua*, page 244).

Where to stay and eat

L'Auberge de Dano (17 rooms) 20 90 81 13. Partner of the Relais Touristique in Boromo, this is an attractive place with pretty *paillotes*, rampant bougainvillea & a wide range of rooms, starting with a small fan single with external loo & bucket shower (4,500f). AC doubles are a little small; you pay more for en suite. Good-looking restaurant menu. **$$–$$$**

LOROPENI RUINS One of only a handful of stone ruins surviving in west Africa, these are older and better preserved than those at Sati and Yoro. They were made a UNESCO World Heritage Site in 2009 – the only one in Burkina. Set amid greenery that has found all manner of ways to launch its assault on the walls, they make for a pleasant leafy wander.

The site (*Entrance costs 1,500f, an additional 500f for a camera and 5,000f for a video; pay at the toll booth & keep your ticket. Young men may offer themselves as official guides; there is no reason to pay extra, but no reason not to if you think they were good*) The most impressive thing about the ruins is their scale. The walls stand up to 7m high and 1.5m thick at the base, enclosing a large space about 50m by 40m. The complex consists of three great compartments, the first of which is the largest.

The bricks are made of rock, rather than mud, which explains the state of preservation. Look out for shea-butter nuts on trees and fallen on paths as you walk through the forest. That's partly the reason the rocks are still standing. They were stuck together using a sweet and sturdy cement of shea butter and honey. If you've attracted any interest from local children, they may show you how to suck the fruits and get at the sweet green fibrous stuffing.

The new theory Until recently, there was an utter lack of knowledge about what these rows of well-ordered bricks are doing in the middle of a forest. There were a range of entertaining theories – some historians said they were built by slaves; others that they were proof that the Egyptians and Phoenicians were hanging around; others still claimed a Portuguese or Moroccan link. Their purpose was much debated, too: a stop-off point for Mande or Dioula traders, an enormous storehouse for slaves...?

It seems almost a shame that the controversy may be at an end. In 2008, two sets of research were carried out by archaeologists from the University of Ouaga. The digs turned up a range of items, such as arrows and bits of pottery, and carbon dating identified the earliest date of occupation as 11th century – earlier than many had thought. The most likely architects, therefore, were the Lorhoron, Touna or Koulango: Lobi clans who were in the region from the 11th century onwards looking for gold. The purpose of the site seems to have been protective: it was a fortress. Which of the three clans were responsible is still unknown.

Despite the evidence, this doesn't chime with local views. According to local sources, when the Gan, Dyan and Lobi arrived in the area they found the great monolith, and decided not to avail themselves of a giant prefab in the middle of the forest. Instead of setting up shop within the ready-made walls, they named the place 'House of Refusal' because, well, they refused to live there.

Whatever the case, the stone bricks carry on standing, implacable, in the middle of a forest glade.

Getting there and away The ruins are signposted about 3km west of the town, 39km west of Gaoua on the decent N11 piste. If you're staying in Gaoua, take a bush taxi or hire a moped. From the sign, follow the track on foot until you hit the ruins, within ten minutes.

Where to stay and eat

Auberge Thangba Thimii (7 rooms) m 78 53 99 05. Set in a pretty building with a neat courtyard, basic but perfectly fine rooms have internal bucket showers, outside loo; some singles, some doubles, all dirt cheap. No electricity, but drinks available. Take the Kampti road, swing left after about 200m towards the phone mast, & head across the footie pitch. **$**

Buvette le Barrage in town serves simple meals and drinks.

GAN COUNTRY

Local history has it the Gan started out around Gaoua, but got pushed further and further west, to the area north of Loropeni. They are thought to be the first occupants of southwest Burkina, and may have arrived from Accra in several stages. They call themselves *kan* (plural *kamba*) and speak *kansa*. Although formally part of the Lobi branch of families, there are several significant differences. Society is more rigidly organised; the Gan have a king, and a centralised system of power. They rely on a diet of yams rather than cereals, and live in distinctive huts with conical straw roofs. Walls are made from bricks of dried earth, joined with clay. Each person has their own house – rectangular for men, round for women – and the roofs of women's houses are plaited, while for men they take the shape of a hat.

OBIRE This is the capital of the Gan and seat of the current king, who came to the throne in 2003. You can request an audience, which is subject to a certain etiquette: he is known not by name but as 'Sa Majesté', and you shouldn't attempt to approach him or to shake his hand. A gift of kola nuts or the money equivalent is expected (1,000f is fine). Despite all this, he's rather young and affable, and open to questions regarding village life, the royal succession, Gan customs and so on. You can even contact him directly to ask about village festivals, which tourists are welcome to attend (m *70 52 61 58, 76 04 28 87;* e *samajesteroigan@yahoo.fr*). There's the harvest festival that takes place sometime in late December, and '*les dernières funérailles*', a week-long memorial event for all who have died in the course of the year. This can take place any time between April and June.

The system of Gan succession is worth noting. Legend has it that, a long time ago, two sister princesses came to live in Loropeni. When their brother the king died, each wanted her own son to succeed him. Finally, after a long quarrel, the older sister won and her son was installed on the throne. But then the two sisters started getting on a bit better and decided that the fairest thing would be to give each side of the family a chance and switch between the two. To this day, the royal line is matrilineal, in that the throne passes to the king's nephew – his sister's son; the reason being, as the current king points out, that you can never be *quite* sure that your wives' sons are your own.

The ancestral tombs Set apart from the royal compound lies a grove of stone huts that were rebuilt in the 1990s with German aid. Within each one sits the life-size clay effigy of an ancestral king, complete with name plaque. They look suitably regal, but also a little sad, and the site seems slightly neglected; one of the kings has crumbled into the dust. Certainly worth a visit, but not a patch on the living king and his compound. Entry is 1,500f, of which half goes to ONTB.

Getting there and away Obire is 8km northwest of Loropeni along a very rough and bumpy track that has tricky patches of sand. Saloon cars can make it, but a 4x4 is better; it's fine by *moto*, but you'll need to know how to handle it.

7

The West

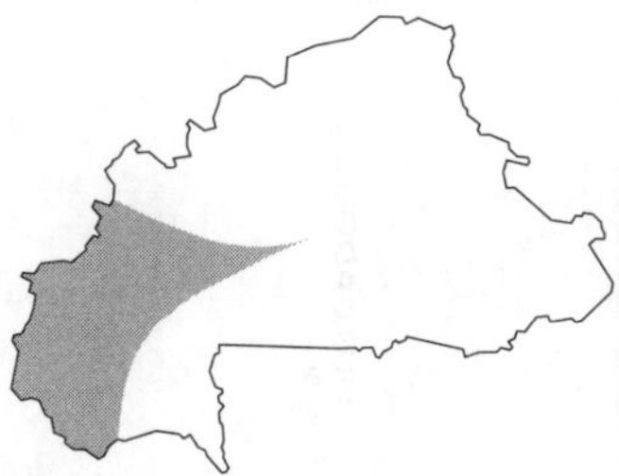

'This must be one of the most beautiful countries in the world,' wrote the French explorer Louis-Parfait Monteil in 1891, awestruck by the verdant beauty in the west of Burkina Faso. He claimed never to have seen anything like it in his travels in west Africa.

The southwest is considered Burkina's touristic highlight. The lush, cooler climate comes as a relief from the fierce heat and dust of the central plateau, and hills, waterfalls and stunning rock formations form the country's most dramatic scenery.

With a name straight out of a Star Wars movie, Bobo-Dioulasso, Burkina's second city, is an ideal base for exploring the region. The architecture and history of the old quarter unfolds along tree-lined avenues, making it a more pleasant place to explore than central Ouagadougou. Surrounded by acres of sugarcane fields, Banfora, 85km further southwest, is one of Burkina's prettiest towns, and the gateway to scenic highlights such as the Domes of Fabedougou, and the hippo lake of Tengrela.

The west is also the cradle of the mask. The Bwaba, who occupy the region between Ouagadougou and Bobo, are master craftsmen, and their fantastic creations can be seen at important mask festivals.

NEAR OUAGA

Within striking distance of Ouaga, there are a couple of good stop-off points on the road to Bobo, ideal for day trips from the capital or to break up the journey southwest. Just make sure you're in the mood for large reptiles feeding on live chickens…

BAZOULE Bazoule is a pretty site and popular weekend spot for Burkinabe families. Well cared for by the **Association Tourisme et Development de Bazoule** (ATDB) (m *76 62 17 59*), a brightly painted artisanal centre fosters bronze workers, woodworkers and weavers, avoiding tourist naffness. The adjacent *campement* has a restaurant serving cool drinks and meals.

Getting there and away From Ouaga take the Bobo road for 23km to Tanguen-Dassouri and look for the sign towards the end of the village. Turn right on to a hard dirt track. It's a lovely drive through Bazoule, with a market every three days. The road winds through the Mossi mud-brick courtyards and straw granaries. Take a moped from Ouaga, or ask any of several stopping coaches headed for Bobo to drop you at the turning. The walk from the main road takes about 20 minutes.

Where to stay

Campement Communautaire Tanga Zugu (9 rooms) m 76 07 27 06, 72 01 35 11; e mareauxcrocodiles@hotmail.fr; www.bazoule-mare-aux-crocodiles.com. Set in spacious grounds, with fun animal-shaped benches sculpted in cement dotted around. Solid stone

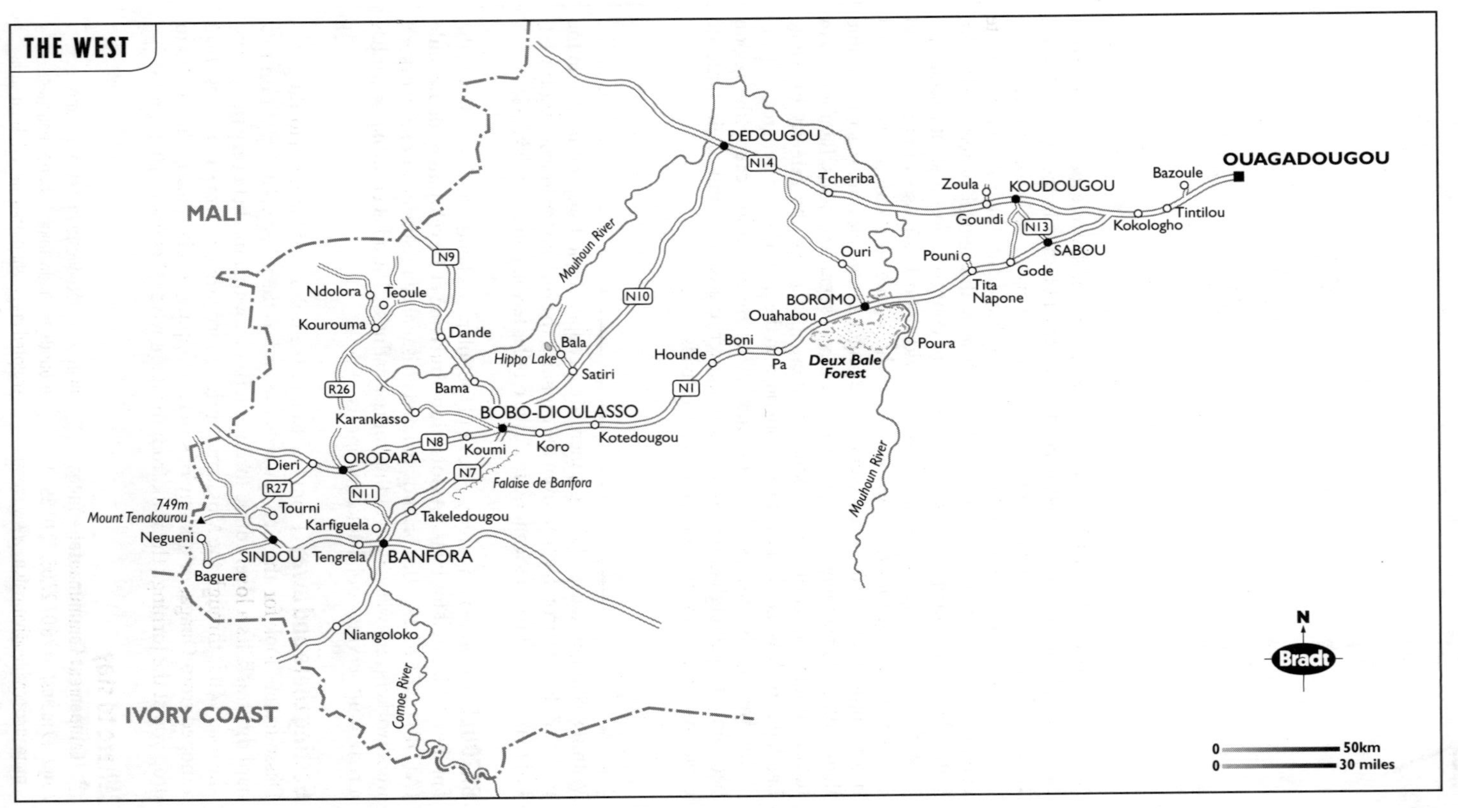
THE WEST
OUAGADOUGOU
Bazoule
Tintilou
Kokologho
KOUDOUGOU
Zoula
Goundi
N13
SABOU
Gode
Pouni
Tita
Napone
Tcheriba
DEDOUGOU
N14
Ouri
BOROMO
Ouahabou
Poura
Deux Bale Forest
Boni
Pa
Hounde
N1
Mouhoun River
Mouhoun River
N10
Bala
Hippo Lake
Satiri
MALI
N9
Ndolora
Teoule
Kourouma
Dande
Bama
R26
Karankasso
BOBO-DIOULASSO
Koro
Kotedougou
N8
Koumi
ORODARA
Dieri
N7
Falaise de Banfora
R27
N11
Tourni
Takeledougou
749m
Mount Tenakourou
Karfiguela
Negueni
SINDOU
Tengrela
BANFORA
Baguere
Niangoloko
Comoe River
IVORY COAST
N
Bradt
0 50km
0 30 miles

huts are nicely painted inside & are decorated with bits of *artisanat*. No electricity, but lamps provided. 3 huts have 3 beds & en suite; 3 have 2 beds and no loo; 3 have 2 beds & no facilities. The restaurant has a big shady *paillote*. **$–$$**

Sacred crocodile lake (*Entry site costs 1,000f for adults, 9,000f for groups of 10; 250f for children. The price includes viewing the tortoises; a chicken costs 1,000f*) The sacred crocodile lake, said to be centuries old, contains more than 100 Nile crocodiles, the most common of 13 croc species throughout Africa. Meeting the crocodiles – although they are fairly small – up close and personal, and entirely unregulated, is quite an experience. Live chickens are often fed to the crocs as a showpiece finale, and the sound of jaws snapping tight around a limp, feathered lump is unforgiving and unforgettable. There is no chewing; only the gulping down of an entire body.

Old tortoise home Bazoule is also home to a tortoise conservation centre, housing nine spurred African tortoises plus more than 15 babies. They are the largest continental land tortoise and threatened with extinction throughout the Sahel. Sometimes killed for their meat in Ethiopia, Sudan and Chad, in Burkina Faso they are a sign of virtue, happiness, fertility and longevity, linking men and the spirits. Living to as old as 150 years and measuring 1m wide, they have status and an aura befitting their years.

Local visits Beyond the crocodile lake is a farm belonging to village chief Naba Kooba, with *agouti*, zebu and porcupine. Follow the path past the lake and take a left. Anyone at the ticket office should be happy to show you. You can also visit the chief's compound (before the crocodile site – look for the arresting horseman statue). Take a small gift as a courtesy.

KOKOLOGHO The **chief's palace** (*na-yiri* in Moore) (*t 50 44 56 03; m 70 76 64 28, 78 79 79 44; e palaisdekokologho@yahoo.fr; www.palaisduroi.com; ⌚ 09.00–12.00 & 15.00–17.00 daily; entry 1,500f*) at Kokologho is an impressive example of Sudanese-style mud-brick architecture. Perhaps keen to show its flock had mastered the mud architecture style as well as its Muslim brothers, the Catholic Mission in Ouagadougou helped Naba Boulga build the palace in 1942, giving it a distinctly non-Islamic twist. His son, Naba Kaonga, lives there today.

The *rap noore* is the main western entry point, reserved for men, while women take the eastern *pagb noore*. Next to the palace, a sacred courtyard contains ten mud-brick huts, each one symbolising one of the villages in this small kingdom. Rituals and sacrifices to spirits and ancestors take place here. Other important buildings inside the court include the *kiims roogo*, never to be opened, containing sacred relics of the kingdom; the *zaongo*, containing a throne on which each deceased *naba* is placed in all his finery for a final council with his ministers; and the *poog kiem rooga*, the house of the queen mother, or the eldest noblewoman of the kingdom, charged with caring for and keeping watch over the *kiims roogo* and *zaongo*. On the last Saturday in January every year, the palace holds a ceremony, *soug pilli*, during which each village comes to look after its symbolic hut inside the traditional courtyard, and to pay homage to the *naba*. Visitors are welcome, and two guides, Thomas and Pascal, can show you around.

Getting there and away Kokologho is on the main Ouaga–Bobo road, 45km from Ouaga. The village sprawls for some distance, but the palace is clearly

THE WISDOM OF CROCODILES

While Bazoule and Sabou offer tourist-friendly versions, you can find sacred caiman lakes throughout the Mossi Plateau – usually well hidden from view and frequented only by elders. The legends may be fanciful, but the respect is real.

One of the best-known stories explains the reverence for the crocodiles at Sabou. A hunter, hungry and parched, came upon the town, feeble from exhaustion. A crocodile saved him, first offering him water with a flick of his reptilian tail, then leading him to Sabou's grand lake. The hunter vowed never again to kill a crocodile.

The story at Bazoule is a little different, hinging on the reign of Naba Kouda (1358–1400). Of his four children, his young son was left with the task of ruling after his father's death. When asked if he was up to the task, the young son replied '*M'pa zolgo ye*' (Since I'm not stupid, I can do it). Over time, the phrase *pa zolog tenga* ('land of the non-stupid') morphed into Bazoule. The sacred crocodiles are said to have fallen from the sky after the rains, during Naba Kouda's reign. They dug a large hole that filled up with rain and from that moment on the village had constant access to water – a population that previously had to go 15km to fetch water was eternally grateful.

Crocodiles and humans are thought to share the same spirit. Were a human to kill a sacred crocodile, that human would also have to die. Likewise, if one of the sacred crocodiles dies, expect to see a villager follow suit.

At festival time, locals make sacrifices and ask the crocodiles for health, fertility, success, fortune and protection against enemies. For the casual visitor perhaps the most relevant aspect of this reptilian reverence is that sacred crocodiles will not go after you. You can eyeball a crocodile within a couple of metres, or even sit on its back at Sabou. This may have as much to do with a chicken diet and habitual human contact as any kind of spiritual bond. Do not expect crocodiles elsewhere to be so accommodating.

signposted on the right. Any of the stopping coach services from Ouaga can drop you off; it's also within striking distance by *moto*.

SABOU Unlike the one at Bazoule, this large lake is full all year round, so crocodiles are usually totally submerged. Someone wades in to drag an unwilling croc by the tail from its afternoon slumber, to be prodded and poked into a display of puissance. The reptiles are bigger than at Bazoule, but more docile, and the demise of the chickens is considerably more barbaric.

Entry to see the crocodiles costs 1,500f each for one to four people; 1,000f each for five to ten people; 750f each for 11 to 20 people; 500f each for more than 20 people. Chicken included.

Getting there and away

By bus Sabou is 82km west of Ouaga and 21km south of Koudougou. Many of the bus companies running the Ouaga–Bobo route stop in Sabou (note that TCV and Rakieta do not). Try TSR, STMB or STAF; Sogebaf is best avoided. STAF's service is the most frequent, leaving from its garage north of the railway tracks in Larle. Departures are at 07.00, 08.30, 10.30, 13.00, 15.30, 18.00 and 22.00; its Gaoua services at 07.00, 14.30 and 15.00 also stop at Sabou. Tickets cost 1,000f. Tickets from Koudougou also cost 1,000f; TZJ-TPW has a Bobo service at 08.30 every day bar Sunday, which stops in Sabou.

By taxi Bush taxis leave from the *autogare* in Koudougou at around 10.00 daily. Moving on from Sabou is easy – you don't have to wait long for transport going in either direction.

Orientation Once in Sabou bus station, turn onto the Koudougou road and look for a sign about 200m ahead on your right. The lake, *campements* and boutiques are a five- to ten-minute walk from there.

Where to stay

Auberge Casani (10 rooms) 50 44 55 11/59. Built by the Zod-Neere Association next door to its colourful workshop, clean en-suite fan rooms & 2 huts with outside shower/loo have mozzie nets & are set in a cosy, picturesque courtyard. A nice little *buvette/restau* serves drinks, simple meals & breakfast. There are 2 6-bed dorms at 4,000f per bed. **$$**

Campement Touristique de Sabou (5 rooms) 50 44 55 01. With new competition up the track, they've tried to pull their socks up here. Huts & rooms have showers & are clean, with new mozzie nets & solar lighting (no fans). The outside so-called flush loos were in dire need of attention, however, so take a look first. Location overlooking the lake is great; there's a pleasant drinks area with thatched shade, & the restaurant does meals. **$**

Local artisanship Local craftwork is the bonus of any trip to Sabou. Three worthwhile local associations have lakeside workshops and boutiques; the first is the **Zod-Neere** 'second-chance' association, for adolescents who have missed out on their primary education. Outside school they train as artisans to help pay school fees, and turn out some excellent, genuinely original jewellery, sculpture, leatherwork and clothing, much of it made at the brightly painted building up the road. Next is the **Association Song Taaba**, which provides training and adapted tools for disabled artisans. It likewise has a beautiful selection of items, and you can watch weavers at work. The third is **Un Metier + Des Outils**, another group that gives training and tools to unemployed young men. They have a bronze workshop on site and you can watch the process.

The Zod-Neere Association (*ask for Lassane Kientore; 50 44 55 11*) also organises the **Rencontre Artistique de Sabou (Renasa)** festival, held every other February (next in 2013).

KOUDOUGOU

Known as a 'town of rebels', Koudougou has a well-worn reputation for making political trouble. The joke goes that there should be a plaque on the way into town simply bearing the words 'watch out'.

Visitors have little to fear, however, and a stay in the town is laid-back compared with the bustle and buzz of Ouagadougou. It has a contrary character all of its own and while not packed with attractions, it makes for an intriguing visit, in particular for its artisans.

As well as housing some of Burkina's noblest errant sons and troublemakers, it is the home of the country's first president. Maurice Yameogo took the helm in 1960, and was semi-exiled to the town following his release from prison. The decaying presidential residence still exists, in a sorry state of repair. Look out for a rather amusing bespectacled statue of him at Place Maurice Yameogo.

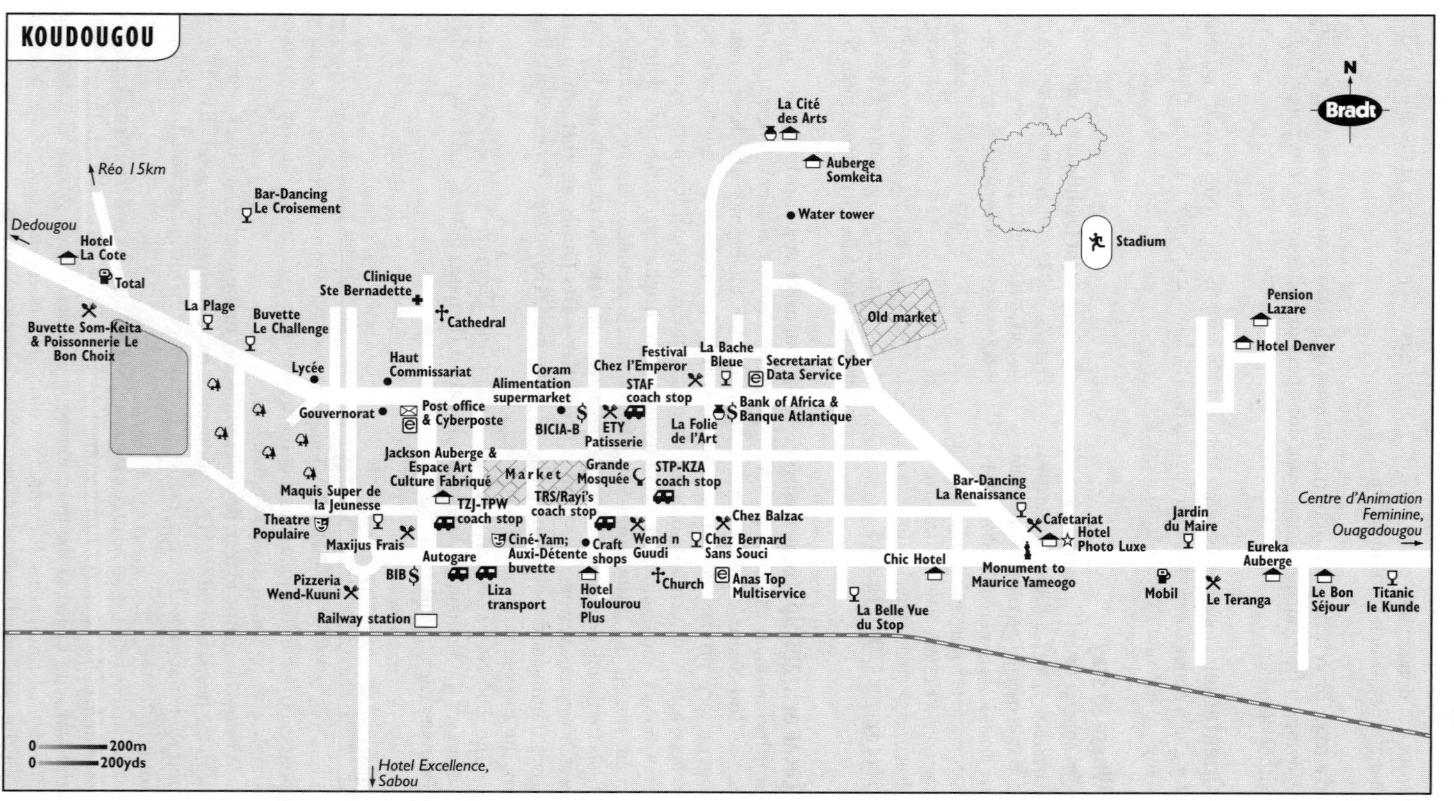
KOUDOUGOU
N
Bradt
Réo 15km
Dedougou
Hotel La Cote
Total
Buvette Som-Keita & Poissonnerie Le Bon Choix
La Plage
Bar-Dancing Le Croisement
Buvette Le Challenge
Clinique Ste Bernadette
Cathedral
Lycée
Haut Commissariat
Gouvernorat
Post office & Cyberposte
Coram Alimentation supermarket
BICIA-B
Festival Chez l'Emperor
STAF coach stop
ETY Patisserie
La Bache Bleue
Secretariat Cyber Data Service
Bank of Africa & Banque Atlantique
La Folie de l'Art
La Cité des Arts
Auberge Somkeita
Water tower
Stadium
Old market
Pension Lazare
Hotel Denver
Jackson Auberge & Espace Art Culture Fabriqué
Market
Grande Mosquée
STP-KZA coach stop
Maquis Super de la Jeunesse
TZJ-TPW coach stop
TRS/Rayi's coach stop
Theatre Populaire
Maxijus Frais
Ciné-Yam; Auxi-Détente buvette
Craft shops
Wend n Guudi
Chez Balzac
Chez Bernard Sans Souci
Autogare
BIB
Pizzeria Wend-Kuuni
Liza transport
Hotel Toulourou Plus
Church
Anas Top Multiservice
Railway station
La Belle Vue du Stop
Chic Hotel
Bar-Dancing La Renaissance
Cafetariat
Hotel Photo Luxe
Monument to Maurice Yameogo
Jardin du Maire
Mobil
Le Teranga
Eureka Auberge
Le Bon Séjour
Titanic le Kunde
Centre d'Animation Feminine, Ouagadougou
0 200m
0 200yds
Hotel Excellence, Sabou

Reflecting the political legacy of Yameogo and his son Herman, now a leading opposition politician, the town has become a hotbed of political dissent against the ruling CDP party and Blaise Compaore's government. Until recently, it was the only municipality in Burkina with a mayor who did not belong to the CDP. He was removed in the summer before presidential and municipal elections in 2005 for alleged irregularities.

His election was partly a result of the death of another of Koudougou's immortals – the investigative journalist Norbert Zongo, in 1998 (see page 31). The sense of injustice surrounding Zongo's death was palpable, expressed in numerous street marches against a government thought to be implicated. Another outspoken human rights activist and critic of the government, the Catholic priest Father Balmans, who has been living in Burkina for almost 50 years, is still based in Koudougou and publishes his regular column in the newspaper *Le Pays*.

In recent years, the town has suffered. The closure of the FasoFani cotton factory, the town's principal employer, ripped out its economic heart. President Compaore promised that FasoFani would start production again in 2006, as part of his 2005 election campaign; since then, the factory has been privatised, but has never regained its former glory.

'All the government has done for Koudougou is to shut the cotton factory,' sniffed one seasoned local.

GETTING THERE AND AWAY

By bus Several bus companies travel between Ouaga and Koudougou daily, usually taking less than two hours. Tickets cost 1,500f one-way; 2,500f return. There's a cluster of stands in central Ouaga that should serve most people's needs: Rayi's and STAF are opposite each other not far from the Hotel de Ville, STP-KZA is tucked down a side entrance to Rood Wooko market, and TZJ-TPW is just behind the *grand mosquée*. Rayi's leaves every two hours 06.00–18.00 daily, as does STP-KZA, which has an extra 20.00 service at weekends.

STAF has slightly plusher coaches for the same fares, leaving Ouaga every two hours 06.00–14.00, then at 16.30 and 18.30. TZJ-TPW leaves at 06.00 then every two hours 07.30–19.30 daily bar Sunday (it has a Protestant owner).

From Koudougou, Rayi's (☎ *50 44 08 32*) and STP-KZA are again near each other by the *grande mosquée*, STAF is up near the BICIA-B bank on the main road, and TZJ-TPW is just next to the Auberge Jackson. Departure times for Ouaga are the same in reverse, though TZJ-TPW has an extra 05.00 service on Mondays. TZJ-TPW also has a service for Bobo, via Sabou, that leaves at 08.30 Monday–Saturday (4,000f).

There are three companies that brave the piste and endless diversions on the road to Dedougou (tar road to be completed by 2013). Liza Transport's stop is near the *autogare*, while EMAF and EDBAF are near the Cine-Yam. All have departures at around 10.00 for Dedougou (2,500f). You can stop off at villages along the way (eg: Tcheriba), and Liza continues on to Nouna (4,000f).

By taxi From the *autogare*, most bush taxis leave in the morning at around 10.00. Common routes include Sabou (1,000f), Leo (2,500f), Yako (2,000f), and Ouahigouya (3,000f). Departures for Toma and Tougan leave in the afternoon.

By train From Ouaga, the train leaves at 08.30 on Tuesday, Thursday and Saturday. From Koudougou, the train leaves at around 20.00 on Wednesday, Friday and Sunday. It costs 1,500f one-way.

GETTING AROUND The town centre is relatively compact, and easily navigable on foot; for excursions further afield it is worth looking into bike or *moto* hire. The best bet is to ask at your hotel. Near the market is a stall bursting with bikes and *motos*, and Mahamadou (m *76 63 95 65*) is happy to rent them out (bicycles 1,500f a day; *motos* 5,000f).

For longer day trips and harder-going roads, hiring a car from Koudougou makes good sense. Marie Madelaine Tiendrebeogo (*50 44 16 56;* m *70 27 41 54*), who runs the women's artisanal centre, can hire out a Nevada station wagon from 30,000f per day with driver or 25,000f without, and can find other vehicles too. If the piste is heavy going, she will prefer you to take a driver who knows the road and thus how best to avoid damaging the car.

WHERE TO STAY While accommodation in central Koudougou is shrinking as more and more places are taken over for student digs, the number of hotels on the fringes is expanding at an almost alarming rate, especially at the higher end of the market. At the time of writing, a new **Hotel Splendid** was under construction on the way in from Ouaga, along with **Hotel Toulourou II**, a massive complex of about 50 bungalows that will hardly befit the term 'annexe'. Happily, there are still a couple of simpler places that stand out from the crowd.

Comfortable

Hotel Excellence (19 rooms) 50 44 02 51/59; e excellencehotel@fasonet.bf. Sister hotel to the one in Ouaga, this has everything you'd expect of a chain – all rooms (set on gloomy grey corridors) are AC with fridge, TV & Wi-Fi. Bed size determines the price, from large single to king size. A swimming pool (1,000f to non-guests) & à la carte restaurant complete the amenities. Off the dirt road to Sabou – follow the signs. **$$$$**

Chic Hotel (33 rooms) 50 44 18 56; e hotel_chic@yahoo.fr. Nothing terribly chic about this place, but en-suite AC or fan rooms have TVs, hot water, Wi-Fi & one outstanding feature: DVD players. There's a bar/restaurant out the back. **$$$–$$$$**

Hotel Toulourou Plus (24 rooms) 50 44 01 70; e sanatandr@yahoo.fr. The hotel has upgraded & expanded with a view to the upper end of the market. Pretty stone bungalows have fridge, TV, hot water & Wi-Fi. Cheaper AC rooms are smaller with TV only; 2 gloomy fan rooms with shower/loo on corridor are 8,000f. There's a pleasant courtyard, but the restaurant has gone downhill. **$$$–$$$$**

Mid range

Hotel Bon Séjour (10 rooms) 50 44 46 80. On the left on the way into town from Ouaga. Clean, although rooms in near perpetual darkness due to the high wall right outside windows. **$$–$$$**

Hotel Photo Luxe (35 rooms) 50 44 00 87/88. Unmissable as you come in from Ouaga, across the street from the bust of Burkina's first president, Maurice Yameogo, the Photo Luxe has a lively atmosphere. Fan rooms with shared indoor bathroom or en-suite AC have good mattresses & solar-heated water (you can go up & see the panels on the roof). Leopard-print divides & garish green kitchen tiles are a feature of the restaurant. **$$–$$$**

Jackson Auberge (28 rooms) 50 44 15 23; m 70 24 58 66; e jacksonhotel@hotmail.fr. An elegant terrace restaurant & swish high-ceilinged reception area front the best-value rooms in the centre of town. En-suite fan rooms are simple, but well-proportioned with mozzie nets & towels; en-suite AC rooms are a bit bigger with TVs. Excellent chef; all they need to do is fill the swimming pool. **$$–$$$**

Pension Lazare (10 rooms) 50 44 03 86. En-suite fan or AC rooms with TV in a homely setting with pretty courtyard; if you're heading this far, it's nicer than Hotel Denver round the corner. **$$–$$$**

Budget/Shoestring

Auberge Somkeita (14 rooms) 50 44 90 99. Opposite La Cité des Arts in Secteur 2. New, spotless rooms arranged around a pleasant courtyard. En-suite AC rooms have TVs; fan rooms have external loo. **$$**

Eureka Auberge (6 rooms) 50 44 22 48. Not much of a discovery; quiet, family-run place with en-suite fan or AC rooms around a scrappy courtyard. **$$**

Hotel Denver (17 rooms) 50 44 18 83. En-suite fan or AC rooms are forgettable but decent enough, & have TVs. A bit off the beaten track – you can look out for signs on the right coming from Ouaga, but the best bet is to ask. **$$**

La Cité des Arts (3 rooms) 50 44 33 35; m 70 71 66 26; e ciarco@fasonet.bf. And now for something completely different... Set on the 1st floor with balcony overlooking the centre's artisans' workshops & exhibition space are 3 delightful en-suite fan rooms, painted in white with touches of brilliant colour. Single beds only, in various combinations up to 3 per room – 5,000f if you're on your own, less for more people. There's a café serving cold drinks & meals downstairs. Bikes (1,000f), P50s (3,000f) & motorbikes (5,000f) for hire. Up behind the water tower near the Trésor Publique. **$$**

Hotel La Cote (11 rooms) m 70 11 01 78. On the road to Dedougou, this once popular place (former Esperance) has fan rooms with inside shower, outside loos. They're grotty with suspiciously crumpled sheets, but the cheapest in town. Bar & restaurant. **$**

WHERE TO EAT Koudougou throngs with great-value joints worth popping into any time of day or night.

Pizzeria Wend-Kuuni 50 44 23 00. On the 1st floor behind the Elikan garage on the Sabou road, we unfortunately spotted this just on leaving Koudougou – but the town's only pizzeria has got to be worth a shot. Locals say it's good, if pricey. $$$

Jackson Auberge 50 44 15 23. Most of the hotels have restaurants, but this is the one that stands out – not only for great food (there's an enthusiastic young Togolese chef), but also for its terrace, set just back from the street. Munch on delicious *steak au poivre* or *salade niçoise* while observing coaches roll in & the odd protesting sheep being loaded onto motorbikes. Wine list was being planned, along with cheaper local menu. $$–$$$

Chez Balzac 50 44 36 73. Doesn't get much beyond the local basics – *riz sauce*, spaghetti & so on – but the hedged garden is attractive & the service excellent. $–$$

La Teranga 50 44 16 16. A gracious bar & restaurant with Senegalese chef, set off the Ouaga road into town. Cool, quiet décor with manicured shrubs in the garden, a smooth-tiled crescent-shaped bar & white pillars. Menu sticks to local favourites. $–$$

Maxijus Frais is *the* breakfast spot in town; the hard-working young staff can barely keep up in the mornings. Open from 06.00, it serves over ten different fresh juices at rock-bottom prices (*bissap*, ginger and papaya, for example), coffee, yoghurt and sandwiches. Later on, it's a laid-back spot to quench your thirst. The **Cafetariat**, next to the Hotel Photo Luxe, can't compete but nevertheless has ice-cold yoghurt, *café au lait* and omelettes, while **ETY Patisserie** by the BICIA-B bank has croissants and *pains au chocolat*. Up on the Dedougou road opposite the Total garage, **Buvette Som-Kieta** is another coffee-and-omelette joint with **Poissonnerie Le Bon Choix** next door, a fish stall care of Madame Zongo, who buys her fish from Mauritania. **Restaurant Wend n Guudi** is a diner serving classic African dishes such as *riz gras*, *riz sauce* and the odd bit of spaghetti; this plastic-covered-table resto has barely changed its prices in ten years. If you're an ardent carnivore, **Festival Chez l'Emperor** is shrouded in roasting meat smoke from mid morning. The proprietor, the self-styled Emperor Naba Loom, who has taken his family name and called himself a chief, makes for an entertaining drinking companion. For a late-night snack, **Chez Bernard Sans Soucis**, run by the jovial, rotund Bernard for the last 30 years, also serves up street-food meat and beer. According to Bernard, that's all you need for a good time.

ENTERTAINMENT AND NIGHTLIFE Koudougou has a profusion of nightspots in a fairly small area, perfect for a bar crawl. Centrally situated on the main road, **La Bache Bleue** is a popular, trendy bar with blue lights and loud music. Head on towards Ouaga to find **Bar-Dancing La Renaissance**, which has dancing every night until late. Next stop is the bar at the **Photo Luxe**, which is much more down 'n' dirty than the hotel next door. There's also a nightclub at the weekends, with a 1,000f entry charge that ensures a well-heeled crowd. Stop off for one more Brakina at the **Jardin du Maire**, an enormous outdoor beer garden, and you may be well-oiled enough to head for the place on everyone's lips these days: the **Titanic Le Kunde**. Known just as 'Le Kunde' around town, it's the unmissable pale-yellow monolith on the left on the way in from Ouaga. Here you can strut your sandals off every night of the week; musicians sometimes play, in which case entry is 500f.

At the other end of town towards Dedougou, **Buvette Le Challenge** is a good spit-and-sawdust roadside bar; a bit further up, just before the *barrage*, you'll find the pleasant **La Plage**. Off to the right in the back streets beyond the cathedral are a number of good *maquis*, the most celebrated of which is **Bar-Dancing Le Croisement**, set in a walled garden with chicken and *brochette* sellers outside. It's well known, so you should have no problem finding it. Closer to town, the **Maquis Super de la Jeunesse** is a leafy affair near the open-air theatre. If you're feeling

BRONZE-MAKING IN FOUR EASY STAGES

Now retired, Koudougou sculptor Amadou Gandema has won national acclaim for the standard of his bronzework, and has exhibited at art fairs across west Africa and in Europe. A star of past editions of SIAO, the grand arts festival in Ouagadougou, he moved to Koudougou in 1950. Amadou's son Abdoulaye, brought up in the same mould, regularly travels to Europe to train students in the arts of bronze modelling and casting, and some artisanally minded visitors come to Burkina simply to learn in his Agamaf *atelier* (*50 44 00 48, 50 44 07 89*). Below is the Gandema family's four-stage guide to bronze.

MODELLING The artistic bit. The masterpiece-in-waiting is first fashioned from beeswax. This is soft, and relatively cheap, so changes to the form can be made quickly and easily. A host of tools and techniques are employed to work the wax into required shapes and textures, to capture the folds of a skirt flapping in the wind, for example, or tightly braided hair. If the model is large, expert model-makers hollow out the chunks of beeswax, to save on the cost of bronze.

MOULDING The wax is coated in a thin casing of clay, mixed with donkey dung to add fibrous strength. While the clay is still soft, a small hole is made in the mould, and it is left to dry in the sun for two days. A second, much thicker layer of clay mixture is added to make the mould as strong as possible. It is left for another two days. The mould is then put on top of hot coals, until the wax inside melts and runs out of the hole – sending all the artistry of the beeswax moulder into a liquid mess.

adventurous (or reckless, some locals would say), head for **La Belle Vue du Stop** near the railway, where the rows of bottled spirits are reflected in the glittering eyes of its clients.

OTHER PRACTICALITIES The **post office** has a Western Union money-transfer point and its **cyberposte** is the biggest internet centre in town. There are at least two other internet centres – **Anas Top Multiservice** on the road to the train station, and **Secretariat Cyber Data Service** near La Bache Bleue. All charge 250f an hour.

There's the usual profusion of banks: **BIB**, **BICIA-B** and **Bank of Africa** all have Visa cash machines, while **Banque Atlantique** has a MasterCard/Maestro facility. Most will change euros; Banque Atlantique will change US dollars too.

SHOPPING Opened in June 2005, Koudougou's permanent red-brick and turquoise-doored **market** is a joy to behold and wander around. Built with Swiss co-operation, it claims to be the best market in Burkina. It's certainly the Covent Garden of the country. Clean and with fewer flies than you are likely to see anywhere else, there are separate areas for meat, fruit and veg, and small boutiques selling African-print materials (*pagnes* of bright cotton imported from Nigeria sell for 1,500f or 2,500f depending on quality), indigo cloth, shoes, handbags, kids' clothes, books and much else. Women in colourful headscarves sit over their tomatoes with their straw-woven fly swats to the ready. Children weave in and out of the crowd with trays of delicious freshly made ciabatta-style loaves for 100f.

Coram Alimentation Supermarket, next door to BICIA-B bank, is a good place to stock up if you are planning a trip into the bush.

CASTING Bronze, an alloy of copper and zinc combined in a 3:1 ratio, is made in a homemade foundry. A hole in the ground with a ceramic pot set inside acts as a furnace. The copper comes from old telephone wires; the zinc comes from the engines of old mopeds. An old fan from the bowels of a car or motorbike acts as a set of bellows to pump air into the bottom of the furnace, and it is connected to a bicycle wheel by a rubber fan-belt. Turning the wheel by hand keeps the temperature up. If the model is to have a darker, non-shiny appearance, a mixture of nitric acid or permanganate and shoe polish is added to prevent oxidisation taking place. The liquid bronze is then poured into the baked clay mould, already hot from resting in a wood fire to ensure the bronze does not cool too quickly. Once filled, the mould is left for two to ten hours, depending on size.

POLISHING The moment of truth arrives with the cracking open of the mould, sending shards of clay across the *atelier*. The bronze figure inside has a rough, pock-marked appearance and the recesses often contain clay, which is scooped out from the innards of the statue. Polishing takes place, to smooth surfaces and shine the metal.

SEEING IS BELIEVING While the theory is interesting, seeing the process in practice takes the breath away. The Koudougou *atelier* receives visitors at any time, and watching a casting session is probably the most dramatic part of the process. Browse the fruits of the red-hot labour at the on-site shop. A selection of bronze animals, figures and candlestick holders comes in a range of sizes and prices and gentle bartering is possible.

Craft boutiques and workshops

Centre d'Animation Feminine (CAF) (*☏ 50 44 16 56; e centrecaf@yahoo.fr*) Trains young women, for free, in arts such as embroidery, batik and soap-making. You can visit and see the women at work – dyeing materials and sewing napkins and tablecloths – and buy at the end. There are about 50 students every year, who are also educated in hygiene, birth control and a spot of business acumen. It was started in 2000 to help girls whose parents could not afford to send them to school. It's off the Ouaga road – look for the CAF sign on the left as you head out of town.

La Cité des Arts (*Secteur 2; ☏ 50 44 33 35; m 70 71 66 26; e ciarco@fasonet.bf*) With its stylish exhibition space, spacious *ateliers* where you can watch artisans at work, a pretty café and tranquil setting, this is a real find. The gallery has bronzes, jewellery, batiks and carvings, all made on site. You can also stay here (see *Where to stay*, page 261). It's up beyond the water tower near the Trésor Publique.

Espace Art Culture Fabriqué (*☏ 50 44 07 89*) A tiny, fashionable boutique, the legacy of one of Koudougou's most famous artisans, bronze-worker Amadou Gandema. His sons regularly give demonstrations in Europe, and have a stand in Ouaga's Village Artisanal. The shop is packed full of bronzes, gleaming gold or weathered black. A small piece, around 12cm high, may set you back 3,500f, while larger pieces go for 17,500f. The friendly owner, Ousmane, can direct you to the family's well-hidden *atelier* (see box, pages 262–3). Another *atelier* worth looking out for is Ousmane Derme's bronze stall opposite the Total station and the Hotel La Cote.

La Folie de L'Art (*m 78 86 23 62; e anolart@yahoo.fr*) Opposite La Bache Bleue are a few craft shops. This one is more of a gallery, run by a young artist from Cameroon, Anolel Pemu, who came to Burkina for its thriving arts scene. There's a lot of life and humour in his work, and he certainly likes to make a statement. He also sells more traditional paintings by local artists – small village scenes start at about 2,500f.

Across the tarmac road from Hotel Toulourou are three great craft shops, crammed full from top to toe. The first belongs to a bronze-worker, Gandema Bourreima, who trains others in the art and sells his work here along with a wide range of masks and other crafts. Next is **Africa Art** (*⌚ Sat–Thu*), with a Senegalese patron, Assane Diall. Simple and stylish leather satchels go for 12,000–15,000f; he also has a range of necklaces from Ghana and Nigeria. Next up is **Bienvenue Aux Beaux Arts**, selling a vast range of *djembes*, hats, bags and satchels, statues, batiks and fabrics; also Tuareg jewellery and *bogolan* cloths from Mali.

Secteur 1 is the place to go to see leatherworkers in full swing and any of these shops can provide directions.

WHAT TO SEE AND DO

Annual festival Koudougou's most famous attraction is also its most fleeting. Les Nuits Atypiques de Koudougou (NAK) is an annual five-day cultural extravaganza, usually held at the end of November. It is Burkina's equivalent of the Edinburgh Festival, showcasing musicians, traditional and modern dance, street theatre, and clowns from Africa and Europe. Organised by a local association, Benebnooma, NAK takes place in a specially constructed complex on the outskirts of town, and performances are complemented by demonstrations from local artisans of their trades, and a circus of temporary restaurants and *buvettes*. Contact Koala Koudbi (*☏ 50 44 03 87/9; e sud.sud@fasonet.bf*) for more information.

Screenings Koudougou's open-air cinema, the **Ciné-Yam**, rarely manages to get hold of film prints these days, but can give you your very own private screening if you negotiate, or supply them with a DVD. Otherwise it will show international football matches on the big screen (100f entry fee for an African game, 150f if it's an international). Next door is the **Auxi Détente Buvette**, hooked up to satellite for avid sports fans. The cinema is run down, but has all the hallmarks of a great night out – disco lights on the ceiling, rows of chairs facing the white-painted wall of a screen and the romance of outdoor movie-going.

Theatre At the **Theatre Populaire** there are open-air concrete pews with stacked seating on three sides. There is no programme of shows, but if a local or touring company is putting on a show while you're there it is well worth a visit. There's sometimes dancing here too – ask locally what's going on.

AROUND KOUDOUGOU

Villages around Koudougou occupy a fertile and pretty part of the country, and offer a window on the realities and activities of farming life that unites most of Burkina. These are best explored on the back of a *moto*, heading west on the unpaved route to Dedougou, and stopping off at any points of interest along the way. Villages hidden from the road are not used to foreign visitors, but with tentative enquiries, you may find yourself led towards a *zaka* (Mossi courtyard), sitting cross-legged sharing a salutary beaker of water with a family, or peering into a granary to consider millet stocks for the year ahead.

A conversation asking for directions can turn into a guided tour of a village, given by someone who would not dream of asking for money. It may be an idea, however, to stock up on kola nuts in Koudougou before setting off, as an appropriate show of thanks to anyone who helps out along the way.

GOUNDI In the early evening, the approach to Goundi, 8km southwest of Koudougou, is swathed in soft, warm yellows and greens, the light reflected in the still waters of its lake, and warmed by a terracotta strand of dirt track passing beneath palm-fronded arches. It is a beautiful introduction to the village, which is celebrated for its pottery. Beneath towering tree trunks that line the route through the village, local women sell onions, guavas and *liannes* (custard apples). The market, after the reservoir, is the best place to look for *canaris*, the all-purpose round terracotta containers. There is also a traditional dance troupe that regularly puts on performances at the Maison des Jeunes.

ZOULA A dirt path on the right, just before Goundi market if you are entering from Koudougou, leads to the village of Zoula, set a few kilometres further back. Here, compounds are more widely spaced, and women also make pottery. During the planting season (when the rains come at the start of July), the craft suffers, because of the need to be out in the fields, although as often as quantities of clay arrive, the bright-eyed women of the village can be seen making and firing *canaris* in their kilns. The village's market is held every two days, where *canaris* can be bought for 700–1,000f.

TCHERIBA This village, 78km west of Koudougou on the way to Dedougou, is a dedicated potting site, where activities continue all year round, no matter what the rain is doing. It is possible to see daily displays of pottery work, and to purchase the results. Tcheriba is known for its distinctive architecture, which eschews customary mud-brick dwellings for pretty, painted houses in a *banco* style built on different levels. You will also see an extraordinary number of granaries. This is because crops are stored before threshing and winnowing here, and therefore take up more room.

DEDOUGOU

A further 49km west of Tcheriba, Dedougou is the capital of Mouhoun province, and with the completion of the fast tar road from Bobo it's on the up and up. Residents already talk casually about popping down to Bobo for the day (the journey now takes less than two hours); when the tar road from Ouaga and Koudougou is also completed (scheduled for 2013), this sleepy town of wide streets and low single-storey brown clay dwellings will really come to life. Look out for grain silos and the royal palace, combining *banco* from 1910 with modern stone cutouts. A meeting place of many cultures – Fulani, Marka, Samo, Mossi and Bwaba – the town's biennial mask festival, Festima, is well worth a visit.

GETTING THERE AND AWAY The town is most easily accessed from Bobo along the new tar road, which has attracted the sleek air-conditioned coaches of TSR (*20 97 70 40*) – much the best option. Departures are at 08.00 and 16.00 (3,000f). Fasowcar also plies the route, leaving at 09.00 (3,000f) and continuing on to Tougan (4,000f). From Dedougou back to Bobo, TSR leaves at 07.30 and 15.00; and Fasowcar leaves at 10.00.

Until the tar is completed, the dirt road from Ouaga beyond Koudougou is somewhat of a trial, and the trip can easily take six hours barring breakdowns. If you don't want to change coaches in Koudougou, LTI, also known as Liza, is your best bet, with an 08.00 daily departure from Ouaga. It passes through Koudougou and Dedougou, and carries on to Nouna. Tickets cost 4,000f. On the way back, Liza passes through from Nouna at about 09.00. EMAF and EDBAF are companies that you can find in the *autogare*, with departures for Ouaga at 08.00 daily.

Djigouya Magna (TDM) has a fleet of small coaches and minibuses that run the Bobo–Ouahigouya route, stopping in Dedougou and Tougan. There are two departures, passing through Dedougou at roughly 12.00 and 16.00 daily in either direction (tickets for both Bobo and Ouahigouya 3,000f).

WHERE TO STAY

Mid range

Hotel Diarra (24 rooms) 20 52 01 48. On the right as you come in from Ouaga. Pleasant atmosphere with restaurant under shady *paillotes*; en-suite AC rooms are fine, but unremarkable. There are a couple of en-suite fan rooms at 7,700f. **$$$**

Hotel Zind-Naaba (23 rooms) 20 52 12 42. A new, elegant establishment between the Ouaga & Bobo roundabouts with swimming pool, restaurant & on-site nightclub. Comfortable en-suite AC rooms are finished to a much higher standard & in better taste than often seen at this level, & are excellent value. Plain pastel linens & – gasp! – duvets. Swimming pool 2,000f to non-guests. **$$$**

Hotel Loba (28 rooms) 20 52 06 48. On the right coming in from Bobo. Lovely shady courtyards & attractive old tiling give this place some character; 1st-floor rooms are off a pretty balcony corridor. There are a few great-value en-suite fan rooms (large single bed) at 4,000f. At the time of writing, Hotel Loba was also constructing a massive annexe of the sort springing up all over the country, with oversized rooms and suites around a swimming pool and restaurant complex. **$$–$$$**

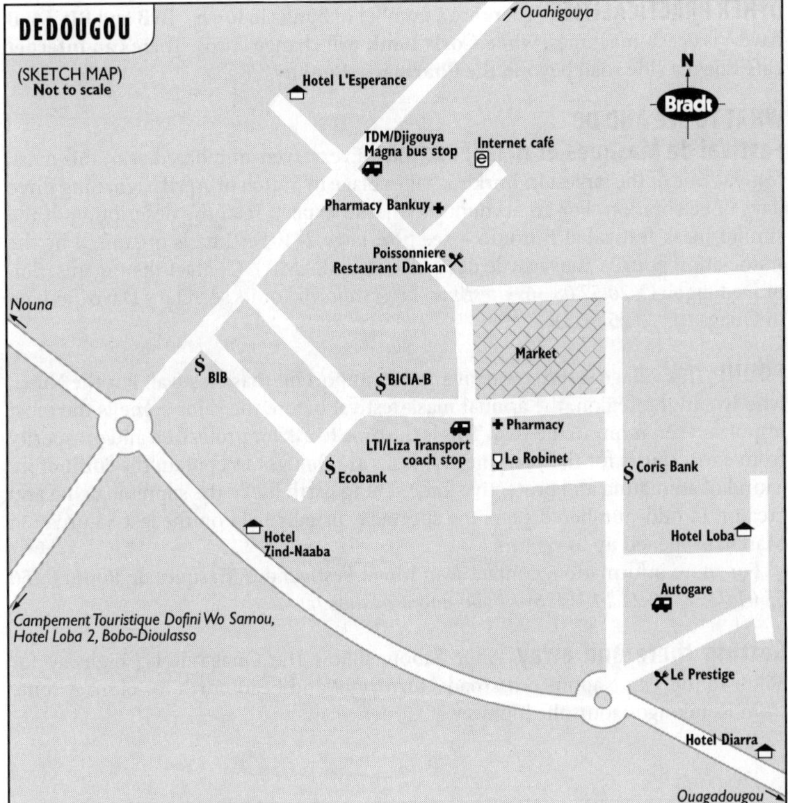

Budget/Shoestring

Campement Touristique Dofini Wo Samou (14 rooms) 20 52 24 90. Set in extensive gardens about 4km out of town on the Bobo road, run by a friendly German/Burkinabe couple. Neat en-suite bungalows with – unfortunately – tin roofs, have mozzie nets & towels; electricity for fans on the way. Restaurant area has pretty *paillotes*. **$$**

Hotel L'Esperance (6 rooms) 20 52 03 15. Good-value en-suite fan rooms will soon be joined by a couple of AC options & a restaurant. Helpful staff. **$**

The **Centre Spiritual** mission is 5km before Dedougou on the road from Ouaga. Opened by French nuns, it is marked by a modest stone cross and small board at the entrance. The beautifully kept compound offers solitude and peaceful contemplation, and an attractive church with stained-glass windows. Rooms are simple and spotless, and the sisterhood can also prepare excellent fresh meals.

WHERE TO EAT AND DRINK **Restaurant Le Prestige** is one of the best in town, serving salads and omelettes as well as the usual dishes. **Poissoniere Restaurant Dankan** is another good option, dishing up a lot more than fish. There's a profusion of street food come nightfall, when the place to be until late is *maquis* **Le Robinet**, near Liza Transport: it's packed every night. There's a nightclub at the **Hotel Zind-Naaba** at the weekends (entry 1,000f), but nobody goes.

OTHER PRACTICALITIES There are a number of **banks** in town – **BIB** and **BICIA-B** have Visa cash machines, while **Coris Bank** will change euros. There's an **internet café** down a side road beyond the **Pharmacie Bankuy**.

WHAT TO SEE AND DO

Festival de Masques et Arts (Festima) Every even-numbered year, this mask festival, one of the largest in Burkina, takes place in March or April, signalling three days of celebration. For an account of what to expect, read the description of the similar mask festival at Boromo – see box, page 271. Festima is organised by the Association pour la Sauvegarde des Masques (ASAMA). Contact the organisation in Dedougou (*20 52 08 36; e festima_org@yahoo.fr*) or its secretary Dayo Tankien in Ouaga (*m 70 25 07 31*).

POUNI This village is the centre of another important mask festival. For the Nuna, who live in the region, the annual mask festival before the rains come is the most important ceremony of the year. This is the time to ask for protection and prosperity from earth spirits for the year ahead. Masks are thought to contain the spirit of *su*, a kind of animating and protective force sent to earth by Yi, the supreme being and creator. In odd-numbered years the spectacle, usually held on the last Saturday in March, is opened up to visitors.

For more information, contact Jean Ido at Festival des Masques de Pouni (*50 35 01 73; m 70 24 14 16/26; e babouidojp@yahoo.fr*).

Getting there and away After Sabou, follow the Ouaga–Bobo highway for 36km to the Tita Napone crossroads, turn right and head north for 6km. A route from Koudougou joins the highway at Gode.

BOROMO

Halfway between the two major cities of Ouaga and Bobo, Boromo has the feel of a frontier town. It is home to one of the smallest ethnic groups in Burkina – the Winye. With some interesting places to stay, talented artisans, nearby Winye villages and the Deux Bales Forest, it is well worth a stopover. Every March a mask festival, Ferimason, takes place at Boromo and three other villages in a four-day extravaganza (see box, page 271).

GETTING THERE AND AWAY

By bus All the major bus companies operating a Ouaga–Bobo service stop in Boromo. One-way tickets are generally 3,000f from either direction with air conditioning, or 2,500f without.

TCV offers the best service – often fully booked, so buy beforehand if you can. Its air-conditioned coaches stop only at Boromo and leave either Ouaga or Bobo at 07.30, 09.00, 10.00, 12.00, 14.00, 15.00, 18.30 and 23.00. Add roughly two hours to this to get the onward times from Boromo. Rakieta (*m 70 52 43 51, 78 00 03 34*) is also pretty good with air-conditioned, non-stop services at 07.00, 10.30, 14.00, 18.30 and 22.45 from Ouaga or Bobo. There are umpteen other stopping services: TSR (*m 70 14 86 11*) has no fewer than 12 departures, three of which are air conditioned; STAF has seven; Sogebaf has five. In short, you won't get stuck in Boromo.

You can also find onward travel to Diebougou (2,500f), Gaoua (3,000f) and Kampti (4,000f) with TSR and STAF (three departures each every day; usually it's only the last one that continues to Kampti), and Koudougou (2,500f) with SPT/KZA.

By taxi The busy coach station also doubles as the bush taxi stop.

WHERE TO STAY

Mid range

Le Relais Touristique (8 rooms) 20 53 80 84. Long established & well looked after, with a choice of clean en-suite AC & fan rooms all with TV; fan rooms a bit overpriced, however. The restaurant is a good bet, & has a wine list (if in festive mood, bottles of Moët are 19,500f). It's on the main drag, about 5mins' walk from the coach stop towards Bobo. **$$$**

Auberge Touristique Belba (10 rooms) m 76 61 31 01; e mkinda@hotmail.com. A delightful cacophony of architectural styles is on show inside the compound's courtyard: an AC 'mini villa' as well as a variety of thatched fan huts with internal or external facilities. On the right just as you come into town from Ouaga. **$$–$$$**

Shoestring

La Voute Nubienne (10 rooms) m 76 04 67 41; www.lavoutenubienne.org. The name comes from the historical/architectural term for building vaulted roofs with nothing but adobe or stone (see box, page 191). This is a training centre for masons in the technique, as well as a lovely *auberge*. The simple vaulted rooms, painted blue, are wonderfully cool. 2 rooms have winding stairs to an upstairs bedroom & terrace with bucket shower downstairs (otherwise it's outside bucket showers & drop loos). Staff can also organise visits to sculptors & puppeteers, or invite *griots* to perform for groups. Nice little bar; meals & breakfast available. Down a road opposite Le Relais Touristique, clearly signposted. **$**

Sama Camp (17 rooms) m 78 89 37 94, 76 08 25 26; www.samacamp.com. Has taken the ideas of La Voute Nubienne & turned them into an exquisite camp; none of the training-centre buzz, but beautifully done in a peaceful setting. Simple adobe huts & rooms have bamboo beds & mozzie nets with outside bucket showers & drop loos. The best room is on the 1st floor with its own terrace & views over surrounding countryside. About 15mins from the coach station (coming from Ouaga, turn right just before it), near École C; best to ask along the way. Meals 3,000f. **$**

WHERE TO EAT AND DRINK The *maquis*-restaurant **La Grace** is a nice eatery with a shady *paillote*, serving up all the usuals – *riz sauce*, couscous – and chicken for 2,000f. For anything beyond the norm, head for the restaurant at Le Relais Touristique. Just opposite there's a whole row of lively looking *maquis*, including **Club de la Foi** and the **Maquis la Solution**. The latter is the place that gets kicking come Saturday night.

OTHER PRACTICALITIES There's an **internet centre** not far from the coach station that charges 500f an hour. There are no bank branches.

AROUND BOROMO

WINYE TOWNS One of Burkina's smaller ethnic groups, about 30,000 Winye live in 19 villages on the western side of the Mouhoun River near Boromo. The sphere of influence extends to a dozen neighboring Bwa, Marka and Nuni villages with whom the Winye maintain economic, ritual and matrimonial ties. They farm millet, maize, rice, peanuts, green beans and more recently, cotton.

The area was first settled towards the end of the 18th century by several ethnic groups (mainly Gourounsi, Nuni, Sisala and Phuo, but also some Dagara, Bwa, Marka and Fulbe). Immigrants mixed with these people to form a new group known as the Winye, whose language bears the same name. They are known as Ko by the Mossi.

In the 19th century, a Marka merchant who wanted to seize the area for its importance as a trade route between Ashanti and the Songhay Empire conducted a *jihad* against the Winye. As a result, they are understandably resistant to Islam, and have preserved the old animist traditions well.

The Winye are typical of the kind of village societies prevalent throughout western Burkina Faso. Society is organised into classes, such as diviners, mask-makers, blacksmiths and *griots*. Initially, because of years of intermarriage and the fact that Winye society was not casted, the tradition of mask-making died out. Skilled Bwaba mask-makers from the west were assimilated into Winye society to carry out this vital function, leading to the development of castes. Mask-makers are not allowed to marry the children of those who cultivate the land, only fellow blacksmiths and *griots* (or their female children).

Ouroubono, 5km southwest, is a kind of spiritual home to the Winye. The pretty village, situated on the edge of a lake of sacred crocodiles, makes a lovely sunset visit. Unlike at Bazoule and Sabou, there are no chickens or guides to pay to entice the crocs out of the water, although you may be able to see them on their way into the water in the morning, or at around 16.00 for a quick sunbathe before returning to the muddy confines for the night. The dirt track to Ouroubono starts just after Boromo's Relais Touristique hotel. Check with the village elders that it is OK to visit before you do so.

The forge at **Ouri** is extensive, mostly working iron. Under cover, it has a subterranean feel about it, and the furnaces generate a fierce heat while young blacksmiths hammer and temper tools and ritual artefacts.

DEUX BALE FOREST (*entry 5,000f, plus 5,000f for an obligatory guide*) A few kilometres south of Boromo, this little-visited park is a worthy stopping point for anyone trying to squeeze in wildlife between Ouaga and Bobo.

Deux Bale is the smallest of Burkina's national reserves, and easily accessible. Its big draw is the chance of seeing elephant. At last count there were 99, and although some of them have since been moved to other parks, three large herds still roam its 81,000ha and are regular visitors to the creeks and banks of the Mouhoun, which flows through the park. The reserve also boasts roan antelope, bushbuck, grey duiker, oribi, jackal, warthog, monkey, baboon and a host of birdlife.

Floods washed away Kaïcedra camp in 2007 (see below), but if you have wheels you should still be able to enter the park. The office is on the Kaïcedra track.

Where to stay

Kaïcedra (8 huts) m 76 62 65 40, 76 65 40 69, 70 74 46 06. The setting of this camp is delightful, alongside the murky, slow-moving waters of the Mouhoun, making it perfect for a close encounter with African elephants. After being washed away by floods in 2007, however, the new camp – of solid concrete huts rather than mud ones – has been beset with problems; when we passed through it was just due to open, but when we called back, it hadn't; the new owners were still awaiting a water supply. For now, there's a glorious *paillote* right on the river itself, which will form the restaurant; the en-suite 2-bedroom huts remain unfinished. There's nothing to stop you visiting the site, though you will be asked for 3,000f entry if there's anyone around (this will be waived for diners & guests once the camp's up & running). A picnic is a splendid idea, & you can also camp. Alternatively, call ahead to check on progress. There's a sign for the camp in Boromo (on the left if you are coming from Ouagadougou). It's along an indistinct & winding dirt track that goes on for a good couple of kilometres further than the 7km the sign

WHIRLING WINYE

Covered from top to toe in raffia outfits, crowned with colourful headdresses that flash teeth and horns, the acrobatic twists, turns and jumps of the dancers at Winye's annual mask festival are an unforgettable sight.

The four-day Ferimason festival tours Boromo and the outlying villages of Siby, Ouri and Oulo starting every morning with the entry of a masked procession into town from the bush, to a cacophony of drums, and short whistles (*sifles*). Once installed in the centre of town, the dancing begins.

The movement is frenzied and heart-pounding and just watching can send you into a state of emotional exhaustion. Troupes from each village come forward to do battle and win the respect of the elders, as *griots* with hourglass drums slung over their shoulders beat maniacally with curved wooden sticks.

Each mask requires a different style of dancing: the crocodile stays close to the ground, with a selection of slinky, languorous shakes and shimmers, all exuding menace; the hyena, its mask locked into an eternal grin, moves in clumsy stops and starts; the monkey fools and prances.

Each dancer is accompanied by an older cohort, who serves as a cross between a boxing trainer, to gee them up, and a schoolma'am, to ensure their moves don't get out of hand. Part of the mentor's role is to ensure that the style of dancing remains correct – it would not do for the buffalo to start dancing like the antelope – and that the dancers do not get too carried away with the moment to forget the animal form they have taken on.

It's not for show. Only certain family lines within the group may wear masks, such as the relatives of diviners, and priests of earth, hunting and war, and for the young men dancing their hearts out in heavy outfits, it is a great honour.

For more information on the Ferimason festival (Festival des Art et des Masques du Son), organised by Action Culturel de Son, contact Issouf Yao (m 76 61 92 05; e yissouf@yahoo.fr).

suggests, so persevere. If you're in any doubt, ask at the police post, or the Total garage in Boromo; if you don't have wheels, you can arrange a ride by moto in town, which should not cost more than 3,000f, plus a litre or so of fuel.

SAFANE If you're grabbed by the adobe architecture bug, you can stay in another example of the all-mud *voute nubienne* building style in the town of Safane, on the road heading north from Boromo to Dedougou. Like its sister *auberge* in Boromo, **Relais de la Colline** (*20 53 78 65*) is all arches and blue-and-white walls.

OUAHABOU It may not look much now, but Ouahabou was the centre of an important Muslim city-state. Mamadou Karanto, originally from Djenne, met the revered Muslim leader Mohamed Ibn Abd El Wahab on a pilgrimage to Mecca, and became a convert to his *wahabi* doctrine. He resolved to create a *wahabi* state (hence Ouahabou) to eclipse the rival Guiriko state (see page 273) for influence and power. He set up at Boromo in 1850, and with the help of his Marka, Mossi and Dioula soldiers embarked on a holy crusade, subjugating the indigenous Winye population and annexing Bwaba territory to the north.

His son, Karamokho Moktar, attempted to extend the territory with forays south into Lobi and Dagara country, but was defeated at the 1887 battle of Djinderme.

The following year, Moktar welcomed the French explorer Captain Binger to Ouahabou. The Frenchman decided that 'this holy man seems to be a downright scoundrel'. Ten years later, Moktar was defeated by the French, with whom he had signed a treaty of protection.

The impressive mosque that still stands in Ouahabou is a handsome example of Sudanese mud-brick architecture, and a testament to this abortive attempt at a *wahabi* empire.

Getting there and away Ouahabou is on the Ouaga–Bobo road, 20km west from Boromo. Coach tickets cost 2,500–4,000f and are available from coach companies on the Ouaga–Bobo route (but not from TCV or Rakieta, which don't stop here).

BONI The small village of Boni, 16km before Hounde, is nestled beneath a large steeply rising hill, and its shaded streets make for a pleasant half a day's exploring. It is home to mask-maker Bonde Yacouba (*20 99 06 53; m 76 61 43 89*), coming from a long line of master craftsmen, who runs an *atelier* and has travelled worldwide to practise and teach his craft. He also made the fantastic mask that forms the entrance to Boni's Catholic church. If you want the real thing without encouraging people to plunder their lofts, you can order a mask from him. A small mask (from 15,000f) takes three to four days; a large mask one to two weeks.

Getting there and away Stopping-service coaches on the Ouaga–Bobo run can also stop at Boni; Ouaga–Boni one-way tickets are 4,000f.

HOUNDE Around two-thirds of the way to Bobo from Ouaga is the sleepy town of Hounde, in the heart of Bwaba country. Each year after harvest time (usually February–March), the town is transformed by its mask festival, famous throughout Burkina, which brings together dancers who tour local settlements on Hounde's market day, every five days, for up to a month. They dance in the coolest parts of the day, 08.00–10.00 and 16.00–18.00.

Getting there and away Coach companies serving the Ouaga–Bobo route – STMB and TSR among others – stop at Hounde. Tickets are generally 4,000f from Ouaga. The *gare routière* is at the Bobo end of town.

Where to stay

Auberge La Colline (5 rooms) 20 99 01 98. The nicest place is happily the cheapest. On the right after entering Hounde, these traditional *rondavels* are squashed into a quiet courtyard & have an authentic feel. Soft mattresses, mosquito nets & straw roofs with open eaves keep the heat out & provide a decent night's sleep. **$**

Auberge Provinciale de Tuy (7 rooms) 20 99 06 03. One of the town's most popular bars, it is unlikely to provide much peace & quiet. The rooms do at least have standing fans to counter the furnace effect of corrugated roofing. Internal showers, outside loos. Turn right just after the Total station and it is on the left after a couple of minutes' walk. **$**

Upapa-Tuy (10 rooms) 20 97 62 19. This Burkinabe–Luxembourg project to promote literacy also has rooms to rent, on the Bobo side of town just before the coach stop. Basic rooms in well-kept grounds, with fans, mosquito nets & showers but external toilet block. **$**

Where to eat and drink The popular **Auberge Provinciale de Tuy** is a much better lunch or nightspot than stay, with good dishes, plenty of cold beer and a pleasant, bustling courtyard. **Restaurant Retrouvaille**, with its jaunty *paillote*, is not far before the coach stop on the main road – the painted guitars, horns and Castel beer signs betray a lively night-time hangout. Just next door to Upapa-Tuy is **Le Rendezvous** with a good menu and a nightclub on Friday and Saturday nights. **Maquis du 3me Millénaire**, almost opposite the Total station at the Ouaga end of town, has garden seating at the back, while **Le Cercle des Amis** on the other side of the road is a good breakfast spot. Just after the coach stop on the left is the **Kiosque Delwende**, with fruit stalls, meat grills and plants outside.

Other practicalities There's a **cyberposte** at the **post office** (500f per hour), and **Cyber Net Solution** opposite the **Total** bank (400f per hour). The **BIB** bank has a Visa cash machine, which is apparently temperamental.

KOUMBIA Just 65km from Bobo there's the option of a village retreat. Take a turning in Koumbia (on the main Ouaga–Bobo road), for the village of Gombele-Dougou about 8km away. Here, a little *campement* lies hidden. **Le Relais du Bouamou** (*20 99 46 20, 20 99 06 57; e romainkani@yahoo.fr;* **$$**), set up by two Frenchmen, has six huts with internal facilities in a rural setting (no electricity). We heard of it too late to visit, but those who've been say it's a tranquil, restful place.

BOBO-DIOULASSO

If you have the time for only a few days in the country, it may make sense to base your stay in Burkina's second city, which is both a great hangout in its own right and within easy reach of a variety of trips. Burkina's live-music capital is a joy for travellers, and much easier to get a feel for than the larger, busier neighbourhoods of Ouaga. The lush landscape brings sweet relief from the arid climate of the central plateau and there are easy links to Mali and Ghana. Because of this, the town has more of an ostentatiously backpacker's feel than other parts of the country and a great range of cheapish accommodation. Correspondingly, there is likely to be a profusion of guides offering their services.

HISTORY OF THE WEST The strategic and economic attractions of Bobo-Dioulasso (meaning 'house of the Bobo and Dioula', after the peoples who settled in the 15th century) have placed it in various tugs-of-war between the competing powers in the region.

For much of the 19th century, it was hotly contested by two opposing families. Famara Ouattara, a prince of the Kong dynasty, established the Kingdom of Guiriko around 1714 with Bobo-Dioulasso as his headquarters. One hundred years later, the Kenedougou state based at Sikasso emerged as a rival and greatly coveted Bobo-Dioulasso. Kenedougou supported the Bobo-Dioula in an unsuccessful revolt against the authority of Guiriko but was decisively defeated by the Guiriko prince Bako-Morou (1839–51) in 1840.

The rivalry resurfaced under the reign of Tieba, Kenedougou's most powerful king, who had managed to repulse even Samory Toure from a grand siege of Sikasso. Wanting to capitalise on what he saw as a weakening Guiriko state, he launched forays into the west and southwest of Burkina, basing himself near Tengrela. After defeating the local chief in the Orodara area, by the end of 1892 he marched on Bobo-Dioulasso, determined to prise the city from Guiriko's control.

Faced with an unprecedented threat, the Guiriko Empire managed to rally the vassal armies under its control for one final struggle. Tieba was defeated and killed in a battle at Bama, about 30km north of Bobo-Dioulasso. Tieba's son, Babemba, returned in 1893 and 1896, but was seen off by spirited resistance from the Turka and other indigenous groups around Banfora. Babemba committed suicide with the fall of Sikasso to the French in 1898, signalling the end of the Kenedougou state.

The Malinke chief Samory Toure also had designs on Bobo-Dioulasso, but a column of his soldiers, led by his son Sarantye Mori, was fought off by Ghana-based British troops in 1896. The column continued to wreak havoc in the region, capturing the powerful Kong Kingdom in 1897. By now Toure was enemy number

COACHES TO AND FROM BOBO

All the principal coach companies, and some complete unknowns, operate numerous daily services from Bobo. Along the Boulevard de la Revolution, interspersed with more useful coach parks, are a plethora of small companies that run down into Côte d'Ivoire – **STIF, SAMA, Molo-Molo, TN Transport, ZST, CTI** and **STN** have services to Bouake; some go on to Abidjan and San Pedro. With unrest ongoing in the country, however, at the time of writing they had mostly been suspended.

FASOWCAR (m *76 79 15 26*) runs to Tougan (4,000f) from Bobo's SONEF garage, via Dedougou (3,000f) and Satiri (1,000f), at 09.00 daily.

RAKIETA (m *20 97 18 91*) has one of only two stations in the centre of town (the other being TCV). An excellent air-conditioned express service to Ouaga leaves at 07.30, 10.30, 14.00, 18.30 and 22.45; times are the same in reverse. Tickets cost 6,000f single, 11,000f return. Departures for Banfora (1,300f single/2,300f return) go at 07.00, 08.00, 10.15, 12.00, 13.00, 14.00, 15.00, 16.00, 17.00, 18.00 and 19.30, with an extra 06.00 service on Sundays. There is also a departure for Hamale, on the Ghanaian border (4,500f) at 14.30, Niangoloko (2,000f) at 07.00, 12.00 and 16.00, Bamako (9,000f) at 06.15 and Bouake (11,000f) at 06.00.

RIMBO (m *75 12 17 43*) runs to Niamey at 17.30 daily (15,000f), but it is best to pick it up in Ouaga. There's also a service to Bamako (10,000f) via Segou (7,000f) at 18.00 daily, and a connecting service to Dakar, Senegal (35,000f).

SKV INTERNATIONAL (*20 98 05 85*) has a twice-daily Ouaga service, at 15.30 and 22.45. It runs to Bamako at 06.00 on Thursday and Sunday (10,000f), via Segou (7,000f); Niamey at 22.45 on Tuesday and Saturday (15,000f); Kumasi, Lome (20,000f) and Cotonou (22,000f) at 22.00 on Saturday. Note that all bar Bamako involve a three-hour wait in Ouaga, so it may be better to pick up the services there instead.

SOGEBAF (*20 96 69 52*) is no longer recommended. Some buses are still running, but the company is slowly winding down.

SONEF (m *78 62 33 34, 74 20 52 88*) is a regional specialist. A coach leaves at 18.00 daily for Niamey (15,000f), going on to Agadez (29,000f) – it is better picked up in Ouaga, as there's a delay in the capital. Another 18.00 daily coach leaves for Bamako (10,000f) via Segou (8,000f), and has connections for Mopti (7,500f), Douenza (11,000f) and Gao (17,000f). There are also connections for Dakar, Senegal (35,000f), Nouakchott, Mauritania (35,000f), and Nouadhibou, Mauritania (40,000f).

one for the colonial powers, who considered his empire-building exploits a constant thorn in their side. In the face of a French and British advance on Bobo-Dioulasso, Samory was forced to retreat to Côte d'Ivoire, where he was later captured by the French and deported to Gabon.

Meanwhile, for the Guiriko state, keeping hold of Bobo-Dioulasso proved a pyrrhic victory. Weakened by a century of debilitating conflicts, Guiriko signed a treaty of protection with the French in 1897.

STAF (*20 98 51 19*) runs to Ouaga at 07.00, 09.00, 10.30, 13.00, 15.30, 18.00 and 22.00 (5,000f – no air conditioning). Times from Ouaga are more or less the same in reverse.

STBF (m *76 79 65 34*) runs to Ouaga (5,000f) and Koudougou (5,000f). Also has a service to Bamako at 08.00 daily (10,000f) via Mopti (9,000f), Segou (7,500f) and San (6,500f). Another minibus service to Bamako goes via Sikasso (4,500f) at 15.00.

STMB (*20 97 08 78*) has stopping services to Ouaga (5,000f single, 9,000f return) at 06.30, 10.00, 13.30 and 22.00. There are also services to Banfora (1,000f) and Nialogoko (2,000f) at 08.00 and 17.00. A service to Bamako (9,000f) via Segou (7,000f) leaves at 12.30 daily.

STP-KZA (m *78 40 70 31*) has a service to Koudougou (4,000f) at 08.00 daily.

TCV (*20 97 75 75*) departs from Ouaga to Bobo in express air-conditioned coaches at 07.30, 09.00, 10.00, 12.00, 14.00, 15.00, 18.30 and 23.00 and costs 6,000f (11,000f return). They're frequently jam-packed, so be sure to arrive at the station at least an hour before the coach leaves to stand a chance of getting a ticket, or buy in advance. Buses doing the return leg leave at the same time. Departures for Banfora (1,300f single, 2,500f return) go at 07.00, 09.00, 11.00, 13.00, 15.30 and 18.00; for Orodara (1,300f) at 08.00, 10.00, 14.00, 16.00 and 18.00. A Bamako service leaves at 06.30 (11,000f), via Segou and Koutiala. It's a good bet for long-distance travel within the region. Its fleet of newish, air-conditioned coaches run to Bouake, Lome, Cotonou and even Lagos.

TDM, also called **Djigouya Magna** (*20 98 26 83*), runs a small coach/minibus service up to Ouahigouya (6,000f) via Dedougou (3,000f) and Toma (4,500f) at 09.00 daily; a second service at 13.00 goes as far as Toma only.

TSR (*20 97 70 40*) runs air-conditioned coaches to Ouaga (6,000f single, 11,000f return) at 07.30 and 14.30 and ordinary coaches (5,000f/9,000f) at 06.30, 09.30, 11.00, 13.00, 16.00, 18.00 and 22.00. It runs to Gaoua (5,000f) at 08.00 and 15.00, along the tar route via Pa. TSR is also the first of the big companies to start running up the new tar road to Dedougou. From another station further along the Boulevard de la Revolution there are departures at 08.00 and 16.00 (3,000f). There are also twice-weekly departures for Lome (22,000f) and Cotonou (23,000f) on Wednesday and Saturday.

ZONNO (m *78 66 91 11*) operates a thrice-weekly departure for Lome, at 22.00 on Tuesday, Wednesday and Saturday (20,000f).

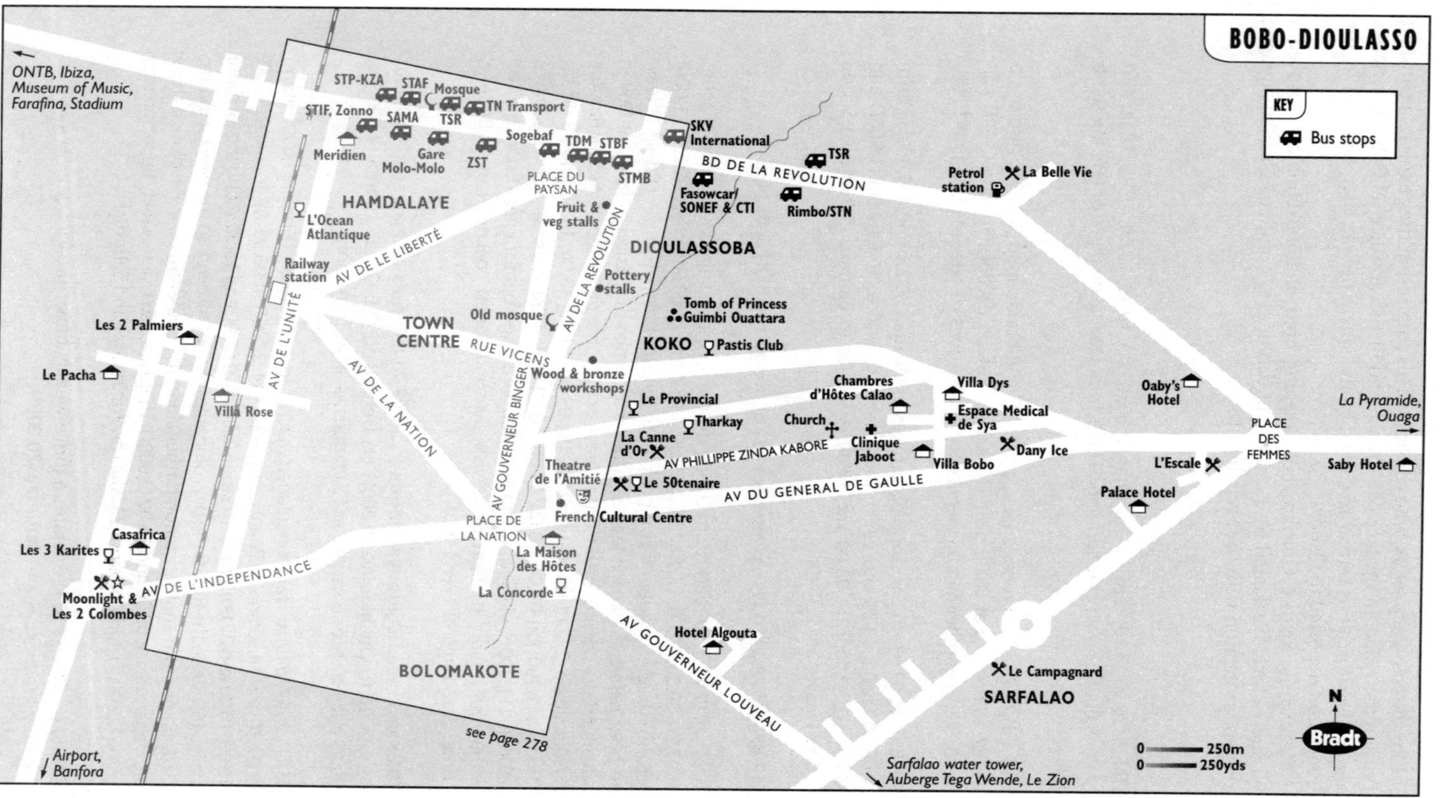

BOBO-DIOULASSO
KEY
Bus stops
ONTB, Ibiza, Museum of Music, Farafina, Stadium
STP-KZA
STAF
Mosque
STIF, Zonno
SAMA
TSR
TN Transport
Meridien
Gare Molo-Molo
ZST
Sogebaf
TDM
STBF
STMB
SKV International
TSR
BD DE LA REVOLUTION
Fasowcar/SONEF & CTI
Rimbo/STN
Petrol station
La Belle Vie
PLACE DU PAYSAN
HAMDALAYE
L'Ocean Atlantique
Fruit & veg stalls
DIOULASSOBA
Railway station
AV DE LE LIBERTÉ
AV DE LA REVOLUTION
Pottery stalls
Tomb of Princess Guimbi Ouattara
Old mosque
TOWN CENTRE
RUE VICENS
KOKO
Pastis Club
Les 2 Palmiers
AV DE L'UNITÉ
Le Pacha
Villa Rose
AV DE LA NATION
AV GOUVERNEUR BINGER
Wood & bronze workshops
Le Provincial
Chambres d'Hôtes Calao
Villa Dys
Oaby's Hotel
La Pyramide, Ouaga
Tharkay
Church
Espace Medical de Sya
La Canne d'Or
AV PHILLIPPE ZINDA KABORE
Clinique Jaboot
Villa Bobo
Dany Ice
PLACE DES FEMMES
L'Escale
Saby Hotel
Theatre de l'Amitié
Le 50tenaire
AV DU GENERAL DE GAULLE
Palace Hotel
French Cultural Centre
PLACE DE LA NATION
Casafrica
Les 3 Karites
La Maison des Hôtes
Moonlight & Les 2 Colombes
AV DE L'INDEPENDANCE
La Concorde
AV GOUVERNEUR LOUVEAU
Hotel Algouta
BOLOMAKOTE
Le Campagnard
SARFALAO
N
Bradt
see page 278
0 250m
0 250yds
Airport, Banfora
Sarfalao water tower, Auberge Tega Wende, Le Zion

GETTING THERE AND AWAY

By car Bobo is an easy drive from Ouaga; sections of the tar road near the capital are undergoing repair, slowing things down somewhat, but after that it's a smooth run and you can get to Bobo in as little as four hours. Allow five hours for coaches. See box, pages 274–5, for coaches to and from Bobo.

By train Bobo makes for a pleasant train ride from Ouagadougou but ongoing security problems in Côte d'Ivoire (the train continues to Bouake and Abidjan, via Banfora) play havoc with the timetable. Trains are supposed to leave Bobo for Banfora (2,000f) at 16.00 every Tuesday, Thursday and Saturday, and for Ouaga (5,000f) every Wednesday, Friday and Sunday, but are frequently delayed. At least in Bobo you can enjoy the architecture of the station building while waiting.

By air Air Burkina (*20 97 13 48*) flies to Bobo-Dioulasso from Ouagadougou. Departures leave at 20.50 on Tuesday; 11.50 on Thursday; and 11.45 on Sunday. Flights to Abidjan cost 104,000f, leaving at 16.50 on Tuesday and 08.20 on Thursday.

GETTING AROUND Pick up shared *taxis verts*, as in Ouaga. Fares cost about 300f around town. For moped and bike hire, ask at your hotel, or scout around the market. At the southern end, Galyam Prestation (m *70 23 04 66, 76 80 72 72*) has bike hire for a slightly pricey 2,000f, P50s for 3,000f and motorbikes for 5,000f. The Algouta and Zion hotels can also sort out moped hire. If you are interested in car hire, Auberge Villa Rose has a couple of excellent 4x4s (one left-hand drive) for 35,000f a day including driver. They also have European mountain bikes for 2,000f a day, town bikes for 1,500f and can sort out *moto* hire. Hotel L'Entente has a list of cars for hire, both saloons and 4x4s, starting from 35,000f a day.

Don't take a moped down an unlit street at night. Theft is common, and Bobo's proximity to Mali and Côte d'Ivoire means vehicles are easily shifted across the border. The unrest in Côte d'Ivoire has brought an increasing number of weapons into Bobo's criminal environment, and theft at gunpoint is increasing.

ORIENTATION The city centre is small enough to be managed on foot; the tightly packed buildings and abundance of greenery provide plenty of shade and you will never have to walk for longer than about 30 seconds to find somewhere serving a cool drink or beer.

The best place to pick up a town map is **Diacfa**, a block north of the market on Avenue de la Republique. The **ONTB tourist office** (*Bd de la Revolution; 20 97 19 86; e ontb@cenatrin.bf; www.ontb.com*), now lost in the grounds of the Ministry of Culture, Tourism and Communication opposite the Museum of Music, is too far out to be of earthly use to anyone: there's a list of guides, a list of sites, friendly smiles and not a lot else.

GUIDES Strolling around central Bobo will inevitably attract the attention of local guides touting for business. Most of the hotels and many of the craft shops have guides attached. An increasing number are receiving training and accreditation from the ONTB, so ask if they have anything to prove their credentials, and trust your instincts. A couple of options to try are **Mamadou Sery** (m *76 63 19 90; e guideamsert@yahoo.fr*), knowledgeable and well-thought of; or **Moussa Ouattara** (m *76 61 12 05, 78 78 98 05; e moussa11076ouattara@yahoo.fr*), who is well organised and has his ONTB badge. Both can arrange a variety of local excursions, within Bobo or to Sindou, the hippo lake at Bala, Lobi and Dagara country.

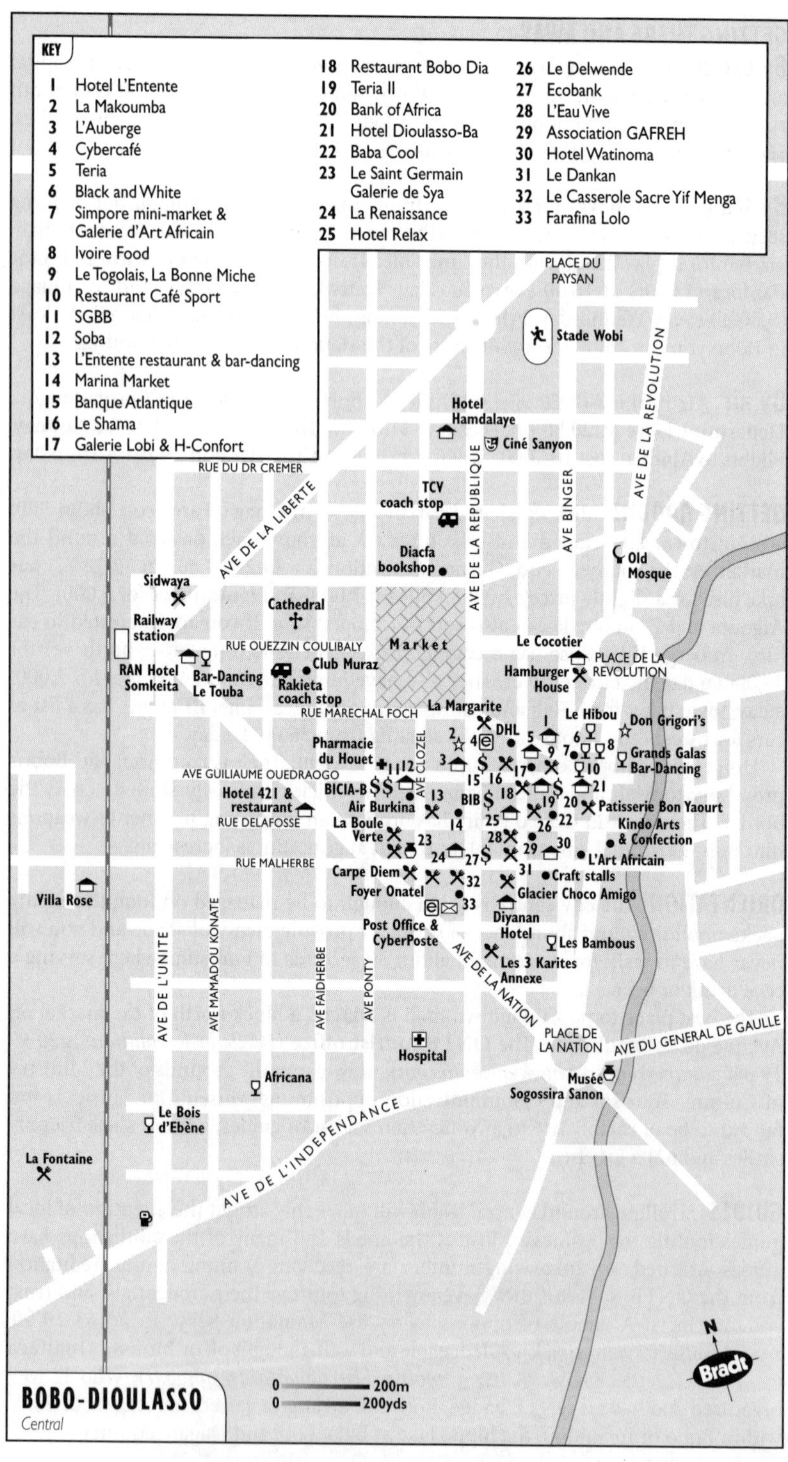
KEY
1 Hotel L'Entente
2 La Makoumba
3 L'Auberge
4 Cybercafé
5 Teria
6 Black and White
7 Simpore mini-market & Galerie d'Art Africain
8 Ivoire Food
9 Le Togolais, La Bonne Miche
10 Restaurant Café Sport
11 SGBB
12 Soba
13 L'Entente restaurant & bar-dancing
14 Marina Market
15 Banque Atlantique
16 Le Shama
17 Galerie Lobi & H-Confort
18 Restaurant Bobo Dia
19 Teria II
20 Bank of Africa
21 Hotel Dioulasso-Ba
22 Baba Cool
23 Le Saint Germain Galerie de Sya
24 La Renaissance
25 Hotel Relax
26 Le Delwende
27 Ecobank
28 L'Eau Vive
29 Association GAFREH
30 Hotel Watinoma
31 Le Dankan
32 Le Casserole Sacre Yif Menga
33 Farafina Lolo
PLACE DU PAYSAN
Stade Wobi
AVE DE LA REVOLUTION
Hotel Hamdalaye
Ciné Sanyon
RUE DU DR CREMER
TCV coach stop
AVE DE LA REPUBLIQUE
AVE BINGER
AVE DE LA LIBERTE
Diacfa bookshop
Old Mosque
Sidwaya
Cathedral
Railway station
Market
RUE OUEZZIN COULIBALY
Le Cocotier
PLACE DE LA REVOLUTION
RAN Hotel Somkeita
Bar-Dancing Le Touba
Club Muraz
Rakieta coach stop
Hamburger House
RUE MARECHAL FOCH
La Margarite
Le Hibou
Don Grigori's
DHL
Pharmacie du Houet
Grands Galas Bar-Dancing
AVE GUILIAUME OUEDRAOGO
AVE CLOZEL
BICIA-B
BIB
Hotel 421 & restaurant
Air Burkina
Patisserie Bon Yaourt
RUE DELAFOSSE
La Boule Verte
Kindo Arts & Confection
RUE MALHERBE
L'Art Africain
Carpe Diem
Craft stalls
Villa Rose
Foyer Onatel
Glacier Choco Amigo
Diyanan Hotel
Post Office & CyberPoste
Les Bambous
Les 3 Karites Annexe
AVE DE LA NATION
AVE DE L'UNITE
AVE MAMADOU KONATE
AVE FAIDHERBE
AVE PONTY
PLACE DE LA NATION
AVE DU GENERAL DE GAULLE
Hospital
Africana
Musée Sogossira Sanon
Le Bois d'Ebène
AVE DE L'INDEPENDANCE
La Fontaine
N
Bradt
BOBO-DIOULASSO
Central
0 200m
0 200yds

WHERE TO STAY Bobo probably has the best selection of backpacker-type accommodation in Burkina. There are several lovely hotels and *chambres d'hôtes*, particularly outside the centre, which hit the spot for both price and ambience.

In the city centre

Luxury/Upmarket

Ran Hotel Somkeita (61 rooms) Av de la Nation; 20 97 09 00, 20 97 27 49; e hotran@fasonet.bf; www.ahrbf.net. Remarkable design makes this at least worth a look if not a stay. The exterior is incredibly ugly, but inside more fascinating than repulsive, like a rejected set from *2001: A Space Odyssey*. What seems to be brown sackcloth is now restricted to the corridors; the rooms have had a lick of paint, but are chokingly overpriced. New rooms near the large pool (2,000f for non-guests) offer garish tiling & frilly curtains. **$$$$$–$$$$$$**

Hotel Relax (43 rooms) Av Almata Diawara; 20 97 22 27, 20 97 00 96; e relax@fasonet.bf; www.groupe-soyaf.com. It has all the mod cons: hot water, TV & fondness for a Visa card, but not only is it characterless, it's also cramped & antiquated rooms are overpriced. The draw is the pool (1,500f for non-guests). B/fast 2,500f. **$$$$$**

L'Auberge (40 rooms) Rue Guillaume Ouedraogo; 20 97 17 67/8; e hoberge@fasonet.bf. A Bobolais institution, the building's distinctive architecture, more Byzantine than Burkinabe, dominates the centre of town. Rooms (& bathrooms) are great, each with a balcony either overlooking the busiest street in town or the good-looking pool area, & have Wi-Fi. However, some guests have found service indifferent, & that restaurant standards have slipped. Swimming for non-guests 1,500f. B/fast inc. **$$$$$**

Hotel Dioulasso Ba (11 rooms) 20 97 75 17; m 70 26 33 37; e hoteldioulassoba@yahoo.fr. New & shiny with a wall of reflective glass, this is soulless conference fodder. En-suite AC rooms all have TV. **$$$$–$$$$$**

Comfortable

Diyanan Hotel (38 rooms) 20 97 07 69. All rooms & bungalows have AC & Wi-Fi & are around a reasonable courtyard, but they're way past their best & overpriced. **$$$–$$$$**

Hotel 421 (27 rooms) 20 97 41 65; e obilys@hotmail.com; www.hotel421.com. Although rooms are spacious, well kept & well equipped, some remarkable décor decisions (frills & purple bathrooms) somewhat spoil the effect. Choice of fan or AC. **$$$–$$$$**

Mid range

Hotel L'Entente (34 rooms) Rue Andre Aubare; 20 97 12 05; e sopresbobo@yahoo.fr. Set in a handsome colonial-style building with attractive courtyard restaurant. There's a range of fan & AC rooms, all with Wi-Fi & good beds. AC rooms have hot water, fridge & TV. Some rooms a bit poky, so ask to see a few. B/fast inc – a rare bonus. **$$$**

Hotel Watinoma (23 rooms) Rue Maherbe; 20 97 20 82; e watinoma@fasonet.bf. An excellent mid-range option that lives up to its good reputation & is particularly well cared-for. AC rooms with Wi-Fi are spick & span, if a bit cramped, & manage to feel tranquil in a great central location. The restaurant's dessert menu is particularly tempting. King-size bed in a more spacious room 26,000f. **$$$**

Hotel Hamdalaye (22 rooms) Av du Gouverneur Clozel; 20 98 22 87. Undergoing extensive renovation work at the time of writing, & therefore had all the ambience of a building site. When it's finished, it should offer clean, comfortable rooms that were once good value – but prices may take a hike. Check first. Choice of en-suite AC, or fan with outside loo. **$$–$$$**

La Renaissance (19 rooms) Av de la Republique; 20 97 86 24; e kasambasalia2005@yahoo.fr. Has gone up a notch with rooms now all en suite, with a few AC options upstairs; the sheets are clean, the mosquito nets reassuring, but somehow the Renaissance never quite shakes off a feeling of dinginess. **$$–$$$**

Soba (43 rooms) 20 97 10 12. Sister hotel to the Entente, but you wouldn't guess it. Staff seem exhausted, & the restaurant's menu has been chewed by mice – an illustration perhaps of how long it's been since a human being ate there. Still, there's Wi-Fi, TVs in some rooms, & you could probably negotiate a bargain. Choice of AC or fan. **$$–$$$**

Teria (24 rooms) Av Alwata Diawara; 20 97 19 72; m 78 04 82 93; e hotelteria@yahoo.fr. Great ambience, positive vibe & comfortable surroundings. All rooms en suite with Wi-Fi; AC rooms are spacious & have a small TV & hot water. The attached café/restaurant offers a great introduction to Bobo life, especially in the mornings, when it's heaving with espresso drinkers. **$$–$$$**

Teria II (31 rooms) Av Guillaume Ouedraogo; 20 98 54 37; m 78 04 82 94; e hotelteria@yahoo.fr. The Teria guys are doing a good job of bringing the former Oasis to life. Rooms are a bit variable, but have been named after staff's villages, & there's a pleasant *paillote* to sit under out the back. All rooms have Wi-Fi; AC rooms have TV & hot water. Attached café is (if possible) even more popular with Bobolais coffee addicts. **$$–$$$**

Budget

Le Cocotier (13 rooms, plus 5 in annexe) 20 98 47 10; e hotelcocotier@yahoo.fr; www.hotel_cocotier.com. A 1st-floor restaurant with *paillote* makes for a tranquil retreat in the middle of town, but rooms are basic & a bit rickety. All fan, with mosquito nets; some have en suite. **$–$$**

Out of the city centre

Upmarket/Comfortable

Les 2 Palmiers (11 rooms) Secteur 9; 20 97 27 59; e hotelles2palmiers@fasonet.bf; les2palmiersbobo@yahoo.fr. The best place to stay in Bobo. Lovely rooms, well decorated & enormous bathrooms in a quiet area of town make for a gloriously tranquil stay. Wi-Fi in all rooms; new rooms have fridge & bigger TV. The only thing that's missing is a pool, but the terrace makes up for it. **$$$$$**

Palace Hotel (12 rooms) 20 97 25 92; e relax.hotel@fasonet.bf. Run by the same people who run the Relax Hotel, this was once a classier option but is beginning to feel run down. Roomy, self-contained villas with fridge & TV are ranged around a pool, but the restaurant has closed. B/fast still available at 3,500f. **$$$$$**

Oaby's Hotel (20 rooms) Bd de la Revolution; 20 97 72 30. An executive-style option offering better value than many hotels of a similar standard in town, with large rooms & lots of white marble, boasting typical accessories including TV & fridge. Most have excellent views of the town laid out below. Even if you're not staying at the hotel, the picturesque pool (1,500f to non-guests) & restaurant area, with wood-fired pizzas, is well worth a visit. The classy bar has billiards for 500f. **$$$$–$$$$$**

Saby Hotel (19 rooms) 20 98 38 57; e seydoul2001@yahoo.fr. On the way into Bobo on the Ouaga road. Clean, tasteful design with some nice features such as Dogon ladders give it some character. AC rooms with TV & fridge are simple but comfortable, & there's a nice garden with bar/restaurant & children's play area. Great selection of juices. **$$$$**

Mid range

Villa Bobo (3 rooms) Secteur 4; 20 98 20 03; m 70 53 78 17; e villabobo@yahoo.fr; www.villabobo.com. There is nowhere quite like Villa Bobo. The lovely rooms with great beds are part of an exquisitely tasteful yet comfortable villa, home to Frenchman Xavier, who assures a warm welcome. As if lovingly tended gardens, swimming pool & *paillote* were not enough, it's also amazingly good value. There's Wi-Fi & a washing machine. Excellent meals available on order. Can also organise excursions to Banfora, Senoufou country & beyond. Choice of AC or fan. B/fast 2,000f. **$$$**

Algouta (18 rooms) Secteur 5; 20 98 07 92; m 78 85 84 42; e hotelalgouta2000@live.fr; www.hotel-algouta.com. Tucked away & a little out of town, but well worth the trek. Light, clean, beautifully decorated rooms have Wi-Fi, en-suite facilities & plenty of space in a leafy setting. Some have an extra bed for 2,000f. Attached restaurant does well-priced food in a delightful dining area, decorated with artefacts & wooden statues. P50 *moto* hire available. **$$–$$$**

Auberge Villa Rose (7 rooms) Rue Malherbe, behind the Comissariat de Konsa; 20 98 54 16; m 70 16 33 00; e villarosebobodioulasso@gmail.com; www.villarosebobodioulasso.com. Tranquil yet upbeat & an easy walk into town, Villa Rose has a great vibe & spacious, good-value rooms around a leafy garden. It's managed by a friendly Dutch/Burkinabe couple who also run education/training projects for young women, which guests are welcome to visit. All rooms en suite with Wi-Fi (internet area for those without computers was under way); choice of fan or AC. Car & bike hire. **$$–$$$**

Chambres d'Hôtes Calao (3 rooms) m 70 65 80 86; e hbadjo@yahoo.fr. Belonging to an avid antiquarian/collector (who lives next door & runs Galerie Le Lobi in town), this simple house & garden are bulging at the seams with his purchases. A cheap twin fan room complements 2 AC doubles, a pleasant sitting/dining area & – a rare find – a well-equipped self-catering kitchen. B/fast inc. **$$–$$$**

Le Pacha (9 rooms) Secteur 9; 20 98 09 54; m 76 61 16 01; e beaudetveronique@yahoo.fr. This friendly, welcoming haven on the edge of town suits most budgets & tastes. The rooms seem a little tired, but are clean & comfortable, & range from fan rooms with external facilities to en-suite with AC. Camping costs 2,000f on foot or with bike, 2,500f with vehicle. **$$–$$$**

Meridien (39 rooms) Av de l'Unité; 20 98 03 42. With so much on offer in this category, it would be a shame to stay here. New en-suite rooms (fan or AC) are clean & spacious, but soulless & overpriced; there's 1 fan room with outside loo for 5,000f, but it's best avoided. **$$–$$$**

Villa Dys (3 rooms) m 78 45 11 69; www.lavilladys.com. Double rooms in a rather dark but pleasant *maison d'hôte* are small but comfy. All have mozzie nets & towels; 1 has en suite. Restaurant & bar area. Fan or AC. **$$–$$$**

Auberge Tega Wende (7 rooms) Sarfalao, opposite water tower; 20 95 26 78. If you get lost *en route* to Le Zion, you could do worse than drop in here. Very friendly, with simple en-suite fan or AC rooms (the latter have hot water & TV). Cold beers too. **$–$$$**

Budget

Museum of Music (5 rooms) Bd de la Revolution; 20 98 15 02; e info@aspac-burkina.com; www.aspac-burkina.com. The museum also has some great accommodation, some at the top of a lovely spiral staircase. Choose fan or AC. Reception can organise numerous tours of Bobo's heritage & much more elaborate tours throughout Burkina. These look a little expensive, but well organised. **$$**

Casafrica (9 rooms) Secteur 8; 20 98 01 57; e casafrica@free.fr; http://casafrica.free.fr. Tucked away between the cemetery & the airport & with a big shady courtyard, this is a travellers' favourite. Fan rooms are simple, but mosquito nets & cleanliness put the mind at rest, which, at this price, makes them excellent value. Some have internal showers; all have outside loo. **$–$$**

La Maison des Hôtes 20 98 34 67. Basically just an accommodation block (not, despite the name, a *maison d'hôte*). Tranquil – feels in the middle of nowhere, but actually not far from CCF & town. Simple rooms have crisp white sheets & mozzie nets. Choice of fan or AC. **$–$$**

Le Zion (7 rooms) Sarfalao; 20 95 17 21; m 78 86 27 25, 78 30 17 01; e didinno2005@yahoo.fr. A true backpackers' favourite with all the features you might expect, plus a few more: simple quirky rooms, good bar/restaurant (serves possibly the only lasagne & tagines in Bobo), rooftop terrace where you can sleep with mattress & mozzie net for 1,500f, washing machine, crafts shop & P50 *moto* hire. No wonder many make the trek. Fan rooms have outside loos; some have showers. Tricky to find, so call ahead. **$–$$**

WHERE TO EAT AND DRINK Most hotel food is adequate, but few have restaurants that you'd bother visiting if you're not staying there. The exceptions are **L'Entente**, **Le Pacha** and **Les 2 Palmiers**.

In the city centre

Expensive

Le Saint Germain Corner of Rues Clozel & Delafosse; 20 97 02 97; m 78 50 49 49; e stgermain.bobo@yahoo.fr. Bobo's swankiest restaurant, set in a beautiful lush garden, comes from the same stable as Les 2 Palmiers & is also an art gallery, music video venue (projected on to back wall) & tapas bar. Too much, perhaps? Soft lighting & tropical greenery sit oddly with blaring music, & the tasteless tapas owe little to Spain. High-class French/African menu, however, so if you like Phil Collins with frogs' legs, you'll be fine. No videos at lunchtime. $$$$

Above average

L'Eau Vive Rue de la Fosse; 20 97 20 86; Mon–Sat; closed Sep. More religious restauranting from the same sisterly order that runs the Ouaga branch. Always worth a look, with good food at reasonable prices (sides included – a rare concession), plus baobab or *karite* ice cream. $$$

Restaurant 421 Av de la Nation; 20 97 41 65. Swish surrounds, if you can handle the animal heads looking down on the food; European & Asian cuisine. $$$

L'Entente Hotel Rue Andre Aubare; 20 97 12 05. Courtyard *paillotes* & an excellent range of juices (baobab, *bissap*) make this a great place to quench your thirst at any time, but there's also a good range of salads & mains. The pizzas are recommended. $$–$$$

Le Dankan Rue Malherbe; 20 98 28 42. Managed by the same people as long-established Le Mande, with the same varied menu but a subtle, clever difference: local dishes 200f cheaper (*riz gras* 600f). So, it attracts more Bobolais & with its buzzing street-side location is a great place to drink as well as eat. Free Wi-Fi. $–$$$

Le Mande Av de la Revolution; 20 98 28 42; e dankan_mande@yahoo.fr. A wide range of mid-price options in secluded surroundings (including local dishes at around 800f) make this a great central dinner option. Delicious fresh juices alone are worth the trip, & can be taken away. $–$$$

Mid range/Cheap and cheerful Espresso coffee, pastries, yoghurt and snacks ensure that **Glacier Choco Amigo** (*Rue Pepin Malherbe*) keeps bustling all morning; ice cream comes later on. **Patisserie Bon Yaourt** (*Av de la Revolution; m 70 24 15 24*) up from Le Mande on the left, serves big tubs of cold, creamy yoghurt for 500f, taken on leather benches. Opposite nightclub Makoumba there's **La Margarite** (*20 96 05 20*), another good breakfast option with croissants at 500f; it does *chawarma* and grills, too, and more expensive pizzas.

L'Entente (*Rue Delafosse; 20 97 03 96*) (not to be confused with Hotel L'Entente), with its wide, raised terrace positioned over a bustling street, is one of the best places in town to watch the world go by. Food is excellent value and the menu varied, including cheap European and African dishes. **Restaurant Bobo Dia** is a well regarded haunt for offal-lovers; liver, heart, kidney and tongue all feature, while **Le Shama** over the road is popular for more standard stuff. **Le Delwende**, also nearby, is not what it used to be, but is still fine for cheap lunchtime nosh, as is **Le Togolais** opposite the Hotel L'Entente; **Restaurant La Boule Verte** (*Rue Delafosse*) is a small, friendly bar serving simple favourites at good prices. **Sidwaya**, by the train station, is a great place for grills and television watching, while **Le Casserole Sacre Yif Menga** on a corner of Avenue de la Republique is packed at lunchtimes as Bobolais pay homage at the altar of well-cooked chicken and rice.

By day it is a typical office block. By night, it is transformed into the **Foyer Onatel**, street bar, grill and culinary revelation. Prepare for the best *poulet rabilet* in Bobo, if not the country. Entire chickens cost 2,000f; sometimes there is *pintade* for a touch more. The earlier you get there, the better the selection of birds you can choose from. Just across the road, **Le Carpe Diem** (m *76 18 29 94*) has a tourist-oriented menu that includes pizza and steak, but everyone ignores it. There's street chicken here too, which you can eat at the *restau* and wash down with wine.

La Bonne Miche (*Av Guillaume Ouedraogo*) is the best place in central Bobo for bread, and often so busy you may need to fight to attract the attention of overworked staff. Buy a thick crusty baguette, pick up meat and cheese from one of the nearby supermarkets and your picnic lunch to accompany a trip to La Guinguette (see page 289) is ready.

Out of the city centre

Expensive/Above average

✕ **Les 2 Palmiers** ☏ 20 97 27 59. Similar high-level European/African menu to the Saint Germain in town, but with a different atmosphere – pleasant terrace or formal AC dining room. Tapas best avoided. $$$$

✕ **L'Escale** Secteur 5; ☏ 20 96 01 63; m 78 20 79 79. Boasting a multi-national menu, this restaurant has the added attraction of feeling like a country club, with a good pool, perfect for night swimming, set among palms, vines & chic background music. There's Wi-Fi, & food is swish, including treats such as steak with gorgonzola or pricey wood-fired pizzas. Whether eating or not, swimming still costs 1,500f. Visa accepted. $$$$

✕ **La Canne d'Or** Av Phillippe Zinda Kabore; ☏ 20 98 15 96; ⊕ Tue–Sun. This nicely decorated restaurant with pretty garden nooks offers some of the best dining in town. The majority of the food is European & African grills, with the odd oriental influence. $$$

✕ **La Fontaine** Off Av de l'Independance; ☏ 20 98 09 01; m 78 00 06 06. Soft lighting & a tinkling fountain offset a fine Lebanese menu, with good-value *meze* & *chawarma* as well as more pricey meat & fish options. The homemade houmous rocks. $$–$$$

✕ **Le Pacha** Secteur 9; ☏ 20 98 09 54; ⊕ Wed–Mon. Lovely tranquil ambience, great wood-fired pizzas & friendly, attentive service makes this a Bobo favourite. The menu is varied, tending towards European; good salads. $$–$$$

Mid range/Cheap and cheerful

✕ **Le Campagnard** m 70 23 89 83, 78 01 05 01. Down in Sarfalao, this places heaves with expats & locals alike, with good reason. As well as the usual suspects (*riz sauce, riz gras*), there are huge, cheap salads, excellent grills (*merguez* is a tasty feature) & cold beers. There's also bushmeat in the hunting season (agouti, porcupine or bushbuck, for instance). $–$$

✕ **Les 3 Karites** m 70 25 70 97. Round the corner from Les 2 Colombes, this place serves a great range of African dishes including *foutou*, *fonio* & *tô* at good prices. It's set in a nice garden & has a good reputation. $–$$

Going for *porc au four* (oven-cooked pork) is something of a tradition among Bobolais, particularly as part of a boozy early lunch at around 10.00. To sustain such shirking, the joints need to be up to the task, and there are a few that are worthy of mention. The first, **La Belle Vie**, is a bit of a hike, just behind the Shell station at the meeting point of Boulevard de la Revolution and Rue Bernard Sibsie. The second, **L'Ocean Atlantique**, is off Avenue de L'Unité up from the railway station; and the third, **Tharkay**, on Avenue Guimbi Oattara, is so popular that it stokes up the oven in the evenings too. Healthy portions cost around 1,000–2,000f.

Les 2 Colombes (*Av de l'Independance*), next door to the Moonlight nightclub, sadly never lived up to its potential; its limited menu is not worth the trek. **Farafina**, up on the Boulevard de la Republique, is a good bet for anyone staying at the music museum; its chicken is a bit pricey, though. **Dani Ice**, on Avenue Charles de Gaulle, is a good ice cream hangout. If you have wheels, head for the Ouaga road to find the best bread and pastries in town at **La Pyramide**. Much-praised, it has the atmosphere of an American roadside diner with pool tables and *baby-foot* upstairs.

ENTERTAINMENT AND NIGHTLIFE Bobo teems with bars and drinking dens. Below is a selection of some local favourites.

Bars

🍷 **Bar-Dancing Le Touba** ☎ 20 97 27 49. On the first Fri of every month, Le Touba, tucked behind the Ran Hotel Somkeita, metamorphoses from a sleepy *maquis* into a hugely popular oldies' night; African/Cuban hits from the 60s, 70s & 80s bring the house down.

🍷 **L'Entente Bar** Rue Delafosse. Next door to the restaurant of the same name, this place has a happy, mellow vibe & the dancing gets going earlier than at many haunts.

🍷 **L'Ocean Atlantique** Off Av de l'Unité. Famous for its weekend matinées, when friendly DJ Mackenzie starts revving things up from 14.00. Get there before 16.00 or you won't get a seat; you'll just have to dance all night. Weekdays get packed from 21.00 too.

🍷 **Pastis Club** Rue Vicens. This is a real old-timers' joint. By midday it's already full of well-oiled pork-pie-hat wearers gearing up for an afternoon session, & has a lovely atmosphere.

Avenue Guimbi Oattara is great for a bar crawl, with a number of worthy *maquis* begging for attention. If you're lucky, you'll catch some live music at **Le Provincial**, from whence you can stagger on until you reach the immensely popular **Le Tharkay**, where the dance floor throbs every night and there's live music at weekends (see below).

Clubs

Moonlight (*Av de l'Independance*) is over the railway lines towards the airport. It's a glitzy, intimate locale that has shot to the top spot in town. Entry is 3,000f, or 4,000f for the VIP lounge with balcony from which you can watch the beautiful people below. Before its arrival, **La Makoumba** (*Av de la Republique; 3,000f entry*) was for many years the most fashionable place to be seen; it's still popular, holding its own against the new pretender, with good air conditioning and uncommonly clean toilets. Wood panelling, a shiny bar that packs bottle after bottle of whisky, and red leather set the 21st-century saloon-bar tone. If you fancy something a little less showy, **Don Grigori's** (*Av de la Revolution*) is another late-night option that comes alive at weekends.

Up on Boulevard de la Revolution lurks **Ibiza**, undergoing renovation at the time of writing, but a massive glitterball of a place that will reopen with a roar. Locals can't wait. 'It has *four* dance floors,' they whisper reverentially.

Live music Friday night is live-music night in Bobo, although many places have a band playing every night of the week. Unfortunately the traditional music scene has taken a hit in recent years in Bobo, as the *cabarets* have turned from *djembes* to DJs in the quest to keep up with the times. So while areas such as Sarfalao and Bolomakote are still great nightlife possibilities, the romance of *cabarets* with regular live-music nights is much rarer than it was. In its place, a number of more central joints fill the gap, listed below.

Bolomakote is the centre of the informal live and traditional music scene in Bobo, where you can find genuine, handmade musical instruments, particularly *balafons*. It is host to numerous smoky *cabarets*, and weekends are especially animated. A good introduction to the neighbourhood is **La Concorde**, a rowdy

BOBO'S LITTLE BRIXTON

There is a street just below City Hall that just refuses to quieten down, whatever the hour. No-one quite knows what it's called, but one clued-up resident has christened it *Petit Brixton*, after the suburb of south London that never sleeps. When all other options have been exhausted, this is the place to come if you still can't bear to tear yourself away from the action. The drag starts with **Black and White**, resplendent in, er, black and white, with a terrace bar to sit and get yourself started. Opposite there's **Le Hibou**, a lively bar, with a collection of late 80s/early 90s arcade games that are a tempting home for 100f coins. Across the road are a couple of *maquis* that blur into one, **Chez Harouna** and **Rue Princesse**; they're obscured by the smoke from **chop stands**, selling delicious *brochette* baguettes or plates of fresh mutton for around 500f. You will also see well-built ladies of the night patrolling their patch in front of the grill stands in the hope of custom. Finally, **Ivoire Food** has more to do with music than food, hosting live bands on Thursday–Saturday nights. If the hour is late and it's food you're after, however, you can head up to the Place de la Revolution, where you'll find **Hamburger House** – a fast-food and take-away joint that keeps going 24/7.

dancing bar that is crammed even on Sunday nights, and easily found on the main road running southwest of Place de la Nation. The **Africana** *buvette*, further in Bolomakote, is also worth seeking out, full of itinerant musicians and artists who are always up for a jam.

There are also several good live-music joints in the centre of town or nearby.

🍸 **Bois d'Ebène** Av de l'Unité; ☎ 20 97 49 62. Popular venue that puts on live music at the weekends. You can eat here, too. Having wine available at what is basically an upmarket *maquis* feels terribly decadent.

🍸 **Le 50tenaire** Av Philippe Zinda Kabore; ☎ 20 95 30 79. A new *bar/restau* that's attracting a lot of chatter & hosts traditional music at the weekends (Fri/Sat). The well-priced food has a good reputation & includes pizza. 'We want this place to do well,' said one local, 'because the owner's a really nice guy.'

🍸 **Les Bambous** m 78 81 58 12; ⌚ Mon–Sat. Lurking behind the roundabout, a policy of live music every night makes it a great destination. It hosts artists from across the region & nurtures local talent on to bigger things, such as the Burkinabe artists Big de Sale & Kantala. There is even accommodation available, for the guest who doesn't mind dark & dingy, and drifting off to sleep with the drums still going. Concerts get under way at 21.00, going on until 00.30; 600f cover charge most nights.

☆ **Le Tharkay** Av Guimbi Oattara; ☎ 20 97 84 38; m 78 01 35 34. To complement its nightly dance sessions, the Tharkay hosts live traditional music on Fri & Sat afternoons, & on into the evening; sometimes on Sun too.

Cinema Bobo now has just one cinema, the enormous, self-enclosed **Ciné Sanyon** in the Hamdalaye district. It shows mostly African films every Thursday–Sunday. Tickets cost 1,000f.

Cultural centres

French Cultural Centre (CCF) (*Av Charles de Gaulle; ☎ 20 97 39 79; e info@ccfhenrimatisse.com; www.ccfhenrimatisse.com*) Refurbished in 2004; has a great variety of shows and exhibitions, and good food in a lively bar area. There is a cinema and a library (⌚ *Tue–Sat*) where you can pick up international newspapers.

Theatre de l'Amitié (*Av Charles de Gaulle; tickets from 1,000f*) When big-name musicians come to town, they play at this open-air amphitheatre. It is also the place for up-and-coming acts – Malian artists Amidou and Mariam were regular performers before they were picked up internationally.

Sport **Club Muraz** (☎ *20 98 01 02*) has tennis courts, badminton, table tennis and a pool available to visitors, for 1,500f.

If spectator sport is more your thing and you're missing Premier League action, head for **Restaurant Café Sport** opposite Hotel Dioulasso Ba. Entry is 100f, and the programme of afternoon and evening matches is chalked up outside. No booze served, however.

SHOPPING

Music To pick up the latest Bobolais and Burkinabe sounds, there are a few music stalls (*discothèques*) to try, selling mostly CDs and some tapes. One is next to Le Makoumba, and another opposite the Hotel Relax. **Nouvelle 302** opposite the SGBB bank may look like a clothes shop, but there's a reasonable range of CDs at the back. To be sure you're not buying a copy, however, it's probably best to head to the **Museum of Music** (see page 289).

Bolomakote is the place for musical instruments. The wood, from Côte d'Ivoire, is good enough to last, and provides resonant sounds.

Arts and crafts It is almost impossible to walk around central Bobo without tripping over a carved wooden bench or knocking over a statue from one of the many curio shops overflowing on to the streets. However, there are few that stand out from the crowd.

Association GAFREH (Groupe d'Action des Femmes pour la Relance Economique du Houet) ☎ 20 98 41 60; m 70 29 05 50; e gafreh@yahoo.fr; www.gafreh.org. This fabulous project takes the ubiquitous chucked plastic bags that adorn Burkina's gutters & recycles them into a huge range of knitted or loom-woven items; there's a stylish range of shoulder/handbags, pencil cases, wash bags, clothing & everything in between. The standards are exceptionally high, the prices amazingly low. You can watch the women at work: find the 'Bureau des Artisans' sign on Rue Delafosse, & go on inside.

Baba Cool Av du Gouverneur Binger; m 70 23 32 44; e bacoolcisse@yahoo.fr; www.lasoupapeailee.org/artistes/seydou-cisse. May look like just another craft shop, but look again – Baba Cool's necklaces are artistic creations that border on fantasy designs. As a result, he has quite a following.

H-Confort Av Almata Diawara; m 76 75 80 86; e hbadjo@yahoo.fr. An enterprising initiative by Honore Kambou, the owner of Galerie Le Lobi next door. Well-made home furnishings & utensils are locally made to a high standard. The crafts shop is also a cut above, as Honore is himself a collector & can explain the history of his items.

Le Saint Germain Galerie de Sya Corner of Rues Clozel & Delafosse; ☎ 20 97 02 97; m 78 50 49 49; e stgermain.bobo@yahoo.fr. Housed in & around the restaurant, the most upmarket gallery in town showcases some of the best-quality crafts & furniture in the country. Almost everything you see is for sale; there are some smaller bits & pieces that may not be as expensive as you'd think. Worth a wander even if you don't buy.

Of the rest, **Farafina Lolo** (m *78 81 01 29*) has a particularly large selection of Malian *bogolan* cloths, along with *pagnes* and batiks; the two stalls opposite Hotel Watinoma – **Bobo Art le Cameleon** and **Galerie Le Kanaga** – both have an attractive range of items and are run by friendly guys. **L'Art Africain** on the corner opposite has a wide selection of *balafons, djembes* and Tuareg jewellery. **Kindo Arts & Confection** (m *70 22 83 03*) just up from Le Mande is good for masks. If you wander up Avenue Almata Diawara and around to the right past L'Entente Hotel, the vendors at a range of shops – **Trésor de L'Art Africain, Burkina Arts & Crafts, Galerie D'Art Africain** among them – will no doubt make themselves known; all worth a nose around. The block behind L'Auberge Hotel is also home to numerous stalls with fabrics, wooden carvings and traditional-style hats.

The best places for contemporary sculpture are the *ateliers* in the Koko quarter. You can see artisans at work, browse the fruits of their labours and commission new work. A few to look out for are **Mamady Conde**'s wood workshop (m *76 67 44 58;* e *cmamady2002@yahoo.fr*), **Kaba Camara**'s wood workshop (m *78 23 14 32, 72 77 17 42;* e *camara_kaba10@yahoo.fr; www.camarakaba-sculpteur.blogspot.com*), and **Douda Traore's** excellent bronze studio.

The **central market** was renovated in 2001, although many of its older features were left intact. It contains decent jewellery, cotton prints, masks and bronzes.

Food There is a lively daily fruit and vegetable market on Avenue du Gouverneur Binger by the stadium, although the best and cheapest place to pick up fresh produce is just by the toll booths on the Ouaga side of town. There are a couple of supermarkets in the centre; **Simpore mini market** is on Avenue du Gouverneur Binger, but Lebanese-run **Marina Market** (*20 97 19 86*) makes a much bigger splash on Avenue de la Republique.

OTHER PRACTICALITIES

Money All the **banks** are represented in central Bobo, and most have Visa machines. As usual, it's **Banque Atlantique** that bucks the trend with a MasterCard/Maestro machine; **BRS** has a MasterCard option too. You may be able to change travellers' cheques at **BICIA-B** or the bigger of the two **Ecobanks**. Both banks will change US dollars and euros, as will **BIB**, which will also change pounds, Swiss francs and Canadian dollars. You can change cash euros at Marina Market.

Communications The main **post office** is about halfway along Avenue de la Nation, but was being renovated; it should have reopened by now. There is also a local **DHL** branch on Avenue Almata Diawara. The **cyberposte**, when it reopens, will probably be the best internet option in town, but in the meantime there's a good place next door to La Margarite restaurant on Avenue de la Republique; it charges 300f an hour.

Emergencies **Pharmacie du Houet** (*Av Ponty; 08.00–12.30 & 16.00–9.00 Mon–Fri, 08.00–2.00 Sat*), opposite the BICIA-B bank, has a list posted in the window of the nightly *pharmacie de garde*. There's a clinic and laboratory next door. Two other private clinics are on Avenue Phillippe Zinda Kabore, both highly regarded: **Clinique Jaboot** (*20 97 30 00*) and **Espace Medical de Sya** (*20 97 00 48;* e *espace.sya@fasonet.bf*). **Clinique St Leopold** (*21 Rue 17-135; 20 97 54 12*), treats Peace Corps volunteers; Dr Yameogo comes highly recommended (consultations 5,000f), as does the doctor at **Clinique Leila** (*918 Av Francois Vilain, Secteur 5; 20 97 33 93*).

WHAT TO SEE AND DO

Dioulassoba (*entry to the old city usually costs 1,000f, plus 1,000f for a guide*) A visit into the old city at the heart of modern Bobo is a must. Huddled on the steep banks of the river that runs through the city, the centuries slide away among the smooth mud-brick walls and tree-trunk ladders of typical Bobo houses. This is the part of Bobo that used to be known as Sya, full of architecture that still serves today as home for thousands of people (for more on Bobo house design, see *Koumi*, page 290). You may even get invited into a courtyard to sample local millet beer, and it is likely you will end up paying homage to the sacred catfish that inhabit the stream, and are the totem animal of the town.

Grande mosquée (*Entry 1,000f*) Across the road from the old city, Bobo's old mosque is the largest in Burkina Faso, and a quintessential example of Sudanese mud-brick architecture. It is the result of both religious devotion and a neat piece of politics by the King of Sya. Menaced by the King of Kenedougou, Sya's monarch sought the help of the Almamy Sidiki Sanou, an Islamic religious leader, who lent his military aid in return for the construction of a town mosque. King Tieba of Kenedougou was stopped 30km short of Sya, and work on the mosque began at the start of the 1890s. Although it recalls the mosque at Djenne, with its distinctive 'sugarloaf' minarets, the *banco* construction here has been whitewashed.

Tourists are allowed to enter; unmarried women may like to reflect on the privilege, which is barred to their Muslim counterparts. If you don't already have a guide, numerous young bucks hang around hoping to play the role, but try instead one of the more knowledgeable *imams*.

Just past the mosque, on the road running north towards the Boulevard de la Revolution, are a number of stalls selling excellent clay pots.

Mausoleum of Guimbi Ouattara (*Entry 1,000f*) A direct descendant of the dynastic Ouattara clan who founded Guiriko, Princess Guimbi Ouattara (1836–1919) has her tomb in this modern mausoleum, located off Rue Vicens (look for the ONTB signs). The eldest daughter of Diori Ouattara and Makogo Ouattara, her father died when she was three, and while her younger brother took power, she went on to play an active role in the politics of the region. Married and widowed three times, she was a larger-than-life figure, much appreciated by French explorers and adventurers passing through for the welcome they received in court. She helped hide the French captain Binger in 1888 on his way to Bobo-Dioulasso, and welcomed Dr Crozat and Captain Monteil.

Railway station In 1934, the railway arrived at Bobo-Dioulasso, completing another stage in the grand French vision for an Abidjan–Niamey transport link, this stage built almost exclusively with Burkinabe forced labour. Owing to spiralling costs and the outbreak of World War II, the railway never got much beyond Ouagadougou, but the impressive terminus at Bobo is the epitome of the colonial interpretation of the Sudanese style.

Musée Sogossira Sanon (*Pl de la Nation; ☎ 20 97 20 80; ⌚ 08.00–12.30 & 15.30–18.00 Tue–Sat, 09.00–13.00 Sun; entry 1,000f*) Formerly known as the Musée Provincial du Houet. Located on one of the city's main roundabouts, this museum is small but well curated, including statues from various groups (Lobi, Dagara, Lela, Mossi and Kurumba). There is a selection of clothes, including war tunics worn by the *sofas* of Samory Toure in his fruitless siege against Sikasso in the 19th century, and Lobi bowls used for mixing arrow poison. There are also traditional Bobo and Fulani homes in the main courtyard.

Museum of Music (*Bd de la Revolution; 20 98 15 02; e info@aspac-burkina.com; www.aspac-burkina.com; Tue–Sun*) Located towards the stadium, this small museum is unrelated to the state-run museum in Ouaga; but its aim, to safeguard musical heritage, is the same, and it organises a programme for emerging artists throughout Burkina. As well as an impressive selection of instruments, there is a listening area where genuine CDs from traditional Burkinabe artists can be heard and bought for 10,000f.

AROUND BOBO

The region is rich in day-trip possibilities, most of which are easily achieved with a moped hired from Bobo.

LA GUINGUETTE (*Entry 1,000f*) One of the most popular of Bobo's nearby attractions, this is a forest-clad body of water forming one of nature's perfect swimming pools in the middle of the river Kou. Also known as *la baignade*, it is usually crowded with bathers at weekends. During the rainy season, the water can be dangerously high, so it's best to check with the ONTB office in Bobo about whether it is safe to visit. About 18km out of town, it can be reached via either a right fork just after Koumi on the Orodara road, or a left fork on the Karankasso road. As well as the main swimming area, you can explore a little upstream if you want somewhere less visited, where you'll find a small but pretty waterfall. A straw hut has snacks.

KORO (*Entry 1,000f*) This village, dramatically perched on a forbiddingly steep stub of granite, has been developed by Burkina's tourist office as a bona fide attraction. It is difficult to know whether this is a good thing or not, as the settlement's evident charm is tainted slightly by the widespread view of visitors as walking cash dispensers. There are four official guides, who make amiable companions and will expect a tip.

It does offer the opportunity to explore a living, breathing village, and scramble about on the enormous, smooth-sided rocks. Views from the top of the village are spectacular, particularly of the escarpment leading to Banfora.

The village is divided into three *quartiers*, for Dioula farmers, Bwaba farmers and blacksmiths. You can see smiths at work, villagers preparing millet and shea butter, fetish sites and the meeting place for elders. Photos are allowed, other than of sacred fetishes, but ask permission if snapping people (who are likely to demand money in return).

There is a refreshment kiosk at the bottom. More exciting is the construction of a camping and eating area just outside the village itself, which looks to be a delightful spot. Take the Bobo road 6km back towards Ouaga. At the well-marked sign, take the turning on the right for 2km.

SACRED FISH POOLS (DAFRA) *Dafra* means 'catfish' in Bobo, and there are two sacred pools where the Bobo come to worship at the scaly altar of these enormous, ugly silurids. The first is in the city centre, and is unremarkable; the second, much more pleasant, is near Koro, a few kilometres out of town. The remains of chicken sacrifices can make for a striking sight. It is difficult to get to, so it's best to take a guide; you'll find unofficial guides there too, who will, of course, expect something for their services.

KOTEDOUGOU An important outpost in the days of Bobo's Guiriko Kingdom, Kotedougou was a religious centre and its Sudanese-style mosque drew Muslim pilgrims from surrounding areas. It was built around 1887, under the rule of Babebini Ouattara. It is also the site of Binger's refuge, when he was hidden in

1888 by the princess Guimbi Ouattara of Bobo-Dioulasso. From Bobo, take the left junction after 20km on the route back to Ouaga, and follow it for 2km.

KOUMI (*Entry 1,000f, not including a tip; 500f for a camera; 100f for parking a moto*) Another ONTB-inspired development, Koumi is an archetypal Bobo village. Of greatest interest are its houses, constructed in a *banco* style with layers of thick red earth rather than mud bricks. To preserve its architectural purity, villagers live with a decree forbidding the use of bricks.

In addition to a stroll around the village, the ONTB has built a replica house that visitors can nose around. A set of shallow steps at the side of the house leads to a roof terrace for sleeping, and, impressively for a house built without bricks, a second-storey room for the husband. A trapdoor from this chamber leads to the room of the first wife below.

For a tourist town, it has an attitude to cameras and photos that we have rarely encountered in Burkina. Perhaps overexposure to camera-wielding visitors has put people off. Generally people demand to have their photo taken and ask for money at the same time.

There are four official guides, and ours, Moussa 'Sylvestre' Sanon (m *76 51 64 65*), was knowledgeable and engaging. From Bobo, take the Orodara road out west for 16km and look out on the right-hand side of the road.

Bobo construction methods The water-earth mix is made over three days, and houses go up in stages, known as *courses*, usually five. If you look carefully at the walls you can see the joins. Palm trunks, resistant to termites, provide support, while fronds are dried, cut and woven together to make wonderful conservatories.

A number of large, mysterious holes in the ground pockmark the outskirts of the village leading down to the river. Each of these is a kind of women-only workshop and gossip stop, where wives, mothers, grandmothers and maidens descend to discuss the secrets of married life, and work on palm-frond baskets – the underground grottos are more humid and stop the fronds from cracking. Each family has its own hole, and the women descend in order of seniority, oldest first.

There are several fetish sites, with the conspicuous dusting of chicken feathers all around, and districts for *griots* and blacksmiths, who you can see at work.

The village has a slight sadness to it, as though everything is done for the benefit of visitors. Some of the houses are long abandoned by villagers who have wanted to move on – residents wanting a more modern design must set up home on the other side of the highway in a less desirable quarter. The village has had no success with cotton, so sorghum is the main crop, along with groundnuts. As an indication of one its most popular pastimes, there is palm wine on sale at the entrance to the village for 100f; you may also see people drinking *sopal*, an extremely toxic moonshine of meths-like strength made from sugarcane.

HIPPO LAKE OF BALA (*Entry 1,000f – if anyone is at the ONTB ticket office*) Around Bala, the course of the Mouhoun River slows so much that the waters flow in both directions, creating a hippo-friendly swampland, hidden in a forest beyond the small village. The hippos are usually under the water for the hotter part of the day, often completely submerged, sometimes with only nostrils and ears breaking the surface. Once you're at the lake's edge, there are boatmen who will take a precarious-looking *pirogue* (wooden canoe) out on to the lake, for 2,500f. Take binoculars for birdwatching too.

The ONTB is in the process of building a campsite alongside the lake.

Getting there and away More difficult to get to than the hippo lake at Tengrela near Banfora, this is a mission, around 60km from Bobo. Head 44km northeast of Bobo on the road to Dedougou as far as Satiri. Both Fasowcar and the smaller Djigouya-Magni (TDM) buses leave Bobo at 09.00 daily (1,000f for Satiri); the latter has an extra service at 13.00. TSR also heads up the tar at 08.00 and 16.00, but check first that it will stop at Satiri for you. Going by public transport leaves you with 22km to cover, so is not really practical unless you pop a bike or *moto* on the bus. If you do this, you should be able to pick up either Djigouya-Magni or TSR on their return runs, at about 16.00 and 17.00 respectively.

At Satiri, head left towards Bala, along a track that passes through lovely rolling countryside. The entrance to the forest is some way beyond Bala. Stick to the main forest path (do not turn left at the payment booth). If in doubt, ask for the *mare aux hippopotames*.

WATERFALLS OF TAKELEDOUGOU The route between Bobo and Banfora passes along the foot of the Banfora Escarpment with bright-green, well-watered sugarcane fields on the flat. Shortly before Takeledougou, there is a dramatic set of falls to your right, about 1km away. The river wends its way towards the road, flowing under the tarmac into another set of falls to the left. These are gentle enough to climb down, and provide some great views of the plains below. You may often find local lads there having a wash and a swim.

A little further along the road is a turning for a track that leads right back towards the first set of falls, and you can walk up from here. There's no need for a guide, although take care not to trespass on any local shrines.

BANFORA

Banfora might just be able to carry off the title of most picturesque town in Burkina. While there is not much to do, the town contents itself with a great setting, among well-watered sugarcane fields and tree-lined hills. There are some glorious accommodation options and the busy Sunday market is one of the best in the country, with artisanal goods from Côte d'Ivoire and Mali mingling with homegrown products. Given how much there is to see and do in the region, Banfora is a great base for exploring.

GETTING THERE AND AWAY

By bus The good road from Ouaga, via Bobo, takes about seven hours by coach including a half-hour changeover in Bobo. A 4x4 would do the 441km in much less. From Bobo it is about 90 minutes by bus. The road east to Gaoua, 197km, is an alternative route, and a way into Lobi country.

From Bobo, either TCV or Rakieta are best, leaving from Bobo town centre. Tickets cost 1,300f. TCV leaves every two hours from 07.00 to 13.00, then at 15.30 and 18.00. Rakieta is even better, leaving almost hourly. To reach Banfora from Ouaga on the same day, take an early service with either company and change coach in Bobo.

From Banfora, there are likewise plenty of services to Bobo. If you'd like to connect with an air-conditioned service to Ouaga (7,000f), take the 06.00, 08.30, 12.00, 16.00 or 19.30 from Banfora with Rakieta (☎ *20 91 03 81*), or the 06.00, 08.30, 11.00, 13.00, 15.30 or 18.00 with TCV (m *75 79 13 08*).

STMB (☎ *20 91 05 61*) also runs a Banfora–Bobo service with a connection to Ouaga. It's less frequent, leaving at 08.00 and 11.45, but cheaper (6,000f for Ouaga) and offers the option of stopping at smaller destinations (Hounde, Sabou) *en route*.

Rakieta also run onward services from Banfora to Niangoloko at 08.30, 14.30 and 18.00. Tickets cost 800f. Both Rakieta and TCV have onward services to Côte d'Ivoire from Bobo that pass through Banfora: given the political situation, check the times beforehand.

Just up from TCV, La Grace has minibus departures for Orodara (1,250f) at 10.30 and 15.30 daily. At the *autogare*, you can find minibus departures for many outlying destinations, notably Sindou, Baguera and Douna in Senoufou country, and Loropeni and Gaoua to the east.

By train The train from Banfora to Bobo costs 2,000f, leaving Monday, Wednesday and Friday evenings.

ORIENTATION AND GETTING AROUND Banfora is a bipolar kind of town. By day, the busy main stretch of road leading to Côte d'Ivoire is frantic, with every kind of trader possible overflowing from the nearby market. After dark this part of town shuts down almost completely and the action moves ten minutes south to the streets around the old, disused cinema, with chop stands, bars and restaurants. To better regulate the town, a new market has been built nearby, but for the moment most traders are resisting the urge to move.

The best way to explore Banfora and environs is by moped. They are easy to track down; the best option is the friendly **Chez Tapissier Ouattara** (m *70 27 75 43*) just down from TCV, which offers daily hire of P50s in good nick for 3,000f, Chinese KTM motorbikes for 5,000f and Yamahas for 7,500f (07.00–18.30), not including petrol.

GUIDES Banfora buzzes with guides, many of whom are pleasant, others over-enthusiastic, some downright hassling and infuriating. Hotels have taken to warning guests of the many *faux types*, so consider your options carefully. Highly recommended, and used by a number of the hotels, is Tiemogo Soulama (m *78 03 44 46*; e *s.tiemogo@yahoo.fr*), who is flexible and goes the extra mile. He has an unusual pricing system, charging 2,500f per site close to Banfora (eg: Tengrela, the Domes), and 5,000f for sites further afield (eg: Sindou). He has a friend who can act as translator into English. Book ahead if possible.

WHERE TO STAY

Luxury

Hotel Cascades Palace (27 rooms) 20 91 28 28; m 78 33 28 28; e cascadespalace@hotmail.fr; www.cascadespalace.com. About 3km outside Banfora on the road in from Bobo, this is an extravagant fantasy of a place with grand white steps leading down to the enormous pool (2,000f to non-guests) & the resort-style accommodation surrounding it. No expense spared: some of the bungalows have top-to-toe wood panelling. Restaurant includes good selection of Lebanese dishes, reasonably priced. **$$$$–$$$$$$**

Comfortable/Mid range

Grand Hotel (20 rooms) There's nothing terribly grand about the rows of boxy rooms here, which are new, clean & very overpriced. Choice of fan or AC. **$$$–$$$$**

Hotel Jackson (15 rooms) 20 91 08 61, 20 91 19 19; e hnebil@hotmail.com. Somewhat of a curiosity: a series of pink bungalows topped with a green hat each, resembling a gated community, with a well-maintained kidney-shaped swimming pool (2,000f for non-guests). Rooms have AC, TV & Wi-Fi, & some frilly finishes. Prices negotiable. **$$$**

Hotel Comoe (16 rooms) 20 91 01 51. Has a courtyard overflowing with plants, wall paintings, chairs fashioned from roughly hewn trees & a hammock swinging free. Spartan, functional rooms complete a travellers' favourite.

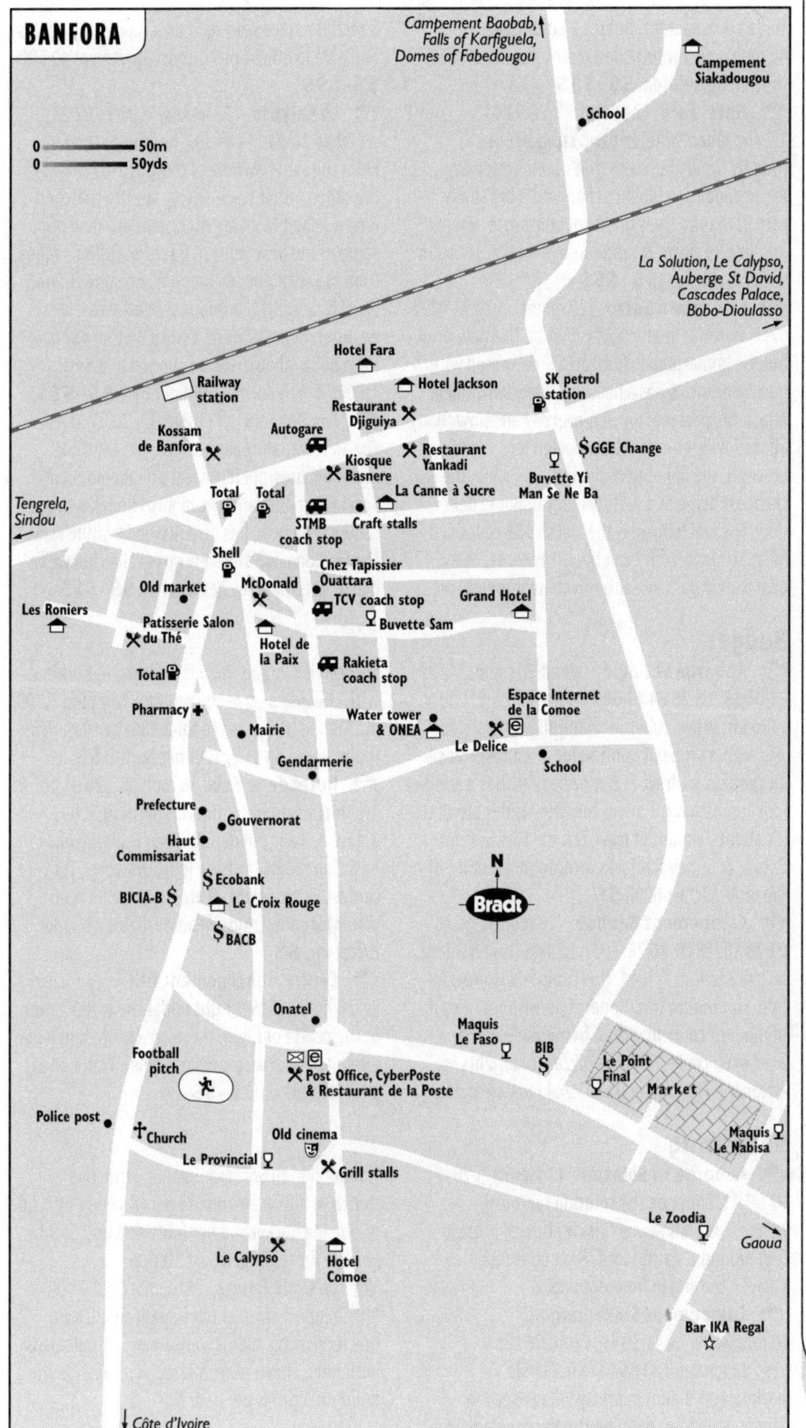

The West BANFORA

7

There's a restaurant, but it's a bit underused. AC rooms are en suite; fan rooms have internal shower, outside loo. **$$–$$$**

Hotel Fara (22 rooms) 20 91 01 17. The oldest hotel in town struggles on, a friendly family business that's seen better days. Accommodation blocks set around a big shady yard of mango trees greet your entrance. Rooms are simple, clean, & range from en-suite AC to fan with outside loo. **$$–$$$**

La Canne à Sucre (20 rooms) 20 91 01 07; e hotelcanneasucre@fasonet.bf. This delightful hotel is immaculately furnished & decorated with teak furniture, & has a beautifully tended garden. A tasteful, personal touch is everywhere. Now that all the lovely en-suite straw-roofed huts are AC, however, the fan options are less appealing, the cheapest being in a slightly dingy building next door. The real bargain is the stylish self-contained AC apartment, with 1 double & 1 twin, set in its own walled gardens with private swimming pool & restful terrace seating. If unoccupied, the pool is available to other hotel guests. Apartment 49,500f. **$$–$$$**

Le Calypso (12 rooms) 20 91 02 29; m 70 74 14 83; e famille_houitte@yahoo.fr. From the same owners of the Calypso *restau* at the other end of town, lovely laterite thatched huts finished to a very high standard now offer some of the best value in Banfora. Options range from fan with outside loo to AC en suite. There's Wi-Fi & delightful outdoor seating areas. Meals on order. Near Palais de Justice on the way in from Bobo, about 1.5km from town. B/fast 1,500f. 6-bed dorm 2,500f per bed. **$$–$$$**

Les Roniers (11 rooms) 20 91 15 16. The annexe to the Canne à Sucre sets the same high standards, but it can feel a disappointment. Spacious, stylish fan or AC rooms/bungalows have comfortable beds, lots of dark wood & white walls. The fan bungalows are very good value, but we've had reports that they get very hot. **$$–$$$**

Budget

Auberge St David (about 20 rooms) 20 91 03 68; m 78 84 17 60; e aubergesaintdavid@yahoo.fr; www.auberge-djatigui.com. Spacious site with a range of good-value en-suite rooms, all spotless with Wi-Fi & mozzie nets. Has a good-looking restaurant menu too. Downsides are that it's about 2km out of town (on the way in from Bobo), & somewhat lacks atmosphere. Choice of fan or AC. B/fast 600f. **$$**

Campement Baobab (10 rooms) m 76 01 28 18, 78 01 86 28. Located 4km from Banfora on the Karfiguela road, this camp is a wonderful find, combining traditional style with just a dash of modern convenience. A homemade wood-fired oven cooks delicious pizzas (order 2hrs in advance). The simple traditional huts are better decorated & maintained than many in Burkina, with cheaper 3- & 4-bed options. Camping 1,700f pp. Moped hire possible for 2,500f per day. *Banji* (palm wine) on sale, 100f per bottle. **$$**

Hotel de la Paix (6 rooms) 20 91 00 16. Outclassed by all the competition, it has a deserted air; the dark & dingy building has basic fan rooms (outside loos). However, it's very central, & friendly staff are happy to heat up water for showering. Meals available on order. B/fast inc. **$$**

Centre Hebergement ONEA (4 rooms) m 70 46 80 85. Set right under the water tower in the centre of town, these are cheap, functional en-suite fan or AC rooms (no nets). Water board staff take priority. **$–$$**

Shoestring

Auberge La Solution (7 rooms) 20 91 00 41. Won't be the solution for most – nondescript fan rooms (inside shower, outside loo) around a scruffy yard. Next up from Le Calypso coming in from Bobo. **$**

Campement Siakadougou (6 rooms) m 74 43 30 49, 78 40 68 28; e s_dandjourouss1@yahoo.fr. Classic backpackers' haunt in pretty village setting, 10min walk from town on the Karfiguela road (follow sign to Sofitex). Simple, attractive thatched huts have mozzie nets & choice of inside or outside bucket shower (outside loos). Shady *paillote* for chilling. B/fast 500f. **$**

Le Croix Rouge (4 rooms) 20 91 04 98. Cheapest place in town, with small, bare but serviceable rooms, containing 2 single beds with nets. Showers are shared, loos outside the building. Price is per bed. **$**

WHERE TO EAT AND DRINK

Above average/Mid range

Canne à Sucre 20 91 01 07. The best & most expensive restaurant in town, although the service can be wanting. Delicious starters including an excellent homemade paté are backed up with solid, filling & pricey main courses. $$$

Le Calypso 20 91 10 28; m 70 26 98 56. One of the best destinations in town, with a diverse menu (including huge portions of excellent fish) served in the comfortable surroundings of a leafy garden. Service is good, if a little slow; if you're at the Calypso hotel, you can order from the menu in advance. $–$$$

Djiguiya 20 91 06 52. On the main road to Bobo, serving reasonable dishes (eg: steak for 1,000f) at a pleasant wooden bar. $$

McDonald 20 91 08 45; half-day Wed. Colourful, lively & a favourite with tour groups, has a good range of juices, yoghurt & crêpes as well as well-priced mains. Whole chicken is 3,000f. $$

Restaurant de la Poste m 70 23 03 04. An enterprising woman has put up shady *paillotes* in the grounds of the post office, & serves possibly the best *riz sauce tomate* in Burkina, featuring bone-free chunks of tender beef. Good range of other dishes too. The locals come in droves. $–$$

By far the best breakfast option is the **Kiosque Basnere** opposite the *autogare*. Decked out in fresh pale greens and blues, it serves espresso coffee & mint tea, omelettes, yoghurt and sandwiches as well as heartier options. **Patisserie Salon du Thé** is an alternative, serving cakes and pastries. **Kossam de Banfora** is a good yoghurt kiosk on the way to the train station, but doesn't do hot drinks; American-themed **Buvette Sam**, near Rakieta, serves up coffee and omelettes at bar stools.

Le Delice is a popular *maquis* set in lovely gardens. It's a real meat-and-beer place, serving up specials such as sheep's-head soup and *porc au four*. There's bushmeat in season. Arrive early, either lunchtime or evening, or many of the best cuts are gone. **Restaurant Yankadi**, on the main road, has cheap African staples all day long, but discerning locals avoid it.

ENTERTAINMENT AND NIGHTLIFE There are a couple of live music venues: French-owned **Maquis Le Nabisa** (*500f entry*) has traditional music every night. **Maquis Le Faso** has live jazz every Saturday and Sunday, along with tasty grills.

For the cheapest beers in town, head to **Buvette Yi Man Se Ne Ba** (Brakina 550f), but if you're up for a long session, the best spot is **Le Point Final** by the new market. There's no dancing, just cold beer and *brochettes*, and it's open till dawn.

If it's dancing you're after, **Bar-Dancing Le Provincial** (*20 88 04 19; 500f cover charge on weekends*) is popular, with tunes every night. Choose between the beer garden and street seating outside that offers a bit of respite. **Bar IKA Regal** (*500f entry*), down past the defunct Videoclub Zoodo, is where the young set hang out, thronging around the rows of shiny motorbikes; there's dancing till the wee hours. *Maquis* **Le Zoodia** is worth a beer *en route*.

SHOPPING **Supermarché de la Paix** is a little store near the Total stations; you can pick up cheap bottles of *bissap* juice here. There are also a couple of **craft stalls** around the Canne à Sucre hotel, selling wooden statues, traditional cotton shirts and bronzes.

OTHER PRACTICALITIES **BICIA-B**, **BIB** and **Ecobank** all have Visa machines. For quick and easy cash exchange go to **GGE Change** (*20 91 00 57*), which accepts euros and US dollars and is open every day. The **post office** features a **cyberposte** at 350f an hour; there's also **Espace Internet de la Comoe** (*20 91 11 07*) next to Le Delice, which charges 300f an hour.

AROUND BANFORA

There are a great number of day trips, walks and excursions in Banfora's rocky green surrounds. If you're travelling by car, or hardy motorbike, a tour west from Banfora via Sindou and back up to Orodara, over a few days is possible, taking side trips at each of the following.

TIEKOUNA This small village is known for its handicrafts, particularly woven baskets made from dried fronds of the *ronier* tree, and pottery. Villagers are happy to show both product and process. On the way to the shady village, look out for more *ronier* palms standing starkly against the sky like a field of abandoned windmills, their pock-marked contours revealing a healthy amount of palm-wine tapping. Head 5km west from Banfora on the Sindou road and take a left fork (signposted) for a few kilometres.

KARFIGUELA FALLS (*Entry 1,000f; parking 300f for cars; 150f for motos; 100f for bikes*) Burkina's most tourist-friendly set of falls (Cascades or Chutes de Karfiguela in French) makes for a lovely picnic-style excursion, with plenty of opportunity to scramble around, to swim or to sunbathe. From the large pool at the base of the falls, set in a pleasantly shaded wooded area, a ten-minute climb brings you to the top. The ascent is helped by steps carved into the rockface, making the going easy enough to carry a generous packed lunch. The reward is great views of the plateau below, a grassy picnic area and a series of natural jacuzzis.

From here, the falls continue on a series of smaller levels, and you can walk the course of the river splashing around, or keep to dry land with a few jumps here and there, until you find a spot you like.

The falls are at their most spectacular in the rainy season, but the drawback is it's more dangerous to climb the trail to the top. If you visit during the dry season, don't expect a raging torrent of water, but throw yourself into the climb.

There is not a guardian or safety rail in sight, so everything is done at your own risk. Pay particular attention to mossy rocks, which can send the most adventurous scrambler flying. When the water is fast flowing there is no risk of bilharzia, and it is safe for swimming.

There is likely to be someone at the entrance keen to accompany you, although having a guide is not necessary, as the route up is obvious, and once there it is possible to explore quite happily alone.

Getting there and away The falls and the Domes de Fabedougou (see opposite) are on the same winding dirt road through sugar plantations and irrigation canals. It takes about 20 minutes to reach the falls from Banfora, and another ten to get to the domes, which at least can be seen from some distance away. At the time of writing, they were both signposted, but if you don't take a guide with you it's worth checking with someone anytime you get to a fork in the road if things aren't immediately obvious.

If you're heading west towards Sindou, look out for a sign for Karfiguela after the turning for Tiekouna that heads right and follow that. It's a lovely route that takes you through the rice fields (impassable during the rains), and local guides know the way. Alternatively, take the road from Banfora towards Bobo. Turn left just after the SK petrol station, cross the railway tracks and keep going, following the dirt road.

Where to stay

Campement Cascades (3 rooms) m 70 43 04 17, 78 54 15 32. A real shame: in an exquisite spot just behind the ticket office, a few simple thatched huts are slowly crumbling to ruin: only 3 are useable. An ambitious bucket shower/drop loo block built by ONTB is reasonably clean. Beer & soft drinks are available, & you can buy fruit, bread & sardines. **$**

Camping de Karfiguela (5 rooms) m 76 59 17 65; e konatou@guideburkinafaso.com; www.guideburkinafaso.com. Another dream that's slowly crumbling; the original owner has gone to France. However, set in the village itself, it has a lovely atmosphere; staff who remain are friendly & doing their best. Huts are basic; there are tents available at 1,750f pp. Food can be ordered. Tricky to find, so ask, or call ahead. **$**

Back towards Banfora, the **Campement Baobab** is a more inviting bush camp option (see *Where to stay*, page 294).

DOMES DE FABEDOUGOU (*Entry 1,000f; parking is 200f for cars, 150f for motos, 100f for bikes*) In western Australia, the bulbous rock formations of the Bungle Bungles draw thousands of tourists every year. Burkina has an almost geologically identical feature, yet it is almost entirely unheard of.

So the magnificent, hauntingly beautiful Domes de Fabedougou rest undisturbed, all the better for their desolation, bar local cows and herders. Better still, they are there for the climbing, and there are some easy ascents up the cracked sides of the domes, which sit side by side like a series of enormous grey igloos.

Geological experts say they date back 1.8 billion years, from the Tarkwaian era. Once upon a time the whole area was underwater, set beneath an ocean packed with free-flowing sediment. Over time, sedimentary rock layers of differing thicknesses have been laid down. Some layers were harder than others, and so were more protected from erosion. Through a process of weathering and fracturing, the rocks were moulded into a combination of giant smooth eggs, craggy fingers pointing skyward and undulating hills that would make more sense if they were coated in green grass and set among the English countryside.

Whatever the geological story, the rocks are giving nothing away, and the ticket office offers up no information about the majestic run of mountains. Visit, and the spirit soars. For directions, see *Getting there and away*, opposite.

TENGRELA This lakeside village is known for its hippopotami, but is also a great hangout for anyone in search of an introduction to rural Burkina. Its accommodation options mean visitors have a chance to stick around for a bit and latch on to timeless rhythms of village life, and pick up crafts such as basket-weaving or *balafon*-playing. Tengrela is also famed for *trembleuses*: young female dancers with cords of cowrie shells jiggling in a trademark Senoufou dance.

Getting there and away From Banfora, take the Sindou road 6km west for the village, and a further 1km to the lake. It's best reached by moped.

Where to stay

Campement du Ciel (6 rooms) m 78 05 33 17, 74 10 43 45, e campduciel@hotmail.nl. On the Sindou road. The 6 huts are very solidly made, spacious with mozzie nets, & painted in rainbow colours. Some have internal shower. There's a shady *paillote* & plenty of entertainment: *baby-foot* & draughts, or *djembe* & *balafon* sessions on request in the evenings. Cold drinks, & meals on order. **$**

Campement Farafina (16 rooms) m 70 24 46 21, 78 17 25 04; e soloisa6@hotmail.com. Also known as 'Chez Solo', this is one of the best rural encampments in Burkina. The colourfully decorated & furnished huts are widely spaced in a large dusty courtyard complete with baby crocodiles, bats & hammocks (although not all in the same place). The owner, Souleymane, is an enthusiastic & knowledgeable host & can organise trips throughout the region. Head of his own troupe of musicians & dancers, he runs courses in African musicianship, dance & cooking, & organises the annual festival (see below). Food is available. Peeking at crocs 1,000f for non-guests. Twin huts 4,000f, 4-bed 12,000f. **$**

Campement Kegnigohi (15 rooms) m 76 42 69 02, 70 24 68 93; e drissatou@yahoo.fr. Reasonably close to the lake, this is pleasant, neat & orderly, although not quite as appealing as its neighbour Farafina. Huts have mozzie nets. Can cook up meals to order. Motorbikes/bicycles cost 4,500f/2,000f per day plus petrol. Twin huts 6,000f. **$**

Campement le Rankart (7 rooms) m 78 25 14 68, 75 13 20 30. Very simple *campement* right next to the lake itself. The circle of huts feels a bit exposed, but you can order food at the little *buvette* under the trees nearby & drinks are available (but may not be cold). Twin hut 6,000f. **$**

Hippo lake (*Entry 1,000f; a 45min canoe trip is 1,000f pp, organised at the pay booth*) Fringed with trees and reeds, the lake hides birdlife and, more importantly, a large hippo herd. Boatmen can take you out on to the lake in a rickety wooden canoe – 'If you even sneeze too hard in the *pirogue* it will go over,' said one visitor of the transport – with apparently nonchalant concern for Africa's most dangerous land animal, whose full range of nasal-hygiene sound effects can be heard as they surface to breathe. The boatmen know what they are doing, however, and will spot where the animals are long before you do. One boatman even talks to the hippos. The best times for a sighting are 07.00–08.00 and after 16.30. Non-early risers are helped by four campsites within walking distance.

Annual festival From 26 December to 1 January every year, Tengrela plays host to a festival of sport and culture. There are *pirogue* and swimming races on the lake, women's cycling races, men's running races, wrestling, football, dancing, music, pottery and more. It's a good opportunity to spot *trembleuses*, too. For information, ask at Campement Farafina.

TOUMOUSSENI This pretty village, home to animist Turka people, hides an extraordinary baobab. If you visit only one sacred tree in Burkina, make it this one. Unremarkable from the outside (if nice and fat), a little hole at its base is just big enough to scramble through; from the inside, the hollow trunk seems suddenly huge, with a shrine, benches, and space for about 20 people. The role of guardian is an important one, and the present incumbent has been in position for over 30 years. Immensely humorous and entertaining, he will tell you all about the tree's history, its resident wildlife, its pool of sacred water and how he was chosen.

When you emerge blinking into daylight, he will show you his compound and hut with its row of ten sacrificial chicken feathers (one for each former guardian). There are a lot of *ronier* palms nearby, and you're unlikely to leave without being offered a bowl of *banji*. There's no fixed fee, but make sure you leave something for the guardian's next sacrifice, and something for the *banji* too.

Getting there and away Toumousseni is about 18km from Banfora off the Sindou road and is best reached by moped. Take a left at the sign, and head towards the village for about 1km. You'll need to ask directions to the tree – or, much better, go with a guide.

SENOUFOU COUNTRY

Squeezed into the west of Burkina and overflowing into Côte d'Ivoire and Mali, the Senoufou are revered as a magical and mysterious people. They are held in such awe that some credulous Mossi are prepared to tell you that cannibalism is still practised among certain sects, if demanded by the chief or the spirits.

The Senoufou believe in a supreme being and creator of the universe, the god Koutyolo. In some versions of the myth he has fallen asleep, in others he was disgusted with his final creation, man – either way, he has withdrawn from the world, leaving it a guideless place. A kinder female god, Katielo, is a mother figure who exerts a more positive influence, overseeing the village and protecting the sacred wood. It is her influence that has enabled man to evolve and learn the arts of farming and music.

There are two other important protecting gods, Komo and Kono, only visible to initiated men. A non-Senoufou village can acquire its Komo cult, so long as it has the permission of a Komo priest. For this, the village must provide two bulls, two goats and a red dog for sacrifice. This latter addition replaces the once-popular human offering.

SINDOU PEAKS (*Entry, with guide, 1,000f; cameras 1,000f; video 5,000f. Basic tours vary from 30mins to 2hrs; for longer tours discuss a guide fee in advance*) A series of monumental sculptures made by the age-old movement of oceans and the beating of the rain and the wind, Sindou's crags have a magical feel. Spindles of sandstone rise into the air like melting sticks of rock. Such is the romance of the peaks that many a Burkinabe director has given them pride of place in film shoots: an abandoned movie set hides among the cliffs on the plateau.

An easy trail up the rocks takes you to a beautiful view from the plateau, perfect for sunset: spookily quiet, even the birds dare not disturb the silence. Get there early, or camp, and you may see monkeys. Take plenty of water, and a torch if you want to explore the nearby cave.

For experienced climbers, some of the 50–80m crags make for good ascents, with natural handholds. It is forbidden to bang in any sort of climbing equipment. You can also take a picnic to a nearby lake, spend the night with local families, or visit a cliffside village with a guide who will accompany you in your transport.

Getting there and away Sindou is 51km from Banfora, best covered by moped or 4x4, although tough in the rainy season. A bush taxi leaves Banfora's *autogare* daily (morning and afternoon) for 1,500f.

Where to stay There's no accommodation at the peaks themselves, but nearby Sindou town (about 1km away) has three good *campements*, or you can camp nearby or stay with a family.

SINDOU The capital of Senoufou country, Sindou is a simple town with little in the way of luxury, but nevertheless always in the mood for a party (see box, page 301). Roadside stalls and kiosks cook up rice with generous lashings of sauce, all at excellent prices.

Getting there and away Transport from the *autogare* in Banfora to Sindou costs 1,500f, with departures at around 09.00 and in the afternoon, daily. Another van regularly takes the same road, passing Sindou for Baguere. Departures for

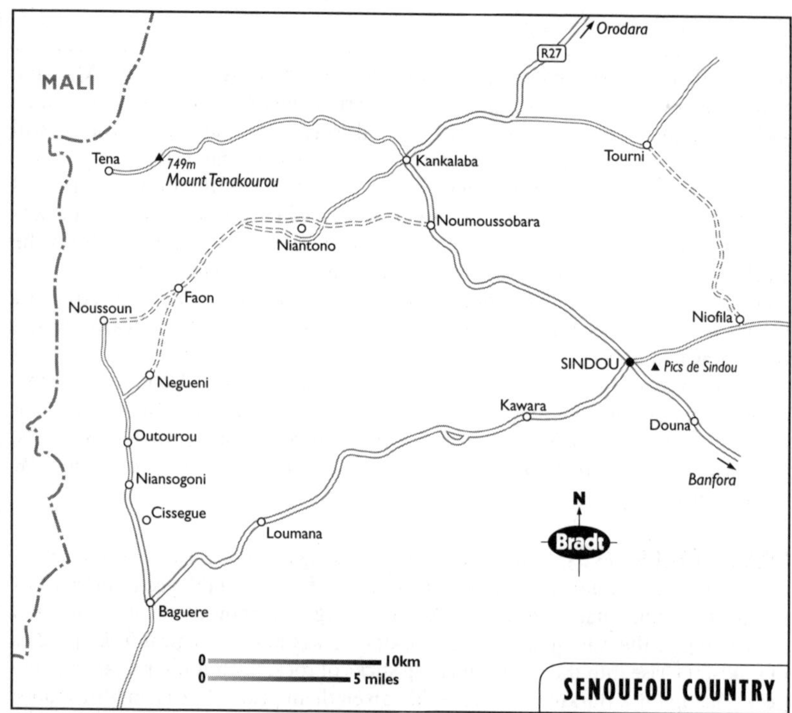

Banfora leave Sindou at 08.00. Market day is Monday, making this a good day for finding a ride.

Where to stay

Campement Djatiguiya (10 rooms) m 76 53 57 95, 79 14 86 44. This is a neat, orderly place with both fan huts & rooms, some with the luxury of en suite. There's a nice *paillote* for eating & drinking (meals available on order). Can also organise excursions. Turn left at the Pic Buvette; it's on the left. **$**

Campement Solidarité (10 huts) m 76 57 19 78, 70 07 97 77; e mokopic@yahoo.fr. On the right on the way in from Sindou, the simplest *campement* is also the prettiest, its attractive huts ranged around shady mango trees. Outdoor bucket showers & loos. Excellent meals on order. A guide & excursions available. B/fast 1,000f. **$**

Campement Terre des Enfants (6 rooms) m 76 08 19 99, 78 54 15 79; e solosindou@yahoo.fr. A portion of the profits goes to the education & care of underprivileged children, & management runs a child sponsorship scheme which pays for schooling, vaccinations, clothes & so on. Spacious huts are solidly built & have fans & showers; some have full en suite. New *paillote* & 4 en-suite rooms under construction. Camping 2,000f per tent. **$**

Where to eat and drink Sindou has few sit-down restaurants, but many street vendors and snack bars with high stools. People are generally very welcoming, so visitors may also be invited to someone's home for dinner, an invitation you should have no hesitation in accepting.

All three *campements* can provide food, and the standards are generally high. The grilled chicken and sweet potato chips at the **Campement Solidarité** are particularly recommended. On the main road, **Maquis Oxygene**, across from the police station, has two pleasant *paillotes* under which to swig cold drinks and beers, and serves up a good lunch. Get there early – before 13.00 – or the locals will have scoffed the lot. Across the street, a stand serves grilled mutton or goat daily. Near the petrol station, a restaurant sells village bread, made day and night, and cold drinks, spaghetti and omelettes. Further down the road across from the *district sanitaire* you can get *riz sauce* and *riz gras*. Towards the far end of town on the right is the **Maquis du Carrefour**, offering cold beers and good simple dishes. Along the road are kiosks and women serving *riz sauce*, fried plantains, fried yams, beans, *riz gras*, oranges, bananas and salads (in the dry season) on any given night. The fish soup at the **Kiosk Kassa** in the middle of town is excellent.

AROUND SINDOU The region around Sindou has some real surprises, with hard-to-reach, abandoned villages perched on and within clifftops usually reserved for *samoe* or 'wild men'. Mud houses and granary lean-tos shelter under the cliffsides, and roads soon become impassable even for 4x4s. If you have time and energy, walking or cycling is the best way to explore (see box, page 303). Moped is a less physically taxing option.

Douna caves The village of Douna is a few kilometres short of Sindou on the road from Banfora. The caves are another 5km or so, off to the right through fields and *ronier* plantations – a route that's a lovely walk or *moto* ride in its own right. Once there, the *grottes* are great for exploring and scrambling around, and are an ideal picnic spot.

Getting there and away To find the caves, you'll need a guide; some of those in Sindou and Banfora know the way. If in doubt, ask at the *campement*. You can only get so far by *moto*; the last 1km or so is soft sand. Allow a good hour to get there from Douna, two hours if you plan to walk all the way.

Where to stay

Auberge Djodouale (7 rooms) m 78 57 62 42. Perched on an escarpment overlooking the rice fields, this is a wonderful spot. It's a pity that the rooms have tin roofs, & that, when we were there, the huts were the only ones in Burkina to actually smell. However, there's a warm welcome, mozzie nets, an enclosure of baby crocs, & cold drinks. Meals available on order. Turn right at the police station coming from Banfora, & follow the signs. B/fast 500f. **$**

Senoufou villages

Niofila This village is 12km northeast of Sindou, with good examples of traditional circular compounds. Entry is through a simple vestibule (*fugago*), with two openings. The main court is filled with round dried-earth huts topped with

PARTY TOWN *Angelique Moss, Peace Corps volunteer, Sindou*

Sindou is very lively and doesn't need an excuse to party. I usually hear *balafons* or drums every night during the dry season for marriages, funerals and other events. There is also traditional dancing all day for two or more weeks around Ramadan and Tabaski. For the ritual dancing, girls dress up in bras and skirts with colourful Christmas garlands. They paint heads, face and body and have their feet hennaed. They dance in a huge circle around trees in the old part of town from sunrise to sunset, with breaks in between. There is also a week or so when the young men are being initiated, and they have their turn around the tree too.

AFRICA'S SAMURAI

Famed for their skills, the Senoufou brotherhood of *dozo* (hunters) is feared and respected. Nowhere is initiation more demanding. Like a kind of African samurai, the *dozo* live according to a strict code of rules and privations necessary to ensure survival in the dangerous, magical world of forest and savanna. They are reputedly in possession of magical powers themselves, including invisibility and invulnerability to arms.

The training, by a master *dozo*, is a complete schooling in the art of hunting and spiritual and moral values. Lying, jealousy and stealing are forbidden, as the *dozo* is the epitome of good and noble conduct. The entry requirement is 12 kola nuts and a chicken – if this pleases the fetishes, the initiate takes a symbolic bath that makes him a *dozo* student.

Dress is instantly recognisable, as is smell: it is forbidden to wash the *dozo* uniform of floppy bonnet and loose-fitting cotton shirt and trousers, usually dyed in earth browns, yellows and greens and adorned with charms for protection and good luck.

Dozo culture draws heavily on the animal kingdom. Cotton masks represent beasts of the bush, while the *sogogbankele* dance is that of the one-horned animal (rhinoceros).

straw. They house shepherds, chicken-keepers, women, single men, elders and fetishes. Husbands have no room of their own, but take their pick of their wives'.

Noumoussobara Further on, 15km from Sindou, and home to a great forging family. Traditionally, blacksmiths commune with spirits, and cut the umbilical cords of newborns (see page 42).

Kawara The rupestral wall carvings here, 5km west of Sindou, were inadvertently graffitied over by a visiting party of primary-school children. Nevertheless, the village's main activity, pottery, continues as it has done for centuries.

Niansogoni Meaning 'between the hills', and 37km from Sindou along a bone-jarring road, this is first in a string of difficult-to-reach Senoufou villages that run north to Negueni. It is a beautiful spot, notable for a dramatic collection of cave dwellings built into the stunning escarpment that looms over the village. Although these dwellings have not been inhabited since about 1980, elders can remember life among the caves, good for protection during Samoury Toure's raids. Relics such as pots, decorated granaries and other cooking tools are still found in the cliffs.

Getting there and away If you don't have your own wheels, you can take a bush taxi from Banfora as far as Baguera. They're not terribly reliable, and breakdowns are common. From there, the *campement* (see below) can pick you up by *moto* – but make sure they know you're coming.

Where to stay

Campement Niansogoni (13 rooms) 20 91 88 11; m 76 48 06 59; e traorichard@yahoo.fr. A lovely circle of traditional huts around a shady *paillote*, just at the foot of the escarpment; all have external facilities. There's a little crafts shop, & cold drinks are available; meals can be ordered, but you need to give a bit of notice. **$**

Climbing the escarpment (*Fee of 1,000f, plus a tip for the guide*) Because some visitors have been tempted to take relics off with them, a guide is compulsory. Richard Traore (*20 91 88 11;* m *76 48 06 59;* e *traorichard@yahoo.fr*) is head of a local association of guides and, if not at the *campement*, can be found at the Catholic mission. A return trip takes about two hours, and the going is fairly steep, so avoid the hottest parts of the day and take water.

Troglodyte villages Continuing north of Niansogoni you can visit the remains of the troglodyte villages of **Outourou**, **Negueni** and **Faon**. The guides' association in Niansogoni can organise three-day camping trips that take in Negueni, Faon and Noussoun; routes are flexible, and are designed to give an introduction to Sama and Wara culture.

Mount Tenakourou It's no Kilimanjaro, but at 749m it's the highest point in Burkina Faso and, tucked up against the Malian border, getting there is quite an adventure. From Sindou, follow the road northwest for 19km as far as Kankalaba. The main road towards Orodara turns sharply to the right, but there should be a large sign directing you to the left-hand fork. Tena village, at the foot of the peak, is 24km away. You'll find a path leading up the side of the hill.

ORODARA Known as the fruit basket of Burkina, Orodara's Saturday market is famed for mangoes. On the tarmac road leading west from Bobo, it makes a good alternative gateway for exploring Senoufou country.

EXPLORING SENOUFOU COUNTRY

The Association Tourisme Solidaire (*20 91 87 00;* m *76 08 46 60*) is working to promote Senoufou culture in the region, and to provide healthcare and educational support for its children.

Its president, Tiemoko Ouattara, brother of Sindou's chief, organises a selection of tours around the region, on foot, bicycle or moped. While prices are not cheap by backpackers' standards, the advantage of signing up for a tour is that you will have a genuine introduction to Senoufou life, and visit villages, routes and sites not normally accessible to visitors. Senoufou country is dotted with sacred sites, much better explored with a guide.

The Senoufou Circuit (four days on foot) takes in Niansogoni, Outourou, Negueni, Faon, Niantono, Kankalaba, Tourni, Niofila and Sindou. The Blacksmiths' Tour (three days on foot) takes in Loumana, Cissegue, Niansogoni, Niantono and Noumoussobara. On foot, fixed-price tours cost 22,500f per person per day; 26,000f by bike; 32,000f by moped (but these take less time), and 35,000f per day for the hire of a car, plus 15,000f per person. Prices are for groups of four; they are slightly more expensive if there are fewer of you.

Family stays, including accommodation, food, guide, programme and washing cost 20,000f per day. Tiemoko can organise a one-off mask party, including *dolo*, kola nuts, goats and chickens. Cultural exchange programmes involve initiation into Senoufou language, pottery, dressmaking, hairstyling, musicianship (*kora, djembe, balafon*) and traditional medicine, for 15,000f a day. They can also arrange other local trips, to Mount Tenakourou, Karfiguela and Tengrela.

Prices include tent, meals, guides, porters, entry passes and a celebration at the end, but not drinks.

Getting there and away TCV runs between Bobo and Orodara every two hours, for 1,500f. Rakieta runs regular services from Bobo for 1,000f. Both stops are at the western (Malian) end of town. From Sindou, the road winds and bumps for about 75km, but the views on the stretch from Kankalaba northeast to Dieri, 8km before Orodara, are fantastic. Or take a bush taxi from Banfora (53km).

Where to stay

Hotel Le Prestige (34 rooms) 20 99 50 16. Best hotel in Senoufou country, it is on the way into town from Bobo, about 1km from the centre, & makes a change from the relative privation of accommodation in the region. Fan or AC rooms are all en suite; there are options for hot water & TV. **$$–$$$**

Le Verger (6 rooms) 20 99 50 27. A cheap, basic *auberge* opposite the Shell station in the centre. Internal showers; outside loos. **$**

Where to eat The **Hotel Le Prestige** does the best food in town, serving up excellent if slightly pricey meals in nice garden surrounds. **Restaurant Le Festin**, with pleasant street-seating next to the Shell petrol station, does a good lunch, as does the *maquis* opposite the Total station. There is a bakery opposite the *gendarmerie*.

AROUND ORODARA Although the Senoufou palace of **Kourouma** is no longer inhabited, with parts falling into ruin, it was a symbol of power under the Kenedougou Kingdom. Wall paintings represent warriors and royal insignia, while there are plans to open a small museum.

Further north still, the mud mosque in the Dioula village of **Teoule** was built around the time Samoury Toure was making raiding incursions from Mali. It is made up of little *banco* bricks, with the top minaret covered and rounded like a smooth ceramic egg. Take the R26, 78km north from Orodara for Kourouma. Teoule is a little further, 5km southeast of Ndorola. Alternatively, take the Mali road north from Bobo for 58km and head west after Dande on a 20km track that ends up at Kourouma. Head right (north) for Teoule.

Appendix 1

LANGUAGE

FRENCH It is essential that visitors learn to speak at least some French before arriving in Burkina, as English-speakers are few and far between. If you want to brush up before you go, the BBC (*www.bbcshop.com*) does an excellent series of audio guides, entitled *The French Experience*, on both CD and tape. These are available at various different levels, and *The French Experience 2* includes voices and characters from across the French-speaking world, including west Africa. Still, if you're rusty, there's nothing like throwing yourself in at the deep end to jog your memory. Burkinabe tend to be pretty forgiving of errors in grammar and accent, so it may be a less harrowing experience than Paris in the spring.

Burkinabe French slang School French will be of little help without some knowledge of the French of Burkina's streets, known as *l'argot*. You can usually pick up what's being said from the tone or context, but we've listed a few of the ones we've picked up below. There are some corkers.

avoir l'oeuf colonial	literally 'to have the colonial egg', meaning to have a beer belly, a caricature of the old colonials
avoir un deuxième bureau	literally 'to have a second office'; euphemism for a mistress
bachée	pick-up truck. In Burkina, this will usually be a Peugeot 404 with some sort of roof covering at the back
bouffer	literally 'to eat', but means to embezzle or engage in corruption
c'est caillou	it's difficult
c'est gâté	it's broken
ca chauffe	it's hot, but also it's kicking (of a bar, for example)
ca fait deux jours	it's been a while since we've seen each other
ca va aller	literally 'it's going to go', meaning it will work, it will be alright
ca va un peu	it's not that great (usually indicating a problem with work, money or health)
char	moped
coin	corner, hangout, bar
colon	a colonialist
en tout cas	used as an enthusiastic term of agreement, meaning for sure, or, ain't that the truth
faux type	a bad sort, con man
gagner petit	to have a baby
je demande la route	not a request for directions, but a polite way of saying to a small gathering that you're off home if that's OK, I'm on my way
je suis en bouille	I am angry, boiling with rage

je suis un vagabond	I'll go wherever you like
laisser tomber	literally 'to let fall', to break up with someone romantically (*pourquoi tu m'a laissé tomber?* means why did you leave me?)
laissez passer	literally 'let you pass', a document allowing you through a checkpoint
laver une pellicule	develop a camera film
le boulot	work
on dit quoi?	what's up
ou bien?	or what? Doesn't really demand a response
pas de quoi	it's nothing, no problem, you're welcome
quoi	often added at the end of a statement for emphasis, and to demand a response, as a sort of 'or what?' (eg *c'est bon quoi*)
sans soucis	no worries
six metres	small, unpaved side-road
tablier	street seller with small wooden box
tantie	meaning auntie, it is said as a sign of respect, not to suggest that you are over the hill
tonton	equivalent to uncle or second father, it is a similar sign of respect as *tantie*
truc	thing

Note on negatives While you may have learned that never is there a 'pas' without a 'ne' somewhere in front of it (eg: *je n'aime pas parler le français*), in Burkina, you pretty much never hear the 'ne'. So listen out especially hard for the 'pas' or 'plus' in phrases such as '*j'ai pas…*' (I don't have) or '*j'en ai plus*' (I don't have any more of them).

Note on articles If you're prone to mixing up your *la* and your *le*, leave it out. Most people do, so you'll be in good company.

Official French The best thing is to take a textbook, and always keep a pocket-sized dictionary on you. We give a few key words and phrases below, but it won't help you with pluperfects or your hopes for a conditional future.

Greetings

good morning	*bonjour*
good afternoon/evening	*bonsoir* (in Burkina, this is used as the usual form of greeting any time after lunch)
good night	*bonne nuit*
hello	*salut*
how are you?	*(Comment) ca va?, comment allez-vous?*
fine thanks	*ca va merci*
very good thanks	*tres bien merci*
my name is	*je m'appelle, je suis…*
glad to meet you	*heureux de faire votre reconaissance*
goodbye	*au revoir*
see you soon	*à bientôt, toute à l'heure*
see you tomorrow	*à demain*
thank you	*merci*
please	*s'il vous plait*
very much	*beaucoup*

(Not) understanding

I don't understand	*je ne comprends pas*
could you repeat that please?	*voulez-vous répéter, s'il vous plait*
do you speak English?	*parlez-vous anglais?*
I don't speak much French	*je ne parle pas bien français*
speak slowly please	*parlez lentement, s'il vous plait*
less quickly please	*moins vite, s'il vous plait*
please can you write it down?	*écrivez-le, s'il vous plait*

Getting there and away

4x4 drive car	*quatre-quatre*	pot-hole	*nid de poule*
50cc moped	*mobylette, moto*	return, round-trip	*aller-retour*
break down	*tomber en panne*	spare part	*pièce de rechange*
can you show me?	*pouvez-vous me montrer?*	station	*gare*
car	*voiture*	stop here	*arrêtez-vous ici*
checkpoint	*contrôle*	straight on	*continuez tout droit*
coach	*bus, autobus, car*	tarmac road	*goudron, route bitumée*
diesel	*gasole*		
dirt track	*six metre*	(green) taxi	*taxi (vert)*
have a good journey	*bon voyage, bonne route*	that's too much	*c'est trop (cher)*
how do you get to?	*pour aller à?*	train	*train*
how much is it?	*c'est combien?*	turn left/right	*tournez à gauche/ droit*
is it far?	*est-ce que c'est loin?*		
motorbike	*motocycle*	unsurfaced road	*piste*
one-way	*aller-simple*	washboard effect when driving	*escalier*
parked	*garé*		
petrol	*essence/carburant*	what time does the train leave/arrive?	*à quelle heure part/ arrive le train?*
please wait for me	*attendez-moi, s'il vous plait*	where is ... ?	*où est ... ?*

Dealing with hassle

excuse me	*excusez-moi*	just a minute	*une minute, un instant*
I'm hungry/thirsty	*j'ai faim/soif*	leave me alone	*laissez-moi tranquille*
I'm in a hurry	*je suis pressé*	no thanks	*ca va merci*
I'm tired	*je suis fatigué*	sorry	*desolé*

Accommodation

air-conditioned room	*chambre climatisée*	ironing	*repassage*
cleaning (of clothes)	*blanchissage*	key	*clef*
courtyard	*cour*	mosquito net	*moustiquaire*
double bed	*un lit à deux places*	room	*une chambre*
fan room	*chambre ventilée*	sheets	*draps*
first/second floor	*premier/deuxième étage*	with shower	*avec douche*
full, no room	*complet*	with en-suite loo	*avec toilette interne*
hot/cold water	*l'eau chaude/froide*		

Eating and drinking

bakery	*boulangerie*	meal	*repas*
the bill	*l'addition, la note*	supermarket	*supermarché*
breakfast	*petit déjeuner*	to your health, cheers	*à votre santé*
dinner	*dîner*		

drinking water	*eau potable*	vegetable and fruit market	*marché de légumes et fruits*
food shop	*alimentation*	well done/medium/ rare/very rare	*bien cuit/à point/ saignant/bleu*
how was it	*c'etait*		
lunch	*déjeuner*		

Health

allergy	*l'allergie*	malaria	*palu, paludisme*
broken	*cassé*	medicine	*les medicaments*
chemist	*la pharmacie*	pain	*la douleur*
cold	*le rhume*	prescription	*l'ordonnance*
doctor	*un médecin*	sore throat	*l'angine, le mal de gorge*
fever	*fievre*		
flu	*la grippe*	sprained	*foulé*
headache	*j'ai mal à la tête*	sunburn	*la coup de soleil*
I feel ill	*je me sens malade*	swollen	*enflé*
it hurts	*ca fait mal*	that hurts	*ca me fait mal*

Money and shopping

bad	*mal*	expensive	*cher*
bank	*banque*	good	*bon*
change	*monnaie*	money	*l'argent*
cheap	*bon marché*		

can you give me some small change?	*pourriez-vous me donner de la monnaie?*
do you cash travellers' cheques?	*acceptez-vous les chèques de voyages?*
how much do I get for a euro/dollar/sterling?	*combien vaut le euro/dollar/livres sterling?*
I'd like to change euros/dollars/sterling	*je voudrais changer des euros/dollars/livres sterling*
what's the exchange rate?	*quel est le taux de change?*
where do I sign?	*où dois-je signer?*

Questions

have you?	*avez-vous?*	what's that?	*qu'est-ce que c'est?*
how?	*comment?*	when?	*quand?*
how much/many?	*combien?*	where?	*où?*
what?	*quoi?*	who?	*qui?*
what do I have to do?	*que dois-je faire?*	why?	*pourquoi?*

Everyday nouns

buvette	mall bar or counter	*griot*	village storyteller
canari	clay pot for water storage	*paillote*	roof for a building or drinking spot, made from straw
charette	hand-pushed or donkey-pulled cart		
château d'eau	water tower	*pièce*	some kind of identification
dolo	millet beer		
forage	well	*pirogue*	canoe
fonctionnaire	civil servant	*ronier*	type of palm tree

Useful words and phrases

early/late	*tôt/tard*	the day after tomorrow	*le lendemain*
fortnight	*une quinzaine*	today/tomorrow	*aujourd'hui/demain*
no/yes	*non/oui*	yesterday	*hier*

MOORE The main local language, which you may also see written as More, Moré or Mooré, is spoken by the Mossi (singular *moaga*), the dominant group in Burkina, of whom there are about six million. The phrases below will get you through pleasant greetings with people on the streets, and are well worth trying on taxi drivers just before you come to discuss price – any showing of local language will help your cause. If you hear something approaching the tail end of *buenos sera* on the streets, it doesn't mean that everyone thinks you're Spanish, they are probably yelling out *nasara*, which means 'white person'. There's much more, best found in a language book picked up locally.

Greetings, conversations and chat-up lines

amen	*ammi*
day after tomorrow	*rayita*
fine	*lafi beme, laafi bala, keemame*
good afternoon	*ne y zaabre*
good dusk	*ne y zi-sobdo*
good evening	*ne y yongo*
good midday (until about 15.00)	*ne y windga*
good morning	*ne y yibeoogo*
goodbye	*wend na taase*
how's it going?	*kibare? yaa lafi? laafi beme?*
how's the harvest?	*y koodo?*
how's your wife?	*y paga?, y pag keemame?*
I am… years	*mam tara yourm…*
I am from…	*mam yita…*
I am happy/sad	*mam suur yaa noogo/mam suura saamama*
I hate you/I love you	*mam kisa foom/mam nonga foom*
I want you	*mam data foo*
I'll be off	*mam na n kulame*
it doesn't rain/it rains	*saga ka niid ye/saga niidame*
it's hot	*yaa tourlgo*
it's the rainy season	*yaa seoogo*
my name is…	*man your la a…*
no/yes	*ayo/nge*
no problems	*yell ka ye*
OK	*woo*
until tomorrow	*wend na kod beoogo*
what's your name?	*fo yourla a boe?*
where are you from?	*fo yita ye?*
how old are you?	*fo tara yourma wana?*
today	*runna, runda*
tomorrow	*beoogo*
will you be my husband?	*fo rat n yum am seerda?*
will you be my wife?	*fo rat n yum am paga?*
yesterday	*zaame*
you're a delightful woman	*fo yaa bi-pugl polle*
you're a good-looking man	*fo yaa ra-sanga*

Market

can you lower the price?	*y toe n barsa me?*
come with me to the market	*wa yaag m raaga*
I want, give me	*m data*

let's go	*ed looge*
money	*ligda*
oh, that's too expensive	*popopo, yaa toog woursgo*
OK	*yaa soama*
thank you	*barka, na possa baraka*
we're here	*taame*

Numbers

1	*ye, yembre, se, sembo*	20	*pisi*
2	*yi, yiibu, si*	25	*pissi la a nu*
3	*ta, taabo*	30	*pis-ta, pis-taabo*
4	*nasse*	40	*pis-naase*
5	*nu*	50	*pis-nu*
6	*yoobe*	100	*koabga*
7	*yoopoe*	200	*kobessi, yiibu*
8	*nii*	500	*kobs-nu*
9	*wae, we*	1,000	*tusri*
10	*piiga*	10,000	*tus-piiga*

Mossi money is counted in clumps of five. That means if you want to say 10f, you need only say two, since it means two fives, which are ten. When counting money out, the 'fives' format is always used, so for 25f, you say five fives (*wakir a nu*); for 100f, you say 20 fives (*wakir pisi*); for 10,000f, you say 2,000 fives (*wakir tusa yi*). Likewise if you are asked for *piiga* (ten) in a marketplace, you must give over 50f, since it means ten fives.

DIOULA Dioula (spelled Jula in the language itself, which is known as Julakaan) is a trading language widespread throughout the region. After French and Moore, it is the most widely spoken language in Burkina. We've tried to write down a few phrases as they might sound in English, avoiding confusing signs and phonetic symbols, but if in doubt sound out every 'e', give everything you're saying a nasal twang and hope for the best. *Toubab* or *toubabou* means 'white person'.

Greetings, conversations and chat-up lines

amen	*amina*
and how is your family?	*somogo-ou do?*
and the children?	*denmisenou do?*
and work?	*baara do?*
and your name?	*i jamu do?*
be my girl/boyfriend	*ke n teri ye*
come and sit near me	*na sigi n kor*
did you sleep well?	*here sira wa?*
family is well	*o ka kene*
fine	*here*
good afternoon (to you)	*(i) ni wula*
goodbye	*ka an ben*
good evening (to you)	*(i) ni suu*
good midday (to you)	*(i) ni tilen*
good morning (to you)	*(i) ni sogoma*
greetings	*foli*
how are you doing?	*i ka kene wa?*
I am called...	*n togo ye...*

I don't like/love you	*n t'i fe*
I like/love you	*n b'i fe*
leave me alone	*fara n na*
let's hang out	*na an bi baro ke*
long life to him/her	*ala m'a balola, ala k'a balo*
my love	*n djarabi*
my name is…	*n jamu ye…*
no	*ai*
say what	*do fo*
thank you	*ami, initche*
thank you, that God may grant the wish	*ami, ala ka duga mina*
that tomorrow may be better than today	*ala ka sni fisaya bii ye*
they are well	*u ka kene*
until another day	*an bi loon were*
until tomorrow	*an bi sini*
welcome	*danse, ala k'a nakan diya*
response:	*nbaa* (if a man); *nsee* (if a woman)
what is your name?	*I togo di?*
yes	*hum*

Market

come with me to the market	*na an ka taga logo ra*
give money	*warri di*
grace of God	*baraji*
how many?	*joli?*
how much are these?	*nin ye djoli ye?*
I want to go to the market	*n bi fe ka taga logo ra*
lower it more	*bariki tugu*
lower the price	*bariki, do bo a ra*
money	*warri*
OK	*n sonna*
that's (too) expensive	*a songo ka gwele (kojugu)*
village, town	*dugu*
voyage, walk	*tagama*
where is the market?	*logofiye be min?*

Numbers

1	*kelen*	20	*mugan*
2	*fila*	25	*mugan ni duuru*
3	*saba*	30	*bisaba*
4	*naani*	40	*binanni*
5	*duuru*	50	*biwooro*
6	*wooro*	100	*keme*
7	*wolonwula*	200	*keme fila*
8	*seegi*	1,000	*waga kelen ou*
9	*kononton*	10,000	*waga tan*
10	*tan*		

As in Moore, every financial number is divided by five: 10,000f, for example, would not translate *waga tan*, but *waga fila* (2,000). So if someone says a pile of peanuts are on sale for *tan*, then you must hand over not 10f, but 50f.

Appendix 2

GLOSSARY

AOF	*Afrique Occidentale Française* (French West Africa) was a federation of eight French territories in western Africa that lasted from 1895 to 1959. It comprised Dahomey (now Benin), French Sudan (now Mali), Guinea, Côte d'Ivoire, Mauritania, Niger, Senegal, and Upper Volta (now Burkina Faso).
atelier	A workshop, often producing the crafts of local artisans
banco	Style of mud architecture common to Sahel region of sub-Saharan Africa
CBMP	*Comptoir burkinabè des métaux précieux:* government body looking after Burkina's mineral rights, setting the buying price for gold
CCF	*Centre Culturelle Française*: French-funded bastion of the arts, a bit like the British Council, dedicated to supporting the best of African and European culture
CDP	*Congrès pour la Démocratie et le Progrès*: the ruling political party, led by President Blaise Compaore since 1996
CDR	*Comité pour la défense de la revolution*: the much-disliked organs of state power instituted during the Sankara era
CFA franc	*Franc de la Communauté Financière d'Afrique* (franc of the African Financial Community): the currency, pegged to the euro, of Burkina Faso and seven other west African states – Benin, Guinea-Bissau, Côte d'Ivoire, Mali, Niger, Senegal and Togo
coutumier	A traditional leader, often a chief of a village, who guards customs and is often believed to have powers of communication with the spirit world
CRN	*Conseil national de la Révolution*: the name of the Sankara-led body that assumed control of the country following the military coup of 1983
ECOWAS	The Economic Community of West African States: a loose alliance of the 15 countries of west Africa – Benin, Burkina Faso, Cape Verde, The Gambia, Ghana, Guinea, Guinea-Bissau, Côte d'Ivoire, Liberia, Mali, Niger, Nigeria, Senegal, Sierra Leone, and Togo
GDP	Gross Domestic Product: measure of national income, calculated by adding the total value of financial goods and services produced within the country within a given year, regardless of ownership
HIV	Human Immunodeficiency Virus (HIV): the virus leads to Acquired Immunodeficiency Syndrome (AIDS) by targeting the immune system, and affects 36–44 million people worldwide, of whom 65% are thought to be in sub-Saharan Africa
IGB	*Institut Géographique du Burkina*: responsible for producing maps of the country
IMF	International Monetary Fund: global organisation of 184 countries, working to foster global monetary co-operation

maquis	Any kind of drinking establishment serving beer; often serves simple food too, and a social mecca for Burkinabe
marabout	Notable religious teacher and leader
MDGs	Millennium Development Goals: the eight targets set down by the United Nations in an attempt to reduce extreme poverty worldwide by half by 2015
naba	Mossi word for 'king', applied to anyone in a position of traditional responsibility at village or town level
NGO	Non-governmental organisation
ONTB	*Office National du Tourisme Burkinabè*: Burkina's national tourist office
paillote	Any kind of roof structure with open walls. Originally roofed with straw but now more often tiled. Used for sheltering and socialising under
RDA	*Rassemblement Démocratique Africaine*: the west African political movement founded by Felix Houphouet-Boigny, who later became President of Côte d'Ivoire. The Burkina branch of the RDA was originally known as the *Union Démocratique Voltaic-RDA* (UDV-RDA). The Burkina branch of the RDA is today known as *L'Alliance pour la Démocratie et la Fédération-RDA* (ADF-RDA).
UEMOA	*Union Economique et Monétaire Ouest Africaine*: in English WAEMU (West African Economic and Monetary Union)

Appendix 3

FURTHER INFORMATION

There is not a great deal of literature about Burkina Faso in English. We've tried to list as much as possible here, although a fair bit of it is out of print and available only via secondhand bookshops. Not all titles deal with Burkina specifically, but all provide a good introduction to life and history in the region. For anyone keen to tackle some French, we've included a section of titles from Burkinabe and French authors.

Skinner's essay on Sankara was a major work of research and we are indebted to it.

DIARIES/BIOGRAPHY/SPEECHES

Barth, H *Travels in North and Central Africa* Frank Cass, 1965; first published in 1857

Park, M *Travels in the Interior of Africa* Wordsworth, 2002

Sankara, T *Sankara Speaks: The Burkina Faso Revolution, 1983–87* Pathfinder, 1988

Sankara, T *We are Heirs of the World's Revolution: Speeches from the Burkina Faso Revolution, 1983–87* Pathfinder, 2002

HISTORY AND BACKGROUND

Chafer, T *The End of Empire in French West Africa: France's Successful Decolonisation?* Berg, 2002

DeCalo, S *Burkina Faso* World Bibliographic Series, 1994

Englebert, P *Burkina Faso: Unsteady Statehood in West Africa* Westview Press, 1989

Fage, J D *A History of West Africa* Cambridge University Press, 1969

Fage, J D (ed) *The Cambridge History of Africa* Cambridge University Press, 1982–84

Hargreaves, J D *France and West Africa: An Anthology of Historical Documents* Macmillian, 1969

Riesman, Paul *Freedom in Fulani Social Life* University of Chicago Press, 1998

Rupley, L and McFarland, D *Historical Dictionary of Burkina Faso* Scarecrow Press, 1998

Skinner, E P *African Urban Life: The Transformation of Ouagadougou* Princeton University Press, 1974

Skinner, E P *Sankara and the Burkinabe Revolution: Charisma and Power*, in the Journal of Modern African Studies, vol 26, no 3, 1988, pp437–455

Skinner, E P *The Mossi of Burkina Faso: Chiefs, Politicians and Soldiers* Waveland Press, 1989

UNESCO *General History of Africa Volume IV: Africa from the Twelfth to the Sixteenth Century* California University Press, 1998

CULTURE

Dagan, E *Man and His Vision: Traditional Wood Sculpture of Burkina Faso* Galerie Amrad African Arts Publications, 1995

Gugler, J *African Film: Re-Imagining a Continent* James Currey/David Phillip/Indiana, 2003

Roy, C *Art of the Upper Volta Rivers* Alain and Francoise Chaffin, 1987
Thackway, M *Africa Shoots Back: Alternative Perspectives in Sub-Saharan Francophone African Film* James Currey/David Phillip/Indiana, 2003
Wise, C *The Desert Shore: Literatures of the Sahel* Lynne Rienner Publishers Inc, 2001

FICTION/NARRATIVE

Achebe, C *Things Fall Apart* Penguin, 1958
Chilson, P *Riding the Demon: On the Road in West Africa* University of Georgia Press, 1999
Fanon, F *Wretched of the Earth* Penguin, 1967
Guirma, Frederic *Princess of the Full-Moon* Macmillan, 1970
Guirma, Frederic *Tales of Mogho: African Stories from Upper Volta* Macmillan, 1971

NATURE

Animals

Collins Guide to Mammals. For real enthusiasts.
Kingdom, Jonathan *Field Guide to African Mammals* Academic Press, 1997. A tried and trusted favourite, which contains most of the information on the animals inhabiting the parks of Burkina Faso that the visitor would wish to know.
Lamarque, François *Les Grands Mammifères du Complexe WAP* Cirad, 2004. More Burkina-specific, this forms the basis of the animals guide at the beginning of this book, providing information on every mammal species in the west African parks of W and Arly (both in Burkina) and Pendjari in Benin.
Stuart, Chris and Tilde *Field Guide to the Larger Mammals of Africa* Struik, South Africa, 1997. Another guide for enthusiasts.

Birds

Borrow, Nik and Demey, Ron *Birds of Western Africa* Christopher Helm, 2001. Represents the entire avifauna of the region.
Serle, Morel and Hatwig *Field Guide to the Birds of West Africa* HarperCollins, 1977. A good bet.
Wilson, Roger and Balanca, Gilles *Les Oiseaux du Complexe WAP* CIRAD, 2007. Contains the fruits of new research on Burkina.

TRAVEL

Ardyn Boone, Sylvia *West African Travels: A Guide to People and Places* Random House, 1974. A fascinating snapshot of Burkina in the 1970s, judged alongside other countries in the region.
Klotchkoff, Jean-Claude *Burkina Faso Today* Jaguar, 1993. This is not a travel guide as such, but full of anecdote and information. The original English translation was so botched it is unreadable, although subsequent editions have improved and it is a lively, idiosyncratic introduction to the country.

IN FRENCH

Binger, G *Du Niger au Golfe de Guinée* Cagniard, first published 1890
Devilliers, G *Putsch A Ouagadougou* Plon, 1984
Dimdolobsom *Les Maximes, Pensées et Devinettes Mossi* 1934
Izard, M *Gens du Pouvoir, Gens de la Terre: Les Institutions Politiques de l'Ancien Royaume du Yatenga* Cambridge University Press, 1985
Ki-Zerbo, J *Le Monde Africain Noir* Centre d'Edition et de Diffusion Africaines, 1963
La Littérature Burkinabe: l'Histoire, les Hommes, les Oeuvres Presses Universitaires de Limoges, 2000

Merlet, A *Textes Anciens sur le Burkina* Sepia ADDB, 1995
Titinga, F *L'Artisan du Burkina* Chez l'auteur, 1987

LANGUAGE

Dioula Facile, Tome I, II and II Dak, 2003
Leroy, A and Balde, AOK *Parlons Poular* L'Harmattan, 2002
Zongo, B *Parlons Mooré* L'Harmattan, 2004

HEALTH

Wilson-Howarth, Dr Jane *Bugs, Bites & Bowels* Cadogan, 2009
Wilson-Howarth, Dr Jane, and Ellis, Dr Matthew *Your Child Abroad: A Travel Health Guide* Bradt Travel Guides, 2005

WEBSITES

Official information

www.cia.gov/library/publications/the-world-factbook US government statistics on Burkina Faso
www.fco.gov.uk British Foreign Office homepage, featuring travel advice
http://hdr.undp.org UN's Human Development index
http://www.peacecorps.gov/index.cfm?shell=learn.wherepc.africa.burkinafaso US Peace Corps page on Burkina Faso
www.primature.gov.bf Official government of Burkina Faso website, with good history section
www.state.gov/g/drl/rls/hrrpt/2004/41590.htm US Human Rights Report on Burkina Faso
www.who.int/countries/bfa/en/ World Health Organisation page on Burkina
www.worldbank.org/bf World Bank entry on Burkina

Current affairs and news

www.fasonews.net News and current affairs
www.lefaso.net Slightly more independent take on Burkina current affairs, with links to a number of Burkinabe newspapers and magazines
www.independant.bf The newspaper of murdered campaigning journalist Norbert Zongo
http://ouaga-ca-bouge.net/ News, culture, tourist information and what's on in the capital
www.ouaganet.com Lively messageboards for Burkinabe diaspora
www.sidwaya.bf State-run daily

Language

www.dictionnaire.com/hachette/ French dictionary
www.french-linguistics.co.uk/dictionary/ French–English dictionary
www.multilingualbooks.com/more.html Can order resources over the internet and have them delivered; not cheap
www.polyglot-learn-language.com Enter 'Burkina Faso' as a search term, and find a teacher online
www.rosettaproject.org/ Online project to provide resources for languages spoken across Africa

Travel related

www.burkina.com/ Site dedicated to tourism in Burkina
www.izf.net/izf/Documentation/Cartes/Pays/Burkinafaso.htm Map of Burkina Faso
www.lonelyplanet.com/thorntree Messageboards on Lonely Planet's website are worth scanning for any on-the-ground updates and issues

www.ontb.bf Official website of Burkina's tourist board
http://struggle.ws/africa/accounts/chekov.html Travel diary kept by an 'Irish anarchist' who travelled through west Africa in 2000, containing long extracts detailing experiences in Burkina

Culture

www.africultures.com Run by eminent French film critic Olivier Barlet, the site has an excellent collection of interviews and reviews of west African and Burkinabe films, many in English
www.culture.gov.bf Visitor-friendly Culture Ministry site
www.fespaco.bf Professional online home of Africa's world-famous film festival
www.modern-african-art.com Showcases the work of artists from Burkina and Senegal
www.musee-manega.bf Cultural explanations of exhibits and Burkinabe life
www.siao.bf Biennial arts and crafts show
www.thomassankara.net New online archive and introduction to Burkina's most charismatic leader
www.uiowa.edu/~africart/ Art historian Professor Christopher Roy's excellent guide to Burkinabe masks, art and culture

Bradt Travel Guides

www.bradtguides.com

Africa

Access Africa: Safaris for People with Limited Mobility	£16.99
Africa Overland	£16.99
Algeria	£15.99
Angola	£17.99
Botswana	£16.99
Burkina Faso	£17.99
Cameroon	£15.99
Cape Verde	£15.99
Congo	£15.99
Eritrea	£15.99
Ethiopia	£16.99
Ghana	£15.99
Kenya Highlights	£15.99
Madagascar	£16.99
Malawi	£15.99
Mali	£14.99
Mauritius, Rodrigues & Réunion	£15.99
Mozambique	£15.99
Namibia	£15.99
Niger	£14.99
Nigeria	£17.99
North Africa: Roman Coast	£15.99
Rwanda	£15.99
São Tomé & Príncipe	£14.99
Seychelles	£14.99
Sierra Leone	£16.99
South Africa Highlights	£15.99
Sudan	£15.99
Tanzania, Northern	£14.99
Tanzania	£17.99
Uganda	£16.99
Zambia	£18.99
Zanzibar	£14.99
Zimbabwe	£15.99

The Americas and the Caribbean

Alaska	£15.99
Amazon Highlights	£15.99
Argentina	£16.99
Bahia	£14.99
Cayman Islands	£14.99
Colombia	£17.99
Dominica	£15.99
Grenada, Carriacou & Petite Martinique	£14.99
Guyana	£15.99
Nova Scotia	£14.99
Panama	£14.99
Paraguay	£15.99
Turks & Caicos Islands	£14.99
Uruguay	£15.99
USA by Rail	£14.99
Venezuela	£16.99
Yukon	£14.99

British Isles

Britain from the Rails	£14.99
Bus-Pass Britain	£15.99
Eccentric Britain	£15.99
Eccentric Cambrige	£9.99
Eccentric London	£13.99
Eccentric Oxford	£9.99
Sacred Britain	£16.99
Slow: Cotswolds	£14.99
Slow: Devon & Exmoor	£14.99
Slow: Norfolk & Suffolk	£14.99
Slow: North Yorkshire	£14.99
Slow: Sussex & South Downs National Park	£14.99

Europe

Abruzzo	£14.99
Albania	£15.99
Azores	£14.99
Baltic Cities	£14.99
Belarus	£15.99
Bosnia & Herzegovina	£14.99
Bratislava	£9.99
Budapest	£9.99
Cork	£6.99
Croatia	£13.99
Cross-Channel France: Nord-Pas de Calais	£13.99
Cyprus see *North Cyprus*	
Dresden	£7.99
Estonia	£14.99
Faroe Islands	£15.99
Georgia	£15.99
Greece: The Peloponnese	£14.99
Helsinki	£7.99
Hungary	£15.99
Iceland	£15.99
Kosovo	£15.99
Lapland	£15.99
Latvia	£13.99
Lille	£9.99
Lithuania	£14.99
Luxembourg	£13.99
Macedonia	£15.99
Malta & Gozo	£12.99
Montenegro	£14.99
North Cyprus	£13.99
Riga	£6.99
Serbia	£15.99
Slovakia	£14.99
Slovenia	£13.99
Spitsbergen	£16.99
Switzerland Without a Car	£14.99
Transylvania	£14.99
Ukraine	£15.99
Zagreb	£6.99

Wanderlust READERS' TRAVEL AWARDS 2011 TOP GUIDEBOOK SERIES

Middle East, Asia and Australasia

Armenia	£15.99
Bangladesh	£15.99
Borneo	£17.99
Eastern Turkey	£16.99
Georgia	£15.99
Iran	£15.99
Iraq: Then & Now	£15.99
Israel	£15.99
Kazakhstan	£16.99
Kyrgyzstan	£16.99
Lake Baikal	£15.99
Lebanon	£15.99
Maldives	£15.99
Mongolia	£16.99
North Korea	£14.99
Oman	£15.99
Palestine	£15.99
Shangri-La: A Travel Guide to the Himalayan Dream	£14.99
Sri Lanka	£15.99
Syria	£15.99
Taiwan	£16.99
Tibet	£13.99
Yemen	£14.99

Wildlife

Antarctica: Guide to the Wildlife	£15.99
Arctic: Guide to Coastal Wildlife	£15.99
Australian Wildlife	£14.99
Central & Eastern European Wildlife	£15.99
Chinese Wildlife	£16.99
East African Wildlife	£19.99
Galápagos Wildlife	£16.99
Madagascar Wildlife	£16.99
New Zealand Wildlife	£14.99
North Atlantic Wildlife	£16.99
Pantanal Wildlife	£16.99
Peruvian Wildlife	£15.99
Southern African Wildlife	£19.99
Sri Lankan Wildlife	£15.99

Pictorials and other guides

100 Alien Invaders	£16.99
100 Animals to See Before They Die	£16.99
100 Bizarre Animals	£16.99
Eccentric Australia	£12.99
Northern Lights	£6.99
Tips on Tipping	£6.99
Wildlife and Conservation Volunteering: The Complete Guide	£13.99

WIN A FREE BRADT GUIDE

READER QUESTIONNAIRE

Send in your completed questionnaire and enter our monthly draw for the chance to win a Bradt guide of your choice.

To take up our special reader offer of 40% off, please visit our website at www.bradtguides.com/freeguide or answer the questions below and return to us with the order form overleaf.

(Forms may be posted or faxed to us.)

Have you used any other Bradt guides? If so, which titles? ....

....

What other publishers' travel guides do you use regularly? ....

....

Where did you buy this guidebook? ....

What was the main purpose of your trip to Burkina Faso (or for what other reason did you read our guide)? eg: holiday/business/charity ....

....

How long did you travel for? (circle one)

weekend/long weekend 1–2 weeks 3–4 weeks 4 weeks plus

Which countries did you visit in connection with this trip?..................

....

Did you travel with a tour operator?' If so, which one? ....

....

What other destinations would you like to see covered by a Bradt guide?

....

If you could make one improvement to this guide, what would it be?

....

Age (circle relevant category) 16–25 26–45 46–60 60+

Male/Female (delete as appropriate)

Home country ....

Please send us any comments about this guide (or others on our list).

....

....

....

Bradt Travel Guides

IDC House, The Vale, Chalfont St Peter, Bucks SL9 9RZ, UK

t +44 (0)1753 893444 f +44 (0)1753 892333

e info@bradtguides.com

www.bradtguides.com

TAKE 40% OFF YOUR NEXT BRADT GUIDE!

Order Form

To take advantage of this special offer visit www.bradtguides.com/freeguide and enter our monthly giveaway, or fill in the order form below, complete the questionnaire overleaf and send it to Bradt Travel Guides by post or fax.

Please send me one copy of the following guide at 40% off the UK retail price

No	*Title*	*Retail price*	*40% price*
1	....	....	....

Please send the following additional guides at full UK retail price

No	*Title*	*Retail price*	*Total*
...	....	....	....
...	....	....	....
...	....	....	....

Sub total ....

Post & packing ....

(Free shipping UK, £1 per book Europe, £3 per book rest of world)

Total ....

Name ....

Address ....

Tel .... Email ....

☐ I enclose a cheque for £........ made payable to Bradt Travel Guides Ltd

☐ I would like to pay by credit card. Number: ....

Expiry date: .../....... 3-digit security code (on reverse of card) .....

Issue no (debit cards only) .....

☐ Please sign me up to Bradt's monthly enewsletter, Bradtpackers' News.

☐ I would be happy for you to use my name and comments in Bradt marketing material.

Send your order on this form, with the completed questionnaire, to:

Bradt Travel Guides
IDC House, The Vale, Chalfont St Peter, Bucks SL9 9RZ, UK
t +44 (0)1753 893444 f +44 (0)1753 892333
e info@bradtguides.com www.bradtguides.com

NOTES

NOTES

Index

Page numbers in **bold** indicate major entries; those in *italics* indicate maps.